The Sexuality Debates

WOMEN'S SOURCE LIBRARY

Series Editors:
Dale Spender and Candida Ann Lacey

This series brings together some of the most important, but still too little known, written sources which document the history of women's struggles for liberation. Taken from the principal women's archive in Britain, The Fawcett Library, and reprinted in full wherever possible, these pamphlets and papers illustrate major debates on a range of issues including suffrage, education, work, science and medicine as well as making the words of individual women widely available for the first time. Each volume contains a historical introduction to the material and biographical details of those campaigners who sought to improve the social, economic and legal status of women. The series was devised in collaboration with Catherine Ireland and David Doughan of The Fawcett Library, both of whom greatly assisted in the selection and compilation of material.

Other volumes in this series:

Barbara Leigh Smith Bodichan and the Langham Place Group edited by Candida Ann Lacey
The Sexuality Debates edited by Sheila Jeffreys
The Education Papers: Women's Quest for Equality in Britain, 1850–1912 edited by Dale Spender

Forthcoming volumes include:

Women's Fabian Tracts edited by Sally Alexander
The Non-Violent Militant: Selected Writings of Teresa Billington-Greig edited by Carol McPhee and Ann FitzGerald
Suffrage and the Pankhursts edited by Jane Marcus
The Lily edited by Cheris Kramarae and Ann Russo
The Revolution edited by Cheris Kramarae and Lana Rakow
Before the Vote was Won: Arguments for and Against Women's Suffrage 1864–1896 edited by Jane Lewis
Sex and Social Order in Britain, 1670–1730 by Carol Barash and Rachel Weil

The Sexuality Debates

Edited by
Sheila Jeffreys

Routledge & Kegan Paul
New York and London

First published in 1987 by
Routledge & Kegan Paul Ltd
11 New Fetter Lane, London EC4P 4EE

Published in the USA by
Routledge & Kegan Paul Inc.
in association with Methuen Inc.
29 West 35th Street, New York, NY 10001

Set in Linotron Bembo, 10 on 11 point
by Input Typesetting Ltd, London SW19 8DR
and printed in Great Britain
by T. J. Press (Padstow) Ltd,
Padstow, Cornwall

Library of Congress Cataloging in Publication Data

The sexuality debates.

(Women's source library)
Bibliography: p.
Includes index.
1. Sex customs—England—History—Sources.
2. Women—England—History—Sources. 3. Sexual ethics—England—History—Sources. I. Jeffreys, Sheila. II. Series.
HQ18.G7S476 1987 306.7'0942 86–26248
ISBN 0–7102–0963–3 (U.S.)

British Library CIP Data also available
ISBN 0–7102–0936–3

Contents

Introduction

Historians have represented the history of sexuality in the last hundred years as a story of gradual but regular progress from the darkness of Victorian prudery to the light of sexual freedom. From a feminist perspective the picture is very different. With the publication of the documents on sexuality collected here it is possible to examine with close and sensitive attention what was really happening in the massive and heated debate around sexuality which took place in the late nineteenth and early twentieth century.

From the 1870s to the 1920s, feminists launched a critique of male sexuality and its effects upon women. Concentrating on areas in which the exercise of male sexuality was particularly damaging to women, such as the use of women in prostitution, the sexual abuse of children, rape in marriage, the spread of venereal disease, women organised to protect women and children. They demanded the transformation of male sexuality. They did not believe that male sexuality was innately different from that of women and asserted that men could take responsibility for their sexual behaviour instead of always blaming women, that men could exercise self-control and did not need the sacrifice of women and children to their pleasures.

Surprisingly, considering the volume of women's activities and theory in this area, collections of documents on women in the nineteenth century have rarely contained much on sexuality. Traditional historians writing of late nineteenth-century feminism have tended to ignore these campaigns entirely. Where they have mentioned the feminist ideas on sexuality they have interpreted them as prudish and puritanical. It may be that these historians were embarrassed by the fact that the women whom they recognised as having quite legitimate aims in other areas, i.e. work, education, suffrage, thought about sexuality in ways which, to minds trained in the sexual ideology of the twentieth century, seemed retrogressive.

The language with which nineteenth-century feminists described sexuality, in terms such as 'sexual excess' and 'continence', has proved a stumbling-block for feminist historians as well. The language available to the women campaigners when they were trying to express their anxieties and their hopes was not created by the women themselves. Similarly today, feminists wrestle to gain some grasp on their feelings about sex within an ideology of compulsory sexual activity, using terms such as 'sexual needs', 'orgasm' and 'frustration' which would have been quite as alien to the feminists of the 1890s and are not necessarily more useful to us today in articulating our experience and hopes about sexuality. The women campaigners against sexual violence and the exploitation of women shared a lack of enthusiasm for sexual intercourse. To understand their work it is important to step outside 'sexual revolution' ideology as much as is possible for those of us who were raised within it.

Part I of this selection contains source material from the male doctors whose work on sexuality has provided historians of the nineteenth century with both horrifying and amusing examples of how sexuality was thought about by middle-class males. Isaac Baker Brown used clitoridectomy to 'cure' women of complaints as various as epilepsy, not wanting to have anything to do with their husbands and painful periods. Clitoridectomy was supposed to cure masturbation and it was this 'self-abuse' which was thought by such doctors to lie at the root of whatever ills might befall women. Such gross mutilation of women who did not conform to the doctors' favoured stereotypes did not cease by the 1870s. In the twentieth century operations are carried out on women in the US and in Britain to make women's vaginas fit their husbands' penises, and to move their clitorises nearer their vaginas on the grounds that this would make them more likely to experience pleasure whilst the husband experienced his own. The difference is that whereas in the nineteenth century operations were carried out on women to prevent them experiencing sexual pleasure, in this century it has been women's failure to experience pleasure when men felt they should which has occasioned these gruesome mutilations.

Feminist concern at men's abuse of women in prostitution began with the campaign to abolish the Contagious Diseases Acts. These Acts of the 1860s, designed to decrease venereal disease in the troops, allowed metropolitan policemen drafted into garrison ports and towns to stop any woman they suspected of working as a prostitute and subject her to examination. Women who refused examination were imprisoned until they agreed and women found (or suspected, since medical knowledge was far from competent) to be diseased were imprisoned until believed by the doctors to be cured.[1]

The documents in section IIA illustrate the politics of the women campaigners in the Ladies' National Association which was set up in 1870 to fight for repeal of the Acts. The Acts were suspended in 1883 and repealed in 1886. Later documents in this section relate to the formation of the organisation which succeeded the Ladies' National Association in 1913, the Association for Moral and Social Hygiene, which combated the international traffic in women and campaigned against renewed efforts to introduce legislation for the regulation of prostitutes.

The energies of the women who had been involved in fighting the Acts went into a continued campaign to transform male sexual behaviour and protect women and girls from sexual abuse. The campaign around the Acts was crucial to women's organising around the issue of sexuality. The campaign allowed women to think, organise and speak on topics previously considered taboo. They built up a passionate sense of grievance at the abuse of women and children by men as evidence about child prostitution and child sexual abuse emerged in the course of the campaign. Some of the campaigners became involved in social purity organisations. Social purity is the name that those men and women who organised for the 'elimination of vice' in the late nineteenth century gave to what became a massive movement. The Social Purity Alliance was founded in 1873 by men who had been involved in the campaign against the CD Acts. Josephine Butler's pamphlet, 'Social Purity', is a classic description of the feminist motivations behind social purity. In social purity men were to organise themselves so that they could learn self-control and work out what they could best do to end the abuse of women in prostitution. Ellice J. Hopkins, whose work appears in this selection, was the leading woman founder of social purity in this period. Whilst she was not a feminist, she made statements such as, 'the man is head of the woman and therefore the servant of the woman', and was a staunch defender of the right of women and children to live without male sexual abuse and exploitation. She placed responsibility firmly upon men for the abuse of women.

Late nineteenth-century feminists defied the myth that the home was a safe place for women and children, and that a woman would be safe in her 'separate sphere'. In section IIB documents have been selected to demonstrate feminist concern with domestic violence. The feminists protested woman-battering and marital rape and campaigned for fifty years against the sexual abuse of children. Material on temperance is included here because much of the strength and fire of women temperance campaigners in this period stemmed from their belief that alcohol was a potent motivator of men's sexual violence and other violence to women.

In the years immediately before the First World War, as the suffrage campaign reached new heights of energy, one of the strongest motivating forces of the campaigners was the belief that the vote would enable women to fight men's sexual violence better, both through getting equal pay which would make sexual exploitation of women more difficult and through making laws more favourable to women in the area of sexual violence. The whole range of suffrage societies published pamphlets on the subject concentrating on sexual abuse of girls, prostitution and the traffic in women. Section IIIC contains a selection of these writings. Ursula Roberts' piece is a fairly typical example of such a work produced by a non-militant suffrage campaigner. Lucy Re-Bartlett provided theoretical justification for this bias in the campaign for the vote. She explained that the suffrage campaigners and, in particular, the militant group, the Women's Social and Political Union, were going to create a new world in which men's sexual violence had ceased to exist. She saw one of their chief weapons as being the 'sex strike', i.e. having nothing to do with men until their behaviour in the sphere of sexuality was transformed. Christabel Pankhurst was in the militant WSPU. Her work, 'The Great Scourge', is an example of what the most radical campaigners in the field of sexuality were saying. Pankhurst thought women should remain spinsters whilst men were unfit to relate to women. She believed that women's anger at men's sexual violence would be sufficient to spur them on to a new and final offensive in the suffrage campaign if it could be roused, and her work is a clarion call to women. Historians have been uniformly hostile to Pankhurst. Alarmed by the strength of her uncompromising attack on men's sexual behaviour, they have represented her as a bitch, prudish or even insane.[2]

Section IIIA contains work from a cross-section of women theorists and writers on sexuality. Elizabeth C. Wolstenholme Elmy was the main feminist theorist on sexuality in late nineteenth-century Britain. She saw men's sexual enslavement of women when they destroyed the matriarchate as the moment when men's sexual violence and their sexual exploitation of women began. She wrote books of sex advice for children and adolescents, campaigned against rape in marriage and promoted the joys of 'psychic love' between men and women which avoided all genitality. She was a main figure in the Ladies' National Association for the Abolition of the Contagious Diseases Acts. The writings collected here range from those of Wolstenholme Elmy and Francis Swiney, whose indictment of men for the abuse of women is fierce, to the piece by Dr Elizabeth Blackwell which includes no feminist analysis of the relations between the sexes, as in describing the evils of prostitution whilst attributing no responsibility to men for the abuse of women in that institution. Annie Besant provides a brilliantly clear description of the way in which the marriage laws reduced married women to a condition of economic and bodily slavery to their husbands. Besant was a believer in 'free love' which she, like other women who practised 'free love' at this time, took to mean avoiding the marriage ceremony because of the terrible disadvantages which women suffered from marriage. 'Free love' did not mean promiscuity or even casualness in relationships as it came to mean in the 'sexual revolution' of the 1960s, but long-term committed relationships without marriage. Ellice Hopkins' piece is in stark contrast. Though a tough and life-long spinster herself, whose attitude towards men's abuse of women in prostitution is as uncompromisingly strong as that of the feminists in the Contagious Diseases Acts campaign, she enjoins women here to acceptance of the necessity for traditional patriarchal marriage.

In the 1890s the sex reform movement developed in Britain. The journal *The Adult* published writings by men and some women celebrating the joy of sexual intercourse and asserting that infrequent sexual intercourse or its absence would cause as many ills as the feminists, who were hostile to that practice, laid at the door of 'excess'. The sex reformers who were campaigning to rehabilitate sex, which they saw as sexual intercourse, denounced prudery and the puritan attitude. There was no place in sex reform for the profound critique of men's sexual abuse of women which the feminists had been developing. The feminists were seen as prudish for failing to appreciate the unalloyed beauty of sexual intercourse with men. Sex reform was fuelled by the development of the 'science' of sexology.

Section IIIB contains an example of sexological writing as well as the writings of women who were influenced or inspired by sex reform and sexology and consequently tended to write about sex in a rather different way from other women theorists. The piece by Havelock Ellis is included here because he is seen by historians as the father of twentieth-century sex advice literature and 'sexual liberalism' and the pioneer of the 'science' of sexology in Britain.

His impact on the way in which sex could be thought about was profound. He prescribed that male sexual behaviour was innately aggressive and sadistic, whereas women were by nature passive and masochistic. Feminist historians have seen sex reform and sexology as constituting a backlash against feminism and feminist ideas on sexuality in this period.[3]

The women sex reformers who read his work were generally hostile to that brand of feminism represented in earlier extracts here, in which women criticised the form of male sexuality and asserted above all the right of a woman to control access to her own body. Women like Stopes and Sanger joined in the conscription of women into compulsory heterosexuality and sexual intercourse whilst striving to provide some relief to women from its most damaging effects, such as unwanted childbearing. When sexual intercourse was being enjoined upon women with such pressure as it was by the male sex reformers, the provision of birth control information became essential. Feminists like Wolstenholme Elmy and Swiney had recommended continence to free women from unwanted childbearing rather than what they called 'artificial' birth control.

The final section IIIC includes three pieces which show how the spinster and the women whose emotional ties were to other women were being stigmatised and marginalised by the sex reformers in the period immediately before and after the First World War. Spinsters had been of enormous importance in the organising of the first wave of feminism and particularly in the campaigns to transform male sexuality. Passionate emotional relationships between women had been seen until the late nineteenth century as acceptable and respectable.[4] The sex reformers attacked spinsters for being manhaters and for being bitter and twisted as the sexologists fought back against the criticism of male sexual behaviour and sought to conscript women into obedient acceptance of their dictates. 'The Spinster' is the lead article in the first issue of a magazine called *The Freewoman*, set up in 1911 by women who accepted the ideas of the male sex reformers and formed a new sex reforming tendency within feminism. The article shows how spinsters were being characterised as dangerous and twisted through lack of sexual intercourse with men.

Ellen Key was enthusiastically seized upon by sex reformers like Havelock Ellis, who wrote the introduction to her book *The Woman Movement*, as the ideal representative of what they called the 'new feminism', i.e. a feminism which promoted motherhood for women and decreed that married women should not work and all women should be married. This was an ideology hostile to the interests of spinsters, lesbians and all women who sought to escape dependence on men. Key represents feminism as 'middle class' and counterposed to socialism. Her work was published all over Western Europe and in America. Her views on motherhood and women's work may be contrasted with those of Christabel Pankhurst in 'The Great Scourge'.

The paper by Stella Browne, given to the British Society for the Study of Sex Psychology, a sex reform organisation set up in 1914, shows how friendship between women or even the love of a woman for children was being categorised in this period as sexual inversion. Browne was a great admirer of Havelock Ellis who created a stereotype of the 'real' congenital as opposed to pseudo-homosexual woman in his 'Sexual Inversion' in 1897. Like Ellis, Browne writes about women she is acquainted with in the form of case studies. Browne felt that sexual repression gave rise to the form of militant feminism which she deplored and was thus not hostile to the idea that women should have sexual relationships with one another. Unfortunately, her unusual, for the time, liberalism in this respect was aimed at undermining the strength of feminism.

The period covered by the papers in this collection was a hugely important watershed period in the history of sexuality. A searching analysis of sexuality and its role in women's oppression was being developed by feminists involved in a massive campaign to change men's sexual behaviour to women's advantage. The new 'science' of sexology and the sex reform movement, despite the immediate practical advantage they brought to women in the provision of birth control information, were hostile to feminism, to women's independence and self-determination.

NOTES

1 For a detailed picture of this period in the history of prostitution see Judith Walkowitz, *Prostitution and Victorian Society, Women, Class and the State*, Cambridge, Cambridge University Press, 1980.

2 For a feminist interpretation of the ways in which Christabel Pankhurst has been denounced by historians, see Elizabeth Sarah, in Dale Spender (ed.), *Feminist Theorists*, London, Women's Press, 1983.

3 Two books which take this approach are, Sheila Jeffreys, *The Spinster and Her Enemies, Feminism and Sexuality 1880–1930*, London, Pandora, 1985 and Lal Coveney et al. (eds), *The Sexuality Papers*, London, Hutchinson, 1984.

4 For a history of women's passionate friendships see Lillian Faderman, *Surpassing the Love of Men: Romantic Friendship and Love between Women from the Renaissance to the Present*, London, Junction Books, 1981.

Part I

Male Doctors on Sexuality

Isaac Baker Brown

from

On the Curability of Certain Forms of Insanity, Epilepsy, Catalepsy and Hysteria in Females

(1866)

Hysteria, with cases

It may, perhaps, be necessary before relating cases which I have treated, suffering from hysteria, to state briefly what I understand by this term. The word Hysteria was doubtless originally used in the belief that it depended on excessive reflex action of the nerves of the uterus and ovaries, when these organs were excited by disease or other causes; but this view is a very limited one, for, as Dr Handfield Jones says, 'it does not appear that females suffering with irritable uterus are more hysterical, often not so much so, as those who have no such disorder'. There is, however, as I have already mentioned, in almost all hysterical patients, an exacerbation at the menstrual periods.

Dr Copland's opinion, that 'increased reflex excitability of the nerves of the female generative organs is one principal causative condition of hysterical affections', appears to me the correct one. Romberg also says, 'from the time when hysteria has taken root, the reflex action preponderates throughout the organism, and renders the individual more dependent upon external stimuli'.

I have alluded in the last chapter to those patients who have no desire to get well. Such I am not considering; and although I believe that all the complaints of an hysterical patient are more or less exaggerated, my experience differs from that of Dr Handfield Jones, who believes that such patients are not '*bona fide* anxious to get well'. In his view he is supported by Dr Prout, who considers that 'the whole energies of the patient's mind are bent on deception'; and by Dr Watson, who says that 'the deceptive appearances displayed in the bodily functions and feelings find their counterpart in the mental'. I am confident that I have met with many instances in which the nerve power has become so weakened that the patient, without having organic disease, really feels all the symptoms she describes, and is only too anxious to be cured. The cases I shall now narrate are a few of a large number that have come under my care and I am not without hope that their relation may show that hysteria, instead of being a term of reproach, does truly represent a curable disease.

The following was the first case that came under my notice, after I had satisfied myself of the correctness of my views on the subject.

Case I Hysteria – Five Years' Illness – Operation – Cure in Two Months

D.E., age 26, single; admitted into the London Surgical Home 12 Oct. 1859.

History. She had been a dressmaker in Yorkshire to all the best families around, but for the last five years had been so ill as to render her unable to do any work, and had been entirely supported by her former customers. When in that neighbourhood, on a professional visit to a lady, I was requested to see, amongst others, this poor *ci-devant* dressmaker. Her physiognomy at once told me the nature of the case; she was much attenuated, having for a long time been unable to retain any food, always being sick, with great pain, immediately after meals. She had constant acid eructations; was so weak as to be at times unable to cross the room; complained of a burning, aching pain, with great weakness at the lower part of the back. Her catamenia were irregular, with much leucorrhœa; bowels generally costive. She was very melancholy, and expressed a most earnest desire to be cured. I advised her admission to the 'Home', and on 15 October, I divided the clitoris subcutaneously. This being my first operation, I did not know the consequences of performing the operation in this manner. For two days the hæmorrhage was profuse and uncontrollable. Sleep was procured by opiates. I ordered olive oil to be rubbed into her chest every night, with a view to nutrition of her attenuated frame. A moderately generous diet was given, *but no stimulants*. She was quite well in two months, and has never since had a day's illness. She resumed her occupation as a dressmaker, and recovered nearly all her former customers. 1865. I have heard almost yearly of this patient, and lately had a letter from the lady to whom I previously referred, saying that my patient is perfectly well and in robust health.

Case II Two Years' Illness – Operation – Cures

P.F., age 21, single; admitted into the London Surgical Home 7 Jan. 1861.

History. Attributes her illness to having strained herself two years ago, when lifting a heavy saucepan from the fire. Has ever since that time suffered great pain in the back and side, much worse when she walks, but tolerably easy in the prone position. Catamenia very irregular, both as to time and quantity. Great pain in defecation. Bowels very constipated. Has been eleven weeks in a metropolitan general hospital, and thirteen weeks in a special hospital for women, from both of which she was discharged as having nothing the matter, because she had no evident disease. She had, however, been treated for uterine disease.

On examination, the uterus was found to be quite healthy; there was, however, evidence of excitation of the pudic nerve.

10 Jan. The clitoris completely excised.

16 Jan. Is much better.

31 Jan. Discharged from the Home, cured. Is quite well in her health, having lost all aches and pains, and being able to defecate without the slightest uneasiness.

Case III Hysteria – Thirteen Years' Illness – Sterility – Operation – Cure, and subsequently Three Pregnancies

S.S., age 33, married; admitted into the London Surgical Home 23 February 1861.

History. Although married several years, has had no children. About a year ago suffered from pain in the right side, which, however, being treated was cured. In April last the pain returned in the back, and at short intervals has recurred. At times the pain is so severe that she is unable to walk. Has for thirteen years suffered from leucorrhœ, globus hystericus, etc.; and has always had distaste for marital intercourse.

Examination confirming me in the diagnosis I had formed of this case, I, on 28 February, operated in the usual manner. Her recovery was retarded by an attack of jaundice, but in May she was discharged cured.

In July 1862, this patient was seen quite well and ruddy, and had long lost all her old symptoms. She had been once pregnant, but miscarried at three months.

In July 1865, she came to town with her youngest child. She was quite well, and had never been ill since the operation.

Remarks. This was the first case of this nature under my care, in which the patient, formerly sterile, became pregnant after removal of the cause of her illness.

Case IV Hysteria, with Sleeplessness – Six Years' Illness – Operation – Cure

H.R., age 55, single; admitted into the London Surgical Home 18 Nov. 1861.

History. For six years has suffered from a feeling of fullness, weight, and heat at the lower part of abdomen, with pain in the back, and 'bearing down'. At this time her menses had just ceased. Has not slept well for three or four years. Wakes every hour. Is always restless and fidgety. Frequent desire to micturate, with pain on doing so, and often desire without power to void it. Bowels costive; digestion indifferent.

She is a nervous, restless woman, with glistening and constantly wandering eye – pupils dilated. Has suffered from peripheral irritation for many years.

21 Nov. 1861. Usual operation performed. A week later, slept well for four hours, the first time for many years.

1 Dec. Has lost the irritability of the bladder, and passes water every four hours only; lost also the bearing-down pain; restless excitement gone.

7 Dec. Eats and sleeps well; is cheerful and grateful; leaves the Home cured, having been in only three weeks.

In 1863 was perfectly well.

Case V Fissure of the Rectum, with Hysteria – Operation for the Former – Relief – Subsequent Operation for Hysteria – Cure

Mrs L., age 55; admitted into the London Surgical Home 9 Dec. 1861.

History. Is a widow. Has for many years suffered from all the inconveniences of a fissure of the rectum, combined with bad digestion, undue nervous excitability, and sleepless nights. Is very anxious to be cured. It being thought that all these symptoms might be due to a painful fissure of the rectum, the ordinary operation for this affection was performed on 12 December. The bowels were opened in a few days without pain, and the fissure was healing well. Being, however, still sleepless, excitable, and irritable, questions were asked which showed that a further operation for removal of another source of irritation was advisable; therefore, on 24 December, I performed my usual operation. The next night she slept well. She became quiet and cheerful, and on 6 January, 1862, she was discharged quite well.

Remarks. This case is very interesting, as it shows that there may exist at the same time more than one irritation exerting inhibitory influence.

Case VI Hysteria, with Epileptiform Attacks in Childhood – Various Ailments for Thirteen Years – Operation – No Benefit

H.D., age 23 single; admitted into the London Surgical Home April 1862.

History. When very young, until ten years of age, had frequent fits. Improved in health till she was fourteen years of age, when she began to suffer from abdominal enlargement. First menstruated at nineteen. Is constantly sick after meals. Has been in nearly every hospital in London. The patient is very hysterical, and is always *talking* religion.

On examination the abdomen was found very tympanitic. Under chloroform this state quite subsided. Walls of abdomen fat and muscular. Body generally well nourished. Evidence of continual irritation of the pudic nerve.

3 April. Operation as usual.

For some time after the operation this patient was much better of the sickness, and great interest was manifested by several visitors in her case; she never, however, received permanent benefit, being a regular impostor, and discovered on several occasions tying handkerchiefs, etc., tightly round her waist to make her abdomen swell. She was discharged as incurable.

Remarks. This case I have inserted as a warning. It is no fault of the operation if it fail in such cases.

Case VII Hysteria – Several Years' Illness – Operation – Cure

Miss M., age 42; admitted into the London Surgical Home 13 April 1862.

History. Has felt ailing for many years, but for the last two has suffered pain in the uterine region, and, on pressure, over the ovaries. This pain is accompanied by bearing down, and a sense of distension. Suffers from considerable leucorrhœa. Menstruation regular, and during the period the pain is absent. Bowels regular. Sleep disturbed. Feels depressed, and is inclined to melancholia.

On examination there was no congestion of uterus or enlargement of ovaries, but there was evidence of peripheral irritation of the pudic nerve.

17 April. Usual operation performed.

She rapidly improved; sleep and cheerfulness returned, and all pain left her. She expressed herself as not having been so well for many years.

13 May. Left the Home, having gained flesh and strength, and being quite cured of all her bad symptoms.

Remarks. Interest attaches to this case, as instead of exacerbation, there was diminution of the symptoms during menstruation.

Case VIII Hysteria – Many Years' Illness – Phantom Tumour – Operation – Cure

A.B., age 24; admitted into the London Surgical Home 16 July 1862.

History. Is a single woman, and procures a living by dressmaking. When younger, was a nurse-maid. Catamenia commenced before she was 13, but she was not regular until she was 19 since when the function has proceeded normally both in time and quantity. Has for many years been ailing, and always had something the matter. Has suffered from intense irritation in the genital region, especially in the bladder, and she has constant pain in the back. For two years has been treated at a dispensary for an abdominal tumour; during this period she has taken much medicine, but without benefit.

On examination the abdomen was found increased in size and universally tympanitic. Under the influence of chloroform the swelling entirely subsided.

17 July. Usual operation performed under the influence of chloroform.

2 Sept. She was discharged quite cured, all her hysterical symptoms having left her, and the tumour never having been seen since the day of operation.

Case IX Hysteria – Five Years' Illness – Sterility – Operation – Cure – Pregnancy – Two Children

Mrs O., came under my care in 1862. She had been ill ever since marriage, five years previously; having distaste for the society of her husband, always laid upon the sofa, and under medical treatment. Evidence of peripheral excitement being manifest, I performed my usual operation. She rapidly lost all the hysterical symptoms which had previously existed; and in about a year came up to town to consult me concerning a tumour, which greatly frightened her, as she feared it was ovarian. I discovered that she was six months pregnant. She was delivered at full time of a healthy child. In 1865 she again called on me to show herself, not only in robust health, but pregnant for the second time.

Case X Hysteria – Irritation of Right Ovary – Menorrhagia – Nine Years' Illness – Operation – Cure

C.M.A., age 28, single; admitted into the London Surgical Home 22 June 1863.

History. Since the age of 10 has been more or less subject to uterine flooding; for the first three years lost blood every day. Has been five times in a metropolitan hospital; always better while there, but as bad as ever as soon as she left. The bleeding is much worse at each menstrual period. She passes large coagula; has constant pain in the back, headache, and palpitation of the heart, and cannot sleep; is dreadfully pale and anæmic.

Examination showed great irritation over right ovary, and there was evidence of long-continued peripheral irritation.

2 July. Usual operation.

7 July. Menstruation came on in a moderate flow.

10 July. Menstruation ceased; is much better, and there is sign of returning colour in the face.

31 July. Has improved considerably, and had no return of the bleeding. To be discharged cured.

Case XI Hysteria – Many Years' Illness – Operation – Cure – Marriage and Progeny

Emma K., age 22, single; admitted 16 September 1863 into the London Surgical Home.

History. Commenced menstruating at 15 years of age, but owing to the use of cold water during a period, the secretion was arrested for six months; the function was then restored, and has ever since continued normal. At 16 she suffered from piles, which occasioned very much irritation and pain after each evacuation, aggravated by constipation and by walking. Though regular as to time, there is always excessive catamenial flow, and it lasts for eight days. Has been under long and varied medical treatment, without benefit.

Examination showed peripheral irritation, as evinced by the abnormal condition of the external genitals.

17 Sept. 1863. The usual operation performed.

1 Oct. Progressing most favourably.

22 Oct. Leaves quite cured.

1866. This lady married, and was delivered August 1865, of a living child. She is still quite well.

It will have been observed that one very prominent symptom in many of the foregoing cases is sleeplessness, or perhaps more properly, frequent wakefulness at nights, and constant restless movements in the day. These are the cases which, if left to go on, are very liable to terminate in insanity. The three following are instances in which the hysteria was verging on this state, and as they can hardly be classed under the head of insanity, I prefer narrating them here.

Case XII Hysteria – Mental Aberration, and Tendency to Melancholia – Eight Years' Illness – Operation – Cure

In December 1861, a single lady consulted me, giving the following history of her illness:

Has not been well for seven or eight years; has felt languid, and not so lively as formerly. For the last two years has menstruated every three weeks, and the flow has lasted four or five days. There is considerable white discharge from the vagina after each period, lasting for a week. Great irritation about vulva, perinæum, and anus before and during each menstrual period. For the last five or six years had had occasional irresistible and unaccountable fits of depression; thinks that it is her mind – if her mind were as strong as her body she would be pretty well: her memory is good, but mind weak. Has suffered from great pain at lower part of the back; says she cannot rise from a chair without great difficulty, on account of a feeling of stiffness in hips and trembling of the legs (this is probably owing to a swelling of the hip-joint, as all the joints of her fingers and ankles are swollen). Says she can sit quietly to crochet or needlework, but cannot sit quietly to think, or compose her mind to write a letter; has not written a letter properly for three years. Has been subject to attacks of melancholy and weeping, without any tangible cause, but which she cannot resist. Suffers from want of sleep, and at night frequently lies awake four or five hours together. Appetite good; bowels costive.

In appearance is fresh-coloured and plump, but she says she is thinner than formerly; dark eyes; large dilated pupils.

On examination there was evidence of great irritation about the vulva, and constriction of the anus, with a very small fissure.

21 Dec. I divided the fissure, and performed my usual operation.

31 Dec. Very much improved; swelling of the joints much less.

1 Jan. She sat up, and feels much better. Her spirits are improved; has no pain in the joints; sleeps well. In another month she returned home quite well, and has continued so to the present time.

Case XIII Extreme Hysteria, verging on Insanity – Five Years' Illness – Operation – Cure

Mrs –, age 32, married; admitted into the London Surgical Home 5 August 1862.

History. Has been married twelve years, but has had no children nor miscarriages. Has always enjoyed pretty good health until about five years ago, when she began to suffer from leucorrhœa and great pain during menstruation. Catamenia regular in time and quantity. Her bladder is so irritable that sometimes she has to pass her water every half-hour; the urine sometimes very much loaded. Suffers from headache and giddiness in the morning. Says that for the last three years the act of coition has been accomplished without the least pleasure, but with pain. Bowels are opened regularly and without pain.

7 August. Having diagnosed the cause of the disease, the usual operation was performed.

9 August. A severe attack of erysipelas came on, and she was very ill for some days, but she made a good recovery.

A few days after the operation this patient was observed to be occasionally very violent and unmanageable, and to have at these times a wild maniacal look. On questioning her husband, it appeared that for several years she had been subject to fits of violent excitement, especially during the menstrual period, and that at such times 'she would fly at him and rend his skin, like a tigress'.

This patient made a good recovery; she remained quite well, and became in every respect a good wife.

Case XIV Extreme Hysteria – Incipient Insanity – Operation – Cure

Mrs R., age 42; admitted into the London Surgical Home 5 Aug. 1862.

History. Has been married, but has been a widow for twelve years. Is companion to a lady. Never had any family. Has been ailing for some years, but has not suffered severely until the last six months. Suffers most from pain in the lower part of the abdomen, and from constant burning and irritation about the vulva. During the last few months has become very nervous and fidgety; never can remain quiet, and says that lately she 'has had a sort of lost feeling, particularly when writing; being unable to compose her thoughts, or concentrate her mental energies'. Has suffered from considerable irritability of the bladder; and her urine is often full of thick deposit. Catamenia regular in time and quantity. Cannot sleep.

On examination is a very nervous woman, her eyes restless and never quiet; constant twitchings of the limbs, and occasionally an appearance almost of insanity about her expression. There is every evidence of a long continued inhibitory influence.

7 August. The usual operation performed.

8 August. Feels very comfortable. Slept better last night than for some years.

9 August. Is improving wonderfully; the expression of countenance completely changed.

9 Sept. Left quite well. Has got fat, and has now a cheerful face and manner. Says she feels a different being, and is quite astonished at her own improvement. Has lost all her nervous twitchings and other uncomfortable symptoms, and has now a comfortable night's rest.

Idiocy and insanity, with cases

As Epilepsy is a much graver disease than hysteria, so is the sequel of the former – dementia or idiocy – much more permanent and difficult to be removed by treatment than insanity, which is the ordinary sequel of hysteria.

I shall give but one case of idiocy, because I regret to say that I have never yet been able to thoroughly restore the mental powers in any patients suffering from this dreadful affliction. Epilepsy is such a chronic disease, and seems to me to produce not only weakening of the mind, but to cause it to be often entirely lost, that, although we may get, as in the following case, a temporary rekindling of the mental energies, I fear we are not yet able to give much hope of complete recovery. Even here, however, I have such faith in the efficacy of perseverance in constant watching, that I am almost inclined to believe that, had this patient been in a condition of life to ensure vigilant medical supervision for a lengthened period after operation, we might at last have succeeded in, if not complete, at least, much greater restoration than in a public institution, or to those in humble circumstances, the surgeon is in a condition to promise.

Case XLII Epileptic Fits, with Complete Idiocy – Operation – Great Temporary Relief, but not Permanent Benefit.

Mary J., age 19, single; admitted into the London Surgical Home 15 Feb. 1864.

This patient was brought to me by Dr Marley, with the following account:

> Has the appearance of a child of 10 or 12 years old; mammæ not developed; has had epileptic fits ever since 12 years of age. Is now almost idiotic; stares vacantly; slobbers at the mouth; passes her motions anywhere, without regard to common decency, and cannot retain her urine. I find from her mother that she is incessantly irritating her genitals. Her fits vary in frequency, from two or three a day to four or five a week. Being satisfied of the cause of her fits, I sent her to you.

History, taken at the Home from her mother. Had perfect health until she reached her eleventh year; was forward in her lessons, and well educated for her age and position. At this time she was suddenly seized with a severe fit, for which no cause could be assigned. A period of two years elapsed before she had a second, when, being placed under medical treatment for eighteen months, she had great relief. Since the expiration of that time to the present she has constantly suffered from fits.

Her intellect did not begin to weaken until two years since, but she ceased growing and learning after the first attack. At this time she does not know her right hand from her left; does not know her mother, and shows no signs whatever of ordinary intelligence. From being cleanly as a child, is now most filthy – in fact, is in every sense an idiot.

Has never menstruated.

On examination – although, as stated by Dr Marley, the mammæ were very rudimentary – there was full development, and indeed abnormal hypertrophy, of the external genitals.

18 Feb. The usual operation performed, under chloroform. The hands to be restrained, and the patient most carefully watched.

19 Feb. Has passed a good night, and is quiet.

23 Feb. Has been very drowsy since the operation. Today asked for food for the first time, and showed some signs of intelligence.

26 Feb. Gave rational answers to several questions which were asked her. Also remembers from day to day any promises of delicacies of diet or money.

1 March. Passed a good night; feels free from pain. Was given some printed cards, which she read – *the first time for nine years.*

2 March. Improving much. Is much more modest in her behaviour, but still passes her excretions without regard to time or place. Notices passing events, and remembers names and faces.

3 March. Has given sensible and somewhat witty replies to various questions asked her in the presence of about twenty medical gentlemen, who today came to see the operation. When moneys were given her, she at once told their different relative value.

4 March. Morning; Seems no worse for the excitement of yesterday. Evening: Had a slight fit.

5 March. A little heavy and stupid today. Somewhat irritable and obstinate.

6 March. Much better. Has a daily clearer notion of right and wrong. Likes books with pictures and large print. When she comes to hard words, she asks the meaning, like a child, but cannot always grasp the meaning of an explanation.

8 March. Not quite so well today. Had a slight epileptic fit this evening, followed by a very severe one in two hours.

9 March. Again much better, but irritable.

12 March. Two fits.

16 March. Not so well: another fit today.

She from this time seemed to retrograde; and on the 4th of April was discharged as incurable.

It will be recollected how, at the end of the chapter on Hysteria, I gave three cases of extreme nervous irritability, with sleeplessness, and tendency to an unhinging of the mental equilibrium. We now come to insanity itself. It would be vain to talk of the varieties of forms in which this state may be seen, when produced by abnormal peripheral irritation of the pudic nerve. It is, however, worthy of notice how each history seems to tell its own explanation of the cause; and after the first few days of treatment, when excitement, caused by irritation from the wound and a natural repugnance to restraint, has passed off, how rapid is the improvement, and how permanent is the result. I have no hesitation in saying that in no case am I so certain of a permanent cure as in acute nympho-mania; for I have never after my treatment seen a recurrence of the disease, whereas, under medical treatment, of how short duration is but too frequently the benefit.

Case XLIII Incipient Suicidal Mania – Many Years' Gradual Illness – Operation – Cure

R.T., age 39, single; admitted into the London Surgical Home 22 Oct. 1861.

History. Has been ailing for many years, and given great trouble and anxiety to her friends. For some time past she has been very strange in her manner, very restless, never quiet, constantly wakeful, threatening suicide, talking to people, even perfect strangers, of her ailments and their causes, of which she is fully conscious. Was formerly modest and quiet.

On examination, she is a fine woman, of restless appearance and manner; eye wandering and unsteady; pupil dilated. The cause of her mental derangement being obvious, on 24 Oct. the usual operation was performed.

The improvement in her mental and bodily health was wonderful: she gained flesh, and became cheerful and modest. She was discharged six weeks after admission.

When heard of in February 1863, this patient continued quite well.

The first case of actual insanity that came under my care was a patient of Dr Warren Diamond, then resident in his private asylum. I cannot do better than transcribe the account which he sent me with the following note:

> Effra Hall, Brixton, S.
>
> Dear Sir, A month having elapsed since you gave up your patient, I forward some particulars of the case, and shall be glad to answer more fully any special time or state you would like to know more about. You will, perhaps, be able to pick something out of this rambling account that may be interesting to you. Hoping you will excuse omissions, etc.
>
> [Believe me, yours faithfully,]
> Warren H. Diamond
>
> I. Baker Brown, Esq.

Case XLIV Several Years' Illness – Two Months' Insanity – Operation – Cure

Miss E.R., age 34, single; no occupation, living with her friends; hair light reddish-brown; face set and vacant, with an occasional pained expression; eyes fixed and dull; extremities damp and cold; stature moderate and well formed. Has for several years past been looked on by her friends as different from others – strange and eccentric. Would go out and walk away into the country alone for miles, and come back exhausted. When friends called, would start up and run round the garden, or to the top of the house and back again, giving no reason for it but that she must do it. Always exceedingly irritable and passionate. Unless some excitement was going on, was listless and unable to rouse herself. When at parties, was so forward and open in her manners, that she was generally avoided by gentlemen. *Never had an offer of marriage.* Her mother died about a year and a half ago, but she took no notice of the occurrence, and was consequently remarked on by her friends. Since then she has been getting more strange and peculiar. About February last, a sister told her, in joke, that if she did not take care she would soon become a fit subject for Dr Diamond, little thinking how soon it would happen. She recently made enemies of old friends, so that her brothers could not make out why they fell off. Would sit or stand without noticing them when they called; and asked them what they wanted that they came to her house (she was the eldest of the family).

I was consulted about her in the end of March, but had then none of her previous history. She was vacant and dreamy; talked of flowers which she called her friends; said 'people's faces were masks; that she was quite unable to rouse or employ herself, as she was changed'; very uncertain in appetite, going a day without her food; not sleeping at night, and for the last few nights showing such great excitement and passion, that her sisters were required to sit up with her.

I recommended change along the south coast, with sea-bathing, etc. She did not improve; and the attendant informing me of a constant irritation of the vulva, lotions were used, but without benefit. Her general health and appetite improved; but not the mind. She could not sleep, and would not bear narcotics; *stimulants acted as narcotics*, but soon lost their effect.

Bowels regular; pulse small and slow; action of heart being irritable, and not corresponding at all times to the power or quantity of the pulse. She sits up in bed, nursing the pillow, and talking to it as if it were a baby; says 'that she died last Sunday' – 'is lost' – 'is buried'.

When out of doors, great difficulty is experienced in getting her in again; she wished to wander away, without aim or purpose. Having given my opinion to her friends, I was authorised to admit her 18 April 1861. Before she left home, she continued calling out, 'Take me to a mad-house! take me quick, or I shall never get well!' She persisted in saying 'she was dead', and 'she felt buried'. Answers in monosyllables. Her pupil is contracted and fixed. At night she does not sleep, and is in such a continual state of excitement that the attendant cannot sleep with her. Has lost all natural modesty in manner and speech. Is not blasphemous. Before me is perfectly reserved and correct in her manner. When I ask questions, she will, after a pause, answer in monosyllables, or repeat the question over and over again, as if trying to grasp the meaning and ally her thoughts. Unless walked about, will stand for hours in one place, gaping, yawning, and throwing her arms about listlessly. She was in this state when you saw her, and from what you told me of your experience of the operation and its results, I was led to infer relief from it in this case, as the delusion of having died on a certain day was movable and could be reasoned away; but the heavy oppressed feeling still made her say, 'But if I am not dead, I am lost, or changed', and naturally led back to the idea. I ascribed the state of her mind to weakening of the body, and general nervous irritation caused by long-continued reflex excitation; and I believed that if the source of irritation could be removed, her mental health would follow as her blood became healthy, and fit to make reparation.

I was led to think more of her uterine state from her expression of pain when she was walked about, and she was reported by the nurse as always complaining of her back, at the lower part, and of great tenderness on pressure over the ovaries.

27 May 1861. You operated on her, she being under the influence of chloroform. She was naturally restless afterwards, not understanding why she was kept in bed. Profuse menstruation came on in the evening, which had not happened for four months previously, and then always very scanty and with much pain. Half an ounce of laudanum, with oil, was rubbed into her chest during four hours; she did not, however, sleep, but continued moaning all night.

28 May. Easier, and more herself – takes her food.

29 May. Slept well last night, without opiates; says she shall now get well and be able to go home; answers questions more readily, and makes longer replies. *Pupil dilated and acts slowly*. Her nurse says she is quite altered in every way, and compares the change in her mind since the operation to 'dividing the tightened strings of a fiddle, and letting them all loose'.

2 June. Left her bed; is still menstruating; appears cheerful; asks questions now, and converses for short periods; has done a few stitches of needlework; says nothing about 'being lost or dead' since the operation. Surface of body and extremities warm. Freaky, anxious look about her eyes and nose gone. Laughs and jokes.

Says 'she has been in a dream', 'that things now seem light', and 'that she means to get well'.

3 July. She has gradually improved and become more natural in her habits and ideas; sleeps soundly every night; takes her meals well; walks about without compulsion; takes a pride in making herself neat, and has washed and dressed herself ever since she left her bed; is perfectly modest in manner and conversation. Her friends remark on the great improvement in her mind, she having had no delusions. Her mental state is, however, weak – what might better be called foolish, with some amount of wilful obstinacy. The family medical attendant, and, in fact, every one who has been in her company, notice the extraordinary change.

A careful perusal of the cases related in the foregoing pages will show that all the theoretical objections mentioned in the introductory chapter, as having been raised against my treatment, have been fully contradicted by facts. Of the permanency of the result, I myself am fully satisfied; and I hope at a future time, by a much larger number of cases, to confirm others in the same opinion.

Issac Baker Brown

from

On Some Diseases of Woman Admitting Surgical Treatment

(1866)

Irritation and hypertrophy of the clitoris

Enlargement of the clitoris, sometimes accompanied by a degree of induration approaching that of cartilage, at others by a relaxed flabby state of its tissues, and always attended by abnormal irritability, is a condition of more frequent occurrence, I believe, than the majority of medical men suspect, and is for the most part brought on by self-abuse. The deplorable effects of this baneful habit, both on the physical and mental health, have been less considered in the case of females than of males, and yet they are of equal gravity, and probably as prevalent. The radical cure of the habit is, however, fortunately in our hands. Long-continued irritation of the clitoris figures among the causes of sterility, for, besides its constitutional effects, the habit acts locally on the functions of the womb, either in the same way, we may presume, as does excessive venery, or by inducing displacement of the organ.

The necessity for the excision or amputation of the clitoris, when much enlarged, has been recognised by surgeons generally; but I would go further and say, that this operation should be resorted to in all cases where that organ is found in an abnormal state, and where constitutional symptoms are traceable to its irritation.

The opinion here expressed has received an abundant confirmation since the publication of the last edition of this work. My further observations have been published at length in a recent treatise, *On the Curability of Certain Forms of Insanity, Epilepsy, Catalepsy, and Hysteria in Females* (1866). In this treatise I think that it is shown conclusively that the diseases named are, in many instances, determined or exaggerated by voluntary irritation of the clitoris; and that in these cases by amputation of the abnormally excited organ the disease may be cured.

The influence of delection in giving rise to mental and convulsive affections of both sexes has long been known, and various moral and physical methods have been recommended to break the bad habit. Among the latter, cauterisation of the clitoris in the female, and vesication of the glans penis, or circumcision, in the male, are chiefly recommended; more rarely excision of the clitoris in the female has been practised.

A long experience of cases in which self-induced irritation of the clitoris was an exciting or aggravating cause of disease, convinced me that cauterisation, actual or potential, could not be depended upon as a remedial agent; and that where it might apparently lead to a good result this was but transitory. Further, in many of these cases the application of caustics, necessarily renewed at intervals, was a source of positive harm. The interference of the surgeon pandered to the morbid appetite of the patient. I was thus led to the more frequent use of excision, and in this course I was confirmed by recent advances in physiological research. The observations of Brown-Sequard and Handfield Jones made it certain that a greater importance must be attached to local sources of irritation, especially about the genital organs, in the causation of nervous and convulsive diseases, than had hitherto been done. What before had been but vaguely present to my mind now became clear, and so far as the opinions of these writers referred to peripheral excitement of the pudic nerve, I determined to subject them to a systematic surgical test. This I have done, and the results are given in detail in the book, already referred to, on the curability of certain forms of nervous and convulsive diseases. Of the happy results of the practice I have no doubt, and the cases I have published will, I think, convince the reader, that several forms of the most painful and distressing diseases of females may be effectually cured by excision of the clitoris.

The operation has, however, been subjected to much adverse criticism, to which it is requisite that I should briefly refer.

First of all, with a forgetfulness of physiology, scarcely credible in these days, the opponents of the operation have declared that 'it unsexes a woman'. The objection is as old as the operation itself, and the phrase in which it has been urged a more free translation from Aëtius, who thus expressed it, *hinc vero sæpe sterilitas exoritur.* Putting aside all theory, the fact that several of my patients have become pregnant after the operation is a complete reply to this objection. (See Cases 3, 9, 11, 19, 48, in my work on the subject.) In the face of the most indisputable evidence that the clitoris is not an essential part of the generative system, the expression 'mutilation of the person', so freely employed, may be passed over as possessing no meaning other than that in which it would be applicable to numerous recognised surgical proceedings.

The author of a recent work on Diseases of Women confesses that, 'If the habit could be overcome, if the mind could be restored to its purity by any mutilation of the person, one would feel no penalty could be too great to pay for such a boon.' Yet he goes on to add, 'The seat of sexual feeling is, however, by no means confined to the clitoris.' If this be the case, wherein consists the author's objection to the practice, or the peculiar force of his words 'mutilation of the person'?

But it has been further alleged, that the operation is unnecessary; that the habit, be it vice or disease, can be met by moral treatment. Indeed, the reviewer of my book, in the *Lancet*, suggests trying to persuade an hysterical patient into the belief that her ailments are imaginary, and that to effect a cure it is only necessary to induce her to 'exert her will', 'to make an effort'.

Now, I ask, who is there of any experience who has not met with cases of masturbation – in the male or female – in which no amount of moral reasoning has sufficed to put a stop to the habit? I myself have met with cases in which months and years of restraint – moral and physical – by medical and other advice, nay, with the utmost endeavours of the patients themselves, have not sufficed to overcome the habit. Are we, then, to forbid that 'surgery shall come to the rescue, and cure what morals should have prevented?' – but, let me add, are so often impotent to stop. I am not ignorant of the value of rousing the patient to efforts at self-control; indeed I have seen many recoveries by the patient's own firm will; but the cases in which moral effort suffices are not those in which I have recourse to the operation.

A still more visionary objection has been propounded in the theory that a recognition of the frequency of self-abuse might suggest its practice to the pure-minded. Such a notion can only be entertained by those who are determined to shirk the question as one for impartial and scientific investigation. Those who employ it may fitly consort with the bigots who refuse the boon of chloroform in labour, on the ground that Providence intended women to bring forth in sorrow.

More reasonable doubts have been expressed respecting those cases of epilipsy in which clitoridectomy has been performed, but in which the bromide of potassium has been employed as part of the treatment. In any individual case this objection would have considerable force; but I have met with many cases in which large doses of this drug had been taken for months without the slightest benefit, nay, even with progressive increase of the disease, and in which the operation has been followed by marked beneficial results; and in the majority of the most successful of my cases bromide of potassium has not been used. In that numerous class of cases comprised under the terms hysteria and spinal irritation, the operation is almost invariably successful, while the bromide of potassium seldom affords the slightest relief.

To return to our subject: the general disorder of the health which arises from self-induced irritation of the clitoris requires to be particularly noted, as well as certain characteristic appearances of the genital organs.

The period when such disorder attacks the patient is about the age of puberty, and from that time up to almost every age the following train of symptoms may be observed, some being more or less marked than others in the various cases.

The patient becomes restless and excited, or melancholy and retiring; listless and indifferent to the social influences of domestic life. She will be fanciful in her food, sometimes express even a distaste for it, and apparently (as her friends will say) live upon nothing. She will always be ailing, and complaining of different affections. At first, perhaps, dyspepsia and sickness will be observed; then pain in the head and down the spine; pain, more or less constant, in the lower part of the back, or on either side in the lumbar region. There will be wasting of the face and muscles generally; the skin sometimes dry and harsh, at other times cold and clammy. The pupil will be occasionally firmly contracted, but generally much dilated. This latter symptom, together with a hard cord-like pulse, and a constantly moist palm, are, my son informs me, considered by Mr Moore, Colonial Surgeon of South Australia, pathognomonic of this condition. There will be quivering of the eyelids, and an inability to look one straight in the face. On inquiring further, disturbance or irregularity in the uterine functions is found, there being either complete cessation of the catamenia, or too frequent periods, generally attended with pain; constant leucorrhea also commonly existing.

To these symptoms in the single female will be added, in the married, distaste for marital intercourse, and very frequently either sterility or a tendency to abort in the early months of pregnancy.

These physical evidences of derangement, if left unchecked, gradually lead to more serious consequences. The patient either becomes a confirmed invalid, always ailing, and confined to bed or a sofa, or, on the other hand, catalepsy, epilepsy, idiocy, or insanity, supervenes. In any case, and more especially when the disease progresses as far as these latter stages, it will almost universally be found that there are serious exacerbations at each menstrual period.

On an examination of the external generative organs, a straight and coarse hirsute growth; a depression in the centre of the perinæum; a peculiar follicular secretion; an alteration of structure of the parts, mucous membrane taking on the character of skin, and muscle having become hypertrophied and generally tending towards a fibrous or cartilaginous degeneration, will all be recognised as characteristic of the habit by the practitioner who has once had his attention drawn to this subject.

Having ascertained the cause and nature of the disease, there are one or two points to be considered before operative measures are decided on.

First, as to age. Although there is no doubt that patients may suffer from peripheral irritation of the pudic nerve from the earliest childhood, I seldom operate or sanction an operation on any patient under ten years of age, which is the earliest date of puberty. In children younger than this, milder treatment with careful watching will usually be found sufficient if it be thoroughly persevered in.

There are again, after puberty, cases which give rise to but slight disturbance, but in which the sufferers are they who love to enlist sympathy from the charitable, and will be ill, or affect to be ill, in spite of any or every treatment.

When I have decided that my patient is a fit subject for surgical treatment, I at once proceed to operate, after the ordinary preliminary measures of a warm bath and clearance of the portal circulation.

The patient having been placed *completely* under the influence of chloroform, the clitoris is freely excised, either by scissors or knife – I always prefer the scissors. The wound is then firmly plugged with graduated compresses of lint, and a pad, well secured by a T bandage.

A grain of opium is introduced per rectum, the patient placed in bed, and most carefully watched by a nurse, to prevent hæmorrhage by any disturbance of the dressing. The neglect of this precaution will be frequently followed by alarming hæmorrhage, and consequent injurious results.

The diet must be unstimulating, and consist of milk, farinaceous food, fish, and occasionally chicken; all alcoholic or fermented liquors being strictly prohibited. The strictest quiet must be enjoined, and the attention of relatives, if possible, avoided, so that the moral influence of the medical attendant and nurse may be uninterruptedly maintained.

A month is generally required for perfect healing of the wound, at the end of which time it is difficult for the uninformed, or non-medical, to discover any trace of an operation.

The rapid improvement of the patient immediately after removal of the source of irritation is most marked; first in the countenance, and soon afterwards by improved digestion and other evidences of healthy assimilation.

It cannot be too often repeated, that this improvement can only be made permanent, in many cases, by careful watching and moral training, on the part of both patient and friends for several months.

In the large majority of cases, I have administered no medicines, trusting entirely, for recovery, to the removal of the source of irritation. Sometimes, however, we may be materially aided by the use of such medicines as the bromides of potassium and ammonium, belladonna, etc.

The following cases may be cited in illustration. Numerous others will be found in my work on the subject.

Case I Hysteria – Five Years' Illness – Operation: Cure in Two Months

D.E., age 26, single; admitted into the 'London Surgical Home' 12 Oct. 1859.

History. She had been a dressmaker in Yorkshire to all the best families around, but for the last five years had been so ill as to render her unable to do any work, and had been entirely supported by her former customers. When in the neighbourhood of her home, on a professional visit to a lady, I was requested to see, amongst others, this poor *ci-devant* dressmaker. Her physiognomy at once told me the nature of the case; she was much attenuated, having for a long time been unable to retain any food, always being sick, with great pain, immediately after meals. She had constant acid eructations; was so weak as to be at times unable to cross the room; complained of a burning, aching pain, with great weakness at the lower part of the back. Her catamenia were irregular, with much leucorrhea; bowels generally costive. She was very melancholy, and expressed a most earnest desire to be cured. I advised her admission to the 'Home', and on 15 October I divided the clitoris subcutaneously. This being my first operation, I did not know the consequences of performing the operation in this manner. For two days the hæmorrhage was profuse and uncontrollable. Sleep was procured by opiates. I ordered olive-oil to be rubbed into her chest every night, with a view to nutrition of her attenuated frame. A moderately generous diet was given, *but no stimulants*. She was quite well in two months and has never since had a day's illness. She resumed her occupation as a dressmaker, and recovered nearly all her former customers. 1865. I have heard almost yearly of this patient, and lately had a letter from the lady to whom I previously referred, saying that my patient is perfectly well and in robust health.

Case II Spinal Irritation and supposed Uterine Displacement – Six Years Illness – Operation – Cure

In 1860 I was requested to see a young lady, age 20, of whom I had the following *history*. For six years she had been confined to a spinal couch, and had also been supposed to suffer from retroversion of the uterus. She had worn a spinal apparatus, attached to which was a steel spring, pressing on sacrum and pubis, and intended 'to support the perinæum, and keep the uterus in position'. Had been treated with caustics and other therapeutic agents for uterine disease. I found the uterus normal in position and healthy in appearance; but on further questioning and examination, I diagnosed peripheral irritation of the pudic nerve. My opinion was strongly contested, as I was told that the young lady was very religious; but as I explained, her illness was to be attributed solely to a physical condition, and was not at all necessarily immoral, I was then met with the objection that, in the event of marriage, my operation might interfere with marital happiness and prevent procreation. I explained how, physiologically, these objections were untenable, but was then unable to adduce actual cases in contradiction of them.

Ultimately I performed my operation in the usual manner. For want of proper attention on the part of the nurse, the dressing was three times displaced; but, nevertheless, at the end of a month this lady was well enough to walk three miles.

Up to this date she has remained quite well.

Case III Nine Years' Illness – Epileptiform Attack – Three Years' Duration – Operation – Cure

G.M., single; admitted into the 'London Surgical Home' 18 December 1860.

History. For the last nine years has suffered greatly and regularly during the menstrual periods. Has been much worse for the last three years, during which time has, at each menstrual period, been frequently taken in a fit, dropping down suddenly and fainting right off; this state lasting for two or three hours. Being in service, this has caused her much trouble, as none of her employers would keep her. For the last six months has suffered severe pain over right ovary, increased by exercise or pressure, and at the menstrual period. Believing that the dysmenorrhea and fits both arose from the same cause, on 3 January the clitoris was cut down to the base. After this operation she never had a fit, and all untoward symptoms left her except the dysmenorrhea; she was therefore re-admitted 27 May 1861, and there being some narrowing of the cervix, it was incised with the hysterotome. 21 June, catamenia came on without pain, and continued to do so regularly. In July she was well enough to return to service.

April 1865. Her mother called at my house to say that this patient had been married some months, and was shortly expecting her confinement. She had remained quite well since the operation.

Case IV Epileptiform Fits and General Hysteria – Four Years' Duration – Operation – Cure

Mrs F., age 44; admitted to the 'London Surgical Home' 23 April 1864.

History. Married sixteen years, but her husband has been abroad for the past seven years. Had inflammation of the womb four years ago, and since that time has continually suffered from bearing-down pains. Frequent desire to micturate. Pain in the loins and spine, sleepless nights, loss of appetite, and other hysterical symptoms. Has slight 'epileptic fits' two or three times a week, more frequently at catamenial periods, which are regular in appearance and not profuse. Has no premonition of fits; is but partially conscious; at first struggles, then becomes rather rigid, and on recovery is always exhausted. Patient is most anxious to be cured of her attacks, of the cause of which she is fully conscious.

25 April. Clitoris excised, under chloroform. 26 April. Had a good night, better than for years. 30 April. Progressing most favourably. Patient expresses great gratitude for the relief she has obtained. She left the 'Home' a month later, looking and feeling quite well; the last note in the case-book being 'a very grateful patient'.

Case V Cataleptic Fits – Six Years' Duration – Operation – Cure

Miss –, age 38, single; admitted into the 'London Surgical Home' 10 August 1865.

History. Was tolerably well until two years and a half ago, but since that time has suffered more or less from menorrhagia, with severe pain in back. Has also severe smarting pain in the bowels, and has frequently lost a considerable quantity of blood *per anum*. Has always been subject to hysterical attacks, but for the last six years has had fits of a much more serious character. They have increased in severity, duration, and frequency, and it is on account of them that she seeks relief. Almost immediately after admission, this patient had a fit, and she was kept a fortnight under observation, that the nature of the attacks might be thoroughly investigated.

She would have a fit sometimes twice a day; but on an average about every other day, either early in the morning or late in the evening. She was most generally attacked when walking about the room, sometimes when sitting; but she was never observed to have one when asleep. She would at the commencement of an attack cease walking, or doing whatever she was employed in; her face would become very pale and set; the eyelids, at first quivering, would be fixed; the eyes wide open and looking upwards, the pupils very dilated. Her mouth would be rigidly shut, and during the attack it was impossible by any means to open it. Her arms would fall straight by her side, and be immovable; the hands unclenched, and fingers extended. If standing, she would be quite upright, and require no support. If sitting, she would always stand up when a fit was coming on. If lying, she would be extended straight on her back. The fit would last for two or three hours, and on a few occasions for as many as six hours. The experiment was frequently made of moving her arms when in the cataleptic state, and on such occasions the limb would remain in the position in which it was placed till the end of the attack. She was always perfectly unconscious, and no kind of stimulant was of the slightest use in restoring her during the paroxysm – time alone was of avail. The attack was sudden, but the recovery to consciousness was but gradual; she would appear as if awoke from a deep sleep, and would be very exhausted, but express no desire for food, wine, or other stimulants. As soon as she recovered, she would sleep for many hours, and awake quite well, but still weak. 14 August. The clitoris was excised, and a painful fissure of the rectum divided. She never had a fit after the operation. Menstruation came on, on the 28th, in moderate flow. 5 October. This patient has improved wonderfully since operation, and now looks extremely well. The wound is quite healed. She takes walks daily, and has had no fits, and is to be discharged as cured. In November she called at the 'Home' to say that she was quite well, and had never had the slightest return of her former illness; she menstruates regularly and normally. February 1866. She remains well.

Case VI Epileptic Fits – Twelve Years' Duration – Operation – Cure

S.F., age 41, single; admitted into the 'London Surgical Home' 16 Dec. 1861.

History. Was always ailing and hysterical for many years. Catamenia appeared early, and always rather profuse. For the last twelve years has suffered from epileptic fits; recurring frequently every week or fortnight, and lately as often as every day. Has constant headaches; is losing memory and all power of concentrating her ideas. Has no premonition of seizure; falls down; is unconscious; has frequently bitten her tongue, and 'froths' at the mouth. Says she has had several attacks of hæmatemesis. She was a dressmaker, and had so frequently, on her way to or from business, fallen in the streets, that she had been carried into almost every hospital in London, and a large number of open surgeries.

On examination, there was found every indication of irritation about the vulva, and also a small polypus of the os uteri, which latter was large and patulous.

19 Dec. Excised the clitoris; polypus uteri also removed.

The recovery of this patient was rapid and uninterrupted. After the operation, she never had a fit, and hardly a headache. She was discharged 20 Jan. 1862, perfectly well, and with greatly increased mental power. At the present time (1866) she still remains perfectly well, and she lately appeared in the operating-room of the London Surgical Home, to satisfy gentlemen present of the permanency of her cure.

Case VII Epileptic Fits – Many Years' Duration – Operation – Cure

N.L.M., age 21; admitted into the 'London Surgical Home' 9 May 1863.

History. Married four years, and had two children; the labours have been bad, and followed by severe hæmorrhage. Had aborted at six weeks, a fortnight previous to admission, and had lost a large quantity of blood. First suffered from epileptic fits at puberty; had several before marriage, and has had four or five since marriage; but has never had a fit when pregnant. Not very regular in menstruation, which is accompanied with severe pain. Has constant pain on right side of head, in back, loins, etc. Great pain in micturating and on defecation. She is always totally unconscious during the fits, and they are followed by extreme prostration. Is of melancholy aspect, excessively anæmic, and somewhat chlorotic; even the mucous membranes (of mouth especially) are blanched. The cause of her fits being diagnosed, the usual operation was performed 14 May.

18 May. Progressing excellently. 20 May. There was great irritability of the bladder, which, however, was immediately relieved by an alkaline and henbane mixture. 31 May. Has not had any return of her bad symptoms until today, when, on being removed to a strange ward, she had a fit, not of violent character, and followed by a heavy drowsiness. 2 June. Is quite herself again. 4 July. Has left quite well in every respect, and when heard of many months later, remained well.

Remarks. The fit following on change of this patient from one ward to another, where there were strangers, shows how important it is for a permanent cure, that visitors and relatives should not be allowed to excite and agitate a patient suffering from these attacks, after an operation is performed, and when the mind is hardly restored to its natural balance.

Case VIII Epilepsy, with Dementia – One Years' Duration – Operation – Cure

A.H., age 17; admitted into the 'London Surgical Home' 28 June 1865.

History. Catamenia first appeared three years ago. They have continued regular to the present time. About twelve months since it was observed, whenever sent on an errand from home, that she would wander about in an absent manner, and return home having forgotten about any message which had been given her. About this time fits were first developed; they increased in frequency and intensity, and she now has them daily, and one or more of less violent character nearly every night in her sleep. When seized, she falls, struggles violently, foams at the mouth, often bites her tongue, and is totally unconscious to all around her. After a fit she sinks into a deep sleep, which lasts for two hours. Has no recollection on awaking of what has taken place. Acknowledges to frequent injurious habits, but is unconscious of their being the cause of her illness. Is vague in all her ideas and conversation, and has almost entirely lost her memory.

Both history and personal examination plainly showed what was the cause of her attacks. On 7 July, the clitoris was completely excised. She had no return of the fits; and on the 23rd the following report appears in the case-book: 'Left her bed today. Is greatly changed; quite rational in all her movements; converses freely and quietly, remembers passing events from day to day, and it is indeed almost impossible to recognise in her the half-idiotic, almost demented girl who entered the "Home" less than a month ago.' She remained in the 'Home' some time longer for observation. Fits never returned: her mind improved daily, and she was discharged as perfectly cured.

Case IX Acute Hysterical Mania – Four Months' Duration – Operation – Cure

Miss –, age 23, was sent to me by Mr Radcliffe, stating that she had been brought over from Ireland as an insane patient, and that everything had been settled for her admission to some asylum, when he was induced to consult me on the last day before her entering one. He stated that the paroxysms always came on at half-past five or six every evening. I replied, if the attacks depended on peripheral irritation, that an operation would at once prevent recurrence of the attacks. She was accordingly admitted into the 'London Surgical Home' 6 Feb. 1864.

When admitted, said she had taken no food for three days, and asked for a cup of tea, which was given her. Enema was also administered. 3.45 p.m. Was seized with a fit, throwing her arms up over her head, and then appearing as if comatose. In about twenty minutes revived; the lips began to quiver, and she gradually became conscious, saying, 'I want a knife – I want blood!' She asked for the matron's hand, that she might bite it off. (The fit coming on earlier on this day was doubtless due to excitement consequent on her removal.) 5 p.m. Mr Baker Brown saw her; as soon as he came near her, she seized his shoulder with great violence; was wild, and would not answer questions; but gradually became soothed, and allowed an examination.

Externally, the abdomen showed signs of a child having been born, and the mammæ had certainly contained milk. The clitoris was enlarged and hard; the nymphæ long and flabby; the mucous membrane roughened and discoloured. Per vaginam, the uterus was found to be retroverted; there was also a fissure of the rectum.

Operation, 5.30 p.m. Was very violent under the first attempts to administer chloroform. She was long in being brought under its influence, but when once thoroughly anæsthetised, bore it exceedingly well. The clitoris was excised, the elongated nymphæ removed, and the fissure of the rectum divided. The wounds were dressed in the usual manner, and the patient, having had two grains of opium administered, was ordered to be constantly watched. In twenty minutes awoke from the chloroform. Was calm, and slept at intervals during the night. 7 Feb., 10 a.m. Visited by Mr B. Brown. Present Mr I. B. Brown, junior, House Surgeon, and

Matron. Pulse quick but steady; tongue brown and furred; breath offensive; gums spongy; pupil natural; countenance rather flushed; skin moist and warm.

The following answers were given to questions asked of her by Mr Brown, seventeen hours after operation, and are in her own words: much, however, of the information was volunteered without questions:

> 'Last March, instead of sliding down a slope, I jumped. This caused displacement of my womb. I suffered great agonies. I was fomented with hot water. I thought it was my back that was hurt. Since then I have been subject to fainting and weakness. I suffer great irritation about my private parts – cannot keep my hands away. The irritation is worse at night. I am obliged to relieve the irritation by rubbing – sometimes for two or three minutes at a time. There is always a discharge. I feel very depressed afterwards. At times I have lost my brain, and felt as if I did not care for living. I would like to have my hands untied: I will be very quiet. Have been separated from my relatives for three years. I shan't tell you how long I have been married – (a pause). I am very rude – I beg your pardon. I have been married three years. I had a baby two years ago: it was not born at the full time – I think five months. I don't know whether it was alive. I left home with my friend when I was 16 (?). It is two years since I left him. I am now 23.'

'After the accident, suffered great pain.' Mr Brown here looked at her gums, and she immediately said:

> 'Oh, yes; I had mercury given me by Surgeon – , in Dublin; he said it was my spine. He did not examine my womb. Dr – examined it, and said there was great displacement. I have been better for treatment at times. My brain has been affected. I have fought very much. I have wanted a child's blood. I have had it sometimes by sucking the wounds of a child. When in a fit, I don't know what is going on around, or what is being said, but I recognise people's voices. I am not regular. Was kept in bed last September for six weeks for flooding; was so for ten days after I was put in bed. Was the same in Paris last year. I was studying in Paris to fit myself for a governess.'

The following are extracts from a letter voluntarily sent to Mr Brown by a lady with whom the patient lived for many months, and left only three weeks previous to admission. Having stated that for some time she was hysterical, and becoming daily more excitable, the letter says:

> On the 13th of September last, she for the first time seemed delirious when going to bed. This was mentioned next morning to Surgeon – who declared it to be nervous irritability of the spine. . . . On the 27th, Dr – was called in, and at once gave his opinion that there was ailment of the womb. He then ordered small blisters on the lower part of the stomach which in less than ten hours relieved her, and removed the mania. She had not any reason for *many* days previous, and was sinking. . . . On the 3rd of October, Dr – fixed an instrument to support the womb; and, except during the time when the intensity of pain caused it, there was no delirium; for a few days she got claret, which seemed to excite her greatly, so it was discontinued; but on the 13th of October I was desired to give her port wine in abundance. She was excessively weak, and mania so dreadful, that she made several attempts to injure herself and me. She got as many as eight large glasses of best port on some days; strong beef-tea, chicken soup, and all the nourishment possible. It was not only suggested, but it was advised to remove her to a lunatic asylum; however, feeling that certainly nine-tenths of her time she was perfectly sane, and could know well where she was and with whom, I did not like the idea of placing so young a creature in an asylum. I kept her here, and watched her day and night; she never was left alone for one moment for three months. . . . I ought to mention that the order for abundance of wine, etc, was from the opinion that 'want of blood to the brain' caused the mania; and that the intense inflammation of all internal organs was relieved by blisters on the lower part of the stomach, and by mercury.

8 February. Lint removed from rectum, and wounds dressed. Is calm and rational; passed a quiet day. 10 February. Very restless; obliged to restrain hands and legs. 11 February. Better; says her head feels heavy; countenance cheerful; manner quiet and rational. 12 February. Very excited and irritable; constantly managing to free her hands; will allow no one near her. 2 p.m. Is quite maniacal; has managed to irritate the wounds, and also the mammæ. To have one grain of opium in pill, and ten grains of bromide of ammonium three times a day. 13 February, 6 a.m. Hands again free; repeat opium. Slept afterwards till 4 p.m., when she awoke calm and rational. 9 p.m. Slept again. 14 February. Very restless, and at times violent. Bandages removed and jacket substituted. 15

February. Much better; rational, and conversing cheerfully. 16 February. Improving. 17 February. At her urgent request, hands were freed, but shortly after she became excited. 19 February. More sensible; had today symptoms of a severe bilious attack, which upset her for some days. 24 February. Much better; allowed to see her sister – the first time since the operation. 1 March. Much improved; has written to her sister, and amused herself knitting and reading during the day. 2 March. Allowed to dress; seemed to enjoy the change, and is very cheerful. 4 March. Visited by her sister; has been quietly cheerful all day. Is certainly improving wonderfully. 20 March. Took a walk, and enjoyed it. 25 March. Spent the day away from the 'Home' with her sister; returning looking quite well, and all the better for the change. 2 April. Discharged quite cured. This patient remained perfectly well, and I hear has since been legally married.

William Acton

from

Prostitution Considered in its Social and Sanitary Aspects

(1870)

I may further observe that prostitution is at once a result produced by and a cause producing immorality. Every unchaste woman is not a prostitute. By unchastity a woman becomes liable to lose character, position, and the means of living; and when these are lost is too often reduced to prostitution for support, which, therefore, may be described as the trade adopted by all women who have abandoned or are precluded from an honest course of life, or who lack the power or the inclination to obtain a livelihood from other sources. What is a prostitute! She is a woman who gives for money that which she ought to give only for love; who ministers to passion and lust alone, to the exclusion and extinction of all the higher qualities, and nobler sources of enjoyment which combine with desire, to produce the happiness derived from the intercourse of the sexes. She is a woman with half the woman gone, and that half containing all that elevates her nature, leaving her a mere instrument of impurity; degraded and fallen she extracts from the sin of others the means of living, corrupt and dependent on corruption, and therefore interested directly in the increase of immorality – a social pest, carrying contamination and foulness to every quarter to which she has access, who

> like a disease,
> Creeps, no precaution used, among the crowd,
> Makes wicked lightnings of her eyes,
> . . . and stirs the pulse,
> With devil's leaps, and poisons half the young.

Such women, ministers of evil passions, not only gratify desire, but also arouse it. Compelled by necessity to seek for customers, they throng our streets and public places, and suggest evil thoughts and desires which might otherwise remain undeveloped. Confirmed prodigates will seek out the means of gratifying their desires; the young from a craving to discover unknown mysteries may approach the haunts of sin, but thousands would remain uncontaminated if temptation did not seek them out. Prostitutes have the power of soliciting and tempting. Gunpowder remains harmless till the spark falls upon it; the match until struck, retains the hidden fire, so lust remains dormant till called into being by an exciting cause.

The sexual passion is strong in every man, but it is strong in proportion as it is encouraged or restrained; and every act of indulgence only makes future abstinence more hard, and in time almost impossible. Some consider that prostitution is the safety valve of society, and that any serious diminution of the number of prostitutes would be attended with an increase of clandestine immodesty. Such a consequence is not one that I think need be apprehended; the insinuation that virtuous women, to be made to yield, require only to be assaulted, is a base and unworthy calumny; nor is it to be supposed that the man who will use a harlot is prepared to insult or injure a modest woman. But intercourse with depraved women debases the mind, and gradually hardens the heart, and each act of gratification stimulates desire and necessitates fresh indulgence; and when grown into a habit, not only breeds distaste for virtuous society, but causes the mind to form a degraded estimate of the sex, until all women seem mere objects of desire and vehicles of indulgence. The prostitute is a sad burlesque of woman, presenting herself as an object of lust instead of an object of honourable love – a source of base gratification, instead of a reason for self-restraint; familiarising man with this aspect of women till he can see no other, and his indulged body and debased mind lead him to seek in them only sensual gratification, and to make, if possible, of every woman the thing that he desires – a toy, a plaything, an animated doll; a thing to wear like a glove, and fling away; to use like a horse, and send to the knackers when worn out; the mere object of his fancy and servant of his appetite, instead of an immortal being, composed, like himself, of body, soul and spirit – his associate and consort, endowed with memory and hope and strong affections, with a heart to love, to feed, to suffer; man's highest prize and surest safeguard; the inspirer of honest love and manly exertion, powerful

> Not only to keep down the base in man,
> But teach high thought and amiable words,

And courtliness, and the desire of fame,
And love of truth, and all that makes a man.

It thus appears that prostitution depends not only on demand and supply, and external causes, but is itself a cause of its own existence, because the possibility of indulgence weakens the force of self-restraint, by creating the idea in the mind of unlawfully and basely gratifying the natural instinct, to which indulgence adds force and intensity, and thus in a measure creates the want, producing from a desire capable of restraints a habit impossible to shake off; while the supply being active, and itself desiring exercise, does not wait for the demand, but goes about to seek it, suggesting, arousing, stimulating evil thoughts and unhallowed passions.

I may now consider more in detail the different causes of prostitution to which I have alluded above. They may, I think, be divided into Primary or Universal, and Secondary or Special. The Primary, comprising mainly the natural instinct, the sinful nature, to which may be added idleness, vanity, and love of pleasure; the Secondary, comprising the remainder of the causes already referred to, may be conveniently grouped under the headings – Artificial, Local, Individual. The existence of the natural instinct I have already referred to as necessarily and inseparably accompanying the divine command, 'Be fruitful, and multiply and replenish the earth.' This is the law of our being, and our instincts accord with the law. It is impossible, therefore, that the sexual passion can ever die out, nor is it to be desired that it should; so long as it continues, however, prostitution is at least possible.

Conceding freely that comparative immunity from disease is secured by the brothel system, to the women who inhabit and the men who frequent such establishments, the question remains whether this freedom from disease is not too dearly purchased? Is it worth while to sacrifice to the pursuit of health every religious and moral consideration? I think not, and I believe that my readers will for the most part agree in this conclusion, especially when it is considered that by a judicious arrangement of health districts, all the prostitutes in the country may be made subject to supervision and the spread of disease infinitely reduced. It is as much my object to raise the fallen as to prevent their injuring society; and I cannot too often repeat that the surest way of completing a woman's degradation, and rendering her reform impossible, is to confine her to the vile companionship and hopeless servitude of a brothel.

Having, in the chapter on 'Causes of Prostitution', referred to the vice bred like filth, from the miserable herding of the lower orders, it becomes me also to number the improvement of their dwellings among preventive measures. The passing of the Common Lodging-house Act of 1851, rendering compulsory the registration of such houses and the compliance of their keepers with certain regulations demanded by decency and cleanliness, was a step in the right direction; and the results thereby obtained are satisfactory as showing how much has been done – painful as showing what is still to do.

It is clear that the whole number have not yet been brought under supervision. This must be a work of time, but enough good has resulted hitherto to encourage us to proceed in what is obviously the way of right.

A step above these common lodging-houses are the so-called private dwellings, where each chamber is let to a separate family. These are subject by law to none but health inspections; but their occupants being generally of a class to whom all decency within their means is as grateful as to the wealthiest, the promiscuous crowding is a source of pain to them that the public would farther its own interest by helping to alleviate. None can feel more acutely than the working classes of all grades the great difficulty of procurring wholesome dwellings near the seat of their labour. Many men live miles away from their work, in order to preserve their growing families from the moral and physical contamination of the crowded courts and alleys, in which only they could find lodgings within their means. The State by itself, or by energetically putting the screw of compulsion upon the municipalities, who are slow to avail themselves of permissive enactments, to love their neighbours as themselves, should hold out a helping hand to the working million, who are, for want of dwellings adapted to their use, drifting to and from among the wretched London 'tenements', or reduced to harbour in the common lodging-house.

This packing of the lower classes is clearly not yet under control, and seems liable to aggravation by every new thoroughfare and airway with which we pierce our denser neighbourhoods. While it prevails, who can impute the defilement of girls, the demoralisation of both sexes, as blame to the hapless parent who does the best he can with his little funds, and procures the only accommodation in the market open to him? It is preposterous, as I have before hinted, to attribute the prostitution so engendered to seduction, or to vicious inclinations of the woman. From that indifference to modesty, which is perforce the sequel of promiscuous herding, it is a short step to illicit commerce; and this once established, the reserve or publicity of the female is entirely a matter of chance.

Among the preventives that we ought to consider before attempting the *cure* of prostitution, should be numbered an altered and improved system of female training. Some remarks on this point published in *The Times* many years ago, are still extremely pertinent:

> When we examine our system of training for girls of the poorer class, we see one very important defect immediately in it, and that is, that they receive no instruction in household work. Girls are taught sewing in our parish schools, and very properly, because, even with a view to domestic service, sewing is an important accomplishment; but they are not taught anything about household work. We do not say that a parish school could teach this, for household work can only be really learnt *in* a house; the schoolroom can provide napkins and towels, but it cannot supply tables, chairs, mantelpieces, and carpets for rubbing and brushing; and, the material to work upon being wanting, the art cannot be taught. But this is only explaining the fact, and not altering it. Household work is not learnt, and what is the consequence? The department of domestic service in this country is hardly at this moment sufficiently supplied, while crowds of girls enter into the department of needlework in one or other of its branches, and of course overstock it enormously. Add to this a sort of foolish pride that poor people have in the apparent rise which is gained in rank by this profession – for, of course, every one of these girls is ultimately to be a 'milliner,' which has for them rather a grand sound. The metropolis, sooner or later, receives this vast overplus of the sewing female population, and the immense milliners' and tailors' and shirtmakers' establishments hardly absorb the overflowing supply of female labour and skill, while, of course, they profit to the very utmost by the glut of the labour-market. A vast multitude of half-starving women is the result of the system; whereas, had household work formed a part of their instruction, besides a better supply of the home field of service, what is of much more consequence, the colonies would take a large part of this overplus off our hands.
>
> What is the natural remedy, then, for this defect in the training of girls of the poorer classes in this country? The remedy is, of course, that they should be taught, in some way or other, household work. At present, in the absence of any such instruction as this, it must be admitted that,

however incidentally, the sewing which is taught in all our parish schools is simply aiding the overflowing tide of needle labour, which is every year taking up such multitudes of young women to the metropolis, and exposing them to the dreadful temptations of an underpaid service. And how is household-work to be taught? Well, that is, of course, the difficulty. There are, as we have said, great difficulties in the way of our parish schools taking it up. The experiment, however, has been tried, in different places, of special institutions for this object; and, in the absence of any formal and public institutions, the houses of our gentry and clergy might be made to supply such instruction to a considerable extent, and without any inordinate demand on private charity. Extra labour, as every householder knows, is often wanted in every domestic establishment; it is even wanted periodically and at regular intervals in a large proportion of our good houses. It would be of great service to the country if a practice, which is already partially adopted, were more common and general – that of taking parish girls by turns for these special occasions. This might be done, at any rate in the country, to a large extent, and even a few days' employment of this kind in a well-furnished house, occurring at more or less regular intervals would be often enough to create a taste and a capacity for household work. The profession of household service might thus be indefinitely widened, and a large class be created that would naturally look to such service as its distinct employment, and be ready, in case of disappointment at home, to seek it in the colonies.

(*The Times*, 6 MAY 1857)

I shudder as I read each jubilant announcement of 'another new channel for female labour'. Each lecture, pamphlet, and handbill, that calls attention to some new field of competition, seems to me but the knell of hundreds whose diversion by capital from their natural functions to its own uses, is a curse to both sexes and an hindrance of the purposes of our Creator. No more impious *coup d'état* of Mammon could be devised than that grinding down against one another of the sexes intended by their Maker for mutual support and comfort.

Free-trade in female honour follows hard upon that in female labour; the wages of working men, wherever they compete with female labour, are lowered by the flood of cheap and agile hands, until marriage and a family are an almost impossible luxury or a misery. The earnings of man's unfortunate competitor are in their turn driven down by machinery until inadequate to support her life. The economist, as he turns the screw of torture, points complacently to this farther illustration of the law of trade; the moralist pointing out how inexorable is the command to labour, too seldom and too late arrests the torture. He only cries enough when the famished worker, wearied of the useless struggle against capital, too honest yet to steal, too proud yet to put up useless prayers for nominal relief at the hands of the community, and having sold even the last but one of her possessions, takes virtue itself to market. 'And thus,' as Parent-Duchâtelet says, 'prostitution exists, and will ever exist, in all great towns, because, like mendicancy and gambling, it is an industry and a resource against hunger, one may even say against dishonour. For, to what excess may not an individual be driven, cut off from all resources, her very existence compromised? This last alternative, it is true, is degrading, but it nevertheless exists.'

But if the national education of women is not to be confined to reading, writing, and needlework, what are we to do with them? The ready answer is – TEACH THEM HOUSEWIFERY; and the rejoinder, how and where, may well met by the sensible and practical suggestion in the newspaper article above quoted, 'that household education should be incorporated to a much greater extent than at present, with the discipline of union houses and schools'.

The parochial clergy and well disposed gentry of the country have ample opportunities, if they would embrace them, of diverting to household pursuits the crowds of young women who annually jostle one another into the ranks of needle-work. The hall, the parsonage, and the parish school would be the best of normal schools for cooking, scrubbing, washing, ironing, and the like. Their owners would gladly, I fancy, impart gratuitous instruction in exchange for gratuitious service, and every housekeeper will bear me out in saying that the knowledge of the business once acquired, the market for properly qualified domestic servants is ample and not half supplied, while that for every description of needlework has long been overstocked. The vanity of girls and mothers must, it is true, be overcome, but the greater economy of the proposed domestic education would go some way to carry the day in its favour; and if a true appreciation of the happiness that wants on colonisation, and of the essentials to its success, were once to get well abroad among our people, their mother wit would lead them soon enough to grasp the comparative value, of the domestic and needlework systems of training.

Prostitution, though it can not be directly repressed, may yet be acted upon in many ways, and in proportion as the social system is wisely administered will its virulence be abated. We cannot put it down, but we can act indirectly on both the supply and demand. A judicious system of emigration will direct into healthy channels the energy that in overpeopled countries finds an outlet in riot, wickedness, and crime. Still, in advocating emigration as helping to prevent the spread of prostitution, I am far from advising that single women should be sent to the colonies alone and unprotected.

Contagious Diseases Act

However much it may be the duty of the State to leave for settlement to the individual conscience all questions of morals and religion, it can hardly be seriously contended that it is right to abandon to the care of the improvident and profligate the restraining of contagious maladies, yet this, except in a few military and naval stations, is virtually the case in England. A woman who knows herself to be diseased, is free to invite all comers to the enjoyment of her person, and to spread among them deadly contagion. The total of venereal beds is, as we have seen, in St Bartholomew's, 75; in Guy's, 58; in Middlesex, 20; in the Royal Free; 26; in the Lock, exclusive of those required by Government, 30. Thus, although, the population of London numbers over 3,000,000, there are only 209 beds given up to females labouring under venereal affections, if we deduct the 120 beds at the Lock Hospital devoted to the Government patients sent there from Woolwich, Aldershot, and other garrison towns.

These figures speak for themselves, and when we remember the deadly character of the disease with which we have to contend, the strong temptations that lead to its contraction, and the vast numbers who yield to that temptation and compare them with the means at our disposal for supplying an antidote to the poison, we may well marvel at the indifference of society and the supineness of Government. But if we can ill excuse the laws, which afford no protection to those who, after all, are comparatively free agents, what shall we say of them, if we find them placing thousands of men every year in the utmost jeopardy, compelling them almost for the convenience of the State, to have recourse to the prostitution by which they are surrounded, and yet providing for them no means of safety or adequate relief? It is hardly credible that, until a few years ago, this was the case in England. At length in 1864 the injury inflicted by this apathy on our soldiers and sailors, and the loss sustained by the public purse, seem to have touched the conscience or the cupidity of the legislature, and in that year an act was passed, the 27 & 28 Vic. c. 85, having for its object the remedy of the evils to which the army and navy are exposed; its provisions, however, proved totally inadequate to meet the requirements of the case, and it was followed in 1866 by a more comprehensive measure, the 28 & 29 Vic. c. 35, commonly called the Contagious Diseases Act.

This act now extends its operation to Canterbury, Dover, Gravesend, Maidstone, Southampton, Winchester, Portsmouth, Plymouth and Devonport, Woolwich, Chatham, Sheerness, Aldershot, Windsor, Colchester, Shorncliffe, the Curragh, Cork, and Queenstown. By the 15th and 16th sections, a justice of the peace, on information being laid before him that a woman, living in any place to which the act extends, is a common prostitute, and on oath before him substantiating such information, may, if he thinks fit, order that the woman be subject to a periodical medical examination by the visiting surgeon appointed under the provisions of the act, for any period not exceeding one year, for the purpose of ascertaining at each such examination whether she is affected with a contagious disease; and thereupon she shall be subject to such a periodical medical examination, and the order shall be a sufficient warrant for the visiting surgeon to conduct such examination accordingly; and by the 17th section any woman, in any place to which the act applies, may, by a submission signed by her, in the presence of, and attested by the superintendent of police, subject herself to a periodical examination under this act for any period not exceeding one year. Any woman found on examination to be diseased, may either go herself, or will be apprehended and sent, to some hospital certified for the reception and detention of government patients. The reception of a woman in a certified hospital by the managers or persons having the management or control thereof shall be deemed to be an undertaking by them to provide for her care, treatment, lodging, clothing and food during her detention in hospital. This period of detention is limited to three months, or, on the certificate prescribed by the act that further detention is necessary, to a further period of six months, making nine months in the whole. If a woman considers herself detained in hospital too long, she may apply to a justice for an order of discharge. Prostitutes refusing to conform to the provisions of this act are liable to be punished by imprisonment and any one permitting a woman who to his knowledge is suffering from a contagious disease, to use his house for the purpose of prostitution shall, in addition to the other consequences to which he may be liable for keeping a disorderly house, be liable to six months imprisonment with or without hard labour. The appointment of the necessary surgeons, inspectors of hospitals, and other officers, is intrusted to the Admiralty and War Offices, by whom also hospitals may be provided and certified for use and all expenses incurred in the execution of the act must be defrayed. The carrying out of the act in the minor details is of course intrusted to the police. It is also provided that adequate provision must be made by the several hospitals for the moral and religious instruction of the women detained in them under this act. We have aready seen that a considerable number of beds have been secured at the Lock Hospital for the use of Government patients. The most admirable arrangements have been adopted at this institution for the examination and treatment of the patients committed to its care, and as the possibility of carrying out an act having for its object the diminution of disease forms an important element in considering the advisability of further extending its sphere of usefulness, I shall offer no apology for relating pretty fully the method pursued in this institution.

Lock Hospital

I was anxious to see the working of the existing Government Lock Hospital, and Mr J. Lane kindly allowed me to accompany him, and explained everything on my visit in October 1868.

The patients (female) are lodged in a new wing; the wards are lofty, and kept scrupulously clean. Each inmate has a separate bed, provided with three blankets, and a hair mattress, an extra blanket being given in winter. Each patient has two pannikins, a half-pint and a pint tin can, with a pewter spoon and a steel knife and fork, and a little box in which she may keep her things, is placed near her bed. The patients are not allowed to go into other wards, but there is an open court in which they take exercise, and they have a sort of hospital dress in place of their own clothes, which are left under the care of the matron. At the head of the bed hangs a towel.

In a little room at the end of the ward water is laid on, and copper basins are hung by a chain to the wall; these basins are kept for the women to wash their faces. This arrangement is specially made to prevent any possible contagion. Fixed to the floor is a bidet, across which the female sits. There is here an admirable device for facilitating the cleansing of the private parts; by which means, a brass syringe, with a long pewter ball, and holding, say six ounces, she injects the lotion, and the waste fluid runs away on opening a plug fixed in the bottom of the bidet. The only improvement I could suggest was that each patient be furnished with two small napkins to dry the organs for injection. The patient always uses an injection before presenting herself to the surgeon, in order that the organs may be in a proper condition for examination, and I must say the cleanliness shown does great credit to the nurses who manage the wards.

The inspections are conducted in the following manner: The women introduced one at a time from the wards by one nurse into a special room containing a properly-raised bed, with feet, similar to the one in use on the Continent. The patient ascends the steps placed by the side of the bed, lays down, places her feet in the slippers arranged for the purpose, and the house surgeon separates the labia to see if there are any sores. If no suspicion of these exists, and if the female is suffering from discharge, the speculum is at once employed. In this institution several sizes are used, and they are silvered and covered with india-rubber. The head nurse after each examination washes the speculum in a solution of permanganate of potash, then wipes it carefully, oils it ready for the next examination, so that the surgeon loses no time, and the examinations are conducted with great rapidity. In the course of one hour and three-quarters I assisted in the thorough examination of fifty-eight women with the speculum.

In this institution the house surgeon examines the women; the surgeon superintending and prescribing the remedies.

Mr J. Lane, in a recent paper, has so well described the method of treatment adopted by him, that I shall give an account of it in his own words:

> Since the admission of patients into this hospital, under the Contagions Diseases Act, from Woolwich and other military districts, the treatment of uterine and vaginal discharges has constituted a large part of its practice. In fact, in 1867, as many as 58 per cent; and in 1868, 65 per cent of the class of patients alluded to, were placed under treatment for this form of disease alone, uncomplicated by any symptom of a syphilitic character, either primary or secondary. These patients are, for the most part, strong, healthy girls, aged from 17 to 25, well fed, and in good condition. Their disease appears to be entirely local, both in its origin and character. It arises, as I believe, in the great majority of cases, simply from the continual irritation and excitement of the generative organs consequent upon their mode of life, though it may be caused, no doubt, occasionally by direct contagion from

urethral discharges in the male. The secretion, when they first come under observation, is of an obviously purulent or muco-purulent character, and evidence of its contagiousness is afforded by the fact (as I am informed) that nearly all of them have been accused of communicating disease before being subjected to examination. It is remarkable how little pain or inconvenience is suffered by these patients; usually they make no complaint whatever, and many of them are unaware that any thing whatever is the matter with them, although, when examined with the speculum, a profuse discharge, derived chiefly from the uterus, is found lodged in the upper part of the vagina. Associated with this, especially in the more chronic cases, abrasions of the epithelium, excoriations, or superficial ulcerations on the vaginal portion of the cervix uteri are very frequently seen. Anything approaching to an inflammatory condition, to which the terms acute gonorrhoea or vaginitis might be applied, is uncommon, and when met with, it is usually in young girls, as yet unseasoned to a life of prostitition. Incidental complications, of a painful character, such as labial abscess, or inflamatory bubo, are occasionally seen, but are not of frequent occurrence.

An external examination alone is quite insufficient for the discovery of these complaints. Purulent secretions from the vulva or lower part of the vagina are, of course, evident enough; but a profuse uterine discharge may be present, and no trace of it be visible until the speculum is employed. There is, however, a considerable difference in women in this respect; in some, the vagina appears to be equally contractile throughout its whole length, and therefore, any secretion formed in it, or entering it, speedily appears externally; while in others, and these are the majority, its contractility is much less at the upper than at the lower part, and discharges are consequently retained in the former situation.

When these discharges are of purely local origin, and there is no constitutional fault, their cure may be speedily effected by local applications. The plan commonly pursued at the Lock Hospital is to make the patients use vaginal injections for themselves three or four times daily. The lotions employed are the diluted liquor plumbi subacetatis, or solutions of sulphate of zinc, alum, or tannin, in the proportion of five grains to the ounce of water. The syringes are large enough to hold six ounces of the lotion, and have a pipe long enough to reach the upper part of the vagina readily. Both these points are important, for the syringes commonly used will not contain sufficient fluid to wash out the canal effectually, and the pipe affixed to them will not admit of its reaching the upper part of the vagina at all. When the vaginal mucous membrane is inflamed and tender, the house-surgeon, when the speculum is used, which is at least twice a week in all these cases, inserts a strip of lint dipped in the lead-lotion, and this is allowed to remain for three or four hours. If the inflamation be acute, the application of the strip of lint is repeated daily through a small speculum. By these means, discharges proceeding from the vagina may usually be cured in a few days, but the injections should be continued as long as any abnormal uterine secretions are observed, for the latter, if not frequently washed away, will be likely to re-excite disease in the vaginal mucous membrane.

But vaginal injections are of little or no use for the care of discharges proceeding from the interior of the cervix uteri – a complication which is almost invariably present in these cases. In the treatment of this condition, success will depend mainly on the amount of personal care and attention afforded by the surgeon himself. At the Lock Hospital, the speculum is used twice a week in all, and three times a week in many of these cases; and through it suitable applications are made to the os and cervix. The nitrate of silver, either solid or in solution, is the remedy most in favour, especially in the earlier stages of the treatment, and when the discharge is purulent; later, simple astringents, such as tannin, alum, or perchloride of iron, are employed. Before using the caustic, all discharge should be wiped away from the os uteri with a piece of dry cotton-wool; and the plug of tenacious matter, which usually fills the cervix, should also be removed, or it will prevent the remedy reaching the diseased surface. The application of a strong solution of alum coagulates this discharge, and renders its removal more easy. The stick of nitrate of silver is then inserted to the depth of about an inch into the canal of the cervix, and is also applied to any abraded or ulcerated surface which may be seen around the os; or, instead of the stick, a solution of the nitrate (a drachm to an ounce of water) may be applied by means of a piece of sponge or cotton wool about the size of a pea, which is passed along the cervical canal with a suitable pair of forceps. I prefer to use the solid nitrate on the first one or two occasions, and afterwards the solution. By these means, the discharge speedily loses its yellow colour, and becomes white or semi-transparent. When this result is obtained, a stringent solution, such as the milder Liquor Ferri Perchloridi of the *British Pharmacopeia*, or solutions of alum or tannin (a drachm to an ounce of water), may be substituted with advantage for the nitrate of silver. The glycerinum acidi tannuci, or acidi gallici, are also frequently used; but they do not appear to possess any advantage over the water solutions.

Other methods of applying remedies to the interior of the cervix uteri have been tried, but the plan above described has been found most convenient and effectual. A very efficient mode is to inject the solutions into the cervix with a syringe; but this has the disadvantage of being sometimes followed by abdominal pains – no doubt, from the fluid penetrating too far into the body of the uterus. I have also used suppositories containing nitrate of silver, sulphate of copper, or alum, incorporated with cocoa-butter, in the proportion, by weight, of one part to four or five, and made into pencils of appropriate size for introduction into the cervix uteri. These answer well enough; but, on the whole, I am disposed to prefer aqueous to greasy applications. The essential point, whatever the substance or solution chosen, is to take care that it is effectually applied along the whole length of the canal of the cervix uteri. There is rarely any pain occasioned by the use of caustics or astringents to these parts. The patients are almost invariably quite unconscious that anything is being done.

In 1867, the number of admissions for this form of disease was 414, and the average period occupied by the treatment was twenty-three days; but 36 per cent were cured in periods of from seven to fifteen days, 21 per cent in from fifteen to twenty days, and 13 per cent in from twenty to twenty-five days. The remaining 30 per cent occupied periods exceeding twenty-five days, the longest being ninety-four days. Many of these latter, however, were suffering from some constitutional condition which may be held accountable for the delay, such as phthisis or some other form of strumous disease or impairment of health from long continual habits of dissipation.

Readmissions for a recurrence of this form of disease are unfortunately too frequent. The 414 *cases* alluded to do not, therefore, represent an equal number of patients; for fifteen women were admitted twice, and four three times, during the year. In fact, as many as eighty-four had been in the hospital previously, some of them as often as six or seven times since October, 1866. When discharged, a large proportion return to habits of prostitution; and, as might be expected, after a time relapse into the same condition. We seldom see them again, however, till after a lapse of several months; so it may fairly be inferred that they remain in a sound state for a considerable period.

The above remarks are founded upon, and refer especially to, cases of *simple* utero-vaginal discharge, in which, as far as can be discovered no syphilitic taint is present. These, of course, are only capable of communicating a simple urethritis of gonorrhœa. Women suffering from constitutional syphilis are, however, very often affected with uterine discharges and ulcerations. Such cases are much less amenable to local treatment; and appropriate constitutional remedies must, of course, be employed at the same time. In any opinion, the uterine ulceration so often concurrent with secondary syphilis is as much a secondary manifestation as mucous tubercles on the vulva, or the analogous condition so often met with on the mucous membrane of the mouth and throat; and its secretion is equally capable of communicating true syphilitic infection.

(*British Medical Journal*, 5 DEC. 1868)

William Acton

from

The Functions and Disorders of the Reproductive Organs (1875)

Masturbation

From the general view of continence and incontinence presented in the previous chapter, I pass on to the consideration of that particular form of incontinence to which children and youths are more especially liable.

Masturbation may be best described as an habitual incontinence eminently productive of disease; its effects are worse than those of most diseases.

The term, like the word *Chiromania*, can properly be applied, in the case of males, only to emission or ejaculation induced by titilation and friction of the virile member with the hand; and in the course of the next few pages such will be the meaning of the term. Use has, however, given it a larger signification. It is now employed to express ejaculation or emission attained by almost any other means than that of the natural excitement arising from sexual intercourse. In children too young to emit semen, friction of the organ is liable to produce that nervous spasm which is, in the adult, accompanied by ejaculation.

This degrading practice in a young child may arise in a variety of ways. The most common is of course the bad example of other children. In other cases, vicious or foolish female servants suggest the idea.[1] In such sexually disposed children as have been described above, the least hint is sufficient, or indeed they may, even without any suggestion from others, invent the habit for themselves. This latter origin, however, is rare in very early life.

The symptoms which mark the commencement of the practice

are too clear for an experienced eye to be deceived. As Lallemand remarks:

> However young the children may be, they become thin, pale, and irritable, and their features assume a haggard appearance. We notice the sunken eye, the long, cadaverous-looking countenance, the downcast look which seems to arise from a consciousness in the boy that his habits are suspected, and, at a later period, from the ascertained fact that his virility is lost. I wish by no means to assert that every boy unable to look another in the face, is or has been a masturbator, but I believe this vice is a very frequent cause of timidity. Habitual masturbators have a dank, moist, cold hand, very characteristic of great vital exhaustion; their sleep is short, and most complete marasmus comes on; they may gradually waste away if the evil passion is not got the better of; nervous symptoms set in, such as spasmodic contraction, or partial or entire convulsive movements, together with epilepsy, eclampsy, and a species of paralysis accompanied with contractions of the limbs.
>
> (VOL. I, p. 462)

Effect of emission in the male

Emission in healthy males is attended with spasmodic excitement, followed by temporary nervous prostration. Lallemand calls this excitement *ébranlement nerveux epileptiforme*. This is seen in a very exaggerated form in the buck rabbit, who, after every copulation, may be noticed to fall on his side in a sort of epileptic fit; the whites of his eyes are turned up; he gives several spasmodic twitches with his hind legs, and lies panting for some moments, until the nervous system recovers itself.

There are some men in whom this sort of epileptiform orgasm takes place every time connection is indulged in. Napoleon I is said to have been subject to epilepsy when, resting from his great labours, he indulged in sexual intercourse. No doubt can exist that deaths which have occurred in houses of ill-fame, as well as on the marriage couch, have arisen from this cause acting upon highly susceptible organisations. Entomological works abound with cases in which the male dies after the act of copulation. The following, which reads almost like romance, may be explained, perhaps, by this epileptiform attack killing the frail insect. It is a brief history of the establishment and growth of a colony of termite ants, as related by Burmeister.

> At the termination of the hot season, the young males and females quit the nest, and appear upon the surface of the earth, where they swarm in innumerable hosts, and pair. The busied workers then convey a chosen male and female back into the dwelling, and imprison them in the central royal cell, the entrances to which they decrease, and guard. Through these apertures the imprisoned pair receive the nutriment they require. The *male now, as amongst all other insects, speedily dies after the impregnation of the female has been effected:* but the female from this period begins to swell enormously, from the development of her countless eggs, and by the time she is ready to commence laying, her abdomen is about 1500 or 2000 times larger than all the rest of her body.

Of course any such epileptic attack in man is only the rare exception. In a young healthy, fully-developed adult, the shock which the nervous system receives is recovered from immediately. Ejaculation is in him a healthy function, from which he rallies directly; and the act may be, and is, repeated with impunity by some men, at very short intervals.

In other instances, however, particularly in those who suffer from any of the severer functional affections spoken of in this volume, the act is followed by intense depression, and a day or two may pass before the system rallies. In such instances, I believe, it will generally be found that the frame has previously been enfeebled by great excesses, and then each act of insemination produces serious depressing effects, far different from the natural ones.

I have been consulted by some few persons, on the other hand, who never appear to suffer from the act, although excesses may be committed to a great extent. This tolerance of the orgasm – which is remarkable in individual cases, and which permits the frequent recurrence of the shock without any ill effect either at the time or later – must depend upon some constitutional difference of nervous system of which we are ignorant.

We may, however, for the present, neglect both of these extremes – the persons who die or seriously suffer from one act of coition, and those who can commit almost satyrine excesses with apparent, though temporary, impunity. The question we have to consider is, what effect the act has upon ordinary men. It is, I conceive, most important to have correct notions upon this subject, to be neither alarmed by vague fears nor led astray by rash ignorance.

It is, of course, the nervous system which is primarily affected.

The ancients had some curious, and I need not say erroneous, notions on these matters. They believed that emission was the actual passage of brain down the spinal cord; and we find them speaking of connection being followed by the *stillicidium cerebri*.

Hippocrates says: 'The humours enter into a sort of fermentation, which separates what is most precious and most balsamic, and this part thus separated from the rest is carried by the spinal marrow to the generative organs.' (De Genitura, *Foesius*, p. 231.)

This popular notion is not yet extinct. It is not long since I heard one man about town coolly asserting to another his entire belief that Lord – , a noted old libertine, was killing himself by inches; that he had long since ceased to emit semen; and under unnatural excitement the substance of the brain was now passing away in the venereal orgasm, as was proved by the great nervous depression which was known to follow each sexual effort. The narrator, moreover, asserted most confidently that his lordship was aware of the fact; but that, in spite of all remonstrance, no sooner did the old debauchee recover from the effects of one loss than he incurred another.

Tabes dorsalis (apparently the ancient term for the disease called by the moderns spermatorrhea) is described by old writers as wasting of the spinal cord. So late as the time of Richerand, we find him, in his 'Physiology,' seriously asking his readers 'if the nervous depression which follows connection depends upon the fatigue of the organs, or, as some metaphysicians have believed, is it caused by the confused and indistinct notion that the soul takes of its own destruction?'

M. Parise also, in his valuable book on the diseases of old age, uses figurative, but no less erroneous expressions to the same effect, which he has gleamed from the old writers.

> Semen is life itself under a fluid form – the vital principle condensed and perceptible. Camus said it was composed of microscopical brains directly emanating from the great brain. The ancients considered this liquid as a discharge from the spinal marrow and brain, and called it cerebri stillicidium.
>
> Its importance is demonstrated by the fact that the smallest quantity contains life in activity, and can communicate it; that its presence and its secretion impress the organisation with an extra quality of force and energy, whereas repeated loss of it enervates and rapidly wears out the body. Nothing costs the economy so much as the production of semen, and its forced ejaculation. It has been calculated that an ounce of semen was equivalent to forty ounces of blood. According

> to Bichat, the secretion of sperm is in an inverse proportion to the secretion of fat; and we at once see the reason, semen is the essence of the whole individual. Hence Fernel has said 'totus homo semen est'. It is the balm of life – one of its best and most powerful stimulants. That which gives life is intended for its preservation.
>
> (Reveillé-Parise, *De la Vieilesse*, p. 415)

Of course these alarming statements are not such as modern science can at all indorse. Nevertheless it should be remembered that the semen, as I shall have occasion presently to show, is a highly organised fluid, requiring the expenditure of much vital force in its elaboration and in its expulsion. Even in the strongest adult, and much more in the youth or the weakly man, the whole of the functions connected with it are most vital and important – the last that should be abused.

Want of sexual feeling in the female a cause of absence of virility

We have already mentioned lack of sexual feeling in the female as not an uncommon cause of apparent or temporary impotence in the male. There is so much ignorance on the subject, and so many false ideas are current as to women's sexual condition, and are so productive of mischief, that I need offer no apology for giving here a plain statement that most medical men will corroborate.

I have taken pains to obtain and compare abundant evidence on this subject, and the result of my inquiries I may briefly epitomise as follows: I should say that the majority of women (happily for society) are not very much troubled with sexual feeling of any kind. What men are habitually, women are only exceptionally. It is too true, I admit, as the Divorce Court shows, that there are some few women who have sexual desires so strong that they surpass those of men, and shock public feeling by their consequences. I admit, of course, the existence of sexual excitement terminating even in nymphomania,[2] a form of insanity that those accustomed to visit lunatic asylums must be fully conversant with; but, with these sad exceptions, there can be no doubt that sexual feeling in the female is in the majority of cases in abeyance, and that it requires positive and considerable excitement to be roused at all; and even if roused (which in many instances it never can be) it is very moderate compared with that of the male. Many persons, and particularly young men, form their ideas of women's sensuous feeling from what they notice early in life among loose or, at least, low and immoral women. There is always a certain number of females who, though not ostensibly in the ranks of prostitutes, make a kind of a trade of a pretty face. They are fond of admiration, they like to attract the attention of those immediately above them. Any susceptible boy is easily led to believe, whether he is altogether overcome by the syren or not, that she, and therefore all women, must have at least as strong passions as himself. Such women, however, give a very false idea of the condition of female sexual feeling in general. Association with the loose women of the London streets in casinos and other immoral haunts (who, if they have not sexual feeling, counterfeit it so well that the novice does not suspect but that it is genuine), seems to corroborate such an impression, and as I have stated above, it is from these erroneous notions that so many unmarried men imagine that the marital duties they will have to undertake are beyond their exhausted strength, and from this reason dread and avoid marriage.

Married men – medical men – or married women themselves, would, if appealed to, tell a very different tale, and vindicate female nature from the vile aspersions cast on it by the abandoned conduct and ungoverned lusts of a few of its worst examples.

I am ready to maintain that there are many females who never feel any sexual excitement whatever. Others, again, immediately after each period, do become, to a limited degree, capable of experiencing it; but this capacity is often temporary, and may entirely cease till the next menstrual period. Many of the best mothers, wives, and managers of households, know little of or are careless about sexual indulgences. Love of home, of children, and of domestic duties are the only passions they feel.[3]

As a general rule, a modest woman seldom desires any sexual gratification for herself. She submits to her husband's embraces, but principally to gratify him; and, were it not for the desire of maternity, would far rather be relieved from his attentions. No nervous or feeble young man need, therefore, be deterred from marriage by any exaggerated notion of the arduous duties required from him. Let him be well assured, on my authority backed by the opinion of many, that the married woman has no wish to be placed on the footing of a mistress.

One instance may better illustrate the real state of the case than much description.

In – , 185–, a barrister, about 30 years of age, came to me on account of sexual debility. On cross-examination I found he had been married a twelvemonth, that an attempt at connection had taken place but once since the commencement of the year, and that even then there was some doubt as to the completion of the act. He brought his wife with him, as she was, he said, desirous of having some conversation with me.

I found the lady a refined but highly sensitive person. Speaking with a freedom equally removed from assurance, or *mauvaise honte*, she told me she thought it her duty to consult me. She neither blushed nor faltered in telling her story, and I regret that my words must fail to convey the delicacy with which her avowal was made.

Her husband and herself, she said, had been acquainted from childhood, had grown up together, become naturally attached, and married. She had reason to consider him debilitated, but – as she was fully convinced – from no indiscrete acts on his part. She believed it was his natural condition. She was dotingly attached to him, and would not have determined to consult me, but that she wished, for his sake, to have a family, as it would, she hoped, conduce to their mutual happiness. She assured me that she felt no sexual passions whatever; that if she was capable of them, they were dormant. Her passion for her husband was of a Platonic kind, and far from wishing to stimulate his frigid feelings, she doubted whether it would be right or not. She loved him as he was, and would not desire him to be otherwise except for the hope of having a family.

I believe this lady is a perfect ideal of an English wife and mother, kind, considerate, self-sacrificing, and sensible, so pure-hearted as to be utterly ignorant of and averse to any sensual indulgence, but so unselfishly attached to the man she loves as to be willing to give up her own wishes and feelings for his sake.

In strong contrast to the unselfish sacrifices such married women make of their feelings in allowing cohabitation, stand out others, who, either from ignorance or utter want of sympathy, although they are model wives in every other respect, not only evince no sexual feeling, but, on the contrary, scruple not to declare their aversion to the least manifestation of it. Doubtless this may, and often does, depend upon disease, and if so, the sooner the suffering female is treated the better. Much more frequently, however, it depends upon apathy, selfish indifference to please, or unwillingness to overcome a natural repugnance for cohabitation.

Other mental conditions may influence the female. Thus, the High Church enthusiast may consider it her strictly religious duty to be separated from her husband during the forty days of Lent; and I have given an instance of a wife refusing to cohabit with her husband because she would not again become a mother. I was lately in conversation with a lady who maintains women's rights to such an extent that she denied the husband any voice in the matter, whether or not cohabitation should take place. She maintained, most strenuously, that as the woman bears the consequences – has all the discomfort of being nine months in the family-way, and thus is obliged to give up her amusements and many of her social relations – considering too that she suffers all the pains and risks of childbirth – a married woman has a perfect right to refuse to cohabit with her husband. I ventured to point out to this strong-minded female that such conduct on her part might be, in a medical point of view, highly detrimental to the health of the husband, particularly if he happened to be strongly sexually disposed. She, however, refused to admit the validity of my argument, and replied that such a man, unable to control his feelings, ought to have married a street-walker, not an intellectually disposed person, who could not and ought not to be obliged to devote her time to duties only compatible with the position of a female drudge or wetnurse.

I am not prepared to say what weight Sir James Hannen would attach to such evidence in the case of a man seeking a divorce, and I am not aware that counsel has as yet urged such conduct on the part of the female in extenuation of immorality on the part of the husband. Of one thing I am quite certain, that many times in the course of the year I am consulted by conscientious married men, who complain, and I think with reason, that they are debarred from the privileges of marriage, and that their sexual sufferings are almost greater than they can bear in consequence of their being mated to women who think and act as in the above-cited instances. I regret to add that medical skill can be of little avail here. The more conscientious the husband and the stronger his sexual feelings, the more distressing are the sufferings he is doomed to undergo, ultimately too often ending in impotence.

Sexual suffering in the married

In speaking of continence, I admitted the difficulties some young men experience in maintaining it, and I furnished some important evidence proving that a strong will, plenty of exercise, and surgical supervision, should enable a man to control his sexual appetites. In the present section I propose devoting a few pages to sexual suffering in the married – a subject which has not met with that consideration from medical men which it deserves.

It often occurs that married men come to me with sad complaints of the intense suffering they have to undergo. I saw one such patient who was a man of strong sexual disposition, married, and the father of several children. In consequence of the rapidity with which his wife (a delicate woman) had brought him a family, she had been suffering severely from uterine disease, for which she was then under treatment, and the medical attendant had recommended separate beds and abstinence from all sexual relations. This patient assures me that no one could imagine what torments he has undergone; warmly attached as he is to a loving, educated, and beautiful wife, yet debarred from all the most cherished advantages of a married man. 'What could I recommend?' was his inquiry.

Let me cite another instance. Such a man as the above came to me with a budget of grievances. Married to a woman of strong animal instincts, she had proved unfaithful to him, and an action for divorce was about being brought by my patient against the lady. *En attendant* my married patient was the subject of most acute sexual suffering, without any immediate chance of becoming legally separated from a woman who, although his wife, had ceased to be a wife to him; yet society had decreed that he must bear his hard lot, without any chance of being speedily released from the most acute sexual suffering. Moving in the best and most fashionable society, much admired by ladies of his acquaintance, he assured me that no one could form any idea of the sufferings or temptations he had hourly to undergo; yet he was chained to this torment, and his every action watched by the most vigilant detective police that the friends of the wife could call to their aid.

I regret to say that in such cases as these, I can do little more than offer my sympathy; still, to persons who are thus situated my remarks on continence are of value; and as a surgeon, I have no hesitation in saying that a man of strong sexual disposition must make many sacrifices. He must eschew much agreeable female society, he should abstain from the indulgences of the table, and he must take more exercise than the indolent are disposed to adopt. The profession can offer him little assistance and but little benefit, unless he be endowed with a strong will – an aid to treatment, often found wanting in strongly-developed animal natures. Is it surprising, then, that so many who, under more favorable auspices, would have continued to make the best of husbands, fall victims to a vicious mode of living, and seek in fornication some alleviation of their sexual sufferings?

These are some of the arcana of social life that are revealed only to medical men, in the hope (often a vain hope) that they may be in a position to suggest some mode of relief.

During the last few years, and since the rights of women have been so much insisted upon, and practically carried out by the 'strongest-minded of the sex', numerous husbands have complained to me of the hardships under which they suffer by being married to women who regard themselves as martyrs when called upon to fulfil the duties of wives. This spirit of insubordination has become more intolerable – as the husbands assert – since it has been backed by the opinions of John Stuart Mill, who in his work on the 'Subjection of Women,' would induce the sex to believe that they are 'but personal body-servants of a despot'. Mr Mill complains that the wife has not even the privilege of the female slave, who he states

> has (in Christian countries) an admitted right and is considered under a moral obligation to refuse to her master the last familiarity. Not so the wife, however brutal a tyrant she may be chained to – though she may know that he hates her – though it may be his daily pleasure to torture her, and though she may feel it impossible not to loathe him – he can claim from her and enforce the lowest degradation of a human being, that of being made the instrument of an animal function contrary to her inclinations.

As opposed to these doctrines, I would rather urge the sex to follow the example of those bright, cheerful, and happily constituted women, who, instead of exaggerating their supposed grievances, instinctively, as it were, become the soothers of man's woes, their greatest gratification apparently being to minister to his pleasures, seeing that woman was created for the purpose of being a help-meet to her husband. Doubtless many a medical man can, like myself, recal the self-condemnation of more than one married woman who, in her repentant moments, has acknowledged that want of sympathy and affection on her part has led first to estrangement and subsequently to a permanent separation from a husband whose merits she has learnt too late to appreciate.

The act of copulation

The physiological explanation of the pleasure attendant on the sexual act is, perhaps, as follows: 'Accumulation of blood', says Kobelt,

> causes, whenever it occurs in the body, a gradual

> augmentation of sensibility; but in this case the glans penis, in passing from a non-erect state to the condition of complete turgescence, becomes the seat of a completely new and *specific sensibility*, up to this moment dormant. All the attendant phenomena react on the nervous centres. From this it appears that, in addition to the nerves of general sensibility, which fulfil their functions in a state of repose and also during erection, although in a different manner, there must be in the glans penis *special nerves of pleasure*, the particular action of which does not take place except under the indispensable condition of a state of orgasm of the glans. Moreover, the orgasm once over, the nerves return to their former state of inaction, and remain unaffected under all ulterior excitement.
>
> They are, then, in the same condition as the rest of the generative apparatus; their irritability ceases with the consummation of the act, and, together with this irritability, the venereal appetite ceases also to be repeated, and to bring about the same series of phenomena at each new excitement.
>
> (Kobelt, *Die männlichen und weiblichen Wollust Organe des Menschen und einiger Säugethiere*, p. 35)

Many foreign writers maintain, and the above observations would seem to corroborate the assertion, that the chief source of sexual pleasure resides in the glans penis. That it has a considerable share in the sensations experienced is very true, but from certain cases that have come under my notice, I cannot help thinking that it has less to do with them than is generally supposed. Some time ago I attended an officer on his return from India who had lost the whole of the glans penis. This patient completely recovered his health, the parts healed, leaving but a stump of the penis two inches in length. I found, to my surprise, that the sexual act was not only possible, but that the same amount of pleasure as formerly was still experienced. He assured me, indeed, that the sexual act differed in no respect (as far as he could detect) from what it had been before the mutilation.

Duration of the Act. It is, indeed, a wise provision that in the human being the act should last but a short time – some few minutes.

In animals the greatest differences in this particular take place.

Thus I read in the 'Description of the Preparations of the College of Surgeons,' that 'the coitus in the kangaroo, and probably in other marsupials, is of long duration, and the scrotum during that act disappears, and seems to be partially inverted during the forcible retraction of the testes against the marsupial bones.' (No. 2477, *Physiological Catalogue*, by Owen.)

The act of copulation, as I can testify, in the moth of the silk-worm is very prolonged. The male is the smaller and darker of the two, and as soon as he leaves the grub state he is ready for the act. He then vibrates his wings with a very singular humming noise, and goes round and round the female. The tails are then approximated, copulation takes place, and lasts for days. As soon as the sexes separate, the same process is repeated, and sexual congress again occurs. It would almost appear as if the short life of these insects was passed in copulation. The female moths died first in all the cases I witnessed, but the males, although surviving the females, were dull and could hardly move, being apparently thoroughly exhausted by their reproductive labours.

In the chapter on erection we have noticed the prolonged copulation of the dog. In some other classes of animals it takes place with wonderful celerity. Among deer for instance, it was at one time stated that coitus had never been observed even by the oldest keepers. Professor Owen mentioned that it may be witnessed in Richmond Park, somewhat in the following way: the buck will be seen to scrape hollows two or three feet deep in certain portions of the park; to these places he leads the does. One by one, they place themselves in these hollows; the buck drives away all other bucks from the neighbourhood, then, with a rush, mounts the doe; in an instant the act is accomplished, and the female retires to be replaced by another. Professor Owen says he cannot explain why these hollows should be made in the ground, as there is nothing in the conformation of the doe to require that she should be placed on a level lower than that which the buck leaps from. However, though the act itself is instantaneous, the premonitory excitement is of long duration. It is possible, therefore, that erection lasts for an instant, and hence the convenience of this preparation and position.

Mr Thompson, the late superintendent at the Zoological Gardens, told me that he has seen copulation take place in the stags both in the wild state and in confinement. He thinks that a peculiar place is not *necessary* for the act. He agrees that it is effected in a few moments, and that in the case of the giraffe, also, no peculiar position is necessary.

The Effect of the Act. The immediate effect of the act on the male deserves some few remarks. Even in the healthiest and strongest person a feeling of fatigue immediately follows.

This nervous orgasm is very powerfully exhibited in some animals. The buck rabbit, for instance, after each sexual act, falls on his side, the whites of his eyes turn up, and his hind legs are spasmodically agitated. The cause of this, and the corresponding phenomena in other animals, is the nervous shock which particularly affects the spinal cord.

The way in which this shock affects a healthy man is, generally, to make him languid and drowsy for a time.

This temporary depression has not escaped the observation of the ancients, who have remarked –

> Læta venire Venus tristis abire solet;

and again

> Post coitum omne animal triste, nisi gallus qui cantat.

So serious, indeed, is the paroxysm of the nervous system produced by the sexual spasm, that its immediate effect is not always unattended with danger, and men with weak hearts have died in the act. Every now and then we learn that men are found dead on the night of their wedding, and it is not very uncommon to hear of inquests being held on men discovered in houses of ill-fame, without any marks of ill-usage or poison. The cause has been, doubtless, the sudden nervous shock overpowering a feeble or diseased frame.

However exceptional these cases are, they are warnings, and should serve to show that an act which *may* destroy the weak should not be tampered with even by the strong.

Lallemand well describes the test which every married man should apply in his own case:

> When connection is followed by a joyous feeling, a *bien être général*, as well as fresh vigour; when the head feels lighter, the body more elastic and ready for work; when a greater disposition to exercise or intellectual labour arises, and the genital organs evince an increase of vigour and activity, we may infer that an imperious want has been satisfied within the limits necessary for health. The happy influence which all the organs experience is similar to that which follows the accomplishment of every function necessary to the economy.

How serious – how *vital* an act, so to speak, that of copulation is, appears from the marked changes which accompany its performance in some animals. It is a well-accredited fact that in the rutting season buck venison is strong, lean, and ill-flavoured. At this time, we are told, the flesh becomes soft and flabby, the hair looks 'unkind'; and in birds, the feathers, after the season of breeding, are in a ruffled state, and droop. The horns of stags (see

Effects of Castration, p. 130) fall off, and the blood is occupied in supplying the consequent demand for new osseous matter.

It is before the spawning season has passed that we prefer the herring, and it is only while it is filled with roe that we care to eat the mackerel. A spent salmon is not fit food for man; and, at this period, as all fishermen are aware, the vivid colours of the trout disappear; and the fish retires exhausted and impoverished, until the vital forces are regained.

Repetition of the Act. Whilst one individual will suffer for days after a single attempt, or even from an involuntary emission, another will not evince the least sign of depression, although the act be repeated several times in succession or on several consecutive nights. Still, as a general rule, the act is and ought to be repeated but rarely. In newly married people, of course, sexual intercourse takes place more frequently, and hence it happens that conception often fails during the first few months of wedlock, depending probably upon the fact that the semen of the male contains but few perfect spermatozoa: in such cases it is only when the ardour of first love has abated, and the spermatozoa have been allowed the time requisite for their full development, that the female becomes impregnated.

This part of my subject will, however, occupy further attention when I come to speak of marital excesses. I may, however, here state that the monthly periods, of course, put a temporary stop to intercourse, while nature provides a further check upon its too frequent repetition, in the effect which pregnancy produces on the female, and through her upon the male.

If the married female conceives every second year, we usually notice that during the nine months following conception she experiences no great sexual excitement. The consequence is that sexual desire in the male is somewhat diminished, and the act of coition takes place but rarely. Again, while women are suckling there is usually such a demand made on the vital force by the organs secreting milk that sexual desire is almost annihilated.[4] Now, as experience teaches us that a reciprocity of desire is, to a great extent, necessary to excite the male, we must not be surprised if we learn that excesses in fertile married life are comparatively rare, and that sensual feelings in the man become gradually sobered down.

It is a curious fact that man and a few domesticated animals are alone liable to suffer from the effects of sexual excesses. In a state of nature wild female animals will not allow the approach of the male except when in a state of rut, and this occurs at long intervals and only at certain seasons of the year. The human female probably would not differ much in this respect from the wild animal, had she not been civilised, for as I shall have occasion again and again to remark, she would not for her own gratification allow sexual congress except at certain periods. The courtezan who makes a livelihood by her person may be *toujours puête*, but not so the pregnant wife or nursing mother. Love for her husband and a wish to gratify his passion, and in some women the knowledge that they would be deserted for courtezans if they did not waive their own inclinations may induce the indifferent, the passionless, to admit the embraces of their husbands. These are truths about which much ignorance and consequently much false reasoning prevails. No portion of my book has more surprised unmarried men than such statements as these. Married men, however, generally confirm my opinion, and not a few have acknowledged that had wives been but judicious and consulted more the feelings of their husbands, the Divorce Court would not have been so often appealed to, nor would women have had cause to complain of there being so many unfaithful husbands.

Besides this kind of natural protection against excesses, arising from the periodical unwillingness of the human female to permit congress, we find that there is not in men, particularly in the intellectual and civilised man, any need for or *natural* impulse towards that excessive periodical indulgence which we notice in the brute creation. The human male is naturally prepared to copulate at all times of the year; he is not, therefore, instinctively required to repeat the act so many times within a short period, as some domesticated animals are, for the purpose of propagating the species. The ram has been supposed to repeat the act from fifty to eighty times[5] in the course of one night. The stallion[6] is, or rather ought to be, always limited to a certain number of mares, but as he takes his mounts during a limited time (two or three months), the act is necessarily repeated very often, and at very short intervals.

Of course, these enormous copulative powers are not only *not* examples, but positive *contrasts* to what should obtain in the human being. As man has no real rutting season (which in animals appears to be a kind of periodic puberty), there is no occasion, and therefore no provision, for the sudden or excessive employment of his reproductive organs, and consequently any such excesses will be fraught with much danger. The brute, moreover, is deficient in the intellectual qualities of man: propagation of his species appears to be about the most important of the objects of his existence. Man is formed for higher purposes than this. To devote the whole energy of his nature to sensual indulgence is literally to degrade himself to the level of a brute, and to impair or totally destroy those intellectual and moral capacities which distinguish him from the inferior creation. Even in the lower animals a limit is placed to sexual indulgence, and we find in some cases very curious physical provisions for attaining this end.

Among the preparations in the College of Surgeons' Museum may be seen the penis of the young tom-cat. It is described by Owen in the catalogue as 'penis of a cat, showing the retroverted callous papillæ of the glans', and it is covered with spinous-looking elevations, which, in connection, must give the female much pain. They disappear in the old tom. The same conformation, and to a much greater extent, exists in the guinea-pig. It is supposed that this rugous state of the male organ excites if not anger, the greatest pain in the female.

NOTES

1 I have heard of a vile habit which some foreign nurses have (I hope it is confined to the Continent) of quieting children when they cry by tickling the sexual organs. I need hardly point out how very dangerous this is. There seems hardly any limit to the age at which a young child can be initiated into these abominations, or to the depth of degradation to which it may fall under such hideous teaching. Books treating of this subject are unfortunately too full of accounts of the habits of such children. Parent Duchâtelet mentions a child which, from the age of four years, had been in the habit of abusing its powers with boys of ten or twelve, though it had been brought up by a respectable and religious woman. (*Annales d'Hygiène Publique*, tome vii, 1832, p. 173.)

2 I shall probably have no other opportunity of noticing that, as excision of the clitoris has been recommended for the cure of this complaint, Köbelt thinks that it would not be necessary to remove the whole of the clitoris in nymphomania, the same results (that is destruction of venereal desire) would follow if the glans clitoridis had been alone removed, as it is now considered that it is the glans alone in which the sensitive nerves expand. This view I do not agree with, as I have already stated with regard to the analogous structure of the penis. I am fully convinced that in many women there is no special sexual sensation in the clitoris, and I am as positive that the special sensibility dependent on the erectile tissue exists in several portions of the vaginal canal.

3 The physiologist will not be surprised that the human female should in these respects differ but little from the female among animals. We well know it as a fact that the female animal will not allow the dog or stallion to approach her except at particular seasons. In many a human female, indeed, I believe, it is rather from the wish of pleasing or gratifying the husband than from any strong sexual feeling, that cohabitation is so habitually allowed. Certainly, during the months of gestation this holds

good. I have known instances where the female has during gestation evinced positive loathing for any marital familiarity whatever. In some exceptional cases, indeed, feeling has been sacrificed to duty, and the wife has endured, with all the self-martyrdom of womanhood, what was almost worse than death.

4 We are apt to believe that in the human female it is almost impossible for gestation and lactation to go on simultaneously. In the mare, however, this occurs. In large breeding establishments the mare is usually put to the stallion, and will 'show to the horse' nine days after a foal is dropped. The object of this of course is that in eleven months she shall again give birth to another foal. This is the surest way to obtain foals, although the produce of a mare after being a year barren is generally stronger and presumably better than on her becoming with foal while suckling. In fact, if left a twelvemonth barren, mares, I am informed by competent men, are stinted with great difficulty.

The late Mr Blenkiron, a well-known breeder of race-horses at Middle Park, kindly looked over this note, and he told me that, although this happens, mares often require some little management 'to show to a horse, although in season', and it is necessary to put the twitch on the nose to distract their attention, otherwise their affection for the foal induces them 'not to show to the horse, although in season'.

5 This statement has been doubted. It is founded on the hypothesis, perhaps somewhat loose, that the chest and abdomen of a ram having been covered with 'ruddle' over night, and the haunches of fifty ewes found smeared with the same composition in the morning, the animal had to such a numerical extent exercised his generative functions. This may or may not be a *sequitur;* but no manner of doubt exists that the sexual power of the animal is, in fact, as well as proverbially, very considerable; but let it be recollected that it is exercised only for a very short time during the twelve months.

6 The late Mr Grey, who had the management of a large breeding establishment at Theobalds, told me that the celebrated stallion 'Teddington', who was then serving mares at his farm, was limited by his owner to forty-five mares during the season, which lasts from February to July, but as it is desirable that mares should foal early in the year, the repeated acts of connection were included in a comparatively short period. In addition to this, the same mare is repeatedly (about every nine days) put to the horse, to secure impregnation. It appears, nevertheless that these stallions do not suffer, and Mr Grey was of opinion that this number, forty-five, is not too much. In reply to my inquiries, he said that nothing but oats and hay are given to these horses; beans are considered to heat them. He seemed not to think that a horse can cover too *much* but admits that he may too rapidly. He did not allow any horse in his establishment to mount more than twice a day. Two trials are generally advisable, as the first leap is often a failure. Country-travelling stallions are said to have stimulants given them, and to have as many as 200 mounts in the season.

Part II
Feminist Campaigns around Sexuality

A *Prostitution*

Harriet Martineau

The Contagious Diseases Acts as Applied to Garrison Towns and Naval Stations

(1863)

(4 September 1863)

The mortality in our Indian army was, as might have been expected, one of the social subjects discussed at the meeting of the British Association at Newcastle; and it is evident that some recent disclosures about existing disease in our army and navy generally were in the minds of the speakers. There was some controversy as to the comparative effects of climate and of vice; and one speaker, who had probably been reading the impressive evidence of Sir John Lawrence in the Indian sanitary returns, urged a relaxation of the restrictions on marriage in the army, as the natural and only effectual check on the vice and consequent disease which are sapping the strength of our armies, destroying the lives of thousands of the men picked for the national defence, and dooming future generations to a life of disease and infirmity.

The anxiety evidenced in the remarks of these speakers at Newcastle is showing itself in other ways, and by signs of great force. There is nothing surprising in this; for in a country where such a state of society exists as at Aldershot, at Shorncliffe, and in our chief ports, all thoughtful and patriotic people must feel the deepest concern and alarm about the present state and future prospects of the public health and morals. There is no question on any hand of the fearful extent of the vice and disease under discussion; the feeling of grief and alarm is common to the whole country; but there is a further pain and dread excited just now by some ways of treating the subject, which, unless openly condemned and repudiated, will sorely aggravate the evil in both its moral and physical effects.

We are told, by a leading contemporary, and in the letters of one of its correspondents, that the country 'will not yet bear' the proposal of a police regulation of the practice of the vice in question, and of the class of women whom it implicates. It is assumed that such police regulation is a good thing, and a thing to which we must come in time, but that our prejudices must be so far respected as that another measure must be tried first, viz., the establishment of hospitals, at the expense of the State, for the sufferers from the special disease. These suggestions have been so often repeated within the last month, so dwelt upon, and urged with such an extraordinary disregard of evidence which is at the command of anybody who chooses to learn the facts of the case, that there is some danger of public sentiment being misguided, unless the truth is told, without disguise and without delay.

The first point evidently is to ascertain whether police regulation effects its object in this case. At present there is not only no evidence that it lessens the amount of either sin or disease but some evidence that it tends to increase both. The Army Medical Reports afford us this evidence. They show the proportion to the strength of the army of soldiers incapacitated by this disease at the various stations abroad and at home; and the comparison between the three foreign stations at which the strictest police regulation has long existed with other stations in the same climate shows that certainly nothing is gained by what is called 'protection'. Taking in nearly the last half century, it appears that, *cæteris paribus*, the 'protected' stations have sent 129 per 1000 of soldiers to hospital annually from this cause, while the 'unprotected' supply 95 per 1000. Now, before any step is taken which the national conscience recoils from, as sanctioning vice by law and authority, and admitting vice to be necessary, it is clearly indispensable to show that the step would answer the purpose for which it is proposed. In the case under our notice this has never been shown, and our present means of knowledge justify us in saying that it cannot be shown. It is to be hoped that every member of the Legislature will keep this in mind, and will ascertain the facts for himself before he gives any sort of countenance to a proposal of a character fatal to the virtue and domestic peace of our country and every family in it.

The truth is, there are frequent and wide diversities in the returns of this disease at military stations; and the causes of these changes are various, as far as they have been traced. More remain to be examined into; but the one point which may be considered more plain than any other is, that police regulation has left the proportions unchanged in one place or time, while other causes were mending matters in another. We shall see the advocacy of this kind of recognition and control going on to assume that the method is effectual, if admissible on other grounds; and we therefore caution the public against allowing any such assumption to pass. It rests with the advocates of police management to prove that it answers its purpose; and they should be made to do it before they are permitted to advance any farther in their scheme for purifying society by giving the sanction of the State to the practice of vice.

In the interval, the State is to support hospitals for the treatment of this disease, in connection with camps and naval stations. It is hoped that while the soldiers and sailors are compelled to enter the hospital, the women who cannot be so compelled may be won by the provision of comfort, the tenderness of treatment, and the prospect of cure. And they will probably be cured morally as well as physically, we are told, and these hospitals may save bodies and souls at once. Such is the suggestion.

Under the Poor-law, however, if strictly enforced, there is provision made for nearly the whole class under notice; and the dispensaries, and hospitals supported by charity, might be abundantly sufficient for the rest. Our medical readers are aware that it is the practice in certain dispensaries for the inspector to discover, in this as in other kinds of disease, the cases which are properly chargeable to the parish, in order to separate them from those contemplated by the charity. It is highly necessary that this should be done on the large scale of our army system before Parliament is asked to grant money for patronising and petting a class of sinners and sufferers already provided for under the visitation of their retribution.

It must not be overlooked that no such system as is proposed could be set up for the army and navy without involving civil society in its trammels, its corruptions, and its snares. The scheme propounded is in fact one which implicates the morality of the whole nation, and which must inevitably produce consequences of the very last importance, whether it should seem to succeed or fail. The step of pronouncing the vice necessary, and of countenancing it on that ground, is one which can never be retraced. As we have shown, there is every reason to believe that it would not avail. If it did appear for a time to check the spread of disease it would foster the growth of the moral evil by which the disease exists. It is not unknown in this country that, according to the test of the best and wisest men in France, the operation of the well-intended system of police repression there is eating into the very heart of the nation.

But, it will be asked, can nothing, then, be done? Can nothing be done by the State? Must we go downwards in the path of destruction as a nation, or become defenceless through the necessity of having a soldiery and naval force of unmarried men, or men who must leave their wives at home? If there must be an army and navy so constituted, and if the calling offers such temptations and facilities as we hear of, what is there to hope? Must we not do something in such a case? – something effectual? – something immediate?

Certainly. There is much that the State can do which has never yet been tried, and much that it should leave off doing, if we are to have a soldiery strong enough and sound enough for its work. There is so much that the State can do that it appears astonishing that any questionable methods should be proposed while so much that is unquestionably good, and directly to the purpose, is disregarded or unappreciated. Another day we may show some of the unused means by which the ravages of disease and vice in our army may be checked or prevented, without offence to the conscience of the nation.

(25 September 1863)

There is no doubt whatever about the ability of the State to do much that has never yet been tried to preclude and to check the vice and disease which, by their effect on the strength of our army, have lately excited so much alarm. There is unquestionably a strong call for zeal and diligence before we commit ourselves to a scheme of special quarantine infinitely more mischievous than any quarantine system that ever was tried. It would be abundantly absurd in any nation to betake itself now to the old quarantine, in the face of all exposures of its constant failure, and before having recourse to sanitary measures of proved efficacy; yet this, and worse than this, is what we should be doing if we now committed ourselves to a system of medical police before exhausting all experiments which might save us from succumbing to the force of a corruption which no manly and pure heart regards as necessary.

There is no phase of this difficulty in which there is not something that the State can do, and that has hitherto been left undone. Under the aspect of physical or moral treatment, with prevention, amelioration, or cure for the aim, unobjectionable methods remain to be adopted.

Let us take prevention first – prevention both of the vice and the disease.

The one thing that seems never to have occurred to the rulers of the soldier's destiny is to apply themselves to preclude *temptation;* whereas on this depends every hope of surmounting the whole difficulty. In a kindred case the action of the State was directed, not against passion but temptation. Lord Campbell's Act against licentious literature is a full recognition of the principle of beginning at the beginning, and forbidding wanton provocation of the passions. So far is the State at present from doing even thus much on behalf of the soldier's self-respect, that it opens the door wide to every evil passion that roams through society, seeking whom it may devour. Our young soldiers have not enough to do; and what they have to do is irksome. The very last tortures of *ennui* are experienced in depôt, in camp, in barrack; and while there is, generally speaking, no provision made for the rational and profitable occupation and pleasant recreation of the soldiers, the whole world of licence is thrown open to men wearied with idleness, desperate with dulness, and craving the relief and luxury of jollity. 'The idle men are always the worst', we are informed on authority; and there is no doubt that the soldiers who were artisans before they entered the army, and who are so fortunate as to be allowed (as some are in India) to occupy their leisure in pursuing their art for their own profit, are steadier, healthier, and happier than the poor fellows who can find nothing to do so attractive as repairing to low drinking-houses, and going the round of unlawful pleasures there. This is a sort of doom to the common run of young soldiers where there are no privileges of school, reading-room, active games in the day and innocent ones in the evenings, harmless refreshment rooms, and a brisk sociality in the midst of comfort, to be had without transgression, and with an actual promotion of respectability.

This is not the only way in which the State may apply itself to deal with temptation rather than passion. It must protect the soldier's health before he has fallen into the abyss, instead of only doing what can be done afterwards. A state of health and vigour such as belongs to pure air, wholesome food, quiet sleep, and due exercise of body and mind, is always and everywhere favourable to respectability; and a languid, restless, and suffering state of body is in itself a temptation to vice when the way is open. As for the other direction taken by precaution – that which deals with passion – the plainest and most pressing duty is to suppress the brothels altogether, and punish with all practicable severity the proprietors and abbettors of that intolerable nuisance. If these houses were treated as Thieves' Homes are, society would have a better conscience than it has, and our soldiers, as well as the rest of the manhood of the country, would have a better chance in life. And there is no evidence – really none whatever – that any new evils would arise, or that any would remain so fatal as what would be got rid of.

So much may be regarded as the moral treatment of the case. In the physical, there is quite as much to be done which is as yet unattempted. That much of the disease which, according to high medical testimony, is the result of dirt (as small-pox and other epidemics are where contagion is out of the question,) ought, of course, to be precluded by good sanitary management. How far a thorough and universal cleanliness might save society from the ravage of various contagious diseases, and this among them, will never be known till the experiment is tried: but it would be better to resort to this experiment on behalf of the army than to that of giving a police recognition and legal protection to vice. Another very important point is to provide the highest professional skill for the whole treatment of the diseased and the endangered. It is said, openly and on high authority, that our army medical officers are unsuccessful in the treatment of this order of disease, and that there is a needless loss of time and strength accordingly. The remedy for this is a better instruction and more effectual study in the Army Medical School. The Director-General ought to see to this, as an improvement immediately and urgently needed. The soldiers thus taken the best care of in their own proper hospitals, their tempters and victims may be consigned to the care provided for them by legal and private charity. To tax the people of England for the establishment of new hospitals for this class in connection with every military and naval station, would be not only unnecessary in itself, but it would inevitably bring after it the establishment of similar hospitals in the service of the rest of society. Farewell, then, to the distinctive honour and privilege of our country and people – the adoption of the family as the basis of society, and the reverence and love for the sacredness of the home as the security for all that, as a nation, we have and hope for.

Those who are now 'sounding public opinion' on behalf of the perilous experiment they advocate, will say that the objects we have held up are exactly those which they are proposing and pursuing. If so, it rests with them to prove that their fresh methods are necessary to the attainment of those objects. Some of the highest authorities, medical and military, are of opinion that the new treatment would aggravate every evil, physical and moral; while it is undeniable that there are means, safe, pure, simple, and manifest, which are much more likely to succeed, and which have never been tried. The present waste of manhood, in the army and out of it, cannot be tolerated – something must be done; but common sense requires that we should undo the evil we have done, and reverse the management by which vice and disease have been fostered, before we resort to any policy from which the moral sense of our people recoils.

Now that this controversy has been ventured upon, any carelessness or levity on the part of the country, and especially of Parliament, would be a crime. When the next session opens, our legislators and their constituents must be prepared to deal decisively with any attempt, open or disguised, to involve us in an experiment which might cost us precisely that for which we most value our lot as the people of England.

(15 September 1863)

The letter which appeared in our columns on Thursday last, on Recreation Grounds for Soldiers, will have been felt by our readers to be well-timed and very sensible. Whatever affords to our soldiers in their leisure hours strenuous bodily exercise, in connection with occupation and exhilaration of mind, is, as far as it goes, an excellent safeguard against the mischiefs which are sure to follow when idle and ignorant men know of no better amusement than sitting drinking in public-houses, where they meet the worst company. The letter of 'N. H. M.' is well-timed in more ways than one. Something is doing, and more is proposed in the way of sedentary amusements for our troops – such as reading-rooms, innocent games, music, etc; and now is the time to urge that a due provision be made for the muscular as well as the intellectual exercise of the men. Athletic games are as favourable to moral as to physical health, and no set of men ever wanted such a preservative more than our soldiers. We are all, no doubt, of Sir C. Trevelyan's opinion, recorded in the evidence of the Indian Sanitary Report, that no sort of recreation can supply the needs of idle men, and that leave and opportunity to work at any trade, outdoor or in-door, by which a soldier may open some prospect to himself, and assist his family, and make some savings, will do more for his health and his morals than the very best provision for cricket and quoits; but till we can get some better arrangement still, and always as an excellent thing in its way, we shall hail the spectacle referred to by 'N.H.M.' of regiments in garrison at Portsmouth playing cricket on Governor's Green, and the Royal

Marine Artillery contending for prizes at their annual games of leaping, running, and throwing weights.

In another way this letter is well-timed. It comes out in the midst of a discussion to which we have before referred, on a subject of the very deepest interest and importance in the eyes of all good citizens. Since we last noticed the new attempt to agitate the proposal to give the sanction of police supervision to the most fatal form of intemperance, a great deal has been said in the columns of the journal which introduced the subject. All the letters and all the articles which have yet appeared there are, however, on one side of the question, although nothing can be more certain or notorious than that the general opinion and conscience of English society are utterly opposed to so fearful an innovation on the national principles of morality as setting up a protection of vice for the sake of controlling it. It is so well known that the country would recoil from such a scheme, if openly and immediately proposed, that the thing is set about in an indirect way, with the cunning of conspiracy; and the chief device of several which are seen through by reasoning and experienced men is – assuming steadily, without pause, intermission, or hint of doubt, that police supervision is, in the case of this vice and disease, a specific safeguard. With reasoning and experienced men this audacious, and yet cautious assumption ruins the whole enterprise; for it is certain that two obligations press upon the innovators, which they must discharge before they can urge their scheme a single step. They must show, first, that no other and less questionable means are available to check the sin and its consequences; and, secondly, that police control would answer the purpose. There has been no attempt on the part of *The Times* or its correspondents to establish either of these points.

Are the conditions of the disease physical, or moral, in the first instance? This is a question nowhere adverted to; yet it is an all-important one when the thing wanted is prevention. In one sense the origin of the disease comes within the range of sanitary care. There was a time when smallpox was a new disease; and we hear the question asked sometimes (as the question 'where did the first brewer get the first yeast?'), how did the first smallpox patient come by the smallpox? The answer, on the part of the highest order of doctors and nurses, is that smallpox grows out of dirt and neglect at this day. It appears where contagion is out of the question. Thus it is, we are told, with other contagious diseases, including the one under notice. So far, it may be precluded by sanitary management. But this goes but a short way. The moral evil through which the disease is engendered separates the case entirely from that of plague and other ravaging diseases which have been placed under police control or sanitary care. In the case under practical contemplation the mischief has a moral origin. It is by intemperance that it spreads, and the remedy is therefore moral reform – the preservation of temperance, and the discontinuance of all incitements to intemperance. Have we tried anything of this sort with our soldiers? The soldiers' case has hitherto been a very hard one; but that of the rest of society seems to be more hopeful, in regard to temperance generally, than it has ever been before. Education and intellectual pursuits are spreading up and down and abroad in society on the one hand; and on the other, the industrial prosperity of the country is favourable to early marriage. It must take long to wear out the immorality about marriage generated by the commercial distresses, the wars and taxes, and dear bread of the early part of the century, by which marriage was discouraged in the most moral class of society, or turned into a pursuit of interest and ambition. A great increase of vice was an inevitable consequence; and we are now suffering, and terrified at the disclosure of, evils originating in a past generation.

Before rushing into any experiment of controlling vice by an express institution of it, we are bound to try the reverse experiment of restoring a habit of temperance throughout society. If ever the evil does decline and pass out of sight, it must be by the elevation of society above this sort of intemperance, as drunkenness has been seen to decline in classes and communities. With intellectual and moral cultivation of the greatest number, and increasing facilities for early marriage, must be joined a vigorous repression of temptation by putting in force the existing law. Our streets must be cleared of the nuisance now so flagrant as to serve as a pretext for a new system of police sanction and control. All dens of infamy should be abolished, whether occupied by thieves, sots, or prostitutes. What we want is not more police sanction, but less police connivance or negligence. When we have tried all means of keeping our people healthy, and occupied, and innocent, and domestic, and have removed from their path of life the grosser incitements which exist in defiance of law and order, we may hear what any advocate of the regulating system may have to say, if any such advocate may then desire a hearing. But we have much to do first.

As for the other point – whether police control answers the desired purpose – the advocates of regulation have produced no evidence of the comparative condition of our own and foreign countries. On their side no ground whatever for a judgment is afforded. On the other hand we have, in the Army Medical Reports, some very instructive facts, only needing to be duly compared and considered to warrant us in steadily setting our faces against any coquetting with the system, which cannot be shown to have done any good, while the mischief it breeds is monstrous and horrible.

In our own colonies, and in military stations at home, there are variations in the vice and the disease which are very remarkable, and at least as striking as any which could be shown to exist in protected and unprotected communities. The amount differs widely in the dragoons, and the artillery, and the infantry, and the military train at one station; and there is a variety as great in another colony, with a reverse proportion of the different arms. In the same place, the returns of different periods differ greatly, and so capriciously as to show that there are influences concerned which we do not as yet understand. We find one-third more in hospital in one term of years; and again, one-half less in another, without being able to account for the difference. Where the regulating system has been vigilantly carried out, we find no good done, as far as can be ascertained. If it is found that, under the same conditions in all respects, there are twelve soldiers in hospital under protection to nine without it, we may be assured that the case is not one for police management, because it depends on causes over which the police have no control.

There is evidence, accessible to all, that the regulation system creates horrors worse than those which it is supposed to restrain. Vice once stimulated by such a system imagines and dares all unutterable things; and such things perplex with misery the lives of parents of missing children in continental cities, and daunt the courage of rulers, and madden the moral sense, and gnaw the conscience of whole orders of sinners and sufferers, of whom we can form no conception here. We shall have entered upon our national decline whenever we agree to the introduction of such a system; and it is only necessary to bring the case fairly before the public conscience to secure us against any such fatal lapse.

The clergy ought to be looking to this, and we trust they are. They are charged, above other classes, with the promotion of education in our country, and with the enlightenment of individual conscience which is the security of all that we care for as a people. Why do not they remonstrate when vile and corrupting proposals are publicly made? or, have they attempted to speak, and been silenced? If they do not feel qualified to form an opinion, why do they not investigate the facts? But if they who can tell us most of the morals of private life will not bestir themselves, there are many more who might and ought; and our belief is, that if those gentlemen of England who have, or can obtain, a conviction as to the course to be taken under present circumstances were to speak their minds, the proposals we have discussed would be scouted, decisively and for ever.

(20 September 1863)

Some incidents which occurred last week render it necessary for us to return to a subject which cannot righteously be shirked while efforts are still made to mislead the judgment of society by false information, and pervert its moral sense by reasoning which is as fallacious as it is profligate. A weekly contemporary, writing of 'the Sin in Scarlet', undertakes to say that the discussion of the social evil which created so much disgust five years ago, has proved to have been very useful, inasmuch as a wide-spread conviction has become apparent that the sin and disease in question can be dealt with only by a system of police regulation; that is, by the establishment of a systematic registration of prostitutes, and inspection for the purpose of preventing the spread of the disease. Not content with this most ominous announcement, the writer further ventures to assert and assume that the opponents of such a system are pious noodles, prudish visionaries, inexperienced theorists, who would let society go to wreck rather than give up moral fancies of their own. The first of these declarations involves such fearful consequences, and the second is so utterly untrue, that those who really understand the history of the difficulty, and can show the falseness of the representation, would be criminal in neglecting to state how the case really stands. The assumption on which the whole argument proceeds – that police regulation has availed before, and will avail again – we have combated already; but it is necessary to point out here a flagrant misstatement, which might do great mischief if allowed to pass. The writer we refer to, while treating the subject of the regulation of the health of our soldiers, says that, according to the Report of the Committee, the effect of protection at Malta for a term was favourable in the highest degree, giving no intimation that the favourable return related not to the soldiers but to the sailors stationed at Malta during that term. Besides that this is quitting one question for another, the fact is precisely opposite to what is stated. At p.25 of the Report (Table N) the numbers are given for both the protected and unprotected periods; and these records show that the proportion of diseased is considerably smaller during the unprotected than the protected years. It is not to be endured that the public mind should be won over to favour the most tremendous of moral and social innovations by a manipulation of figures so negligent, or so dishonest, as this. The incident so speaks for itself that we need say no more on this head. We will only observe that we should long ere this have heard of the effect of such facts on the minds of the Committee if the facts had been true.

And what is it that everybody but pious noodles and impracticable sentimentalists is declared to be ready to do? What is it that we are to involve our country and people in, against the judgment of some of the first physicians and surgeons in the world, and in the face of disclosures of a corruption in some foreign countries so deep-seated, so ghastly, and so fantastic and unimaginable that even our own fearful ills are not to be named with it? What is it that we are to do, by the way of experiment, while there is strong ground for supposing that it must fail? Even where police regulation seems to reduce the mischief for a time, we invariably find it ceasing to operate after a longer or shorter period, and then the last state of things is infinitely worse than the first. New ways are tried as the old ones fail; disappointment ensues sooner or later, and then what can be done? The vantage ground which we still hold is lost to those unhappy people, and can never be regained. We may well try every honest and sensible method with courage and hope, before being tempted to a rashness which will leave us at length bewildered with despair.

But what is it that we are supposed to be eager to do? What is it that we are assumed to be thinking and believing? The case of the army is the one immediately in question. What is that case?

Our soldiers enter the army as youths, for the most part; and when they complete their term of service (ten years) they are under thirty. Artisans and labourers are, as a class, ready and willing to wait till thirty to marry; and there is no supposition prevalent in society that they must be vicious in the interval. Why should there be such a supposition in the case of the soldier – an assumption so confident as to cause him to be regarded and treated as a gross animal instead of a respectable man? Every soldier *can* marry, if he chooses. Six (besides sergeants) of every hundred are allowed to have their wives with them at the public expense. The remainder are advised not to involve themselves and others in poverty and difficulty by marrying without countenance and aid; but if they choose to run the risk, nobody can prevent it. What prevents the unmarried from being as temperate and well-conducted in their personal habits as the young men in civil life who await the time when they may fitly and reasonably marry? The sanitary reports of our armies at home and in India show but too plainly why the soldier is more likely to sink into gross animalism then men of other callings. The first step unquestionably should be to give him opportunity and inducement to be, like his old comrades the artisans and labourers, a self-respecting man.

But while favouring the element of brutality in him we had not need go further, and assume in practice that his animalism is a necessity which must be provided for. This is the fatal step which it is now hoped that the English Parliament and the English people may be induced to take. If the soldier is more immoral than his contemporaries of the working class, it must be because the standard of morality is lower in the army than out of it. Shall we then raise it to what we clearly see it might be, or degrade it further by a virtual avowal that vice is in the soldier's case a necessity, to be provided for like his need of food and clothing? This admission of the necessity of the vice is the point on which the whole argument turns, and on which irretrievable consequences depend. Once admitted, the necessity of a long series of fearful evils follows of course. There can be no resistance to seduction, procuration, brothels, disease, and methods of regulation, *when once the original necessity is granted*. Further, the admission involves civil as well as military society, and starts them together on the road which leads down to what the moralists of all ages and nations have called the lowest hell.

Further, what is necessary cannot be a sin. Any man, in the army and out of it, can see this; and every man who is treated as an animal will be sure to insist on it. Under such an arrangement it is no wonder that the officers of the continental system, police authorities and agents, and medical attendants in Lock Hospitals, everywhere complain that 'the labours of Sisyphus are entailed upon them'. There can be no repressive power in a system which treats a voluntary moral evil as a fate, and then proposes to take care of its consequences.

The writer we have referred to pretends to ridicule this gravest consideration of all by saying that we do not sanction nor legalise murder and other crimes by 'recognising' them, and cannot therefore be said to sanction this vice by 'recognising' it as a subject to control in its consequences. It seems scarcely credible that such nonsense as this should be adventured with a public which reads newspapers. We do not provide for the indulgence of murderous and thievish propensities, nor undertake the charge of reducing their horrors within endurable bounds, nor relieve and heal the perpetrators of the sin at the public expense – making them comfortable, and then sending them forth, well aware that they will sin again, and 'entail the labours of Sisyphus' on us. Nor, on the other hand, do we provide for the punishment of the sinner, in order to the protection of society. The cases are so radically different and so conspicuously alike, that it is not easy to understand the audacity of any attempt to confound them.

'The other course' proposed is to treat soldiers (and all other men) as moral agents, and not as animals. What men (soldiers and others) are reputed and expected to be, that they are sure to be. It is a national disgrace that our people should even have been asked to regard and treat their soldiers and sailors as predestined fornicators. Before this 'course' is adopted we shall be wise to try any and every other change – even to having our army stationary at home, and composed of married men. This, however, cannot be necessary, and it ought not to be imagined necessary while the young manhood of the working classes requires no such insulting management as our soldiery is supposed to demand.

We have no misgivings about the rectitude of public sentiment and the national conscience on this matter. What we fear is that false information, fallacious representations, and impudent assumptions should perplex our citizens and put them off their guard, so as to allow the moral sceptics who are trying to undermine our domestic purity and peace to obtain an advantage which it would be difficult to wrest from their grasp.

Annie Besant

The Legalisation of Female Slavery in England

(1876)

The first annual meeting of the 'British, Continental and General Federation for the Abolition of Government Regulation of Prostitution' was lately held at the Westminster Palace Hotel, and was largely attended by friends of the movement from all parts of England, from France, and from Switzerland. M. Loyson better known as Father Hyacinthe, was to have been present, but a severe attack of bronchitis chained him to his room; M. de Pressënsé, another well-known French speaker, was, however, there to take his place, together with M. Aimé Humbert, a gentleman whose talent appears to lie in organisation and in work more than in speech. The long-sustained labor of the Society of the Repeal of the Contagious Diseases Acts is well-known to our readers; many of them may not, however, be aware of the late extension of the sphere of their work, consequent on the thought and toil of their noble-hearted missionary, Mrs. Josephine E. Butler. The narrative of her crusade through Europe in the bitter cold, through France, into Italy, into Switzerland, over the Jura in the depth of winter, now lies before us, and is the record of a heroism equalled by few women, or by few men either. (The title of the book is *The New Abolitionists*, price half-a-crown, and it well deserves careful perusal.) Undaunted by failure, unwearied by defeat, loyal in spite of taunts, brave in spite of threats, gallant-hearted in face of a misery and and evil which might well drive the boldest to despair, Mrs. Butler sets us all an example by which we should strive to profit. Societies have been formed in all directions in France, Switzerland, and Italy, and these are now federated together into one body, sworn to destroy the recognition and encouragement of prostitution by the State.

Reaction from Christian cant upon this subject, and the rightful recognition of the sacredness and dignity of human nature, physical as well as mental, have to a great extent prejudiced many of the Secular party against the society agitating for repeal; the unwise and indelicate proceedings of scattering wholesale – so that they fell into the hands of the youth of both sexes – a number of tracts and leaflets dealing with medical details and with terrible crimes, the perusal of which by young girls and boys is about as wholesome as the reading of the *Police News*, roused a feeling of bitter indignation against those whose names appeared as leaders of the repeal movement, although they were very likely utterly ignorant of the follies perpetrated by unwise coadjutors. This phase fortunately seems to have disappeared; and it is hardly necessary to say that there is nothing in the speeches made at the meetings of the society to which the most prudish could object, unless, indeed, they object to the question being dealt with at all. Should this position be taken, surely it is then well to remind such that the discussions to which they object only become necessary through the existence of the evil attacked, and that the lack of modesty lies in the commission of the evil, and not in the endeavor to rescue the victims of it. When men of the world angrily object to women touching such a subject, they should remember that if they really respected the modesty and purity of women no such subject would be in existence, and that to those who gain nothing by the perpetuation of prostitution their loud indignation looks very much like the angry dread of a slave-owner who fears that the abolitionist preacher may possibly, sooner or later, deprive him of the services of his human property. I assert that the Secular party, as a whole, has a duty with regard to this subject, which it sometimes fails to discharge; a duty towards the promotion of national morality, or national health; and a duty also of asserting the sacredness of the individual liberty of women as well as of men, the inalienable rights of each over his or her own person.

It is perfectly true that marriage is different as regarded from the Secularist and from the Christian point of view. The Secularist reverences marriage, but he regards marriage as something far higher than a union 'blessed' by a minister; he considers, also, that marriage should be terminable, like any other contract, when it fails in its object, and becomes injurious instead of beneficial; he does not despise human passion, or pretend that he had no body; on the contrary, reverencing nature, he regards physical union as perfecting the union of heart and mind, and sees in the complete unity of marriage the possibility of a far higher and nobler humanity than either man or woman can attain in a state of celibacy. But, surely in proportion to our admiration for this true marriage, and our reverence for the home which it builds up, and which forms the healthy and pure nursery for the next generation of citizens, must be our pain and our regret when we come face to face with prostitution. By prostitution I mean simply and solely physical union sold by one sex and bought by the other, with no love, no respect, no reverance on either side. Of this, physical degradation and mental degradation are the invariable accompaniments; just as intoxication may be sometimes indulged in without leaving perceptible and permanent bad effects, but, persisted in, destroys body and brain, so may sexual irregularity be practised for a time with little apparent injury, but, persisted in, destroys as fatally as intoxication. This is no matter of theory, it is simply a matter of observation; individuals whose lives are irregular, nations where prostitution is widespread, lose stamina, virility, physical development, the whole type becoming degraded. It is urged that 'man's physical wants must be satisfied, and therefore prostitution is a necessity'. Why *therefore?* It might as well be argued, man's hunger must be appeased, and therefore theft of food is a necessity. The two things have no necessary connection with each other. Does prostitution promote the national health? If so, why this necessity for legislation to check the spread of contagious diseases? Those diseases spring from sexual irregularities and are an outraged Nature's protest against the assertion that prostitution is the right method of providing for the sexual necessities of man. As surely as typhoid results from filth and neglect, so does the scourge of syphilis follow in the wake of prostitution. These unfortunate women who are offered up as victims of man's pleasure, these poor white slaves sold for man's use, these become their own avengers, repaying the degradation inflicted on them, and spreading ruin and disease among those for whose wants they exist as a class. Mrs Butler truly writes:

> You can understand how the men who have riveted the slavery of women for such degrading ends become, in a generation or two, themselves the greater slaves; not only the slaves of their own enfeebled and corrupted natures, but of the women whom they have maddened, hardened, and stamped under foot. Bowing down before the unrestrained dictates of their own lusts, they now bow down also before the tortured and fiendish womanhood *which they have created*. . . . They plot and plan in vain for their own physical safety. Possessed at times with a sort of stampede of terror, they rush to International Congresses, and forge together more chains for the dreaded wild beast they have so carefully

> trained, and in their pitiful panic build up fresh barricades between themselves and that womanhood which they proclaim to be a 'permanent source of sanitary danger'.

Mrs Butler was writing from Paris, where the system is carried out which we have in England in only a few towns. If any one doubts the reality of this natural retribution, let him go and watch the streets where many of these poor ruined creatures may be found, and there see what women are when transformed into prostitutes – a source of disease instead of health, of vice instead of purity. Each one might have been the centre of a happy home, the mother of brave men and women who would have served the Fatherland, and we have made them *this*.

National morality and national health go hand-in-hand; a vicious nation will be a weak nation, and when a government begins to deliberately license women for the purposes of prostitution, it has taken the first step towards the ruin of the nation it administers. Louis Napoleon made Paris a sink of impurity; when the struggle came, the working-classes only – whose circumstances preserved them from gross excesses – were fit to fight for France. When the license system has had a fair trial, and the danger spreads and spreads, the government finds itself burdened with a class of women it has formed and certificated; and despairing of repressing disease by simple licensing, it begins to gather the women into houses, licensed also by itself; abroad, in England's colonies, these houses are licensed by England's rulers, and in France, in Italy, and elsewhere, they are found in most cities. Thus government becomes saddled with the supervision of a vast and organised system of prostitution, and struggles vainly against the evils resulting from it. In Italy, the government draws money from this source, and the shame of Italy's daughters and the profligacy of her sons are made a source of national revenue. And what is the result? simply that these houses become *foci* of vice, demoralising the youth of the country. 'Pastor Borel testified to having seen schoolboys entering these haunts of patented vice, with their satchels on their backs.' Well might we ask, with the old Roman Consul, Postumius: 'Can ye think that such youths are fit to be made soldiers? That wretches brought out of the temple of obscenity could be trusted with arms? That those contaminated with such debaucheries could be the champions for the chastity of the wives and children of the Roman people?' Profligates can never be made into sturdy citizens; muscles enervated by the embraces of purchased women will never be strung to heroism; a vicious nation will never be a nation of freemen. Then, in the name of the liberty we have won, of the glory of England, in the hope of the coming Republic, we are surely bound to protest against the introduction of a system among us that had degraded every nation in which it has been tried, which has only got, as yet, one foot upon our shores, and which, if we were true to our duty, we might easily drive from our English soil before it has time to sap the strength of our men and to destroy the honor of our name.

It still remains to see how this legislation is consonant with individual liberty; how it is touched by the question of a standing army, and how the evil of prostitution may be met and overcome.

I have already urged that no repressive Acts will destroy disease in a community where prostitution is encouraged, and that the wide prevalence of prostitution is ruinous to the physique of a nation; the admitted failure of regulation abroad, and the more and more complete control demanded for the police over the unfortunate women sacrificed to the 'necessities of men', prove, beyond the possibility of denial, that no eradication of disease is to be hoped for unless the registered women be given over thoroughly to continual supervision, and be literally made slaves, equally obedient to the call of the doctor who heals and to that of the man who infects, holding their bodies at the hourly order of each class, with no right of self-possession, no power of self-rule permitted to them. I challenge this claim, made in the name of the State, over one class of its citizens, and I assert that the sacred right of individual liberty is grossly and shamefully outraged by this interference of government, and that, therefore, every soldier of liberty is bound to rise in protest against the insult offered to her. No more inalienable right exists than the right of the individual to the custody of his own person; in a free country none can be deprived of this right save by a sentence given in open court, after a jury of his peers has found him guilty of a crime which, by the laws under which he lives, is punished by restriction of that liberty; so jealously is this right guarded, however, even in the criminal whose full exercise of it is temporarily suspended, that the limits within which it may be touched are carefully drawn; even in the prison-cell the felon has not lost all right over himself, and his personal liberty is only restricted on the points where the law has suspended it. No official may dare to compel a criminal to labor for instance, unless compulsion to labor is part of the judicial sentence. Firm and strong lies the foundation stone of liberty. *No citizen's personal liberty may be interfered with, unless proof of guilt justifying that interference be tendered in open court, and every citizen has a right to demand that open trial if he be arrested by any officer of the law.* This is the foundation stone which is rudely upset by the Contagious Diseases Acts. Under them women are arrested, condemned, and sentenced to a terrible punishment, without any open accusation or public trial; by simple brute force they are compelled to submit, despite their pleading, their cries, their struggles; they have no redress, no assistance; they are degraded both in their own sight and in the sight of all who deal with them; a free woman is deprived by force of the custody of her own body, and all human right is outraged in her person – and for what? in order that men may more safely degrade her in the future, and may use her for their own amusement with less danger to themselves. A number of citizens are deprived of their natural rights in order that other citizens may profit by their loss; and the State, the incarnation of justice, the protector of the rights of all, dares thus to sacrifice the rights of some of its members to the pleasures of others. It is idle to urge that these women are too degraded to have any rights; the argument is too dangerous for men to use; for if the women are too degraded, the men who make and keep them what they are are partners of their degradation; if the women are brutalised, only brutalised men can take pleasure in their society; every harsh word cast at these poor victims recoils with trebled force on the head of those who not only seek their companionship, but actually pay for the privilege of consorting with them.

But not only is liberty outraged by this intrusion on individual self-possession, but it is still further trampled under foot by the injustice perpetrated. Two citizens commit a certain act; the law punishes one by seizure, imprisonment, disgrace; it leaves the other perfectly free. No registration of women would be necessary if the other sex left women to themselves; no disease could be spread except by the co-operation of men. By what sort of justice, then, does the law seize one only of two participators in a given action? If it be pleaded the individual liberty may be overborne by social necessities – an argument which does not really admit of being used in this matter – then the 'good of society' demands the arrest, imprisonment, and examination of both parties; it can serve no useful purpose to allow unhealthy men to propagate disease among healthy women. If men have the right to demand the protection of the law, why should women be deprived of that same protection? If so necessary for the safety of men, why not necessary for the safety of women? Is it not, really, far more needed among the men, for, if a married man should contract disease, he may infect his innocent wife and his unborn children? Surely the State should interfere for the protection of these; and any man found in a house of ill-fame, or consorting with a prostitute, should be at once arrested, be compelled to prove that he is not married, and has no intention of being so; and, failing such proof, should be examined, and kept in hospital, if need be, until perfectly cured. The Acts would be very rapidly repealed in St Stephen's if all their provisions were carried out justly, on both sexes alike. 'Men would not submit to it.' Of course they would not, if one gleam of manhood remained in them; and neither would women, with any sense of womanhood, submit to it, if they were not bound hand and foot by the triple cord of ignorance, weakness and starvation. Poor, pitiful sufferers, trampled on by all, till the sweet flower of womanhood is crushed out for evermore, and only some faint breath of its natural fragrance now and then arises to show how sweet it might have been if left to grow unbruised. In the name, then, of Liberty outraged, in the name of Equality disregarded, we claim the repeal of these one-sided Acts, even if the bond of Fraternity prove too weak to hold men back from this cruelty inflicted on their sisters.

But, it is urged, with a celibate standing army, prostitution is a physical necessity. Then, if an institution lead to disease, deterioration of physique, and moral and mental injury, destroy the institution which breeds these miseries, instead of trying to kill its offspring one by one. A large standing army is unnecessary; the enforcement of celibacy is a crime. Of course, if a number of young and healthy men are taken away from home, kept in idleness, and deprived of all female society, immorality must necessarily result from such an unnatural state of things. The enforcement of celibacy on vigorous men always results in libertinage, whether among celibate priests or celibate soldiers. But the natural desires of these men are not rightfully met by the State supplying them with a number of licensed women; to do that is to treat them simply like brutes, and thereby to degrade them; it is to teach them that there is nothing holy in love, nothing sacred in womanhood; it is to change the sacrament of humanity into an orgie, and to pollute the consecration of the future home with the remembrance of a parody of love. With a celibate standing army prostitution *is* a necessity, and I know of no reason why we should look at facts as we should like them to be, instead of facts as they are; but a celibate standing army is *not* a necessity. The true safeguard of a free nation is not a large standing army; rather it is a well-organised militia, regularly drilled and trained, whose home-ties and home-interests will, in case of honorable war, nerve each arm with double strength, and string each muscle with the remembrance of the home that is threatened by the foe. The hero-armies of history are not the armies which idle in peace, and have nought in common with the citizens; such armies are the pet toys of aristocratic generals and are easily turned against the people by tyrants and by ambitious soldiers; but the hero-armies are the armies of citizens, less dainty in dress, less exact in marching, less finished in evolutions, but men who fight for home and wife, who draw sword in a just quarrel, but to please no prince's whim; men like Cromwell's Ironsides, and like Hampden's yeomen; men who are terrible in war because lovers of peace; men who can never be defeated while living; men who know how to die, but not how to yield.

What remedy is there for prostitution other than that attendent upon a celibate standing army? So far as the women are concerned, the real remedy for prostitution is to give women opportunities of gaining fairly paid employment. By far the greater number of prostitutes are such *for a living*. Men are immoral for their amusement; women are immoral for bread. Ladies in the upper classes have no conception of the stress of agony that drives many a forlorn girl 'on the streets'. If some of them would try what life is like when it consists of making shirts at three halfpence each (cotton not provided), and starving on the money earned, they would perhaps learn to speak more gently of 'those horrid women'. Lack of bread makes many a girl sell herself, and, once fallen, she is doomed. On the one side are self-respect, incessant toil, starvation; on the other side prostitution, amusement, plenty. We may reverence the heroic virtue that resists, but we can scarcely dare to speak harshly of the frailty that submits. Remunerative employment would half empty the streets; pay women, for the same work, the same wage that men receive; let sex be no disqualification; let women be trained to labour, and educated for self support; then the greatest of all remedies will be applied to the cure of prostitution, and women will cease to sell their bodies when they are able to sell their labour.

The second great remedy, as regards the women, is that society should make recovery more possible to them. Many a young and loving girl is betrayed through her love and her trust; having 'fallen' she is looked down upon by all; deserted, she is aided by none; everybody pushes her away, and she is driven on the streets, and in despair, reckless, hopeless, she becomes what all around call her, and drearily sinks to the level assigned her by the world. Meanwhile her seducer passes unrebuked, and in the families where she would not be admitted as scullery-maid he is welcomed as fit husband for the daughter of the house. That which has ruined her and many others is only being 'a little wild' in the circles where he moves. A public opinion which should be just is sorely needed. The act so venial in the man cannot be a crime in the woman, and if, as it is said, men *must* be immoral, then those who are necessary to them ought not to be looked down upon for their usefulness.

We ask for justice equal to both sexes: punishment for both, if their intercourse be a crime against society; immunity for both, if it be a necessary weakness. We hold up one standard of purity for both, and urge the nobility of sexual morality on man and woman alike.

More reasonable marriage laws would also tend to lessen prostitution. Much secret immorality is caused by making the marriage tie so unfairly stringent as it is today; people who are physically and mentally antagonistic to each other are bound together for life, instead of being able to gain a divorce without dishonor, and to be set free, to find in a more congenial union the happiness they have failed to find with each other. Reasonable facility of divorce would tend to morality, and would strengthen the bond of union between those who really loved, who would then feel that their true unity lay in themselves more than in the marriage ceremony, and was a willing, ever renewed mutal dedication instead of a hard compulsion.

But at the root of all reform lies the inculcation of a higher morality than at present prevails. We need to learn a deeper reverence for nature, and therefore a sharper repugnance for all disregard of physical and moral law. Young men need to learn reverence for themselves and for the physical powers they possess, powers which tend to happiness when rightly exercised, to misery and degradation when abused. They need also to learn reverence for the humanity in those around them, and the duty of guarding in every woman everything which they honor in mother, wife, and daughter. If a man realised that in buying a prostitute he was buying the womanhood of those he loved at home, he would shrink back from such sacrilege as from the touch of a leper. Woman should be man's inspiration, not his degradation: woman's love should be his prize for noble effort, not his purchased toy; the touch of a woman's lips should breathe of love and not of money, and the clasp of the wife should tell of passionate devotion and supremest loyalty, and never be mingled in thought with the memory of arms which were bought by a bribe, or caress that was paid for in gold.

Elizabeth Blackwell

Rescue work in Relation to Prostitution and Disease

(1881)

Ladies,
The letter inviting me to take part in your deliberations proposed many important subjects for discussion, and, amongst others, the subject of venereal disease amongst the fallen. On this point I was asked more especially to give information. I esteem it a privilege to aid in any way your very important work. I will begin by stating certain propositions which are fundamental in rescue work, and which are susceptible of ample proof.

First, by prostitution is meant mercenary and promiscuous sexual intercourse, without affection, and without mutual responsibility.

Second, its object is on one side pecuniary gain, on the other side the exercise of physical lust. It is the conversion of men into brutes, and of women into machines.

Third, so far from its being necessary to humanity, it is the destruction of humanity. It is the production of disease, of gross physical cruelty, of moral death.

Lastly, it should be checked by legislative enactment, and destroyed by social opinion.

Now to amplify and enforce the foregoing propositions would require a longer space than it would be right for one person to claim in a general conference, and would prevent the special consideration of the subject of disease. I will, therefore, simply offer them for consideration as fundamental propositions. I will only beg you to observe the distinct statement in the above, that it is sexual intercourse without affection and without responsibility that I have spoken of. I say nothing about the exercise of the sexual faculties in legitimate or illegitimate single unions, where affection and responsibility may enter as elements. However injurious, therefore, illegitimate but single unions may be to the welfare of society, I leave them entirely aside in these remarks, as not coming under the head of prostitution. I speak of the conversion of soulless lust into a business traffic – of the system of brothels, procurers, and so-called Contagious Diseases Acts – the system which provides for, not checks, vice. I solemnly declare that so far from this system being a necessary part of society, it is the greatest crime that can be committed against our common humanity.

Let me now lay bare to you the root of the whole evil system, because, as a physician acquainted with the physiological and pathological laws of the human frame, and as one who has lived through a generation of medical practice amongst all classes of the community, I can speak to you with a positive and practical knowledge rarely possessed by women. The central point of all this monstrous evil is an audacious insult to the nature of men, a slander upon their human constitution. It is the assertion that men are not capable of self-control, that they are so inevitably dominated by overwhelming physical instincts, that they can neither resist not control the animal nature, and that they would destroy their mental or physical health by the practice of self-control. Now it is extremely important that you should understand exactly the nature of this dangerous falsehood. It is that most dangerous of all kinds of falsehood – the perversion of truth. I think it was Swedenborg who said: 'I saw a truth let down into Hell, and forthwith it became a lie.' I have often thought of this bold image, when observing in the present day the audacious *lie* which is announced as truth, in relation to that grand and universal force of humanity, the sexual power.

When you see a poor drunkard reeling about the streets, when you recognise the crimes and misery produced by intemperance, you do not say that drunkenness is necessary to men, and that it is our duty to provide clean and attractive gin shops and any amount of unadulterated alcohol to meet the craving appetites of old and young. On the contrary you form a mighty crusade against intemperance. And how do you go to work? You recognise the absolute necessity which exists in human nature for amusement, social stimulus, refreshment, change, and cheeful hilarity; and so you provide bright entertainments, bands of hope and excursions for the young, attractive coffee palaces and clubs for the adults; in your entertainments you substitute wholesome drinks for 'fire-water'; you repress the sale of alcohol by legislative enactments, you arrest drunken men and women, and you establish inebriate asylums for their voluntary cure. You recognise that drunkenness is a monstrous perversion of legitimate human necessities, and you set to work to reform public opinion and social customs. Whilst on the one hand you legislate, on the other hand you educate. You perceive that the distinctive feature of humanity is its power of intellectually guiding life, and you train boys and girls in the exercise of this specially human faculty, moral self-control.

Now, my friends, lust, unchecked, untransfigured by affection, is like fiery alcoholic poison to the human constitution. It constantly grows by indulgence, the more it is yielded to the fiercer it becomes; an instinct which at first was governable and susceptible of elevation and enlightened direction and control, becomes through constant indulgence a vicious domination ungovernable and unrestrainable. When unsubdued it injures the health, produces disease, and grows into an irresistible tyrannical possession, which converts human beings into selfish, cruel, and inhuman devils. This is what the great universal force of sexual passion becomes, when we resolutely ignore it in childhood and youth; refuse to guide it, but subject it to accumulated vicious influences in manhood; and when even our churches and religious organisations are afraid or ashamed to deal with this most powerful force of our God-created human nature, we suffer lust to grow into a rampant evil – a real drunkenness – and then we have the audacity to say in this nineteeth century: 'This is the nature of men; they have not the human power of intelligent self-control; women must recognise this fact, and unbridled lust must be accepted and provided for.'

Now, I say deliberately, speaking as a Christian woman, that such a statement and such a belief, is blasphemy. It is blasphemy on our Creator who has brought our human nature into being; and it is the most deadly insult that has ever been offered to men. Do not accept this falsehood. I state to you as a physician, that there is no fact in physiology more clearly known, than the constantly increasing power which the mind can exercise over the body either for good or evil. If you let corrupt servants injure your little children, if you allow your boys and youth to practice self-abuse and fornication at school and college, if you establish one law of divorce for a man and another for a woman, if you refuse to protect the chastity of minors, if you establish brothels, prostitutes, and procurers, you are using the power of the mind over the body for evil. You are, indeed, educating the sexual faculty, but educating it in evil. Our youth thus grow up under the powerful influence of direct education of the sexual instincts in vice; but so far, even in our so-called Christian civilisation, we are ashamed to attempt direct education of those faculties for good.

I have made the above remarks as bearing directly on the subject of disease, as well as to call your attention to the proper place which 'rescue work' must occupy in humanitary work. As prostitution is the direct result of unbridled licentiousness, you may as well attempt to 'mop up the ocean' as attempt to check prostitution, unless at the same time the root of the evil, viz., licentiousness, is being attacked. Let it be distinctly understood, however, that I would encourage, not discourage, rescue work. I honour the self-denial and beneficence even of those who cannot see the source of the evil they are trying to mitigate; but I would much more strongly encourage those, who, being engaged in this work, do at the same time clearly recognise that the warfare against licentiousness is the more fundamental work; and who, whilst themselves engaged in rescue work, bid God speed and give substantial encouragement to all others who are directly engaged in the great struggle against every form of licentiousness, against every custom, institution, or law, that promotes sexual vice. Such earnest rescue workers are not simply mopping up the ocean, they are also helping by their encouragement of other fundamental work to build up a strong dyke which will resist the ravages of destructive evil forces. Thus, any efforts that can be made to teach personal modesty to the little boys and girls in our Board schools all over the country, form a powerful influence to prevent prostitution. Attention to sexual morality in educational establishments everywhere, in public and private schools and colleges, amongst young men and young women, is of fundamental importance. Also, efforts to secure decency in the streets, in literature, in public amusements, form another series of efforts which make a direct attack upon licentiousness, and cut away another cause of prostitution. Again, the abolition of unjust laws and the establishment of *moral* legislation forms another series of effort, and a vital attack upon the roots of prostitution. Always remember that the laws of a country possess a really terrible responsibility through the way in which they influence the rising generation. Inequality between the sexes in the law of divorce, tolerance of seduction of minors, the attempt to check sexual disease by the inspection of vicious women, whilst equally vicious men are untouched, all these striking examples of the unjust and immoral attitude of legislation, will serve to show how law may become a powerful agent in producing prostitution, through its direct attitude towards licentiousness. Now, every encouragement afforded by those engaged in rescue work to fundamental efforts to check licentiousness, either through subscription of money, through expressed sympathy or through active work, is also aid to rescue work, because such fundamental efforts attack the causes of prostitution.

Having thus stated distinctly the aspect under which rescue work must always be regarded – as a precious out-growth of Christian charity, but not as a fundamental reform – I will speak more fully on those points upon which my opinion has been more particularly asked for, viz., the question of venereal disease as affecting individuals and posterity, and the effect of late legislation on prostitution.

This subject of venereal disease is a very painful one to the non-professional mind, and I would not bring it before an ordinary audience. But this is an assembly of experienced women dealing directly with the vicious classes of society. I think such persons are bound to inform themselves on this subject. It is needed to their effective work, and I consider it an honourable duty to furnish what necessary medical knowledge I can.

Venereal disease, syphilis, gonorrhœa, are all names distinctively used for the diseases of vice, which exist in various forms. All forms of these diseases are injurious to the health of the diseased individuals. All forms also, are injurious to the health of the partner in sexual intercourse. But only one form of such disease is transmissable to offspring. I shall not enter upon the question of the extent to which these diseases endanger the health of the community. My long public and private medical observation lead me entirely to concur in the opinion of Mr Simon (formerly Medical Officer of the Privy Council), as to the exaggerated statements that have been made respecting the extent of these diseases. I fully recognise, however, the very grave character of venereal disease, and as a hygenist, I consider that *any* danger from such a cause should be checked.

These diseases are called the diseases of vice, because they spring directly from the promiscuous intercourse of men and women. Syphilis never arises from the single union of a healthy man and woman. We do not know the exact conditions under which promiscuity produces these diseases. Dirt, and excess of all kinds, favour their production; but we also know that, however apparently healthy the individuals may be who give themselves up to indiscriminate debauch, yet these diseases will speedily arise amongst them. Now, I wish to point out with emphasis (to you who are engaged with the criminal classes) this chief originating cause of disease – viz., promiscuity. It is a cardinal fact to notice in studying this subject, for it furnishes a solid basis of observation from which you may judge legislation, and all proposed remedial measures. If you will bear in mind that unchecked licentiousness, or promiscuity, contains in itself the faculty of *originating* venereal disease, you will possess a test by which you may judge of the good or evil effects of any proposed measure. Ask yourself whether any particular legislative act tends to check licentiousness in men and women; if not, it is either useless or injurious to the nation because it does not check that source of constantly increasing danger – viz., promiscuity. The effect of brothels and Contagious Diseases Acts, of establishments and laws which do not tend to check promiscuous intercourse, is to facilitate, not stop such vice, and cannot eradicate the diseases of vice which spring from such intercourse. The futility of any system which leaves the causes of disease unchecked and only tries to palliate its effects, is evident. The futility of such a false method would remain, even if it compelled the inspection of vicious men as well as women. But when a system attempts only to establish an examination of women, leaving men uninspected, and allowing free scope to the licentiousness of all, it becomes a direct encouragement to vice. It tends to facilitate that brutal custom of promiscuous intercourse without affection and without responsiblilities, which is the disgrace of humanity – the direct source of physical disease, as well as of measureless moral evil.

But I do not advocate letting disease and vice alone. There is a right way as well as wrong way of dealing with venereal disease. I consider that legislation *is* needed on this subject. It is unwise to propose to do nothing because legislation has unhappily done wrong. It is out of the question to suppose that in this age, when we justly boast of the progress of hygiene or preventive medicine, that so great an evil as the unchecked spread of venereal disease should be allowed to continue. It was the necessity of providing some check to the spread of disease, which operated a few years ago, when the unjust and immoral Contagious Diseases Acts were so unhappily introduced into England, by those who certainly could not have realised their injustice and immorality. All legislation upon the diseases of vice which can be durable, i.e., which will approve itself to the conscience of a Christian people, must be based upon two fundamental principles – the principles, viz., of equal justice, and respect for individual rights. These principles are both overturned in the Contagious Diseases Acts, Acts which are, therefore, sure to be abolished in a country which, however many blunders it makes, is equally distinguished for its love of justice, and its love of liberty. Respect for individual rights will not allow compulsory medical examination and treatment. The right of an adult over his or her own body is a natural fundamental right. We should uproot our whole national life and destroy the characteristics of the Anglo-Saxon race, if we gave up this natural right of sovereignty over our own bodies.

Society, however, has undoubtedly the right to prevent any

individual from injuring his neighbour. Interference to prevent such injury is just. The same sacredness which attaches to individual right over one's own person, exists for one's neighbour over his or her own person. Therefore no individual suffering from venereal disease has a right to hold sexual intercourse with any other person. In doing so, he goes outside his individual right and injures his neighbour. The wise principle on which lesgislation should act in dealing with venereal disease is therefore perfectly clear. Society has a right to stop any person who is spreading venereal disease; but it has not right to compel such a person to submit to medical treatment. It is of vital importance to recognise the broad distinction between these two fundamental points, viz., the just protection which society must exercise over its members, and the inherent right of self-possession *in* each of its members.

Accepting, therefore, one essential legislative principle so strongly emphasised by the Contagious Diseases Acts, viz., that the State has a right to interfere with sexual intercourse when its vicious action injures society – what we must strive for, is an enlightenment of public opinion, which will insist upon a *just* practical law upon this subject. The contagious diseases legislation indicates that the time has arrived when the intervention of law is needed, to place greater restraint upon the brutal lust which tramples on the plainest social obligations. A law, wisely enforced, making the communication of venereal disease by man or woman a legal offence, would place this necessary check on brutal appetite. Such a law would not be the introduction of a new principle into legislation. The principle of regulating sexual intercourse for the good of society, has always been recognised, and must necessarily be developed with the growth of society. It was reaffirmed, but in an injurious manner, a few years ago.

It is the just and moral application of this principle that must be insisted on, instead of an unjust, immoral, and tyrannical perversion of the principle. The necessary safe-guards in the working of such a law, the special inquiry, the protection of innocence, the avoidance of public scandal, etc., must be sought for with care. But the people have a right to require that legislators shall seek for, and find the right method, of enforcing any law which is just in principle, and necessary for the welfare of society. It is not only a duty, it is the greatest privilege of enlightened statesmen, to embody the broad common sense and righteous instinct of a Christian people, in the institutions of a nation.

A law which makes it a legal offence for an individual suffering from venereal disease to hold sexual intercourse with another person, and a ground for divorce, is positively required, in order to establish a true principle of legislation, a principle of just equality and responsibility, which will educate the moral sense of the rising generation, and protect the innocent. Any temporary inconveniences which might arise before the wisest methods of administering the law had been established by experience, would be as nothing compared with the elevating national influence of substituting a right method of dealing with the disease of vice, for the present unjust and evil method. The first direct means therefore, for checking venereal disease, is to make the spreading of this disease a legal offence.

Secondly, a necessary regulation to be established in combating the spread of this disease is its full treatment in all general dispensaries and hospitals supported by public and charitable funds. Such institutions have hitherto refused to receive persons suffering from disgraceful diseases, or have made quite insufficient provision for them. This refusal or neglect has left venereal diseases more uncared for than ordinary diseases. It was a perception of this neglect, which induced the establishment of special institutions for the cure of such disease. But no general hospitals supported by charitable funds given to cure the sick, have a right to refuse to make adequate provision for any class of curable suffering which is not infectious, i.e., dangerous to the health of the other inmates. The rigid exclusion in the past of venereal diseases from our general medical charities, on the ground of their disgraceful nature, has done great mischief by producing concealment or neglect of disease. This mischeif cannot be repaired in the present day by establishing special or so-called Lock hospitals. A strong social stigma will always rest on the inmates of special venereal hospitals, a stigma we ought not to insist upon inflicting; but no such stigma rests on the inmates of a general hospital. These hospitals are established for the purpose of relieving human suffering, and such suffering constitutes a rightful claim to admission not to be set aside.

Whilst thus advocating the careful framing of a law to make communication of venereal disease by man or woman a recognised legal offence, and whilst insisting upon the claim of this form of physical suffering to free treatment in all general medical charities, I would most earnestly caution you against the dangerous sophism of attempting to treat prostitutes as such. Never do so. Never fit women for a wicked and dangerous trade, a trade which is utterly demoralising to both men and women, and an insult to every class of women. The time is coming when Christian men and women will see clearly that this hideous traffic in female bodies, this frightful danger of promiscuous intercourse, must be stopped. Men themselves will see that they are bound to put a check upon lust, and forbid the exercise of physical sex to the injury of another individual. Serious consideration will then be given to the ways in which sexual power may be rightfully exercised, and preserve its distinctly human features of affection and mutual responsibility. Whilst social sentiment is growing towards such recognition, it is our duty as women, unflinchingly to oppose prostitution – mercenary indiscriminate sexual intercourse – and to refuse utterly to countenance it. The tenderest compassion may be shown to the poor creature who *ceases* to be a prostitute; the most beneficient efforts may be exerted, and sympathy for the individual human soul shown in the merciful endeavour to help every woman to leave this vile traffic, but never fit her for it.

Let no one countenance this human trade in any way by assisting to make vice itself attractive and triumphant over our human nature. I therefore earnestly counsel all those engaged in rescue work to keep this rule clearly in mind. Plead earnestly and affectionately with the prostitute to leave her vile trade. Offer her remunerative occupation; every rescue worker should be able to do this.[1] If she has children whom society may justly remove from her deadly influence, work upon her maternal feelings to induce her to become worthy of the care of the innocent, and regain her children; but do nothing to raise the condition of prostitutes as such, any more than you would try to improve the condition of thieves as thieves.

There is, however, another suggestion which I will present to you, because it bears directly upon our way of dealing with the vicious, and enforcing law, and I believe that its acceptance is only a question of time. I refer to the introduction of a certain number of superior women into the police organisation, to act amongst other duties, as heads of stations where women offenders are brought. I know the scenes which station houses witness. I know that policemen themselves often dread more to arrest a half-drunken woman than a man, and that it requires more than one man to overpower the maniac who, with tooth and nail, and the fury of drink, fights more like a demon than a human being. I know that such wretched outcasts rage in their cells like wild beasts, filling the air with shrieks and blasphemy that make the blood run cold. Nevertheless, wherever a wretched woman must be brought, there a true woman's influence should also be brought. When the drink is gone, and only the bruised disfigured womanhood remains, then the higher influence may exert itself, by its respect for the womanhood which still is there.

There are many special advantages to be derived from the

introduction of a few superior women into the police force. I think that the services of a lady like the late Miss Merryweather, for instance, would be invaluable, both for the actual service such a woman would render in the management of female offenders, and also for the higher tone that such appointments would infuse into the police force itself. It is only the appointment of a few superior women that I should recommend, and these must be solely responsible to the highest head of the organisation. The introduction of ordinary women corresponding to the common policeman, or in any way subordinate to lower officials, would be out of the question, and extremely mischievous. But to secure the insight and influence of superior and proved women in dealing with female offenders, by placing them in positions of authority and responsibility, would be a great step made towards the solution of some of the most difficult problems of society. The problems which grow out of the relations of the sexes have hitherto proved insoluble – the despair of legislation. With the most conscientious endeavour to act wisely, even our ablest statesmen do not know how to deal with them. It is impossible that men alone can solve these sexual problems, because there are two human elements to be considered in such questions, which need the mutual enlightenment, which can only result from the intelligent comparison of those two elements. The necessary contribution of wise practical suggestion which is needed from the intelligence of women, can only come through the enlarging experience gained by upright women. The reform now suggested is one of the steps by which this necessary experience may be reached, viz., the placing of some superior women in very responsible positions in the police organisation; positions where their actual practical acquaintance with great social difficulties may enlighten as well as stimulate their intelligent devotion in the search for remedies.[2]

Let me in conclusion heartily bid God speed to the noble efforts of your rescue societies and to all those engaged in re-instating our fallen womanhood. I hail with deep satisfaction the meeting of this Conference. It is a brave and sincere action on the part of Christian women to meet together and hold serious counsel, upon the wisest method of overcoming the deep practical heathenism of our society – the heathenism of tolerating and protecting mercenary promiscuous sexual intercourse.

NOTES

1 The necessity of being able to offer fair remunerative occupation is becoming more and more evidently a necessary condition of rescue work. The pitiful response, 'It is my bread', is now often addressed to those many noble-hearted young men who, instead of yielding to, remonstrate with, the street-walkers.

2 I cannot now enter upon a subject most difficult and important, a most prolific source of prostitution, viz., a standing army. I will only state to you for a special reason that my observation on the Continent of Europe has convinced me that the prevalence there of the system of universal military conscription, i.e., the compulsory enrolment of the entire male youth of the nation in the military service of a great standing army, is the greatest barrier that can exist to the gradual humanising of sexual life. Let us, therefore, most gratefully recognise that in our own country we have not the gigantic evil of military conscription to overthrow; and let us ever hold in honour the memory of our ancestors who have preserved us from that measureless curse.

Josephine Butler

An Appeal to the People of England on the Recognition and Superintendence of Prostitution by Governments

(1870)

Fellow Countrymen,

I trust you will pardon me for somewhat abruptly addressing to you the following appeal, which I do under a deep sense of responsibility, and with a sorrowful heart.

I write in the name of the thoughful and Christian women of England, and I beg leave to draw your attention to the attempt now being made by a vigorous and active association, calling itself an 'Association for promoting the extension of the Contagious Diseases Act to the Civil Population', to bring into action generally throughout the country measures which provide for the legislation of prostitution. We are deeply convinced that such legislation is opposed to the interests of morality; while it will prove, as it has proved in other countries, ineffecutal to stamp out disease. Its effect upon those large classes of men to whom, in default of religious principle or a high moral training, the laws of the country are a guide to conscience, is to teach them to look upon fornication not as a sin and a shame, but as a necessity which the State takes care that they shall be able to practice with impunity. In increasing the facilities to vice, you must certainly increase its noxious results. Such is found to be the consequence of the systemising and recognition of prostitution in Paris, and in many Continental cities. Special disease is not less prevalent at the present day in Paris than in London, and this may be easily accounted for; for while contagion on the one hand, may be to a *certain extent*[1] diminished by the surveillance exercised upon fallen women, on the other hand so many more men are induced, by fancied security from the danger, to indulge in illicit intercourse with these women, that the risks run by the community at large, and the contagion actually spread are in the one case as great as the other – nay, it would seem they are greater, since some even of the promoters of the extension of this system, together with high medical authorities in Paris, pronounce the state of Paris, in respect to this disease, to be most terrible; and in every place where such a system prevails, men are encouraged to become fornicators by having presented to them for their use, openly, and with the sanction of the State, women with the government stamp upon them, warranting them healthy and sound. Such vice is common in all classes in Paris, it is thought no shame, and the almost universal prevalence of it increases largely the demand for these unhappy women, so that in order that the existing staff of prostitutes should not be 'overworked', it is reported by witnesses from Paris that fresh relays of healthy women have to be continually drafted in from the provinces. (The women of certain provinces are in great request, as being found by the *Agents de Mœurs* to be peculiarly strong and healthy.) Dr Leon Lefort lately replied in answer to the question why venereal disease is not greatly diminished in Paris 'It would require the French police to enrol thirty thousand women to *make the system complete*, and to give any hope of coping with the spread of the disease.' And the history of every Continental town where this system prevails, show a constant increase in the number of prostitutes from year to year, this increase being out of all proportion to any increase in the population in general; it is a gulf into which women are flung by thousands, but which never closes. Such are the effects which inevitably follow the introduction of a '*system*' by which the souls and bodies of tens of thousands of women are deliberately, and under the direction of the government, sacrificed to a supposed necessity.

While the public acknowledgment of such a supposed necessity is deeply degrading to men, both as an avowal that they are utterly and hopelessly the slaves of their own passions, and as an incentive to increased immorality, it is utterly destructive to the hopes of all good women for a purer and better state of society. The happiness and character of all virtuous women throughout the land must eventually suffer from the consequences of such measures, while upon the poor women, on whom the proposed Law takes immediate effect, there falls a blight and a destruction more complete than anything they can in its absence experience – heavy as their punishment in any case is.

The women who are terrified to submission again and again to the ordeal which this law requires them to submit to, are reduced by it to the character of wild beasts, in whom every trace of womanhood, and all hope of recovery are deadened and crushed out. The last lingering light of conscience is extinguished in them by the direct official sanction, which, under this law they cannot but believe they possess for the practice of their vocation.

Further, the proposed measures, politically considered, are without precedent in the history of our country in their tyranny, and their defiance of all which has ever been considered by Englishmen as *justice*. If you will study the provisions of the Acts of 1866 and 1869, and the evidence given last session before the Select Committee of the House of Commons, you will see how distinctly the introduction of such a law tends to the creation of a bureaucracy in England, which would be intolerable to a free people. It resembles the Spanish Inquisition in its system of paid spies, and the admission of anonymous whispers as evidence not to be rebutted. Contrary to the entire spirit of English Law, the whole burden of proof is thrown not upon the accuser, but upon the accused; there is a complete absence of all fair and open court – to say nothing of jury; and the accused, in this case, are the weakest, the most helpless, and most friendless of the community.

By this law a crime has been *created* in order that it may be severely punished; but observe, that has been ruled to be a crime in women which is not to be considered a crime in men. There are profligate men who are spreading disease everywhere, but the law does not take effect on *these*.

I have said that a crime has been created – which is to be severely punished. The alternative for every woman accused is either to appear before the Magistrates, or to submit to a torture which to any woman with a spark of feeling left in her is worse than death. Refusing to submit to the torture she is imprisoned. There is no escape from the one penalty or the other. An innocent woman who is accused may escape the torture, but she cannot escape the appearance before the Magistrates, and that very appearance means ruin to the character and prospects of a poor and virtuous woman. The tortures to which these poor fallen women (to whom, if there be an acknowledged *necessity* on the side of men for their existence, the State ought to be grateful and tender) are subjected by this Law, has no parallel except in the darkest and foulest forms of persecution practised on helpless women in the cruelest ages of history. This and none other is the character of the inquisition imposed by this Law, albeit it is advocated and practised in the name of humanity. Insensibility engendered by custom, and ignorance of the nature of women alone can account for the fact that men should be found to practice such horrors in the name of humanity. It is sometimes said that to *these* women it is no torture.

Perhaps it is to women rather than to men that they *confess* the shame and the anguish. I will only say, from a large and intimate experience of women of this pitiable class, that I never found one among them, except those very few who are degraded so far as to be beyond the pale of human nature, who did not shrink with horror from that torture, and who would not rather endure any amount of bodily pain than that which is so intolerable to womanhood, violence done to the deepest and the most indelible instincts of her nature. How, then, must the better and more tender, – the very young, the still womanly among them, regard it? It is a solemn question, whether it be lawful for the State to inflict torture of so cruel and indecent a nature upon any of its subjects for *any given end whatsoever*, or for *any crime that can be named* – to say nothing of the lawfulness of the infliction of such torture for a crime which it treats as a crime *only* in one sex, and *only* among the *poor* of that sex. For the torture, be it observed, is to be inflicted for the crime of being a prostitute, (a crime to which thousands are on the evidence of witnesses before the Parliamentary Committee, driven by absolute starvation) while the crime for refusing to submit to the torture (which is the second crime *created* by this law), is punished by imprisonment with hard labour.

It may be objected that these are not criminal proceedings – that the ordeal is imposed without the assumption of criminality, prostitution not being a crime against the State. But disobedience to a law is a crime against the State, and this ordeal being in fact as great a punishment as any criminal could be subjected to, and being regarded as such by women, a woman will naturally if possible refuse to obey it, and is thus forced to become a criminal, and may be imprisoned. Again, this law does not clearly define a prostitute. It is the strangest, the most indefinite law that was ever made, since it does not define that to which it is applicable, but leaves it to be defined by those who in each case are to apply it. Nay, it is most awful in its indefiniteness, for the definition of a woman to whom this law is applicable is to be the *suspicion of a policeman*. There is no woman, then, however virtuous, to whom this law is not applicable, for there is no woman on whom the *suspicion of a policeman may not fall*. The quality of 'suspiciousness' will be vastly stronger in some policemen's minds than in others, so that the definition above is wide and varying. I do not wish to make too much of individual cases which have occurred, of arrest and outrage practised on virtuous women; but let us look at this law in its broad sense, in the indefiniteness of its terms, dangerous alike to virtue and to freedom, and in the awful conclusion by which at best it must be advocated, and say if it is not a blot on the legislation of any nation. It is a fouler blot on the legislation of England than even it might be elsewhere; for in England always, except in this case, are the rights of *habeas corpus* respected. Is this a law for Englishmen to sanction? Is this a law to be made in a country where individual liberty has been so carefully guarded? Nay, it is a law for a country of slaves. Are Englishmen to benefit, and our country to become greater, if English women are to be deprived of the rights hitherto inherited by all who are born in her? There are few civilised countries in which people are not brought forward to a fair trial when under suspicion of having done wrong. Individual liberty in most lands is in the *generality* respected, but that which constitutes the freedom, which is the birthright of Englishmen and women, is not the knowledge that *for the most part* individual freedom will be respected, but the knowledge that *in all cases it must be respected.* Freedom, in this sense, is gone from every individual English woman, while the individual liberty of a large class of women is continually violated, and while she herself may run the chance, though it may be but the ten thousandth part of a chance, of having *habeas corpus* disregarded in her own case. I do not speak too strongly. Freedom is the gift of God, and man has only a right to deprive his fellow man of that gift when he is guilty of *crime;* and if immoral women are to be accounted criminals, what shall we say of immoral men? Again if 'prostitution is a necessity', which the chief abettors of the Act assert is the basis of the whole measure, then what shall we say of the justice of treating those as criminals, who minister, to their own loss, to this social necessity? A remarkable book has just been published in Paris, from which I extract the following:

> If the number of female prostitutes is considerable, that of male prostitutes is much greater. The latter, being subjected to no medical inspection, quietly infect our population with their corruption, are a permanent danger to public security, and propogate debauchery, blackening even the imagination of the honest and pure, obliged to take account of their existence, and to endure encounters with them; but the man in this case, is irresponsible. By a strange anomaly, he, declared a major, is irresponsible; she (the woman), declared a minor, is responsible.

A reviewer of this book, in one of the Paris journals, remarks, 'I think these just and contemptuous words are conclusive, without dispute, and prove how iniquitous and how illogical is the relative position of man and woman in regard to morality.'

We must believe that the promoters of this Act have been actuated by a humane desire to arrest a terrible physical scourge, that many of them have forced themselves to look at the question as a purely sanitary one, and while one cannot but feel that the plan of the enquiry was skilfully and carefully framed to exclude the moral question involved, one cannot fail to observe in the evidence that several Members of Committee found a difficulty in excluding it from their own minds and consciences. Disgust with the details which it was needful to hear, may have deterred some from forcing themselves to a candid examination of the matter from all sides. It is impossible to think of our legislators as acting, in such a matter, except under a deep sense of responsibility, but for the law itself we dare not utter one word of excuse. It is not a law for Englishmen to endorse: it is a law worked out in secrecy, mystified by indefiniteness, upheld by violence. When it is unveiled it will be seen to stab at the very heart of freedom. It is a fatally retrograde step. It is called a crusade against sin and misery. It is a crusade against freedom, and to promote the more safe and convenient practice of vice. It is an insult to God and to man.

It is not in England alone that the battle concerning such sinister laws will be fought out with the bitterness of death, and with the intensity of a crucial and final decision. In England it is perhaps little known that a social revolution is pending on the Continent, turning upon this very point, the superintendence of prostitution by Governments, based on the assumption that prostitution is a necessity. I have lately been present at some meetings on the Continent, at which there were representatives of Germany, France, Russia, Switzerland, and Italy. The feeling expressed on this subject was unanimous and strong. It is supposed by many people in England that Parisians at least are universally satisfied with the system in Paris; but it is not so. There are men and women in Paris, (their number is increasing every day) who, in their earnest efforts for moral and social progress, point to this shameful system as the first obstacle to be removed. A petition has lately been addressed to the French Chamber for the removal of the great 'Plaie Sociale', the 'dedication by the Government of a large section of the female population to purposes of immorality' and in a short time petitions will be addressed to every Government in Europe on this subject. A lady at one of the meetings I allude to, spoke thus:

> The first hope which I conceived in beginning this work was that of causing this shameful grievance to come to an end. In the name of *morality* I demand it. Those who refuse us, are those who desire to profit by the advantages which this

> abuse secures them. Everywhere we meet with opposition. This will not cease until the *laws* are changed.

And an Italian lady of high character writes thus, on behalf of those women upon whom destruction is brought by such a system: 'Truly it is time that women should absolutely refuse to submit to this vile tyrannical inquisition upon their persons, and that they should pronounce themselves universally and energetically against this perpetual outrage on decency.' And wherever there are, as there are in every country in the world, high-minded, intelligent, and honourable women, ready to head a protest against this tyranny, there are also invariably to be found just men to aid them; and though women may be weak, justice is strong, and the desire of justice in the hearts of these men is all the more powerful a passion, because those who are suffering the injustices are the weakest. There is a progress of opinion in these days which no legislature can resist, and in the heart of that progress will be found working that inextinguishable instinct of womanhood which refuses that a large portion of her sex shall be systematically outraged for the supposed good of the rest of the community; an instinct which has been implanted in woman, by whom? – by God himself; and of which it might be said to those who act in violation to it: 'Take heed lest ye be found to fight against God.' If our legislators should succeed in imposing upon our country laws, which are already beginning to create a secret revolution abroad, they will shortly be obliged to confess themselves far behind the progress of the age, and to perceive that they have been guilty, however benevolent their aim, not only of a great cruelty, but of a great blunder.

You have perhaps been told that this Act is not identical with the French system. The difference, such as it is, is of detail only, and not of principle. You are perhaps aware that the Prussian Government derives some portion of its revenue from the payments of the prostitutes under its control. Our Government has not yet proposed to do the same: but the expenses incident to the working of the Act are to be paid out of the national purse. Now it is affirmed by the supporters of the Act that the present staff of the special police, (woman hunters) for the localities where the Act already operates, is very insufficient, and that it must be greatly increased. If the provisions of the Act are to become universal, the taxation throughout the country must be enormously increased to meet the demand; and it is most probable that the unpopularity of such an increase of taxation would oblige

Government to fall back on the expedient of helping itself through the earnings of harlots.

The following quotation from the Parliamentary evidence shows how naturally to the minds of some of the Promoters of the Act, this expedient must follow for the perfecting of the system. A witness says, in reference to a question as to the distinction to be drawn between common street-walkers who openly solicit, and a superior class of women who more artfully practise their vocation:

> 797. Q. Do you not think that it would be difficult to draw the line in an Act?
>
> *A.* I do not consider that necessary; I think that every common prostitute should be registered, and a day named for medical examination. It would be desirable to classify, as far as possible, the women for this purpose, a certain day in the week being set apart upon which medical examinations would be made *by payment*; this would enable the better class of women to classify themselves, *and would partly defray the expense of putting the Act in operation.* Great discretion, however, is necessary in carrying out an Act such as that contemplated.

(This injunction to discretion and caution occurs constantly in the evidence. It would appear that the minds of some of the examiners and witnesses were alive to the prospect that the 'common sense' and justice of the English public at large might become a serious obstacle to the carrying out of the measure.)

It is mere quibble to dwell on the absence, for the present, of a *formal* license. What else is the system of registration by which women are compelled to obey the periodical summons? It must be remarkable to everyone who will go carefully through the evidence how plainly the committee speak of 'the system', thus admitting its substantial identity with Continental measures. The essence of all the Acts is the compulsion under which women are placed in regard to the dreaded and cruel ordeal I have alluded to: to secure this it seems that legislators, who support the Act will do almost anything, and in order to enforce this over the civil community they must inevitably adopt the French system in its entirety, and they must back it up with an enormous weight of compulsion. Duchâlelet,[2] in his faithful and terrible history of the growth of this system in France, describes the lull which succeeded its first introduction. Surprise, ignorance, terror, kept the victims of it quiet, and to some extent submissive at first; but there succeeded to this an agitation, a rebellion; '*recalcitrantes*' increased every day, women, even the most depraved, cried out against this tyranny in the streets; minute directions were given to the police as to how to deal with the women when they flew, like enraged tigresses, at their throats; girls had to be driven to the place of torture at the point of the bayonet; many fainted *before* the ordeal; every kind of stratagem was invented and circulated among them for evading the police, and every form of espionage and tyranny was superimposed by Government upon the original Act to prevent such evasion. Hunted down, terrified, imprisoned, and despairing, the women at last succumbed, and again there succeeded a period of death-like submission, the effects of which can only be truly estimated by one who is thoroughly acquainted with the cold, passionless vice of Paris, the effeminacy of its men, the rapid, steady increase of prostitution, together with the decrease of virtuous marriages since the introduction of the system, the dissolution of family life, the fears of the Emperor lest the population should die out, and the utterly brutalised condition of its *filles de joie*, who represent a type of animal as yet unknown in England.

The Secretary of the noble 'Rescue Society' in London, says:

> The English fallen women who frequent the Haymarket and other similar resorts will be found to speak with the utmost abhorrence of the greater degradation of the foreign women perambulating the same neighbourhoods; and the Committee have known more than one instance where the loathing produced by a knowledge of the habits of these women has led some English girls to desire to escape the abominations incidental to a continuance in a career of sin.
>
> Moreover, the wheedling, shameless pertinacity of the solicitations of the foreign women who abound in certain quarters of the metropolis is rarely, if ever, followed to a like extent by English girls; and this difference has often been noted and commented on at the time by the members of this Society. It seems impossible in conversation to touch the heart or conscience of a French fallen girl, and the arguments which are found most successful with an English girl are found entirely inoperative to produce any compunction or feeling of shame in the former.
>
> There is another noticeable feature in connection with this subject. The French woman cooly speculates in her course of infamy as if in regular trade, saves money, and retires: the English fallen woman rarely, if ever, saves; but rids herself as soon as possible of the ill-gotten gain, as if it were

> contaminating, or its possession a curse. In fifteen years' experience the managers of this Society – one, considering the number of cases dealt with, unequalled by any similar committee in this country, have not met with more than one or two English women who have made a persistent effort to save money. It is one thing, therefore, to eradicate physical disease, assuming (which is shown to be the merest assumption) that such will be the result, and, whilst doing so, to damn the soul. It is another and preferable one to avoid – strenuously to avoid – any course which tends to harden and sear the national and personal conscience.

In my own experience I have met with several unfortunate women who habitually gave all they earned in their hateful trade to the relief of the poor. One of these said to me, 'I know I am *very* bad, but I will be as good as I *can* be.' Another said 'I am a wicked girl, but I love little children.' This girl bestowed all her earnings, (as I learned after her death) on little children, and very old people who were in distress. She also nursed tenderly, till it died, the child of a wicked and cruel procuress by whom she was engaged, and could scarcely be torn away from its coffin, wildly wishing to 'follow that child whither it had gone'. I could multiply instances of this kind of agonised grasping at scraps of virtue in these outcasts, of whom so large a proportion are driven by a combined force of circumstances, which only the strongest virtue could resist, into this rank. And these are the persons whom Dr. Davies, medical officer, at the late meeting at Bristol, pronounced in one fearfully sweeping and inclusive sentence to be '*dead*' to virtue.

A lady in a great seaport ventured into a house filled with these unhappy girls. Sitting down among them, she opened her Bible, and without preface, read that beautiful chapter of St John's Gospel, (a strange one to choose, some would say, for such an occasion), 'Let not your heart be troubled, neither let it be afraid; In my Father's house there are many mansions.' One, and then another of the girls sat down on the floor round the feet of the reader, listening with awe and softened faces. At the close, one said to another, 'I will go this day to a Penitentiary. Lizzie, will you go?' and they went, another and another followed, and maintained through the years of discipline the resolution then formed. Persons capable of conceiving an aspiration after holiness and peace on the hearing of those matchless words, which many a Pharisee hears time after time in Church with a stony heart, cannot be wholly devoid of a lingering self-respect. The greater includes the less.

But it is of such that Dr Davies and his *confrères* say, 'In that class of women self-respect is dead.'

This view, no doubt it is which enables such men to regard the persons of these poor girls as mere carcases for the dissecting room. A gentleman, full of indignation against this assertion, said, 'these helpless girls are considered by such men it would seem as created only for death and the dunghill here, and perdition hereafter'. In France there was lately an exposure of cruelties practised by vivisection in the cases of horses and other animals. Let us suppose the case of a horse which the operator, *believing to be dead*, proceeds to dissect: the approach of the knife to some sensitive nerve reveals, by the quiver which runs through the poor creature's frame, and its spasmodic effort to escape, that it was *not* dead, and that the operator has been guilty, through the falseness of his own conclusions as to its state, of *vivisection.* Such is precisely the case of the thousands of women (creatures at least originally as noble as a horse) whose womanhood the majority of the medical faculty seem to agree with Dr Davies in pronouncing to be *dead*, and whom they treat accordingly. And mark the result! The horse is killed by that very stroke of the knife which revealed that there was life in him; and the last remnant of modesty in these human victims is killed by the infliction of that bitterest agony induced by the revival under the process of vivisection of the strong instincts of womanhood. But such agony cannot last. The very process which aroused into existence the whole sensitiveness of that most sensitive of God's creatures, a woman, has in the same moment dealt its death-blow. One of the officers appointed by the French Government to carry out the provisions of its system, said to an English gentleman, 'The women betray strong emotions at first, but very soon they care *not a sou for anything.*' The streets of Paris are to the eyes of a foreign visitor, orderly, bright and beautiful, like a magnificent whited sepulchre; but what a Golgotha within, thanks to the wisdom and the ingenious legislation of man!

We are constantly told that the French system renders the women orderly, quiet, and submissive, while it greatly lessens their misery by the care taken of their health. To the legislators, who have brought about such a state of things, we may apply with force the words of Tacitus 'Solitudinem faciunt; pacem appellant.'

Appeals are constantly made to our feelings in support of the Act. We are told of the thousands of innocent women and children in the better as well as the lower classes, who are at this moment the victims of the terrible disease which it aims at suppressing. Now an appeal to our human tenderness is not likely to be received with indifference by the women and mothers of England, who, for the most part, are not unfamiliar with the sight of suffering, and who are not generally idle in the work of alleviating or removing it. We surely mourn, if any do, over the 'slaughter of the innocents'; and those among us who have ministered in Lock Hospitals and other receptacles of the sick and miserable, are sufficiently aware of the prevalence and virulent nature of the disease in question. Let it be understood that we at least as much as any, desire to arrest disease, to rescue every evil-doer, man or woman, from the present and future consequences of sin. The question therefore to all of us, is of the most vital consequence, 'how is this best to be done?' We believe that from a medical point of view alone (having forced ourselves to examine the subject, though preferring to leave the arguments connected with it to be dealt with by others) these regulations proposed are futile. And we are profoundly convinced that *wherever moral principle is loosened, and evil deeds are consequently multiplied in a community, there will inevitably, by a law of God and of nature, follow increased bodily disease.* In a *material* as well as spiritual sense it is universally true that, 'The wages of sin is death.' 'Fornicators and adulterers God will judge.' The judgment may not immediately succeed transgression, but, given a generation or two after the passing of such an Act as we are considering, with its tacit license granted to vice, we shall see that the inevitable judgment is not to be averted by any scheme whatsoever that man can devise, except one which is based firmly upon a recognition of the moral law, and of the harvest of results to be reaped in the future. While writing the above the post has brought to me a letter from the Editor of a Paris journal; he, being one of those who are of opinion that the medical surveillance exercised in Paris does lessen disease among those *who come under* that surveillance, and not regarding the question with any over-sensitive predjudices on moral grounds, is in a position to speak dispassionately of the facts before him. His testimony is therefore of no small value as to facts. He says that since these regulations were in force they have seen prostitution in Paris develop greatly:

> It is no longer possible to walk a step in Paris without being jostled by a crowd of unfortunates. Whilst protection therefore may have advantages, it has also inconveniences. Precisely because the public health is less exposed, men, finding a greater security, are less restrained. Thus, legislation has ministered to the health of the prostitutes, and by a *contre-coup*, has augmented the number of those who are devoted to it, and the number of men who seek the society of prostitutes. To render debauchery less dangerous is to

encourage it, to extend it. Here is my personal view of the matter.

Where is the judgment, where are the powers of reasoning of Englishmen, if they can look upon the testimonies which crowd upon us from abroad, and from the contemplation of human nature generally to this particular case, and not see that such a result as this must inevitably sooner or later eat into the heart of that which is at present their chief concern, the *physical* well-being of the community. *Inevitably wide-spread disease must follow wide-spread immorality*. Science, religion, and experience all alike teach that lesson.

Some of the appeals made to us on behalf of the innocent who suffer amaze one by their impudence. I must be excused for making use of so harsh a word, but I can call it nothing else. These appeals assume that the only remedy of this slaughter of the innocent is the making safe for married men the path of the fornicator. They continually speak as though there were but two sets of persons to be considered – fallen and contagious women on the one hand, and pure women and children on the other. It is curious to observe how they ignore in their arguments the existence of that intermediate class, who convey contagion from the one to the other. Certain persons resent, as if it were an indelicacy, any allusion to that most important link, the adulterous husbands and fathers, who are dispensing disease and death in their families. Yet to a truth-loving mind the question must occur, 'would not the abstinence from fornication on the part of these husbands and fathers be at least as direct a mode of hindering disease, as that of reducing a vast proportion of the female population to a condition worse than that of the lower animals for their convenience?' But, it is objected, it is not for married men chiefly that this safe provision needs to be made, but for youths who will afterwards be married; and there is an affecting case in point always ready for citation, of some young man upon whom life-long suffering has been entailed by a single lapse of his youth, and not only on himself but on his wife and children. We, mothers of England, are not less concerned for our sons than for our daughters. Assuredly we do not fail in compassion towards anyone upon whom retribution falls so heavily; and undoubtedly the penalty for a single offence in a man is sometimes very heavy; in the case of a woman it is invariably overpoweringly heavy. Such a case as this is one which is continually cited as an argument appealing at once to our reasons and our compassion for the establishment of these public regulations. But let us look at the matter a little more closely, and see whether it is wholly compassionate either to the erring or the innocent to set this Act into operation. Does it not occur to those who use this argument that under the operation of this Act such lapses among young men, who would afterwards be married, would be somewhat more frequent, nay that they would become so much more frequent as altogether to counterbalance the advantages said to be gained by the one-sided expedient which we deprecate. We know what human nature is, and the very prevalence of this terrible disease proves a state of morality among men which warrants us in saying that the moment the double restraint is withdrawn – the moral and physical – by means of the recognition by Government on the one hand of the veniality or necessity of such offences, and by the supposed removal of a material risk, young men in England will plunge into vice as freely as they do in countries which have adopted this system. I have dwelt at some length on this part of the subject, but I beg to be excused for doing so, since the testimony which pours in from foreign countries,[3] while I write, is of such weight and significance that I cannot but feel that the advocates of the measure at home have failed to look at this part of the matter calmly, and with a wise consideration. Before leaving this part of the subject I must say, with shame and grief, that it is well known to those women whose charity leads them to seek out their unhappy sisters in their haunts of sin, that these incautious young men are not in fact the only persons in whose interest this Act proposes to work; that it is not the young and unmarried alone who support these abodes of infamy.

We are asked what we have to offer in place of the proposed Government interference. We have much to offer – much to suggest; and this is the most important part of my subject. Within the limits of this appeal I can only state generally what will be brought forward carefully and in detail hereafter.

At the late meeting at Bristol, an advocate of the Act spoke as follows:

> It appears to me that the cure of these unhappy women of their bodily disease is so naturally connected with the attempt to reclaim them from the course of life on which they have entered, that it is almost impossible in a country like England to dissociate the one from the other.

Now with these words we entirely agree; this speaker has accidentially indicated the basis upon which the measures *we* advocate must be built up. We believe that any considerable mitigation of disease throughout the country can only take place when associated with direct, large-handed, and enlightened efforts for the reclamation of the fallen and still more for the *prevention* of prostitution itself; we believe also that the mitigation of disease can only be attained when government has recognised the necessity of dealing out equal justice to all classes and human beings alike, and taken account of the inextinguishable instincts implanted by God in the nature of woman. We believe that result can only be attained when the means for that end have been once and for ever dissociated from legal enactments, and from that inhuman ordeal, to which by such legal enactments women are driven. Now let us look at the words of this speaker and at the matter of which he speaks, and see whether there is not something very important which he has omitted to mention, something which, under the system he advocates, is so intimately a part of that care of the bodies of these unhappy women which he says must go hand in hand with the care of their souls, as to render *nil* the good which might under other circumstances result from this union. His words would have had a closer relation to the facts of the matter before us, and would apparently have represented more correctly the views of the medical men who are eager for this Act, if they had run thus:

> It appears to me that certain repeated outrages on the persons of those unhappy women, to which they shall be compelled under the fear of imprisonment to submit, are so naturally connected with the attempts to reclaim them from the course of life on which they have entered, that it is impossible to dissociate the one from the other.

Now on this very dissociation I shall chiefly insist as the first and most important means by which any progress can be made towards the ends we aim at, the lessening at once of disease and of the great evil of prostitution itself. And here I must pause to express my amazement at the blind and unscientific manner in which men, generation after generation, have tried to combat this disease in the face of an obstacle which is superable, and which to this day they have failed to perceive the real essence of, and therefore have failed to surmount. What is it which has made women continually evade and rebel against the arbitrary provisions of all government enactments? What is it which has made needful the immense background of coercion and terror, the enormous police force and taxation needful to maintain such coercion? Why is it that women in all countries where such measures are in operation refuse to obey until this expensive machinery, and this cowardly terrorism brought to bear on them by men, forces them to obedience? Is it because they love to suffer, that they prefer to be unmolested when sick, that they do not value the comforts of a hospital, and shelter, and nursing, but choose rather to let disease run on till it kills them? Assuredly not. Most of them are very poor, and when the first symptom of illness comes on, their thoughts would naturally turn to the hospitable door of any asylum where alleviation of suffering or the arrest of disease was promised. The answer is plain enough to all who have had any intercourse with them, who have reasoned with them on the disastrous consequences to others of their carrying on their trade while afflicted with disease, and who have heard the scornful bitter answers to such reasonings. And if, under the pressure of disease and with the hope of cure, they cannot, without this expensive coercion be forced to endure the public outrage, it is not strange that they should resist it while in health, and this Act, as you are aware, inflicts the hideous penalty of women in health equally with the diseased. It is strange that so little of the truly scientific spirit should have entered into experiments so momentous as these – that an end should have been aimed at by means which have left wholly out of account the essential peculiarities of the subjects of the experiments. It is as if men had laboured to solve some problem in chemistry or in any other material science, while blindly and persistently leaving out of account the essential qualities of the most important of the ingredients to be dealt with; and as if French and German chemists having failed, after great expense and labour wasted, to solve the problem, English chemists were about to take it up and to blunder on in the same way, leaving out of account some physical truth as important, for example, as that water or air expand when heated. Is there no one who has science enough to look into this matter, and to proclaim the futility of this proposed enormous and expensive coercion of women, while women remain what God made them? Pascal said, 'La tyrannie est, de vouloir avoir par une voie, ce qu'on ne peut avoir que par une autre.' 'Tyranny is, to seek to do in one way what can only be done in another.' The present is a particular example of this general statement. Most certainly such government tyranny seeks to accomplish what *may* be accomplished, but *never* by such means as it designs to use.

I have spoken of the instincts of womanhood. While these continue to be outraged the beneficent results aimed at will for ever remain as far out of our reach as they now are; while on the other hand the taking into account of these instincts and letting them to some extent guide us, instead of working in defiance of them, would go far towards the solution of a problem which has remained till now unsolved. For God has given to woman, for good and wise ends, an *absolute sovereignty over her own person, and of this no man, no legislation on earth has any right to deprive her* – no not even if she becomes a criminal. And our laws, until lately, have recognised this. Any outrage on the person even of a prostitute has been punished as an 'assault'. No male criminal is for any offence, however serious, subjected to indecent personal outrage perpetrated (to add to its horror) in the presence of persons of the other sex. If the Government were to sanction torture beyond the limits of legitimate punishment in the case even of a few of the lowest and most depraved of *men*, a popular tumult would soon arouse it to the consciousness of what it had done. A single 'indecent assault' upon a woman by a subject of the Government is punished by law. What shall we think of a Government which brings in a system for *wholesale and legalised indecent assaults upon women?* Truly, if we are driven to our last resources, we shall not despair, for *then* will our power be proved to be the greatest, inasmuch as we women of England shall be found to be the representatives of truth and morality when we rise up in open rebellion, and declare that we *will not* be so outraged, that we will not endure to see women deprived of jury trial, or consent that they shall be indecently assaulted by Government officials any more than by some obscure son of Belial. I repeat that while this right bestowed by God on woman – this absolute sovereignty over her person – is disregarded by man, no efforts of his will avail to lessen that blight under which nations, cursed for their own sins, are now groaning. I speak with a force of conviction which I feel confident, even were I alone in my conviction and all the world against me, would by itself and by its own force ultimately win the day. But I am not alone. I express the conviction of the intelligent women of England, of France, of Germany, of Sweden, of Prussia, of Italy, of our Colonies. It has begun to be felt in England that there are *some* social questions coming now within the range of legislation, in regard to which it would not be amiss to have some expression of the feelings of women. Surely on a question which *directly strikes* at the physical and moral life of tens of thousands of women, and profoundly affects the morality of the whole population, which threatens the purity and stability of our homes, which stabs at the very heart of pure affection, which degrades all womanhood through foul associations of thought and feeling, and which murders chivalry and generosity towards women in the hearts of our sons and brothers, surely on such a question as this the voice of the women of England should be heard; and undoubtedly it will be heard; for we live under no Imperialism in England, and to a Parliament – a future if not a present one – fairly and truly representing the people, we shall fearlessly appeal. Of such a Parliament, we shall claim that it let this matter alone. Meanwhile a great and important duty falls upon the community at large to fulfil.

The accommodation in Voluntary Hospitals for persons venereally diseased has been and is utterly inadequate, insomuch that the voluntary system cannot be said to have had by any means a fair trial, while at the same time the results accompanying the trial, as far as it has gone, have been successful. The Report of the Rescue Committee says:

> It is within the knowledge of this Committee that no case is at present admissable to hospital in an incipient stage of disease, and that at least three out of every four which should receive hospital treatment are refused on that ground alone, there being only room now for the worst cases. Here is a state of things – while only one poor creature in every four can be received and placed under treatment, a proposal comes forth for a wholesale scheme to prevent the spread of contagion.

Secretaries of Refuges inform us of poor outcasts wandering from hospital to hospital, and being rejected by each in turn for want of room to receive them. Such then have been forced back *against their will* into circumstances wherein they spread contagion, and are now supposed to be only amenable to coercive measures of the most horrible kind. It is well to mention here certain customs which act as obstacles to the poorest class of outcasts seeking treatment when ill. These customs are not needful, and may and ought to be dispensed with. They prevail in the Lock wards of the Workhouse Hospitals. It is to these wards that the persons most dangerous to the lower classes of the community must resort. The Secretary of the Rescue Society writes on this head, 'The accounts forced upon us, and the bitter complaints made to us by fallen women themselves cannot be presented to the public, but we earnestly hope that the evils we refer to will ere long be obviated.' Those who cannot look beyond existing conventions, however shallow and cruel, will reply that it is necessary nevertheless that we should continually be educating young doctors, that the persons of the poorest of our population best afford the needful scope for medical tuition and clinical practice. To this I reply that no voice of nature or of experience has ever ordained that the persons of women of any class should afford scope for the practice of boys. It is needful to speak plainly of this obstacle as well as of the other; for so long as it acts in any degree as a deterrent to the seclusion of diseased persons, the voluntary system cannot be said to have had a fair trial throughout the country. But there are hospitals where no such practices are allowed, and there is nothing to prevent the immediate disuse of them in others. That such customs do act as a deterrent is beyond all dispute.

Further, I am impelled to suggest here that if a lessening of the great social evil itself be an object with the country, as well as the prevention of contagion, the principle announced by the speaker at Bristol must be carried further than it has yet been carried. It is the same hand which searches out the hidden causes of suffering and ministers to the diseased body which must lead the sufferer back to the paths of virtue, and none but women can effectually combine these two offices. I do not deny the excellence of many kind Christian doctors, and that their efforts for the moral restoration of their patients are sometimes successful. But there is a peculiarity in the case, both physical and mental, of a suffering outcast woman. Such require human tenderness as well as the announcement of God's forgiveness. It is not the reading out of exhortations by a chaplain only which will restore the wrecked nature to health, and deliver the crushed heart from the bitter hatred of human beings, which so often enchains it: especially is this the case when the patient is a *prisoner*, previously outraged by command of the Government, and maddened with the sense of wrong or hardened into fiendish impudence. A poor repentant girl said to me one day,

> Shall I tell you the first thing that softened my hard heart, which had withstood all the prayers and all the preaching? It was that day that you came into the ward and to my bed, and stroked back my hair with your hand, and kissed my forehead again and again: I did not speak to you, but I wept all that night, and thought, "O if I could be loved *once* with a pure love before I die!"

To be loved with a pure love, and to desire such a love is salvation for these. How can this human kindness be safely exercised towards them in the degree that they require it, by the present healers of their bodily ailments? Ladies who superintend hospitals are well aware of what is too often involved in the expression on the part of medical students of a natural kindness towards such patients. I am not lodging any serious complaint at the door of our youthful medical staff. I take a favourable view of the natural modesty of boys, while I deprecate the early hardening and destruction of pure and tender feeling in them by the processes to which they are subjected. What mother of a pure young son entering the medical profession can read the following unmoved? They are the words of a lady who had had many years of experience at the head of one of our great Hospital Training Establishments.

> No one can feel more strongly than I do on the subject of the extension of the Contagious Diseases Act. I shall be glad in any way to express my conviction that all good women should oppose it. We deplore extremely the deterioration in the health and character which takes place after a short time in almost every young student who enters our Hospital, and probably the undue familiarity with the persons of poor women may have something to do with this. It is very sad, and many who have entered healthy and happy, and, as I believe, good lads, have become anything but what they should be. I wish from the depths of my woman's heart something could be done to make this evil result less frequent; certainly if this Act passes into law, it will become *worse* and not better.

It will scarcely be maintained, at this day, that women are not as capable as boys of being trained in the delicate discrimination, and mechanical skill required for the detection and treatment of a subtle disease. For their own sex their faculties will assuredly be found peculiarly available. In what, to them, would be a work calling forth all their sympathies and all their womanly tact, their perceptions would be fully roused, and their skill exercised to the utmost, while their moral influence would be incalculably beneficial. For the establishment of a sufficiency of voluntary measures, and especially in the provision of female medical officers, whose presence alone would add a great attraction to the voluntary hospital, above that which it now possesses for the poor outcast, we must necessarily encounter some delays, but much may be done at once, if the public were fully awakened to the urgency of the case, and aware of the success of the partial voluntary agencies already at work. Delay, however, if inevitable on the one hand, is as much so on the other; for as Mr Simon has well shewn in his report, it would be a task neither easy nor of speedy accomplishment for Government to impose its proposed regulations on every town in England. A long time must elapse before the populations in certain localities could be persuaded or coerced into adopting a system which they abhor, and until the system became universal, any benefits resulting from it of a physical kind, would, as Mr Simon shows, be inappreciable. Disease cannot be arrested at once, nor is there any one grand specific for the diminution of the present evil under which our country is suffering. The evil must be met from many sides at once, and with a largeness of aim, a patience and a prescience, in which we cannot but think that the promoters of the act have been wanting.

Meanwhile when we shall have done away with compulsory legislation as utterly insufficient, through the direct encouragement given by it to the practice of vice, for the *ultimate* diminution of disease; when we shall have established voluntary hospitals, voluntary not only as being separate from the State, but in the sense that the stricken are at liberty to enter and to leave, making the continued residence not a matter of punishment, but an occasion of gratitude for kindness experienced and benefits received; when we shall have set on foot a sufficient missionary agency to search out the fallen and induce the diseased to seek timely aid in these hospitals, and with this, coupled proportionate measures for their complete moral reclamation; when the pure women of England shall in earnest have taken up the matter; when the verdict of society shall cease to require that an impassable gulf shall for ever separate virtuous and Christian women from their fallen sisters, and shall grant these Christian women leave to exercise in an infinitely smaller degree the grace and magnanimity which the Saviour of the world showed forth when He Himself bridged over the gulf between God and fallen human nature; we shall have made no inconsiderable step towards the solution of the physical problem, which can never be solved while it continues to be considered and treated apart from the moral and spiritual influences and principles with which it is inseparably united. The measures we propose in place of Government interference it will be seen admit of none but moral suasion: it will probably be allowed by most persons that persuasion is better than compulsion, if persuasion will effect what we aim at. I repeat, then, that we confidently believe that it will effect – not the *extinction* of disease, nor the final up-rooting of the great social sin, but far more then compulsory measures can ever effect. I have dwelt strongly on this, for the amazing blindness is not easily overcome which has for so many years hindered men from seeing that it is vain as well as immoral to endeavour to stamp out the instincts in women which ever will continue to make them resist, and justly resist, the compulsory system. That perversion of sentiment and of judgment is not easily rectified, which has so long and so strangely overlooked the essential nature of the tacit and dogged resistance on the part of women, which renders inevitable on the part of men and rulers such a background of indecent and tyrannous coercion and costly machinery in order to overcome it.

Mr Simon closes his admirable Report, drawn up for the Privy Council, with the following words:

> I cordially agree with those persons who deplore the extreme insufficiency of Hospital (voluntary) accommodation provided among us for prostitutes venereally affected. The defect may not be for legal remedy, but not the less is it real, and I sincerely hope it may be dealt with by agencies appropriate to its nature. But considering how large a proportion of society has responsibilities of causation or connivance in that sphere of suffering and shame, and considering what cause for compassion, even those who are purest from such responsibilities, may recognise in states of human life so estranged and so bitterly punished, I should suppose that dictates of justice on the one side, and impulses of charity on the other, would respond, and not parsimoniously, to any well-considered appeal in the matter.

The first practical step to be taken is here clearly indicated. Another writer says, 'The public may be assured that the check and diminution of the disease (which is all that can be hoped for) may be best secured by voluntary provision for the cure of persons afflicted with it, extended either by benevolence alone, or by benevolence subsidised by Government aid.' It has been objected by a writer in a local newspaper, who is in favour of the Act, that what is here stated about the aversion of women to obey its requirements is not true, and that that is evidenced by the fact that some have voluntarily come from districts not under the Act and applied to be admitted under medical supervision when suffering from disease. Now before we can estimate the amount of repugnance which such a poor woman may have had to overcome in herself before taking such a step, we must consider the nature and the number of the influences on the other hand which drove her into taking it. The writer himself unconsciously indicates one. He says, they hoped to be cured 'without going to the Workhouse Hospital, which they naturally dread'. Why do they dread the Workhouse Hospital? It is in the Lock Wards of the Workhouse Hospital that, as I have said, the freest use is made of living subjects for purposes of medical tuition. The case of this poor woman then is that of one who only has a choice of evils, and who flees from one she knows to one she imagines *may not* be so bad. The alternatives presented to her are death from disease in some miserable lodging or in a ditch, the Workhouse Hospital with its horrors, or entrance into the Lazaret created by Government with its far greater horrors. To apply to a Refuge she knows to be useless, for Refuges cannot receive diseased applicants. What wonder that we should have heard some poor wanderer say, when racked with pain and without the means to support life, that she would go and try the new kind of Hospital? Has a Christian country no more merciful alternative to offer to a suffering outcast than any of these which I have described as surrounding her?

The association for carrying out the Act have spoken much of the good moral effects, which they say have accrued to the women subjected to it; and the fact of the reclamation from vice of a certain number of the women under surveilance was dwelt upon at the Bristol meeting by advocates of the Act. These things deserve our grave consideration. Before entering more minutely into the matter, I wish first to observe that there is an essential incompatibility in general between the objects of the Act and the objects of a Rescue Society, which labours to reclaim from public use the persons whom the Act declares (and to be logical it must declare) to be a necessity for the public. So incompatible have the two ends in view been found in every country where the system under consideration has been tried, that it has been found needful to discourage, as far as possible, the return to virtue of the women leaving hospitals with certificates of health. An English gentleman went over to Paris, a year or two ago, to try to trace out a young English girl who had been persuaded to go to Paris, and whose excellent parents had continually mourned her as worse than dead. He found her in the Hospital of St Lazare. She was fully minded to return to her home, but communicated in a whisper to her deliverer that she would not be permitted to leave the hospital until she had given a written promise to return to her former mode of life. This, on enquiry, he found to be true, and the refusal was boldly defended as a matter of necessity. 'She is cured, many are wanted; we cannot dismiss the diseased for this purpose. The ranks of those who pursue this *métier* must be filled up from other sources if you take away those whom we have now in use.' Such is the answer given. This girl could only escape by giving the required promise, and breaking it as soon as she left the hospital. It may be said that we English are not so likely to forget moral aims in our pursuit of a physical one as the French are. But I think we shall be ultimately disappointed if we trust to our general sense of morality for guarding us against results which have accompanied such a system in every other case. Let the matter be searched into. Let evidence be sought out of every country as to the *numbers*[4] of '*filles publiques*' registered and unregistered in each succeeding year since the establishment of these regulations. Numbers will convince sometimes when arguments will not; and in places where a strict account is kept there cannot be any serious mistake in the matter of numbers. When we find, therefore, as we do, that such a system inevitably and rapidly increases the number of women devoted to the uses of debauchery, we are justified in asserting generally that the tendency of such a system is in direct opposition to the aim and tendency of a reclaiming society, which seeks the reduction of the numbers of these women. We can scarcely fail to observe a hidden significance in the following wording of the Report of the Association for promoting this Act: 'A collateral but not unimportant result which inevitably follows the establishment of these measures is the improvement in the moral and social condition *of the women*.' Of what women? Of the women who by it are delivered from a life of sin and restored to home or to a refuge? No, these are not the women alluded to. This sentence has reference to the prostitutes, who are subjected to Government control, and carrying on their vocation. Now let me ask, what moral improvement can take place, by any possibility, in the character of the harlot, which is not evidenced by an immediate effort to quit a life of sin and shame? I know not how the case may be with men, but certainly I know enough of the heart of women to affirm that conscience in them does shed so oblique a light as to allow the profession of an improved general moral tone unaccompanied by the renunciation of vicious habits. The effort may be spasmodic, and frequently repeated without success, so many are the forces combining to press them back again to evil, and to keep them out of society; but wherever there is the smallest progress there will be the struggle, and where it is again and again defeated, the pangs of conscience will produce a wild uneasiness of conduct, an alternation of hope and despair, and a recklessness or sullenness of manner, which would not entitle them to the designation of orderly and well-conducted prostitutes. To my mind the above words of the Association's Report contain the strongest condemnation of the system that could have been uttered, proving appallingly that wherever moral ends are postponed to purely physical ends the moral sense concerning the relative importance of the two is quickly blunted: so blunted is it in this case that it becomes possible for men to conceive of and report publicly moral improvement in women who are persevering in a life of the deepest ignominy. It indicates in the women the sleep which precedes death, the collapse succeeding fever, from which it is so hard to arouse them. It takes us at once in the imagination to the well-mannered, well-drest, desperate, or conscience-heardened *fille de joie* of Paris. An improvement in the moral and social condition of publicly disciplined, recognised harlots, forsooth! it is a washing of the outside of the cup and platter, a whitening of the sepulchre; it is the deadliest symptom which presents itself to the eyes of one who is versed in the characters and histories of these unhappy women. A picture of such may suffice to enable us to compute the 'moral and social improvement' alluded to.

> She has not the troubled expression of countenance she once had, but looks as if she regarded herself as of some importance. She, and I hear many others, whose repeated reports of good health cause them to be looked upon as prizes, are much sought after. There is no need now for solicitation in the streets, for her lodging is constantly frequented by uninvited guests.[5] She is better dressed, more orderly in person, better fed evidently, and on the whole satisfied with herself and her present life. She is one of those who resented at first the police control, but who now is beyond all sense of shame. Those who like herself are submissive to the regulations and orderly in their houses, receiving crowds of male visitors, and complimented by the police, begin to feel themselves popular persons, pets, in fact, both with the garrison and with the medical staff, and the notions they formerly had about right and wrong, about God and about sin, are all, as it were, turned upside down. I could scarcely regard her as any longer a woman, and as you may imagine, left her, feeling that it was utterly hopeless to try any more to influence her for good. It is evident that the poor souls, when they reach this state of hardness, believe they have the sanction of the *Queen* for the continuance of their profession – for Government to them means the Queen – and that so long as they are clean and orderly in their profession they have satisfied the Queen and thus they satisfy what remains to them of conscience.

Mr Simon says in his Report,[6] that he believes it to be unquestionable that the women, who have come under the Act, have become more cleanly in their persons, and that 'brothels inspected by police are less apt than they were to be scenes of riotous disorder; changes, on which no doubt the *users* of those persons and places may congratulate themselves; but which cannot without extreme abuse of terms be described as of any moral significance'. An Inspector of the Special Police, questioned before the Parliamentary Committee, bears evidence with much apparent satisfaction to the fact that at Devonport and Portsmouth, where the Act is in operation, the women look healthier, neater, and are more decent in demeanour; also, 'that the greater cleanliness of the brothels is something very remarkable'. Upon this an experienced and humane friend of the poor remarks:

> The public are not accustomed to hear houses of ill-fame spoken of as other than places that must be unrecognised by parish authorities or police; or else, say they, these dens would at once be rooted out, and their keepers prosecuted. Has it come to this, that the heads of police can inform us of the existence of these places, with a congratulating speech on their improved appearance and more orderly management?

It may be needful to guard our arguments from misapprehension as the the freedom we claim for all who are not criminal before the Law. That the Law should deal far more stringently than it has yet done with public soliciting in the streets, with procurers and procuresses, and with houses of ill-fame, is much to be desired. And it seems probable that the Act we are considering will practically nullify those Acts under which brothel-keepers are at present liable, as such, to penal consequences. Section 36 of the Act we are considering, provides that penalties shall be inflicted on brothel-keepers harbouring women who are *diseased*, and the whole bearing of the Act has reference, not to the offence of prostitution, but to the offence of being in a diseased condition. When the police agent employed in carrying out this Act finds diseased women living in houses of notoriously evil fame, he ought at once to take steps to suppress that house; but this he does not do, nor does this Act require him to do so. His active and official interference then with such houses, stopping short of measures for their suppression, is a practical admission of their necessity, and we can scarcely wonder to hear him giving a congratulatory report on the more orderly and cleanly condition of such places of resort. This principle will naturally develop into the French system of publicly licensing such houses. It is indeed the openly avowed wish of some of the advocates of the Act that it should be so. The Rev. W. Clay is reported, in the newspaper reports of the Bristol Meeting, to have said that 'he maintained that prostitution was a necessity, but he hoped that the time would soon come when we should sweep the streets of those girls, and if they would ply their trade they should do it in *licensed* houses'.

The Act moreover does not directly forbid solicitation in the streets. The lessening for the present of that evil is to be accounted for therefore, as I have said, by diminished need for solicitation, in other words by the popularity bestowed by Government on certain women at regularly recurring occasions. But let the Act work for a few years, and see then the result. In Paris as we have seen, the streets are crowded to excess with women of one character. People conversant with some Continental towns know well what is meant by the saying that 'no respectable woman can walk alone in the streets there'. It not only implies a danger of being accosted by dissolute men, but a danger of being arrested, as two elegant ladies, strangers to Paris and all its evils, were lately in the Champs Elysées, by the *Agents de Mœurs* with the demand 'Vos billets, Mesdames', and on failing to produce the certificate of a prostitute, to be driven off, as they were, in a cab to the Hospital of St Lazare. The promenaders of the streets of cities which long have been subjected to these Government measures may not perhaps have the coarse manners of some others, nor do they so openly solicit, but are the temptation and the danger lessened for young men by the orderly and elegant appearance of the crowds of unfortunates, or by the fact so well-known that virtuous women are almost excluded from the thoroughfares by them? That system has the contrary effect to what Mr Clay desires, that of 'sweeping these girls off the streets', for it effectually clears the streets of all other women *except* these. So much for the lessening of temptation of this open nature for the pure and the young. It seems however that there are persons who would rather their sons should fall again and again into gross sin, provided they suffer no physical inconvenience from it, than that they should incur the smallest risk of suffering the penalty which God has attached to a breach of the law of purity.

One of the supporters of the Act, at Bristol, when asked whether provision had been made for the restoration to virtue of the women coming under it, replied – and there is much significance in his reply – that that end had been kept in view *as far as it was consistent with the spirit and intentions of the Act to do so*. It will be found that only the minimum of effort for the reclamation of the fallen is consistent with the spirit and intention of the Act, experience of the Act proving to those who work it the necessity, according to their logic, of a supply proportioned to the invariably increasing demand. It is worth while to consider carefully the figures contained in the evidence, on the subject of the reclamation of the women. Let us look at clause 12 (page 9) of the Report, and compare it with the abstract given on page 94 of the Evidence. Between June 1868, and April 1869, 17,161 women have been under the regulations. Of these, 391 have quitted the profession of prostitutes, and are computed as restored to virtue. This is urged as so great a success as to justify the extension of the Act, while no reference is made to the fact shown by a writer in the *Westminster Review*, and known to every one experienced in the history of prostitution that, about a sixth of this unhappy class do in any case quit their dreadful trade year by year – not by death, but by voluntary reclamation of one kind or another. (It must not be supposed that we assert that this sixth become virtuous members of society for the rest of their lives. From my own experience of this matter I should say that many of these are again, after a time, ensnared by sin, through many causes, while on the other hand I should say that of *more* than a sixth of these unhappy people, it may with truth be said, that *they do not practice continuously their degrading profession;* disgust and many other motives drive them out of it for a season at least; in not a few cases, for ever.) If then we look at it in this light, these Government measures *hinder* recovery frightfully. According to statistics in the *Westminster Review* (which are undoubtedly within the mark) more than 2000 would have been reclaimed without the help of the Act: under its provisions only 391 are restored.

Supposing that many of the cases for the four quarters are the same women, or even supposing that all are, and that the last quarter represents the real number of cases, the disproportion is still very considerable, and the number of reclaimed cases does not increase in proportion to the number brought under the Act.

	Under the Act	*Reclaimed*
For the first quarter	2,212	68
For the second quarter	6,974	99

The statistics before the Select Committee are opposed to the conclusions drawn by the Committee.[7] Probably few among them have compared these tables with the evidence. A reference also to page 94 (Aldershot) reveals that the case is pretty much that of compelling the women back to their miserable life, as in Prussia, Austria, and France, where it would seem Governments have pledged themselves by the superintendence they have undertaken, and by the regulations they have set on foot, not to allow the supply to fall below the demand, the demand being continually increased by these very regulations. The following are Mr Simon's words on this subject:

> The clause of the statement (that women are reclaimed by the Act) cannot fail to seem morally important to anyone who accepts it without reserve. I fear, however, that such hopes as it at first sight would seem to justify, as to possible moral result of a government superintendence of prostitution, would on any large scale show themselves *essentially delusive;* not, perhaps, as regards individual reclamations to be

> affected, even from brothels, by pure and kindly contact, but as regards the statistics of prostitution, broadly and practically considered. For I apprehend that the concubinage market, like other markets, tends to be fed according to demand; and that, if prostitution is really to be diminished, the principles of those who would diminish it must be *preventive*.

We are told by promoters of the Act that the spiritual wants of the poor women have been taken into account, and that accordingly a chaplain has been appointed in some of the large Hospitals, and that at Plymouth a subscription of £150 has been voted by Government to a 'Samaritan Fund' for the aid of those who wish to escape from their evil life.

This is well, but when we consider that hospital accommodation for London alone under the Act, would cost £100,000 a year, and that £20,000 have already been expended at Plymouth for the carrying out of the material provisions of the Act, it is impossible to look upon the £150 bestowed for the moral reclamation of the women, as a magnificent outlay; and it may also be said that the omission of the appointment of chaplains to Lazarets of such magnitude, would have had an appearance so invidious, that mere regard for public opinion would have made such appointments desirable.[8] The promoters of the Act have become too suddenly zealous for the conversion of the fallen not to force us, however charitably inclined, to question a little the nature of their zeal. Can they be ignorant of the voluntary efforts on behalf of the fallen, which have been made for years past in London and in other cities, and that some of the refuges in the neighbourhood of great military stations have, after a brave struggle, been obliged to close their doors to the outcast, *for want of funds;* that the Rescue Society numbers 5000 rejected applicants since its establishment, from the same cause; and that many other Refuges throughout the country record similar forced rejections of these poor wanderers? It has been said,

> To compound with conscience for the omission of active efforts for the ingathering of strayed sheep to the fold, by a reliance on extraneous and legislative compulsion to secure their return, may be a social and religious snare incidental to some persons and to some places, but to affirm without hesitation that 'no other way can be so effectual' for the reformation of lost women, as their arrest for the calamity of physical disease, and that they can be reached by no other plan, is entirely opposed, at least, to the experience of persons deeply interested in the welfare of this unhappy class.

To anyoone well acquainted with the temper of the humbler classes in some parts of England, it appears inevitable that the attempt to impose such a Law upon the whole country will be attended with far greater difficulty than has ever attended it in other countries, or as yet in the military and naval towns where it has been carried out. I allude to the opposition of the women themselves, the victims of it. It is well known that the wretched women who haunt such localities as Aldershot, Plymouth, etc., are the lowest, most ignorant and debased of their unhappy class; compulsion would therefore not be so difficult in their case. In spite of this, however, it is stated by Mr. Sloggett (visiting surgeon) before the Select Committee, that 143 women in Plymouth manage *every week* to evade the requirements of the Act. But let the Act be tried in the case of any of these numerous civil populations of our great towns, especially those of the North of England, where the spirit of the people is more independent, and then the real difficulties of the matter will be in a position to be truly estimated. Vast numbers of these fallen women are by no means of the lowest class. Many have fallen from a much higher grade than that in which they now are. They are, moreover, by no means wanting in acuteness of intellect, independence of feeling, and a disposition to enquire into the causes of all they see around them. They begin already to enquire the meaning of this Act, as applied to military stations: numbers of them are asking; 'if we are *necessary* to the country, why are we to be persecuted by such a torture as this Act inflicts on us?' A refined looking woman of this class was lately informed of the provisions of the Act, and replied, with an apparent deep conviction of the truth of her words, 'Such treatment of women will never be allowed in England while the Queen lives.' And this is the conviction of most of them.

A servile rebellion, of an unusual and awkward kind, is what our Government must expect to have to deal with if it should fall into the error of attempting to maintain this law. And it must expect also that the sympathies of the great majority of respectable citizens will be with the poor rebels, who would gain courage from the knowledge of that sympathy, however careful the virtuous might be to conceal that it was felt for them. The police force which would have to be brought to bear in this case would be in a position of antagonism to the feeling of the rest of the public, and a struggle would ensue, the like of which I trust will never be seen in England – a wholesale persecution of women by men! Whatever may be said of the faults of our countrymen, we do know that the English are not yet a nation of cowards, and most certainly none but cowards could look calmly on and see such a struggle as this going forward, at such fearful odds, and with such a sinister significance. It may be needful in great popular rebellions, when the mob proceeds to acts of violence and aggression, to turn out the police or the soldiery upon men and women alike, and that women rioters should take their chance of being shot down with the men. But in such a conflict as we anticipate, if this Act should be pressed on the civil community, of what acts of violence or aggression are the women guilty? of what crime are they accused? Painful as it is to speak so plainly, I must say the truth – the only crime of which they would be guilty is that of protecting themselves from personal violation, and this is a self-protection, which under any other circumstances whatever, it would be a discredit and a reproach to any woman, fallen or not, to fail to exercise. And 'why', these women themselves ask; 'Why, if under all other circumstances we must and ought to protect ourselves from forcible outrage, are we justified in submitting to it in this case?' They cannot be made to see that the protection of their own persons from indecent violence, is not an inalienable right of womanhood, and in this view of the matter they are not alone.

I observe in the evidence before the Select Committee the following question and answer. The Secretary to the Admiralty says:

> 489. I think it very important that anything that is done should be quite gradual. I think it would offend, and prevent the Act being carried into effect, if it were forced upon any place.
>
> 490. Q. If the Act were really resisted by any popular force, it would be impossible to enforce it?
>
> *A.* Quite impossible.

The Select Committee, in framing their report to the House of Lords, after bringing their labours to a close, use these words:

> All the witnesses examined before the Committee are agreed as to the practicability of extending the Act, *but all recommend great caution in doing so.*

What! have the rulers of England altogether forgotten that there is a truth couched in the familiar words 'Vox populi vox Dei?' Have they forgotten that we are supposed to be governed by a Parliament *representing the people*, and is it possible that they are able to assert with one breath that the Act will probably be obnoxious to the people of England, and yet that it is desirable to impose it, and *for the good of that people?* Surely it is not among members of the present Government that such inconsistency will be found. Surely it is not by men so true to the nation as they have been, that an attempt could be made to impose upon the nation by stratagem and extreme caution what members of their own committee have confessed it will be impossible to carry out if the people should once be roused even to a clear knowledge of the matter! I extract the following from the evidence:

> 190. Q. Has it ever occurred to you to hear the religious objection, to which reference has just been made, raised in conversation by any persons of the civilian class; I mean the objection that interference of this kind was a sort of recognition of the existence of the class?
>
> *A.* I have heard that.
>
> 192. Q. By persons of what class or position?
>
> *A.* The middle class; superior tradesmen and persons of that class generally with whom I have casually come into contact.

All honour to the middle class of England! To them chiefly our appeal is directed; on their efforts mainly our hopes are fixed. The over-refined, and the luxurious of the easy-going classes of society will not encounter the disgust and annoyance of dealing in any way with this matter. Mere theorisers there are who will dabble in it, but from whom no practical help can be hoped for. Nevertheless there is virtue yet in England.

A few words I must say on the subject of the wide indirect moral effects of such measures. First as to the demoralising effects of it on the large police and medical staff required. The Warden of a well known House of Mercy, a gentleman not unknown to the public, writes, 'This Act will tend to degrade the medical profession. It ought to revolt every feeling of a surgeon's better nature to subject a poor woman to such an ordeal *against her will*, and I do not see how men can do it without themselves being the worse for it.' On this subject the testimony of Parent Duchâtelet is fearfully instructive, wherein he describes, in pages which it is scarcely possible to read, the demoralisation of the medical staff employed under this system. Respectable men relinquished the office one by one, in disgust, and the work was left to medical students of inferior grade and reckless character, upon which succeeded a state of things too nearly approaching Pandemonium for human words to express. But as to the general effect on public morals we need to recall to our minds the meaning of some of the provisions made and the laws given by Moses to the Jewish nation; 'Thou shalt not seethe the kid in his mother's milk?' This might seem a waste of tenderness, for neither the kid nor the mother could be aware of the supposed outrage of natural instinct. This and similar laws were given for the sake of the *people*, among whom the Lord would not sanction even that amount of hardness or cruelty which would succeed in the popular mind familiarity with an outraged sentiment in regard to the maternal instincts of a poor goat. But alas! what comparison can such an outrage bear to that practised on the feelings of tens of thousands of women, being tenderly fashioned, and possessing human affections and immortal souls? (That offence *will come* through the frailty and corruption of human nature we know, but it is an awful thing for a Government to sanction such offences). By our laws cruelty to animals is punished; the flaying alive of a cat is an offence punishable by imprisonment; but those laws are not so much for the sake of the poor animals, as for the preservation of public morals, it is the effect on the feelings of the people of the *knowledge of the perpetration* of such cruelty that is the main thing considered, and justly so. But surely it is a mere sentimentalism to punish an outrage on a dumb animal, to shut up the serpent house in the Zoological Gardens from the public view, in order that the terror of the poor rabbits destined to be devoured should not become a familiar and heart-rending sight to the visitors of the gardens, while there is the remotest prospect of the sanctioning among us of the constant and periodical torture, in a far more subtle and cruel fashion, of beings susceptible not only of bodily pain but of the cruellest rendering and scourging of their natural instincts and human emotions: beings whom God made physically weaker than man, and spiritually his equal, not that they should be despitefully and shamefully handled, but that they should be reverenced, even at their lowest estate, even as man claims to be reverenced. Now these terrible inquisitorial proceedings cannot be kept from the knowledge of the whole population. Not only the mature among us, but our young men and maidens must all know of what is being constantly enacted. The imagination of the young and the pure will be tainted by such knowledge far more than it could be by the possible knowledge of anything which now exists. The conscience of men will become seared, and their feelings blunted. Cruelty is perhaps the most horrible of all vices, and one which everyone agrees needs to be watched against in boys and young men of the Anglo-Saxon race. But what refining or tender influences will avail with our young men if they become familiar with the horrible adjuncts of an Act such as is under discussion, with the utter contempt implied in them of the persons and feelings of women? The Hebrew Law-giver did not permit that the instincts of the mother goat should be outraged, and this was because of his regard of the moral education of the people. But in these days the instincts of a much worthier creature are recklessly and unhumanly outraged for an end doubtful of attainment, and including consequences to the male community solemnly to be deprecated.

On the subject of measures for the prevention of the great social evil the limits of this appeal will not allow me to speak. It is of such importance as to deserve to be treated alone, and drawn out carefully. I will only mention that Duchâtelet, after a careful examination of the matter, attests that at the beginning of the present system in France, out of 3000 lost women in Paris, only thirty-five were in a position in which they could be any means gain a livelihood otherwise than by their base traffic. If statistics on this head could be had in England, they would reveal a pitiful state of things. Among the lowest class sheer hunger, among the better the denial to women of the admission to trades and professions, their wretched education, their frequently orphaned and utterly friendless state, the severe judgment of society on a single lapse, are among the causes which make it humanly speaking *impossible* for many to escape the worst fate. A member of the Moonlight Mission addressed a poor girl on the moral and spiritual aspects of her life of sin: She looked up at him with her haggard face, and said earnestly, 'I know all that sir, but *I am very, very hungry*.' These then are the persons of whom it has been coarsely said, 'if they will make a trade of their own persons, they deserve to be outraged'.

It remains for me only to express our conviction that this our appeal will not fall upon barren hearts. We profoundly believe in the existence of purity among Englishmen, we have seen something of the anger which the knowledge of the existence of this Act has aroused in the minds of just, tender, and clear-thinking men, an anger almost as great as a woman can feel, and we believe that this noble indignation will not be unfruitful.

Coruage is needed to take up the subject, and your practical aid, fellow countrymen, is needed at this crisis. Working men ought to be fully alive to the dangers which threaten their innocent wives and daughters through mistakes inevitably made by the special police, in all places where prostitution is superintended by the State. Young women working in mills or otherwise in manufacturing towns must be warned of the danger which there would be in walking abroad, if this Act were put in operation. Thoughtful and maternal women of the better classes should now take courage and do what they may by quiet influence in this matter, and lastly upon ministers of religion of every denomination, a grave responsibility rests. Some articles on this subject appeared in the *Daily News*, in 1863, when these proposals were first made in connection with garrison towns, from one of which I extract the following:

> There is evidence, accessible to all, that the regulation system creates horrors worse than those which it is supposed to restrain. Vice once stimulated by such a system imagines and dares all unutterable things; and such things perplex with misery the lives of parents of missing children in continental cities, and daunt the courage of rulers, and madden the moral sense, and gnaw the conscience of whole orders of sinners and sufferers, of whom we can form no conception here. We shall have entered upon our national decline whenever we agree to the introduction of such a system; and it is only necessary to bring the case fairly before the public conscience to secure us against any such fatal lapse.
>
> The clergy ought to be looking to this, and we trust they are. They are charged, above other classes, with the promotion of education in our country, and with the enlightenment of individual conscience which is the security of all that we care for as a people. Why do not they remonstrate when vile and corrupting proposals are publicly made? or, have they attempted to speak, and been silenced? If they do not feel qualified to form an opinion, why do they not investigate the facts? But if they who can tell us most of the morals of private life will not bestir themselves, there are many more who might and ought; and our belief is, that if those gentlemen of England who have, or can obtain a conviction as to the course to be taken under present circusmtance were to speak their minds, the proposals we have discussed would be scouted, decisively and for ever.

One word on the utter uselessness of the proposed measures. It is precisely on the material side that experience at home and abroad most fully proves the advisers of the adoption of this measure to be wrong. The assertion of all these men is, 'the material advantages of such a measure are unquestioned and unquestionable, if only they can be carried without moral evil'. The reply is, 'the material advantages are not only not proved, they are absolutely disproved by the facts and statistics of all countries'. The application of a Sanitary Act to one sex alone, is, I believe, without parallel in the history of England. It is impossible to stamp out disease where half of those who are conveying the contagion are under no surveillance or control whatever. A woman dismissed with a certificate of sound health may become diseased within an hour after such dismissal, and is from that time till the next periodical summons in a condition to contaminate many. This is precisely the point on which medical witnesses from Paris are staggered, and on which they have no answer to give. On this head Parliament has statistics enough to refer to. Let them learn from those statistics the uselessness of the proposed measures. We are willing that the matter should be fairly fought out on the material ground only, for on this ground we have nothing to fear, appealing as we do to the incontestible logic of facts. We have nevertheless thought it right and needful to remind you, fellow countrymen, of the weighty moral considerations which are involved in the present question.

In conclusion, let it not be supposed that it has cost us little to break through the rule of silence imposed by society upon women, when such matters are to be treated; nor that it has been at a small cost to ourselves that we have gone into the matter in all its details. We will say as little as possible of our own mental sufferings, but we would say to other women 'Let none enter *this* chamber of horrors except to aid the fallen and to set the captive free.' Charity, and anger against wrong are however at times motives more powerful than the desire to conform to conventional rules, and to avoid all risk of offending the fastidious. A lady expresses the feelings of many of us in writing thus: 'God knows, it is no blasphemy to say it, there are many Gethsemanes on earth to sad and suffering souls. I think sometimes we drink of that cup, and are baptised into that baptism, and if we believe in good at all, we must believe that Infinite love is suffering and pitying with us.' While enduring censure, as we must, for daring to speak, and while suffering much secret anguish of soul, we are yet sustained by the conviction that we have fulfilled a solemn and painful duty.

An English Mother

Postscript

The following is an extract from a letter received since the above appeal was written. It is from the author of a book which is well worthy of study, *La Femme pauvre au XIX*ME Siècle.* These words, written by a person in experience and research not inferior to Parent Duchâtelet himself, ought to convey a serious impression to English legislators as to the necessity at least of prolonged deliberation, and of far more extensive enquiry than has yet been made into the moral and political as well as physical effects of that legislation in foreign countries, which some persons advocate for England.

> Paris, 7 November 1869
>
> Prostitution ought undoubtedly to be governed and repressed: If your Parliament would forbid and punish provocations in the public ways, keep a watch against places of ill-fame, and proceed with rigour against the persons who frequent them, it would act wisely: but let it beware of imitating official France, who is the *prostitute* of nations! (Mais qu'il se garde d'imiter la France officielle, qui est la prostituée des nations!) Belgium, Austria, and even Italy have fallen as low as ourselves by reason of having become our imitators. This law has so infamous a character as the protector of the disorders of men, that the contempt which exists among us for the executive authority can only be attributed to the disgust which every honest man feels for every individual police functionary. In your cities the social evil arises from a general insufficiency of the means of subsistence among women, from the exemption of seducers from legal penalties, from *la recherche imparfaite de la paternité*, and other causes. Attack then resolutely the evil in its beginnings, and take care always to see in men and women who corrupt society companions who ought to be *equally* punished. Morality, logic, the preservation of society admit of no other apprehension of the matter. You have the inexpressible happiness of having a moral government, responsible functionaries, and a Queen who is the model of every virtue of public and private life. Supplicate that honourable and single-hearted woman to take in hand the cause of human dignity, of conscience and of virtue; and obtain from the wisdom of your Parliament a solemn affirmation of the authority of reason over subversive passions. Truly if you cannot withdraw women from the batons of those policemen, who herd them like droves of cattle in the interests of debauchery, you may abandon all hope for the general elevation of your women of England. But allow me to hope better things from the good sense of the English. Accept my sympathy in your couragious efforts.
>
> Yours, etc., J. V. Daubié

Alexandre Dumas, (fils) writing on the same subject, winds up a sketch of the decline of his country during the years of this official regulation of morals, with the following mournful and indignant words:

> Maladroits! When a nation, Christian, catholic even; when a people which invokes continually its revolution of '89, which proclaims its desire for justice, liberty, equality, not only for itself but for others, is so hypocritical, so cowardly, and so stultified as to permit that millions of girls, young, healthy, beautiful, of whom they could make intelligent fellow workers, faithful companions and fruitful mothers, should be used for nothing but to be made into degraded, dangerous, and barren prostitutes; such a nation deserves that prostitution should devour it completely; and this it is which is now coming upon us!
>
> *Alex. Dumas*

Again, many such letters as the following have been received:

> Eglise Reformée, Paris, December 1869
>
> Dear Madam – I can tell you my own impression, and that of Christian physicians on this subject. I *abhor* our system, the object of which is to protect debauchery against the natural consequences of debauchery, and to legalise vice. The effects of such an immoral system cannot be good. My brother, who is one of our first physicians, writes to me that the French system is morally detestable. ('Certainly', this physician says, 'it shuts the door of hope to the poor women and hardens them in vice.') Another physician tells me that it is a fact that the standard of morals is lower in countries where vice is under police control, though one might expect the contrary. Another consequence of the French system is, that Christian efforts to reclaim the poor victims of vice are not free as in your country.
>
> I remain, dear Madam, Yours truly in Christ,
>
> G. *Monod*

NOTES

1 Even this is doubtful, and is asserted by some of the highest medical authorities to be so.

2 This careful collator of statistics was himself an advocate of the system, yet details with a scrupulous fidelity all its horrors and all its cowardliness as exercised by the strong upon the weak. He cannot suppress at times a burst of indignation and pity, and of regret that such a terrible coercion should have been brought to bear upon a class whom he, out

of his intimate knowledge of them, declares are never without virtue and modesty in the *first* months of their trade. He tells many incidents, such as one of a poor girl who was permitted on a summer day to walk into the yard of the prison in which she was confined, and who gazing with wide open eyes of admiration at the blue sky above her head, exclaimed with arms outspread, and in a voice of adoring gratitude – 'Oh how good our God is, how good our God is, to give us this beautiful sky to look at.' – Yet she was classed among the *lowest*.

3 And not only from foreign countries, but from the Military Depots at home where this Act is in force. On the authority of a medical man, and of officers of high standing at Aldershot, it may truly be stated of the soldiers there that since the passing of the Act, they (in the terrible words of the Hebrew prophet) 'assemble themselves by troops in the harlot's houses', and it is instructive to listen to the tone in which the men speak of the kind, fatherly, and protecting attitude of Government towards themselves in this matter, together with their increased brutality of feeling towards the women.

4 M. Le Cour, 'Chef du Bureau' of this department in Paris, and other authorities, show us, statistically, that when the number of registered women *decreases*, there is an enormous increase of the unregistered, whose power of evasion of the police is insuperable by any means that can be devised.

5 It is insisted by upholders of the Act, that the fact of the women not holding their own certificates makes the system more moral than that of France. But it is evident that the women are quite as able to make a trade of their dismissal from the medical room, as if they had the certificate in their own hands; for the periods of such dismissal are known to the whole neighbourhood of *male* prostitutes, and every woman knows that her dismissal means sound health. Moral men, who have been accosted by women in the localities where the Act is in force, say, that the form of solicitation runs thus: 'Superintendent So-and-So has my certificate', or 'I was discharged this morning: the fact of my being at large shows you that I am safe.' The certificate which lies in the policeman's pocket, is capital to a woman as much as if it were in her own.

6 See the Blue Book containing the Eleventh Annual Report of the Medical Officer to the Lords of Her Majesty's most Honourable Privy Council.

7 Since this Appeal was first written, the persons engaged in carrying out the Act have laid claim to a much greater number of reclamations. Their claim will be strictly and searchingly investigated. I will not comment upon the boast they make until the results of this investigation are before the public.

8 In the estimate for 1869, for the purpose of extending the operation of the Contagious Diseases Act to a few additional towns, the sum of £43,460 was granted; viz.: For buildings, £18,500; for general expenses, £18,700; for police, £3,260; for the colonies, £3,000. There will shortly be in England and Ireland 507 beds in various hospitals for the use of

women under this Act. The average cost per bed per annum is £33, involving an annual expense of £16,731, which estimate does not include cost of police or buildings.

Josephine Butler

Letter to my Countrywomen, Dwelling in the Farmsteads and Cottages of England

(1871)

I

My Dear Friends,

There is a law now in force in this country which concerns you all, and yet of which many among you have never even heard. I want you to listen to me for a little, whilst I try to explain it to you, and when you have heard and understood, you will, I think, feel about it as I do.

I daresay you all know that there are women, alas, thousands of women, in England who live by sin. Sometimes, when you have been late at your market-town, you may have passed one such in the street, and have shrunk aside, feeling it shame even to touch her; or perhaps, instead of scorn, a deep pity has filled your heart, and you have longed to take her hand, and to lead her back to a better and happier life. Now, it is the pity and not the scorn which I would fain have you feel towards these poor women, and when you have read what I have to tell you about them, I think it will not be hard for you to be merciful to them in your thoughts.

In the first place, you must understand that very few ever begin to lead a bad life from choice. Thousands of the miserable creatures whom we call *fallen* have really not fallen at all, for they never stood upon any height of virtue or knowledge from which it was possible for them to descend, and if they love darkness, it is because no light ever shone upon them; no tender mother ever spoke to *them* of God or Christ; no kind father ever shielded *them* from temptation; no pure examples ever encouraged *them* to resist evil, and to seek after that which is good; rather, they have been sold

– yes, sold – into their life of bondage by those who ought to have died to save them from such misery.

I daresay you will hardly believe it, yet it is but too true. It is said that there were in one large seaport town, only a few years ago, 1500 prostitutes under fifteen years of age, some of them mere children of eleven or twelve; and of these many had been sent upon the streets by their own parents, who lived upon the wages of their sin and shame.

Again, many girls are led astray when very young – sometimes most shamfully deceived and betrayed – then, finding the doors of their relatives and friends shut against them, they are driven by despair into recklessness and vice.

A still larger number, in fact far more than half of all the women who live by prostitution, fall into it through lack of food, and clothes, and shelter. Are we sure, you and I, that, in like case, we should not have done the same? Hunger and cold are hard to bear; it needs the courage of a martyr to die rather than to sin – and not only a martyr's courage, but a martyr's faith also; and how should those who find this world so cruel and so sad, place their trust in the God who made it?

To show you how much want has to do with prostitution, I will just mention here that a French doctor, who inquired carefully into the histories of 3,000 fallen women in Paris, found that of those 3,000 only thirty-five had had any chance of earning their bread honestly.

Now, if you were to add together all the women who are trained to sin from their cradle, all those who are betrayed into it by deceit, or driven into it by despair, and all those who sink into it through real starvation, you would find very few left whom you could justly call bad – doing evil because they love evil; very few, therefore, to whom you have any right to deny your pity and your help.

Perhaps you will say, 'if all that this lady tells us about these women is true, we are very sorry for them, but we don't see how we can help them; the Government to whom we pay so much money that it may take care of the people ought to do that. Surely it is trying to save some of the poor creatures.'

To this I answer: the Parliament and the Government of England have done nothing *for* these women, what it has done *against* them you now shall hear.

I have taken it for granted that you all know that there is such an evil as prostitution in the land; but perhaps some of you are not aware that those who lead vicious lives are liable to certain painful and dangerous diseases, called *contagious*, because it is supposed that one person can only take them from another by *contact*, or *touch*. A healthy man, by merely walking down a street where there is small-pox or fever, may sicken and die; but with these contagious diseases it is quite different, all men are safe from them so long as they live virtuous lives. Therefore, as I daresay you will think, every man can preserve himself from them if he chooses, and if he does not choose, he deserves to suffer, and ought not to be saved from suffering, because through it he may, perhaps, learn to be wiser and better.

But as regards certain men, at least – I mean soldiers and sailors – our Government judges otherwise.

You know it costs a great deal of money to train a man to be a soldier or sailor, and if he is often ill and unfit for service that money is as good as lost. Now, when the Government found that very many soldiers and sailors were constantly in hospital, owing to contagious disorders, they asked themselves what they could do to prevent such a waste of the public funds, and such a weakening of the forces on which the country has to depend for safety in time of war, which was quite right; but instead of teaching or helping them to lead pure lives, they resolved to protect them against contagious diseases – in other words, to make it safe for them to sin.

So they took counsel with doctors and officers high in the army, and high in the navy, and they drew up a Bill – that is to say the plan of a new law – and brought it to Parliament to pass, but this they did not do until the beginning of August, when the business of Parliament was supposed to be over for the year, and many members of the House of Commons had already left town and gone to Scotland or abroad. They called the Bill a Contagious Diseases Bill, and because the Bills about the Cattle Plague were also called Contagious Diseases Bills, some of these members who might have returned to speak and vote against it, mistook it for one of these and stayed away – for which they were afterwards sorry; and because the newspapers gave no account of the Bill, nor any proper report of the speeches made about it Parliament, it became law without the knowledge and consent of the people.

The particular measure of which I am writing was passed in 1869. There had been laws to protect soldiers and sailors against contagious diseases since 1864, but as they were milder in their provisions, and their operations confined to a very few places, little had been thought or said about them.

Now, the men who drew up these different Acts say that they kept them so quiet because they thought the matter with which they had to do indecent and disgusting, and unfit to be talked of or read about. But when I have told you what was written in the Act of 1869 – for which the Acts passed in 1864 and 1866 prepared the way – I think you will agree with me that they were afraid to let Englishmen and Englishwomen understand the new laws lest they should cry out against them.

The Contagious Diseases Act of 1869 provides that in fifteen towns where there are always many soldiers and sailors – such as Canterbury, Aldershot, Portsmouth, and Plymouth – there shall be surgeons appointed to examine with certain instruments the persons of all prostitutes, to see in what state they are, and those whom they find to be healthy they are to allow to go away, having given them a notice of when they are to come to be examined again, and so long as a woman appears on the stated days for examination, the police do not arrest or otherwise interfere with her; but those whom the surgeons find to be diseased, they are to send to what are called hospitals, but are really prisons, to be cured, and when they are well, they are dismissed to follow their former pursuits, their certificates of health being put into the hands of the police.

Further, this Act gives power to certain police inspectors, to watch all women and girls. The Act does not specify the age. As a matter of fact, girls of most tender years are brought under it, and the police-officers say that they especially watch seamstreses, labourers' daughters, and domestic servants, in those towns, and for fifteen miles round each, and if one of these paid spies – for since they wear plain clothes, so that people cannot tell they belong to the police-force, they are really spies – *suspects* any woman of being a prostitute, or of *intending* prostitution, he can go to her and say, 'Come to Mr So and So', naming the Examining Surgeon, 'and sign the paper'. Now this paper is called the Voluntary Submission, and by signing it a woman agrees to submit for a whole year (it might, under the Act, be a shorter time, but the police have *always* filled it up for a year) to be examined whenever she is called upon to be so, but it is so carefully worded that an ignorant girl might put her name to it without knowing that by so doing she was signing away her liberty for twelve months, her character for ever.

If, however, she does understand this, and refuses to go to the surgeon, then the police spy can take her before a single magistrate, and that one magistrate, on the oath of that one policeman, who only needs to swear that he *suspects*, not that he knows her to be leading a vicious life, may order her to submit to the examination, periodically for twelve months, and if she does not obey can send her to prison for three months, and when the first three months are over, if she still refuses to be examined by the surgeon, the magistrate can commit her for three more, and so on again and again.

So, if a woman is ignorant or frightened, and goes to the surgeon, she is put on the list of common women, and if she is well informed and brave, and goes before the magistrate, she may be imprisoned for life, without ever having been properly tried; and the examination to which she is ordered to submit is so cruel and indecent, that it is shameful even to speak of it; and those who have undergone it a few times, become so hardened and degraded, that almost all hope of saving them is lost. The object for which they are thus brutalised, is that the men who share their guilt and often tempt them to it, may go on sinning as much as they like, without any danger to their health; for in the eyes of *generals and admirals*, the souls of English women are of less consequence than the bodies of English men – if those bodies happen to be clothed in a red coat or a blue jacket.

Now, I beg you to think first with what awful dangers such a law surrounds innocent women. Remember, a policeman can accuse a girl, or even a child, of prostitution merely on suspicion, and there is no rule laid down to fix the signs which shall be held to give him a right to think evil of her. Each policeman is to judge of them for himself; and it is clear that they do not all agree, for of several witnesses who were examined on this point before a committee of the House of Commons, one said that the police suspected a woman who was seen 'larking' about the street, and talking to men; and that when the police saw a woman out late of an evening, they were very liable to jump to the conclusion that she was a prostitute. A surgeon under the Act said that the ground of suspicion was more a question as to mannerism than anything else. But if to be out of doors alone at night, or to be seen talking to men in the streets, is to be looked upon as a sign of a bad character, and to give a policeman the right to accuse a girl of prostitution, what woman will not fear to leave her house after dark, or to exchange a greeting with a friend?

And if the oath of one policeman is enough to condemn a girl, how will she be safe even in her own house? For supposing that a policeman has a spite against her, or any of her people, what is there to prevent his accusing her falsely, since he cannot be punished, even if the accusation be proved false, if he swears that he believed it to be true?

And the danger is not only from the paid spy; every man if he is angry with a woman, perhaps because he has tried to seduce her, and she has resisted him, can write to the police, not even signing his name to the letter, since he will not be called upon to appear as a witness, saying – 'such a person is a prostitute', and without even knowing who her accuser is, she can be brought before the examining surgeon, or the magistrate, and so may be doomed to sin and shame for life, because some wretch envied her her innocence. Think, too, how the threat of such a false accusation might be used to extort money from the timid and weak.

I do not say that women would often be falsely accused, nor yet that money would often be extorted from them by the threat of such false accusation; but I do assert that whilst the Contagious Diseases Acts continue the law of the land, such things might happen, and that no innocent woman, however poor or ignorant, ought for a single day to be exposed to so frightful a risk; and I want you also to understand that it is just the poor and ignorant who are endangered by these Acts, since no police spy, or any other man, would dare to accuse a woman of wealth and position, able to protect herself, or with friends strong enough to protect her, unless he had the most certain proofs of her guilt, and perhaps not even then.

I feel sure you will see directly how cruel these laws are to good women, but I want you to see, too, how unjust they are to sinful ones. For when a woman sins, does she sin alone? Rather for one sinful woman are there not fifty – ay, a hundred – sinful men? And which of them, the ignorant, half-starved prostitutes, or the men, often well-taught and well-fed, who consort with them, are they that carry disease to virtuous wives, and transmit it to unconscious infants? Surely the men. Then they are not only more guilty, but also more dangerous in their guilt. Yet the punishment of the sin of *two* is made by these laws to fall upon *one* alone, and that one the least to be blamed, and the most to be pitied.

But even if a woman be utterly vile – the tempter not the tempted – ought she to be deprived of all her rights and liberties? It has always been the boast of Englishmen that the law of England treats every accused person as innocent until he has been proved to be guilty. The burglar, the murderer is not asked to accuse himself; he is tried in open court, so that all his countrymen may know what has been said for and against him, and judge whether he has been fairly treated; he has lawyers to defend him, twelve men to listen to the evidence, and a judge to help them to understand the law, and to remind them that they must not condemn him upon suspicion, but only upon proof; and he cannot be found guilty unless the whole jury is convinced that he really is so. All these safeguards against injustice and oppression the Law of England gives to the man accused of the darkest crime, but for the last two years Parliament has denied every one of them to women only charged with sin, whose accomplices it not only does not punish, but even tries to protect against those penalties which God himself has attached to vice.

And this brings me to the third charge which I have to make against the Contagious Diseases Acts, namely, that they tend to encourage men in vicious habits.

This they do in two ways; directly, by affording them opportunities of sinning safely; appointing for them, as it were, cities of refuge, to which they can flee, and in which they can indulge their evil desires without fear; and, indirectly, by accustoming them to think that vice is so natural, so necessary, that no one expects them to be virtuous; for they must see that those who framed these Acts despaired of ever improving mankind, since if they had had any hope of being able to reform it, instead of building hospitals in which to cure prostitutes, so that there may be always healthy women for soldiers and sailors (and of course all other men living in or near the subjected towns), to consort with, they would surely have founded schools and reading rooms, and clubs, and workshops, and other like institutions, where they might spend their idle time in learning good, instead of in doing evil.

But we have other proof that the Contagious Diseases Acts are founded on the belief that human nature is hopelessly brutal. Many writers, in newspapers and elsewhere, openly say that this is why they were passed, and this is why they must be maintained, and some doctors – not all, many are virtuous themselves, and believe that others can be virtuous too – go so far as to tell their patients that vice is good for their health.

And that these Acts have really increased vice among men is proved by the fact that on the nights after the prostitutes have been examined by the surgeons, and when it is *supposed* that there is no danger in approaching them, since all who were found to be diseased had been sent to the hospitals, the bad houses in the fifteen towns are crowded, especially by young lads and married men.

Supposed, I say, for the promise of safety contained in the fact of a woman being at large just after having been examined, often proves false, in truth it has not been shown that contagious disorders have diminished in England among soldiers and sailors, since the Contagious Diseases Act became law; and in France, where like laws have been in force for many years past, they abound so frightfully that persons, capable of forming an opinion on the subject, believe that it is to them that the French owe the terrible defeats of the late war, for they could neither march nor fight like the healthier and more virtuous Germans; and if this opinion is correct, it deserves to be carefully considered, since it is for the avowed purpose of keeping the army and navy healthy that our Contagious Diseases Acts were framed and carried.

In speaking of the hospitals in which prostitutes are cured, I have called them prisons, and it is right, therefore, that I should prove to you that they deserve the name.

They are prisons; firstly, because a woman can be sent to them against her will, on the word and at the mere pleasure of an examining surgeon; secondly, because she can be kept there against her will, for any length of time, not exceeding nine months, on the word and at the mere pleasure of the house surgeon, whose interest it is not to let her go, till some other unfortunate comes to take her place, because the Government pays a large sum to the hospital funds for every bed that is full, but much less for the beds that are empty; thirdly, because once within their walls, she can be forced to do any work which the governor and nurses may think fit to demand of her; lastly, because whilst she remains in them, she cannot see any of her friends, or even the clergyman of her parish, or her own lawyer, without the permission of the said house surgeon, much of whose power over the women in his charge is given him, not by the Acts which have at least been passed by Parliament, and are therefore the law of the land until such time as they are altered or repealed, but by the Admiralty – that is to say, the board of gentlemen who are appointed to manage the affairs of the navy and of the navy only, and who, therefore, have no legal right to interfere with, or make rules for, any person who is not a sailor.

I believe some of the points I have mentioned are true only of the Royal Albert Hospital at Devonport, but all the others are real prisons, in so far as women are sent to them and confined in them against their will.

Now, I think, I have made you understand what the Contagious Diseases Acts are, and the purpose for which they were passed; and I hope I have succeeded in convicting you of their cruelty, injustice, and immorality. In a second letter I will tell you what has been done towards forcing Parliament to undo its evil work, and will show you how you too can help to rid the country of these bad laws. But before concluding this I must just point out that all these police spies, and examining surgeons, and hospitals for diseased women, who are to be cured, not that they may be saved from their vicious life, but that soldiers and sailors may share it without risk, cost a great deal of money, and that all that money comes out of the pockets of the people.

I am, my dear Friends,
Yours very faithfully,

An English Lady

II

My Dear Friends,

In my first letter I explained to you the nature and object of the Contagious Diseases Acts; it remains for me still to give you the history of the efforts which have been, and are still being made, to bring about their repeal.

You must know that there are many good men and women in our country who have devoted their lives to the work of reclaiming prostitutes, and of offering protection and aid to women and young girls who through poverty, ignorance, or evil companionship are in danger of falling into sin. And because several persons by joining together can do more than by each working alone, societies have been formed for this purpose, one of which, the Rescue Society, has in the last seventeen years opened the doors of its various Homes to no less than 6,722 fallen women and girls, of which number seventy out of every hundred have been restored to a virtuous life, whilst lack of funds has compelled it reluctantly to refuse admission to many others who implored its aid.

Now, as it was well known that there were in London such associations for the rescue of fallen women, does it not seem to you that the first thing the Government ought to have done when it began to think of passing laws to diminish the diseases arising out of the vice of which such women are at once the victims and the ministers, should have been to consult the men who had laboured among them for years, and to hear and weigh all the information they had to give and all the plans they had to propose? So far, however, from doing this, Government prepared its measures so quietly – asking only the advice and aid of men whom it knew to be in favour of the laws against contagious disease in force in France and in other continental countries – and when prepared brought them so secretly into Parliament that neither the Rescue Society nor the managers of any similar institutions seem to have known anything about the Act of 1864, and only to have heard of the Act of 1866 after it had passed both Houses and become law. Then, indeed, the members of those societies lifted up their voices against it; but with little effect, for the men in high places to whom they wrote expressing their horror and indignation at what had been done, took no notice of their letters, and the newspapers shut their pages against them.

Still they persevered; and by spreading abroad papers containing their reasons for objecting to laws to protect men in the practice of vice, they so alarmed the party in favour of the Contagious

Diseases Acts, that in the spring of 1869 a Bill which would have extended them to every town in the land was withdrawn from the House of Lords. Yet, but a few months later, Parliament suddenly and secretly increased the number of towns in which they were to be enforced to fifteen, at the same time adding greatly to the severity which might be used to compel women or children suspected of prostitution to submit to examination.

Now, we ought to feel very grateful to these Rescue Societies for having been the first to speak out boldly against so great and cruel a wrong, and for having at least saved the manufacturing and country towns from being placed under the Acts; but we have the evidence of their secretary, Mr Cooper, that he and his friends would not have been able to arouse public feeling on the subject sufficiently to render it impossible for the Government to maintain the laws already passed, had they not unexpectedly received help; and that help, you will be glad to hear, came to them from women.

Of all the faithful followers of Christ who have striven to show their love for Him by saving their weak and erring sisters, none, of late days, has done more than Mrs Butler, the wife of the Rev. George Butler, 280, South Hill, Park Road, Liverpool, who delicately nurtured, highly educated, refined and sensitive in every thought and feeling, has yet never shrunk from entering the vilest dens of vice, nor ever scorned to take the hand of any woman, however fallen, if by clasping it she can only draw her back to the paths of virtue and peace.

Now, in August 1869, just when Parliament was busy passing the last and worst of the Contagious Diseases Acts, this Mrs Butler was in Switzerland, and there she attended a meeting of ladies who had come together from various countries of Europe to talk over the condition of women in their several lands, and to take counsel together how they could secure for themselves and their sisters all over the world a larger measure of justice, freedom, and well-being.

Very earnestly they considered the many evils under which the female sex had still to suffer, and many were the old laws and customs pressing unfairly upon women, which they resolved to strive to have altered; but whether they came from France, or Germany, or Italy, one and all declared that their labours would be fruitless so long as laws were made *against* women to protect *men* in the indulgence of their animal appetites.

> What is the use of our labouring to improve the position of our sisters and ourselves whilst thousands amongst us are subjected to the vilest and most brutalising treatment, for the

avowed purpose of keeping the bodies of vicious men in good health. When that great cruelty and injustice is done away with, all the lesser cruelties and injustices will come to an end also; but not until then; for the very existence of such laws encourages men to believe that women are their playthings or their slaves, born to minister to their pleasures or their wants, and to laugh at them when they ask for equal rights and liberties.

Now you may fancy that the words of these foreign ladies would go to the heart of the English woman who, in her own country, had been working so patiently to help and reform her fallen sisters; and you can picture to yourselves how she would think about them as she journeyed homewards. Well, she landed at Dover to find a letter waiting for her at the hotel, which told her of the passing of the new Contagious Diseases Act, and implored her aid to resist and overthrow it.

That letter, following upon what she had so lately heard in Switzerland, was like a voice from heaven, and Mrs Butler began at once to write to and consult with other ladies whom she knew to be labouring for the virtue and welfare of women; and so it came to pass that an association of ladies was formed, pledged to work in every possible way against the laws which they condemned; and on 1 January 1870, this association published the following protest:

Protest

We, the undersigned, enter our solemn protest against the Contagious Diseases Acts.

First, because, involving as they do such a momentous change in the legal safeguards enjoyed by women in common with men, they have been passed, not only without the knowledge of the country, but unknown to Parliament itself; and we hold that neither the representatives of the people, nor the press, fulfil the duties which are expected of them, when they allow such legislation to take place without the fullest discussion.

Second, because so far as women are concerned, they remove every guarantee of personal security which the law has established and held sacred, and put their reputation, their freedom, and their persons absolutely in the power of the police.

Third, because the law is bound in any country, professing to give civil liberty to its subjects, to define clearly an offence which it punishes.

Fourth, because it is unjust to punish the sex who are the victims of a vice, and leave unpunished the sex who are the main cause both of the vice and its dreaded consequences; and we consider that liability to arrest, forced surgical examination, or (where this is resisted) imprisonment with hard labour, to which these Acts subject women, are punishments of the most degrading kind.

Fifth, because, by such a system, the path of evil is made more easy to our sons and to the whole of the youth of England; inasmuch as a moral restraint is withdrawn the moment the State recognises, and provides convenience for the practice of a vice which it thereby declares to be necessary and venial.

Sixth, because these measures are cruel to the women who come under their action – violating the feelings of those whose sense of shame is not wholly lost, and further brutalising even the most abandoned.

Seventh, because the disease which these Acts seek to remove has never been removed by any such legislation. The advocates of the system have utterly failed to show, by statistics or otherwise, that these regulations have in any case, after several years' trial, and when applied to one sex only, diminished disease, reclaimed the fallen, or improved the general morality of the country. We have, on the contrary, the strongest evidence to show that in Paris and other continental cities where women have long been outraged by this forced inspection, the public health and morals are worse than at home.

Eighth, because the conditions of this disease, in the first instance, are moral, not physical. The moral evil through which the disease makes its way separates the case entirely from that of the plague, or other scourges which have been placed under police control or sanitary care. We hold that we are bound, before rushing into the experiment of legalising a revolting vice, to try to deal with the *causes* of the evil and we dare to believe that with wiser teaching and more capable legislation, those causes would not be beyond control.

Nine hundred ladies attached their names to this protest, and the first to sign it were two women of whom England is justly proud – Harriet Martineau, the noblest female writer of our day, and Florence Nightingale, the soldier's faithful nurse and friend. It soon spread far and wide, and the struggle between the supporters of the Acts and those who cried out against them as wicked and unjust began in earnest.

There was work of all kinds to be done, and all over the country men and women came forward to do it. Some who lived in the towns where the Acts were in force went amongst the prostitutes and encouraged them to go before the magistrate rather than sign the 'Voluntary Submission', or inquired into the cases of women who had been condemned under the Acts to imprisonment or examination, and succeeded in proving that some, at least, had been unustly accused. Others took up their pens and wrote to the newspapers; and when the editors of all the more powerful journals refused to publish their letters, they established a newspaper of their own, which they called *The Shield*, because its object was to protect women against oppression; or wrote tracts and pamphlets to teach the people what had already been done, and what was likely still to be done, if steps were not quickly taken to check the men who wanted to extend the Acts to the whole country; others collected money to pay for the printing and spreading of such papers; others drew up petitions to Parliament, praying for the repeal of the Acts, and went from house to house colecting signatures to these petitions.

But the most difficult part of the work on which these ladies had entered, Mrs Butler undertook. In order that the opposition to the Acts might be rapid and general, it was necessary to hold public meetings to protest against them, and that some one should speak at those meetings and explain why they had been called. This she did. In Birmingham, Nottingham, Liverpool, Manchester, Leeds, Glasgow, and other cities, she addressed large meetings, some of women, others of men, and others of both men and women; and I leave it to you to think how painful it must have been to a delicate and pure minded woman to speak on such a subject in public; but the solemn conviction that she was speaking for God, as well as for her fellow-women, gave her courage and strength, and her noble words won over thousands to the cause for which she pleased. Eminent men of all sorts, clergymen, dissenting ministers, doctors, writers, declared themselves on the side of the Ladies' Association. But still the greater number of men and women of the upper and middle classes held aloof, either approving the Acts, or shrinking from the disagreeable task of opposing them, or thinking selfishly 'such laws will never touch *us*, why should *we* trouble ourselves about them'; and all the newspapers which write for and are supported by those classes, were either altogether silent about the Acts, or else only printed letters and speeches in their favour, whilst some few among them heaped ridicule and abuse upon the brave women who were labouring for their repeal. Therefore the Ladies' Association and their helpers turned to the working classes, knowing that if their support could be secured, success was certain, since by the Reform Bill, passed only two years before, the working men in the towns at least had almost all obtained votes, and being far more numerous than any other class, they have it now in their power, if they only stand by each other, to return to Parliament what candidates they please.

And, thank God, they were not appealed to in vain. They could not say 'these laws do not concern us', for they knew that if they were to be extended to all towns, as their authors desired, no working man's wife, or sister, or daughter would be safe from false accusation and the dread of being falsely accused; and they had no sympathy with the new doctrine that men are by nature brutes and cannot be cured of their brutal ways, for what they were striving for was not liberty in indulge their lower appetites, but light and knowledge to enable them to control those appetites, and rise to a higher life. They felt too, and felt deeply, the injustice of these one-sided laws, which, of two sinners, punish only one; for the sense of fair play was still strong among them, and they saw clearly that to allow the weakest, because the most despised class in the community, to be oppressed was to give up the country to be ruled by might and not by right; to be governed by laws framed by a class for the benefit of that class, the very thing against which they and their fathers had been struggling for years. 'We will have no more class legislation; England shall be governed *by* the people *for* the people' – this had been long their watchword, and they could not therefore stand coldly by and permit laws for the advantage of the vicious few to be forced upon the virtuous many. No, this was impossible; and so, instead of the scorn or indifference which Mrs Butler and her friends met with from persons of rank, education, and position, the operatives of England received them with the honour and sympathy which their unselfishness and courage deserved; and it soon become clear from the public meetings which they held to discuss the Contagious Diseases Acts, from the numerous petitions which they sent up to Parliament against them, and from the questions which they put to their representatives, that at the next general election the supporters of the Acts would be rejected by the people.

Week after week the agitation against the Acts grew and strengthened, and at last Mr Fowler gave notice of his intention to ask for leave to bring in a Bill for their repeal, and the country waited anxiously to know what would be said for and against them in the House of Commons. But when the day fixed for the debate on

Mr Fowler's motion, 20 July 1870, arrived, one of the gentlemen in favour of the Acts, availing himself of a right which all members of Parliament possess, but which for years had never been used, turned out all the people who had come to listen and all the newspaper reporters also, and so the public learned very little of what passed in the House that night, except the speech which Mr Jacob Bright, the member for Manchester, made against the Acts, which was afterwards published by the Ladies' Association. However, it was by this time clear to Government that something would have to be done to satisfy the people; but, as they were still unwilling to do away with the Acts, they proposed that a Royal Commission should be appointed to inquire into their working. The Ladies' Association, the National Association, and all the local committees throughout the country, disapproved of this step, partly because they knew it would put off repeal for a year at least, and partly because they thought it did not matter whether the Acts could, or could not, be shown to have diminished contagious disease. 'These laws are immoral and unjust, whether they succeed in their object or fail' said they, 'and if they really do enable men to sin without having to suffer for it, we shall only oppose them all the more, because we foresee that they will in the end destroy virtue, first among men and afterwards among women.' However, they were not strong enough in Parliament to get their views accepted, and so a Royal Commission of twenty-five gentleman was appointed to examine witnesses, and to learn all that could be learned about the effects of the Acts on the soldiers, the prostitutes, and the public at large. This Commission finished its work on 13 May, and it will very shortly present to Parliament what is called a Report, that is to say, a paper containing a short account of the information they have obtained and the opinion which they have formed. Of course we cannot tell beforehand whether that report will be in favour of or against the continued existence of the Acts, but, however that may be, the question will still have to be decided by Parliament itself, and as the day of decision is drawing near, it becomes more and more necessary for all those who believe them to be wicked and unjust, to take every means to let their views be known. Fresh petitions against them will be presented both to the House of Lords and the House of Commons, and the more numerously these petitions are signed the more weight they will carry with them. I feel sure you will all be eager to put your names to these protests against a cruel wrong. But it is not sufficient that you should sign yourselves, you must use your influence with your fathers and brothers, husbands and sons, to induce them to do the same, for Parliament will pay more respect to a petition signed by fifty men that to one signed by 500 women. Perhaps you will wonder I should say this, and think to yourselves: 'but these Acts concern us women far more than they concern men; it is we who suffer from them, therefore it is only just that we should be the first to be listened to when we protest against them.' My friends, in this world things are not always as they should be; of course the ears of the powerful ought to be ever open to the voice of the oppressed, crying for justice, but, in fact, the exact contrary is the case. If individuals or classes are weak, they may complain as they will, and yet not gain redress for their wrongs, unless those who are stronger than they take up their cause, and insist upon their demands being attended to. We women, are weak, therefore we must win over men to speak for and work with us. But why are we weak? Are we not half, more than half the nation, and do we not add to its wealth by our labour? Yes, but we have no votes; we are not represented in Parliament; and it matters not what we think since we have no means of compelling the Government to take our thoughts into account. You will, perhaps, be told that we have no need of votes because men vote for us and represent us. But do they really represent us? Why, if women had had a voice in the election of members of Parliament, would the Contagious Diseases Acts ever have become law? No one can believe it after the way in which, during the last two years, women have toiled and striven for their repeal; and there are many other laws and customs still in force in this country which would perish to a certainty the day women became possessed of political rights. About some of these I may, perhaps, tell you another time; now I only want to impress upon you the importance of gaining over the men of your families to the side of the Association for the Repeal of the Contagious Diseases Acts; and I think you will not find it difficult to do this, for the interest of all good men is, in this case, at least, clearly the same as the interest of all women. None but the vicious, or those who, though virtuous themselves, have lost all faith in the possibility of raising others to virtue, can desire the maintenance of laws which aim at rendering vice more common, because more safe; and they must be looked upon with anger and fear by every decent man who has a wife, or sister, or daughter, who, sooner or later, might become their victim.

I am, my dear Friends,
Yours very faithfully,

An English Lady

P.S. Since closing my letter, it has unhappily become probable that the Report of the Royal Commission will not be ready until too late for Parliament to take any steps this session towards repealing the Contagious Diseases Acts, which will thus remain in force another year.

The friends of those measures hope, doubtless, to weary out their adversaries by delay, or at least to gain time to devise some plan by which, whilst giving up their outward form, they may still keep their substance; but they will find themselves mistaken in their hopes. It is not only to the Acts themselves that we, who are working against them, object, but also and chiefly to the principles on which they rest – the principle that vice is necessary, as men cannot be healthy without it, that of two sinners the *lesser* alone is to be punished: and punished solely that the *greater* may be free and safe to repeat his offence – and agains these we mean to fight, until, if men are not ashamed to hold them in their hearts, they shall, at least, blush to proclaim them with their lips, until every trace of them has vanished, for ever, from our laws.

Universal repeal of the Contagious Diseases Acts

Since the second of my two letters went to press, it has become known that the Royal Commission will report in favour of the Repeal of certain clauses of the Contagious Diseases Acts of 1866 and 1869, by a majority of 13 to 6. Yet I would earnestly beg my country-women not to suppose that the struggle is at an end. Endeavours to reimpose the first Act, that of 1864, will undoubtedly be made by those who cannot be brought to see that the principle on which our agitation has been founded, binds us to accept no measure embodying, in any degree, ideas of human nature, degrading to man and insulting to his Creator.

However much their provisions may differ, all the three Acts were born of the belief that vice is necessary to man, and that Government is bound to protect its male subjects from the natural consequences of their vicious self-indulgence, by depriving women of their rights and liberties, placing them, as regards character, at the mercy of the police, and rendering them liable to a painful and degrading examination.

It matters not to us whether that examination is made because a policeman swears that he believes a woman to be a prostitute, as by the later Acts, or that he believes her to be suffering from a contagious disease, as by that of 1864; nor yet, whether the term of imprisonment in hospital is limited to nine months or to three. It is against *all* compulsory examination, *all* oaths of suspicion, *all* hospital prisons that we protest; but, above all, against all punishment of sin, all cure of disease, by force, in one sex, and not in the other. Equal justice is what we claim – equal justice for high and low, rich and poor, man and woman, and nothing less will ever content us.

Yet the existence of contagious disease is to the full as painful to us, as it can be to naval or military officers, and our hopes of rooting it out of the land as great, and far better founded, for we mean to attack it in the vicious passions which are its source.

So far as statistics can be procured, we find that three-fourths of the prostitutes in England fall before they are 19 years old; more girls are seduced at 16, than at any other age. Do not these figures say plainly that sin, in women, is mainly the fruit of youth and ignorance? Do they not call aloud to us to insist upon the enactment of laws, which shall protect our daughters until they are old enough, and wise enough to protect themselves?

At present it is a felony to seduce a child under 10; a misdemeanour to seduce one under 12; but after that age it is no offence, my friends, to ruin your little ones. To this state of the law we know that a large part of female error can be traced; this state of the law, therefore, we will endure no longer. Make it felony to seduce a girl below 17; a misdemeanour to seduce one under 19, and I venture to foretell that we shall soon hear no more of towns with 1,500 prostitutes under 15 years of age.

What we need to put down prostitution, and so to lessen contagious disease, are, first: laws to hinder men from leading children astray, before they can have any knowledge of the gulf of misery and sin into which they are being plunged; secondly, education, true moral education, to teach every boy and girl in the land that vice is mean, and selfish, and unmanly; that their passions are not their rulers, but their servants; that they are allied to God as well as to the brutes, and that it lies with them to choose with which of the two they will claim kinship.

For such laws then, and for such education must we work, when our first duty of destroying every shred and tatter of the Contagious Diseases Acts has been accomplished; but, remember, that when we have swept them out of England our work will not be done, for they are in force in India, and the Colonies also, where, to the evils inherent in them, is added the danger of their turning against us the hearts of those over whom it is, at present, our privilege and responsibility to rule.

In India, a land to which, with its two hundred million inhabitants, our island is, but as a single county to the whole United Kingdom, this danger is greatest, not only from the multitudes touched by the Acts, but also from the religious and moral convictions of the people, which lead them to regard the instrumental examinations with such horror that when the Acts were applied to Bombay, Dadoba Pundersung asserts that 3,000 women fled into the surrounding country, where many died of exposure or hunger.

Remember, my friends, what is just for one man or one woman is just for all men and all women: the rights and liberties which the mother country asks for herself she owes to all her children.

Differences of creed or of tongue make no difference of conscience or of heart; and what is a shameful wrong to a white woman is no less shameful when its victim happens to be black. And the claims of our Indian sisters upon us are all the stronger because, owing to the inferior position held by the female sex in the East, they are powerless to help themselves, since it is not possible for them to join together, as we in England have done, to resist injustice and oppression.

Our task, then, will not be accomplished till the Acts for whose downfall we have toiled in our own country, have been swept away in every part of the British dominions; nor even then, whilst women in France, and Germany, and Italy, and Spain, stretch out their hands imploring our aid to obtain from their Governments the same measure of justice which we have won from ours.

Petitions to both Houses of Parliament are in course of preparation, for which we shall ask the support of your names.

An English Lady

Josephine Butler

Social Purity

(n.d.)

I am asked to speak to you on the subject of *Social Purity*. I felt some difficulty in accepting your invitation, when this title to my Address was put before me. Under such a title, it seemed to me my address to you might come to be of a nature somewhat vague and unpractical; and this is just what I wish it should not be.

On the other hand, I felt a difficulty in regard to answering the question which may be and is asked by you, 'What can we *do* practically to promote Social Purity, and to combat the evil around us?' The part in this work which belongs to men launched into the world, to fathers of families, to mothers, to women in general, and to the mass of the working classes, is not exactly the part which you can take at present. To all these classes of persons I have been more accustomed to speak than to persons of your age and your position.

Yet, at all ages, and in all positions, there is a moral responsibility in regard to this question, even though the time or the call to action may not have yet come. I have endeavoured to think carefully what is the nature of the responsibility laid upon you – what the nature of the active effort, if any, which is demanded of you; and I venture to give you the result of my thoughts. Observe, so far as I take upon myself to indicate to you your own part, I do it with reserve, and am subject to correction: but when I speak of principles in this matter – when I tell you of what men and women generally ought to be and do in regard to it; when I speak of justice and injustice, of selfishness and cruel wrong, and of the redress of that wrong – I speak with no reserve, with no hesitation, but with immoveable conviction, and from a somewhat deep and wide experience. As a woman, addressing men on the subject most vital to us next to our relations with God, I speak also with authority.

It will be useful to consider first what it is that lies at the root of the evil which we are gathered together here today to consider, with a view to opposing it. The root of the evil is the unequal standard in morality; the false idea that there is one code of morality for men and another for women – which has prevailed since the beginning, which was proclaimed to be false by Him who spoke as the Son of God, and yet which grew up again after His time in Christian communities, endorsed by the silence of the Church itself, and which has within the last century been publicly proclaimed as an axiom by almost all the governments of the civilised and Christian world.

This unequal standard has more or less coloured and shaped the whole of our social life. Even in lands where a high degree of morality and attachment to domestic life prevails, the measure of the moral strictness of the people is too often the bitterness of their treatment of the erring *woman*, and of her alone. Some will tell me that this is the invariable rule, and that the sternest possible reprobation of the *female* sinner as being the most deeply culpable, has marked every age and all teaching in which the moral standard was high. No! – not every age, nor all teaching! There stands on the page of history one marked exception; and so far as I know, one only – that of Christ.

I will ask you the question today, therefore, in this connection, 'What think ye of Christ?' Come with me into His presence. Let us go with Him into the temple; let us look at Him on the occasion when men rudely thrust into his presence a woman, who with loud-tongued accusation they condemned as an impure and hateful thing. 'He that is without sin among you, let him first cast a stone at her.' At the close of that interview, He asked, 'Woman, where are those thine accusers?' It was a significant question; and we ask it again today. Where, and *who* are they! In what state are *their* consciences? Beginning from the eldest even to the youngest, they went out, scared by the searching presence of Him who admitted not for one moment that God's law of purity should be relaxed for the stronger, while imposed in its utmost severity on the weaker.

Almost as soon as that holy Teacher had ascended into the heavens, Christian society and the Church itself began to be unfaithful to his teaching; and man has too generally continued up to this day to assert, by speech, by customs, by institutions, and by laws, that, in regard to this evil, the woman who errs is irrevocably blighted, while the man is at least excusable. As a floating straw indicates the flow of the tide, so there are certain expressions that have become almost proverbial, and till lately have passed unchallenged in conversation and in literature, plainly revealing the double standard which society has accepted. One of these expressions is, 'he is only sowing his wild oats'; another is, that 'a reformed profligate makes a good husband'. The latter is a sentiment so gross that I would not repeat it, if it were not necessary to do so – as a proof of the extent of the aberration of human judgment in this matter.

Here we are at once brought into contact with the false and misleading idea that the essence of right and wrong is in some way dependent on sex. We never hear it carelessly or complacently asserted of a young woman that '*she* is only sowing her wild oats'. This is not a pleasant aspect of the question; but let us deal faithfully with it. It is a fact that numbers even of moral and religious people have permitted themselves to accept and condone in man what is fiercely condemned in woman.

And do you see the logical necessity involved in this? It is that a large section of female society has to be told off – set aside, so to speak, to minister to the irregularities of the excusable man. That section is doomed to death, hurled to despair; while another section of womanhood is kept strictly and almost forcibly guarded in domestic purity. Thus even good and moral men have so judged in regard to the vice of sexual immorality as to concede in social opinion *all* that the male profligate can desire. This perverse social and public opinion is no small incentive to immorality. It encourages the pernicious belief that men may be profligate when young without serious detriment to their character in after-life. This is not a belief that is borne out by facts. Marriage does not transform a man's nature, nor uproot habits that have grown with his years; the licentious imagination continues its secret blight, though the outward conduct may be restrained. The man continues to be what he was, selfish and unrestrained, though he may be outwardly moral in deference to the opinion of that 'society' which having previously excused his vices, now expects him to be moral. And what of that other being, the partner – his wife – into whose presence he brings the secret consciousness, it may be the hideous morbid fruits, of his former impurity? Can any man with any pretension to true manliness, contemplate calmly the shame – the cruelty – of the fact that such marriages are not exceptional, especially in the upper classes?

The *consequences* of sins of impurity far outlast the sin itself, both in individuals and in communities. Worldly and impure men have thought, and still think, they can separate women, as I have said, into two classes, – the protected and refined ladies who are not only to *be good*, but who are, if possible, to *know* nothing except what is good; and those poor outcast daughters of the people whom they purchase with money, and with whom they think they may consort in evil whenever it pleases them to do so, before returning to their own separated and protected homes. They forget that, even if they could by the help of modern impure legislation, leave all the *physical* consequences of their evil deeds behind them, they cannot so leave the moral consequences. The man's whole nature is lowered and injured who acts thus. But the evil does not stop with his own debasement; he transmits a degraded nature to his children. The poison is in his soul. His children inherit the mixed tendencies of their parents – good and bad; and what security has this prosperous man of the world that the one who is to inherit foul blood and warped brain may not be his *daughter!* Have these successful sinners ever thought of Nemesis coming in such a shape as this?

The double standard of morality owes its continued existence very greatly to the want of a common sentiment concerning morality on the part of men and women, especially in the more refined classes of society. Men are driven away at an early age from the society of women, and thrown upon the society of each other only – in schools, colleges, barracks, etc; and thus they have concocted and cherished a wholly different standard of moral purity from that generally existing among women. Even those men who are personally pure and blameless become persuaded by the force of familiarity with male profligacy around them, that this sin in *man* is venial and excusable. They interpret the ignorance and silence of women as indulgent acquiescence and support.

Women are guilty also in this matter, for they unfortunately have imitated the tone and sentiments of men, instead of chastening and condemning them; and have shown, too often, very little indeed of the horror which they profess to feel for sins of impurity. Now we have the profound conviction that not only must as many men and women as possible severally understand the truth concerning their relations to each other, but also that they must learn the lesson in each other's presence, and with each other's help. A deeply-reaching mutual sympathy and common knowledge must (if we are ever to have any real reform) take the place of the life-long separation and antipathetic sentiments which have prevailed in the past.

Obviously, then, the essence of the great work which we propose to ourselves, is to Christianise public opinion until, both in theory and practice, it shall recognise the fundamental truth that the essence of right and wrong is in no way dependent upon sex, and shall demand of men precisely the same chastity as it demands of women. It is a tremendous work which we have on hand. Licentiousness is blasting the souls and bodies of thousands of men and women, chiefly through the guilt of the men of the upper and educated classes. The homes of the poor are blighted – the women among the poor are crushed – by this licentiousness, which ever goes hand-in-hand with the most galling tyranny of the strong over the weak. The press and the pulpit, apparently dismayed by the enormity of the evil, the one sometimes in sympathy with it, the other losing faith in the power of God and in spiritual revival, *have ceased altogether to administer any adequate rebuke*. In our homes and in social circles, mistaken delicacy has come to the aid of cowardice, and the truth is betrayed even in the house of its friends. The warnings of God are concealed, and young men and women are left to be taught by sad and irremediable experience the moral truths which should be impressed upon them early in life by faithful instructors.

You ask, What can we do? It appears to me that the direct work of rescuing women is not altogether suitable for you. Such work attempted by young men seems to me often to involve an element not favourable to the end desired. You must not refuse, if you can do it, to save one who crosses your path, any more than to save a drowning man if you saw one in the water; but I do not think direct rescue work is precisely that to which you are at present called. As to active work among yourselves – among other men – you can judge perhaps better than I. But *for you this is the great time of preparation*. It is *now* that you must attain to that strength of principle and clearness of conviction which will enable you to act when the time comes, and to act *aggressively* against this evil.

Having attained to a just judgment in this matter, there is one thing you can do; that is, to help to form a just public opinion around you. We know how strong public opinion is in school and universities – how misleading it often is. Public opinion is to the community what conscience is to the individual; it may be warped or it may be enlightened. You will thus be preparing both the written and the unwritten law of the future, by forming right opinions around you; for laws are to a great extent the outcome of public opinion. It is public opinion which gives sense to the letter, and life to the law.

Learn first, and above all things, to be *just*. Never even mentally endorse any hasty or unjust assertion which you may hear on this subject of the relations of men and women. Accustom yourselves even rather to doubt every assertion which you may hear made in masculine society concerning women and concerning the subject before us. I ask you most earnestly to do this, because, as I have said, there are many falsehoods current in society on the whole subject of the relations of the sexes, and of the possibility of virtue – falsehoods which are honestly repeated by honest people, in the belief that there is some foundation of truth in them. These falsehoods and unequal judgments are at the root of so much of grievous practical cruelty and wrong, that, when once seen to be false, we must have no mercy for them, though we must be gentle and patient with those who are misled by them.

Men have asserted for ages past that on this subject of the 'social evil' women cannot judge, because they do not know the strength of men's natures, etc. Now I do not assert that the judgment of women taken alone would be complete or wholly just. But neither is the judgment of men on this subject complete or wholly just. It is impossible that it should be so. The verdict of both halves of humanity must be heard. Men alone have spoken hitherto. Never have they honestly asked the counsels of women on this subject, nor (till now) has the verdict of women been heard. The judgments you commonly hear expressed are still those judgments formed by men alone; therefore it is that I ask you, when you hear them expressed, to hold your own judgment in abeyance, and to wait. I urge it also, because it is so good and so strengthening a habit of mind for you to cultivate. Learn to dread the harbouring even of an unjust or untrue thought on this question. Learn to doubt carelessly-expressed current opinions uttered by men about women, and echoed by women. Each time you endorse by repetition in words, or even in your inmost thoughts, an unjust and untrue opinion on this question, you have given a slight warp to your own mind; and you are on the road, if you do not take care, to injustice in act as well as thought.

Let me remind you of Christ's words: '*Why do ye not of yourselves judge that which is right?*' You are young, and you think older men must judge more wisely? By all means seek the opinion of older men; but having sought it, then once and again, *judge ye for yourselves that which is right.*

Nothing can acquit you of your responsibility for the free and independent exercise of those powers of judging with which God has endowed you. '*Prove* all things; hold fast that which is good.' 'Believe not every spirit; but try the spirits whether they are of God.'

I believe that the sense of justice has grown weak among my countrymen, not only on this question, but generally. With the enfeebling of the sense of justice, the love of freedom, and consequently *public spirit,* have greatly decayed. The decay of public spirit is a bad sign. I speak of this to you, for many of you may hereafter be in public positions; you will at least – all of you – be able to influence public opinion more or less.

The Christian and the Christian minister have gone as far from this sense of justice as other men. In the best times of our country, the sense of justice and the love of freedom have been in the greatest vigour. But now we find men, in the full profession of Christianity, and often sincere and devout believers in Christ, yet daily false to great principles. God is certainly just as well as merciful. His mercy continues to be preached; but the great principles of justice, of which He Himself is the source, are practically forgotten; and in many men the sense of justice is enfeebled almost to extinction.

I would entreat you therefore not to be too much guided on this vital question of human life which we are now considering, by the verdict of certain cliques, or sets of men, however high a scientific, philosophical, or ecclesiastical authority they may seem to possess. Sets of men, cliques, and professions, are extremely apt to go wrong, through the preponderance in their judgments of vital questions, of the interests or special points of view of their particular set or class. They pull each other into wrong views; and here the strong re-assertion of the *individual conscience*, enlightened from above, is often the only thing to save men from continued and dangerous error.

In illustration of how far sets of men may depart from principle, I may mention that the Church in America was at one time the bulwark of slavery; children were torn from the arms of their mothers, and sold as slaves for the support of missions to the heathen; theological colleges were endowed by legacies in slaves, and men quoted Scripture in support of the deed. The Rev. Thomas Wotherspoon said, 'I draw my warrant from the Scriptures to hold the slave in bondage; the principle of holding the heathen in bondage is recognised by God.' The Rev. Robert Anderson wrote, in an epistle to the Presbytery of West Hanover,

> Now, dear Christian brethen, I humbly express it as my earnest wish that you quit yourselves like men. If there be any stray goat of a minister among you tainted with the dangerous principles of Abolitionism, let him be ferreted out, silenced, excommunicated, and left to the public to dispose of in other respects. Your affectionate brother in the Lord.

The Right Rev. Bishop Hopkins, of Vermont, said, in a public lecture:

> From its inherent nature slavery has been a curse and blight

> wherever it exists; yet it is warranted by the Bible. What effect had the Gospel in doing away with slavery? – none whatever. Therefore as slavery is recognised by the Bible, every Christian has a right to own slaves, provided they are not treated with *unnecessary* cruelty.

There are men in our own day who attempt to throw the sacred mantle of the Scriptures over the vile thing against which we are leagued. Mr Lecky dwells with a poetic sentiment upon the tragic figure which ever appears upon the page of history – the 'priestess of humanity charged with the mournful office of bearing the sins of the people', whose sacrifice to the demon of lust is the necessary preservative of the purity of our homes! More than one modern writer has endeavoured to prove that harlotry is an institution in harmony with the Divine economy of the world, and is glad to quote Augustine and other fathers of the Church who expressed their admiration of the apparently stern but really benevolent design of the Eternal Father in the setting apart, from age to age, of a class of women, predestined to wrath, to be ministers to those passions in man which would otherwise bring 'disturbance into society, confusion of off-spring, and other inconveniences'.

I have heard that in heathen times there were temples of Venus, where there were priestesses who were also the victims of shameful lust. But I believed that eighteen centuries ago Eternal Love had appeared upon the earth.

Is it not time that the woman's voice should be heard in this matter – that she should have a veto upon that immoral claim which men have passed on to their descendants, generation after generation, to the sacrifice, in the interests of impurity, of vast armies of her sisters, women born with capacities, as others, for honourable relationships and spiritual perfecting? Women *have* at last spoken, thanks be to God! These blasphemies have at last been called up for judgment before the tribunal of the public conscience, and an open denial has been given to the 'old and chartered lie'.

I have asked you not to be too much guided by class opinion or the verdict of particular professions. It is well, however, that the voice of those sections of society who suffer the most directly and sorely from organised impurity should be heard with respect, more especially when uttered after a long compelled silence, or forced out by the pressure of exceptional pain or wrong. Next to the women who most directly suffer, in fact or through sympathy, from this social wrong, the working classes in general are they whose position in respect to it most urgently claims for them a hearing. They are not the class who make themselves heard by writing books and articles.

In your future life, some of you will no doubt come in contact more or less directly with the industrious poor; and it may not be premature to possess yourselves of the point of view from which they almost universally regard this grave question. We have had special opportunities during the last ten years for gauging the opinion of the working classes on this subject, and we have found their verdict almost unanimously in accord with justice. No doubt it is the most *truly* educated class which has supplied to this cause its most high-minded and powerful workers. But speaking generally, it cannot be said that the highly educated and privileged classes have shown either discernment or zeal in this matter. The following letter was written by an Italian working man to the journal *Emancipazione*, in Rome:

> Worthy Editor – You will surely allow a little space in your paper to a working man to state his opinion upon this beautiful emanation of our national wisdom – Regulated Prostitution! and observe, that what I write would be written by thousands of my companions. Men of education tell us that the social evil is a necessity. No doubt we shall have a revised dictionary composed by these gentlemen some day. Meanwhile, I ask you the favour to be allowed to tell these persons what the working men think. Tell them, then, that if gentlemen who have nothing better to do than to eat and drink and enjoy themselves, believe that evil to be a necessity, we working men do *not* believe it. If they think that they ought to spend not only the money, but the morality of the nation, to maintain a healthy standing army by the sacrifice of the honour of our daughters, we working men do *not* think this. These gentlemen who make such a noise about the necessity of this vice, too often forget, I think, that in order to satisfy that necessity, the *dishonour of the daughters* of the people is indispensable; for as yet no society of worshippers of these medical theories has been found ready to sacrifice their own daughters to satisfy this necessity. Tell these gentlemen that we working men know what is lawful and what is unlawful, what is moral and what is immoral, better than they do. We answer them that God and conscience existed before their science, and that if their high education produces such fruits, the sooner they get *un*educated the better it will be for their own souls, and for the souls of those whom they endeavour to influence. We poor fellows, who

> are constrained to labour twelve or fourteen hours a day, know too well that food *is indeed* a necessity, but we do not forget that it is a duty to satisfy that necessity lawfully. Yours, for justice' sake,
>
> *A Working Man*

Another working man of Southern Europe says:

> What an outcry there would be among these gentlemen were we to seize their property for our common use, and get Parliament to legalise that robbery. But they have taken our daughters for their common use, and have legalised *that* robbery and outrage.

In regard, then, to this question, which may be called a question of *life and death* for the nations of the world, I would say to you, use your present time of preparation wisely. 'Get wisdom, and with all thy getting, get understanding.' I know not what 'wisdom' is, if it be not that illumination of the intellect, that holy light in the understanding which, together with every other good and perfect gift, cometh down from the Father of lights. It is a light which does not necessarily come through high education, nor is it won by the unaided exercise of the reasoning powers, though it implies and demands the faithful cultivation and exercise of those powers. It must be asked of God. In this, and other great questions of human life we frequently find men of kind hearts and honest intentions going far astray, for want of that illuminated intellect which is the gift of God. The benevolent heart is not a sufficient guide in matters of justice.

But in order to arrive at the truth in these great subjects, in order to attain a clear insight and immovable conviction in these matters of principle, there is one thing which I am convinced is indispensable, i.e., a certain amount of solitude. You must learn courageously to isolate your own soul, and to retire from the presence of your fellow men. No deep inspiration was ever won, no truly great character was ever formed without solitude: as Lacordaire has said, 'The heart suffers, if it is not lost, by continual contact with men; man forms himself in his own interior, and nowhere else.'

It is not out of place, perhaps, when asked to suggest what you can do, to urge upon you the present thoughts. I do so the more earnestly because in a place like Cambridge, where you are living so near together, there is a great temptation to be always dropping into each other's rooms. The facilities for hearing what so-and-so thinks are so readily in your reach, that it is natural to seek in intercourse with your friends, rather than in solitude, to clear up your own views and strengthen your convictions. Nothing is more helpful or more useful as a corrective for our own defects, and at its best, nothing is more elevating than communion with men and women who are enlightened and wise; but I believe that not only is this good missed, but a positive evil is encountered when this habit of conferring with man takes the place of communion with God. There is far too much talk in these days.

Do not be surprised if I beg you to avoid the habit of much talk even on grave questions. 'In all labour there is profit; but the talk of the lips tendeth only to poverty.' It requires a degree almost of heroism, when pressing business and voices on all sides seem to be claiming us, to close our chamber door and lock out, not only our fellow men, but their opinions and judgments and every-day sayings, which are so apt to follow us into our retirement. When we can so easily get the advice of good men, it requires some force of character to determine to work out *alone* the problems which trouble us. And yet *it must be done*, if you are to rise to the full stature of your individual manhood, and if you are to have any influence for good. Resolve then to bring these subjects into the presence of God, and, asking him to illuminate your intellect, and to free your mind from all weakness and prejudice, ponder them, wrestle with them if need be, having none but God as witness of your effort.

It was suggested to me that I should speak to you on the all-important subject of *Social Purity;* and that it might be better to postpone the consideration of the subject of that legislation for regulating vice against which a great international 'league' is now contending. I understand the feelings which prompted this suggestion; but when I shall have explained myself, I think those who made the suggestion will also understand my feeling about the matter.

The truth is, I should not deem it to be perfectly honest in me to stand before you today to speak of these vital questions, and at the same time to be silent concerning that special work to which God in his providence has called me. I should be guilty of a kind of infidelity to the special charge I received from God, were I to deal only with the subject of *Social Purity*, and not speak plainly to you of the attitude the State has assumed towards organised vice. Probably you will some day be in positions of trust, perhaps some of you in Parliament; in any case all of you will be able, more or less directly, to influence the public mind, if you desire to do so. I have undertaken to suggest to you what you may now be preparing yourselves to do practically in the future, rather than what you should do during your University career; and in this view of the matter I should deeply regret any omission on my part which might prevent your joining some years hence the 'noble army', of which I shall now speak to you.

You should know then, that never, till we dared to challenge the public authorities of the world as we have now done, was this question brought fully into the light of day, and the public conscience in any measure awakened, as we now see it to be.

In 1869, our Parliament passed those Acts – under a misleading title – which organise and regulate prostitution in the manner in which it has been organised for nearly a century in many parts of the Continent. The system had been previously introduced by our Government into our Colonies, and a certain revenue has continued to be derived by the Government from the licenses sold by it to traders in debauchery.

Now I wish you to try to realise that these Acts introduced into England not only an immoral principle and demoralising procedures, but the most violent infringement of all the first principles of just law and of jurisprudence, legalising that which in all lands, until recent times, has been held to be illegal. The danger for the whole community is imminent when the safeguards of law and constitutional right are swept away for any portion of that community. This is far too large a part of the subject for me to enter on here; it has called forth the efforts of the ablest jurists on the Continent, and learned books have been written in condemnation of this unnatural, this bastard law enacted in England.

But God overruled for good the enactment of this masterpiece of tyranny and immorality. It awakened the slumbering conscience of our people. It is to this that you owe it, my friends, that there is now a 'holy war' being waged openly against impurity, in which you are invited to join: how then could I be silent on this point?

Our public appeal, and our open war against the Government establishment of vice, has been fruitful for social rousing and reform, as no movement which we know of in this direction has yet been. It has forced the enemy to come forth from the ambush in which he had lurked, concealed but destructive, for so many centuries. Our open defiance of governments, and of that false public opinion which made it possible for governments to enact such a law, has done what years – even centuries – of more silent and private work had never done, and could never do. It compelled the enemy to show himself; and to declare his nature and principles. It forced men once more to call things by their right names. The upholders of this law were obliged openly to declare as their belief, and as the basis of this legislation, the doctrine of the *necessity of vice* for man, and of the impossibility of self-restraint; and then was called forth the public denial of that doctrine. For the first time in the world's history *women* came to the front in the controversy. The whole cruelty of the law falling on their own sex for the fancied preservation of the health of men, woke up the womanhood of this land, and now of the world, in a way which reminds us of the words of sacred prophecy, 'When the enemy cometh in like a flood, the Spirit of the Lord shall raise up a standard against him.' It is the weak hands of women which bear up this standard. Never till the woman's public defiance of this law, and of the evil principles which underlie it, was heard – never till this sacred cry of revolt was uttered aloud, did this war against impurity begin in earnest. How then should I be silent on this topic?

Some may still fail to see how the aim of the abolitionists of the State regulation of vice is at all a direct blow at the root of the evil. There is a great significance in the bitter opposition and the personal hostility we have aroused. No amount of 'rescue work' among women, no quiet propagandism of social purity among men, would ever have excited this hostility. The opposition we meet is a cheering token – a proof that we have struck a vital point in the evil thing. The pioneers in this crusade had somewhat to bear: nor must you imagine that you, entering later this field of battle, will have an easy time of it.

You will not find great people coming forward, eager to give their names to this crusade, or to have the honour of crowning the edifice, as they do in the cause of Education and some social reforms, when others have patiently and laboriously laid the foundations. The highly educated (though there are many noble exceptions), the refined and fastidious of the more privileged classes, will continue to oppose us with silent scorn and avoidance. Yet, though some of us may say with St Gregory Nazianzen, 'More stones were thrown at me than other men had flowers', there is a great reward in this work; and not the least part of that reward is the humble and courageous indifference to the world's censure and the world's praise, to which it surely educates us. No work with a less definite aim or of a less militant character will ever thus excite the hostility of the enemy. This is too well proved by the patronising approval of ordinary 'rescue work' given even by the most violent partisans of State regulation of vice.

The saving of the female victims of vice is, after all, not a thorough reform, in the *largest* view of this sorrowful question.

During the present hopeful agitation in Paris against State regulation, many articles have appeared in leading Parisian journals imploring the abolitionists to turn their efforts to the excellent work of 'rescue'. *Le Temps*, in a leading article, ardently entreats all good men and women to rally round a work (the work of rescue), which 'not only will *wound no one*, but will receive protection in high quarters, and the assistance of influential individuals'. It beseeches them 'to occupy themselves with repentant women, and to leave the Government freely to act in its own province'. M. Humbert, our Continental secretary, commenting on this, says, with a stern irony:

> Thus each set of persons will have a well-defined task assigned them. The one will precipitate victims wholesale into the gulf, while the other will draw a few of the same victims with difficulty, one by one, out of that gulf.

Immoral men know that for every victim you save, they can easily get another to fill her place, so long as public opinion is unchanged, and male profligacy is condoned.

Our work is world-wide. Let me introduce you to it a little. These are days of international action. No nation now 'liveth to itself or dieth to itself', any more than the individual. This campaign of ours has taught us English more than any other previous event, to lay aside our insular character and prejudices, and to love our foreign neighbours as if they were our own compatriots. As you have asked practical suggestions from me, I would suggest that you should learn to be quite familiar with some modern languages, more especially French, and that in foreign travel you should seek, not health and enjoyment alone, but an acquaintance with the efforts and conflicts of reformers of other lands. You will thus find an *élite* of men and women to whom we can introduce you, acquaintance with whom will greatly enrich your experience, and stimulate you to action.

England holds a peculiar position in regard to this question. She was the last to adopt this system of slavery, and she adopted it in that thorough manner which characterises the actions of the Anglo-Saxon race. In no other country has the social vice been regulated by a law. It has been understood by the Latin races, even when morally enervated, that the Law could not, without risk of losing its majesty and force, sanction illegality, and violate justice. In England alone, the regulations are *law*. Their promoters, by their hardihood in asking Parliament to *decree* illegality and injustice, have brought on, unconsciously to themselves, the beginning of the end of the whole system throughout the world.

The Englishman is a powerful agent for evil, as for good. In the best times of our history my countrymen possessed pre-eminently vigorous minds in vigorous bodies.

> But, when faith decays (religious and moral faith together), and when the animal nature has grown as strongly as the moral nature, and along with it the animal appetites, and when appetites burst their traditionary restraints, and man in himself has no other notion of enjoyment save bodily pleasure and the accumulation of wealth, he passes (and, above all, the Englishman passes) by a quick and easy transition into a mere powerful brute.

There is no creature in the world so ready as the Englishman to destroy, to enslave, to domineer, and to grow fat upon the destruction of the weaker human beings whom he has subjected to his bold and iron will.

But, together with this development towards evil, there has been in our country a counterdevelopment. Moral faith is still strong among us, especially in certain sections of society. It was in England, then – in England which adopted *last* the hideous slavery – that there arose *first* a strong and national protest and opposition to that slavery. English people rose up against the wicked law before it had been in operation three months. English men and women determined to procure its abolition, and, by God's help, to effect a moral revival, not at home only, but abroad; and they promptly carried their crusade to every country on the Continent of Europe.

The progress of our cause has been truly marvellous. Yet, on the other hand, it is obvious that the partisans of this evil legislation have recently been smitten with a kind of rage for extending the system everywhere; and that they are on the watch, with an activity and adroitness almost superhuman, to introduce it wherever we are off our guard, or not strongly represented. This fact seems to point to a more decided and bitter struggle on the question than we have yet seen.

We now need to call up among us – to pray for and beseech Heaven to grant us – more of *aggressive and militant virtue* than we yet see among us. To live purely and blamelessly ourselves is not now enough; we must have the fibre of soldiers; the courage, if need be, of leaders of a forlorn hope, over whose dead bodies our fellow-soldiers will march to victory.

An energetic member of our executive committee, M. Pierson, of Zetten, in Holland, says:

> I look upon legalised prostitution as the system in which the

> immorality and incredulity of our age are crystallised; and that in attacking it we attack in reality the great enemies which are hiding themselves behind its ramparts. But if we do not *soon* overthrow these ramparts we must not think our work is fruitless. A great work is already achieved: sin is once more called sin instead of "*necessary evil*"; and the true standard of morality, as an *equal* standard for men and women, for rich and poor, is once more lifted up in the face of all the nations.

These are times, it would appear then, in which we, in all lands, seem summoned to join hands with all who call upon the name of the Lord – with all who love justice – in order that by our combined strength we may be able to oppose the evil which 'cometh in like a flood'. What we have to do seems to me now to be this: *to form a nation within the nations* – a nation which will recognise the supremacy of the moral law, and which will contend for the dignity and autonomy of the individual, against the Socialism (whether represented by imperialism or democracy) which takes too little account of the individual, and is too ready to coerce, oppress, or destroy the human being in the supposed interests of an aggregate of human beings which it calls *Society*, or *The State*. The soul of each human being was created free and responsible before God; and every human law which has in it any of the Divine character of His law, recognises the inviolability of the individual. The 'nation within the nations' will have to labour, by holding fast its faith in God, to hold fast those great principles of justice towards man, which are slipping away from us.

This legalisation of vice, which is the endorsement of the 'necessity' of impurity for men, and the institution of the slavery of women, is the most open denial which modern times have seen of the principle of the sacredness of the individual human being. It is the embodiment of Socialism in its worst form.

An English high-class journal confessed this, when it dared to demand that women who are unchaste shall henceforth be dealt with 'not as human beings, but as foul sewers', or some such 'material nuisance', without souls, without rights, and without responsibility.

When the leaders of public opinion in a country have arrived at such a point of combined scepticism and despotism as to recommend such a manner of dealing with human beings, there is no crime which that country may not presently legalise, there is 'no organisation of murder – no conspiracy of abominable things – that it may not, and in due time will not, have been found to embrace in its guilty methods'. It is for the newly-born 'nation within the nations' to protest that there is no such thing as a *political whole*, which is entitled to violate or dispense with the smallest right of the meanest worm that crawls its floor; that there is no such thing as a national unity of so splendid a tradition that the smoke of *one* personal wrong may not quench it.

Were it possible to secure the absolute physical health of a whole province, or an entire continent by the destruction of *one* – only one – poor and sinful woman, woe to that nation which should dare by that single act of destruction, to purchase this advantage to the many! It will do it at its peril. God will take account of the deed, not in eternity only, but in time; it may be in the next, or even in the present generation.

I have now told you something of our vast league against this great evil; and I earnestly invite you to join it. It appears to me that God has been pleased in a special manner to bless that work, in bestowing upon it a marked, vivifying and fructifying power. The attitude of those who entered this conflict was (and needed to be) very aggressive and very courageous; and I think this may teach us that if we fear not, but go forward in the power of God to the direct and open attack of any instituted evil, He will so give us His blessing that we shall see the spiritually and morally dead arising around us, and energies quickened on all sides for true reform. Numberless societies and moralising agencies have taken their rise from ours. The 'Social Purity Alliance' which you are invited to join, and of which some of you are now members, took its rise from the energy awakened by the central attacking phalanx. Economic agencies in connection with the employment of women, 'Preventive' and 'Rescue' societies, 'Leagues' among students and other men, etc., are now formed on the Continent in connection with our work; and almost all are, in some sort, the offspring of the parent movement.

I dare to hope that after this appeal it will be impossible for any one of you individually and personally to wrong or sin against any woman. Even in some future moment of strong temptation and of weakness of will, the memory of this hour will have a restraining influence. You will not so sin against your mother, your sister, against one whom you may in future win as your wife – one whom perhaps you even now love. You will not so sin against me, who, as the exponent of the long-endured sufferings and wrongs of women, stand and plead with you today.

But even if there were a man here present in whose mind there dwells some bitter memory of the past, or who feels himself unworthy to pronounce the name of *Purity*, I would say to him, not from myself alone, but for all my fellow-workers in this cause, that every such man, honestly regretting the past, becomes doubly my brother, as every repentant woman is doubly my sister. If I could not say this, in vain should I have learned for myself the glad tidings of perfect and everlasting forgiveness and oblivion for sins past; and most unworthy should I be to confess my own and only hope to be in Him who, once from his cross on Calvary, and now from his throne in heaven, says: 'Thy sins and thine iniquities shall be remembered no more for ever': they shall be 'cast into the depths of the sea', they shall be 'no more mentioned to thee again for ever'. We invite all without exception, whatever their judgment of themselves, whatever their past may have been, to accept this full redemption, and to join us in this holy war.

> He that today shall shed his blood with me,
> Shall be my brother: be he ne'er so vile,
> This day shall gentle his condition.

Lastly, suffer me to say one word more. I believe the secret of true manliness lies, more than in anything else, in humility; and yet the true nature of humility is often imperfectly understood. It is so far from implying a cringing attitude before our fellow-men, that it induces the very opposite – a courageous independence of character, and (what often seems to those who do not understand the secret) a bold self-reliance. It is a virtue not easy of attainment. When the young escape the graver moral perils, they sometimes fall into other errors which they do not suspect, a certain conceit and want of simplicity which are not beautiful in the sight either of God or man. I beg you to bear with me if I entreat you to avoid that characteristic which we sometimes call 'priggishness', which arises from the absence of true simplicity. Why is it that this fault is so odious that one can hardly love the person who is tainted by it, be he ever so pure and blameless in his life? I think it is because we all recognise readily in others the beauty of simplicity, and feel the absence of it to be a fundamental defect in the character. 'Simplicity' implies truth, and honesty, and modesty, and the absence of any mental or moral swagger, or self-conceit.

I can feel very leniently towards young persons who fall into this or any other error, because of the respect and tenderness I have for youth; but I imagine this pedantic tone of mind is very little likely to commend the good principles of any young man infected by it to persons of his own age. There are persons of all ages in whom it is so ingrained that it seems to require some great and overwhelming sorrow, or some grievous self-knowledge, to bring them to an attitude of perfect and absolute simplicity before

God, and to destroy the root whence all affectations of character and manner take their rise.

There is a tendency in these days to undervalue the grace of humility; or rather, its true nature is misunderstood. Humility, so far from destroying moral force, increases it; it destroys, or at least sternly represses that petty egotism which assumes such a variety of subtle forms, and through which the strength of the soul evaporates.

> It keeps even a John the Baptist waiting in the desert till his appointed time; and then, when the hour is come, it opens upon the world the whole force of a soul which is strong because it is humble.

True humility is not a want of enterprise nor a subtle resource of idleness; it is not a lack of courage, nor is it the meekness which shrinks from a rude encounter; it is not the abandonment of responsibility; it is not hostile to the claims of civil or public interests, nor is it the parent of political incapacity.

> It implies the greatest of all victories within the human soul; it is the full recognition of the insignificance of self before the power and majesty of God; the force which is apparently forfeited by the casting down of self-reliance in the character, is more than recovered when the soul rests in perfect trust on the strong arm of God.

In fact, that which is commonly called 'self-reliance' is simply (in the spiritually instructed) this perfect trust in Another; and the lowliest attitude of the soul before God, if sternly and absolutely sincere, is that which brings down the richest blessings to earth.

I invite you to ponder well these things. And when the time comes for you to go forth more actively into the world, I beg you to join yourselves to this great work in some branch or other of it. We need to make common cause against so gigantic an adversary. Many will welcome you with outstretched hands and joyful hearts.

I sometimes think, looking at the gathering multitude of our fellow-workers at home and abroad, that the words descriptive of the abolitionists of negro slavery in America, are not inapplicable to some of these opponents of a still greater and more widely-spread slavery.

> It was said, one must experience. Something of the soul-sickness caused by public opposition and hatred, to enter fully into their trials. Those who are living in peace can form

> but a faint conception of what it is to have no respite, no prospect of success within any calculable time. The grave, whether it yawns beneath their feet, or lies on the far horizon, is, as they well know, their only resting-place. Nowhere but among such people as these can an array of countenances be beheld so 'little lower than the angels'.

Ordinary social life is spoiled for them; but another life, which is far better, has grown up among them. They had more life than others to begin with, as the very fact of their enterprise shows: and to them that have, more shall be given.

> They are living fast and loftily. The weakest of them who drops into the grave, worn out, has enjoyed a richer harvest of time, a larger gift out of eternity, than the octogenarian self-seeker, however he may have attained his ends.

We never have been, and may never be, called to suffer as these martyrs of America suffered; but I love to read and think of their labours and their fortitude. It is very strengthening to do so, in connection with a struggle, which has so many of the essential features of all the great and noble conflicts of the past; and it is good to hold communion of spirit with the confessors and martyrs of other times, 'who stretched out their strong arms to bring down Heaven upon our earth'.

Ladies' National Association

What It Is, and Why It Is Still Needed

(n.d.)

The Ladies' National Association for the Abolition of Government Regulation of Vice was formed in the year 1869, with the object of securing the Repeal of the Contagious Diseases Acts of 1866–1869.

Those Acts introduced into this country the Continental system of regulating and licensing vice. They were applied to eighteen naval and military districts in England and Ireland, and their object was to enable men, especially soldiers and sailors, to practice immorality without risk to their health. To this end, women were to be registered, medically examined and certified, and, in fact, a Government trade in vice, of a peculiarly degrading kind, was established.

It was against this immoral system that Mrs Josephine Butler led her great Crusade thirty-eight years ago. It is hard to realise now the forces that were arrayed against her and the odium incurred by all who joined in the movement. But Mrs Butler had the courage and enthusiasm which give the power to lead. It was said of her: 'She saw and obeyed the vision.' In her character there was that which inspired men and women alike. As Prof. Stuart wrote of her after her death: 'She was one of the great people of the world.'

Thus her gifts fitted her to lead the fight, not only as Hon. Secretary of the Ladies' National Association, but in the wider struggle for Repeal throughout the world, and it is not too much to say that it was owing to her work and influence that the Contagious Diseases Acts were first suspended in 1883, and finally abolished in 1886. The Ladies' historic Protest against the Acts, signed by Florence Nightingale, Harriet Martineau, Mary Carpenter, and other women of influence throughout the country, is given in full at the end of this paper, together with a comprehensive resolution passed by the Ladies' National Association in 1895.

After the passing of the Repeal Bill, several of the Associations were disbanded, among them the 'National Association' and the 'Working Men's League' with its 50,000 members. It proved, as Mr Benjamin Scott says in his valuable work, *A State Iniquity*,

> unwise in the extreme for so many divisions of the great army to throw down their arms because of a successful victory which did not end the campaign, and considerable pressure was needed before it was realised that a principle of Government adopted at home must be carried abroad.

Thus, in the very year (1886) in which Repeal was gained in England, a document known as the 'Infamous Memorandum' was issued by military authorities in India. It became known through private channels to Abolitionists in this country, and questions were asked in the House of Commons. The Memorandum, which was printed as a Parliamentary paper, aroused such profound indignation that, after a brilliant speech by Mr Walter McLaren, then MP for Crewe, on 5 June, 1888, the House of Commons passed the following resolution:

> That in the opinion of this House, any mere suspension of measures for the compulsory examination of women, and for licensing and regulating prostitution in India, is insufficient; and the legislation which enjoins, authorises or permits such measures ought to be repealed.

On 24 July, 1888, the C.D. Acts for India were repealed in Council at Simla, the repealing Act receiving the Viceroy's assent on 5 September 1888. It was evident, however, that, in spite of professed Abolition, Regulation was still carried on in Indian cantonments, and renewed agitation became necessary. The British Committee for dealing with Abolition in the British Empire, and especially in India, was constituted in May 1890, and in the autumn of 1891 this body arranged with Mrs Andrew and Dr Kate Bushnell to make a thorough investigation of the actual state of affairs in India. This was accomplished in 1892, and in April 1893, those ladies gave their evidence before a Departmental Committee, at the India Office in London. The result was the passing in India of Act V., 1895, which prohibited the examination of women for the purposes of prostitution. An agitation was at once set on foot by medical and military authorities in England, advocating a return to Regulation. The Government yielded to pressure and panic, and the result was the Repeal in 1897 of the above Act in order to make way for the new 'Cantonment Rules', under cover of which it is possible to carry on a modified form of Regulation in Indian cantonments. Later evidence goes to show that this is still being done in many military stations. Thus the position of affairs in regard to India is very similar to what it was in 1890, and the work needs to be done over again.

Similar laws and ordinances exist in some of our Colonies and in other Dependencies, and there are many people who would gladly see the old Acts, in some disguised form, re-introduced into the British Islands.

In attempts to bring about Notification of Disease and Detention of Women in Hospitals, there lurk dangers not suspected by those who are ignorant of the insidious nature of such efforts, and who, in their anxiety to save innocent people from the ravages of disease, fail to see that such legislation imperils the liberty of the subject and violates the principles of morality.

This is the answer to the question at the head of this paper – 'Why should the Ladies' National Association still exist?' It is as necessary today as it was in the past that the women of England should be alive to the facts connected with such legislation at home and abroad; it is the more necessary because of the loss, one after another, of those who bore, both in and out of Parliament, the burden of the conflict, a loss which culminated in the death of the beloved leader herself. We appeal today to an awakened womanhood to remember, in the midst of the social reforms for which they work, this cause which still urgently needs their active support and which is always in peril as long as immoral legislation exists and flourishes. Such legislation constitutes a grave danger to ourselves, whether enacted in Colonies and Dependencies, or in foreign countries.

In the enormous increase of military expenditure and the threats of enforced military service that startle us from time to time, there are not wanting signs which to the watchful heart repeat the lesson taught by experience – 'The price of liberty is eternal vigilance.'

Protest of the Ladies' National Association Against the C.D. Acts

(*Published on New Year's Day, 1870*)

We, the undersigned, enter our solemn Protest against these Acts:

1 Because, involving as they do, such a momentous change in the legal safeguards hitherto enjoyed by women in common with

men, they have been passed, not only without the knowledge of the country, but unknown to Parliament itself; and we hold that neither the representatives of the people nor the Press, fulfil the duties which are expected of them when they allow such legislation to take place without the fullest discussion.

2 Because, so far as women are concerned, they remove every guarantee of personal security which the law has established and held sacred, and put their reputation, their freedom, and their persons absolutely in the power of the police.

3 Because the law is bound, in any country professing to give civil liberty to its subjects, to define clearly an offence which it punishes.

4 Because it is unjust to punish the sex who are the victims of vice, and leave unpunished the sex who are the main cause both of the vice and its dreaded consequences; and we consider that liability to arrest, forced surgical examination, and (where this is resisted) imprisonment with hard labour, to which these Acts subject women, are punishment of the most degrading kind.

5 Because, by such a system, the path of evil is made more easy to our sons, and to the whole of the youth of England; inasmuch as a moral restraint is withdrawn the moment the State recognises, and provides convenience for, the practice of a vice which it thereby declares to be necessary and venial.

6 Because these measures are cruel to the women who come under their action – violating the feelings of those whose sense of shame is not wholly lost, and further brutalising even the most abandoned.

7 Because the disease which these Acts seek to remove has never been removed by any such legislation. The advocates of the system have utterly failed to show, by statistics or otherwise, that these regulations have, in any case, after several years' trial, and when applied to one sex only, diminished disease, reclaimed the fallen, or improved the general morality of the country. We have, on the contrary, the strongest evidence to show that in Paris and other continental cities where women have long been outraged by this forced inspection, the public health and morals are worse than at home.

8 Because the conditions of this disease, in the first instance, are moral, not physical. The moral evil through which the disease makes its way separates the case entirely from that of the plague, or other scourges, which have been placed under police control or sanitary care. We hold that we are bound, before rushing into the experiment of legalising a revolting vice, to try to deal with the causes of the evil, and we dare to believe that, with wiser teaching

and more capable legislation, those causes would not be beyond control.

Resolution passed at the Annual Meeting of the Ladies' National Association in July 1894

That this meeting, regarding the existence of the State Regulation of Vice in any form as a violation of the Common Law, and consequently a sentence of outlawry proclaimed against women, a denial of the unity of the moral law and an encouragement to vice, and a hygienic mistake and a danger to the public health, hereby records its continued hostility to the system in any form, and pledges itself to maintain constant vigilance against its re-introduction into Great Britain, to use every effort to obtain its entire abolition in India and the Crown Colonies, and further, as far as possible, to help the Abolitionist movement throughout the world.

Resolution passed at the Annual Meeting in April 1907

In view of the fact that the system of State Regulation of Vice, which this Association was founded to oppose, still exists in several of our Colonies and Dependencies, this meeting of Subscribers is of opinion that the Ladies' National Association should be strengthened to continue its protest against all such legislation.

Ladies' National Association

Compulsory Detention in Lock Wards

(n.d.)

Of all the problems relating to public hygiene which confront the social reformer, that of the prevalence of what are called the venereal diseases is one of the most insistent. The problem shapes itself differently to different minds – on a large scale or a small one – according to their different preoccupations. Some, with a fine scorn of details, ask for a large and valiant scheme for 'stamping out' the mischief. Others are content to ask only a little – the first thing that comes to hand – as, for instance, compulsory powers to detain such patients as have already found their way to the lock wards of the workhouse until they are sufficiently cured to be no longer a danger to others.[1] In this case the advantage, limited as it is in scope, at first sight *seems* obvious enough.

Few persons today would propose to revive the attempts made in past years to deal with these diseases by applying compulsion only to women. But the fallacy which led to such attempts is not quite dead. The man, it was said, seeks his pleasure occasionally, at the risk of contaminating one women, while the woman will be receiving visitors every night of the week, so that there is no possible comparison as to the extent of the danger to the public health. Quite so: but if the one woman contaminated by the man is a prostitute, the whole of the infection conveyed to her many customers is due to him. Equally with her, and not less so, he is a pest and a danger to society; and it is he, and not she, who is the direct purveyor of venereal disease to innocent women and children. These facts are too commonly ignored, and though no formal distinction is intended to be made between the two sexes by the advocates of Poor Law detention, it is practically certain that there would be a tendency to apply the rule much more strictly in the case of women than of men.[2] Moreover, if the man is a bread-winner, considerations of expense would come in, since his detention would mean that not only himself, but also those dependent on him would come on the rates for months or years.

Let us consider more fully the case of the women, as it appears to be simpler. Here is the Women's Lock Ward. Thirty beds, let us say, generally full. A certain number are old cases, incurables. We may leave them out of count; they have no wish to leave. A certain number, say half, are actual prostitutes. Their disease has reached a point at which it becomes a hindrance to the practice of their calling, and they have come in to get 'patched up', and go out again as soon as possible. Another is a servant, a nursemaid, with an extremely infectious syphilitic throat. Until her condition was discovered she was sleeping with her mistress's children. She hopes and intends to be out in two or three weeks, and will go into service again, probably resuming at the same time a course of clandestine immorality. Two or three are comparatively decent girls, seduced by their sweethearts. One is quite innocent; she has syphilis on the lip from a kiss. Two or three are respectable married women with children at home.

All these came in of their own accord. All require a much longer course of treatment than they are at all inclined to submit to. The married mother grows every day more anxious as to what may be happening to her uncared-for children. At the worst, her secret thought is that she cannot trust her husband. At last she can bear it no longer, and out she goes. The rough girl of the streets finds the dulness of the ward more irksome every day. Suddenly she, too, takes her discharge and is gone. Another is only staying till a certain ship comes home, bringing a certain sailor. He is no chance customer, but was her faithful pal the whole of his last year's leave. When they parted he charged her not to get ill and not to marry, and he would see her again on his return. She has got ill, nevertheless, and has come here on purpose to be ready when his ship arrives. That ship will be her motive for leaving, in spite of all persuasions to remain; but it must be remembered that it was also her reason for coming in at all. She would never have come if she had doubted her liberty to go when she would. As things are at present, each of these when she leaves the ward probably drops all treatment, and perhaps all precautions too. This is a serious defect in the present system.

Now let us consider what will be happening outside, if they are compulsorily detained. The tedious time 'while mother was in hospital' suffices for her two daughters of 14 and 15 to turn wild, under the leadership of an abandoned girl two or three years older, and is thus responsible for the creation of two young prostitutes, soon to become venereal patients themselves, and a curse to the neighbourhood for many a year to come. The girls newly seduced, at first bitterly distressed and holding themselves aloof from the foul talk of the ward, harden gradually in its poisonous atmosphere, and sink to a lower moral level; and when discharged at last, they carry its evil influence into their homes or work-places. These, and such as these, are amongst the things that must be taken into account by those well-meaning persons who think to confer a public benefit by detaining women in lock wards. They are serious drawbacks when the length of stay depends on the patient's own will and conscience and knowledge of circumstances. But a medical authority armed with compulsory powers would, it is to be feared, very seldom take into consideration these counterbalancing evils.

But, it may be answered, the compulsory powers can be used with some discrimination. Decent married women, or even girls once fallen, are not likely to be spreading contagion far and wide as soon as they are released. But who can doubt the advantage of detaining until all danger of infection is past, the reckless prostitute who uses her liberty only to spread moral and physical devastation? True, it is an advantage as far as it goes. But how far does it go?

These women all know each other, and we can easily imagine their talk. 'What's become of So-and-so? I haven't seen her about for a week.' 'Gone to the Union.' 'More fool she! whatever did she go in there for?' 'Too bad to keep on.' 'Well, she's done for herself. Fancy giving herself away like that! Why couldn't she go to So-and-so' (the chemist) 'or So-and-so' (the woman quack), 'they'd soon have given her something to put her right.' Or, 'What's the matter with you? You look pretty bad.' A pause, an exchange of nods and lifted eyebrows. 'Oh, is it *that?* Well, don't go on the parish, whatever you do, or they'll get you into the infirmary, and there you may stop till your hair's grey.'

Actually and practically, this is what would be the effect of what is called 'compulsory detention'. It might rather be called compulsory freedom. Rather than risk their liberty many would go without the treatment they would otherwise gladly have obtained, and thus, for one whose prolonged detention protects the public health, there might be ten or twenty who, through the well-meant action of the authorities, will be persistently endangering it. More especially, it would drive into concealment those early stages of the disease which every competent medical authority emphatically insists it is most important to treat as the only hope of securing a speedy and permanent cure. This speedy cure is important, not only for the patient's own sake, but for the avoidance of danger to others.[3]

At least one experiment in detention of this kind has already been made in this country, even in the absence of legal compulsory powers. Some forty years ago the Managers of the Glasgow Lock Hospital required these patients, as a condition of admission, to sign an undertaking to remain until discharged. Some refused to sign, and went away; others signed but broke their pledge. The experiment was a complete failure, and was abandoned within a twelvemonth. A more successful method was found in letting the girls feel themselves perfectly free to leave when they liked, but reasoning with them, and putting before them the advantages of remaining. It is just the same in a Rescue Home. The recognition of a girl's right to go is the best way of detaining her. The fact that she can leave tomorrow if she likes makes it easier to stay in today, and so the crisis passes.

In the male Lock Wards the conditions are not altogether dissimilar. Many of the inmates are of a lawless class, and their premature discharge may seem to constitute a public danger. But in the case of men, as of women, we have to reckon with the deterrent effect of any threatened loss of liberty, an effect becoming more marked as the inconveniences of prolonged detention, if actually enforced, become more widely known. The project is intended to ensure a greater amount of isolation and treatment of venereal disease. But surely its natural effect will be to drive these cases out of reach of any control or treatment at all. Doctors and Guardians get impatient at finding so small a proportion of the patients respond to their persuasions. What would they think if they found themselves left at last with no patients at all to persuade?

This gives rise to a further question. Venereal disease is by no means confined to the pauper class, and it will not be appreciably diminished by compulsory measures applied to that class only. Some persons therefore urge that it should be placed on the same footing as other infectious diseases, i.e., under the Notification Act. This is a matter for the Public Health Department rather than the Poor Law Authority, but it may be well briefly to indicate some reasons against it which are as strong as those against detention. In view of the strong motives for concealing venereal disease, and of the ease with which this can be done in many cases, it would be impossible to enforce notification universally; while the usual corollary – isolation during the whole contagious period – is neither possible nor necessary for most of those affected. These considerations would probably be fatal to the scheme, even if the doctors gave their assistance, which is more than doubtful. 'Will anyone show me a doctor who will denounce his own patient?' said Professor Fournier, the great Paris specialist.

Suggestions and recommendations

Is there, then, nothing to be done? Far from it. The first thing necessary is adequate and convenient gratuitous treatment, that is to say, local facilities adequate to the local requirements, which, of course, may vary from time to time; consultations at convenient hours, not involving loss of working time for working men and women; proper correlation of outdoor and indoor treatment, and sufficient arrangements for the case, comfort and, so far as necessary, privacy of patients, so as to prevent the receipt of this kind of medical assistance from being regarded as an intolerable ordeal.

As regards in-patients, it must be remembered that their willingness to remain will largely depend on a multitude of miscellaneous conditions. The cheerfulness or discomfort of the ward, the work, exercise and recreation required or permitted, the amount and kind of supervision, the rules as to admission of visitors, the patience or roughness of the nurses, their sympathy or contempt, the confidence inspired by the doctor, or the reverse, will all have their share as motives for staying or going. In short, if the ward is regarded as a place of punishment the patients will not stay longer than they are compelled; if, on the other hand, they can be convinced that it is really a place where they can find cure and human compassion, they will usually respond by consenting to stay as long as may be needful. Attention to details like these, too often neglected or mismanaged, will, therefore, have a real and potent influence in the actual prevention of disease.

But here, again, amongst the means of effectual prevention we must emphasise the absence of any sort or appearance of compulsion in the matter of detaining unwilling patients. The dread of detention would almost certainly neutralise the effect of the most favourable conditions and defeat the most well-meant efforts.

They very important semi-official International Conference on Venereal Diseases held in Brussels in 1899 gave striking evidence of the general tendency in favour of non-coercive measures even in those countries where the theory of the necessity of coersion has taken the deepest root. The very doctors of the prison hospital of St Lazare, where the refractory prostitutes of Paris are immured for treatment, urged the opening of purely voluntary dispensaries where patients might come without fear of detention. They hoped thus to get at some of the women who at present escape all the vigilance of the police.

In our own country the Army Medical Advisory Board 'has come to the conclusion that in the United Kingdom, at any rate, an attempt to grapple with the problem by methods of compulsory isolation and treatment is neither practicable nor expedient'. They add that 'better results are likely to be obtained by the diffusion of the knowledge of the serious consequences of these diseases, and the provision of effective treatment for both sexes under conditions to which no penal stigma is attached'.

Above all, it must never be forgotten that the crux of the problem, and the key to it, are essentially moral. The amount of disease depends most of all on the amount of vice. Vice commonly implies concealment, and concealment implies powerlessness of the authorities. Those who complain that nothing is being done to arrest venereal disease ignore the fact that Land Bills and Housing Bills (so far as they pass into law and practice), and all improvements in sanitation generally, and in material conditions favourable to physical and moral health, are actually combining towards the solution of the problem, along with many items of criminal law legislation from 1885 onwards, and an ever-increasing mass of philanthropic effort, including the work of such voluntary associations as the National Vigilance Association, the International Bureau for the Suppression of the White Slave Traffic, Homes and Colonies for the Feeble Minded, all the various Purity and Temperance Societies, the Mothers' Union, Girls' Friendly Society, Boys' Brigades and Scouts, and innumerable others. These and all practical and progressive religious work are so many active agencies for the diminution of venereal disease.

Along these lines, every step in advance is a step in the direction of unmitigated social good. Along the lines of coercive administrative action the cry has constantly been that success is just ahead, and a little more coercion is all that is needed; and the result has always been that the amount of vice and its power of concealment have kept well ahead of the more and more drastic efforts which have only tended to defeat themselves.

NOTES

1 Similar proposals are made in regard to inebriates and the feeble-minded. In their case other considerations may be advanced, and the present pamphlet only deals with the case of ordinary venereal patients who are not feeble-minded.

2 The Majority Report of the Poor Law Commission, which repeatedly and with insistence recommends compulsory powers of detention for venereal cases, suggests that able-bodied men under detention (it does not say whether inebriates, consumptives or venereal patients are intended) should be allowed out occasionally, to see how they behave! One would like to ask if the Commissioners have any idea how the test is to be applied, or what the result is likely to be. The patient, if a venereal case, is to be subjected to prolonged detention because he occasionally becomes a danger to society; but the occasion is to be furnished all the same.

3 A new drug has lately been introduced by which it is claimed that syphilis can be cured in a few weeks. As to the real value of the discovery no assured verdict can yet be given, and meanwhile many of the leading specialists are very sceptical. In any case the argument of this pamphlet is unaffected, for the drug in question has no effect on gonorrhœa, which is by far the commoner form of disease.

Katherine Dixon

A Straight Talk to Men by a Woman: Address to Soldiers

(1916)

Introduction

I am going to ask you to let me speak quite straight to you. Sometime ago when I was in India, I was much amused at the criticism of two soldiers upon a sermon they had just heard in the Garrison Church. One said to the other, 'He do speak straight don't he?' 'Yes!' said the other, 'it ain't waste of time listening to a bloke like that preaching.' I agree with that soldier. It is waste of time listening to people when you can't make out what they want to say, and I will try not to fail in that way, so that I may not waste your time, or my own.

Six hundred years ago there lived a man of the name of Raymond Lull, who did not believe in the crusades against the Saracens that were then going on. He believed that there was only one thing that could conquer the world, and that was love. So he went and lived amongst the Mahomedans and tried by his life of love to win them to his faith. His motto was, '*He who loves not lives not.*' I believe that he was right, and that the whole of religion is contained in that one word *love*. 'Thou shalt love God with all thy heart and mind and soul and strength, and thou shalt love thy neighbour *as thyself.*'

But what does it mean to love one's neighbour *as oneself?* It means never doing anything to, or saying anything to, or of, anyone that you would not like done to or said to, or of, yourself. It means doing the disagreeable jobs that have to be done *yourself*, rather than letting anyone else do them. It means, in fact, sacrificing youself rather than sacrificing anyone else.

That is what loving your neighbour *as yourself* means, and what a different place the world would be if we all did it.

'*But who is my neighbour?*' That is a very old question, it is the question that the lawyer asked Christ 2,000 years ago, and the world has been asking it ever since – even the followers of Christ have been asking it, and we haven't yet grasped the answer. We find it so difficult to realise that every man, woman and child upon the face of this earth is our neighbour. The whole of history is the story of the *Good Samaritan* repeated over and over again.

You remember how the poor, wounded man lay there, and the good and learned people passed by saying, 'Oh! this is no business of mine, I am too much occupied with other things to attend to that man.'

I don't suppose the Priest or the Levite were bad men. They had simply not grasped the fact that the misfortunes of that particular man were their concern. They had not learnt who their neighbour was. Is it not extraordinary to think of all the evils from which *our neighbours* have suffered all these centuries since Christ lived on this earth, evils in which good people have acquiesced, or have, like the Priest or Levite, 'passed by on the other side'?

Slavery and serfdom

Look how the world tolerated the evils of slavery for hundreds of years, believing that it was quite right for certain men to own a large number of other men and women and to make them do exactly what they wanted, regardless of the wishes of the slaves themselves.

Now we are slowly beginning to understand that every man has a right to be free and to order his own life himself and that all slavery is an abomination.

In France, before the French Revolution, the position of the serfs – the French peasants – was little better than that of the negro slaves before the abolition of slavery. They were at the mercy of their masters, the nobles, and their lives were of little account if they interfered with the pleasure or the whims of their lords. You will understand what I mean when I tell you that there was a disgraceful old French law allowing nobles to kill two of their serfs, if, when returning from the chase, their feet were cold and they wished to warm them in fresh blood.

Look at the evils that Charles Dickens exposed and that existed in England at the beginning of last century; horrible conditions of life and labour, especially amongst children.

Look at the treatment of native races by so-called Christian countries, even in our time, or at the sweating in our large towns today, or at the way private owners of land, even in England, have been content to house their tenants. The other day a friend was reading me the manuscript of a book he had written. He had succeeded to an estate in – shire, and the book describes the conditions under which he found the tenants of that property. They were living in little hovels without air or light. My friend pulled them all down, and built new ones, though by doing so he has impoverished himself too much to live on the place; but he has made some kind of attempt to love his neighbour as himself.

It is not a question of any particular class, or nation, or race, because men who have suffered from oppression have frequently oppressed others when their turn came. No! We have *all* believed that certain members of the community (always the weak and friendless) could be put outside the pale of society and 'passed by on the other side'. As Tolstoy said, 'We are always thinking that some human beings can exist without love and consideration, and there are no such human beings.' No, there are *no* such human beings, however low they may have sunk, and however poor and friendless they may be.

Slaves of the prostitution market

And today I want to arouse in you a sense of responsibility towards a slavery that still exists amongst us, and which we all help either to destroy or to encourage. I can begin best to tell you what I mean by telling you a story.

A few month's ago a woman friend of mine was dining in a London restaurant, and into the restaurant came two outcast women. You know the kind of women I mean; they are to be seen in every large town. They sat down at a table and were going to order their dinner, but there was a stir throughout the room, a movement of disgust and annoyance, that the women should dare to come in there. Someone rang for the manager, the manager spoke to the waiter, and the waiter went up to them and asked them to leave the restaurant. The elder of the two women got up and marched out of the room, trying to look as if she didn't care. The other one, who was only a girl, sat on alone, covered her face with her hands and began to cry. My friend went over to her and said, 'Will you come and dine with me?' and the girl went.

Why are there outcast women in the world today? These women are slaves, who are bought and sold, because there is a demand for them. It was only slaves whose bodies could be bought as theirs are, who could be treated as chattels as they are today. This it is that sets them apart from other women, that brands them with the mark of slavery. The fact that they are treated as *things*, not as human beings; this is of the very essence of slavery.

I ask you men to remember that nothing that any woman can do alters the fact that she is a human being with the rights and privileges of a human being: those who ignore that fact suffer for it in character more even than the woman herself. Do you suppose it was not better to be a slave than a slave-owner? Yes, these women are slaves because there is still a demand for slaves.

Lately I have been doing what is called rescue work in – , helping to free some of these poor women, and I will tell you what the rescue worker there said to me. She said, 'What is the good of my rescuing a few of these girls, whilst the demand for them always goes on? There will always be the supply. If I could speak I would give it up and go to men and attack the demand.' That is the only way to stop slavery, to make people see what it is. Do you understand? We are trying to destroy the slavery of prostitution, which ruins men and women body and soul. We are trying to help these neighbours of ours – these sisters of ours – so that they may cease to be slaves and outcasts.

France and 'Red Light' slavery

Do you know that in France and other counties there are registered slave houses for these women, houses which are under the control of the police, who have the power to arrest any woman suspected of leading an immoral life, so that she may be shut up in one of these houses and forced to submit to various kinds of humiliation and degradation. These women are slaves indeed.

In England a woman who has gone wrong can be helped to make a new start; but what chance do you suppose a girl has of starting a new life, when she is in one of the registered houses? Who will help her?

I would like you men to understand this. *Every man who goes to one of those houses is helping to keep up a system of slavery which our descendants will look back upon with as much disgust as we regard any of the evils of the past.*

In England, as you know, there are no registered houses of vice; on the contrary these houses are unlawful here, because, thank God, England generally stands for freedom.

But alas! we have a very similar system in India, and some of us are trying to rouse public opinion, so that it may be abolished.

Protection in wrong-doing

Do you know why these houses exist? They are allowed so that by the medical examination of the women, the health of the man may be protected. Protected from the consequences of his own act! Protected in doing what every honest man knows he ought not to do. But it is a false protection which has proved a failure, medically, in every country, and has ruined many a man who trusted to it.

A quarter of a century ago these slave houses spread all over Europe; now one by one the towns are giving them up, they are, as I say, a failure, (there is more disease in the countries where they exist, than in those where they do not) and public opinion once it begins to think, hates them, just as the public conscience always hates slavery once it begins to wake up.

Yes! and it is the same with this, as with every other form of slavery. Slaves have always been exploited not for their own benefit, but for someone else's. Why should men be protected and not the women?

A 'Necessary Evil?'

But the oppression always re-acts on the oppressor, and it is the same here. We are fighting this system of 'regulation' as it is called, as much for the men as for the women. It has a brutalising effect on both, and it makes men look upon this sin as a 'necessary evil' which Governments condone. A necessary evil! Have you ever met a man yet who was the worse for leading a straight life! and haven't you met many who were the worse for not leading one?

What is meant by 'necessary evil'? How can it be 'necessary' for one human being to injure another, or for one set of human beings to profit by the degradation of another? What right has one human being to profit by injuring another? How *can* one human being benefit by injuring another? Some day we shall see that the worst, the most permanent harm, we can do to ourselves is when we injure someone else. At present the world thinks of the physical effects of prostitution and ignores the still more important effect of vice upon life and character. As a man wrote to me the other day, 'You are right in saying that we have got hold of the wrong idea that it is disease and not vice which is to be feared and avoided.' Men still fear – in fact – only that which destroys the body instead of that which has power to destroy both soul and body.

I long for every man to understand that in entering a home of vice, whether a clandestine house in England or a 'tolerated' house abroad, he injured *at least* three people beside himself.

1 He injures the woman because he makes it more difficult for her to rise. He is keeping her in slavery.
2 Through that woman he harms his future wife, and, indeed, all women, for we are all one, and an injury done to the weakest amongst us is an injury done to us all. He is raising between himself and his wife the barrier of a past of which he will someday be ashamed. He also *always* runs the risk of infecting his wife with a terrible disease.
3 He injures his future child by unfitting himself in body and soul to be a father. For the sins of the fathers are indeed visited on the children, and until a man has seen this so-called 'necessary evil' in its true light as individual selfishness, he is not fit either for the joys or for the responsibilities of fatherhood.

Do you think it is worth it? If men thought these matters out, I believe the demand would cease.

Slavery or freedom?

Men, I ask you by your lives and your influence to help us to get rid of the demand for slaves and the supply of them. Why should we have women who are outcasts, when men who commit the same deeds are not? There is only one moral law for both men and women, and only one rule for all of us. 'Thou shalt love thy neighbour *as thyself.*'

I ask you to think of the lives these women lead – outcasts, without home or children, without self-respect or the respect of anyone else, without, in fact, anything that makes life worth living to you and me. I know that, once you begin to think, you are *not* willing that it should go on. God has roused us to fight the evil of prostitution:

1 So that the world may become what He wants it to be.
2 So that our children may be free in body and soul from the taint of this sin.
3 So that there may be no more slaves, no more outcasts, amongst His children.

The cure for all the evil in the world, is to love your neighbour as yourself. To sacrifice yourself rather than to sacrifice anyone else. Will you do it? Remember, '*He who loves not lives not.*' Whether then you go to France or Egypt, India, Mesopotamia, wherever you go, we ask you to try, with God's help, so to live that you may help to lift men and women out of lust, out of degradation, out of slavery, into the glorious liberty of the children of God.

Helena M. Swanwick

Committee of Inquiry into Sexual Morality

(1918)

Introduction

Origin and Scope of the Inquiry

1 In the years immediately preceding the outbreak of war in August 1914, British people had been increasingly concerned about the question of sexual morality, its effects upon the status of women, on the birth-rate and general health, as well as about the existence (and some thought the increase) of commercialised vice.
2 Lord Gorell's years of experience as President of the Probate, Divorce and Admiralty Division of the High Court of Justice had led him to the conviction that our Marriage Laws tended to increase rather than diminish sexual promiscuity, and on his retirement from the Bench he secured the appointment of a Royal Commission to inquire into the Divorce Laws, of which Commission he was the Chairman. Its recommendations were published in 1912.
3 The movement for the enfranchisement of women had brought into great prominence the degrading effect of the venality of some women upon the status of all, and the growing Labour movement among women led to the same discovery. Investigations, especially in America,[1] revealed the organisation of an international market, with procuration agents, a system of finance, of advertisement, and of corruption by means of alcohol, treating and seduction of quite young girls.
4 The tragic death of W. T. Stead on the *Titanic* gave impetus to a movement for the amendment of the Criminal Law Amendment Act 1885, and on 13 December 1912, an Act was passed, of which the main provisions were to increase the powers of police

in apprehending suspected procurers, and magistrates in imposing the penalty of flogging on men who lived by the immoral earnings of women. In the course of the agitation in support of this Bill very sensational stories were told, with the object of proving a widespread system of kidnapping and of otherwise procuring innocent girls for immoral purposes, especially abroad.

5 At the same time, public opinion began to be very much alarmed at the prevelance and consequences of Venereal Diseases, and at the general effect of sexual promiscuity on the birth-rate. In France, the plays of M. Brieux were calculated to startle the ignorant. In Great Britain, it was from suffragists that the move for public agitation began. In 1908 Dr Louisa Martindale, at the request of the National Union of Women's Suffrage Societies, wrote a courageous little book entitled *Under the Surface*, which was the occasion for a furious onslaught on the National Union in the House of Commons by a Member, who held the book to be injurious to morals. This proved a great advertisement: the book was sent to every Member of both Houses of Parliament, and its candour and moderation were widely acknowledged. A book which further aroused women to the hitherto unsuspected dangers of marriage came from America, entitled *Social Diseases and Marriage*. It was by a high authority, Dr Prince Morrow; though it was first published in 1903, it was not till some five years later that its facts and conclusions were widely spread in this country by suffragist speakers.

6 Then the medical profession began to agitate. The International Medical Congress in London (1913) recommended the appointment of a Royal Commission on Venereal Diseases, which issued its final report in March 1916. As a result, the National Council for Combating Venereal Diseases was founded.

7 Meanwhile an unofficial Commission inquired into the birth-rate and published its first report in June 1916.

8 The outbreak of war thus found the public peculiarly alert, even alarmed, on the question of sexual immorality. It was a subject that had been very prominent, and the conditions of mobilisation brought it into scandalous prominence. Young men were taken from their homes and from the society of women of their own families; young women were made to feel in the first months of the war that they were of very little importance in this great business of winning the war; their status was lowered in their own eyes, they held themselves cheap, while enthusiasm for the volunteers ran high, and many girls spent all their leisure in running after them, or in hanging about camps. Many of the cinemas and theatres pushed in the direction of sexual licence, and then the Press exploited the scandal by gross exaggeration about its extent.

9 Signs of panic appeared. Wild stories of thousands of war-babies got abroad, but the health of the army was the first consideration with the authorities as well as with the public generally. Magistrates were encouraged to detain for medical examination girls charged with loitering or accosting; the police were urged to deal drastically with the women; powers were taken under the Defence of the Realm Act to exclude women from camp areas; and at last, after the failure, in 1917, owing to popular opposition, of a Criminal Law Amendment Bill, Regulation 40D, was promulgated under the D.O.R.A., making it an offence for a woman affected with Venereal Disease in a transmissible form to have, solicit, or invite sexual intercourse with any member of H.M. Forces. Little was done to protect the soldier's wife from being infected by her husband should he return diseased from abroad. Underground agitation was always making itself felt for the adoption in England of the system of 'tolerated houses', under which British soldiers abroad were living, and a counter-agitation arose, and was only partially successful, to put 'tolerated houses' abroad out of bounds for the British soldier.

10 Various well-intentioned efforts were made to cope by legislation with what was felt to be a growing evil. The Bill of 1917 has been mentioned. In April 1918 two Bills were introduced in the House of Lords (the *Sexual Offences Bill* by Lord Beauchamp; the *Criminal Law Amendment Bill* by Lord Sandhurst).

11 These Bills covered some of the ground of the 1917 Bill, and some clauses were supported by various reformatory and philanthropic organisations, in which women took an active part. Many of the clauses were, however, keenly opposed, among the most contentious being, in the Sexual Offences Bill, Clause 1, sub-section (1), making it penal for a person suffering from venereal disease in a communicable form to have, solicit, or invite sexual intercourse with another, or wilfully to communicate such disease; Clause 1, sub-section (3), giving the court power, under certain conditions, to order the medical examination of persons charged with certain offences; Clause 2, increasing the penalties upon 'every common prostitute, or night-walker loitering or being in any thoroughfare or public place for the purpose of prostitution or solicitation'. In the Criminal Law Amendment Bill, exception was taken to Clause 3, providing for the detention, for a possible period of three years in a reformatory, of girls under 18 found guilty of disorderly conduct, etc.; and to Clause 5, which was similar to Clause 1 sub-section (1), of the Sexual Offences Bill.

12 These two Bills both reached the Committee stage, and on 7 May 1918, were referred to a Joint Select Committee of both Houses of Parliament: the function of the Committee being to take evidence and draft a measure which should embody the agreed portions of both Bills. This Committee did not meet till August 1918, and it was not until 15 October that it began to take evidence. Before its work was completed the General Election in December 1918 terminated it. Many meetings for protest and for discussion, as well as the evidence of the working of the D.O.R.A. regulations, had revealed difficulties and complexities which led thoughtful people to the conclusion that more harm than good was done by panic legislation. After the introduction of the Criminal Law Amendment Bill 1917, the Association for Moral and Social Hygiene in March of that year passed the following resolution:

> This Association, believing that the duty of the State towards young people who are drifting into criminal courses is to restore and reform rather than to punish them, calls for the appointment of a Commission to inquire:
>
> 1 How far the present methods of prisons, courts and police help or hinder such restoration;
> 2 How the Laws and their administration can be improved;
> 3 Whether the co-operation of voluntary, educational, and reformative agencies can be more largely utilised.
>
> The Association is convinced that in the absence of such inquiry any extension of repressive legislation is likely to do more harm than good. All experience shows that moral reformation of individuals is more likely to be brought about by voluntary methods than by compulsion; therefore the Association urges that the Government should endeavour to improve and co-ordinate existing agencies, whether official or voluntary.

13 Nothing was done by the Government except the passing of 40D and the introduction of further proposals for 'repressive legilsation'. There was also talk of the introduction of a one-clause Bill prohibiting sexual intercourse of venereally diseased persons, and another establishing compulsory notification. Therefore, at a meeting of representative women's organisations, convened on 27 June 1918, by the Association, the following resolution was unanimously passed:

> This meeting urges that the Association for Moral and Social

Hygiene shall promote the establishment of a Commission of men and women to be appointed by the organisations hitherto associated together in opposing penal legislation directed against prostitutes. That this Commission should have power to add to its number, and to invite expert evidence, and should consider the whole question of legislation and remedial treatment dealing with the social evil and venereal disease in accordance with scientific knowledge and fundamental morality.

14 The Association for Moral and Social Hygiene took the necessary steps, and the Commission (which called itself a Committee of Inquiry) started work on 14 October 1918. The Joint Select Committee, referred to above, began taking evidence the same week, but it was felt that, valuable as this Committee was, there was still room for an independent inquiry by a Committee upon which women were represented, and having wider terms of reference.

15 Those who had been for many years associated in adversely criticising proposed repressive legislation as well as the existing law felt that it was incumbent upon them to consider:

1 What existing or proposed legislation they could support; and
2 Methods other than legislative by which not only individuals, but associations, institutions, and the Government itself might promote sane and healthy sex relations.

The Report will be issued in two parts, corresponding to these two categories of considerations.

16 The Committee has no desire to appear in perpetual opposition. There is plenty of constructive work for all to do in meeting the social evil. But so long as legislators and administrators act on no intelligible principle of justice or equality on the one hand, and on no scientific basis of the connection of effects with causes on the other, the panic cry, 'For God's sake let us do something – anything!' must be resisted.

17 It is clear to the Committee that, in dealing with relations so intimate, so sensitive and so individual as those of sex, the attempt to suppress vice by penal legislation directed against it can accomplish very little good. Such legislation has, on the other hand, increased immorality by taking away the hope and the opportunity of recovery. Indirectly, by providing means of recovery, and by the improvement of general conditions of life, Government can do much. Individual and associated understanding and effort can do more.

NOTE

1 The brothel system is described in *Commercial Prostitution in New York*, by George J. Kneeland (1913), and in *The Social Evil in Chicago*, by the Vice Commission of Chicago (1911). In 1916 there was published in England a little book called *Downward Paths*, whose object was to state some of the causes of prostitution.

B *Domestic Violence*

Frances Power Cobbe

Wife-torture in England

(1878)

It once happened to me to ask an elderly French gentleman of the most exquisite manners to pay any attention she might need to a charming young lady who was intending to travel by the same train from London to Paris. M. de – wrote such a brilliant little note in reply that I was tempted to preserve it as an autograph; and I observe that, after a profusion of thanks, he assured me he should be 'trop heureux de se mettre au service' of my young friend. Practically, as I afterwards learned, M. de – did make himself quite delightful, till, unluckily, on arriving at Boulogne, it appeared that there was some *imbroglio* about Miss – 's luggage and she was in a serious difficulty. Needless to say, on such an occasion the intervention of a French gentleman with a ribbon at his button-hole would have been of the greatest possible service; but to render it M. de – would have been obliged to miss the train to Paris; and this was a sacrifice for which his politeness was by no means prepared. Expressing himself as utterly *au désespoir*, he took his seat, and was whirled away, leaving my poor young friend alone on the platform to fight her battles as best she might with the impracticable officials. The results might have been annoying had not a homely English stranger stepped in and proferred his aid; and, having recovered the missing property, simply lifted his hat and escaped from the lady's expressions of gratitude.

In this little anecdote I think lies a compendium of the experience of hundreds of ladies on their travels. The genuine and self-sacrificing kindness of English and American gentlemen towards women affords almost a ludicrous contrast to the florid politeness, compatible with every degree of selfishness, usually exhibited by men of other European nations. The reflection then is a puzzling one –

How does it come to pass that while the better sort of Englishmen are thus exceptionally humane and considerate to women, the men of the lower class of the same nation are proverbial for their unparalleled brutality, till wife-beating, wife-torture, and wife-murder have become the opprobrium of the land? How does it happen (still more strange to note!) that the same generous-hearted gentlemen, who would themselves fly to render succour to a lady in distress, yet read of the beatings, burnings, kickings, and 'cloggings' of poor women well-nigh every morning in their newspapers without once setting their teeth, and saying, 'This must be stopped! We can stand it no longer'?

The paradox truly seems worthy of a little investigation. What reason can be alleged, in the first place, why the male of the human species, and particularly the male of the finest variety of that species, should be the only animal in creation which maltreats its mate, or any female of its own kind?

To get to the bottom of the mystery we must discriminate between assaults of men on other men; assaults of men on women who are not their wives; and assaults of men on their wives. I do not think I err much if I affirm that, in common sentiment, the first of these offences is considerably more heinous than the second – being committed against a more worthy person (as the Latin grammar itself instructs boys to think); and lastly that the assault on a woman who is *not* a man's wife is worse than the assault on a wife by her husband. Towards this last or *minimum* offence a particular kind of indulgence is indeed extended by public opinion. The proceeding seems to be surrounded by a certain halo of jocosity which inclines people to smile whenever they hear of a case of it (terminating anywhere short of actual murder), and causes the mention of the subject to induce rather than otherwise to the hilarity of a dinner party. The occult fun thus connected with wife-beating forms by no means indeed the least curious part of the subject. Certainly in view of the state of things revealed by our criminal statistics there is something ominous in the circumstance that 'Punch' should have been our national English street-drama for more than two centuries. Whether, as some antiquarians tell us, Judas Iscariot was the archetypal Policiello, who, like Faust and Don Juan, finally meets the reward of his crimes by Satanic intervention, or whether, as other learned gentlemen may, the quaint visage and humour of the Neapolitan vintager Puccio d'Aniello, originated the jest which has amused ten generations, it is equally remarkable that so much of the enjoyment should concentrate about the thwacking of poor Judy, and the flinging of the baby out of the window. Questioned seriously whether he think that the behaviour of Punch as a citizen and *père de famille* be in itself a good joke, the British gentleman would probably reply that it was not more facetious than watching a carter flogging a horse. But invested with the drollery of a marionette's behaviour, and accompanied by the screeches of the man with the Pan-pipe, the scene is irresistible, and the popularity of the hero rises with every bang he bestows on the wife of his bosom and on the representative of the law.

The same sort of half-jocular sympathy unquestionably accompanies the whole class of characters of whom Mr Punch is the type. Very good and kind-hearted men may be frequently heard speaking of horrid scenes of mutual abuse and violence between husbands and wives, as if they were rather ridiculous than disgusting. The *Taming of the Shrew* still holds its place as one of the most popular of Shakespeare's comedies; and even the genial Ingoldsby conceived he added a point to his inimitable legend of 'Odille', by inserting after the advice to 'succumb to our she-saints, videlicet wives', the parenthesis, 'that is, if one has not a "good bunch of fives" '. Where is the hidden fun of this and scores of similar allusions, which sound like the cracking of whips over the cowering dogs in a kennel?

I imagine it lies in the sense, so pleasant to the owners of superior physical strength, that after all, if reason and eloquence should fail, there is always an *ultima ratio*, and that that final appeal lies in their hands. The sparring may be all very well for a time, and may be counted entirely satisfactory *if they get the better*. But then, if by any mischance the unaccountably sharp wits of the weaker creature should prove dangerous weapons, there is always the club of brute force ready to hand in the corner. The listener is amused, as in reading a fairy tale, wherein the hero, when apparently completely vanquished, pulls out a talisman given him by an Afreet, and lo! his enemies fall flat on the ground and are turned into rats.

Thus it comes to pass, I suppose, that the abstract idea of a strong man hitting or kicking a weak woman – *per se*, so revolting – has somehow got softened into a jovial kind of domestic lynching, the grosser features of the case being swept out of sight, just as people make endless jests on tipsiness, forgetting how loathsome a thing is a drunkard. A 'jolly companions' chorus seems to accompany both kinds of exploits. This, and the prevalent idea (which I shall analyse by-and-by) that the woman has generally deserved the blows she receives, keep up, I believe, the indifference of the public on the subject.

Probably the sense that they must carry with them a good deal of tacit sympathy on the part of other men has something to do in encouraging wife-beaters, just as the fatal notion of the good fellowship of drink has made thousands of sots. But the immediate causes of the offence of brutal violence are of course very various, and need to be better understood than they commonly are if we would find a remedy for them. First, there are to be considered the class of people and the conditions of life wherein the practice prevails; then the character of the men who beat their wives; next that of the wives who are beaten and kicked; and finally, the possible remedy.

Wife-beating exists in the upper and middle classes rather more, I fear, than is generally recognised; but it rarely extends to anything beyond an occasional blow or two of a not dangerous kind. In his apparently most ungovernable rage, the gentleman or tradesman somehow manages to bear in mind the disgrace he will incur if his outbreak be betrayed by his wife's black eye or broken arm, and he regulates his cuffs or kicks accordingly. The dangerous wife-beater belongs almost exclusively to the artisan and labouring classes. Colliers, 'puddlers', and weavers have long earned for themselves in this matter a bad reputation, and among a long list of cases before me, I reckon shoemakers, stonemasons, butchers, smiths, tailors, a printer, a clerk, a bird-catcher, and a large number of labourers. In the worst districts of London (as I have been informed by one of the most experienced magistrates) four-fifths of the wife-beating cases are among the lowest class of Irish labourers – a fact worthy of more than passing notice, had we time to bestow upon it, seeing that in their own country Irishmen of all classes are proverbially kind and even chivalrous towards women.

There are also various degrees of wife-beating in the different localities. In London it seldom goes beyond a severe 'thrashing' with the fist – a sufficiently dreadful punishment, it is true, when inflicted by a strong man on a woman; but mild in comparison of the kickings and tramplings and 'purrings' with hob-nailed shoes and clogs of what we can scarcely, in this connection, call the 'dark and true and *tender* North'. As Mr Serjeant Pulling remarks,

> Nowhere is the ill-usage of woman so systematic as in Liverpool, and so little hindered by the strong arm of the law; making the lot of a married woman, whose locality is the 'kicking district' of Liverpool, simply a duration of suffering and subjection to injury and savage treatment, far worse than that to which the wives of mere savages are used.

It is in the centres of dense mercantile and manufacturing populations that this offence reaches its climax. In London the largest return for one year (in the Parlimentary Report on Brutal Assaults) of brutal assaults on women was 351. In Lancashire, with a population of almost two millions and a-half, the largest number was 194. In Stafford, with a population of three-quarters of a million, there were 113 cases. In the West Riding, with a million and a-half, 152; and in Durham, with 508,666, no less than 267. Thus, roughly speaking; there are nearly five times as many wife-beaters of the more brutal kind, in proportion to the population, in Durham as in London. What are the conditions of life among the working classes in those great 'hives of industry' of which we talk so proudly? It is but justice that we should picture the existence of the men and women in such places before we pass to discuss the deeds which darken it.

They are lives out of which almost every softening and ennobling element has been withdrawn, and into which enter brutalising influences almost unknown elsewhere. They are lives of hard, ugly, mechanical toil in dark pits and hideous factories, amid the grinding and clanging of engines, and the fierce heat of furnaces, in that Black Country where the green sod of earth is replaced by mounds of slag and shale, where no flower grows, no fruit ripens, scarcely a bird sings; where the morning has no freshness, the evening no dews; where the spring sunshine cannot pierce the foul curtain of smoke which overhangs these modern Cities of the Plain, and where the very streams and rivers run discoloured and steaming with stench, like Styx and Phlegethon, through their banks of ashes. If 'God made the country and man made the town', we might deem that Ahrimanes devised this Tartarus of toil, and that here we had at last found the spot where the Psalmist might seek in vain for the handiwork of the Lord.

As we now and then, many of us, whirl through this land of darkness in express trains, and draw up our carriage windows that we may be spared the smoke and dismal scene, we have often reflected that the wonder is, *not* that the dwellers there should lose some of the finer poetry of life, the more delicate courtesies of humanity, but that they should remain so much like other men, and should so often rise to noble excellence and intelligence, rather than have developed, as would have seemed more natural, into a race of beings relentless, hard, and grim as their own iron machines – beings of whom the Cyclops of the Greek and the Gnomes of the Teuton imaginations were the foreshadowings. Of innocent pleasure in such lives there can, alas! be very little; and the hunger of nature for enjoyment must inevitably be supplied (among all save the few to whom intellectual pursuits may suffice) by the grosser gratifications of the senses. Writers who have never attempted to realise what it must be to hear ugly sounds and smell nauseous odours and see hideous sights, all day long, from year's end to year's end, are angry with these Black Country artisans for spending largely of their earnings in buying delicate food – poultry and salmon, and peas and strawberries. For my part, I am inclined to rejoice if they can content themselves with such harmless gratifications of the palate, instead of the deadly stimulants of drink, cruelty, and vice.

These, then, are the localities wherein Wife-torture flourishes in England; where a dense population is crowded into a hideous manufacturing or mining or mercantile district. Wages are usually high though fluctuating. Facilities for drink and vice abound, but those for cleanliness and decency are scarcely attainable. The men are rude, coarse, and brutal in their manners and habits, and the women devoid, in an extraordinary degree, of all the higher natural attractions and influences of their sex. Poor drudges of the factory, or of the crowded and sordid lodging-house, they lose, before youth is past, the freshness, neatness, and gentleness, perhaps even the modesty of a woman, and present, when their miserable cases come up before the magistrate, an aspect so sordid and forbidding that it is no doubt with difficulty he affords his sympathy to them rather than to the husband chained to so wretched a consort. Throughout the whole of this inquiry I think it very necessary, in justice to all parties, and in mitigation of too vehement judgment of cases only known from printed reports, to bear in mind that the women of the class concerned are, some of them wofully unwomanly, slatternly, coarse, foul-mouthed – sometimes loose in behaviour, sometimes madly addicted to drink. There ought to be no idealising of them, *as a class*, into refined and suffering angels if we wish to be just. The home of a Lancashire operative, alas! is not a garden wherein the plants of refinement or sensitiveness are very likely to spring up or thrive.

Given this direful *milieu*, and its population, male and female, we next ask, What are the immediate incitements to the men to maltreat the women? They are of two kinds, I think – general and particular.

First, the whole relation between the sexes in the class we are considering is very little better than one of master and slave. I have always abjured the use of this familiar comparison in speaking generally of English husbands and wives, because as regards the upper orders of society it is ridiculously overstrained and untrue. But in the 'kicking districts', among the lowest labouring classes, Legree himself might find a dozen prototypes, and the condition of the women be most accurately matched by that of the negroes on a Southern plantation before the war struck off their fetters.[1]

To a certain extent this marital tyranny among the lower classes is beyond the reach of law, and can only be remedied by the slow elevation and civilisation of both sexes. But it is also in an appreciable degree, I am convinced, enhanced by the law even as it now stands, and was still more so by the law as it stood before the Married Women's Property Act put a stop to the chartered robbery by husbands of their wives' earnings. At the present time, though things are improving year by year, thanks to the generous and far-seeing statesmen who are contending for justice to women inside and out of the House of Commons, the position of a woman before the law as wife, mother, and citizen, remains so much below that of a man as husband, father, and citizen, that it is a matter of course that she must be regarded by him as an inferior, and fail to obtain from him such a modicum of respect as her mental and moral qualities might win did he see her placed by the State on an equal footing.

I have no intention in this paper to discuss the vexed subject of women's political and civil rights, but I cannot pass to the consideration of the incidental and minor causes of the outrages upon them, without recording my conviction that the political disabilities under which the whole sex still labours, though apparently a light burden on the higher and happier ranks, presses down more and more heavily through the lower strata of society in growing deconsideration and contempt, unrelieved (as it is at higher levels) by other influences on opinion. Finally at the lowest grade of all it exposes women to an order of insults and wrongs which are never inflicted by equals upon an equal, and can only be paralleled by the oppressions of a dominant caste or race over their helots. In this as in many other things the educating influence of law immeasurably outstrips its direct action; and such as is the spirit of our laws, such will inevitably be the spirit of our people. Human beings no longer live like animals in a condition wherein the natural sentiments between the sexes suffice to guard the weak, where the male brute is kind and forbearing to the female, and were no Court of Chancery interferes with the mother's most dear and sacred charge of her little ones. Man alone claims to hold his mate in subjection, and to have the right while he lives, and even after he dies, to rob a mother of her child; and man, who has lost the spontaneous chivalry of the lion and the dog, needs to be provided with laws which may do whatever it lies with laws to effect to form a substitute for such chivalry. Alas! instead of such, he has only made for himself laws which add legal to natural disabilities, and give artificial strength to ready-constituted prepotence.

I consider that it is a very great misfortune to both sexes that women should be thus depreciated in the opinion of that very class of men whom it would be most desirable to impress with respect and tenderness for them; who are most prone to despise physical infirmity and to undervalue the moral qualities wherein women excel. All the softening and refining influences which women exert in happier conditions are thus lost to those who most need them – to their husbands and still more emphatically to their children; and the women themselves are degraded and brutified in their own eyes by the contempt of their companions. When I read all the fine-sounding phrases perpetually repeated about the invaluable influence of a good mother over her son – how the worst criminals are admitted to be reclaimable if they have ever enjoyed it – and how the virtues of the best and noblest men are attributed to it, as a commonplace of biography – I often ask myself, 'Why, then, is not something done to lift and increase, instead of to depreciate and lower, that sacred influence? Why are not mothers allowed to respect themselves, that they may fitly claim the respect of their sons? How is a lad to learn to reverence a woman whom he sees daily scoffed at, beaten, and abused, and when he knows that the laws of his country forbid her, ever and under any circumstances, to exercise the rights of citizenship; nay, which deny to her the guardianship of *himself* – of the very child of her bosom – should her husband choose to hand him over to her rival out of the street?'

The general depreciation of women *as a sex* is bad enough, but in the matter we are considering, the special depreciation of *wives* is more directly responsible for the outrages they endure. The notion that a man's wife is his PROPERTY, in the sense in which a horse is his property (descended to us rather through the Roman law than through the customs of our Teuton ancestors), is the fatal root of incalculable evil and misery. Every brutal-minded man, and many a man who in other relations of life is not brutal, entertains more or less vaguely the notion that his wife is his *thing*, and is ready to ask with indignation (as we read again and again in the police reports), of any one who interferes with his treatment of her, 'May I not do what I will *with my own?*' It is even sometimes pleaded on behalf of poor men, that they possess *nothing else* but their wives, and that, consequently, it seems doubly hard to meddle with the exercise of their power in that narrow sphere![2]

I am not intending to discuss the question of the true relation between husbands and wives which we may hope to see realised when

"Springs the happier race of human kind"

from parents 'equal and free' – any more than the political and social rights of women generally. But it is impossible, in treating of the typical case wherein the misuse of wives reaches its climax in Wife-beating and Wife-torture, to avoid marking out with a firm line where lies the underground spring of the mischief. As one of the many results of this *proton pseudos*, must be noted the fact (very important in its bearing on our subject) that not only is an offence against a wife condoned as of inferior guilt, but any offence of the wife against her husband is regarded as a sort of *Petty Treason*. For her, as for the poor ass in the fable, it is more heinous to nibble a blade of grass than for the wolf to devour both the lamb and the shepherd. Should she be guilty of 'nagging' or scolding, or of being a slattern, or of getting intoxicated, she finds usually a short shrift and no favour – and even humane persons talk of her offence as constituting, if not a justification for her murder, yet an explanation of it. She is, in short, liable to capital punishment without judge or jury for transgressions which in the case of a man would never be punished at all, or be expiated by a fine of five shillings.[3]

Nay, in her case there is a readiness even to pardon the omission of the ordinary forms of law as needlessly cumbersome. In no other instance save that of the Wife-beater is excuse made for a man taking the law into his own hands. We are accustomed to accept it as a principle that 'lynching' cannot be authorised in a civilised country, and that the first lesson of orderly citizenship is that no man shall be judge, jury, and executioner in his own case. But when a wife's offences are in question this salutary rule is overlooked, and men otherwise just-minded, refer cheerfully to the *circonstance atténuante* of the wife's drunkenness or bad language, as if it not only furnished an excuse for outrage upon her, but made it quite fit and proper for the Queen's peace to be broken and the woman's bones along with it.

This underlying public opinion is fortunately no new thing. On the contrary, it is an idea of immemorial antiquity which has been embodied in the law of many nations, and notably, as derived from the old Roman *Patria Potestas*, in our own. It was only in 1829, in the 9th George IV, that the Act of Charles II, which embodied the old Common Law, and authorised a man 'to chastise his wife with any reasonable instrument', was erased from our Statute-Book. Our position is not retrograde, but advancing, albeit too slowly. It is not as in the case of the Vivisection of Animals, that a new passion of cruelty is arising, but only that an old one, having its origin in the remotest epochs of barbarian wife-capture and polygamy, yet lingers in the dark places of the land. By degrees, if our statesmen will but bring the educational influence of law to bear upon the matter; it will surely die out and become a thing of the past, like cannibalism – than which it is no better fitted for a Christian nation.

Of course the ideas of the suffering wives are cast in the same mould as those of their companions. They take if for granted that a Husband is a Beating Animal, and may be heard to remark when extraordinarily ill-treated by a stranger – that they 'never were so badly used, no not by their own husband'. Their wretched proverbial similarity to spaniels and walnut-trees, the readiness with which they sometimes turn round and snap at a bystander who has interfered on their behalf, of course affords to cowardly people a welcome excuse for the 'policy of non-intervention', and forms the culminating proof of how far the iron of their fetters has eaten into their souls. A specially experienced gentleman writes from Liverpool: 'The women of Lancashire are *awfully fond* of bad husbands. It has become quite a trusim that our women are like dogs, the more you beat them the more they love you.' Surely if a bruised and trampled woman be a pitiful object, a woman who has been brought down by fear, or by her own gross passions, so low as to fawn on the beast who strikes her, is one to make angels weep?

To close this part of the subject, I conceive then, that the common idea of the inferiority of women, and the special notion of the rights of husbands, form the undercurrent of feeling which induces a man, when for any reason he is infuriated, to wreak his violence on his wife. She is, in his opinion, his natural *souffre-douleur*.

It remains to be noted what are the principal incitements to such outbursts of savage fury among the classes wherein Wife-beating prevails. They are not far to seek. The first is undoubtedly *Drink* – poisoned drink. The seas of brandy and gin, and the oceans of beer, imbibed annually in England, would be bad enough, if taken pure and simple, but it is the vile adulterations introduced into them which make them the infuriating poisons which they are – which literally *sting* the wretched drinkers into cruelty, perhaps quite foreign to their natural temperaments. As an experienced minister in these districts writes to me, 'I have known men almost as bad as those you quote (a dozen wife-murderers) made into most kind and considerate husbands by total abstinence.' If the English people will go on swallowing millions' worth yearly of brain poison, what can we expect but brutality the most hideous and grotesque? Assuredly the makers and vendors of these devil's philtres are responsible for an amount of crime and ruin which some of the worst tyrants in history might have trembled to bear on their consciences; nor can the national legislature be absolved for suffering the great Drink interest thus foully to tamper with the health – nay, with the very souls of our countrymen. What is the occult influence which prevents the Excise from performing its duty as regards these frauds on the revenue?

2 Next to drunkenness as a cause of violence to women, follows the other 'great sin of great cities', of which it is unnecessary here to speak. The storms of jealousy thence arising, the hideous alternative *possession* of the man by the twin demons of cruelty and lust – one of whom is never very far from the other – are familiar elements in the police-court tragedies.

3 Another source of the evil may be found in that terrible, though little recognised passion, which rude men and savages share with many animals, and which is the precise converse of sympathy, for it consists in anger and cruelty, excited by the signs of pain; an impulse to hurt and destroy any suffering creature, rather than to relieve or help it. Of the widespread influence of this passion (which I have ventured elsewhere to name *Heteropathy*), a passion only slowly dying out as civilisation advances, there can, I think, be no doubt at all. It is a hideous mystery of human nature that such feelings should lie latent in it, and that cruelty should grow by what it feeds on; that the more the tyrant causes the victim to suffer the more he hates him, and desires to heap on him fresh sufferings. Among the lower classes the emotion of Heteropathy unmistakably finds vent in the cruelty of parents and step-parents to unfortunate children who happen to be weaker or more stupid than others, or to have been once excessively punished, and whose joyless little faces and timid crouching demeanour, instead of appeals for pity, prove provocations to fresh outrage. The group of his shivering and starving children and weeping wife is the sad sight which, greeting the eyes of the husband and father reeling home from the gin-shop, somehow kindles his fury. If the baby cry in the cradle, he stamps on it. If his wife wring her hands in despair, he fells her to the ground.

4 After these I should be inclined to reckon, as a cause of brutal outbreaks, the impatience and irritation which must often be caused in the homes of the working classes by sheer *friction*. While rich people, when they get tired of each other or feel irritable, are enabled to recover their tempers in the ample space afforded by a comfortable house, the poor are huddled together in such close quarters that the sweetest tempers and most tender affections must sometimes feel the trial. Many of us have shuddered at Miss Octavia Hill's all-too-graphic description of a hot, noisome court

in the heart of London on a fine summer evening, with men, women, and children 'pullulating', as the French say, on the steps, at the windows, on the pavement, all dirty, hot, and tired, and scarcely able to find standing or sitting room. It is true the poor are happily more gregarious than the rich. Paradoxical as it sounds, it takes a good deal of civilisation to make a man love savage scenery, and a highly cultivated mind to find any 'pleasure in the pathless woods' or 'rapture in the lonely shore'. Nevertheless, for moral health as much as for physical, a certain number of cubic inches of space are needed for every living being.

It is their interminable, inevitable propinquity which in the lower classes makes the nagging, wrangling, worrying women so intolerably trying. As millers get accustomed, it is said, to the clapping of their mill, so may some poor husbands become deaf to their wives' tongues; but the preliminary experience must be severe indeed.

These, then, are the incentives to Wife-beating and Wife-torture. What are the men on whom they exert their evil influence?

Obviously, by the hypothesis, they are chiefly the drunken, idle, ruffianly fellows who lounge about the public-houses instead of working for their families. Without pretending to affirm that there are no sober, industrious husbands goaded to strike their wives through jealousy or irritation, the presumption is enormous against the character of any man convicted of such an assault. The cases in which the police reports of them add, 'He had been bound over to keep the peace several times previously' or 'He had been often fined for drunkenness and disorderly behaviour' are quite countless. Sometimes it approaches the ludicrous to read how helplessly the law has been attempting to deal with the scoundrel, as, for example, in the case of William Owen, whom his wife said she 'met for the first time beside Ned Wright's Bible-barrow', and who told the poor fool he had been 'converted'. He was known to Constable 47 K as having been convicted *over sixty times* for drunkenness and violent assaults; and the moment he left the church he began to abuse his wife.

The pitilessness and ferocity of these men sometimes looks like madness. Alfred Stone, for example, coming home in a bad temper, took his wife's parrot out of its cage, stamped on it, and threw it on the fire, observing, 'Jane! it is the last thing you have got belonging to your father!' In the hands of such a man a woman's heart must be crushed, like the poor bird under his heel.

Turn we now from the beaters to the beaten. I have already said that we must not idealise the women of the 'kicking districts'. They are, mostly, poor souls, very coarse, very unwomanly. Some of them drink whenever they can procure drink. Some are bad and cruel mothers (we cannot forget the awful stories of the Burial Clubs); many are hopelessly depraved, and lead as loose lives as their male companions. Many keep their houses in a miserable state of dirt and disorder, neglect their children, and sell their clothes and furniture for gin. Not seldom will one of these reckless creatures pursue her husband in the streets with screams of abuse and jeers. The man knows not where to turn to escape from the fury. When he comes home at night, he probably finds her lying dead drunk on the bed, and his children crying for their supper. Again, in a lesser degree, women make their homes into purgatories by their bad tempers. There was in old times a creature recognised by law as a 'Common Scold', for whom the punishment of ducking in the village horse-pond was formally provided. It is to be feared her species is by no means to be reckoned among the 'Extinct Mammalia'. Then comes the 'nagging' wife, immortalised as 'Mrs Caudle'; the worrying, peevish kill-joy, whose presence is a wet blanket – nay, a wet blanket stuck full of pins; the argumentative woman, with a voice like a file and a face like a ferret, who bores on, night and day, till life is a burden.[4]

These are terrible harpies. But it is scarcely fair to assume that every woman who is accused of 'nagging' necessarily belongs to their order. I have no doubt that every husband who comes home with empty pockets, and from whom his wife needs to beg repeatedly for money to feed herself and her children, considers that she 'nags' him. I have no doubt that when a wife reproaches such a husband with squandering his wages in the public-house, or on some wretched rival, while she and her children are starving, he accuses her to all his friends of intolerable 'nagging', and that, not seldom having acquired from him the reputation of this kind of thing, the verdict of 'Serve her Right' is generally passed upon her by public opinion when her 'nagging' is capitally punished by a broken head.

But *all* women of the humblest class are not those terrible creatures, drunken, depraved, or ill-tempered; or even addicted to 'nagging'. On the contrary, I can affirm from my own experience, as well, I believe, as that of all who have had much to do with the poor of great cities, there are among them at least as many good women as bad – as many who are sober, honest, chaste, and industrious, as are the contrary. There is a type which every clergyman, and magistrate, and district visitor will recognise in a moment as very common: a woman generally small and slight of person, but alert, intelligent, active morning, noon, and night, doing the best her strength allows to keep her home tidy, and her children neat and well fed, and to supply her husband's wants. Her face was, perhaps, pretty at eighteen: by the time she is eight-and-twenty, toil and drudgery and many children have reduced her to a mere rag, and only her eyes retain a little pathetic relic of beauty. This woman expresses herself well and simply: it is a special 'note' of her character that she uses no violent words, even in describing the worst injuries. There is nothing 'loud' about her in voice, dress, or manners. She is emphatically a '*decent*', respectable woman. Her only fault, if fault it be, is that she will insist on obtaining food and clothing for her children, and that when she is refused them she becomes that depressed, broken-spirited creature whose mute, reproachful looks act as a goad, as I have said, to the passions of her oppressor. We shall see presently what part this class of woman plays in the horrible domestic tragedies of England.

We have now glanced at the conditions under which Wife-beating takes place, at the incentives immediately leading to it, the men who beat, and the women who are beaten. Turn we now to examine more closely the thing itself.

There are two kinds of Wife-beating which I am anxious the reader should keep clearly apart in his mind. There is what may be called *Wife-beating by Combat*, and there is Wife-beating properly so called, which is only wife, and not wife-and-husband beating. In the first, both parties have an equal share. Bad words are exchanged, then blows. The man hits, the woman perhaps scratches and tears. If the woman generally gets much the worst of it, it is simply because cats are weaker than dogs. The man cannot so justly be said to have 'beaten' his wife as to have vanquished her in a boxing-match. Almost without exception in these cases it is mentioned that 'both parties were the worse for liquor'. It is in this way the drunken woman is beaten, *by the drunken man*, not by the ideal sober and industrious husband, who has a right to be disgusted by her intoxication. It is nearly exclusively, I think, in such drunken quarrels that the hateful virago gets beaten at all. As a general rule she commands too much fear, and is so ready to give back curse for curse and blow for blow, that, in cold blood, nobody meddles with her. Such a termagant is often the tyrant of her husband, nay, of the whole court or lane in which she lives; and the sentiments she excites are the reverse of those which bring down the fist and the clogs of the ruffian husband on the timid and meek-faced woman who tries, too often unsuccessfully, the supposed magic of a soft answer to turn away the wrath of such a wild beast as he.

One word, however, must be said, before we leave this revolting picture, even for that universally condemned creature, the drunken wife. Does any save one, the Great Judge above, ever count how many of such doubly-degraded beings have been *driven* to intemperance by sheer misery? How many have been lured to drink by companionship with their drunken husbands? How many have sunk into the habit because, worn out in body by toil and child-bearing, degraded in soul by contempt and abuse, they have not left in them one spark of that self-respect which enables a human being to resist the temptation to drown care and remembrance in the dread forgetfulness of strong drink?

The second kind of Wife-beating is when the man alone is the striker and the woman the stricken. There are the cases which specially challenge our attention, and for which it may be hoped some palliative may be found. In these, the husband usually comes home 'the worse for liquor', and commences, sometimes without any provocation at all, to attack his wife, or drag her out of the bed where she is asleep, or has just been confined. (See cases p. 237.) Sometimes there is preliminary altercation, the wife imploring him to give her some money to buy necessaries, or reproaching him for drinking all he has earned. In either case the wife is passive so far as blows are concerned, unless at the last, in self-defence, she lays her hand on some weapon to protect her life – a fact which is always cited against her as a terrible delinquency.[5]

Such are the two orders of Wife-beating with which a tolerably extensive study of the subject has made me familiar. It will be observed that neither includes that ideal Wife-beater of whom we hear so much, the sober, industrious man goaded to frenzy by his wife's temper or drunkenness. I will not venture to affirm that that Ideal Wife-beater is as mythical as the griffin or the sphinx, but I will affirm that in all my inquiries I have never yet come on his track.

I have insisted much on this point, because I think it has been strangely overlooked, and that it ought to form a most important factor in making up our judgment of the whole matter and of the proper remedies. It will be found, I believe, on inquiry that it is actually surprising how very seldom there is anything at all alleged by the husband against the wife in the worst cases of wife-torture – except the 'provocation' and 'nagging' of asking him for money; or, as in the case of poor Ellen Harlow, of refusing him twopence out of her own earnings when he had been drinking all day and she had been working. In thirty-eight cases taken at random, five were of the class of drunken combats; and in thirty nothing was reported as alleged against the victims. In many cases strong testimony was given of their good conduct and industry: e.g. the wife of William White, who was burnt to death by the help of his paraffin lamp, was a 'hard-working, industrious woman'. The wife of James Lawrence, whose face bore in court tokens of the most dreadful violence, 'said that her husband had for years done nothing for his livelihood, while she had bought a shop, and stocked it out of her own earnings'. The wife of Richard Mountain had 'supported herself and her children'. The wife of Alfred Etherington, who has been dangerously injured by her husband kicking and jumping on her, had been supporting him and their children. The wife of James Styles, who was beaten by her husband till she became insensible, had long provided for him and herself by charwork; and so on.

Regarding the extent of the evil it is difficult to arrive at a just calculation. Speaking of those cases only which come before the courts – probably, of course, not a third of the whole number – the elements for forming an opinion are the following:

In the Judicial Statistics for England and Wales, issued in 1877 for 1876, we find that of Aggravated Assaults on Women and Children, of the class which since 1853 have been brought under Summary Jurisdiction there were reported,

In 1876	2,737
In 1875	3,106
In 1874	2,841

How many of these were assaults made by husbands on wives there is no means of distinguishing, but, judging from other sources, I should imagine they formed about four-fifths of the whole.

Among the worst cases, when the accused persons were committed for trial or bailed for appearance at Assizes or Sessions (coming under the head of Criminal Proceedings), the classification adopted in the Parliamentary Return does not permit of identifying the cases which concerned women only. Some rough guess on the matter may perhaps be formed from the preponderance of male criminals in all classes of violent crime. Out of sixty-seven persons charged with Murder in 1876, forty-nine were men. Of forty-one charged with Attempt to Murder, thirty-five were males. Of 157 charged with Shooting, Stabbing, etc. 146 were men. Of 232 charged with Manslaughter, 185 were men; and of 1,020 charged with Assault inflicting bodily harm, 857 were men. In short, out of 1,517 persons charged with crimes of cruelty and violence, more than five-sixths were males, and only 235 females. Of course the men's offences include a variety of crimes besides Wife-beating and Wife-torture.

The details of the crimes for which twenty-two men who were

capitally convicted in 1876 suffered death are noteworthy on this head. (Criminal Statistics p. xxix.) Of these:

Edward Deacon, shoemaker, murdered his wife by cutting her head with a chopper.
John Thomas Green, painter, shot his wife with a pistol.
John Eblethrift, labourer, murdered his wife by stabbing.
Charles O'Donnell, labourer, murdered his wife by beating.
Henry Webster, labourer, murdered his wife by cutting her throat.

Beside these, five others murdered women with whom they were living in vicious relations, and three others (including the monster William Fish) murdered children. In all, more than half the convicted persons executed that year were guilty of wife-murder – or of what we may term *quasi*-wife-murder.

A source of more accurate information is to be found in the abstracts of the Reports of Chief Constables for the years 1870–1–2–3–4, presented to the Home Secretary, and published in the 'Report on Brutal Assaults' (p. 169, et seq.). In this instructive table Brutal Assaults on Women are discriminated from those on men, and the total number of convictions for such assaults for the whole five years is 6,029; or at the average of 1,205 per annum. This is, however, obviously an imperfect return. In Nottinghamshire, where such offences were notoriously common, the doings of the 'Lambs' have somehow escaped enumeration. 'The Chief Constable states that he is unable to furnish a correct return.' From Merionethshire no report was received in reply to the Home Office Circular; and from Rutland, Salop, Radnor, and Cardiganshire, the Chief Constables returned the reply that there were no brutal assaults in those counties during the five years in question – a statement suggesting that some different classification of offences must prevail in those localities, since the immunity of Cardiganshire and Salop for five years from such crimes of violence would be little short of miraculous, while Flint alone had sixteen convictions. Thus I conceive that we may fairly estimate the number of brutal assaults (*brutal* be it remembered, not ordinary) committed on women in England and Wales and actually brought to justice at about 1,500 a year, or more than four *per diem;* and of these the great majority are of husbands on wives.

Let us now proceed from the number to the nature of the offences in question. I have called this paper English *Wife-torture* because I wish to impress my readers with the fact that the familiar term 'wife-beating' conveys as remote a notion of the extremity of the cruelty indicated as when candid and ingenuous vivisectors talk of 'scratching a newt's tail' when they refer to burning alive, or dissecting out the nerves of living dogs, or torturing ninety cats in one series of experiments.

Wife-*beating* is the mere preliminary canter before the race – the preface to the serious matter which is to follow. Sometimes, it is true, there are men of comparatively mild dispositions who are content to go on beating their wives, year after year, giving them occasional black-eyes and bruises, or tearing out a few locks of their hair and spitting in their faces, or bestowing an ugly print of their iron fingers on the woman's soft arm, but not proceeding beyond these minor injuries to anything perilous. Among the lower classes, unhappily, this rude treatment is understood to mean very little more than that the man uses his weapon – the fists – as the woman uses hers – the tongue – and neither are very much hurt or offended by what is either done by one or said by the other. The whole state of manners is what is to be deplored, and our hope must be to change the bear-garden into the semblance of a civilised community, rather than by any direct effort to correct the special offence. Foul words, gross acts, drink, dirt, and vice, oaths, curses, and blows, it is all, alas! *in keeping* – nor can we hope to cure one evil without the rest. But the unendurable mischief, the discovery of which has driven me to try to call public attention to the whole matter, is this – Wife-*beating* in process of time, and in numberless cases, advances to Wife-*torture*, and the Wife-torture usually ends in Wife-maiming, Wife-blinding, or Wife-murder. A man who has 'thrashed' his wife with his fists half-a-dozen times, becomes satiated with such enjoyment as that performance brings, and next time he is angry he kicks her with his hob-nailed shoes. When he has kicked her a few times standing or sitting, he kicks her down and stamps on her stomach, her breast, or her face. If he does not wear clogs or hob-nailed shoes, he takes up some other weapon, a knife, a poker, a hammer, a bottle of vitriol, or a lighted lamp, and strikes her with it, or sets her on fire; and then, and then only, the hapless creature's sufferings are at an end.

I desire specially to avoid making this paper more painful than can be helped, but it is indispensable that some specimens of the tortures to which I refer should be brought before the reader's eye. I shall take them exclusively from cases reported during the last three or four months. Were I to go further back for a year or two, it would be easy to find some more 'sensational', as, for example, of Michael Copeland, who threw his wife on a blazing fire; of George Ellis, who murdered his wife by pitching her out of a window; of Ashton Keefe, who beat his wife and thrust a box of lighted matches into his little daughter's breast when she was too slow in bringing his beer; and of Charles Bradley, who, according to the report in the *Manchester Examiner*,

> came home, and after locking the door, told his wife he would murder her. He immediately set a large bulldog at her, and the dog, after flying at the upper part of her body, seized hold of the woman's right arm, which she lifted to protect herself, and tore pieces out. The prisoner in the meantime kept striking her in the face, and inciting the brute to worry her. The dog dragged her up and down, biting pieces out of her arms, and the prisoner then got on the sofa and hit and kicked her on the breast.

But the instances of the last three or four months – from September to the end of January – are more than enough to establish all I want to prove; and I beg here to return my thanks for a collection of them, and for many very useful observations and tabulations of them, to Miss A. Shore, who has been good enough to place them at my disposal.

It is needful to bear in mind in reading them, that the reports of such cases which appear in newspapers are by no means always reliable, or calculated to convey the same impressions as the sight of the actual trial. In some of the following instances, also, I have only been able to obtain the first announcement of the offence, without means of checking it by the subsequent proceedings in court. *Per contra*, it should be remembered that if a few of these cases may possibly have been exaggerated or trumped up (as I believe the story of the man pouring Chili vinegar into his wife's eyes proved to have been), there are, for every one of these *published* horrors, at least three or four which *never are reported at all*, and where the poor victim dies quietly of her injuries like a wounded animal, without seeking the mockery of redress offered her by the law.

James Mills cut his wife's throat as she lay in bed. He was quite sober at the time. On a previous occasion he had nearly torn away her left breast.

J. Coleman returned home early in the morning, and, finding his wife asleep, took up a heavy piece of wood and struck her on the head and arm, bruising her arm. On a previous occasion he had fractured her ribs.

John Mills poured out vitriol deliberately, and threw it in his wife's face, because she asked him to give her some of his wages. He had said previously that he would blind her.

James Lawrence, who had been frequently bound over to keep the peace, and who had been supported by his wife's industry for years, struck her on the face with a poker, leaving traces of the most dreadful kind when she appeared in court.

Frederick Knight jumped on the face of his wife (who had only been confined a month) with a pair of boots studded with hobnails.

Richard Mountain beat his wife on the back and mouth, and turned her out of her bed and out of their room one hour after she had been confined.

Alfred Roberts felled his wife to the floor, with a child in her arms; knelt on her, and grasped her throat. She had previously taken out three summonses against him, but had never attended.

John Harris, a shoemaker, at Sheffield, found his wife and children in bed; dragged her out, and, after vainly attempting to force her into the oven, tore off her night-dress and turned her round before the fire 'like a piece of beef', while the children stood on the stairs listening to their mother's agonised screams.

Richard Scully knocked in the frontal bone of his wife's forehead.

William White, stonemason, threw a burning paraffin lamp at his wife, and stood quietly watching her enveloped in flames, from the effects of which she died.

William Hussell, a butcher, ran a knife into his wife several times and killed her. Had threatened to do so often before.

Robert Kelly, engine-driver, bit a piece out of his wife's cheek.

William James, an operative boilermaker, stabbed his wife badly in the arm and mouth, observing afterwards, 'I am sorry I did not kill both' (his wife and her mother).

Thomas Richards, a smith, threw his wife down a flight of fourteen steps, when she came to entreat him to give her some money for her maintenance. He was living with another woman – the nurse at a hospital where he had been ill.

James Frickett, a ratcatcher. His wife was found dying with broken ribs and cut and bruised face, a walking-stick with blood on it lying by. Frickett remarked, 'If I am going to be hanged for you, I love you.'

James Styles beat his wife about the head when he met her in the City Road. She had supported him for years by char-work, and during the whole time he had been in the habit of beating her, and on one occasion so assaulted her that the sight of one of her eyes was destroyed. He got drunk habitually with the money she earned.

John Harley, a compositor, committed for trial for cutting and wounding his wife with intent to murder.

Joseph Moore, a labourer, committed for trial for causing the death of his wife by striking her with an iron instrument on the head.

George Ralph Smith, oilman, cut his wife, as the doctor expressed it, 'to pieces', with a hatchet, in their back parlour. She died afterwards, but he was found Not Guilty, as it was not certain that her death resulted from the wounds.

Alfred Cummins, tailor, struck his wife so as to deprive her of the sight of an eye.

Thomas Paget, laundryman, knocked down his wife in the street and kicked her till she became insensible, because she refused to give him money to get drink.

Alfred Etherington, shoemaker, kicked his wife in a dangerous way, and a week later dragged her out of bed, jumped on her, and struck her. He said he would have her life and the lives of all her children. He gave no money for the support of his family (six children), and he prevented her from keeping the situations she had obtained for their maintenance. She had summoned him six or seven times.

Jeremiah Fitzgerald, labourer, knocked down his wife and kicked her heavily in the forehead. He had been twice convicted before. The woman appeared in court with her face strapped up.

Patrick Flynn, violently kicked his wife after he had knocked her down, and then kicked a man who interfered to save her. Had already undergone six months' hard labour for assaulting his wife.

Here is a case recorded from personal observation by a magistrate's clerk:

> I attended a dying woman to take her deposition in a drunkard's dwelling. The husband was present in charge of the police. The poor wretched wife lay with many ribs broken, and her shoulder and one arm broken, and her head so smashed that you could scarcely recognise a feature of a woman. She, in her last agony, said that her husband had smashed her with a wooden bed-post. He, blubbering, said, 'Yes, it is true, but I was in drink, or would not have done it.'

And here is one that has come in while I have been writing:

> At the Blackburn police-court, yesterday, John Charnock was committed for trial on a charge of attempted murder. It was stated that he had fastened his wife's head in a cupboard

> and kicked her with his iron clogs, and that he had deliberately broken her arm. (3 Feb 1878)

And here another (reported in the *Manchester Courier*, 5 February) so instructive in its details of the motives for Wife-murder, the sort of woman who is murdered, the man who kills, and the sentiment of juries as to what constitutes 'provocation' on the part of a wife, that I shall extract it at length:

> Manslaughter at Dukinfield
>
> Thomas Harlow, 39, striker, Dukinfield, was indicted for the manslaughter of his wife, Ellen Harlow, 45 years old, at Dukinfield, on 30 November 1877. The prisoner was committed by the magistrates on the charges of wilful murder, but the grand jury reduced the indictment to that of manslaughter. Mr Marshall prosecuted; and the prisoner, who was undefended by counsel, stated, in his plea, that he had no intention of killing his wife when he struck her.
>
> The prisoner, who was employed in and about Dukinfield, lived with his wife and three children in Waterloo Street, in that town. On the morning of the 30th November the deceased went out hawking as usual, and returned shortly after twelve o'clock. On her return she busied herself in preparing dinner, and the prisoner went out for a short time. In the afternoon the prisoner laid himself down, and slept for two or three hours. About five o'clock the deceased, and a lodger named Margaret Daley, and several others, were sitting in the house, when the prisoner came in and asked his wife for twopence. She replied that she had not twopence, and that she had had trouble enough with being out hawking all day in the rain and hungry. He then began to abuse her, and asked her for something to eat. She gave him some potatoes and bacon; after eating the greater part of which he again began to abuse her. He once more asked her for twopence, and Margaret Daley, seeing there was likely to be a disturbance, gave him the twopence, and told him he had better get a pint of beer. Instead of getting beer, however, he sent a little girl to purchase a quantity of coal, and then recommenced abusing his wife. Shortly afterwards he was heard to exclaim, 'There will be a life less tonight, and I will take it.' At this time the persons who were sitting in the house when the prisoner came in went out, leaving Harlow, his wife, and their son Thomas, and Daley together. The prisoner had some further altercation with his wife, which ended with him striking her a violent blow under the right

> ear, felling her to the floor. She died in a few minutes afterwards, the cause of death being concussion of the brain. The prisoner subsequently gave himself into custody, and made a statement attributing his conduct to the provocation his wife had given him.
>
> The jury found the prisoner guilty, and recommended him to mercy *on account of the provocation* he received. Sentence was deferred.

I think I may now safely ask the reader to draw breath after all these horrors, and agree with me that they cannot, *must* not, be allowed to go on unchecked, without some effort to stop them, and save these perishing and miserable creatures. Poor, stupid, ignorant women as most of them are, worn out with life-long drudgery, burdened with all the pangs and cares of many children, poorly fed and poorly clothed, with no pleasures and many pains, there is an enormous excuse to be made for them even if they do sometimes seek in drink the oblivion of their misery – a brief drama of unreal joy, where real natural happiness is so far away. But for those who rise above these temptations, who are sober where intoxication holds out their only chance of pleasure; chaste in the midst of foulness; tender mothers when their devotion calls for toilsome days and sleepless nights – for these good, industrious, struggling women who, I have shown, are the chief victims of all this cruelty – is it to be borne that we should sit patiently by and allow their lives to be trampled out in agony?

What ought to be done?

First, what has been done, or has been proposed to be done, in the matter?

In June 1853, an Act was passed (16th Victoria, c. 30) entitled 'An Act for the Better Prevention and Punishment of Aggravated Assaults upon Women and Children, and for Preventing Delay and Expense in the Administration of the Criminal Law'. In the preamble to this Act it is stated that 'the present law has been found insufficient for the protection of women and children from violent assaults'; and the measure provides that assaults upon any female or any male child – occasioning actual bodily harm – may be punished by summary conviction before two Justices of the Peace in Petty Sessions, or before any Police or Stipendiary Magistrate. The penalty to be inflicted is not to exceed imprisonment for six months with or without hard labour, or a fine not exceeding £20. The offender may also be bound to keep the peace for any period not exceeding six months from the expiration of his sentence. Failing to enter into recognizances, the offender may be kept in prison for a period not exceeding twelve months.

Since this Act was passed twenty-five years ago, no further legislation has taken place on the subject except the Consolidating Act (24 and 25 Vict c. 100), which simply re-enacts the Act as above stated.

Beside this Act on their behalf, wives are able to obtain relief in certain cases, under the Divorce Act. That is to say, those women who are able to apply to the Divorce Court may obtain, under section 16 of the Act (20th and 21st Vict. c. 85), on proof of cruelty, a sentence of Judicial Separation, which shall have the effect of a divorce *à mensâ et thoro*.

In the case of the ignorant, friendless, and penniless women, who are the chief victims of Wife-torture, such relief as this court affords is practically unattainable; but another clause of the same Act (the twenty-first) is of great value to them. It provides that a wife deserted by her husband may, at any time after such desertion, apply to a Police Magistrate in the metropolitan district, or to Justices in Petty Sessions if in the country, for an order to protect any money or property she may acquire; and if any such Protection Order be made, the wife shall, during its continuance, 'be in all respects in the same position, with regard to property and contracts, and suing and being sued, as she would have been under the Act if she had obtained a decree of Judicial Separation'.

For reasons to be hereafter noticed, this clause in the Divorce Act is of the utmost importance in establishing the principle that a Police Magistrate, or two Justices of the Peace in Session, may pronounce, on proof of the minor offence of desertion by the husband, a sentence which is tantamount, so far as property is concerned, to a Judicial Separation. The clause is, I am informed, brought very frequently indeed into action, and the magistrates not unfrequently interpret 'desertion' to signify an absence of three months without cause, albeit in the Divorce Court such absence must exceed two years to enable the wife to obtain a judicial separation.

It was doubtless believed by the benevolent promoters of these Acts that their provisions would have done a good deal to check the ill-usage of wives. But the offence appears to have diminished very little, if at all, during the twenty years which have since intervened, and at last one well-meaning, though somewhat eccentric member of the House of Commons felt himself moved to speak on the subject.

On 18 May 1874, Colonel Egerton Leigh made a vehement appeal for some increased punishment for aggravated assaults on women. He said that England had been called the Paradise of Women, and he brought forward his motion to prevent it from becoming a Hell of Women. After a speech, in which Colonel Leigh appeared overcome by emotion, he ended by saying that he 'was sure the women of England would not appeal in vain to the House of Commons', and Mr Disraeli answered him in the same vein of cheerful confidence which that Honourable House always expresses in its own eagerness to do justice to women. The House 'must have sympathised', he said, 'with Colonel Leigh, for it was a subject on which there could not be any differences of opinion'. He hoped

> his honourable and gallant friend would feel he has accomplished his object in directing the attention of the country to the subject, and that he would allow his right honourable friend, the Secretary of State for the Home Department, whose mind is now occupied with this and similar subjects, time to reflect as to the practical mode in which the feeling of the country can be carried out.

Colonel Leigh was requested to be 'satisfied that after the address he has made, Her Majesty's Government will bear in mind what is evidently the opinion of the House'; and, of course, Colonel Leigh expressed himself as perfectly satisfied, and withdrew his amendment (authorising flogging) with one of the jokes, which are so inexpressibly sickening in connection with this subject, about 'fair play for the fairer sex'.

On 15 October 1874, six months after Colonel Leigh had thus broken a lance in defence of the tortured women, the Home Office issued a Circular inquiring the opinion of the Judges, Chairmen of Quarter Sessions, Recorders, Stipendiary Magistrates of Metropolitan Police Courts, and Sheriffs of Scotch Counties, respecting five points connected with brutal assaults, the principal being whether the existing law was sufficiently stringent, and whether flogging should be authorised, 'especially in cases of assaults on women and children'.

The replies to these questions were published in a Parliamentary Blue Book entitled 'Reports on the State of the Law relating to Brutal Assaults', in 1875, and the following is a summary of the results:

There was a large consensus of opinion that the law as it now stands is insufficient to effect its purpose. Lord Chief Justice Cockburn says, 'In my opinion the present law against assaults of brutal violence is not sufficiently stringent' (p. 5), and Mr Justice Lush, Mr Justice Mellor; Lord Chief Baron Kelly, Baron Bramwell,

Baron Pigott, and Baron Pollock, express the same judgment in almost the same words (pp. 7–19).

Several of these, and also other judges, who do not directly say that they consider the present law insufficient, manifest their opinion that it is so by recommending that (under various safeguards) the penalty of flogging be added thereto. The agreement of opinion of these great authorities on this point appears (to the uninitiated) as if it must have been sufficient to carry with it any measure which had such weighty recommendation.

The following are the opinions in favour of flogging offenders in cases of brutal assaults:

Lord Chief Justice Cockburn, Mr Justice Blackburn, Mr Justice Mellor, Mr Justice Lush, Mr Justice Quain, Mr Justice Archibald, Mr Justice Brett, Mr Justice Grove, Lord Chief Baron Kelly, Baron Bramwell, Baron Pigott, Baron Pollock, Baron Cleasby, and Baron Amphlett. The opinions of Lord Coleridge and Mr Justice Denman were hesitating, and the only decided opponent of flogging at that time on the judicial bench in England was Mr Justice Keating.

The Chairmen of Quarter Sessions and magistrates in Sessions were in *sixty-four* cases out of the sixty-eight from whence responses came to the Home Office, in favour of flogging: Leftwich, Oxford (county), Stafford (county), and the North Riding being the only exceptions.

The Recorders of *forty-one* towns were likewise in favour of flogging, and only those of Lincoln, Nottingham, and Wolverhampton were opposed to it. The Recorders of Folkestone and of Newcastle-on-Tyne added the recommendation that a husband who had been flogged for a brutal assault on his wife should be divorced from her.

On reading this summary it will doubtless to many persons appear inexplicable that three years should have elapsed since so important a testimony was collected at the public expense, and at the trouble of so many eminent gentlemen whose time was of infinite value; and that, so far as can be ascertained, absolutely nothing has been done in the way of making practical use of it. During the interval scores of Bills, on every sort and kind of question *interesting to the represented sex*, have passed through Parliament; but *this* question, on which the lives of women literally hang, has never been even mooted since Lord Beaconsfield so complacently assured its solitary champion that 'Her Majesty's Government would bear in mind the evident feeling of the House on the subject.' Something like 6,000 women, judging by the judicial statistics, have been in the intervening years 'brutally assaulted' – that is, maimed, blinded, trampled, burned, and in no inconsiderable number of instances murdered outright – and several thousand children have been brought up to witness scenes which might, as Colonel Leigh said, 'infernalise a whole generation'. Nevertheless, the newspapers go on boasting of elementary education, and Parliament busies itself in its celebrated elephant's trunk fashion, alternately rending oaks and picking up sixpences; but *this* evil remains untouched!

The fault does not lie with the Home Office – scarcely even with Parliament, except so far as Parliament persists in refusing to half the nation those political rights which alone can, under our present order of things, secure attention to any claims. We live in these days under *Government by Pressure*, and the Home Office *must* attend first to the claims which are backed by political pressure; and Members of Parliament *must* attend to the subjects pressed by their constituents; and the claims and subjects which are not supported by such political pressure *must* go to the wall.

Nevertheless, when we women of the upper ranks – constitutionally qualified by the possession of property (and, I may be permitted to add, naturally qualified by education and intelligence at least up to the level of those of the 'illiterate' order of voters), to exercise through the suffrage that pressure on Parliament – are refused that privilege, and told year after year by smiling senators that we have no need whatever for it, that we form no 'class', and that we may absolutely and always rely on men to prove the deepest and tenderest concern for everything which concerns the welfare of women, shall we not point to these long-neglected wrongs of our trampled sisters, and denounce that boast of the equal concern of men for women as – a falsehood?

Were women to obtain the franchise to-morrow, it is normally certain that a Bill for the protection of Wives would pass through the legislature before a Session was over. I have yet hopes that even before that event takes place, some attention may be directed to the miserable subject, and that it may be possible to obtain some measure, holding out a prospect of relief to the wretched victims – if not of repression of the crime of Wife-torture. What measure ought we to ask for the purpose?

Of the desirability that any step should be taken in the direction of inflicting the lash for aggravated assaults on women, I shall not presume in the face of such authorities as have been cited above, to offer any opinion whatever.

One thing is manifest at all events. It is, that if flogging were added to the present penalties of wife-beating, the great difficulty which meets all efforts to stop the practice would be doubled. That difficulty is the inducing of the women (whose evidence is in most instances indispensable) to bear testimony against their husbands. It is hard enough to lead them to do so when the results will be an imprisonment to end in one month or in six, after which the husband will return to them full of fresh and more vindictive cruelty, and when in short, bringing him 'up' means abandoning the last ray of hope of ever making a happy home. This sentiment, half prudence, half perhaps in some cases lingering affection, cannot be overcome (even were it desirable to do so), as the law now stands, and causes endless failures of justice and perplexity to the always well-meaning magistrates. As a general rule it is said the wives will often tell their stories to the constables at the moment of the arrest, and can frequently be induced to attend in court the day or two after their injuries and while still smarting from their blows, and kicks, and 'cloggings'. But if a week be allowed to elapse, still more if the case be referred to the Quarter Sessions or Assizes, the wife is almost certain in the interval to have relented, or to have learned to dread the consequence of bearing testimony, and, instead of telling her true story, is constantly found to narrate some poor little fable, whereby the husband is quite exonerated, and, perhaps the blame taken on herself, as in the pitifully ludicrous case cited by Colonel Egerton Leigh in the House of Commons – of the woman who appeared without a nose, and told the magistrate she had *bitten it off herself!* On this subject, and on the defects of our whole procedure in such cases, some just remarks were made by Mr Serjeant Pulling in a paper read before the Social Science Congress at Liverpool, published in the Transactions for 1876, p. 345. He says:

> No one who has gained experience of wife-beating cases, can doubt that our present system of procedure seems as if it were designed not to repress crime, but to discourage complaints. A woman after being brutally assaulted by her husband, and receiving a sufficient number of kicks and blows to make her think she is being murdered, calls out for the aid of the police; and if her statements were there and then authentically recorded, and afterwards, on the commitment and trial of the aggressor, allowed to form part of the formal proof against him (subject of course to the right of the accused to refute it by cross-examination), there can be little doubt that the ends of justice would oftener be attained. In practice, however, the course is for the police to hear the loose statements of the scared victim and bystanders; and the subsequent proceedings are left very much to depend on the

> influences brought to bear on the poor wife in the interim (before the trial). She may relent before morning comes, or be subjected to so much sinister influence on the part of the husband and his friends as to be effectually prevented from disclosing the whole truth at all; or if doing so in the first stages of the proceedings she may be easily made so completely to neutralise its effect, that conviction becomes impracticable. The lesson taught to the ruffian is that if he ill-uses his dog or his donkey he stands a fair chance of being duly prosecuted, convicted, and punished; but that if the ill-usage is merely practised on his wife, the odds are in favour of his own entire immunity, and of his victim getting worse treatment if she dare appear against him.

To avoid these failures of justice, and the consequent triumph of the callous offenders, magistrates are generally very anxious to have these cases summarily disposed of, and to strike while the iron is hot. But of course there hence arises another evil, namely that the greater offences, which ought to be tried in the higher courts, and were intended to receive the heaviest penalty which the law allows, are punished only to the extent of the powers of the summary jurisdiction, of which the maximum is six months' imprisonment. Occasionally there is reason to believe the magistrates mend matters a little by the not unfair device of ordering the offender to find security for good behaviour, which, as he is generally unable to discover anybody foolish enough to give it for him, involves his incarceration in jail, possibly for a year. And, again, magistrates kindly endeavour to make the period of detention serve the process of reclaiming the man to better feelings about his wife, by allowing her entreaty to weigh importantly in any application to curtail his sentence, and letting him know that any repetition of offence will be closely watched and doubly severely punished. But all these humane devices, though sometimes, it is to be hoped, successful, yet leave the mournful fact patent to observation that the existing law, even worked with the extremest care and kindness, cannot and does not prevent the repetition, year after year, of all the frightful cruelties, beatings, burnings, cloggings, and tramplings of which we have given some pages back a few awful samples.

The relief which I most earnestly desire to see extended to these women, and from which I would confidently hope for *some* alleviation of their wretched condition, though its entire cure is beyond hope, is of a very different sort. It is this. A Bill should, I think, be passed, *affording to these poor women by means easily within their reach, the same redress which women of the richer classes obtain through the Divorce Court.* They should be enabled to obtain from the Court which sentences their husbands a Protection Order, which should in their case have the same validity as a judicial separation. In addition to this, the *Custody of the Children should be given to the wife*, and an order should be made for *the husband to pay to the wife such weekly sum for her own and her children's maintenance as the Court may see fit.*

The following are the chief clauses in a Bill, which has been prepared by Alfred D. Hill, Esq., J.P., of Birmingham, and the principle of which has been approved by many eminent legal authorities:

BILL

Intituled *An Act for the Protection of Wives whose Husbands have been convicted of assaults upon them.*

Whereas it is desirable to make provision for the protection of wives whose husbands have been convicted of assaults upon them: Be it enacted by the Queen's Most Excellent Majesty, by and with the advice and consent of the Lords Spiritual and Temporal and of the Commons in this present Parliament assembled, and by the authority of the same, as follows:

1 In any case where a husband has been convicted summarily or otherwise of an assault upon his wife, and has been sentenced to imprisonment therefor without the option of a fine in lieu of such imprisonment, it shall be competent for the Court by which such sentence has been pronounced, either at the time of such conviction or at any time afterwards, upon proof thereof, to make and give to the wife upon her application an order protecting her earnings and property acquired since the date of such order from her husband and all creditors and persons claiming under him; and such earnings and property shall belong to the wife as if she were a *feme sole;* and if any such order of protection be made, the wife shall, during the continuance thereof, be and be deemed to be in the like position in all respects with regard to property and contracts, and suing and being sued, as she would be if she had obtained a decree of judicial separation from the Court for Divorce and Matrimonial Causes.

2 The police magistrate or justices shall include in such order as aforesaid an injunction restraining the husband from going to or visiting the wife without her consent; and if any husband against whom any such injunction shall be made

shall commit any act of disobedience thereto, such act shall be deemed to be a misdemeanour, upon due proof of which any Court which would have been competent to make such order and injunction may commit him to the common gaol or house of correction of the city, borough, or county within the jurisdiction of such Court for any period not exceeding three months with or without hard labour.

3 And any Court which would have been competent to make such order as aforesaid may further include in such order a provision that the wife shall have the legal custody of the children of her husband and herself. And the same Court which would have been competent to make such order may further include in such order a provision directing that the husband shall pay to the wife a weekly sum for the maintenance of herself and of such children, which provisions of the order shall, if the payments required by it be in arrear, be enforced in the manner prescribed by the Act of the 11th and 12th Vict. c. 43, for the enforcing of orders of justices requiring the payment of a sum of money.

4 Every such order as aforesaid shall, within ten days after the making thereof, be entered with the registrar of the county court within whose jurisdiction the wife is resident, and a copy of such order shall, within such ten days, or within a reasonable time in that behalf, be served upon the husband. And it shall be lawful for the husband to apply to the Court for Divorce and Matrimonial Causes, or to the magistrates or justices by whom such order was made, for the discharge thereof, and they may (if they think fit) discharge the same. And the said Court for Divorce and Matrimonial Causes, or magistrate, or justices, is or are hereby authorised to discharge such order if it, he, or they shall deem fit.

(Here follows Schedule)

The reasons which may be urged on behalf of this measure are manifold. They rest at all points on admitted principles of legislation.

In the first place, the Divorce Laws offering to women *who can avail themselves of them* the remedy of Judicial Separation in cases of the cruelty of their husbands, it is a matter of simple justice that the same remedy should be placed within the reach of those poor women who are subjected to tenfold greater cruelties than those which the court always rules to constitute a ground for divorce. At the same time, except by some such machinery as has been suggested – namely, that the police magistrate or petty sessions court be given the power to pronounce the separation – it is difficult to conceive of any way in which the very humble and ignorant class of women, with whom we are concerned, could ever obtain the decree which is *in principle* at present their *right*.

A second reason for such a measure is that, as above stated, Magistrates are already empowered, in cases of *desertion*, to give Protection Orders which are expressly stated to be (so far as property is concerned) equivalent to a Judicial Separation – and which (very frequently given as they are) practically act as Judicial Separations in all respects. The objection which has been raised by some hasty readers of the Bill, that it proposes to give an unheard of power to one or two Magistrates, thus falls to the ground. They already practically exercise the same power every day in the minor case of desertion. The husband is also afforded by the Bill every facility for obtaining a discharge of the Order should it appear to have been unjustly given.

Finally, a most important reason for adopting such a measure is, that it – or something like it – is indispensable to induce the victims of such outrages to apply for legal redress.[6] The great failure of justice which has so long gone on in this matter, is chiefly due, as I have said before, to the fact that the existing law *discourages* such applications – and in like manner must every projected law do so which merely adds penalities to the husband's offence without providing the suffering wife with any protection from his renewed violence when that penalty has been endured. Under the Wives Protection Bill, should it become law, the injured wife would have the *very thing she really wants*, namely, security against further violence, coupled with the indispensable custody of her children (without which, no protection of herself would offer a temptation to the better sort of women), and some small (though probably precarious) contribution to their maintenance and her own. With this real relief held out to them by the law, I should have little doubt that we should find the victims of brutal assaults and of repeated aggravated assaults very generally coming forward to bear testimony and claim their release, and the greatest difficulty attendant on the case would be at an end.

Even were there but a few who availed themselves of the boon, I still think it would be fitting and right that the law should hold it out to them. In many instances no doubt the mere fact that the wife had such a resource open to her would act very effectually on the husband as a deterrent to violence.

As to the justice and expediency of giving the custody of the children (both boys and girls of all ages) to the wife, there can be,

I should think, little hesitation. The man who is, *ex hypothesi*, capable of kicking, maiming, and mutilating his wife, is even less fit to be the guardian of the bodies and souls of children than the lord and master of a woman. They are no more safe under his roof than in the cage of a wild beast, and the guilt of leaving them in the one place is little less than that of placing them in the other. When a child is killed by one of these drunken savages – as the illegitimate child of George Hill, whom he knocked on the head with a hammer in revenge for having an affiliation order made on him; or as the child of six years old whom James Parris murdered because its mother failed to keep an appointment – or when a child is cruelly injured, as the poor little girl into whose breast Ashton Keefe thrust a box full of ignited matches because she had been slow in fetching his beer – when these outrages occur we are indignant enough with the offenders; but, if they had previously betrayed their tiger instincts, is there no guilt attaching to those who *left* these defenceless creatures in their dens? For both the children's sakes and the mothers' this clause of the Bill, then, appears of paramount importance – in fact, *a sine quâ non* of any measure possessing practical value.

Lastly, as regards the alimony for the wife, and the maintenance for the children, to be paid by the husband after the term of his imprisonment, I presume the justice of the provision will not be disputed. The man obviously cannot wipe away his natural obligations by the commission of a deed of cruel violence, and it would be a most dangerous lesson to let him think he could do so. The difficulty of course lies in enforcing such an order in the case of those lowest classes of artisans and labourers who can move freely from place to place, obtaining employment anywhere with the help of a bag of tools, or tramping the country from workhouse to workhouse. In the case of affiliation orders it is, I understand, found pretty uniformly that the small tradesmen, and men having a fixed business, pay their weekly dole fairly regularly, thereby minimising the scandal; but the lower and looser sort of men decamp, and are lost sight of sooner or later, the Poor-law authorities rarely troubling themselves to look after them. The same resource of escape will undoubtedly be sought by not a few separated husbands should the Bill before us become law. The evil is serious, but perhaps not so serious or irremediable as it may appear. The Poor-law authorities or the police might surely be stirred to put in motion the machinery which lies ready to hand in case of greater crimes.

NOTES

1 Let it be noted that while they *were* slaves, these negroes were daily subjected to outrages and cruelties of which it thrilled our blood to hear. Since they have been emancipated their white neighbours have learned at least so far to recognise them as human beings, that these *tortures* have become comparatively rare.

2 Stripped of the euphemisms of courtesy wherewith we generally wrap them up, it cannot be denied that the sentiments of a very large number of men towards women consist of a wretched alteration of exaggerated and silly homage, and of no less exaggerated and foolish contempt. One moment on a pedestal, the next in the mire; the woman is adored while she gives pleasure, despised the moment she ceases to do so. The proverbial difficulty of introducing a joke into the skull of a Scotchman is nothing to that of getting into the mind of such men that a woman is a *human being* – however humble – not a mere adjunct and appendage of humanity; and that she must have been created, and has a right to live for ends of her own; not for the ends of another; that she was made, as the old Westminster Catechism says, 'to glorify God and enjoy Him for ever', not primarily or expressly to be John Smith's wife and James Smith's mother. We laugh at the great engineer who gave as his opinion before a Royal Commission that rivers were created to feed navigable canals; and a farmer would certainly be treated as betraying the 'bucolic mind' who avowed that he thought his horse was made to carry him to market, and his cat to eat his mice and spare his cheese; yet where women are concerned – beings who are understood to be at least *quasi* rational, and to whom their religion promises an immortal life hereafter of good and glory – the notion that the Final Cause of Woman is Man seems never to strike them as supremely ridiculous.

3 Old English legislation embodied this view so far as to inflict the cruelest of all punishments – burning to death – on a woman guilty of *petty treason*, i.e., the murder of her husband, while the husband was only liable to hanging for murdering his wife. A woman was burned to death under this atrocious law at Chester, in 1760, for poisoning her husband. The wretched creature was made to linger four months in jail under her awful sentence before it was executed.

4 I have seen a woman like this tormenting a great, good-natured hobbledehoy, who unhappily belonged to Carlyle's order of 'Inarticulate ones', and found it impossible to avoid being caught every five minutes in the Socratic *elenchus*, which she set for him like a trap whenever he opened his mouth. At length when this had lasted the larger part of a rainy day, the poor boy who had seemed for some time on the verge of explosion, suddenly sprang from his chair, seized the little woman firmly though gently round the waist, carried her out into the hall, and came back to his seat, making no remark on the transaction. Who could blame him?

5 Such was the case of Susannah Palmer, a few years ago, whose husband had beaten her, and sold up her furniture again and again, blackened

her eyes, and knocked out her five front teeth. At last on one occasion, with the knife with which she was cutting her children's supper, she somehow inflicted a slight cut on the man while he was knocking her about the head. He immediately summoned her for 'cutting and wounding him', and she was sent to Newgate. I found her there and afterwards received the very best possible character of her from several respectable tradespeople in whose houses she had worked as a char-woman for years. Friends subscribed to help her, and the admirable chaplain of Newgate interested himself warmly in her case and placed her in safety.

6 Mr. W. Digby Seymour, Recorder of Newcastle-on-Tyne, in giving in his opinion on the desirability of adding flogging to the penalties of wife-beating, says – 'If you flog the husband you will for ever degrade him as a married man. Let him be flogged by all means; but why not amend the laws of divorce, and in cases of a conviction for "brutal violence," entitle the wife, on simple proof of conviction, to a divorce *á vinçulo?'* – Returns, p. 90.

Mr. Lonsdale, Recorder of Folkestone, says practically the same: 'I would not authorise flogging in cases of assaults upon wives unless that punishment were allowed to have the effect of a judicial separation.' – Ibid., p. 82.

Ellen Webb

Temperance in the Home

(1881)

Home is a centre from whence radiates an influence extending to all eternity. Its features are perpetuated in the homes of the children who pass forth from its shelter; for they, creating homes for themselves, carry with them the moral atmosphere with which they have been surrounded in their youth. This is especially the case with the daughters, and the young bride who, in a well ordered home, has been trained by a wise mother to 'guide the house', will go forth to her duties as mistress of a household to carry on the work begun by that mother which will thus extend from generation to generation. Woman is the pivot round which home life revolves, and as a rule, it is woman who makes its comfort or its misery.

To the Christian wife who has married 'in the Lord' the husband relegates the government of the household. She it is who, in the middle or upper classes, engages servants, regulates the expenditure, arranges for entertaining guests, teaches her children, or selects their governess or their schools. She decides who shall be their companions, and in most cases what ministry the family shall attend. She watches over the health of all the inmates of the house deciding (generally) when it is advisable to call in a medical man, and who that medical man shall be. To her her children come as to one who can sympathise with them in any trouble, who will deal gently though firmly with their faults, and if in after years one goes astray, it is the thought of the loving mother that will recall the erring one to the paths of virtue and peace. With such a woman as a mistress, servants remain for years, or, if they leave to marry and make homes for themselves, they will form them on the model of the one they have left, carrying the habits of order, punctuality, probity, sobriety, Sabbath-keeping, and neatness into the sphere to which they belong. A well ordered home in any class is a blessing to a neighbourhood, while a household in which disorder reigns is a cause of annoyance to all around. The noisy dissipation, the quarrelling amongst children and servants, the Sunday excursions, the eye sore of ragged blinds and dirty door-steps are a source of discomfort to those who are unfortunate enough to be living near; and the inmates themselves are only too glad to escape from their miserable surroundings and seek some comfort in other places.

Now, of all the sources of discomfort and disorder in a home 'strong drink' is the most fruitful, and it is that which most frequently severs the bonds which hold its members together. If the Master of the house 'drinks' misery will enter the door, and though in some cases the fact remains hidden for a while (the wife alone being the unhappy victim of the inebriate's folly or violence, and loyally hiding the wretched secret) the servants soon detect the evil, and ere long, visitors are also aware that 'Mr So and so drinks'. The effect on him is to paralyse his brain power, and destroy his judgment; ere long his business or his profession is neglected, his money is squandered aimlessly; and in some cases, unconsciously, ruin at last overtakes him, his home is broken up, and his poor wife and children are driven forth to earn as best they can a precarious livelihood, while he who should have been the 'houseband' loosens all the ties that bound the family together, and so destroys his home. This is a sad and melancholy picture, but, alas, one which is drawn from life, and one which is too common in this drink cursed country. But if this picture is sad, what if 'strong drink' overcomes the Mistress of the house! Alas, no words can depict the miseries which follow so sad a case as that when the wife and mother again and again inebriated affects illness, and permits her unsuspecting children to sympathise with her in her frequent attacks of 'faintness', or 'giddiness', or 'headache', which disguise the truth from their innocent eyes. Servants, if good, refuse to live with a woman so degraded, and, if bad, take advantage of her incapacity to rob and injure her. In vain her husband remonstrates, pleads, argues, or exerts his authority. If once the craving is formed drink she will have, and no barriers seem strong enough to bar the way to the indulgence of this horrible craving. Again and again the wife promises amendment, bitterly she repents today, but tomorrow she is again under the sway of this monster. Her house neglected, her children running wild, her husband driven away from his comfortless home. What is the end? One more potent draught than usual and death comes in to release the man wedded to a living death, and to consign an immortal soul to a drunkard's eternity; or perchance a lunatic asylum delays the end for a few years, during which the desolate husband and the un-mothered children struggle against the disorder created by her, who should have been the beneficent ruler of the home, blessing and being blessed.

How many homes there are in which at family gatherings one is absent, and why? Has not strong drink been the cause in very many instances. Where is the young man once the bright, eager, merry lad whose fun brightened the whole home circle. Is he not banished as a ne'er do-weel? Did he not frequent music halls and theatres, and did he not 'take to drinking'. Where is the fair haired girl, whose graceful form moved so pleasantly about the old home? Alas! she is under the care of a lady who receives inebriates. See that melancholy man who occupies a seat near his aged mother: he is not a widower, but where is the bright, gay daughter-in-law who was welcomed so lovingly into the family circle? Alas, strong drink has driven her from his house, and he knows not where she is. Thus and thus the 'ruthless enemy' goes on destroying happiness and severing family bonds, and *yet* wine and beer are still on the tables! Welcomed as friends whilst they are doing the cruel work of foes. When will English men and women arise and cast forth this treacherous alcohol, banishing it from their homes as they would banish the father of evil.

Mothers and wives! stand up in your own personal abstinence, and free your homes from its blighting influence. Never have it in the house, never offer to procure it for your visitors. Never allow your servants beer money, but tell them frankly your position in the matter; you can give an increase of wages if you choose, but let it be understood it is not to supply them with beer. Teach your children to abstain on principle, tell them why you do not have it on the table, and why you wish them to decline it when at other people's houses. Get them to work with you. Proclaim your total abstinence principles to your friends, and let them know that at your table no one will be tempted to partake of 'wine the mocker', or the 'strong drink which is raging'. And, mothers, let your selection of a medical adviser be a wise and prayerful one. Beware of calling in a man who trusts to the virtues of decoctions of whose properties he is ignorant, and who sends his patients to the wine merchant and brewer for their medicine. Decline firmly to allow your children to be dosed with port wine or brandy. If a mother is firm the prescription will probably be withdrawn and a substitute provided, but if your doctor refuses to attend unless his vinous prescriptions are swallowed, accept his resignation, and seek another, who will abide by your decision that your children shall be treated without alcohol.

Happy is that home where alcohol never enters, where husband, wife, children and servants abstain from it on principle and are all water drinkers.

Zoedone, Hedozone, Vin-sante, or sparkling Hygeia may be useful sometimes, but water is the beverage which God has given us. 'Man has sought out many inventions', but nothing can take the place of that pure element which is absolutely essential to life. Let not your children's palates be vitiated by alcoholic beverages, and water will afford them as gratifying and refreshing a draught as could the finest wines of France, Spain or Germany.

Thank God that in England water can be had for a mere nominal price, and even where it is not supplied perfectly pure, filters can easily be obtained which will render it so.

In the management of her household surely the Mistress should avoid all useless expenditure, and although the wine department is generally but partially under her control, she could effect a material saving by herself becoming an abstainer, even if she could not *at once* banish alcohol from the house. How few women calculate what the wine costs which they themselves consume; one glass of Sherry a day, at the low price even of 2/6 the bottle, costs £4 10s. a year; Port (say at 3/6), one glass a day, £6. Many a lady who calls herself a 'moderate drinker' takes two glasses of Sherry at luncheon, and three at her dinner, which at the low price named amounts to £22 10s. per annum, besides which there is an occasional glass of Champagne, Port, or Claret to be added to the score, bringing it probably up to £25. A bottle of Claret a day at 2/– costs £36 10s. a year, and yet many a man thinks *that* a very moderate allowance if taken at luncheon and dinner. In a family where there are three or four grown-up sons and daughters at home, the wine becomes a very serious item of expenditure, and where dinner parties and balls are given, the amount of money wasted in this way is one which few people realise; even where the greatest difficulty is experienced in meeting the expenses of schooling, wages, rent and taxes, the idea of curtailing the wine bill seems rarely to be entertained, and yet how easily it may be done by a firm self-denial on the part of the Mistress, who should set the example of abstinence, and thus win over to her side her children, her servants, and her husband. The money saved in this way will add immensely to the comforts of the home, and where the struggle has been hard to make the income meet the expenses, an easy consciousness of reduced expenditure to meet the income will save many a heartache, many a weary forecast, many a painful brooding over difficulties, and a light heart will give a cheerful countenance with which to brighten hearth and home.

But even where such a retrenchment is not needed, is it sufficiently considered what an immense amount of good might be done with the money saved by abstinence from this 'delightsome poison'? Is it generally known that a pension of £20 per annum is a boon so coveted that from 800 to 1000 persons, most of them well educated men and women, are each year straining every nerve to obtain it from such Societies as the National Benevolent Institution; the United Kingdom Beneficent Association; the British Home for Incurables; the Royal Hospital for Incurables; and the National Hospital for the Paralysed? Were the sad sad lists of these candidates carefully studied by those who unthinkingly sip their four or five glasses of wine a day, without regarding the cost, and they were to realise that the sacrifice of that wine would enable them to maintain some aged governess, some suffering cripple, some helpless paralytic, or some desolate orphan, is it not probable that that sacrifice would be made, and the money thus saved be devoted to such a purpose?

And if the banishment of alcohol from the houses of the upper classes is attended with such marked advantage, in the lower classes the difference betwixt the home of the abstainer and that of the drinker is even more marked. The wages which they receive may be the same, the number in the family may be equal, but the comforts and even luxuries which are to be found in the home of the abstainer render it so superior that a stranger would guess that he received double the wages of the other; few people who have not worked in the cause of temperance have any idea of the frightful amount of money spent by the working classes on strong drink, and those who would confer the greatest possible boon on a workman and his family, should induce them to become total abstainers. Houses destitute of every comfort are quickly furnished, and even adorned, where the wages are diverted from the till of the publican to those of the honest tradesman of the neighbourhood; they then indeed become worthy of the name of home, and there the sober workman seeks his rest, surrounded by his tidy children, while his neat and smiling wife provides the comfortable meal from which the poisonous alcohol is banished; his boys, preserved from many snares by being abstainers, avoid the public houses, and either enjoy some healthy out-door sports as recreation, or by attending Lectures, Reading Rooms, and Institutes, seek that knowledge which will help them on in after years; his daughters, trained in abstinence and going out as servants under Christian abstaining mistresses, either attach themselves to the family, or, after years of honest service, marry men like-minded with themselves, and create homes which continue to dispense blessings on all around. Strong drink has been the bridge over which thousands of young girls have passed to their ruin, and it is a fact that rigid total abstinence is a barrier to a life of sin and shame. Our jails and workhouses are peopled by drinkers, whilst a life abstainer has hardly ever been known amongst their inmates.

Why then should this monstrous source of evil be tolerated? Why does not the Church of Christ arise and in *His* mighty power cast out this emissary of Satan, which is driving men and women forth from the sanctities of home life to dwell 'among the tombs'. He has told us that in His Name we should do greater works than He did. Let us then take the power which He offers, and destroy this Juggernaut whose victims are flinging themselves by thousands under its crushing weight, which is bearing them down to Hell.

Women of England! purify your homes from this unholy thing, this demon of discord and strife, this element of all unrighteousness. Forsake not the 'cold flowing waters' (emblematic of spiritual life) for that 'strong drink' which 'shall be bitter to them that drink it'; your children, taught by you to shun its snares, will, in after years, rise up and 'call you blessed', your husbands will praise you, and though you may never go forth, like your American sisters, to the 'holy war', it will be said of you, 'she that tarried at home divided the spoil'.

Frances Swiney

Alcohol

(1917)

> Alcoholism is chronic poisoning resulting from the habitual use of alcohol, even when this is not taken in amount sufficient to produce drunkenness. . . . Alcoholism is one of the most frightful scourges, whether it be regarded from the point of view of the health of the individual, of the existence of the family, or of the future of the country.

In these words the French Government in 1902 thus publicly, by official placards, warned the people of the dangers of alcohol.

For, as regards the use of alcohol, a complete revolution has taken place in the opinion of the medical profession during the last twenty years. Alcohol is now recognised as a narcotic and a poison, that has a cumulative action on the system, and is therefore almost discarded medicinally as being considered distinctly harmful.

'On grounds both of fact and theory,' writes Dr Saleeby, 'there is every reason to recognise in alcohol, as in syphilis and in lead, a racial poison, originating racial degeneration, which, in accordance with generally recognised principles, shows itself in the latest, highest, and therefore most delicate, portion of the organism.'

Nature of alcohol

Alcohol is a waste-product in the activity of the yeast plant, its action on the yeast cells being to limit their growth. A strong percentage of alcohol entirely prevents the growth of the yeast; thus, 'when the proportion of alcohol reaches about 14 per cent, the organism, like bacteria, being killed by their own life's product, alcohol'.

Alcohol will prevent the growth of plants if these are treated with only 1 part of alcohol in 100 parts of water. It will also destroy the green colouring matter of plants.

Alcohol is emphatically first and last a protoplasmic poison; that is to say, it is deleterious to cell-growth, leading eventually to degeneration of the cells themselves, and thus affecting with disease all the organs of the body, whether formed of animal or vegetable protoplasm. It has, indeed, a 'fatal influence on the processes of life'.

Effects of alcohol

The effects of alcohol in even the smallest doses are at once apparent in the nervous system. Alcohol attacks like wildfire the nerve centres; first, the higher psychical functions of the brain; second, the emotional functions of the brain; third, the nerve centres of the brain, which initiate and control voluntary motions; and fourth, the cerebellar apparatus of the brain, which regulates these movements. As Dr Clouston states:

> From the medical and scientific point of view, we have this great physiological fact before us – that the first thing alcohol does in 99 cases out of 100 is to effect the mental working of the brain of the man who imbibes.

While Professor Sikovsky declares that

> alcohol diminishes the rapidity of thought, makes the imagination and power of reflection commonplace and deprived of originality, acts upon fine and complex sensations by transforming them into coarse and elementary ones. Alcohol perverts the moral nature, affects the judgment, and impairs the memory.

Persons who habitually take alcohol between meals gradually develop nerve changes, showing loss of energy, lessened capacity for business, and diminished attention to detail. In Professor Macdougall's investigations with workers he found that '3 ounces of whisky caused 53 per cent more errors than when the brain was under normal conditions'. Alcohol also affects injuriously automatic work, rendering it less trustworthy and accurate, as shown by the experiment of Professor Kraepelin at his psychological school at Heidelberg, when the capacity for adding up figures and mental arithmetic were prejudicially affected by small doses of alcohol. Memory was distinctly hampered; untruthfulness and inexactitude increased; association of ideas and the formation of judgments slowed down in activity. Thus, mental fatigue is increased by alcohol, and it is the greatest error to believe that alcohol dispels fatigue; on the contrary, it is not a stimulant, but only acts as a drug, as a deadening agent to normal sensation. It is, therefore, more than any other factor the cause of the nervous debility and of the nervous exhaustion so prevalent at the present day. 'Alcohol in all its forms has a prolonged depressant after-stage, and insidiously sets up widespread tissue degeneration, for which reason it is a misuse of terms to call it a stimulant.'

When we consider the effect of alcohol on the emotions, we are brought face to face with the chief source of the world's immorality, crime, disease, and misery; for the first effect of alcohol on the emotions is to render them less under the control of the individual's will-power, reason, and judgment. 'Thus love, joy, ardour, courage, hate, fear, rage, passion, all seek expression which, unless directed by reason may become a danger, love degenerating into passion, joy into orgy, ardour into impatience, and courage into recklessness.'

Alcohol and morality

Alcohol and syphilis and venereal disease, generally are boon companions. Dr Iwan Block, in his *Sexual Life in England*, has shown how

> the new, the excessive consumption of meat and of alcoholic beverages has unnaturally stimulated the sexual impulse, and has conducted it into devious paths. From the standpoint of medical experience and observation I am prepared to term alcohol the evil genius of the modern sexual life, because in a malicious and underhand manner it delivers its victims to sexual misleading and corruption, to venereal infection, and to all the consequences of casual sexual intercourse.

In truth, 'the continued increase in the consumption of alcohol leads to a further diffusion of venereal diseases', with the after-effects of a resulting increase in illegitimate births, seduced girls, a higher rate of suicides, and a degenerate people. 'I am firmly convinced that if drink were eradicated,' declares Sir Gorell Barnes,

President of the Divorce Court, 1906, 'this court might shut its doors, at any rate for the greater part of the time.'

Alcohol and crime

The connection between alcohol and crime is appalling.

> We know beyond dispute that in countries like France, Italy, and Belgium the progressive curve of crime and that of madness regularly follow the ascending curve of the consumption of alcohol. In Norway, where defence against alcoholism has been strongly and rigorously organised, criminality has immediately declined.

In England and Wales, according to criminal statistics for 1903, drunkenness accounts for 230,180 offences; while out of 200 male offenders convicted of murder 60 per cent of the cases were directly due to alcoholism.

The reason for this affinity between crime and alcohol is not far to seek. Neither the drunkard nor the criminal is in a normal state.

Alcohol and insanity

It may be said that every criminal is insane i.e., that a lesion in the brain is the cause of an immoral, unethical, subnormal act. The mind is not in a healthy state that can instigate a crime. Therefore we find drunkenness and insanity go hand in hand. 'It is certain,' writes Dr Clouston in his official report, 'that for every man in whom excessive drinking causes absolute insanity there are twenty in whom it injures the brain, blunts the moral sense, and lessens the capacity for work in lesser degrees.' Alcohol is accountable for fully 20 per cent of the cases admitted into the asylums today. In France, out of 57,000 lunatics, 78 per cent were drinkers and 88 per cent of violent cases were drunkards. In Ireland, where insanity is on the increase, half of the inmates of the asylums owe their disease to drink. In England it is computed that six out of every ten lunatics were made such by alcohol. According to Dr Forbes Winslow there are 128,787 registered lunatics in England and Wales today – i.e., one lunatic in every 278 of the population. He considers that in a few years 'there will be more insane persons in the world than sane'. The habitual drinker, though not actually insane, is subject to insane delusions, to unfounded suspicions, jealousies, hatreds, dislikes, and extraordinary fancies.

Alcoholic dementia rapidly ends in deaths, as every organ of the body is affected, and the moral nature of the individual undergoes a complete change as the disease advances; in fact, in the mental ruin it is not possible to recognise the original character. Under the influence of alcohol a fond husband will become a selfish, brutal, and murderous tyrant; a devoted mother will take the blankets off her children's beds and pawn them for drink; a modest woman will become indecent, and an honest man a thief. Memory goes, and no statement of an habitual drunkard is reliable.

Alcohol is responsible for many cases of epilepsy, as it excites into activity the inherited latent tendency. Chronic alcoholic patients often become hopeless epileptics, while neuritis and paralysis are due to the same cause in a number of cases among comparatively young people who have become addicted to the drink habit.

Alcohol and organic disease

By poisoning the cells of the brain and diminishing their number and their efficiency, we find that alcohol thus attacks first the highest centres and functions, only later overwhelming those of organic life. The whole digestive system invariably suffers from the consumption of alcohol. 'It creates want of appetite, nausea, irregular and insufficient nutrition, indigestion, and consequently a faulty elaboration of the food.' It attacks and irritates the delicate mucous membrane of the stomach, tending to more or less general physical deterioration through a diseased, worn-out digestive system. Taken with or without food, the action of alcohol on the muscular movements of the stomach is the same, rendering them sluggish, weak, and impaired. Especially has alcohol a peculiarly deleterious effect upon the digestion of women.

In the opinion of Dr J. M. Whyte, 'liver disorders are probably in all cases prejudicially influenced by alcoholic beverages. In kidney diseases alcohol should be withheld. Alcohol in moderate quantities irritates the kidneys.' We must never forget that alcoholism is a cell disease; if, therefore, alcohol be taken in very large quantities, so as to produce fatty degeneration of the liver cells, death occurs rapidly. But diseases of the liver result more frequently from the frequent taking of small doses of alcohol at short intervals, between meals, nips, etc. Thus, publicans and commercial travellers are the greatest sufferers from liver and kidney diseases. Chronic Bright's disease ensues as the kidneys become more and more affected.

Alcohol and epidemics

A drunkard is ever an easy prey to epidemics, as alcohol has a most deleterious action upon the white blood-cells, the life-preservers of the body against infective microbes. It is proved that alcohol, even in the smallest doses, paralyses the white cells, and prevents the exercise of their microbe-destroying function. Thus, the life of the drunkard is endangered from the first lapse into excess. Moreover, it is well-known in the medical profession that the man who imbibes frequently is extremely likely to contract syphilis and gonorrhœa. Lead poisoning, mercurial poisoning, and other industrial diseases affecting the lungs, are found most among the inebriate workers. Dr Scott declares that 'he cannot recall a single case of a total abstainer ever being attacked by lead poisoning'. A drunkard has little chance of recovery if attacked with pneumonia, typhoid fever, erysipelas, bloodpoisoning, or cancer. Alcohol deprives him of natural resistance to disease. Alcoholism is the enemy to longevity, as the records of life-insurance companies prove.

It is a great fallacy to suppose that a weak heart is strengthened by alcohol; on the contrary, 'alcohol has a somewhat similar effect on the heart to that produced by the typhoid toxin' is the verdict of Sir James Barr, M.D. 'It has yet to be proved that the heart muscle can be stimulated by alcohol,' writes Dr Munro, of the Glasgow Royal Infirmary, while Dr Crile has shown by direct experiments that in cases of 'shock' alcohol only aggravates the conditions.

Alcohol and body temperature

The body temperature is actually lowered by alcohol. 'The greater the cold, the more injurious is the use of alcohol,' wrote Dr John Rae, the Arctic explorer; and it is well known that Nansen would not allow any alcohol to be used in his two great Arctic expeditions. Alcohol is the true cause of many deaths from exposure, as its action is to send a flow of blood to the surface of the body and the ends of the nerves, whereby a sensation of warmth is conveyed to the brain, but in reality the blood parts on the surface with valuable heat which should be retained in the vital parts of the body. Alcohol all through is a false friend and a relentless enemy to the human system.

Hereditary effects

But if the drunkard suffers in his lifetime, the race suffers for generations from his vicious indulgence. 'Of all hereditary taints,' says Dr E. Laurent,

> 'alcoholism is undeniably the most frequent. . . . It is the most common cause of degeneration, and our prisons are peopled mostly with degenerates or with the children of drunkards. When, in the ancestry of any criminal, we cannot find insanity, or epilepsy, or hysteria, we shall find, nine cases out of ten, that alcohol has been the cause of all the trouble. The other taints may often skip a generation, but this is rarely the case with alcoholism. Alcohol is a poison which pardons not.'

In reformatory asylums for inebriates, out of 2,554 admissions Dr Eugene Trousson found that 41 per cent were the offspring of drunken parents – i.e., 933 had drunken fathers, 80 had drunken mothers, and 40 had both parents drunkards.

'There is today no doubt whatever that chronic alcoholism modifies profoundly the brain and nervous system of both parent and offspring. Some of the most characteristic cases of instinctive criminality are solely or chiefly due to alcoholism in one of the parents.' Dr Kerr and Professor Warner, in *American Charities*, p. 62, give instances in which temperate parents have had a number of healthy children, and then, becoming intemperate, have had grossly defective and diseased children. Thus, in one family the first son and daughter were sound in mind and body, but four other children born after the father became an habitual drunkard were complete idiots in three cases, and one was mentally deficient. In Norway the close connection between drunkenness and idiotic offspring has been proved by the marked increase in ten years in intemperance among the people after the removal of the spirit duty in 1825 and the increase of 150 per cent in the production of congenital idiots. 'Idiocy,' says Dr McKim, 'is the lowest manifestation of human degeneracy.'

One half of the idiots in England are of drunken parentage, and the same is true in Sweden and other European countries. 'If the father has been a drunkard, the son is likely to be insane or idiotic,' declares Dr J. H. Kellogg.

> Only an insignificant number of drinkers' children are physically and mentally normal – 17.5 per cent, according to Legrain. . . . Arrive found tuberculosis in 10 per cent of drinkers' children, but only in 1.8 per cent among the children of healthy parents.

'The unborn child of a drunken and pregnant mother is practically another drunken person as liable, or more liable, to suffer from the effects of drink.'

Alcohol and motherhood

Alcohol is known to pass in considerable quantities, as such, into the fœtus, devitalising the growing organism, and injuring every cell in the body. The increase of drunkenness among women is thus a question of national importance. Alcoholism in the father is a grave danger to the race and a curse on future generations. Alcoholism in the mother spells the extinction of the race, as she loses, through the effects of the poison in her system, the creative powers of maternity. The germ cells deteriorate, and, after conception has taken place, the impoverishment of the mother's vitality during the subsequent pregnancy precludes all healthy normal growth in the embryo. Consequently at birth the child possesses for its start in life an enfeebled, nervous, and diseased organisation.

Dr Sullivan, through personal investigation, ascertained 'that of 600 children born of 120 drunken mothers, 335 died in infancy or were stillborn, and that several of the survivors were mentally defective, and as many as 4.1 per cent were epileptic'.

Now in the United States alone there are about 135,000 helpless epileptics; and as epilepsy is essentially a brain disease, it follows that the brain-cells of these unfortunates are malformed and degenerate – spoilt, in fact, in the making. No person *becomes* epileptic. The tendency to the disease is inborn and inherited. Syphilis and alcohol share between them the onus of causation for one of the most terrible of human afflictions. The mother especially is the chief agent in the hereditary transmission of epilepsy; for the conclusions drawn by medical observation of homes for epileptics is that the habitual use of intoxicating beverages by a mother during gestation is the prime cause of the disease; 12 to 15 per cent of the surviving offspring of alcoholic mothers become epileptic. As Dr Saleeby truly states: 'Parental alcoholism as a true cause of epilepsy in the offspring is now generally recognised.'

'The characteristic mental trait of the child of the inebriate mother is a warped or stunted intelligence accompanied by impulsive, uncontrolled actions.'

Alcohol and feeble mentality

Feeble-mindedness among children is on the increase, and in solving the problem of the feeble-minded experts regard alcohol as the main cause of that deterioration of brain-tissue which lies at the root of the feeble mentality of so many human beings at the present day. For instance, there were in England, Scotland and Wales in 1908, 149,628 feeble-minded persons, apart from certified lunatics. Of 55,000 school children examined in New York, 58 per cent were below the required standard of intelligence; 53 per cent of these children had drinking parents. 'It is my strong conviction that a large percentage of our mentally defective children including idiots, imbeciles and epileptics, are the descendants of drunkards,' states Dr Fleek. Verily 'there is a generation that curseth their father, and does not bless their mother' (Prov. XXX. 11).

These conclusive facts point to imperative action. 'Parenthood,' declares Dr Saleeby, 'must be forbidden to the dipsomaniac, the chronic inebriate, or the drunkard, whether male or female.' More especially must the woman who so disgraces her womanhood as to become a drunkard be denied the prerogative of motherhood. 'Today,' writes the authority quoted above, 'many of the children who make our destiny are born drunk, owing to maternal intoxication during labour.' Moreover, the drunken mother poisons her child after birth, when she nurses it; for it has been proved that alcohol is found in the milk, and thus the unfortunate babe receives alcohol as a food, and is nourished on a rank poison. As the effect of alcohol is greatest upon immature cells it is no matter for wonder that the children of drunkards are stunted, undeveloped, and weakened in all the organs of the body. They are handicapped from conception and at birth. They are imperfectly nourished after birth, first, through the poisonous ingredients in the mother's milk; second, through the insufficiency of the supply. No fallacy is more pernicious than that which supposes the flow of milk is increased through the consumption of alcohol. On the contrary, in the end the supply is lessened; no drunkard is able to nurse her child without supplementing artificial food for her maternal deficiency, and soon the source of the milk is dried up. This inability to suckle is carried on to the second and third generation, and thus explains the constant increase of this inability through inheritance. Another remarkable fact has come to light through investigation of the laws of heredity. 'The rule is, that if the father is a drunkard, the daughter loses her power of suckling', and thus bequeathes her deficiency to her daughter even when both women are temperate or non-drinkers. The women in the upper classes who are unable to nurse their children are the daughters of the three-bottle men of the last century. But the majority of women must recognise that it lies in their own will-power to eschew alcohol in all its forms. If womanhood realised the responsibilities of motherhood there would be no drunken mothers nor drunken fathers, nor miserable diseased offspring.

'Though I have served forty years in the army, and seen every nation worth looking at', declares Surgeon-General Evatt, C.B., 'I have never at any time or place seen womanhood so degraded as it is in "Christian England". We don't respect motherhood. It is supremely sacred. Yet women are to be seen drinking everywhere in your pot-houses. Where is the sacredness of motherhood?' Ah! Where? You may go the length and breadth of India, and among the native women you will see no drunkard. Among the Japanese, the Chinese, the North American Indians, the Maories and the Polynesians generally, drink may disgrace the men, but it is still an inconceivable shame for a woman to be intoxicated.

With the nation that remains sober is the future of the world. Is it possible that the mothers of the great Anglo-Saxon race are allowing the heritage of their children to be jeopardised by a vice that digs deep and fast the graves of its victims?

The economics of drink

The drunken nation, any more than the drunken family, is never rich. However great may be its material wealth, it is poor even to destitution of the factors that constitute true wealth. The people of the United Kingdom in 1916 spent 182,000,000 sterling on alcoholic drinks, or £500,000 a day. That vast expenditure brought no return. It was sheer and absolute waste. It made, however, '124 widows and orphans in England every day, or more than 45,000 per annum'. It destroyed life in the adult, the minor, the infant, and the unborn babe. It ravaged the home and emptied the house, the wardrobe and the larder; it drove into the street the unemployed and the unemployable; it replenished the ranks of the prostitute; it beguiled to destruction, physical and mental, the young man in his strength and the girl in her prime; it filled our prisons, work-houses and lunatic asylums; it ruined the health of thousands, and numbered among its victims an army of lost and despairing souls. Modern civilisation is now on its trial. If it is a drunken civilisation, its doom is fixed. For the people 'have given a boy for a harlot, and sold a girl for wine, that they might drink'. 'Shall I not visit them for these things? saith the Lord. Shall not My soul be avenged on such a nation as this?'

Maria Adelaide Lowndes

Child Assault in England

(n.d.)

Child assault is a terrible crime which would seem at first sight to be rather an atavistic throw-back to a period of uncivilised savagery than an ordinary evil common to uncontrolled human nature. But what can we say when we find it, apparently, increasing as civilisation advances, and becoming if anything more prevalent in England in recent years than formerly?

Something surely is very wrong with our method of dealing with the offence, and with the criminals who perpetrate it.

Mr Justice Greer in his charge to the Leeds Grand Jury in July last, animadverting on the fact that statistics showed crime in that part of the country was increasing, drew special attention to the fact that one class of offence never seemed to diminish, i.e., indecent attacks on young girls, young boys and young women. For his own part he declared that he regretted exceedingly that the only weapon for dealing with such cases given to Judges was sending the accused to prison.

Three grave difficulties stand in the way of reform: (1) the general ignorance of women, at any rate, of the whole subject; (2) the comparative rarity of convictions when cases are brought into Court; and (3) the inadequate sentences quite commonly pronounced on the offender when convicted.

If it came to be understood by the community at large that such crimes were intensely resented by society, and branded the perpetrator for life; that men suspected of such acts were held under police observation, that when charged before the Magistrate a real effort would be made to obtain evidence; and lastly, that if they should be convicted the sentence would be adequate and exemplary; then, indeed, we might hope for comparative safety for our little children, now threatened with such terrible ills and dangers.

In view of the general experience of women engaged in dealing with criminally assaulted children, that the crime is in no wise less prevalent of recent years, some figures supplied by the Home Secretary in reply to a recent question in the House are distinctly disquieting. Mr Briant, MP, recently asked for information regarding the number of prosecutions and of convictions for criminal assaults on girls under 13 during the five years 1912, 1913, 1914, 1920 and 1921 (figures for 1922 not then being available). From the Government's reply we gather that whereas in 1912 the number of prosecutions was 125, with convictions 73; in 1921 the prosecutions undertaken were but 69, with convictions at Assizes 37; and 2 by Summary Jurisdiction.

Why, we must ask, are there fewer prosecutions?

In this article it is proposed to state quite plainly what is meant by the expression 'Child Assault', and also some of its more terrible aspects; for the question can no longer be left unexplored in the darkness that veils evil deeds.

The most horrible forms of this crime are the cases in which it is complicated with incest, and involves the violation (often for a long period) of little girl children – say under the age of 10 – and also of course much younger. A case, indeed, has lately occurred in the North of England of a father who criminally assaulted his baby girl of under one year old, causing her death.

Are Magistrates and Judges beginning to awaken to the horror of these abominable crimes, and to the necessity for sternly suppressing the evil by exemplary punishment?

We doubt it. For though, probably due to the animadversions of Mr Justice Darling, the crime of incest need no longer be tried in camera, there are as yet no signs that when the victim is a little girl any grave attempt is being made to bring down condign punishment upon the head of the criminal who has assaulted her.

Mr Briant, MP for North Lambeth, in his important speech on Child Assault in the House, in July last on the Home Office Vote emphasises this fact:

> My chief grievance is that the Courts of Magistrates who have power to inflict at least six months will not do so, and they impose penalties which would be ridiculous, if they were not tragic in their leniency, for the most horrible offences.

He then went on to instance cases of wholly inadequate punishments that he was cognizant of – adding,

> Few people ever raise their voices for the sake of these children who are being practically murdered, body and soul. These outrages are going on more than people know. Some of the assaults are almost too horrible to relate. I have not exaggerated in anything I have said.

The failure to provide at the public expense any veritable refuge or help for the greater part of these unfortunate little ones thus injured is also a crying scandal. This is said advisedly. When such a case has been tried in Court and *a conviction secured*, the victim of the outrage should be sent by the Judge or Magistrate, as the case may be, to a Certified Home for such luckless children, and there kept, at the charges of the State, for a term of years, being paid for at the rate of about 17s. 6d. a week. Such Houses are inspected periodically by Government officials, and are expected to be kept in a high state of efficiency. The only certified Industrial Home in the Northern Midlands of England is St Winifred's Home, Wolverhampton, worked by the Horbury Sisterhood. The Home takes children from all parts of the country, and yet not more than two or three cases *per annum* are sent there by the Courts. The payment for such children is made in part by the Home Office, and in part comes from the Local Authority of the place to which the child concerned belongs, as provided in the Children's Act. The terrible fact is plain – for this crime Magistrates and Juries will not convict; and innumerable cases are shuffled out of on the plea of 'no evidence': while not infrequently, it is feared, pressure may be brought to bear against commitment by Local Bodies who do not want to be charged with the child's maintenance.

But if the Home Office has no cases to provide for – or so few – it may well be asked what evidence is there that the victims of this crime are comparatively numerous? The plain fact is that the Homes that exist for the treatment and care of such children are wholly inadequate to the need, and are always absolutely full unless the failure of subscriptions should make this impossible. The Mother Superior of the Horbury Sisterhood, who has devoted seven years of her life to the study of this question, and the care of the child victims, is inundated with letters on the subject from all parts of the country. The Home at Wolverhampton is full, but of cases paid for by private generosity or out of money raised with infinite difficulty from the general public. No children are taken in over 13, neither are mental cases received, nor acute cases of syphilis, yet many are turned away for lack of funds; and surely this is a crying shame. Nearly all the work of the Home, including education, is voluntary work, and it can receive about fifty cases, but as much as £400 a year from the outside public is absolutely necessary for keeping the institution going on its present scale. With shame be it said this very modest sum is not forthcoming. In a speech made recently in aid of funds the Bishop of Lichfield said: 'and for this work . . . the whole of the North of England contributes £150!'

There are other certified Homes in the South – St Mary's, Buxted, worked by the Wantage Sisters, St Monica's, Croydon, under the care of the Church Army, and St Faith's Home, Teddington. All may be said to be in continual difficulty for lack of funds, under the increased expenses of the time. In this great country there are four struggling institutions where women give their lives and themselves to the heart-breaking work of trying to mend the young lives evil men destroy and ruin, and through the length and breadth of the land men know of these things, and practically make no money contribution of any sort to stem the evil or bind up the broken lives.

There are four Homes, and I am told there should be fifty; but there is not the money to keep the four out of debt.

A terrible case bearing on this question has recently occurred in Chelsea which secured considerable attention locally. A young girl of 15, small and ill-grown, living with her parents in some Model Buildings, died after giving birth to a child on 21 August 1922. No doctor had been sent for, or any skilled attention secured. It was obvious from enquiries made that the unfortunate little mother had spent a night of agony; and all night her father had refused to go for a doctor. In the morning (Sunday morning) a midwife was fetched; the child was born, and an ambulance conveyed mother and babe to the Infirmary. Here it was found that the poor girl was suffering from a rare and horrible internal complaint: it was too late to do anything for her, and she died on the Monday morning (the baby a week or two later). An inquest was held the following Monday (28 August); here the Chelsea Coroner, with a jury of men only, after taking the deposition of the Infirmary officials, decided that the enquiry must be held *in camera*, and – surely inadvisedly – had the Court cleared. Then for an hour-and-a-half the mother was examined, she maintaining that neither she herself nor her husband had the least idea till the Saturday night that her daughter Gladys was *enceinte*.

The inquest was adjourned for a week; and in the meantime it transpired that the second child, Grace, a little girl of 11 was found to have been criminally assaulted. The adjourned enquiry opened on 4 September, and proceeded *in camera* as before, the child Grace being called and examined for an hour; after her, two aunts and one or two neighbours were called as witnesses, and after them the girls' father was called, and examined at length.

The adjourned inquest having lasted two-and-a-half hours, the jury retired, and after being absent a minute or two returned a verdict of 'death from natural causes', adding they considered the father and mother of the children should be censured, 'we do not accept their evidence as true'.

The parents were then recalled, and the Coroner addressing them said:

> You both of you deliberately and systematically lied in the Courts. The conditions under which you and your family live are horrible in the extreme. It is dreadful to contemplate the way you and your family are associated together in that flat. You, [addressing the man] are to blame. You could have got medical assistance; you had ample opportunity; but that you did not do so because you wished to conceal the matter as long as you possibly could the jury are abundantly satisfied.
>
> *Discharged.*

As is so usual the whole matter was dismissed on the plea of lack of evidence.

In this case, however, the neighbours were scandalised – the true situation was very well understood, and it was in fact well known that the father was the criminal. Public clamour demanded a further inquiry, and the case of the young mother, who would seem to have died from neglect, was taken up by the NSPCC. A warrant was issued for the arrest of the father, which he succeeded in evading for some little time. Presently, however, he was brought before the Magistrate and the case was proceeded with, the depositions taken at the Coroner's inquest having been produced by the police.

'That man will get twenty years,' said the mothers of the Buildings, convinced that the question of the outrages on the children was at last being considered in Court. Nothing of the sort occurred, of course. In fact the Society for Prevention of Cruelty to Children is precluded in London from touching incest cases; they must either be undertaken on the part of the police or at the instigation of the Attorney-General or the public prosecutor. It is a Crown prosecution.

The Chelsea case was finally dismissed by the Magistrate, after being several times adjourned. It transpired in Court that for years past the man had been in and out of prison, chiefly for dishonesty, but that on the other hand the mother had a good record. She seems to have been a hard-working woman, but of weak character and terrified of her husband. The Magistrate, for reasons difficult to understand, appears to have glossed over the case, remarking that neglect of the type alleged 'was one of those matters which in circumstances of poverty often occurred without bad consequences', and adding 'that in those circumstances he would not punish either defendant'. Addressing the man, his Worship added: 'I hope you will feel some sense of responsibility towards your wife, who is a hard-working woman. . . . Go away, and take care of your wife.'

Of his dead daughter and his outraged child of 11 – no word. Thus the father, after weeks on remand at Brixton Prison, was liberated on 1 January 1923.

Five days afterwards he died suddenly. 'Heart failure' was the medical verdict, and the Coroner, reviewing the case, remarked: 'There were serious suspicions with regard to this man concerning his daughter's death. An inquest was held at the time, but there was not sufficient evidence to bring any charge against him except that of neglect.'

But I fully believe evidence might have been secured.

In cases where the evidence is so clear and unmistakable that it is impossible to dismiss the case, there is very little done as a rule to ensure that the way of such transgressors should be hard. Lady Astor, speaking in the debate on the Home Office Vote already referred to, recalled a case tried some years ago in what is now her own constituency of Plymouth.

> A man was brought up for a most horrible and ghastly assault on a little girl of 7, and another man was brought up for stealing. The man for stealing got two years' imprisonment, and the man for the child assault got six weeks: and the Judge remarked "This is the kind of thing that might happen to any man".

'That made an ardent Women's Suffragist of the late Member for the Sutton Division of Plymouth' added Lady Astor.

The Laws of England are not lenient to such evil-doers. The Incest Act, 1908, provides that males criminally and incestually assaulting young girls under 13 are guilty of felony, and liable to a punishment of from five years' imprisonment to penal servitude for life.

Cases of incest, however, are terribly common. Often it is a grandfather who victimises a child. The Sisters at Wolverhampton had a case to deal with where the grandfather had assaulted a little child nightly for three years. She was paid 1d. a night 'not to tell'.

Usually children's mouths are closed by terrible threats of what will happen to them if they say a word. It is not difficult to terrorise little children.

Another form of this evil is the case of those social pests – often old men of 70 or 80 – who bribe little girls with sweets to come to their rooms or some private spot with others, when the whole number are assaulted.

Attention must also be drawn to the fact that it is by no means only in the lowest class that these shocking crimes occur. They occur in all classes: and mothers should bear this in mind. Big brothers home from school or perhaps a school friend will go into the rooms of little sisters; and find their own means of silencing them. There are also terrible stories of lodgers, and the social ruin that has been spread by them in families.

It is pitiable to hear of the condition of many of these poor little children when they reach the care of a Home, more especially if they have gone through the ordeal of the Police Court or the Assize. 'It is often years before they recover,' I am told. And when the outrage upon them has been committed in very tender years, and it is hoped all is forgotten, often as they grow older, and suddenly understand what has been done to them, they pass through a terrible time of agony and horror; feeling in their secret souls that they belong to the outcasts of society and are doomed for life. It should be remembered that the conviction or not of a particular man for such a crime against a young child makes no difference as to the need for after care in all such cases.

One of the Homes mentioned above, that receives children under the age of 10 only, recently read in Committee a notice from the Local Education Authority suggesting that all children in the Home who were normal should be sent to the provided school of the place instead of being educated in the Home. During the discussion that ensued the Medical Attendant of the Institution, who was present, declared that out of the thirty child inmates he doubted if there was one who could be accounted normal, so greatly had they suffered from the treatment to which they had been subjected.

In the meantime what is done in the Courts where such offences are tried to redeem matters? In the first place, as a rule, all women are turned out of the Court, and the unfortunate child stands unsupported and terror-stricken among a number of strange men; for only a very small percentage of our few women police are told off to take statements from little girls who are the victims of these offences. If the case is serious she is subjected to a horrible and terrifying cross-examination by the attorney for the defence, with often enough none to aid or stand by her. At the end of this terrible ordeal – the usual verdict having been secured – the unfortunate little girl, to begin with nerve-wracked and broken, now almost demented, has nowhere to go. Magistrates, more humane than others, may 'recommend' her for a Home, but if not 'committed' there is no public money for her support, and probably no charity available. The criminal meanwhile – the man who is almost a murderer – goes unpunished.

Some little while ago a brave Police Court woman, having been turned out of the Magistrates' Court during the hearing of such a case, petitioned the Home Office for leave to be present at all such trials. She obtained an official warrant later on, and stood by a little child, helping her when cross-examined, soothing her terrors and generally supporting her. A conviction was secured. As Sir A. Steel-Maitland admitted in the House of Commons, reinforcing the appeal made by Viscountess Astor to the Home Secretary in regard to the Women Police: 'There are some kinds of police work which can better be effected by trained women than by any male constable that exists.'

To sum up. These cases must not be heard *in camera*. There must be women in Court. If tried before a Jury there must be some women jurors; and since no Magistrate can give an exemplary punishment they should by rights be taken to a higher Court. This, however, for the moment would seem hopeless of attainment, since it is often impossible to secure a sentence of even six months' imprisonment at present.

Two men coming out from such a trial were overheard saying to a woman who deplored there had been no conviction, 'What nonsense! Men should not be punished for a thing like that. It doesn't harm the child.'

Yet we cannot forget that a terrible verdict has been pronounced on such criminals. One who knew the issues of life has said: 'It were better for such a man that a millstone were tied round his neck and he drowned in the depths of the sea.'

It is difficult to persuade oneself that it is not in pursuance of this idea, '*men should not be punished for these things*', that all over the country the Women Police, who have done such wonders for the protection of young women and little girls, are being reduced in numbers, 'to save expense'. Has great England really come to this, that she cannot spend a few thousand pounds for the safeguarding of her children![1]

But in very truth a new day has dawned, though the sun has not broken through the clouds. In former years we might have said: 'Surely ten righteous men in higher places might arise and remedy these horrors.' They have not arisen. Now we say: 'Ten million women voters can deal with these questions.' As knowledge of the true situation grows, more and more they will stand behind Lady Astor, Mrs Wintringham and their supporters, in the House urging the Home Secretary 'to look into this matter and to act'. If he would act quickly and strongly, he would have the whole of the awakened public conscience behind him.

NOTE

1 In the Police Reports (*Counties and Boroughs of England and Wales*) for 1921 and 1922 one may learn that on 29 September 1920, we had thirty-three Police Women attested as Constables – (i.e., with power of arrest) and ninety-three not attested (133 in all).

On 29 September 1921, thirty-one attested and seventy-four not attested (105). While in addition, during that year there had been 111 not attested Police Women in the Metropolitan Police District, whose appointments had been determined by the Home Secretary.

On 29 September 1922, we find thirty-six attested and fifty-one not attested (eighty-seven), with besides twenty not attested Women Police for the Metropolitan Police District, retained by Mr. Bridgeman in response to protests.

These few women (for 1922, eighty-seven) to be spread about among the sixty Counties and the 125 Boroughs of England and Wales; with in addition, twenty women to work among the millions of London.

(During 1923 these twenty women have been sworn in as members of the force, and given powers of arrest.)

C *Suffrage and Sexuality*

Ursula Roberts

The Cause of Purity and Women's Suffrage

(1912)

It is often asserted – and seriously asserted by people whose opinions carry weight – that Women's Suffrage would not help to do away with prostitution. There are many women who regard the Suffrage movement from an academic point of view, seeing that the refusal to extend the franchise is logically indefensible, but not understanding why any one should make a fuss about the matter and drag in the question of morals. It is primarily to such as these that this pamphlet is addressed.

Some people think that prostitution is necessary: that so long as good women remain good and virile men virile, so long must there exist a class of degraded or 'fallen' women to safeguard the interests of the former and satisfy the needs of the latter. There is nothing to be done with such arguments save to denounce them as utterly false and pernicious. All the authority of modern medical science goes to controvert the old heresy that chastity is physically harmful to men. From the moral, as distinguished from the scientific, point of view it is surely incredible that the exercise of functions which ensure the physical life of the race should involve the destruction of a great part of its life spiritual. It should be unimaginable that any one believing in a God of love, in the Fatherhood of God, and in the Resurrection of the Body, should speak of prostitution as 'a regrettable necessity'. If we believe that man cannot live a natural life without sexual self-indulgence, we cannot believe in the Incarnation: we cannot believe that God became man, and that all Christ's brothers may follow in His steps.

Demand and supply

Other people admit that prostitution should be put a stop to, but deny that legislation can help to solve the question. So long as there is the demand, there will be the supply they say, and 'you can't make people good by Act of Parliament'. Let us consider for a moment the question of demand and supply. Surely it is clear that in this case supply stimulates demand. Not only is there the obvious temptation put in men's way by the solicitation of the streets, but there is the more subtle working of the belief that a fallen woman can't get up again. There must be hundreds of men who will control themselves when the object of their desire is an unspoilt girl, but will visit a brothel with no sense of responsibility, because they regard a prostitute as sunken too low to be capable of sinking lower. Again consider the effect of the mere knowledge that the trade exists. It must seem to put the whole sex-question on a different footing. Indulgence is given the sanction of public acquiescence: society by providing a field ready ploughed invites the sowing of the traditional wild oats.

The assertion that 'you can't make people good by Act of Parliament' is true in a sense. 'It's a choice between compulsory religion and no religion at all,' said Dr Christopher Wordsworth once in urging the advisability of enforced attendance at chapel for undergraduates. 'The distinction is too subtle for my mental grasp' was Connop Thirlwall's wise and witty answer. But any one who considers may see how misleading the current saying is in connection with legislation affecting prostitution. It is largely force of circumstances that makes us what we are, and prevents us from being what we might be. If legislation can affect the circumstances of our lives, it can affect us. We must seek to understand how the majority of prostitutes come to carry on their trade.

The wages of working women

There is a wide-spread notion among sheltered women that prostitutes carry on their trade to satisfy their own lust. Let us see what Charles Booth has to say as the result of many years' searching investigation of social conditions in London:

> The sole aim of prostitution is the satisfaction of male sexual passion without the responsibilities of marriage or anything that can be called social relationship. The female share in

> the matter is strictly professional. The woman's passions are hardly involved at all, she is moved neither by excitement nor by pleasure. She merely seeks her living in the easiest way open to her, or is induced to follow this course of life by the desire for fine clothes and luxuries not otherwise attainable.

Prof. Forel, the great Swiss authority on sexual questions, a man to whom sentimentality is obnoxious, states clearly that in his opinion

> poverty is one of the most powerful auxiliaries of prostitution. . . . Poverty compels the proletariat to live in the most disgusting promiscuity. . . . It urges parents to exploit their children. Among small tradespeople also poverty is an indirect agent of prostitution. In certain occupations which leave the girls free evenings the proprietor only pays his employees an absurdly small salary because they can add to it by prostitution. For this reason many saleswomen, dressmakers, etc., are obliged to content themselves with a minimum wage. When they complain, and specially when they are good looking, they are often given to understand that with their attractive appearance it is very easy for them to increase their income, for many a young man would be glad to 'befriend' them, to say nothing of other insinuations of the same kind.[1]

He also points out that 'waitresses are used as baits in certain taverns', and tells us that about 80 per cent of the prostitutes in Paris have some other occupation. He alludes to the low wages given to women as compared with those given to men, and concludes: 'Is it to be wondered at that they have recourse to prostitution?'[2] The Rev. G. P. Merrick in his 'Work among the Fallen' states that out of 100,000 cases known to him he had not found 100 who did not loathe the life.

The evidence of such diverse men as the three quoted receives abundant corroboration from those responsible for rescue-homes and penitentiaries. Almost all are agreed that the lust which creates the trade is the lust exclusively of men. Why then do women become prostitutes if not to satisfy their own lust? The passage quoted from Prof. Forel suggests that the answer to this question must deal in part with economics. Let us quote some statements of facts showing the rate of women's wages, and the condition of their labour in this country. We are only concerned with women workers who are grossly underpaid, and we may divide these into three classes: (*a*) home-workers, (*b*) workers in factories and workshops, (*c*) shop assistants, clerks, waitresses.

(*a*) Miss Clementina Black in her 'Sweated Industry and the Minimum Wage' classes the first division as the poorest of all. She tells us that match-box making is one of the poorest trades, 2¼d. a gross being the ordinary rate of pay. A typical worker, helped by her four children, earned at this trade from 10d. to a 1s. a day. A young deserted wife is described as trying to support herself and two young children by making shirts at the rate of 1s. 2d. a dozen; she completed the shirts with the exception of sewing on buttons and making button-holes, and succeeded in earning 5s. 8d. a week, finding her own cotton, machine needles, and oil. Another woman was paid 9½d. a dozen.

Paper bags are made at the rate of 3d. to 5d. per thousand. A woman working steadily for eleven or twelve hours a day earns about 5s. a week by covering racket-balls at 2s. per gross. Brush-makers can earn about 6s. by working seventy-two hours a week.

'Ill-health,' Miss Black tells us, 'is the chronic state of the woman home-worker. If she depends upon her own exertions, she will inevitably be ill-fed and ill-clothed. . . . The half-starved apathetic human creature cannot maintain a high output of work.' Thus we see that the more a sweated woman-worker needs good food the less able is she to obtain it.

(*b*) An analysis of pay-sheets showing the wages received in two consecutive weeks by girls employed in a confectionary factory shows an average of slightly over 7s. 6d. a week. The custom of reducing wages by fines and deductions is a very common one, and must be taken into account in considering the question of wages. In a provincial stay-factory the nominal wages varied from 5s. 3d. to 10s. 2½d, but the actual wages were between 3s. 11d. and 8s. 8½d. These deductions are often outrageously mean. One ingenious employer extracted 30s. a week from his workers for cleaning the work-room, and paying the cleaner only 15s. kept the balance. Factories actually exist in which there is a fine of 6d. for washing the hands! In one factory a foreman frequently deducted 1s. or 2s. from a week's wages merely on the ground that the girl who should have received it was 'earning too much'.

(*c*) Deductions also play an important part in the lives of shop-assistants, clerks, and waitresses. The following deductions seem almost incredible, but are quite authentic: £10 from £30, £8 from £28, £23 from £35. Not only must we take into account the actual monetary loss these deductions involve, but also the constant chafing and irritation such persecution must give rise to. Heart-rending as are the lives of sweated home-workers and factory hands, the appalling monotony and narrowness of the daily round of shop-assistants seems almost more pitiful. The home workers or factory-hands may have some human links – half-starved baby or an invalid husband, though they double burdens, may at the same time lighten the woman's load of woe. To the shop-assistant who 'lives in' the voices of humanity must seem well-nigh dumb. They are kept, in the words of a provincial draper, 'to sell people what they don't want'. And what remains a part from this maddening and degrading intercourse with customers? 'Standing in groups, gossiping, fine 2d.' Miss Robinson may work, eat, sleep beside Miss Brown week in week out with about as much natural human interchange of thought and feeling as exists between the double-yoked oxen in the plough.

The life of waitresses is perhaps less desperately monotonous, but it obviously provides more direct temptation to immorality. As we have seen, Prof. Forel speaks of waitresses being used as baits in certain taverns. The finer senses of barmaids in public-houses and station refreshment-rooms must very soon become blunted by enforced endurance of familiarity and coarseness from customers. The average wages of waitresses are reckoned as from 7s. to 14s. a week, less 8d. or 9d. for washing and 1s. 9d. or 1s. 10d. deductions for breakages.

It is clear from this brief résumé that the average woman-worker can barely support herself on her wages. We ought deliberately to picture ourselves what it means to her to clothe, feed, and house her body on 7s. or 8s. a week. Even when she is comparatively well and strong, and has no one dependent or partially dependent upon her, it must mean unceasing self-denial and discomfort – a cup of tea and a bun when others whom she knows are faring sumptuously at restaurants – last summer's faded blouse and shabby skirt when she could have gay dresses for the asking. And if illness comes or loss of employment, what alternatives are there for the unprotected girl save destitution or prostitution?

'Out of a job', 'no hands wanted', no one ready to accept the services she is willing to exchange for a little food and clothing, a little bit of shelter – 'the labour-market is overstocked', they say. But it is always 'market-night in the Haymarket'; there are always purchasers for pretty goods in Piccadilly.

A certain proportion, then, of London's 60,000 prostitutes are driven to the trade through poverty; some directly, i.e. when starvation and prostitution are the only alternatives, more indirectly i.e. when conditions of labour are so bad that the temptation to escape them prevails over the natural shrinking from immorality common to all save a very small proportion of women.

The feeble-minded

Perhaps next in importance to the question of low wages and bad conditions of labour comes the problem of the feeble-minded. The recent report of the Royal Commission on the Care and Control of the Feeble-minded tells us that the existing machinery for dealing with feeble-minded women and girls is hopelessly inadequate. The guardians have no power of detention. Union Infirmary records show case after case of feeble-minded women coming in to be confined of their fourth, fifth, sixth, or even seventh illegitimate child. The Magdalen and Rescue Homes show an average of feeble-minded girls and women varying between 30 and 50 per cent. Feeble-minded girls are peculiarly liable to be seduced. In some cases there is a positive tendency to immorality, in more it is a negative quality that ruins them – they are too feeble to make any resistance to the demands of unprincipled men. Once they are seduced, the downward path is easy.

Depraved homes

A third source from which prostitutes are drawn is that of the depraved homes, in which little girls are violated by their own fathers, step-fathers, or brothers. Records of prosecutions show that these cases are not rare, and experience goes to prove that offences are very much more frequent than are prosecutions for them. Intimidation is often exercised to prevent the poor children from 'letting on', and when discovery is made it is often too late for anything to be done, since recourse to the law must be taken within six months of the offence. Initiated into vice at the age of ten or eleven, or even earlier, it is small wonder that these poor little girls should go from bad to worse till they reach the streets, and finally the Lock Hospital.

The white slave traffic

A fourth source is that of the white slave traffic, that is the organised trade in girls who are forced by entrepreneurs, or procurers, into entering upon a life of vice under the delusion that they are to be given respectable employment. It is impossible to estimate with any degree of accuracy the extent of this hideous traffic, since it is naturally carried on by methods which, so far as possible, ensure secrecy. The secretary of the National Vigilance Association states that no less than 17,000 cases have been dealt with within seven years at either railway-stations or ports by this society alone. Investigations recently carried on in America by Mr Edwin W. Sims, District Attorney at Chicago, give reason to believe that about '65,000 American girls and about 15,000 aliens are being entrapped yearly for the trade'. The procurers get girls into their power by various ingenious tricks. A really attractive girl can be sold for as much as £100, so that it pays to expend time and trouble on her capture. Many apparently innocent advertisements in the daily papers are really white slave traps. Here are two examples chosen at random from among many quoted in the M.A.P. publication 'The White Slave Traffice' (price 6d.):

> Professor 40 years old, with money, wishes to make the acquaintance of a Christian young lady who may be poor, with a view to marriage.
>
> Nursery governess required immediately for London for boy of 4 years old. Must be gentlewoman, good needlewoman, musical, not over 25. Salary £30 all found.

Practically all the theatrical advertisements beginning 'amateurs wanted' are traps, as are many of those for masseuses.

Another method of capture is to enter into casual conversation with any pretty girl who happens to be alone, and to lead her by apparently innocent stages into a position which makes it impossible for her to resist her captor's final demands. Once dishonoured, she is usually bound to him either by the promise of marriage or by the fear of blackmail. It becomes impossible for her to get away, and she finds herself sent abroad and established in a brothel without a chance of communicating with her friends. Here she is kept deeply in debt to the proprietor and is closely watched, never being allowed out of the house without the 'protection' of a man who keeps her within sight to see that she solicits satisfactorily, and does not run away. Since the entrepreneurs do not care about any save quite young girls, and since the average working life of a prostitute is about six years, she probably ends her days in a Lock Hospital before she is thirty, and her place is ready for another victim.

Legislative possibilities

The horrors are told, and the cry goes up 'Something must be done: these shameful deeds must cease.' We must now state the case for remedy by legislation and demonstrate that there is a sense in which people can be 'made good by Act of Parliament', or at least be prevented from becoming bad. We will consider the proposed legislation under five heads, in relation to prostitutes (*a*) who have been impelled into the trade by economic stress, (*b*) who have drifted into it through feeble-mindedness, (*c*) who have been violated as children and have grown up in vicious surroundings, (*d*) who have been forced into the trade as white slaves, (*e*) who have a natural tendency towards vice.

(*a*) This class is the hardest to deal with briefly, since the question really involves a sweeping criticism of the whole existing social system. So long as there is unemployment there will be prostitution. The suggested remedies for unemployment resolve themselves into two, viz., Socialism, and Tariff Reform. We must not discuss these now, but it is quite clear that neither can come about apart from legislation

We may also point out that since the male franchise has been extended wages have risen. This is mainly due to the power which labour, forming itself into trades unions, has over capital when labour is backed by the vote. So far women's trades unions have not been able to accomplish much. Experts assure us that this is to a great extent due to women's lack of political power.

(*b*) This class is best dealt with by reference to the suggestions in the report of the Commission on the Care and Control of the Feeble-minded (1904–1908), which have been adopted by the subsequent Commission on the Poor Law – both majority and minority reports are agreed on this point. Segregation for life is recommended as the only means of preventing feeble-minded girls from doing great harm to the community. It is obvious that sporadic measures taken by voluntary agencies must be inefficient for dealing with this problem, since compulsory detention in private institutions is out of the question.

(*c*) Legislation affecting this class is badly needed. Obviously the restriction of prosecution to within six months of the offence must be abolished. The length of the sentence should not be allowed to depend so much as at present upon the leniency or strictness of individual magistrates or judges. At the last Northampton Assizes in two cases of offences against children, aged 14 and 7 respectively, the sentences were for one month in the former and four months in the latter case. That such cases should be tried by juries exclusively masculine is surely outrageous.

(*d*) So long as the white slave traffic exists, it is worse than absurd to argue that women have no concern with affairs of imperial or international importance. Since this traffic forms a highly complicated network which extends its meshes all over Europe and America, no number of isolated private efforts will effect a remedy. Any scheme dealing with the question must be drawn up not merely on national, but on international lines. Under existing conditions it has been proved possible for an entrepreneur, arrested in Bordeaux and found guilty of having incited minors to debauchery and of falsifying certificates, to be acquitted solely on the ground that his offences were committed not in France but in Switzerland. A woman prosecuted in England for bringing girls from Belgium for immoral purposes was acquitted on the ground that the offence of procuration was not included in the Anglo-Belgian extradition treaty.

It is commonly agreed by disinterested students of the question that state regulation of vice as practised in certain foreign countries is a direct encouragement to the white slave traffic. If the sporadic efforts of individuals can do little to modify the affairs of their own land, it is obvious that they can do still less to affect conditions in foreign countries. What can be done must be done officially through governments.

The question of repatriation is also one to which this assertion applies. It is believed that if men and women of disreputable life are not allowed to reside in foreign countries, exportation for immoral purposes would become unprofitable. For obvious reasons the victim of a procurer seldom leads so hopelessly servile a life in her own country as in a foreign land, and a very great improvement might come about through international action on this question.

Among the legislative measures which have been taken in other countries and might with advantage be put into force in our own, the following may be mentioned:

(1) In Italy medical men have been circularised with a view to obtaining their co-operation in the work of stamping out vice.

(2) In Norway the Minister of Religion has issued a circular to the clergy requesting that young girls preparing for their First Communion should be warned of the dangers they run in seeking employment with strangers abroad. The Scandinavian-American line has had placed on its vessels

women officials to safeguard the interests of possible victims. It is noticeable that these two eminently practical steps have been taken by a country in which women are enfranchised.

(*e*) This is very much the smallest of our five classes. Legislation could probably do little to affect it directly, though it is possible that authority might be given to the Board of Education to arrange for special control of children showing a strongly marked tendency to vice. Such cases are frequently pathological, and action could probably be taken in connexion with the medical inspection of school children. Obviously this would be more effective when the school age is raised. Probably most of these pathological cases are hereditary and a better general standard of morals would affect this class in the next generation.

Reasons for present apathy

We have touched briefly upon certain legislative measures which would affect the circumstances of women's lives. It is, of course, true that none of the proposed measures would materially help the present generation of prostitutes. But the majority of prostitutes working today will have died off within half a dozen years. We could and we must prevent another supply from taking their place. Why have not measures been taken long ago? There are many explanations, hardness, apathy, ignorance, prudery among women: selfishness and more or less conscious acquiescence among men: the system of party politics: and the futility of much that has been done in the name of Christianity.

One can hardly trust oneself to speak of the women who are hard – the women who are bitter, and will not let their hearts ache and their tears flow for those who have sought the ever-open market with their wares. It is want of imagination that keeps them hard. Books may help them. Can a woman read of Rossetti's 'Jenny' and afterwards, when she meets her in the street, pass with cold scornful eyes?

> If but a woman's heart might see
> Such erring heart unerringly
> For once! But that can never be.

It must be: we must prove Rossetti wrong there: we must 'love roses better for her sake'. Yes, even though she seem but

A cipher of men's changeless sum
Of lust past, present, and to come.

Can any woman steel her heart against the sob in Francis Adams' 'One Among so Many'?

O my poor Darling, O my little lost sheep
Of this vast flock that perishes alone
Out in the pitiless desert!

And what is more, can every 'virtuous' woman shut her ears to the sting of bitter reproach in the same poet's 'Edgware Road'? Prostitution of the body for money or position is no less degrading, but rather more so, when the mockery of the 'Church's blessing' professes to hallow it.

It is not only the 'Jennies' who needs must quail before

The pale girl's dumb rebuke,
Whose ill-clad grace and toil-worn look
Proclaim the strength that keeps her weak.

It is only those to whom some knowledge of the miracle of love has been revealed that cannot rest until their part is played in the battle against lust. Perhaps one explanation of the apathy of many sheltered women is the lowness of their own ideal of love. 'Men can't help being lustful, and unless our own daughters are to be sacrificed there must be a class of low women to satisfy men's lust.' Now that the spread of medical knowledge is killing the belief in this old heresy, even the selfish sheltered women must cease to acquiesce in prostitution. It is time that the average woman began to realise such facts as these:

(1) That numbers of married men each year infect their wives and children with venereal disease;
(2) That no disease has such a murderous influence upon offspring as syphilis. It is said to kill 20,000 children annually in France alone;
(3) That 80 per cent of infantile blindness is due to venereal disease.
(4) That 45 per cent of sterile marriages are due to the same cause; and finally
(5) That the breeding-place of all venereal diseases without exception is the social institution called prostitution.

When the knowledge of these facts has penetrated into our homes, women will surely rebel against the loathsome conditions they have tolerated so long. The women who have winked at the evil while it seemed to their interest to do so will rake the evil out when the recognise in it a source of peril to their children and themselves.

Prudery must be laid aside, if this evil is to be raked out. We must make it impossible for a woman to say in the future 'I could not bear my sons to know that I so much as suspect the existence of immorality.' We must make it impossible for boys to get into bad habits simply because their mothers are too ignorant or too prudish to help them. Above all, we must make it impossible for children to be brought up in an atmosphere that encourages the double standard of morals for men and women.

It is impossible to do more here than briefly to allude to the evils of the present Parliamentary methods which are responsible for the deadlock in various branches of social reform. That the grounds for dissatisfaction are not the figments of women's brains is apparent from the admission of so acute an observer as Mr C. F. G. Masterman, M.P. At last year's Church Congress at Cambridge Mr Masterman remarked that a measure to which no one in the House could take exception stood very little chance of exciting enough interest to be carried into law. In other words, governments draft bills less in the interest of the people they represent than with a view to the advancement of their own party interest. It is impossible to believe that women, if granted political power, would tolerate such an outrageous sytem.

'Women will be the last thing civilised by man,' says *The Pilgrim's Scrip*. Man has been so dilatory over the task that woman must take the matter into her own hands and set to work at the civilisation of his sex as well as her own.

NOTES

1 *The Sexual Question*, English Translation by C. F. Marshall, M.D. F.R.C.S., pp. 309f. This book is only supplied to members of the medical and legal professions. It should be mentioned that the author advocates certain measures which are quite incompatible with Christian morality; but this fact does not weaken his witness to the importance of the economic aspect of prostitution. His scientific authority is of the highest.

2 Cf. the case of a tobacconist who, it was recently stated in the Leeds County Court, paid his employee seven shillings a week for ninety-three and a half hours' work, and told the magistrate that he would not regard this as anything remarkable if he knew the ordinary wages in the city. Another tobacconist, when asked if he thought a girl could live on such a wage, answered 'Of course not, but look at the chances she gets in our business.' (*The Common Cause*, 2 Feb. 1911).

Lucy Re-Bartlett

from
Sex and Sanctity

(1912)

II
Militancy: its place in our century

(This essay though written in March 1912, is given here unaltered, for the increasing gravity of militancy together with the mutilation of the White Slave Traffic Bill seem only to call the more urgently for the interpretation it attempts.)

In judging the recent action of the militant branch of the women's suffrage movement many people have failed to grasp its true significance through seeing it as action having effect upon the vote alone and judging of its value by its immediate efficacy. 'Madness' has been amongst the kinder of the judgments expressed, and judging by the standard of immediate utility, the word is perhaps not out of place. But the deeper significance of this 'madness' and its effect not only as manifested in the suffrage movement but as shown in many other lines of action today, is something which the majority of people have quite failed to grasp.

It represents the new spirit of a new age, appearing with all the crudity with which new things do appear – battling with terrible difficulties, and through these, as through its own immaturity, of necessity for the moment failing, but no more to be stamped out by failure than any other power which humanity slowly, through the centuries, has elaborated.

The enormous power of these women militants to suffer and to sacrifice themselves for an impersonal Cause is the one thing which thoughtful people at this moment should be finding worthy of consideration – all that this means should be the one reflection – all that it has ever meant in history. To go no further back than the last half century, was it not this spirit alone which worked out that marvel of modern times – the freedom of Italy? The parallel is not out of place, for none who have studied the war of Italian Unity can see in it mere military achievement: it was the soul of a people which rose up, and across many mistakes, and many failures, conquered finally every obstacle in the face of a marvelling and largely hostile Europe. '*But these were men*,' some may respond, '*and this was patriotism!*' True, but it is something akin to patriotism – the love of a 'new country' which their hearts foreshadow to them – which is stirring in many women today. And as to being 'women', there are moments of great tension in which human beings lose for a time the limitations of sex and become simply souls, with the common force of souls.

This is what is not generally understood in regard to woman's militancy today – that whatever immature expressions it may sometimes take, it is yet a spiritual uprising, and for that reason cannot be suppressed. It marks all over the world the awakening of a new soul in woman, and could it be suppressed today, it would but rise stronger tomorrow, for it forms part of a new social conscience which all the progress of the times is serving to augment.

There are three factors which lie behind the new militancy of woman, and they are wider *knowledge*, wider *power*, and wider *love*. In days gone by, most women of the better classes did not know of many of the social cancers which a wider education has revealed to them today: they did not know, and so they did not suffer, and did not burn. But today many know, and for those who together with knowledge have attained to the power of independence and to a love which reaches beyond ties purely personal, it has become an impossibility to sit still. And could we wish this otherwise? For women who do not *know*, today, as in the past, there is excuse, but can we wish that the women of any country should remain indifferent when the first time perhaps the horrors of the White Slave Traffic are revealed to them, the ruin of little children, and the total inadequacy of the law and general indifference of the legislator in face of these and other horrors? Is it any wonder if some women feel called by God Himself to take their part in legislation? Called by their womanhood and by their motherhood – and that even should they *prefer* the purely private life, to many, once these things have broken on them, it can seem only a terrible selfishness, while such wrongs continue unredressed? Just as for man there are certain elementary duties of manhood, such as honour and courage, which come ahead of any special ties, so for woman there are the claims of pity, protection, and purity, which are inborn with her womanhood and which she *may* not silence if she is to be worthy of the name of woman. 'Unwomanly' is a word very often applied to the suffragettes, but perhaps it belongs more truly to those women who can listen coldly to tales of wrong and suffering, and still more to those who can permit themselves a jibe at sister women who, whatever their errors, at least are struggling and suffering in a noble cause, while they, the critics, too often are doing nothing.

The *spirit* of militancy is something which requires to be understood and reverenced, whatever reserves society may permit itself to make regarding certain forms of expression chosen. And if this spirit were once comprehended, it would at the same time be seen how totally useless, and worse than useless, are all the coercive measures brought against it. The 'madness' which has led to window-breaking would be seen as having many other expressions, far further reaching, and totally beyond the power of police or magistrate to deal with.

We have said that it forms part of a new conscience in women, and this conscience is living and moving in many women, who either by reason of the country in which they dwell, or because of some particular quality in their own nature, are often not moved to make any special struggle for the vote. But the same new perceptions and new passion are working in them as are making their sisters in England go to prison for it. They too feel linked by their womanhood to every suffering woman, and every injured child, and as they look around upon the great mass of men who seem to them *indifferent*, there is growing up in the hearts of some of these women a great sense of *distance*. This is a thing far more tremendous than window-breaking, which society will do well to realise. Again it is the soul of woman speaking, and this time in a way which no 'law' can oppose. It is moved by some, as an objection to giving the vote to women, that it will cause dissension in the home, through differing opinions. There is no fair difference of opinion which can have power to rouse anything like the feeling which is rising in some women now as they feel the awfulness of certain wrongs, the indifference of men, and their own helplessness to bring any remedy. It is the sense of *helplessness*, more than any other thing, which brings the touch of 'madness' to many women. By some women it cannot be accepted. Not all are moved to window-breaking, but some are moved to things far deeper and more tremendous. In the hearts of many women today is rising a cry somewhat like this: 'If I cannot *help*, at least I will not *acquiesce. . . . I will know no man, and bear no child, until this apathy be broken through – these wrongs be righted!*' There are women both married and single who with differing degrees of consciousness, with varying intensity, are feeling thus, and acting thus today. It is the 'silent strike', and it is going on all over the world. In a recent article in the *Hibbert Journal*, the increasing celibacy of women was noted and bitterly commented on. It was attributed to degeneracy and dislike to motherhood. Instead, if society could only understand, it is a newly awakened conscience, and a far deeper motherhood, which in most cases lie behind it. It is the new soul in woman crying out to a new soul in man – crying out to him to be her soul's mate as well as her body's mate – to fight shoulder to shoulder with her against the evil and the cruelty in the world – telling him that till he can do this she cannot feel he *is* her mate, and cannot feel God's permission to their union.

This is the essence of woman's militancy today, and it will be seen that 'window-breaking' is only as one wave breaking from a great sea: that particular wave – with difficulty – may perhaps be stemmed, but there can be no stemming of the sea behind.

Yet these things do not represent sex antagonism in any fundamental way, nor, as some mistakenly imagine, the weakening of sex attraction. They represent only a 'strike' – a temporary protest – an appeal. They constitute woman's revolt, not against man, but against certain false social conditions which her soul has grown too large to let her any longer tolerate. Her revolt, far from being a menace to sexual love, is the first step towards a sexual love far higher – all that is needed is that man should understand, and should build the new conditions in which this higher love and higher woman will have room to breathe.

Right down at the bottom there is something fundamentally true in the idea that woman should always be gentle, just as there is in the idea that marriage should be always indissoluble, and that man should be the guiding factor in creation. They are all things deeply and fundamentally true, but in an absolute, ultimate, and ideal way. They imply a society in which marriage will be always true and holy, in which the spiritual power in man will be always equal to his physical force, above all, a society in which weakness will never be tortured, and strength never called upon to spring to its defence. This is the society of the future, and when it dawns it will perhaps be seen that the type of woman today most militant is then the type most gentle. But it will also be seen that her militancy in this age of evil was one of the forces which brought the new order in. And in judging then of the women who lived in the terrible transition period which is our present time, posterity will not ask regarding them, '*Were they always wise – were they always balanced,*' but rather, '*Did they belong to the old order or the new – did they feel the wider love struggling for expression, and help its utterance, or were they amongst the blind who lagged behind?*' That is all that posterity will care to question. In those days the 'sword of Christ' will be better understood, and pity will be felt for the weak woman hands which first tried to lift it, and all errors will rouse only reverence, not blame. Whatever the path these militants took – whatever mistakes they made – if they were channels for the new and wider love, posterity will say, '*God bless them*'. Something of their loneliness will be measured – something of their pain – and the 'militancy' which today, the world over, is their crown of thorns, may then be seen as their crown of glory.

III
Forces behind the vote

Beneath the great struggle for woman's suffrage, with all that is revealing of the most noble and ignoble, there are few who realise what we may call the underlying situation, or few, at least, who realise it in all its magnitude and inevitability. The public roughly seems to be divided between people who deny to the struggle any sexual significance at all, and those who, seeing this significance, attribute it to sexual morbidity and hysteria, while the truth, in fact, lies in neither of these extremes.

The situation with which we are face to face represents indeed a sex war of a certain kind, but not a war, as some would have us think, arising from a morbidity which must be stamped out. It is a war which signifies vitality, not decadence – which is simply the outward sign and inevitable accompaniment of the transition of men and women from a state which we must call 'spiritual childhood' to a better state of spiritual adulthood. Of the three great stages of human development, the instinctual, the mental, and the spiritual, humanity, in large numbers, is now struggling in the second stage. And this of necessity means complications, for the uncritical simplicity of instinct has been left behind, and the peace and wisdom of the spirit not yet gained.

If this interpretation of our times could even provisionally, as a theory, be accepted, many puzzling phenomena would find their explanation, and whilst continuing to be momentary problems to be dealt with, would lose their alarming and seemingly unnatural aspect. The increase of feminine celibacy for instance – a phenomenon which alarms some people so greatly – finds in great part its explanation here, while all the conflicting elements in the suffrage struggle find fully and completely their *raison d'être*.

The divergencies so noticeable in the suffrage field between constitutional and militant suffragists on one side, and again between them and their 'anti' opponents on the other, are ascribable to the fact that however fine all these types may be when seen at their best, they are yet types belonging always to distinctly different periods. The anti-suffragist, however cultured, represents with her ideals the purely affectional woman of the past, the constitutional suffragist, in most cases, is the average intellectual woman of the present, and the militant – in imperfect form – is the inspirational woman of the future. Behind each type is breathing the spirit of a totally different age, and this it is which makes their divergencies so inevitable, and yet at the same time makes each type an indispensable element in the working out of a struggle which is to give us ultimately, yes, a new order of woman, but an order which must include all that is best of the past and present, as well as the new powers of the future.

This is what the suffrage struggle means to those who look behind it – it appears just as a great exercise ground on which men and women of the past, the present, and the future are showing themselves clearly – a stage on which those masculine and feminine forces which have got to blend in so many deeper things than politics, are coming into the open, learning to know each other as they have not yet done, and through harmony and discord alike, acquiring at least the possibility of passing onward to a fuller life.

This fuller life, which depends upon a truer co-operation between the sexes, finds its symbolic expression in the vote which facilitates co-operation by affirming equality. It is indeed only a tiny beginning of the fuller life, but it is a true beginning. More and more, as an intimate sense of their equality develops in the minds of both men and women, the one-sidedness and immaturity of many social institutions will give place to completeness and maturity.

But this can only be if the sense of equal value which the vote should symbolise is intimately felt and continually maintained. The mental slavery of woman is a far more subtle thing, and far more difficult to change, than her external subjection. To teach woman to think in terms of womanhood, clearly, bravely, pursuing her own feminine lights without imitation or subjection, is a thing far harder than to set her politically or economically free. The mental suggestion of centuries is still behind her, and the average woman of today frees herself at one moment only to fall captive the next. Yet the ability of woman to reach to this power of independent and essentially feminine thought is the only thing which can give real value to feminine suffrage. And it is here, we submit, that the militant – that element in the suffrage field at present least appreciated – is showing her indispensable value.

She is showing it precisely by that intensity of feeling which, because of the momentary expressions it is finding, is bringing down on her such blame. Few have paused to note that these particular expressions will pass, and the power they indicate alone remain. And it is this power, drawn from intensity, which alone can safely 'bring the ship to port'. By that expression we do not merely mean obtain the vote, but safeguard this stage of evolution, and bring forth the new woman in all her completeness of feeling, thought, and inspiration. So much do we see this intensity as the central thing that we do not hesitate to say that if women had not shown themselves in large numbers as possessing it, it would not seem to us to matter very much whether they got the vote or not, because, without such intensity, there would be no sufficient power behind it when gained. Something would be obtained, of course, but not that deeply significant something which belongs to the introduction of a new spirit – that new spirit which only the 'new woman', complete and strong, can bring.

The suffragists have told us, both the constitutional party and the militants alike, that it is towards social purity and the protection of woman and child life that their forces will be principally turned when the vote is gained. But we all know what forces of resistance will oppose them when they attack any one of these questions. They are battles, these, which will never be fully gained save in a changed or changing social atmosphere. And it is here that passion, the special passion of the 'new woman', counts. These battles will be partly won in private life, and partly in Parliament, but always and only with that force behind them which is passion, be it quietly or otherwise expressed. To bring any lesser force into this arena is about as futile as it would be to bring a penny squirt against a conflagration. These questions are not talked out – they are bled out, wrung out, lived out. New laws will help, and the vote will help, but only with this force behind them. And where do we find this force today? Only in the militant – the militant as known through the Women's Social and Political Union, or through that still larger body of more private militants whom the world does not always know, but who are largely influencing and changing the social atmosphere of our time. The average woman has a different place – she means the reassurance of society, and her good judgment and manifold usefulness are no small forces. But alone she cannot suffice – she has not the driving force which this special moment asks for. The moderation which is her special characteristic is of inestimable value in times of peace, but moderation alone never worked out a revolution, nor swung humanity across a transition crisis.

And now let us look at the militant for a moment in her private relation – we continue with our study of her in preference to the constitutional, or anti-suffragist, because both those types are already well understood and need no comment: the 'militant' is the mysterious figure, yet a figure which should not remain mysterious, for in comprehension of this type of woman lies truly the key to the situation – not merely the suffrage situation but also that tumultuous moment of male and female evolution which lies behind it.

The 'militant' is often accused of great bitterness towards man, and few people seem to have realised that a period of this kind must needs be passed through before the old relations between men and women can be set aside and the new and nobler ones established. Woman cannot truly struggle for the new order until she hates the old. Just as we said that passion was needed in the public field, so is it needed here. Mere new conceptions are not enough: when love is in question, woman will not have strength for being true to her new principles unless together with her longing for the higher things which she is struggling towards, there burns in her also a hatred for those things of the past which she is seeking to leave behind. Then only will she have strength to be faithful, and being faithful, will mount rapidly from strength to strength until she reaches the point where bitterness can be left behind, because the things against which it was levelled lie also far behind. This is the new woman 'arrived'. For her the transition stage is finished, and from out the calm of the new life attained she will show forth all that gentleness which has been the crowning grace of woman in the past, and which together with a new strength and wider vision will assuredly crown equally the woman of the future. But the gentlest women who attain this point, if they look back and tell the truth will nearly all require to say, '*There was a point where had I not been bitter, I doubt – if sufficiently – I had been brave!*'

Bitterness is only a temporary thing, but it must be recognised as having its place in the transition period, and more patience must be brought to dealing with it. Adolescence is frequently ungraceful, but we do not blame the girl of fourteen because she has lost the charm of childhood, and not yet reached the greater charm of her full womanhood. We wait and help her grow. Let us try to meet the spiritual development of woman with something of the same patience and comprehension, even if it have to take the temporary expression of celibacy in many women. Let us recognise that they may be offering their highest service to society in this celibacy – that this form of protest may be the only thing in many cases which can call out the 'new man', as well as give birth to the 'new woman'. There are many factors behind celibacy, and it is so large a subject that it requires a separate treatment. But it should be noted here that it is at least intimately connected with the *Sturm und Drang* period which humanity is at present passing through, and must be met with patience.

And in conclusion there is one aspect of the woman's movement, apparent throughout the whole moevement, but especially amongst the militants, to which we should wish to draw especial notice. We allude to the new and wonderful *solidarity* which is springing up amongst women of the new type all over the world. There is no need to point out how lacking women have been in this quality in the past – it is unfortunately a well-known stain, and has often won for woman the well-deserved scorn of man. And still today the old-fashioned woman will frequently 'give away' her sisters – even the so-called 'good' woman will join in an ungenerous judgment, especially if it mean putting herself in line with male opinion. In the 'new' woman alone, whatever her faults, this meanness is never found. She loves instinctively her sister women, known and unknown, and stands by them. And is not this alone enough to make us recognise her as a new creation, and open our hearts to her, and bless her? There is no other thing which could mark equally woman's new condition – her passage from slavery to freedom – from smallness to greatness – from darkness to light. And the new love is man's gain as much as woman's, for until women can fully and passionately love her sister woman, she cannot properly love man. A strange saying this may seem to many, but some men and women will know it true. And this new love which we say is springing up all over the world, where has it been so clearly shown as amongst the condemned and derided suffragettes? Again and again they tell us why they go to prison – or women's greatest sufferings, and greatest wrongs. But not for their individual wrongs, for many of them belong to the happy and protected levels of society. It is the suffering of others which inspires them – the suffering of collective womanhood – in many cases of unknown womanhood. These women have put in practice very literally and simply the words of the great Apostle, '*Bear ye one another's burdens, and so fulfil the law of Christ.*' And just because we think some of their actions mistaken, we are not letting ourselves recognise this great force which we are dealing with – we are letting ourselves criticise, when we should be humbly asking for light to see. The times are strange, and many things are hard of understanding. But let us try to understand at least. For some who have so tried, the glimmering of the dawn is very clear, and it is under the inspiration of that light that they say to others, 'Look ye too behind the shadows of the moment, and catch the vision of the coming day'.

IV
Feminine celibacy: its meaning today

Feminine celibacy and its increase is a question which is engaging the attention of a considerable number of people today, yet amidst all that is written and spoken in regard to it, the deepest causes remain generally undefined. We hear a good deal about unequal population, and economical difficulties, but those deepest internal causes which are resident in the changing nature of woman herself, are either not set forth at all, or are set forth falsely. It is our intention therefore to limit ourselves entirely in this essay to the discussion of these latter causes – the causes which we believe will be chiefly responsible for the maintenance and increase of woman's celibacy in the future unless a wider comprehension can be forthcoming.

For many reasons may it be said that the women who today decline marriage offer a much greater problem than those to whom the chance of it does not come. For one thing because we know that there are already many plans for opening up new careers to women in the colonies, and were the purely external cause of inequality of numbers all that lay behind feminine celibacy in England at this moment, the solution of the difficulty, in great part at least, would already be appearing along those lines. It is pretty well known that a girl stands an excellent chance of marrying if she goes to Canada, and we may fairly argue that if a larger number of the single women of England were really set on marrying, a larger number would be seizing this opportunity – amongst women already engaged in earning their living, and therefore accustomed to buffeting with the world, such a venture would require no great temerity. But emigrants of this type so far are few, and we may conclude from this that the wish for marriage amongst our so-called 'surplus' women is at least no burning desire. So much may be said for even those celibate women of England to whom marriage in the Home isle does not offer itself. And that want of desire is really the principal factor with which we have to deal is still more clearly shown when we consider the ever-increasing number of women to whom the chance does come, and who decline it, or those again to whom no actual proposal perhaps may come, but whose attitude of mind and choice of life constitute what we may call an initial refusal. This last class of women is very numerous, and we may profitably commence our study with them.

They have of course their earliest origin in the education of the day, which even when it does not go beyond the High School is yet training girls to think with a clearness never even approached in the female education of the past. It may be said that this is an external cause and could be changed. But we question in what way. Many middle-class parents are obliged to train their girls to earn their living, and this means of necessity the High School, and even in many cases the University. There was only one way of preserving the old-fashioned, uncritical woman, and that lay in not developing her power of thought. But education has entered into the necessities of the time – the very State compels its commencement, and the struggle for existence ensures its furtherence. And apart from the education which is definitely imparted, there is that which is in the air. If we could imagine a father withholding his daughter from ordinary High School instruction, privately or otherwise imparted, it would still be impossible for him to keep her as ignorant as was the woman of fifty years ago. There would always be the chance play, the chance book, the chance speech of a friend. He would require to segregate her altogether to keep her from imbibing the quickened mental atmosphere of the times. If education belongs in one sense to external things, it yet belongs to those which cannot fundamentally be changed, because it has become also part of the atmosphere of the time and, in that sense, belongs to the inner and directing things – it may be modified, but it can no longer be eliminated.

And since the case stands thus, it seems so foolish to be resenting and regarding as an unnatural thing that new critical spirit in woman which is an inevitable result of her wider education. What if the bright High School girl of eighteen does look about her and say that marriage today is 'not good enough', and decide for college with subsequent independence? Her mode of expression may be immature as are her years, but her attitude holds nothing of decadence. For if she thus sets aside the largest things in life, she only does so, be it noted, because of the very imperfect form in which they offer themselves, and this holds the seeds of vitality.

The difficulty arises through the fact that we are not educating our boys and girls at this moment in such a way as to make their agreement easy. In boys' schools the old idea of a profound inequality of sex still continues – they are not growing up with any idea of the equal dignity of women, their equal intelligence, or the need for new standards of moral conduct in themselves. In girls' schools, on the other hand, the new spirit is beginning to breathe strongly – along with the new development of brain is going also a great development of the moral life – woman's value, woman's independence, woman's dignity, are all things which the modern school girl is beginning to feel strongly. There is enthusiasm often for the mistresses, and mighty enthusiasm for those older scholars who go on to Girton or Newnham and do brilliant things. It is with her whole personality quickened with this new moral and mental life – this sense of new posibilities – that the High School girl leaves her school today and faces society. And there she meets generally only the average modern man, brought up on the old ideas. Is it any wonder that the cleverest, and the brightest, and the strongest of these girls do not find him 'good enough', and that they turn their faces college-wards, and freedom-wards?

This is the state of the case in regard to a large number of women who choose the single life today, and it is this position amongst other things, we would indicate in passing, which makes so mistaken all continued resistance to feminine suffrage, For the vote in its deepest significance is an educational factor, and the deepest problem with which Parliament is face to face is not one of broken windows, but one of discordant education, and, in consequence, of quietly, steadily growing, feminine discontent. Parliament of course may withold the vote from women if it pleases, may keep the marriage and divorce laws of the country as they are, and through these and many other factors may continue to teach to the male population of the country that the sexes are not equal in value, and that woman is subordinate to man. But the trouble is that the modern woman will no longer assimilate the doctrine. And thus more and more, while conditions continue as they are, we shall have the finest women in the country declining marriage, with all the loss to the country which that means. And it is society which is responsible, be it noted – society, which from Parliament downwards is not training up its men to meet its women.

It is often said of women of this type that they are very selfish, and that mere vanity – the thirst for a wider individual life – is making them neglect their highest social duties. But it is difficult to understand how true development of the individual can be in conflict with social interests. Surely in the deepest sense there can be no social progress which does not include individual progress, and vice versa. We are told that at a lower point in evolution it is only the instinct of self-preservation which preserves the species. If this is selfishness, as of course it is, it is yet a selfishness which the world has needed. May it not be that the mental and moral life of woman today has need of something of the same fierce instinct of self-preservation if it is to be preserved to do its ultimate work in society, and that the women who feel this new life stirring in them are being only true and faithful in not bowing to conditions which would crush it? The new life is not stirring in all women, nor nearly all – there are plenty of the old type left for carrying on the existing order until a better order can be born. But if we wish that this better order *shall* be born, must we not be content to accept with blessing more than blame the women who demand it, wait for it, and work for it? There is a discontent, let us remember, which is holy discontent, and which no society can afford to be without.

Yet discontent with external conditions, such as unfair laws, or the attitude of the average man, is not the only nor the deepest force which is driving woman into celibacy today. This is the force which is working in the type which we may call the 'mental woman', and inasmuch as her new mentality has been bestowed upon her by society, we would repeat that it is particularly foolish on the part of society to fight with the obvious fruits of its own work: the power of criticism has been roused in woman, and this criticism can now only be allayed by the removal of its chief causes. Yet if these causes, social and political, were removed tomorrow, it would only be the 'mental woman' who could respond immediately to the change. That would already be a great gain, and it surely behoves society to work towards it. Yet we point out that there would still remain a category of women not to be affected by these changes, or at least not directly or immediately – women whose celibacy has a deeper origin, and one entitled to an even deeper respect.

It is not only the form, but also the spirit of society which is passing through a time of upheaval just now, and just as the 'mental women' of whom we have been speaking are connected with the changes in form – just as their celibacy, springing largely from false forms, is for the thoughtful person a continual protest and call for better forms – so is there another type of woman whose protest runs along the lines of the spirit – whose whole energy is running out towards the changing and uplifting of that.

To understand the celibacy of women of this type it is necessary that we have a clear idea of just how great is this change in spirit which is seeking to work itself out. It is nothing less than the change from bondage to freedom, from strife to peace, and from peace to power. And in many other social relationships besides those of sex, do we find the struggle for this change of spirit going on today. It is fighting itself out between class and class, and between nation and nation. Never have strikes been more terrible, nor war more imminent. And for some the moment spells only anarchy, violence, and egoism, whilst for others much at least of this upheaval points to the breaking-up of apathy, and the influx of new life. But by all alike, whatever the interpretation given, the moment is admitted to be one of great changes and great strain – it is recognised that a new spirit is working in the air, which for better or for worse must take its course. Now is it strange that this new spirit which is producing revolution in the outer world, should be working also in the inner – should be taking up its abode in the soul of woman, and there also, for better or for worse, should be requiring to work itself out to its conclusion?

Put crudely, it is more breathing room which humanity is fighting for today. This makes the war of nations, and the war of class. In the inmost soul of woman, it means the struggle between sense and spirit. For so soon as she reaches to any depth of insight, woman recognises that her chief battle-ground lies here – that laws of men at best can only aid her, and it is nature's laws which have decreed her subjection, and will maintain it, until she is mistress of herself. These large and fundamental facts of life the spiritual woman grasps very early on her spiritual pilgrimage – grasps them very often intuitively, before her mind has been able to present them to her clearly. And this it is which gives us the second class of celibate – the young girl who living in the social world will yet not go beyond friendship with men – who hates sentiment, and draws back from the first touch of love-making. Yet who puzzles people often, because they recognise that she is not the least masculine, nor the least cold, and apparently is not turning aside towards another life, like her more intellectual sisters. Unknown to her, and unknown to those who surround her, they are the wings of liberty – true spiritual liberty – which are beginning to faintly agitate in the soul of this type of girl. And all uncomprehended – through that most difficult period of early girlhood when nothing almost is comprehended – this force is great enough to keep her single, even often across much loneliness, and opposition, and pain.

It is the soul struggling for its liberty with the same blind desperation with which man has often struggled for it in the outer world: struggling as a drowning person might struggle to keep his head above the water – struggling almost with the instinct of the animal – that instinct blind, yet so unerring. Is the thing so hard to understand? It is simply the struggle for existence – that struggle which all humanity has waged – lifted to the spiritual plane. It is the soul here which is crying out for room to breathe, but just as all humanity has cried out in the physical world.

When this type of girl marries – and she does sometimes – there is always tragedy. And then society shakes its head, and says, '*There are women who should not marry*', and those who want to be scientific, talk about 'incompleteness'. But nobody sees that the greatest incompleteness lies with those who did not understand, and the blame with those who, often against her will, have driven this girl into marriage.

She was a little bit of the new soul of the world – the new soul which is struggling to break through and bring us better things. And if those in authority had but left her to grow strong – to bring to maturity the new life struggling in her – she might have married later in such way as would have brought blessing both to herself and the man she married, and anyway, married or single, she would have brought her special note and value to the world. But because society has little imagination, little insight, and little reverence, it all too often crushes out this type of woman – it marries her where marriage is not right, and where there should have been great value, places tragedy.

Tragedy always, without exception. For, however much humanity may ignore them, or fail to understand them, the laws which are the most unfailing in this working are the laws of the spiritual life. And it is spiritual law which decides that once the wings of liberty have begun to beat within a soul, they will not cease their beating till there is death or victory.

But what does this mean in the life of man and woman? Not the ending of love, surely, but only the introduction of a wider love – the beating free from the lower levels where the dominion of sense brings bondage, into the higher levels where the freedom of the spirit brings health to the life entire. When this point is reached, it is the most restive girl who will make the completest wife. But the pilgrimage from the old love to the new is not a short nor easy one. We are told that the kingdom of heaven must be taken with 'violence', and in no field is that more true than in the love of man and woman.

There must always be a period of violence when the love which is called human, but is so often less than human, is cut suffering and bleeding away. When because of those beating wings in her soul, woman fights desperately with herself and with man: fights her own vanity, and man's appeal to it – fights smallness, and domination, and all passion which is just the blood, because so soon as any of those things touch her, she feels the new wings within her droop and cease to beat. And their beating has become as very life – life which must be defended even at the cost of human life, if need be. So is the new soul of the world speaking within the new woman. And she stands away from man until he understands. But the life she is struggling to defend is new life for him as much as for her, and therefore does love grow only higher and tenderer through all the fierceness, and far from separating them, it is across the fire of that fierceness that the souls of men and women first learn to meet.

The woman of this type – not she who is crushed by life, but she who resists its crushing – recalls the legend of Brunhilde surrounded by her wall of flames. If she be gained by trickery or violence, the fate of her husband is likely to be that of Gunther, but if the true Siegfried can present himself, able to pass through the flames – then there is Brunhilde on the other side.

It may be said that there are few women of this type in the world today, but whosoever believes that is much in error. All over the world, in ever-increasing number, they are springing up. They are not always recognised, but that is another matter. Let those who count them few, remember this – that like only shows itself to like, and no secrets are so jealously guarded as the secrets of the soul. The 'warrior maid' is with us in the world today, and greatly is she needed, and great will be the gain when she is better understood. When she is not understood, she sometimes dies, and sometimes turns to window breaking, or all that stands for, but when she is comprehended, she becomes the guardian of the greatest treasures of the race.

The day has passed in which the purely gentle woman was she who could do most for man – at the point where humanity stands today, when a new love is seeking to break through and join class with class, and nation with nation, and soul with soul, it is a larger, braver, stronger woman whom the world requires. One who can help man to tear the veils from his own soul, and reach that inmost spirit which alone knows no privilege of sex, or class, or race, and knowing none, and claiming none, alone can bind the world in unity. Here, in this inmost sanctuary of truth, the wings of liberty may cease their anxious beating and fold themselves in peace – here 'warrier maid' and 'warrior man' may join their lives, and celibacy pass to union. But not before – not for those souls in whom the new love has stirred – on whom has dawned the vision of the wider life. And this is the deepest meaning of woman's celibacy today – we do not say the msot common, but the deepest meaning. It is an offering to a new life, dimly felt, and passionately reached towards – an offering sometimes conscious, sometimes just instinctive, blind, and desperate. But always, in women of this type, an *offering*. Something so far from egoism – so far from coldness. Something that in proportion as it draws down the spiritual forces towards which it reaches, is *maternity*, in all its agony, and all its glory – a force which is linked with the 'mystery of mercy', and the love which is redemption. But that is a separate subject, calling for separate treatment. Enough here if we have but shown the place of these single women among the servants of the world, and won for them, in the hearts of some few at least, a truer comprehension and a deeper sympathy.

Christabel Pankhurst

from

The Great Scourge and How to End It

(1913)

The end of a conspiracy

Forty of the most prominent doctors recently signed a manifesto demanding the appointment of a Royal Commission to inquire into the subject of veneral disease – the disease, that is to say, which is caused by sexual vice.

The Government have since appointed a Royal Commission, but out of fifteen of its members, only three are women. Nor has representation been given to the Woman's Movement in its more modern aspect. It is an intolerable insult that women should be in a minority on such a Commission. They ought to have at least equal representation with men. The secret nature of this inquiry is also to be condemned.

The doctors point out that tuberculosis, insanity, scarlet fever, typhoid, cancer, and other diseases are being fought by State and private enterprise, but, they continue 'in all this organised effort there is one noteworthy omission: there has always been a conspiracy of silence as regards venereal disease'.

The Suffragettes are, according to the judges, not unacquainted with conspiracy of one sort, but we would point out that it is long since they refused to be a party to the conspiracy of silence regarding venereal disease. For a long time they have been clamouring for something to be done to stamp out this frightful plague.

The time has come, say the doctors, when it is a national duty to face facts and to bring them prominently to the notice of the public. They state as follows the terrible problem with which the public has to deal:

> The worst form of venereal disease is highly contagious, and

> dire in its effects. It claims its victims not only from those who have themselves to blame for contracting it. It is one of those diseases that may be transmitted from parent to child, so that the offspring of a sufferer is born with the virus actually in its tissues, to cause, it may be, hideous deformity, or blindness, or deafness, or idiocy, ending often in premature, though not untimely death.

Truth to tell, further inquiry is hardly necessary, though a Royal Commission ought to be the means of enlightening women as to the nature and extent of this terrible evil. Men already know a great deal, and doctors know most of all. No Royal Commission is needed to discover the cause of venereal disease. Its cause is perfectly well known. As one writer has well expressed it,

> the breeding-place of all venereal diseases without exception is in the social institution called prostitution, or sexual promiscuity; in the debasement and degradation of what should be the highest of physical powers – those involved in the act of generation.

The doctors urge that both the cure and prevention of venereal disease shall be considered. Women will lay stress upon prevention, because even if cure were possible in the physical sense, it is impossible in the moral sense. A community which tolerates prostitution is a community which is morally diseased. The man prostitute (for why should we give this name only to the woman partner in immorality?) has his soul infected as well as his body.

We repeat that where these terrible diseases are concerned prevention is better than cure. It is not only better than cure, but it is the only cure, for whether these diseases are curable even in the narrowest sense of the term is very doubtful, and even when cured they can be contracted again. Everybody admits that one attack of gonorrhœa does not give immunity against subsequent attacks, and the idea that one attack of syphilis gives immunity from other attacks is not very seriously entertained by experts. As one authority says: 'The reason why so few cases of reinfection are seen is because so few cases are really cured, they are syphilitic and cannot be reinfected.'

As the hope of curing venereal diseases is so illusory, prevention is obviously the true policy. No individual can hope to avoid these diseases except by abstaining from immoral sexual intercourse, and similarly a nation cannot remain unaffected so long as prostitution exists.

Therefore prostitution must go! At this shrieks of protest will be raised. We shall hear the usual balderdash about 'human nature' and 'injury to man's health'. Human nature is a very wide term, and it covers a multitude of sins and vices which are not on that account any the more to be tolerated. It is human nature to rob and to kill. Cannibalism itself is in the nature of certain human beings. Robbing, killing, and cannibalism are nevertheless all forbidden, and the people who venture to let go their 'human nature' in these directions are comparatively few!

Why is human nature to have full scope only in the one direction of sexual vice? The answer to that question is that men have got all the power in the State, and therefore make not only the laws of the State, but also its morality.

According to man-made morality, a woman who is immoral is a 'fallen' woman and is unfit for respectable society, while an immoral man is simply obeying the dictates of his human nature, and is not even to be regarded as immoral. According to man-made law, a wife who is even once unfaithful to her husband has done him an injury which entitles him to divorce her. She can raise no plea of 'human nature' in her defence. On the other hand, a man who consorts with prostitutes, and does this over and over again throughout his married life, has according to man-made law, been acting only in accordance with human nature, and nobody can punish him for that.

One is forced to the conclusion, if one accepts men's account of themselves, that women's human nature is something very much cleaner, stronger, and higher than the human nature of men. But Suffragists, at any rate, hope that this is not really true. They have more faith in men than men have in themselves, and they believe that a man can live as pure and moral a life as a woman can. The woman's ideal is to keep herself untouched until she finds her real mate. Let that be the man's ideal, too!

Men's health can be preserved only at the price of prostitution – such is the ridiculous and wicked theory advanced by many men and some doctors. The truth is, that prostitution is the greatest of all dangers to the health of men. In the first place there is the risk amounting to certainty of infection by the terrible disease we are considering. Not only so, but prostitution involves a futile and wasteful expenditure of men's energy – energy which they greatly need to enable them to hold their own in science, art, athletics, industry, and commerce.

And what of women's health? No longer will they accept the theory that their health and dignity are to be sacrificed to the health of the other sex. Merely to state the proposition that women should suffer physically and spiritually for the benefit of men is to show its falsity. Nature certainly never intended so monstrous a thing! Indeed, it is very plain to anyone with the smallest intelligence that the ruin of women means the ultimate ruin of men.

It did not need the doctors' manifesto to warn the more instructed amongst women that prostitution and the diseases caused by it are a menace to themselves and their children. But vast numbers of women are still without this knowledge. Innocent wives are infected by their husbands. They suffer torment; their health is ruined; their power to become mothers is destroyed, or else they become the mothers of diseased, crippled, blind, or insane children. But they are not told the reason of all this. Their doctor and their husband keep them in ignorance, so that they cannot even protect themselves from future danger.

Healthy girls enter into marriage without the smallest idea of the risk they are incurring. Nobody tells them, as Dr John W. Barrett tells us in his article in the *Bedrock*, the scientific review, that 'we know, from very careful insurance medical records, that the great majority of men put themselves in the way of infection before marriage'.

Those who read this statement will have their minds prepared to receive the further appalling statement, widely accepted by medical authorities, that 75 per cent to 80 per cent of men have before marriage been infected with one form of venereal disease. Some of these men may seem to be cured, but we have seen how little cure in this connection means. Very sad cases are on record of men who marry when apparently cured, and yet infect their wife. It is therefore hardly too much to say that out of every four men there is only one who can marry without risk to his bride. Such facts are terrible indeed, and the sooner they are grasped the better for the individual and for the race.

Even after marriage, danger arises over and over again unless the husband abstains from immoral acts. In future chapters we shall show more fully what venereal disease means to a woman.

We may point out in passing that prostitution and its evils are largely a medical question, and must be dealt with by medical men. Prison doctors administer medicine which keeps under control the 'human nature' of men prisoners who have no natural self-control. Apart from that, to instruct men in sex hygiene is the doctors' primary duty.

It would indeed be an extrordinary thing if the medical profession, which has discovered means of regulating every other bodily function, should be unable to tell men how to regulate the sex function, and to prevent that excessive sex activity which, as they themselves admit, is fatal to the health of the race.

We look to the medical profession, therefore, to come to the rescue of men whose willpower fails them; to come to the rescue of wives whose life will otherwise be blighted by disease; to come to the rescue of children yet unborn, who, unless help is forthcoming, will enter into a cruel inheritance. A high privilege it will be to rid humanity of a most awful scourge.

A woman's question

The Prime Minister has been heard eloquently discussing the prevention of tuberculosis. A most desirable thing, but it is even more desirable that the Prime Minister shall talk about another and even more terrible form of disease, and that he shall try to prevent it – that he shall strike at the cause of sexual disease.

The cause of sexual disease is the subjection of women. Therefore to destroy the one we must destroy the other. Viewed in the light of that fact, Mr Asquith's opposition to votes for women is seen to be an overwhelming public danger.

As we have said, sexual disease – or venereal disease, as it is commonly called – is more to be dreaded than even tuberculosis. It must first be remembered that the whole truth about the effects, direct and indirect, of venereal disease is not yet known. New discoveries are being made every day, and each discovery reveals fresh reason for the belief that venereal disease is humanity's greatest enemy.

As everybody knows, the more serious forms of venereal disease are two, namely, syphilis and gonorrhœa. One authority says that among the causes of death syphilis comes next to tuberculosis in frequency. This statement must be supplemented by others before we can realise the full gravity of the matter.

Firstly, owing to the campaign of silence now breaking down, medical certificates for the cause of death are often so arranged as to conceal the part played by syphilis, and therefore the available statistics do not fully represent the facts.

Secondly, the syphilitic character of various ailments formerly supposed to be non-syphilitic is now being recognised. Various other ailments are coming under suspicion, and this suspicion that they are syphilitic is only too likely to be established by further medical research.

Thirdly, syphilis, by diminishing the power of resistance of the organism, renders the effect of all illnesses and accidents more serious.

There is also this to be noted in drawing the comparison between tuberculosis and syphilis. Syphilis is a powerful predisposing cause to tuberculosis. Moreover, there is also a form of consumption which is definitely syphilitic. We may also add that syphilis is now recognised as being a strong predisposing cause to cancer.

Even in the present imperfect state of knowledge, it is safe to say that syphilis, which is one only of the venereal diseases, ousts tuberculosis as the most potent single cause of physical degeneracy and of morality.

For women the question of venereal disease has a special and a tragic interest. It strikes at them in their own person and through their children. A woman infected by syphilis not only suffers humiliation and illness which may eventually take the most revolting form, but is in danger of becoming the mother of deformed, diseased, or idiot children. Why are such children born into the world? women have often cried in despair. The answer is – Syphilis! Miscarriage is frequently caused by the same disease. Indeed nothing, as one doctor says, is so murderous to the offspring as syphilis.

Rather different, though hardly less terrible where women are concerned, is the effect of gonorrhœa. In future chapters we deal more fully with this matter. Here we may say that gonorrhœa is one of the most prevalent of all diseases. It is acquired before marriage by 75 per cent or 80 per cent of men, and it is very often contracted after marriage by such men as are not entirely faithful to their wives. To men the disease gives comparatively little trouble, and in the old days the doctors made very light of it.

But to women, owing to their physiological structure, it is one of the gravest of all diseases. A very large number of married women are infected by their husbands with gonorrhœa. The common result is sterility, which prevents the birth of any child, or may prevent the birth of more than one child. Race Suicide!

Generally speaking, the female ailments which are urged by some ignoble men as a reason against the enfranchisement of women are not due to natural weakness, but – to gonorrhœa. Women – and there are so many of them – who 'have never been well since they married' are victims of gonorrhœa.

An enormous percentage of the operations upon women are necessitated by this disease, which in many cases so affects the organs of maternity as to necessitate their complete removal. Race Suicide again.

These are awful truths, so awful that the woman's instinct is to keep them hidden, until she realises that only by making these truths known can this appalling state of affairs be brought to an end.

Women have suffered too much from the conspiracy of silence to allow that conspiracy to last one minute longer. It has been an established and admitted rule in the medical profession to keep a wife in ignorance of the fact that she has become the victim of venereal disease. A bride struck down by illness with a few days, or within a few weeks, of her wedding day is told by her husband and the doctor that she is suffering from appendicitis, and under cover of this lie her sex organs are removed without her knowledge. Women whose husbands contract syphilis, and are in turn infected, are kept in ignorance of this, and are thus unable to protect themselves and to do their duty by the future.

Here we have the woman question in perhaps its most urgent and acute form. Have the Anti-Suffragist women any idea of what the wrongs of women really are? We beg them to realise that so long as the subjection of women endures and is confirmed by law and custom, so long will the race be injured and degraded, and women be victimised.

Sexual disease, we say again, is due to the subjection of women. It is due, in other words, to the doctrine that woman is sex and beyond that nothing. Sometimes this doctrine is dressed up in the saying that women are mothers and beyond that nothing. What a man who says that really means is that women are created primarily for the sex gratification of men, and secondarily, for the bearing of children if he happens to want them, but of no more children than he wants.

As the result of this belief the relation between man and woman has centred in the physical. What is more, the relation between man and woman has been that of an owner and his property – of a master and his slave – not the relation of two equals.

From that evil has sprung another. The man is not satisfied to be in relation with only one slave; he must be in relation with many. That is to say, sex promiscuity has arisen, and from that has in its turn come disease.

And so at the beginning of this twentieth century in civilised Britain we have the doctors breaking through the secrecies and traditions of long years, and sounding the note of alarm. This canker of venereal disease is eating away the vitals of the nation, and the only cure is Votes for Women, which is to say the recognition of the freedom and human equality of women.

The effect of women's enfranchisement will, where this question of redeeming the race is concerned, be manifold. There are three sets of people mainly responsible for dealing with the problem –

the ordinary man, the ordinary woman, and the medical profession. The medical profession has until now viewed the question of venereal disease chiefly from the standpoint of the man. As woman's influence increases, her interests and the interests of her children – in a word, the interests of the race – begin to take their due place in medical consideration. This process will not be complete until the equality of women is recognised and enacted by the law. Then we shall have doctors taking the sound, balanced view that the moral and physical health of the race transcends their 'obligation' to foolish individuals who, for the sake of indulgences of which they themselves are ashamed, would wreck the lives of themselves, their wife, and their children. We shall have doctors applying themselves to the task of helping men, if need be by medicinal means, to live as befits a highly-evolved and self-respecting human being.

The outcome of enfranchisement will be to make women hate more than anything else in the world the very thought of selling themselves into slavery as under the conditions of the present day so many of them do sell themselves. The weapon of the vote will enable them to break down existing barriers to honest livelihood.

Upon men the effect of women's enfranchisement will be to teach them that women are their human equals, and not the subhuman species that so many men now think them; not slaves to be bought, soiled, and degraded and then cast away.

We know to what bodily and spiritual corruption the subjection of woman has brought humanity. Let us now see to what cleanness and nobility we can arrive through her emancipation!

How to cure the great pestilence

The re-education of men upon sexual matters is one of the most urgent needs of the day. At present their minds are chokeful of ignorant and unclean superstition as to their own sex nature, and they entertain beliefs on this question which are directly contrary to medical opinion, and produce the most deplorable results so far as themselves, women, and the race are concerned. Although doctors affirm that a pure and continent life is never the cause of disease, whereas immorality is the greatest of all foes to health, still the opposite theory is maintained by millions of men.

It is because of men's ignorance and superstition that prostitution is so widely thought to be inevitable. Immoral intercourse with prostitutes men are pleased to term 'the exercise of their natural functions' and now that a determined crusade is being waged against prostitution, those who wage that crusade are accused of defying Nature. Nature, indeed! As though Nature had not decreed a punishment for sexual immorality such as she imposes in respect of no other sin.

The horrible disease against which doctors are crying out at the present day is the direct outcome of prostitution, which must henceforward be classed with the other unnatural vices.

What every woman believes, who is not diseased or else morally corrupted by acute poverty on the one hand or excessive luxury and irresponsiblity on the other, is this: sexual intercourse where there exists no bond of love and spiritual sympathy is beneath human dignity. That such intercourse is forbidden by Nature herself, and more strictly forbidden and more harshly punished than any other sin, we have already said. Until men in general accept the views on the sex question held by all normal women, and until they live as cleanly as normal women do, the race will be poisoned, as it is today, by foul disease.

Very reluctant are men to receive and act upon this truth. Always they want to sin and escape the consequences. To persist in sexual immorality and to remain free from sexual disease is their impossible ideal. Even now, when the health and sanity of our race are at stake, men are trifling with a great peril, and are pretending that immorality can be made safe.

In the first place, they proclaim that they have found at last the cure for which they have been seeking throughout the centuries. A cure for sexual disease, which is of all diseases the most incurable! – as though Nature had not willed that there should be no way of escape from this scourge except one, and that one way the way of purity. This boasted new cure is called Salvarsan, and men are speaking of this supposed remedy as though its discovery were a licence to them to go and sin in safety.

But what is the truth of the matter? This cure is by no means proved to be a cure. The doctors are disagreeing about it, and with the best will in the world to believe that Salvarsan will cure syphilis, they cannot shut their eyes to the very ominous facts which manifest themselves in connection with the use of this remedy. Quite recently an inquest was held in London upon a man of forty-two, who died after an injection of Salvarsan. Dr Willcox, the expert in poisons, who was called to give evidence, expressed the opinion that death was due to delayed poisoning caused by the arsenic in injection. But a little while ago, he said, a woman died in a similar way. A French medical expert, M.Hallopeau, in a treatise on the eradication of syphilis, says:

> Salvarsan is not without serious drawbacks. In the first place, its efficacy is far from being absolute. In a number of cases, which vary according to the statistics from one-tenth to a quarter, the disease is not cured, and at the end of a few months new symptoms appear. In the second place, the remedy is not harmless when administered, for one has seen up to the present a large number of cases of death admittedly due to its action, and this figure must necessarily be smaller than the number of deaths that actually occur, for these intimate dramas have only two witnesses – the patient and the doctor, and if the patient disappears it is so much to the doctor's interest to be silent that he must almost necessarily succumb to this temptation.

Dr Marshall, surgeon to the British Skin Hospital, at a conference held some months ago, refused to admit that the curative power of Salvarsan has been proved, because, as he said,

> In such a disease as syphilis the value of a new drug cannot be estimated till it has been tried for at least ten years. The chief tests of the efficacy of such a drug are its powers in preventing tertiary or parasyphilitic manifestations and the transmission of disease to the offspring. This remedy appears to be liable to cause severe toxic effects, sometimes ending fatally. No doubt many of the deaths after Salvarsan were due to faulty technique and like causes, but a certain number are difficult to explain, except by arsenical poisoning.

These opinions concerning Salvarsan are entertained by many other medical authorities; even the discoverer of Salvarsan, Dr Ehrlich, now claims no more for it than that it is 'a valuable adjunct to treatment'. It is obvious, even to the lay mind, that a remedy whose advocates allege that it can swiftly destroy one of the most virulent and prolonged of maladies, must be itself a dangerous substance – a veritable two-edged sword. In fact we are brought back again to the obvious truth that the only certain cure of sexual disease is prevention.

The next method by which men hope to secure immunity from the consequences of ill-doing is that of the State regulation and recognition of vice. Some would disguise this system by calling it by another name. But one man, at any rate, has had the courage of his convictions. He is Major French, of the Royal Army Medical Corps. Whether or not as a representative of the Government is as yet unascertained, he read a paper before the International Medical Congress. He recommends that the State should assume 'the effectual control of openly-practised prostitution by the localisation of irreclaimable women into certain areas or streets'. These women would be periodically inspected, perhaps once or twice a week, in order to see whether they were diseased, and if diseased they would be isolated and treated, and then men would again begin the task of making them diseased.

Anticipating the objection that the maintenance and medical treatment of these women victims of immorality would involve a very heavy charge upon the public funds, Major French makes the extraordinary and mendacious statement that prolonged treatment is only necessary in the case of syphilis, and that one or two months' adequate treatment and isolation would be sufficient in the case of gonorrhœa. Considering that persons apparently cured of gonorrhœa have three or four years later been known to infect another healthy person, the dangerous character of Major French's false statement will be seen.

There is, according to Major French's scheme, to be no compulsory medical inspection of men, because, he says,

> men infected with venereal disease are not so dangerous as women, because a woman practising prostitution usually associates with numerous men, and a man could not and does not associate with a like number of women.

We maintain that, on the contrary, a diseased man is far more dangerous than a diseased prostitute, because every man is free to abstain, and knowing the dangers involved he is a fool if he does not abstain, from intercourse with a prostitute, whereas the man who is diseased can, and in innumerable cases, does, communicate his disease to his unsuspecting wife and to his children.

The plea for State regulation of vice is, according to Major French, based on 'the cardinal fact that prostitution has always existed, and unfortunately must continue to do so for all time'. What this means, put into other words, is that men will always sacrifice their own self-respect, and the health of their wife and family, on the altar of immorality. We think better of men than this, provided that the necessary work of education and reform is done amongst them. Major French must really speak for himself, and not for other men!

It is contended that since the system of regulated vice was established in connection with the Indian Army the percentage of the cases of syphilis in that army has been reduced. Major French in saying this ignores the fact that of late years those at the head of the Indian Army have enjoined upon the soldiers the possibility and the necessity, from the health point of view, of a moral life.

Thus Lord Kitchener issued a memorandum to every soldier, in which he said:

> It is necessary that those who are serving their country in India should exert to the utmost those powers of self-restraint with which every man is provided, in order that he may exercise a proper control over his appetites.

Lord Kitchener further declared 'that every man can by self-control restrain the indulgence of those imprudent and reckless impulses that so often lead men astray'. Sir George White and Lord Wolseley have issued statements to soldiers on the same lines. The soldiers who become infected by disease are punished by loss of promotion, forfeiture of first-class pay, and in other ways, and this has obviously a salutary effect.

It is to be noticed, too, that a decline in venereal disease has also taken place in the Home Army, although there is no State regulation of vice where the Home Army is concerned.

Another point to be noticed is that, in spite of the regulation of vice in Berlin, a high medical authority is of the opinion that in that city every man who reaches the age of thirty has, on an average, had gonorrhœa twice, and every fourth or fifth man has had syphilis! State regulation of vice has been tried in many countries, and always it has failed – its failure being now almost universally admitted by medical men.

But it is not the opinion of medical men or the opinion of women which will necessarily prevail, if things are left to take their course, and there is danger that an attempt may be made, under cover of what will be called 'notification of disease', to establish some form of State regulation of vice and State control of women of a certain class.

Against any such system women will fight to the very death. No woman-slavery of that kind can be tolerated at this time of day. If men venture to re-establish in this country a system according to which certain women will be segregated, controlled, and medically examined for the purposes of vice, that will mean the establishment of a sex war. It will mean that women in general, not only for the sake of the slave women but for their own sake, will regard men as contemptible and degraded beings.

Even though, by the degradation of a slave class of women, men could keep their bodies clean, they could not keep their minds clean, and the modern woman, emancipated as she already is spiritually, and as she soon will be politically, will have nothing to do with men who are foul in mind.

The great pestilence, this sexual disease which is ravaging the community, makes a problem that has got to be solved. And now that we all know what is wrong, none of us can rest until it is put right. But the quackery of regulated vice must be put aside once and for all. Also, while medical treatment will, and ought to be, fully available to those diseased, there can be no reliance upon remedies as a substitute for clean living.

The real cure of the great plague is a twofold one – Votes for Women, which will give to women more self-reliance and a stronger economic position, and chastity for men.

The dangers of marriage

Women have always known that marriage, viewed as a spiritual union, is not without its risks; that either on the man's part or the woman's part love may fail, or that the clash of temperament or opinion may threaten happiness. Hence the old saying that marriage is a lottery.

But what women have not known is that marriage as a physical union is (apart from the natural risk of childbirth, which also they foresee) a matter of appalling danger to women.

The danger of marriage is due to the low moral standard and the immoral conduct of men. Men before marriage, and often while they are married, contract sexual disease from prostitutes and give this disease to their wives.

'The infection of pure women in marriage is, says Dr Prince Morrow, 'the crowning infamy of our social life.' He says further:

> Statistics show that the majority of men who marry have contracted disease, and that many are the bearers of contagion to the women they marry. We witness the effects in the women who suffer ill-health, sterility, mutilation of their bodies, and permanent invalidism. Society's only solicitude is that they suffer in silence. In addition, many of them are compelled to suffer the sight of their babies blinded at birth, children aborted or if they survive, compelled to bear in their frail bodies the stigmata of degeneration and disease which are the heritage of the prostitute. . . . No one can deny that these facts, the saddest facts of human experience, are of common occurrence, and they will continue so long as society shuts its eyes to the existence of this danger to the family, and from a false sense of prudery or a fastidious nicety refuses to be enlightened.

There we have a clear statement, and if anything, an *under*-statement, of the risks attendent upon marriage.

What women must realise is that sexual disease communicated to them by their husbands is the cause of the special ailments and the poor health by which so many women are afflicted. Women are not naturally invalids, as they have been taught to believe. They are invalids because they are the victims of the sexual diseases known as syphilis and gonorrhœa.

Let every woman not yet married remember that the vast majority of men contract sexual disease in one of its forms before they are married. Let every woman learn that to cure a man of such disease is long and difficult, and strictly speaking impossible, since no doctor can give a guarantee that his patient is cured, and will not immediately or in years to come, infect his wife.

The unmarried woman, whereas now she is well and strong, may within one day of her marriage lose her health for ever. This is a hard saying, but it is true, and women have a right to the protection that knowledge gives.

Never again must young women enter into marriage blindfolded. From now onwards they must be warned of the fact that marriage is intensely dangerous, until such time as men's moral standards are completely changed and they become as chaste and clean-living as women.

A clear statement of the case is given by Dr Prince Morrow, when he says:

> The conditions created by the marriage relation render the wife a helpless and unresisting victim. The *vinculum matrimonii* is a chain which binds and fetters the woman completely, making her the passive recipient of the germs of any sexual disease her husband may harbour. On her wedding night she may, and often does, receive unsuspectingly the poison of a disease which may seriously affect her health and kill her children or, by extinguishing her capacity for conception, may sweep away all the most cherished hopes and aspirations of married life. She is an innocent in every sense of the word. She is incapable of foreseeing, powerless to prevent, this injury. She often pays with her life for her blind confidence in the man who ignorantly or carelessly passes over to her a disease which he has received from a prostitute. The victims are for the most part young and virtuous women – the idolised daughters, the very flower of womankind.

It is not only the men notoriously and obviously immoral who are dangerous as husbands. As Dr Morrow says:

> Who are responsible for the introduction of venereal diseases into marriage and the consequent wreckage of the lives of innocent wives and children? As a rule, men who have presented a fair exterior of regular and correct living – often the men of good business and social position – the men who, indulging in what they regard as the harmless dissipation of 'sowing their wild oats' have entrapped the gonococci or the germs of syphilis. These men, believing themselves cured it may be, sometimes even with the sanction of the physician, marry innocent women, and implant in them the seeds of disease destined to bear such fearful fruit.

In previous articles it has been shown that an overwhelming majority of men put themselves in the way of infection before marriage by having intercourse with prostitutes, and that 80 per cent of these men become diseased. These facts give warning to women that the chances are strongly against the man who offers himself to them in marriage being healthy.

The frequency with which married women are infected by sexual disease is very great. Noeggerath, the great authority, stated that three out of five married women are infected by gonorrhœa.

Writing on Gonorrhœa and Puerperal Fever Tausig says that 'every pregnant woman should be examined with a view to detecting a latent gonorrhœa'.

A great many men claim that before marriage they are cured of the sexual disease they have contracted, but this, as we have said, is more than they can prove and more than any doctor can certify. Dominant characteristics of the sexual diseases are the length of their duration, and their tendency to become chronic, and to recur years after every symptom seems to have disappeared.

As Marshall, a great authority on the question, says: 'The duty of the medical man ends after pointing out to his patient the possible eventualites in case of his marriage.'

The point vitally important to women to bear in mind is that unless their husbands are completely chaste and faithful to them after marriage, this same danger that they themselves will be infected arises.

'Unfortunately,' as Dr Prince Morrow says, 'in many cases it is the unfaithful husband and father who receives the poison from a prostitute in an extra-conjugal adventure, carries it home, and distributes it to his family.'

We have in the past referred in general terms to the effects produced by gonorrhoea and syphilis respectively, and now we will address ourselves to this matter in more detail.

Syphilis is the prime cause of race degeneration. Insanity, statisticians declare, is on the increase. The cause of that is syphilis. Nerve trouble is also on the increase, we are told – the rush of modern life, telephones, and motor cars being, as people fancy, the reason of it. The true cause again is syphilis.

This poison of syphilis working in the race and being over and over again reintroduced is producing results that are the despair of doctors and sociologists.

The definition of syphilis as given by Marshall is, that it is 'a contagious disease, chronic in evolution, intermittent in manifestations, and indefinite in duration, caused by a specific microbe'.

Syphilis is hereditary and can be transmitted to the offspring, being, as Marshall expresses it, 'the hereditary disease *par excellence*'. Syphilis is not so prevalent as gonorrhœa, which is contracted by 80 per cent of men, but complete statistics are unavailable, and it is possible that as many as 20 per cent contract it. This ailment being fiercely contagious, a syphilitic husband almost certainly infects his wife.

The disease passes through three stages – primary, secondary, and tertiary. The aim of a doctor is to prevent the disease reaching the tertiary stage. As the appearance of tertiary symptoms is sometimes delayed for many years he can have no assurance that he has been successful.

It used to be thought that syphilis was contagious only in the primary and secondary stages, but the latest opinion is that it is contagious even in its tertiary stage. Certainly it can be communicated to the offspring in the tertiary stage, and what may happen is this, that an expectant mother is infected by her unborn child, who, having inherited syphilis from its father, in turn infects its mother. Many syphilitic children fall vitims to their disease before birth. If they survive birth then they are a source of contagion to nurse and to mother.

In the tertiary stages of syphilis any part of the body may be affected – nose, lips, tongue, throat, lungs, joints, digestive organs, heart, sex organs, eyes, and ears. Above all the brain, spinal cord, and nervous system are liable to be affected. Inherited syphilis causes mental deficiency, idiocy, malformations of all kinds, and other diseased conditions.

That syphilis causes loathsome skin disease is well known. Sometimes it manifests itself in the form of ulcers resembling lupus, but more rapidly destructive in their effect. Terrible disfigurement of the face, and especially of the nose, may be caused by syphilis.

Syphilis is an important cause of anæmia, as it acts on the blood by diminishing the number and power of the red blood corpuscles, by diminishing the proportion of hæmoglobin, and by increasing the number of the white corpuscles.

Syphilis is also a very important cause of heart disease. Says Marshall:

> Syphilitic disease of the heart is more common than is generally supposed; in fact, syphilis must be regarded as the chief factor in heart disease, apart from rheumatism. It may be insidious in onset and remain latent a considerable time without giving rise to symptoms, and then cause sudden death in persons apparently in the prime of life. True Angina pectoris must in most cases be due to syphilis, since this is the most frequent cause of the disease of the coronary arteries and aorta.

'Probably no disease is more productive of arterial degeneration than syphilis,' says Mott. The veins and the glands are particularly subject to damage by syphilis.

Syphilis sometimes produces trouble resembling gastric ulcer and disorders of the stomach. Professor Fournier regards inherited syphilis as likely to constitute a favourable soil for the development of appendicitis.

There are syphilitic forms of pneumonia and pleurisy. That syphilis is a predisposing cause to tuberculosis is now admitted.

The sex organs are naturally very subject to attack by syphilis, and much suffering is endured by women on this account. Syphilis is also the chief cause of miscarriage. Its effect in destroying and deforming the next generation is particularly great.

Syphilis is now known to be the cause of Bright's disease, diabetes, hysteria, eye trouble, producing blindness. It is also recognised as a predisposing cause of cancer. 'If the inclusion of sarcoma and carcinoma among the parasyphilitic affections seems to be transgressing the limits of pathological knowledge,' says Marshall, 'we must admit that no other satisfactory explanation of the origin of malignant tumours has yet been brought forward.'

'Syphilis,' says Fournier, 'is a veritable poison to the nervous system.' It is a cause of paralysis, neuralgia, neuritis.

'One of the principal causes of insanity is syphilis,' says Marshall. Epilepsy and idiocy are referable to the same cause.

These consequences are not only suffered by the persons who wantonly contract syphilis in the course of immoral living. They are suffered by innocent wives, and as the Bible tells us, the sins of the fathers are visited in the form of syphilitic maladies upon their children and their children's children.

In a future article we shall have more to say as to the hereditary aspect of this question, but we may here quote the opinion of Marshall that the generative effects of syphilis are frequently transmitted to the third generation, and possibly further, only to die out with eventual sterility.

Thus, apart from the women infected in marriage, there are numbers of women who have inherited from their forbears the terrible legacy of suffering – and there are men who also suffer, though they have learned so little by it that they seek in immoral intercourse new infection, which they in their turn transmit to generations yet to come.

The medical profession is constantly discovering more about syphilis, and every new discovery teaches them to dread it more as one of the worst enemies of the human race.

The knowledge we already have, as summed up in the facts given above, bears out the saying of a doctor who affirms that syphilis is the principal cause of death occurring before the natural term, and that 'If syphilis and gonorrhœa were eliminated, you would have, from the medical point of view, almost a new world to deal with.'

Syphilis and gonorrhœa can be eliminated in two ways. One is that men shall lead chaste lives. If they refuse to do this, then the only other way in which syphilis and gonorrhœa can be exterminated is by exterminating the race itself.

What women think

For generations women have been very silent. but they have thought the more, and the time has come to put their thoughts into words.

It is now the turn of men who have hitherto done all the talking to listen to what women have to say about life and its problems.

In a world peopled with men and women, the question of the relationship between the sexes is naturally one which occupies a large place in the minds of women as well as of men.

One of the thoughts of women which has now come to the point of expression is – that prostitution must go! They will be told, they *are* told, that such a thing is impossible. But in answer to that they say again, with the utmost firmness – prostitution must go.

They are assured that in the past attempts have been made over and over again to get rid of prostitution, and that such attempts have failed, and always will fail, so long as the world lasts.

Women have a very simple answer to that argument, and it is:'You have never tried to abolish prostituion, and so, of course, you have not succeeded.'

Certainly, efforts have been made to cover up all outward trace of the existence of this loathsome thing, but the real cure for it has never been applied. Beneath all the surface appearance of attacking prostitution, men have cherished the belief that prostitution is necessary, and that immorality and incontinence are legitimate for them.

The true cure for prostitution consists in this – the strengthening of women, and the education of men.

To strengthen women means, in the first place, to fill them with a higher sense of their own importance as the transmitters of life. Nature, in giving to women the chief share in continuing the race, has singled them out for special honour. It is certainly not the less developed and less powerful sex to whom the great task of maternity has been entrusted.

Their capacity for maternity is, therefore, an evidence of woman's vitality and special human worth. If only for this reason, women must feel a special pride in being women. They must, and they do, condemn every law and custom which belittles and condemns to social and political inferiority the mother sex to which they belong.

In short, the disfranchisement of women is an insult to motherhood, which can no longer be tolerated. Prostitution is to be condemned on the same grounds. This is so, not only because prostitution makes slaves and outcasts of the women slaves used for purposes of vice, and degrades their high sex function, but also because the further effect of prostitution is to poison men's idea of the sex-relationship, even where all the other women are concerned.

And again, as we have so often pointed out, in prostitution is bred the sexual disease which is communicated to wives, whose health and power of maternity are in consequence injured or destroyed. When maternity holds its rightful place in the world's regard prostitution will exist no more. But that day will not come until women are valued as individuals and as human beings, and not merely as sex beings.

The idea that women exist only for race and sex purposes is

held by a great many men who wish to be considered as having in view the interests of women and of the race, but it is an idea that is very largely responsible for prostitution and vice. 'If women are sex beings and nothing more,' argue the immoral men, 'then those women who are not occupied with child-bearing are fit for nothing more than to satisfy our vices.'

What men, including eugenists and social reformers of all kinds, must realise, is this: The power of maternity is something which women have in addition to their other powers. The power of maternity corresponds with the power of paternity, and not to some other power or quality in men. It is true that to give birth to a child makes a great demand upon the vitality of women, but the answer to that is that the vitality is hers, given to her by Nature to meet the need of that vitality.

The belief that women are naturally weak is the greatest of all delusions. It is true that many women's strength is now, owing to artificial causes, less than it ought naturally to be, but these artifical causes must be done away with. One of them is, as we have already shown, the great prevalence of sexual disease, which directly attacks the sexual health and vitality of women. Want of exercise, unhygienic dress, and other such circumstances contribute to make a great many women weaker than they are by nature.

Yet, even as things are today, we find women, in addition to bringing children into the world, doing some of the hardest and most unremitting toil. It is only when the question of wage-earning arises, or when women claim the right to be active in the higher fields of human activity, that it is argued that maternity unfits them for equality with men.

We repeat, then, that for women to establish their freedom and equality with men, apart from any question of maternity and sex, is a necessary step towards the abolition of prostitution. It is largely because men have been too much persuaded of women's unlikeness to themselves, that they have wanted to put and keep them in subjection and exploit them for purposes of vice. For the abolition of prostitution, it is necessary that men shall hold women in honour, not only as mothers, but as human beings, who are like and equal unto themselves.

Another aspect of the problem is economic. More and more women are becoming persuaded of the fact that, both in marriage and out of it, they must be economically independent, and that there must be no question of living by the sale of sex. For sex is degraded by any hint of sale or barter.

As regards the unmarried woman, there must be a security that she can live by selling the work of her hand or brain. It is notorious that an enormous percentage of white slaves are forced into slavery by economic pressure, by the impossibility of earning more than a starvation wage, or by the impossibility of earning anything at all. Women's right to work and to live by their work is, therefore, one of the chief points in their charter of liberty.

Nor are things different where the married woman is concerned. The fact that a wife depends upon her husband for the necessities of life leads, as everybody knows, to a great deal of unhappiness in marriage. Social reformers, who attach so great an importance to the economic side of every problem, ought to be the first to realise that in the reforming of social conditions it is not enough to put the husband in possession of larger means; and that to every adult individual – man or woman, wife or maid – must be secured economic independence. And yet it is often they who uphold the reactionary theory that married women ought not to be economically independent.

The system under which a married woman must derive her livelihood from her husband – must eat out of his hand, as it were – is a great bulwark of sex-subjection, and is a great reinforcement to prostitution. People are led to reason thus: a woman who is a wife is one who has made a permanent sex-bargain for her maintenance; the woman who is not married must therefore make a temporary bargain of the same kind.

It is not as though a married woman does not earn her keep by the work she does. Here are some of the avocations which married women pursue: cooking, laundrywork, dressmaking, marketing, mending, scrubbing and cleaning; bathing, dressing, and general care of infants, house-management, sick nursing, social entertaining, husband's career-making. This varied work, if done by married women, has a money value. It is right, therefore, that a married woman shall get the same monetary payment for her work as is received for the work done by the rest of the community. Nor is it enough to solve the problem at issue, for a wife to have a legal claim upon a share of her husband's earnings. That may work well enough in practice where the husband is possessed of large means, but in the vast majority of cases something more than that is needed. Merely to give a woman half her husband's earnings is to make one person's wage or salary meet the needs of two persons, and perhaps of a family into the bargain. By way of illustration, we may take the case of husband and wife who are both doctors, or actors, or industrial workers. Each earns an independent income, and both should contribute equally to the maintenance of the family. If, on the other hand, the wife is earning nothing, then the family circumstances are greatly reduced, and the wife can never be in the same sense economically independent. Co-operative housekeeping, which not only lightens women's work by organising it and scientifically directing it, but also brings wage-earning within the reach of every wife without impairing domestic comfort, is a system to be heartily encouraged by those who desire the full emancipation of women. Of course, married people will always be free to make such arrangements as suit their own case, but the type of marriage will in days to come be one in which the wife is economically independent.

More important than everything else as a means of strengthening women's position is, of course, the gain of the Parliamentary vote. The vote is the symbol of freedom and equality. Any class which is denied the vote is branded as an inferior class. Women's disfranchisement is to them a perpetual lesson in servility, and to men it teaches arrogance and injustice where their dealings with women are concerned. The inferiority of women is a hideous lie which has been enforced by law and woven into the British Constitution, and it is quite hopeless to expect reform between the relationship of the sexes until women are politically enfranchised.

Apart from the deplorable moral effect of the fact that women are voteless, there is this to be noticed – that the law of the land, as made and administered by men, protects and encourages the immorality of men and the sex exploitation of women. As an illustration of this, we have only to refer to the Piccadilly Flat Case, in which male offenders were screened from punishment, and the woman who had ministered to their vice was punished so much more leniently than are women who destroy property for the sake of the vote. As a further illustration, we may point to the bastardy laws, which make it shamefully easy for a man to escape due responsibility for his children born out of marriage, and the fact that the law does not protect young girls after the age of sixteen, and not even up to that age, if a male offender against a girl pleads that he thought her to be over the age of consent. The unequal divorce laws are another illustration of the way in which a Parliament elected only by men protects the immorality of men. The scandalous leniency shown in regard to assaults upon infant girls provides another example of the evil caused by the outlawry of women.

There are speeches, pamphlets, and books by the hundred on 'motherhood', 'mothercraft', the 'ignorance of mothers', and so forth. What women think is that the public attention ought now to be directed less to the education of women than to the education of men. Fatherhood, father-craft, and the duties and responsibilities of paternity are, or rather ought to be, the question of the day.

There are men who urge that almost before she herself leaves the cradle, a girl should be put in training for motherhood. When, and in what way, a girl's mind should be directed towards motherhood can best be decided by women themselves. What men ought now to do is to train the young of their own sex. As things are at present women are certainly more fit for maternity than men are for paternity.

We have already said that if men were conscious of their paternal duty prostitution would be at an end, because by intercourse with prostitutes a man endangers his own power to become a father, endangers the health of his wife, and endangers the health and sanity of his offspring. There is no doubt whatever that boys at a very early age ought to be taught their responsibility to the next generation. It is quite futile for women to prepare themselves for motherhood unless men at the same time are preparing themselves for fatherhood. To have wise and healthy mothers avails nothing if there are not also wise and healthy fathers.

One of the lessons that men have to learn is that their sex powers are given to them as a trust to be used, not for the purpose of immorality and debaucher, but to be used, reverently and in a union based on love, for the purpose of carrying on the race.

The rightness and possibility, and the imperative necessity of an equal moral standard for men and women, is what every man should be taught from youth upwards. This women think, and upon this women will more and more insist.

They will be told, of course, as they have always been told in the past, that an equal moral standard for men and women is an impossible dream. Such statements have lost all their power to deceive women, who have by this time taken care to arm themselves with the necessary medical knowledge. Women know that, as one doctor has expressed it, man's physical nature is accurately adapted to the needs of his moral being, and that the rule of chastity observed by women can also be observed by men to their great advantage in point of health and vigour. In a previous chapter, called 'Chastity and the Health of Men' there appears the testimony of many medical men, which testimony gives overwhelming proof that prostitution and immorality are not in accordance with Nature, but are a violation of Nature's laws. Chastity and continence for men are natural and healthful; it is unchastity and incontinence which destroy men morally and physically.

Now that women are aware of these facts, they treat with contempt the gross cant about men's sexual needs, by which it is sought to excuse prostitution and vice. The truth is that the desires of men are inflamed to an unnatural degree by impure thought and action, by excess in the way of meat and drink, and by physical and mental indolence.

Sexual disease is also responsible for exaggerated sexual desire. It is most important that men and women shall have a knowledge of this fact, which is brought out very clearly in the following quotation from the writings of James Foster Scott, M.D.:

> It is well to remember that at certain stages of gonorrhœa the voluptuous desires of some patients are inordinately intensified. The point of importance in this connection is that a most dangerous class of diseased men, with abnormally strong sexual appetites, are going about without conscience, supervision, or legal restraint, and using these very women whom so many men feel safe in patronising. . . . Diseased men get reckless in the indulgence of their passions. Not only have they lost their *morale*, strong in the belief that there is little more for them to acquire, but also the inflammation in the deep urethra morbidly stimulates their passions, so that these men are most highly dangerous to human society, being in fact poisonous men seeking to poison others. Excessively lustful, and governed by no moral restraint, they actively seek to gratify their passions at the expense of any available woman's health and life, and at the expense of those foolish men who follow in their tracks.

When it is reflected that from 75 to 80 per cent of men contract gonorrhœa, the part which this disease plays in connection with the problem of vice is obviously a very large one.

The truth is that, owing to disease and other causes, the sex desire in men is stronger than is warranted by the interests of society. When some aspiration towards greater liberty and towards self-development on the spiritual plane is concerned, women are often, quite unreasonably, exhorted to sacrifice themselves to the supposed interests of society as a whole. Now, with great reason, men are called upon, in the interests of themselves and of women and of society as a whole, to keep their desires under due control.

The excuses offered by men for not doing this are many and various. Thus, one man makes his protest in the name of art, and asks indignantly, 'Do you think that any artistic manifestation could come out of chastity and normality?' Now it is very natural that inspiration should come through a union which is one of love, but that vice and uncleanness are a way to inspiration, is a fallacy with which M. Jean Finot deals very trenchantly in his *Problems of the Sexes*. He says: 'How many great minds, irremediably destroyed by misguided voluptuousness, are cut down before having expended for the human race one-tenth of their knowledge'; and he quotes Sainte-Beuve, as follows:

> Who shall say how, in a great city, at certain hours of the evening and the night, there are periodically exhausted treasures of genius, of beautiful and beneficent works, of fruitful fancies? One in whom, under rigid continence, a sublime creation of mind was about to unfold, will miss the hour, the passage of the star, the kindling moment which will nevermore be found. Another, inclined by nature to kindness, to charity, and to a charming tenderness, will become cowardly, inert, or even unfeeling. This character, which was almost fixed, will be dissipated and volatile.

Art is creative. Sexual excess is a waste of man's creative energy.

Another grotesque idea which men have entertained, is that by immoral life they excite the admiration of women, and that women think immoral conduct 'manly'. On the contrary, women think it altogether unmanly and contemptible. Strength and cleanliness and self-control – and even more than self-control a mind which is too big and fine to harbour immoral ideas and intentions – are what women admire in men. Women are in agreement with Forel, who says:

> Sexual intercourse which is bought and sold has no relation to love. As a mode of gratifying the sex instinct it stands even lower in the moral scale than the habit of self-abuse. Prostitution is a hot-bed of sexual vice and abnormal practices. By its means, the sexual instinct is perverted and led astray into every imaginable bypath, while women are degraded in the basest of all slaveries.

Women are aware that excessive sexuality, as manifested in prostitution, is unnatural, and that it leads inevitably to other unnatural practices. Far from regarding immorality as manly, women regard it as a terrible blemish upon character – as a disqualification for fatherhood, a disqualification for husbandhood.

The normal woman regards the sex act as the final pledge of her faith and her love. The idea that her husband may take a lower view of it is repulsive to her. The thought that, before or after his marriage, prostitution can enter his mind as an alternative to marriage, is intolerable. A woman's knowledge of psychology tells her that a man who is, or has been, immoral inevitably has his sex ideals tainted, and cannot therefore regard marriage as she herself regards it. Thus the black cloud of prostitution necessarily darkens the legitimate sex union.

Another of women's thoughts born of the more developed sense of comradeship among women, is that so long as there exists a huge class of slave women, the more fortunate women cannot live peaceably and contentedly as though all were well. If some women are corrupted and outcasts, and sacrificed to immorality, this concerns all women, and those who are responsible must be called to account. Besides, as we have seen, womanhood as a whole suffers in health and happiness as the result of the maltreatment of the slave class.

It would seem that certain men are alarmed by the dangers of prostitution, and, of course, they find it expensive. At any rate, we detect a tendency in many quarters to preach to women the observance of a looser code of morals than that they have observed hitherto. 'You are asking for political freedom,' women are told.

> More important to you is sex freedom. Votes for women should be accompanied, if not preceded, by wild oats for women. The thing to be done is not to raise the moral standard of men, but to lower the moral standard of women.

To this proposal the women reply by a firm and unqualified negative. Votes they certainly intend to have, and that quickly, but they know too well what is the harvest of wild oats, and having that knowledge, they refuse to sow any.

When women have the vote, they will be more and not less opposed than now to making a plaything of sex and of entering casually into the sex relationship.

In the opinion of the Suffragettes sex is too big and too sacred a thing to be treated lightly. Moreover, both the physical and spiritual consequences of a sex union are so important, so far-reaching, and so lasting, that intelligent and independent women will enter into such union only after deep consideration, and only when a great love and a great confidence are present.

And here we may, perhaps, deal with the statement made by some men, that women suffer who are not mated with men, and that what they are pleased to term 'the unsatisfied desires' of women are a problem. Now, in the old days when marriage was the only career open to women, those who did not marry regarded themselves, and were regarded, as failures – just as a lawyer might who never got a brief, as a doctor might who never got a customer. But nowadays the unmarried women have a life full of joy and interest. They are not mothers of children of their flesh, but they can serve humanity, they can do work that is useful or beautiful. Therefore their life is complete. If they find a man worthy of them, a man fit physically and morally to be their husband, then they are ready to marry, but they will not let desire, apart from love and reason, dominate their life or dictate their action.

It is very often said to women that their ideas of chastity are the result of past subjection. Supposing that were so, then women have the satisfaction of knowing that their subjection has brought them at least one great gain – a gain they will not surrender when the days of their subjection are over. The mastery of self and sex, which either by nature or by training women have, they will not yield up.

Warned by the evils which the tyranny of sex has produced where men are concerned, women have no intention of letting matter triumph over mind, and the body triumph over the spirt, in their case.

This being the point of view of the Suffragettes, the most modern of all modern women, it will be seen that out of the present impasse in sex matters, there is only one way – chastity for men, guaranteed and confirmed by the greater inependence which the Vote will give to women.

Part III

Feminism, Sexuality and the Impact of Sex Reform

A *Before Sex Reform*

Elizabeth C. Wolstenholme Elmy

from *Phases of Love*

(1897)

> A self-poised royal soul, brave, wise, and tender,
> No longer blind and dumb;
> A Human Being of an unknown splendour,
> Is she who is to come.
>
> *Charlotte Perkins Stetson*

> Man owes all his superiority over the brute to the moral power of love; wherever he fails to recognise that power his superiority vanishes.
>
> *Menville de Ponson*

Yet saw we, from our rest beneath the pine trees – and were glad – that the time of this darkness is drawing to its end; for that man is learning to know – and, knowing, to prize – the psychic rather than the physical in his fellowship with the partner of his earthly pilgrimage, and is realising that the journey, hitherto so somber for either may, with the simple aid of justice, become for both an ever brighter pageant of life and light and love.

Clearly marked we this as we meditated the story of man's progress, his mental evolution – from the animal scarcely yet human, and the savage with carnal qualities and desires only – through intermediate grade and race – to the combined high intellect of head and of heart, which elevates to psychic place and purpose our comradeship of the sexes.

Rare, yet sure, have been its foreshadowings in earlier history; more and yet more rapidly in our present time is this higher phase of our advance becoming manifest. Youthful students, male or female, of newer generation, shudder to recognise within how recent a period in our own language the word 'love', as applied to human passion, denoted but a sensual appetite, scarcely touched by psychic motive. Let them not be depressed; but rather take courage by the approach their own emotions thus show toward 'sweeter manners, purer laws' than when, a bare lifetime agone, one of the noblest of England's poets could only haltingly describe 'the existence of Love as not identical with Friendship, and yet distinct always and *very often* divided from Lust'.

Older languages and civilisations were steeped in the grossness: continually the carnal oppression and the low esteem of womanhood, with ensuant debasing effects, physical and moral, upon man and upon the offspring, till it seems the rational conclusion that all distinctively human evils had their primal source in the indulgence of a blind and selfish sensuality. Repeated and widespread had been the retribution; nation after nation had risen to somewhat of height but had again fallen; the one constant in their internal polity was that from sensual motive they treated their women as slaves; the one constant and consequent in their own fate was that their children were bred slaves also, in blood, in spirit, in idea: the baseness of their heredity was upon them; what people might so endure? It is the brightest and surest augury for the future of certain younger kinsmen of ours on American and Australasian shores, that their institutions are abolishing all distinctions of sex in civic right; while Britain's 'wisdom' still 'lingers' to come to full fruit!

The consideration of the piteously unjust human status of the womanhood – the motherhood – of the race, involved our yet further backward glance into man's past, and to the periods when in him, as in his fellow animals, the actions were those of the developing and inherited unconscious instincts; little more than mechanical functions as yet, but affording a basis for physical faculties and psychic affections, soon to be evoked by the further incidents of life and surroundings.

Modern biology is well agreed in regarding the manifestations of affection or sympathy in the human, and in various other types of animal life, as so many transmitted outcomes from the maternal instinct primarily; that instinct itself having been developed in the continual struggle for existence, 'by the survival of those types which have best fulfilled the most fitting maternal functions'. Even very low down in the rank of being, the psychic advance of the mother beyond consideration for her own simply physical and individual well-being is traceable in her action concerning the offspring; to such psychic and altruistic conduct being solely due in many cases the preservation of the species.

Supplementary to the maternal condition, and apparently as an inheritance or reflection from it, is seen in many types a paternal care also, exercised conjointly with, or separately from, that of the mother – and including sometimes a guarding of her or the young during their most unprotected period; while, in yet other species, we witness a regulated community of action of the whole group of individuals for the general welfare of themselves and progeny.

Some part or compound of one or more of these qualities is observable in most types of animal life; as are also manifest the elements of sexual attraction and affection – again in varying degrees of vividness, reciprocity, and permanence. In some types the affection between the parents is but transitory, ending with the mutual concern for the young; while in yet other species, though parental care may be conspicuous in the mother, the father may show no sign of feeling for any other than himself in the whole of the possible relation. But in birds generally, and of both sexes, parental and conjugal affection are well marked; the latter being, in given species, of life-long duration. Man may take shame to himself when he reflects how many of his fellows, even, now, compare anything but favourably in psychic conduct with some of our winged little sisters and brothers in Nature's family.

Thus saw we that at no very high level of animal feeling could be appraised human passion generally, in the times of which was earliest historic record; and that, moreover, unpleasing survivals of the same primitive condition are still extant, even in our civilised life. Yet, happily, saw we also, in the world's present age, a swiftly advancing and ever loftier concept of the newer and higher faculty – the psychic emotion and impulse between two human beings of different sex, to which the name of 'love' is specially and worthily applied.

Is it only a coincidence that connected written record seems to have originated almost contemporaneously with the dim dawn of that which was to be the juster, purer phase of human sexual emotion? Thus, in the Rig-Veda 'the most ancient of books in the library of mankind', where continually the very 'phase of thought as well as of language' is so primitive and strange as to be scarcely amenable to present translation, (for thought and language have also had their crude origin and development), there is little suggestion of aught that even the most willing might dignify with the title of psychic love as between the sexes. So, too, with the primitive poets, philosophers, or historians, of any nation, and what incidents of marital or family life and relations they may casually present.

But although, in early time, the thinkers and narrators chronicled the passion – if at all – scarcely as other than a simply fleshly incident, yet we soon find them rendering – sometimes involuntary, but presently a conscious – testimony to a deeper than physical element in the emotion; an element whose gradual evolution may be noted in subsequent history, until we reach its accelerating growth and development in our own more happy day of the advance of psychic capacity in both sexes; an advance mainly brought about by the growing emancipation and autonomy of woman – her fuller measure of intellectual culture and physical strength, of social status and individual freedom.

It is sometimes reproached to woman that previous measures of freedom conceded to her were not fully availed of, or were permitted to lapse. But her bodily servitude had never been relaxed, and the unjust bondages of femininity and maternity still held and crippled her. Cursory writers have thus overrated the degree of social equality of the sexes in ancient Egypt; calmly forgetful of the incompatible facts of polygamy, concubinage, and slavery, as also of the compulsory liability to motherhood of even the legitimised wife. So that Mrs Farnham's words, in conclusion of the passage quoted on a previous page, are amply justified:

> There was neither the sentiment, philosophy, nor moral feeling in the brightest days of Egypt, that could save an individual woman of any rank from the grossest injustice which man chose to inflict on her, or her sex from the shame and degradation of absolute slavery to his lusts.

By this we hold: No man is wholly great,
  Or wise, or just, or good.
Who would not dare his all to reinstate
  Earth's trampled womanhood.

Thomas Lake Harris

A nation rises no higher than its mothers.

Thus our saddest spectacle in all the long history of the evolution of love was man's blind cruelty in the misuse of woman; not alone by positive physical oppression and excess, but also by the restriction of her native individuality of mental power and action, at incalculable loss to humanity thereby. Through all known time and peoples has this male policy so prevailed that to read the history of one nation in this matter is to comprehend generally that of all. Greece and Rome, intellectually great as they were deemed, afford prominent example.

There, as elsewhere, man usually sought in woman the sensual only, and all her training was ordered to that end. At an unnaturally early age was her carnal servitude initiated – some words of

Epictetus, the latest of the Grecian philosophers, showing tersely the common fate allotted to woman in both countries about that time. He enunciates, calmly and unmoved as in any other of his aphorisms:

> Girls, so soon as they reach the age of fourteen years are called women. Thenceforth, seeing that there is nothing else for them but only to be bedfellows to man, they proceed to beautify and adorn themselves; placing all their hope therein. Wherefore it is well to take care that they should understand that no honour can accrue to them but in gentle demeanour, with bashfulness and chastity.

Here is epitomised the relative social condition of woman, not only in ancient civilisation, but also late on into modern life and thought – or thoughtlessness. Still flagrant is the 'double code of morality', which demands chastity in woman, and yet condones a sensual licence in man, – indulged by his robbery of that very chastity from luckless woman victims, whom society forthwith execrates.

The early writings of all nations bear tacit or active witness to this unequal social treatment of the sexes. In the Iliad and the Odyssey may be found plentiful instance of conjugal fidelity in the wife, with far from reciprocal conduct on the part of her husband; laches by a man, married or unmarried, being treated as utterly venial (unless in approaching another man's wife), while unmeasured condemnation follows the fault of any woman.

This difference was doubtless largely owing to the wife being simply considered as the husband's property or slave; a condition in which no love worthy of the name could bloom; though, perhaps, some factitious emotion might be evoked in a wife, in response to an illusive regard – as much jealousy as kindness – on the part of the husband. But the element of intellect or mental companionship was piteously wanting. As an acute observer remarks:

> Throughout the Eastern Countries of Europe and in Asia men have considered themselves to be the lords of creation, and looked upon woman as made for their gratification. The pleasure sought for in their society was simply sensual. It is difficult to believe that Solomon with all his wives and concubines had one intellectual friend amongst them all.

Readily predictable consequences ensued; woman, being sought for less worthy purposes only, was less worthily esteemed. A caged morality, moreover, is notoriously uncertain, and was so much the object of insidious attempt by other men themselves, that woman was defamed as an object of frailty and general suspicion by the very sex that betrayed her; insomuch that, except in the one relationship of mother, the occasions are rare where early writers credited woman with a purpose of her own other than a sinister one. Thus we find Hesiod – next only in antiquity to Homer – in his poem of 'Works and Days', delivering 'general maxims, inculcating industry, honesty, and expediency, together with a *mistrust of women*'.

The shallow maligning of woman is common not only in the ancient literature of Greece and India, but also in the Jewish scripture of approximate date. This latter work begins the assumed history of mankind by a mythical story imputing a specific reproach to woman – as usual – and attributing to her wilful act certain evil results which, as far as they do exist, modern science is ever more clearly showing to be but consequences or aspects of human ignorance on the part of both sexes. A graphic testimony to the physical character of sexual affection at the period is also supplied by a song (considerably tempered by later translators) ascribed to the polygamous monarch already mentioned, and written in the gross style general to Oriental productions of that class; while further works dubiously attributed to the same author, and most other of the Hebrew books, biblical or otherwise, are deeply tinctured with the then prevalent depreciation of womanhood.

So, incidentally and from various sources, has been fomented the feud of sexual misunderstanding, in the presence of which was slight holding for the intelligent sympathy and mutual respect that afford the only root and growth for the enduring regard of psychic love. Yet, under all the repression and bondage and evil report of woman, the results of the psychic attributes in motherhood showed through from time to time, and compelled a recognition, even from masculine prejudice. So that the classic authors in general, while affecting the conventional reviling of the character of woman, did yet continually endow their idealisations of her – possibly reconstructed from impressions of their own gentle mother or sister – with finer and purer soul qualities than were the masculine equipment; attributes which did undoubtedly exist and find development in woman, and, by reflection and inheritance, prepared and established the way to high love in man also.

Thus the Greek dramatists, Aeschylus, Euripides, and Sophocles, portray in their heroines, Alcestis, Antigone, Iphigenia, and others, not only a noble personality and a courage above death, but also ascribe to them the purest of womanly nature and the tenderest of altruistic – and thereby psychic – affection. And the masculine mind was moved, if not reformed; the men of Athens signified their appreciation of Sophocles' presentment of Antigone, by demanding the repetition of that drama thirty-two consecutive times. Love was indeed struggling hard for psychic height, but the base weight of fleshly lust still held too dominant sway in man; truly

> He rode a horse with wings, that would have flown,
> But that his heavy rider kept him down.

The reasonings of the deepest of thinkers, moreover, supported the position of the poets; advancing Indian philosophy had recognised woman's lofty intuitions by declaring that 'every book of knowledge known to Oosana or Vreehaspatee is by nature implanted in Woman'. And Greece's sage, Socrates, could yet learn from the native feminine intellect of Diotima; whose influence is doubtless traceable in his own exalted conclusion that

> Love is a spirit which spans the abyss between earth and heaven; not the mere desire of beauty, but an instinct of immortality.

Thus his disciple, Plato, reports the words; and confirms them by emphasising in his own ideal of love the essentially spiritual or intellectual requirement, and 'making manifest that the strongest and closest attachment might be free from any sensual taint'. While himself the writer of one of the prettiest and purest of human love messages –

> Thou gazest at the stars, my own Star: I would be Heaven, that with thousand eyes I might gaze back at Thee!

– it is clear that his was no passion born of solely physical attraction, from his words in a further place:

> I call a vicious man the common-place admirer who loves the body rather than the soul; for his love can be of no duration, seeing that he loves a thing which does not itself endure. As soon as the bloom of the beauty which he loved is past, he flies away elsewhere, oblivious of his sweet phrases, his dulcet promises; but it cannot be so with him who loves a noble soul: he remains faithful all his life, for that which he loves knows no change.

This was a distinct advance upon the lower phase of passion, which had sufficed to a lower phase of intellect only: and practical testimony to this evolving higher intellectual passion and its prominence, is to be gathered from the example of the yet two other philosophers who may claim also the position of greatest among the minds of Greece: Pythagoras, who, a generation previously, had married the exceptionally learned Theano; and Plato's own pupil, Aristotle – expousing the equally noble-souled Pythias, whom he so loved, that after her death he ceased not to offer to her memory such homage as was usually accorded to the gods.

> Love? First give wisdom – intelligent care,
> That shall help to bring out all the good that is there.
> Love? First give justice! There's nothing above! –
> And then you may love!
>
> *Charlotte Perkins Stetson*

> Perfect love and perfect trust have never yet existed except between equals.
>
> *Helen H. Gardener*

Blind, truly, to his own highest interests, had been the general vision in man; seeing and seeking in woman her lower and physical qualities only; holding her comfort, her health, or her life, as at best but a due offering to his own sensual propensities; and checking and crushing out any effort or aspiration of hers to a fuller mental status or personal independence, which might prove not so submissive to his baser scheme.

Hence his efforts to retain woman in a perpetual childhood of intellect; while bodily she was early subjected to his purposes, remaining, moreover, in the legal power of some male relative, – father, or husband, or brother, or son – during the whole of her life. Little recked of in former history but as a subordinate and insignificant personality; a slave, a spoil in warfare, a concubine; a daughter or sister – to be used as a convenient item for matrimonial sale or barter – and thus to attain the dubious dignity of a wife; and the general position has been continued with but little of cardinal change through succeeding ages.

During all this time of man's cruder passion, woman also had often striven to satisfy her soul with the unjust ethical and physical conditions enjoined by him; she being taught that even a painful acceptance on her part was a fitting sacrifice to the assumed need of man, a duty to the race, or a passport to divine favour. In some cases, doubtless, her character became infected with the debasement, so that the blind subserviency to which she had been trained penetrated even into her own philosophy or frame of thought, with the evil result that – sinking to, or striving not beyond, the feeble and baser standard of mental and physical action assigned to her by man – he, in turn, misled by woman's acquiesence, judged such behaviour to be her normal and spontaneous disposition, and even pretended to excuse his own reckless excess thereby.

With the advent of freer intellect in our later time, woman at once repudiated this tame acceptance of the degrading masculine teaching. Mary Wollstonecraft protests:

> Indignantly have I heard women argue in the same track as men, and adopt the sentiments that brutalise them, with the pertinacity of ignorance.

She points regretfully to the source of the ignorance, in the fact that

> Females, who are made women of when they are mere children, and brought back to childhood when they ought to have left the go-cart for ever, have not sufficient strength of mind to efface the superinductions of art that have smothered nature.

And she deplores the procured subserviency of intellect, and specially the 'fear of departing from a supposed sexual character', that have 'made even women of superior sense' adopt and echo man's erroneous judgments and language concerning woman. Eliza W. Farnham says later, and yet more forcibly

> It is no matter that the victim may have become callous by use, to the most unnatural and repulsive features of her lot; no matter that she may even have reached such a depraved state of the sensibilities and the whole nature, that a better condition would be rather dreaded as a restraint than desired as a right; we equally feel that it ought not to have been so with her, and that her love of the wrongs she is in, is only a proof of their enormity and long continuance.

Similar protest is repeated in our own day, by one who tells her sisters:

> The willingness to accept a degraded and subordinate status in the world, and the assertion that they like it, are the lowest depths of degradation to which human beings can be reduced.

It is futile to apply the title of 'love' to any passion existent under conditions so condemned. And it is in woman's own repudiation of her artificially unequal position that is seen the first fertile hope of the higher humanity, in which alone, as man favours and furthers her claim, lies for him and for her the capacity for worthy love, and for its potentialities yet to come.

For, from woman's enforcedly restricted mental and physical condition, not only herself but man and the race have suffered and lost incalculably; woman has never been permitted to follow the promptings of her native intellect – to discover, and cultivate (*in her own manner*), and enjoy, and impart to a lacking world the fruits of her own specific genius; the child has missed the benefaction practicable from a truly intelligent motherhood; and only on rarest occasion till within this modern time of woman's advancing freedom and education has it been possible for man to even taste or estimate the elevated and lasting delight and sympathy and strength of her equal psychic fellowship.

Transitory only could be the excitation of the physical phase of passion; and its indulgence contrary to the dictates of justice naturally tended to weaken and soon extinguish any higher emotion. Poets had at times lamented this fleetingness of the psychic element of love after marriage; or, in shallower mood, had held it as of the inevitable habit of the passion: the truth and the remedy involved have been left for these later years to recognise – that true love admits of no physical expression but as sanctioned by the equal will and psychic purpose of both parties.

It was in the neglect of this condition, and the consequent infliction on woman of unacceptable approaches and undesired maternities, that had lain the main hideousness of civilised 'marriage' hitherto; and only with the full recognition of the wife's continuing right of physical inviolability will the institution be accepted by either party in the near future. Under no other condition can a true love exist; marriage without such love is but a degrading bondage, and childbirth a wrong to the dreaded offspring. True psychic love will, indeed, neither contemplate nor assent to parental possibility but under circumstances calculated to secure not only justice to the mother, but the health and happiness of the child itself, and thereby of advancing humanity.

Frequently, however, and shamefully, woman is left to enter upon marriage without true knowledge or any warning as to the real nature of the wife's so-called 'duties' therein; its possible physical relations, of perhaps the most repugnant or even perilous character to herself – abuses and excesses, resultant often in misery and suffering or premature death – but which she finds to be assumed as part of the 'iron contract'. With a husband of gross nature the continual unwelcome intimacies may only be ended by her own flight, in which event our law is sufficiently civilised to no longer enforce her return to the husband's house. Should, however, percuniary circumstances, or the fear of scandal, or the counsel of 'friends', or love for her children and pain in leaving them, beguile her into an unwilling conjugal tolerance, little happiness can follow. For in unjust marital conduct the allotted psychic purpose of the relation is shattered; the gentle grace of the lovers is lost in the boorishness of the husband, the disillusionment of the wife: the early psychic affection on either side withers away; all semblance of a true companionship is at an end; and thus marriage, which should be the temple of a consecrated love, becomes but too generally its living tomb.

Yet saw we that it was not to marriage itself – 'the marriage of true minds' – but rather to its past and present unjust conditions, personal, social, and legal, that the continually attendant wrongs and miseries were to be attributed. And, with the developing intellectual sympathy of both sexes, purer conditions for this highest of human alliance were rapidly approaching. In our memory rang the clear words of one of England's greatest in wisdom:

> What marriage may be in the case of two persons of cultivated faculties, identical in opinions and purposes, between whom there exists that best kind of equality, similarity of powers and capacities, with reciprocal superiority in them – so that each can enjoy the pleasure of looking up to the other, and can have alternately the pleasure of leading, and of being led in the path of development – I will not attempt to describe. To those who can conceive it there is no need: to those who cannot, it would appear the dream of an enthusiast. But I maintain, with the profoundest conviction, that this, and this only, is the ideal of marriage; and that all opinions, customs, and institutions which favour any other notion of it, or turn the conceptions and aspirations connected with it into any other direction, by whatever pretences they may be coloured, are relics of primitive barbarism. The moral regeneration of mankind will only really commence, when the most fundamental of the social relations is placed under the rule of equal justice, and when human beings learn to cultivate their strongest sympathy with an equal in rights and cultivation.

Following this song of man's aspiration through our minds, came the cry of equal intellect and psychic yearning from a woman,

> The possibility of a constantly growing blessedness in marriage is to me the very basis of good in our mortal life.

Thus spoke the voices of a score of years ago: while in yet more recent days some of the indispensable means of attainment of their ends are indicated by two conjoint masters of physiology and psychology, who teach the worthy control of lower passion by higher purpose, as essential to any intellectual and just condition of marriage:

> We would urge, in fact, the necessity of an ethical 'prudence after marriage', of a temperance recognised to be as binding on husband and wife as chastity on the unmarried. It is no new nor unattainable ideal to retain, throughout married life, a large measure of that self-control which must always form the organic basis of the enthusiasm and idealism of lovers.

Elizabeth Blackwell

from
The Moral Education of the Young in Relation to Sex

(1879)

On the physiological laws which influence the physical and mental growth of sex; and on the social results of neglecting these laws

Age after age brings forward varying phases of thought, when some particular facts of life are thrown into unusual prominence, such special devlopment of thought serving to mould the society of that generation, giving it a special stamp, and thus advancing the progress of humanity one step forward. Of all the ideas gradually worked out and gained as the permanent possession of human society, the slowest in growth, is the idea of the true relations of the sexes. The instinct of sex always exists as the indispensable condition of life, and the foundation of society. It is the strongest force in human nature. Whatever else disappears, this continues. Undeveloped, no subject of thought, but nevertheless as the central fire of life, nature guards the inevitable instinct from all possibility of destruction. As an idea, however, thought out in all its wide relations, shaped in human practice in all its ennobling influences, it is the latest growth of civilisation. In whatever concerns the subject of sex, customs are blindly considered sacred, and evils deemed inevitable. The mass of mankind seems moved with anger, fear, or shame, by any effort made to consider seriously this fundamental idea. It must necessarily come forward however, in the progress of events, as the subject of primary importance. As society advances, as principles of justice and humanity become firmly established, as science and industry prepare the way for the more perfect command of the material world, it will be found that the time has come for the serious consideration of this first and last question in human welfare, for the subject of sex will then present itself as the great aid or obstacle to further progress. The gradually growing conviction will be felt, that as it is the fundamental principle of all society, so it is its crowning glory. In the relations of men and women, will be found the chief cause of past national decline, or the promise of indefinite future growth.

The family, being the first simple element of society – the first natural product of the principle of sex – the whole structure of society must depend upon the character of that element, and the powers that can be unfolded from it. Morality in sex will be found to be the essence of all morality, securing principles of justice, honour and uprightness, in the most influential of all human relations, and as it is all-important in life, so it is all-important in the education which prepares for life. A great social question lies therefore, at the foundation of the moral education of youth, and influences more or less directly each step of education. It is indispensable to consider the relation of this subject to the various stages of education, and the methods by means of which education may guide and strengthen youth, in their entrance into wider social life.

The principles which should guide the moral education of our children – our boys and girls – must necessarily depend upon the views which we hold in relation to their adult life, as men and women; these views will unavoidably determine the course of practical education. Two great questions therefore, naturally present themselves at the outset of every careful consideration of moral sexual education.

First, what is the true standard for the relations of men and women – the type which contains within itself the germ of progress or continual development?

Second, is this standard attained, or how can it be attained by human beings?

It will be seen that the answer we give to these two important questions, will guide every step in the education of youth. The endeavour to ascertain the true answer, in its bearing upon the growth of the young, and the welfare of family life, is the object of the present work.

The very gradual growth of mankind from lower to higher forms of social life, makes the study of the relation of the sexes a very complicated one; but a sure guide may be found in the great truths of physiology viewed in their broad relation to human progress; and it is on the solid foundation of these truths, that correct principles of education must be based. The tendency of our age, in seeking truth, is to reject theories and study facts – facts, however, on the largest and most comprehensive scale. Every physician knows that nothing is more stupid than routine practice; nothing more unreliable than theories unsupported by well-observed facts; and at the same time, nothing more misleading than partial facts. The laws of the human constitution itself, as taught by the most comprehensive investigations of science, must be carefully studied. We must learn what reason, observing the facts of physiology, lays down as the true laws which should govern the relations of men and women – laws whose observance will secure the finest development of our race, and serve as a guide, in directing the education of our children.

The relations of human beings to each other, depend upon the nature and requirements of individuals. It is, therefore, essential to know what the nature of the individual human being really is; how it grows, and how it degenerates. Such knowledge must necessarily form the basis of all true methods of education. The following physiological facts, however abstract they may seem to be at the first glance, are really indispensable to a broad comprehension of the subject of Moral Education.

We find, throughout nature, that every creature possesses its peculiar type, towards which it must tend, if it is to accomplish the purpose of its creation. There is a capacity belonging to the original germ, which, if the necessary conditions are presented, will lead it through the various stages of growth, and of development, to the complete attainment of this type.

This type or pattern, is the true aim of the individual. With the process by which it is reached, it constitutes its nature.

In order to determine the nature of any creature, both the type it should attain, and the steps by which alone that type can be attained, must be taken into consideration, or we are led astray in our judgment of the nature, of the individual. Thought is often confused by a vague use of the term 'nature'. The educated man is more natural than the savage, because he approaches more nearly to the true type of man, and has acquired the power of transmitting increased capacities to his children. What is popularly called a state of nature, is really a state of rudimentary life, which does not display the real nature of man, but only its imperfect condition.

Striking instances of unusual imperfection may often be observed in the physical structure of the individual, for there are blind as well as intelligent forces at work, in the long and elaborate process of forming the complete human being. Thus, sometimes we find that the developmental process of the body goes wrong, and produces six fingers instead of five through successive generations; or the formative power of some organ runs blindly into excess, producing the diseased condition of hypertrophy. Arrest of development also, may take place at any stage of youthful life as well as before birth, the consequence being deficiency of organic power, or even defective organs, although in such cases growth and repair continue, and even long life may be attained. These conditions are not natural, although they exist, because they are contrary to the type of man. For the same reason the cannibal must be regarded as unnatural.

In studying the individual human type, we find some points in which it resembles the lower animals, some points in which it differs from all others, and some temporary phases during which it passes from the brute type to the human. If it stops short at any stage of the regular sequence or development, it fails in its essential object, and although living, it is unnatural. When we seek for the distinguishing type of the human being – the type for which the slow and careful elaboration of parts is necessary – we find it in the mental, not in the physical, capacity of Man. Physical power, and the perfection of physical instincts, are attained by the lower animals, in a higher degree than by man. It is only when we observe the uses and education of which the physical powers are susceptible, and the development of which the mental powers are capable, that we perceive the immense superiority of the human race, and recognise the type – viz., the true nature of man, towards the attainment of which all the elaborate processes of growth are directed. The more carefully we examine the intellectual growth of the lower animals, tracing the reflex movements and instinctive actions of the invertebrata, through the intelligent mental operations of the dog or the elephant, the more clearly we perceive the distinguishing type of man. This type is that union of truth and good, which we name Reason. Reason is the clear perception of the true relation of things, and the love of their harmonious relations. It includes judgment, conscience – all the higher intellectual and moral qualities.

Reason, with the Will to execute its dictates, is the distinguishing type of man.

It is towards this end that his faculties tend, in this consists his peculiarity, his charter of existence. Any failure to reach this end, is as much an arrest of development, as is a case of spina bifida, or the imperfect closure of the heart's ventricles. We cannot judge of the Nature of man, without the clear recognition of this distinctive type; and it is impossible to establish sound methods of education, without constantly keeping in view, both the true nature of man, and the steps by which it must be reached. These steps – i.e., the method by which man grows towards his distinctive type in creation – constitute the fundamental question in the present inquiry.

One distinguishing feature of human growth, is its comparative slowness. No animal is so helpless during its infancy, none remains so long in a state of complete dependence on its parents. During the first few years, the child is quite unable either to procure its own food, or to keep itself from accidents, and it attains neither its complete bodily nor mental development, until it is over twenty years of age. We find this slow growth of faculties, to be an essential condition of their excellence. It is observed to be a law of organised existence, that the higher the degree of development to be reached, the slower are the processes through which it is attained, and the longer is its period of dependence on parental aid.

The forces employed in the elaboration of the human being, differ in their manifestation at various stages of its growth. There are two marked forces to be noted, often confounded together, but important to distinguish – viz., the power of growth, and the power of development; the former possessed throughout life, the latter, at certain epochs only. The capacity for growth and nutrition, by means of which the human frame is built up and maintained out of the forces derived from food and other agents, is shown until the last breath of life, by the power of repair, which continues as long as the human being lives. All action of the organism, every employment of muscular or nervous tissue, uses up such tissue. The body is wasted by its own activities, and it is only by the exact counterpoise of these two forces – disintegration and repair – that health and life itself are maintained. In youth, in connection with very rapid waste of tissue, exists a great excess of formative power, which excess enables each complete organ, to enlarge and consolidate itself. The reduction of this excess of formative power to a balance with the waste of tissue, marks the strength of adult life. Its diminution below the power of repair, marks the decline of life. The force of development however is shown, not in the enlargement and maintenance of existing parts, but in the creation of new tissues or organs or parts of organs, so that quite new powers are added to the individual. After birth these remarkable efforts of creative force belong exclusively to the youth of the individual. They are chiefly marked by dentition, by growth of the skeleton and the brain, and still more by the addition of the generative powers. With this work of development, the adult has nothing to do, it is a burden laid especially upon the young, it is a work as important and exclusively theirs, as child-bearing is the exclusive work of the mother.

One of the first lessons then, that Physiology teaches us, in relation to the healthy growth of the human being, is the slow and successive development of the various faculties. Although the complete type of the future man exists potentially in the infant, long time and varying conditions are essential to its establishment, and the type will never be attained, if the necessary time and conditions are not provided.

The second physiological fact to be noted, is the order observed in human development. The faculties grow in a certain determined order. First, those which are needed for simple physical existence; next, those which place the child in fuller relations with nature; and lastly, those which link him to his fellows. As digestion is perfected before locomotion, so muscular mobility and activity exist before strength, perception before observation, affection and friendship before love. The latest work of nature in forming the perfect being, is the gift of sexual power. This is a work of development, not simply of growth. There are new organs coming into existence, and the same necessary conditions of gradual consolidation, and long preparation for special work exist, as in the growth of all the organs of animal life. At the age of puberty when the special life of sex commences, the other organs of relation – skeleton, muscles, brain – are still carrying on their slow process of consolidation.

> At eighteen, the bones and muscles are very immature. Portions of the vertebrae hardly commence to ossify before the sixteenth year. After twenty the two thin plates on the body of the vertebrae form, completing themselves near the thirtieth year. Consolidation of the sacrum commences in the eighteenth year, completing after the twenty-fifth. The processes of the ribs and of the scapula are completed by the twenty-fifth year, those of the clavicle begin to form between eighteen and twenty, those of the radius and ulnar, of the femur, tibia, and fibular, are all unjoined at eighteen, and not completed until twenty-five. The muscles are equally immature, they grow in size and strength in proportion to the bones, and it is not until twenty-five years of age, or even later, that all epiphyses of the bones have united, and that the muscles have attained their full growth.

As a necessary consequence of this slow order of natural growth, the individual is injured when sufficient time for growth is not allowed; or when faculties which should remain latent, slowly storing up strength for the proper time of unfolding, are unduly stimulated, or brought forward too soon. The writer above quoted remarks, 'It is not only a waste of material, but a positive cruelty, to send lads of eighteen or twenty into the field.' The evil effect of undue stimulation to a new function, is two-fold. The first effect is to divert nature's force, from the consolidation of faculties already fully formed, and second, to injure the substantial growth of the later faculty, which is thus prematurely brought forward. Thus the child compelled to carry heavy burdens will be deformed or stunted; the youth weighed down by intellectual labour, will destroy his digestion or injure his brain. So if the faculty which is bestowed as the last work of development, that which requires the longest time, and the most careful preparation for its advent – the sexual power – be brought forward prematurely, a permanent injury is done to the individual which can never be completely repaired.

The marked distinction which exists between puberty, and nubility should here be noted. It is a distinction based upon the important fact, that a work of long-continued preparation takes place in the physical and mental nature, before a new faculty enters upon its complete life. Puberty is the age when those changes have taken place in the child's constitution, which make it physically possible for it to become a parent, but when the actual exercise of such faculty is highly injurious. This change takes place, as a general rule, from fourteen to sixteen years of age.[1] Nubility, on the other hand, is that period of life when marriage may take place, without disadvantage to the individual, and to the race. This period is generally reckoned, in temperate climates, in the man, at from twenty-three to twenty-five years of age. About the age of twenty-five commences that period of perfect manly vigour, that union of freshness and strength, which enables the individual to become the progenitor of vigorous offspring. The strong constitution transmitted by healthy parents, between the ages of twenty-five and thirty-five, indicates the order of Nature, in the growth of the human race. The interval between these two epochs, of puberty, and confirmed virility, is a most important period of rapid growth, and slow consolidation. Not only is the life-long work of the body, going on at this time, with much greater activity than belongs to adult life – i.e., the work of calorification, nutrition, and all that concerns the maintenance of the body during its unceasing expenditure of mechanical and mental force – but the still more powerful actions of development and growth, are being carried on to their last and greatest perfection. Although, as will be shown later, the influences brought to bear upon the very young child, strongly affect its later growth in good or evil; yet this period between fourteen and twenty-five is the most critical time of preparation for the work of adult life.

Another important fact, announced by physiological observation, is the absolute necessity of establishing a proper government of the human faculties, by the growth of intelligent self-control. Reason not Instinct, is the final guide of our race. We cannot grow, as do the lower animals, by following out the blind promptings of physical nature. From the earliest moment of existence, intelligence must guide the infant. At first this guiding intelligence is that of the mother; and through all the earlier stages of life, a higher outside intelligence, must continue to provide the necessary conditions of growth, until the gradual mental development of the child, fits it for independent individual guidance. The great difficulty of education lies in the adjustment of intelligence, for there are antagonisms to be encountered. There is first of all to be considered the adaptation of parental intelligence to the large proportion of indispensable physical instinct, with which each child is endowed by nature. There is next the adjustment of the two intelligences – the parental and filial. These relations are constantly changing, and the true wisdom of education consists in meeting these changes rightly.

It is very important to observe, that each new phase of life, each new faculty, begins in the child-like way – that is to say, there is always a large proportion of the blind instinctive element, which absolutely needs a higher guidance. The instinctive life of the body always necessarily exists, and therefore constantly strives to make itself felt. This life of sensation will (in many different ways) obtain a complete mastery over the individual, if Reason does not exist, and grow into a controlling force. This danger of an undue predominance of the instinctive force, is emphatically true of the life of sex. It begins, child-like, in a tumult of overpowering sensations – sensations and emotions which need as wisely-arranged conditions, and as high a guiding influence as does the early life of the child. At this period of life, an adjustment of the parental and filial intelligence is required, quite as wisely planned as in childhood, in order to secure the gradual growth of intelligent self-control in the young life of sex. If we do not recognise this necessity, or fail to exercise this directing influence, we do not perceive the crowning obligation of the older to the younger generation. However much parents may now shrink from this obligation, and owing to incorrect views of sex, be really unable to exercise the kind of influence required, the necessity for such influence, nevertheless exists as a law of human nature, unchangeable, rooted in the human constitution. It is Nature's method, that every new faculty requires intelligent control from the outset, but only gradually can this guidance become self-control.

This necessity is seen more clearly as we continue our physiological inquiry. The preceding considerations refer chiefly to the slow processes by which the various parts of the body must be built up step by step, under the guidance of outside intelligence, which furnishes the proper conditions of physical growth. Equally certain, and in the legitimate scope of true physiology, is the influence which the mind of the individual exercises upon the growth of the body. This difficult half of the subject presents itself in increasing importance as science advances. The particular theory of mind held by individuals does not affect our inquiry. Everyone understands the term, and gives to its influence a certain importance. Our perception of the degree of power exercised by the mind over the body, and the importance of that power, will continually grow as we observe the facts around us. It is a fact of every-day experience, that fright will make the heart beat, that anxiety will disturb digestion, that sorrow will depress all the vital functions, whilst happiness will strengthen them. How often does the physician see the languid, ailing invalid converted, from mental causes – through happiness – into a bright, active being! Medical records are full of accumulated facts showing the extent to which such mental or emotional influence may go; how the infant has been killed when the mother has nursed it during a fit of passion; or the hair turn grey in a single night through grief or fright.

We find that the mind, acting through the nervous system, affects not only the senses and muscles – the organs of animal life, under the direct influence of the cerebro-spinal axis – but that it may also extend its influence, to those processes of nutrition and secretion which belong to the vegetative life of the body. Emotion can act where Will is powerless, but a strong Will also can acquire a remarkable power over the body. It has been remarked 'that men who know that there is any hereditary disease in their family, can contribute to the development of that disease, by closely directing their attention to it, and so throwing their nervous energy in that direction'. It was a remark of John Hunter, 'that he could direct a sensation to any part of his body'. The mechanism of this action has been so clearly expressed by an able physiologist, and bears so directly upon our subject, that it may be studied with advantage by every parent.

> The nervous power of every segment of the spinal cord, and every one of the sensory ganglia in their state of perfect integrity, and complete functional activity, are all in such

subordination to the brain, that they only minister to *its* actions, except in maintenance of organic functions, as breathing and swallowing. With regard to every other action, the Will, if it possesses its due predominance, can exercise a determining power, keeping in check every automatic impulse, and repressing the promptings of emotional excitement. This seems to result from the peculiar arrangement of the nervous apparatus, which causes the excitor *impression* to travel in the upward direction, if it meet with no interruption, until it reaches the brain, without exciting any reflex movements in its course. When it arrives at the sensorium, it makes an impression on the consciousness of the individual, and thus gives rise to a sensation; and the changes thus induced, being further propagated from the sensory ganglia to the cerebrum, become the occasion of the formation of an *idea*. If with this idea any pleasurable or painful feeling should be associated, it assumes the character of an emotion; and, either as a simple or an emotional idea, it becomes the subject of intellectual operations, whose final issue is in an act of the Will, which may be exerted in producing or checking a muscular movement, or in controlling or directing the current of thought. But if this ordinary upward course be anywhere interrupted, the impression will then exert its power in a *transverse* direction, and a 'reflex' action will be the result, the nature of this being dependent upon the part of the cerebro-spinal axis, at which the ascent had been checked.

As in the case of other sensations, the sexual, when moderately excited, may give rise to ideas, emotions, and desires, of which the brain is the seat; and these may re-act on the muscular system through the intelligence and Will. But when inordinately excited, or when not kept in restraint by the Will, they will at once call into play respondent movements, which are then to be regarded as purely automatic. This is the case in some forms of disease in the human subject, and is probably the mode of operation in the lower animals. In cases in which this sensation is excited in unusual strength, it may completely over-master all motives to the repression of the propensity, and may even entirely remove the actions from volitional control. A state of a very similar kind exists in many idiots, in whom the sexual propensity exerts a dominant power, not because it is in itself peculiarly strong, but because the Intelligence being undeveloped, it acts without restraint or direction from the Will.

The mental power exercised by the Will, is strikingly shown in the control exerted by human beings over the strongest of all individual cravings – the craving of hunger. The exigencies of human society have caused this tremendous power of hunger, to be kept so completely in check, that the gratification of it, except in accordance with the established laws (of property, etc.), is considered as a crime. In spite of the terrible temptation which the sight of food offers to a starving man, society punishes him if he yield to it. Still stronger than the established laws, are those unwritten laws which are enforced by 'public opinion', in obedience to which, countless people, in all civilised countries, suffer constant deprivation – even starving more or less slowly to death – rather than transgress universally accepted principles, and subject themselves to social condemnation, by taking the food which does not belong to them. Another curious and important illustration of mental action, is shown in the accumulating instances of self-deception, of contagious hallucination, and of emotional influence acting upon the physical and mental organisation, so strikingly depicted by Hammond, and other writers, in the accounts of pretended miracles, ecstasies, vision, etc.

Of all the organic functions, that of secretion is the one most strongly and frequently influenced by the mind. The secretion of tears, of bile, of milk, of saliva, may all be powerfully excited by mental stimuli, or lessened by promoting antagonistic secretions. This influence is felt in full force by those of the generative system, 'which' writes a distinguished author,

> are strongly influenced by the condition of the mind. When it is frequently and strongly directed towards objects of passion, these secretions are increased in amount, to a degree which may cause them to be a very injurious drain on the powers of the system. On the other hand, the active employment of the mental and bodily powers on other objects, has a tendency to render less active, or even to check altogether, the processes by which they are elaborated.

That the mind must possess the power of ruling this highest of the animal functions, is evident, from its uses, and from the nature of man. The faculty of sex comes to perfection when the mind is in full activity, and when all the senses are in their freshest youthful vigour. Its object is no longer confined to the individual, it is the source of social life, it is the creator of the race. Inevitably then, the human mind (the Emotions, the Will) must control this function more than any other function. It assumes a different aspect from all other functions, through its objective character. The individual may exist without it – the race not. Every object which addresses itself to the senses or the mind, acts with peculiar force upon this function. Either for right or for wrong the mind is the controlling power. The right education of the mind, is the central point from which all our efforts to help the younger generation must arise. It will thus be seen that the stand-point of education changes in childhood and in youth; the first period being specially concerned with the childhood of the body, or of the individual, the second period representing more particularly, the childhood of sex, or of the race. In neither childhood nor youth must either of the double elements of our nature – mind and body – be neglected, but in childhood the body comes first in order, in youth, the mind.

The higher the character of a function and the wider its relations, the more serious and the more numerous are the dangers to which it is exposed. A physiologist remarks, 'In youth, the affinity of the tissues for vital stimuli, seems to be greater, when the development is less complete.' That which the strong adult may endure with comparative impunity, destroys the growing youth, whose nature from the very necessities of development, possesses a keener sensitiveness to all vital stimuli. This important remark is true of mental, as well as physical youth, and applies with especial force, to the prevention of the dangers of premature sexual development. More care is needed to secure healthy, strengthening influences, for the early life of sex, than for any other more simply physical function.

In the preceding considerations, the faculty of sex has been regarded chiefly in its individual aspect, and the principles laid down, by means of which the largest amount of health and strength can be secured for each individual. But this half view is entirely insufficient in considering those physiological peculiarities of the function of sex, which must determine the true aim of education. There are two other physiological facts to be considered – viz., the Duality of Sex, and its Results.

The power we are now considering enters into a different category from all other physical functions, as being first, the faculty of two not of one only, and, second, as resulting in parentage. Directly a physical function is the property of two, it belongs to a different class from those faculties which regard solely the individual. That very fact gives it a stamp, which requires that the relations of the two factors should be considered. No faculty can be regarded in the light of simple self-indulgence, which requires two for its proper exercise. The consideration of such faculty in its imperfect condition, as belonging to one half only, is an essentially false view. It is unscientific therefore, to regard this exceptional faculty simply as a limited individual function, as we regard the other powers of the human body. Its inevitable relations to man, to woman, and to the race, must always stand forth as a prominent fact in determining the aim of education. If this be so, the moral education of youth with the necessary physiological guidance given to their sexual powers, must always be influenced by a consideration of these two inevitable physiological facts – viz., duality and parentage, and the training of young men and women, should mould them into true relations towards each other, and towards offspring.

The question of the hereditary transmission of qualities, of the influence of both mind and body, in determining the character of offspring, is a question of such vital importance, that it cannot be disregarded, even in the narrowest view of family welfare; and still less in any rational view of education, which lies at the base of national progress. This great question is still in its infancy, collected facts comparatively few, and the immense power of future development contained in it, hardly suspected by parents and philanthropists. We know already, that various forms of disease, physical peculiarities, and mental qualities, may all become hereditary; also, that the tendency to drunkenness and to sensuality, may be transmitted as surely as insanity or consumption. If we compare the mental and moral status of women in a Mahommedan country, with the corresponding class of women in our own country, we perceive the effect which generations of simply sensual unions, have produced on the character of the female population. The Christian idea of womanly characteristics is entirely reversed. The term 'woman' has become a by-word for untruth, irreligion, unchastity, and folly.[2]

The same observation may be made in so-called Christian countries under Mahommedan rule, in independent countries in close proximity to this degrading influence, and whenever the influence of unions whose key-note is sensuality, prevails. The woman is considered, morally, inferior.

> She is man's help, but not his helpmate. He guards and protects her, but it is as a man guards and protects a valuable horse or dog, getting all the service he can out of her, and rendering her in turn, his half-contemptuous protection. He uncovers her face, and lets her chat with her fellows in the court-yard, but he watches over her conduct with a jealous conviction, that she is unable to guard herself. It is a modification, yet a development, of the Mussulman idea, and he

seems to think if she has a soul to be saved, he must manage to save it for her.

Every one who has observed society in eastern Europe, must be aware of the constant relation existing between the prevalence of sensuality, and this moral degeneration of female character. This influence on the character is due, not only to the customs, religion, and circumstances, which form the nation, but also to the accumulating influence of inherited qualities. The hereditary action, produces tendencies in a particular direction in the offspring, which renders its development easier in that direction. It is only gradually, through education and the influence of heredity in a different direction, that the original tendency can be removed. But if all the circumstances of life favour its development, the individual, the family, and the nation, will certainly display the result of these tendencies in full force.

A striking illustration of this subject has lately been published in the report of the New York Prison Association for 1876. An inquiry was undertaken by one of the members of the association, to ascertain the causes of crime and pauperism, as exhibited in a particular family or tribe of offenders, called 'The Jukes', which for nearly a century has inhabited one of the central counties of the State. The investigation is carried back for some five or six generations, the descendants numbering at least 1200; and the number of persons whose biographies are condensed and collated, is not less that 709. The facts in these criminal lives, which have grown in a century from one family into hundreds, are arranged in the order of their occurrence, and the age given at which they took place, so that the relative importance of inherited tendencies and of immediate influences, may be measured. The study of this family, shows that the most general and potent cause, both of crime and pauperism is the habit of licentiousness, with its result of bastardy, and neglected and miseducated childhood. This tribe was traced back on the male side, to two sons of a hard drinker, named Max, living between 1720 and 1740, who became blind in his old age, transmitting blindness to some of his legitimate and illegitimate children. On the female side the race goes back to five sisters of bad character, two of whom intermarried with the two sons of Max, the lineage of three other sisters being also traced. In the course of the century, this family has remained an almost purely American family, inhabiting the same region of country, in one of the finest States of the Union, largely intermarrying and presenting an almost unbroken record of harlotry and crime. 'The

Jukes,' says the report, 'are not an exceptional race; analogous families may be found in every county of the State.'

Conspicuous facts, such as these, display in a striking manner, the indubitable influence of mind in the exercise of the highest – the parental – function. We see as a positive fact that mental or moral qualities quite as much as physical peculiarities, tend to reproduce themselves in children. The mental quality or character of the parent must then be considered physiologically, as a positive element in the parental relation; thought, emotion, sensation, are all mental qualities. In human unions this great fact must be borne in mind. Any sneer at 'sentiment' proceeds from ignorance of facts. Happiness is as vivifying as sunshine, and is a potent element in the formation of a child. Hence arises the necessity of love between parents – love the mental element, as distinguished from the simple physical instinct. The divorce of these two elements is fearfully illustrated in those hideous scenes lately occurring in the east of Europe, which have held every person capable of a human sentiment in shuddering horror. Happily we have reassuring proof of the power of love to triumph in the human heart, in the noble instances of conjugal devotion, which observation of private life affords.

To understand the true relations of men and women in their bearing upon the race (relations which must determine the moral aim of education), the duality of sex and the peculiarity of the womanly organisation must be recognised. Woman having a special work to perform in family life, has special requirements and sharpened perceptions in relation to this work. She demands the constant presence of affection, an affection which alone can draw forth full response, and she possesses a perception which is almost a special instinct for detecting coldness or untruthfulness, in the husband's mental attitude towards her. The presence of unvarying affection has a real, material, as well as a moral power, on the body and soul of a woman. Indifference, or neglect, is instantly felt. Sorrow, loneliness, jealousy, all constantly depressing emotions, exercise a powerful and injurious effect upon the sources of vital action. This physiological truth, and the necessity of securing the full assent of the mother in the joint creation of superior offspring, are important facts bearing on the character and happiness of one half of the human race, and influencing through that half the quality of offspring, which have never received the attention so weighty a subject demands.

In pursuing the physiological inquiry, we are met by one remarkable fact which it is impossible to ignore, and which remains from age to age as a guide to the human race. This guide is found in the physiological fact of the equality in the birth of the sexes. This is a clear indication of the intention of Providence in relation to sexual union; a proof of the fundamental nature of the family group. Boys and girls are born in equal numbers all over the world, wherever our means of observation have extended; a slight excess of boys alone existing. The Registrar-General's last report shows a proportion of 106 boys to 100 girls born throughout Europe. Sadler writes:

> The near equality in the birth of the sexes is an undoubted fact; it extends throughout Europe, and wherever we have the means of accurate observation, the birth-rate being in the proportion of twenty-five boys to twenty-four girls.

The injurious inequality which we so often find in a population is not Nature's law, it is evidence of our social stupidity. It proves our sin against God's design, in the existence of brutal wars, and our careless squandering of human life. All rational efforts for the improvement of society must be based upon Nature's true intention, viz.: the equality of the sexes in birth and in duration of life, not upon the false condition of inequality, produced by our own ignorance. It is essential always to bear in mind this distinction between the permanent fact, and the temporary phenomenon.

The foregoing facts illustrate fundamental physiological truths. They show the Type of creation, towards which the human constitution tends; and the distinctive methods of growth by which that type must be reached. In brief recapitulation, these truths are the following, viz.: The slowness of human growth; the successive development of the human faculties; the injury caused by subverting the natural order of growth; the necessity of governing this order of growth by the control of Reason; the influence of Mind – i.e., Thought, Emotion, Will – on the development or condition of our organisation; the necessity of considering the dual character of sex; the transmission of qualities by parents to their children; the natural equality in the creation of the sexes.

These truths, which are of universal application to human beings, furnish a Physiological Guide, showing the true laws of sex, in relation to human progress. We find that the laws of physiology point in one practical direction, viz.: to the family, as the only institution which secures their observance; they show the necessity of the self-control of chastity in the young man and the young woman, as the only way to secure the strong mental and physical qualities, requisite in the parental relation, whilst they also prove the special influence exerted by mutual love, in the great work of Maternity. The preparation therefore of youth for family life, should be the great aim of their sexual education.

Experience, as well as Reason, confirms the direct and indirect teaching of Physiology; they both point to the natural family group as the element out of which a healthy society grows. It is only in the family that the necessary conditions for this growth exist. The healthy and constantly varying development of children, naturally constitutes the warmest interest of parents. Brothers and sisters are invaluable educators of one another, they are unique associates, creating a species of companionship that no other relation can supply. To enjoy this interest, to create this young companionship, to form this healthy germ of society, marriage must be unitary and permanent. A constantly deepening satisfaction should exist, arising from the steady growth together through life, from the identity of interest, and from the strength of habit. Still farther we learn that such union should take place in the early period of complete adult life. Children should be the product of the first fresh vigour of parents. Everything that exhausts force or defers its freshest exercise, is injurious to the Race. Customs of society, or incorrect opinions – which obstruct the union of men and women in their early vigour, which impair the happiness of either partner, or prevent the strong and steady growth of their union – impair their efficacy as parents, and are fatal to the highest welfare of our Race.

The wide bearing and importance of the truths derived from physiology will become more and more apparent, as we examine another branch of the subject, and ascertain from an observation of facts around us, how far the present relations of men and women in civilised countries are based upon sound principles of physiology. It is necessary to know how far these principles are understood and carried out from infancy onward, whether efforts for the improvement of the race are moulded by physiological methods of human growth, and what are the inevitable consequences which result from departure from these principles.

According to a rational and physiological view of life, the family should be cherished as the precious centre of national welfare; every custom therefore, which tends to support the dignity of the family, and which prepares our youth for this life, is of vital importance to a nation. Thus the slow development of the sexual faculties, by hygienic regime, by the absence of all unnatural stimulus to these propensities, by the constant association of boys and girls together under adult influence in habitual and unconscious companionship, the cultivation in the child's mind of a true idea of manliness, and the perception that self-command is the distinctive peculiarity of the human being, are the ordinary and natural conditions which rational physiology requires. On the contrary, every custom which insults the family, and unfits for its establishment; which degrades the natural nobility of human sex, which sneers at it, and treats this great principle with flippancy, which tends to kill its divine essence and reduce it to a great idiot body – all such influences and such customs are a great crime against society, and directly opposed to the teaching of rational physiology.

An extended view of social facts, not only in different classes of our own society, but also in those countries with which we are nearly related, is of the utmost value to the parent. Physiological knowledge would be valueless to the mass of mankind, if its direct bearing upon the character and happiness of a nation could not be shown. So in considering the sexual education of youth according to the light of sound physiology, the social influences which affect the natural growth of the human being are an important part of applied physiology.

The tendencies of civilisation must be studied in our chief cities. The rapid growth of large towns during the last half century, and the comparatively stationary condition of the country population, show where the full and complete results of those principles which are most active in our civilisation must be sought for. London, Paris, Vienna, Berlin, New York, are not exceptions, but examples. They show the mature results towards which smaller towns are tending. Those who live in quiet country districts often flatter themselves that the rampant vice of large towns has nothing to do with villages, small communities, and the country at large. This is a delusion. The condition of large towns has a direct relation to the country.

In these focal points of civilisation, we observe, as examples of sexual relationship, two great institutions existing side by side. Two institutions in direct antagonism, viz., Marriage and Prostitution – the latter steadily gaining ground over the former.

In examining these two institutions, the larger signification of licentiousness must be given to prostitution, applicable to men and women. Marriage is the recognised union of two, sharing responsibilities, providing for and educating a family. Prostitution is the indiscriminate union of many, with no object but physical gratification, with no responsibilities, and no care for offspring. It is essential to study the effects, both upon men and women, and upon mankind at large, of this great fact of licentiousness, if we are to appreciate the true laws of sexual union in their full force, and the aims, importance, and wide bearing, of Moral Education. We shall only here refer to its effects upon the young.

We may justly speak of licentiousness as an institution. It is considered by a large portion of society as an essential part of itself. It possesses its code of written and unwritten laws, its sources of supply, its various resorts from the poorest hovel to the gaudiest mansion, its endless grades, from the coarsest and most ignorant to the refined and cultivated. It has its special amusements and places of public resort. It has its police, its hospitals, its prisons, and it has its literature. The organised manner in which portions of the press are engaged in promoting licentiousness, reaching not thousands, but millions of readers, is a fact of weighty importance. The one item of vicious advertisements falls into distinct categories of corruption. Growing therefore as it does, constantly and rapidly, licentiousness becomes a fact of primary importance in society. Its character and origin must be studied by all who take an interest in the growth of the human race, and who believe in the maintenance of marriage and the family as the foundation of human progress.

Every one who has studied life in many civilised countries, and the literature reflecting that life, will observe the antagonism of these two institutions; the recognition of the greater influence of the mistress than the wife, the constant triumph of passion over duty and deep steady affection. We see the neglect of the home for the café, the theatre, the public amusement; the consequent degradation of the home into a place indispensable as a nursery for children, and for the transaction of common every-day matters, a place of resort for the accidents of life, for growing old in, for continuing the family name; but too tedious a place to be in much, to spend the evening and really live in. Enjoyments are sought for elsewhere. The charm of society, the keener interests of life, no longer centre in the household. It is a domestic place, more or less quiet, but no home in the true sense of the word. The true home can only be formed by father and mother, by their joint influence on one another, on their children, and on their friends. The narrow, one-sided, diminishing influence of Continental homes, amongst great masses of the population, from absence of due paternal care, is a painful fact to witness. That there are beautiful examples of domestic life to be found in every civilised country, homes, where father and mother are one in the indispensable unity of family life – no one will deny who has closely observed foreign society. Indeed any nation is in the stage of rapid dissolution, where the institution of the family is completely and universally, degraded; but the preceding statement is a faithful representation, of the general tone and tendencies of social life in many parts of the Continent. That the same fatal principles, leading to the like results, are at work both in England and America, will be seen as we proceed. Licentiousness may be considered as still in its infancy with us, when compared with its universal prevalence in many parts of the Continent; but it is growing in our own country, with a rapidity which threatens fatal injury to our most cherished institution, the pure Christian home, with its far-reaching influences – an institution which has been the foundation of our national greatness.

The results of licentiousness should be especially considered, in their effects upon the youth of both sexes, of both the richer and poorer classes; also in their bearing upon the institution of marriage, and upon the race. In all these aspects, it enters into direct relation with the family, and no one who values the family, with the education which it should secure, can any longer afford to ignore what so intimately affects its best interests. It is to the first branch of the subject that reference will here be chiefly made.

The first consideration, is the influence exerted by social arrangements and tone of thought, upon our boys and young men, as they pass out of the family circle into the wider circles of the world, into school, college, business, society. What are the ideas about women, that have been gradually formed in the mind of the lad of sixteen, by all that he has seen, heard, and read, during his short but most important period of life? What opinions and habits in relation to his own physical and moral nature, have been impressed upon him? How have our poorer classes of boys been trained, in respect to their own well-being, and to association with girls of their own class? What has been the influence of the habits and companionships of that great middle-class multitude, clerks, shopkeepers, mechanics, farmers, soldiers, etc.; what books and newspapers do these boys read, what talk do they hear, what interests or amusements do they find in the theatre, the tavern, the streets, the home, and the church? What has been the training of the lad of the upper class – that class, small in number but great in influence, which being lifted above any sordid pressure of material care, should be the spiritual leader of the classes below it, a class which has ten talents committed to it, and which inherits the grand old maxim, 'Noblesse oblige?' How have all these lads been taught to regard womanhood and manhood? what is their standard of manliness, what habits of self-respect and of the noble uses of sex, have been impressed upon their minds? Throughout all classes abundant temptation to the abuse of sex exists. Increasing activity is displayed in the exercise of human ingenuity for the extension and refinement of vice. Shrewdness, large capital, business enterprise, are all enlisted in the lawless stimulation of this mighty instinct of sex. Immense provision is made for facilitating fornication – What direct efforts are made for encouraging chastity?

It is of vital importance to realise how small at present is the formative influence of the individual home, and the weekly discourse of the preacher, compared with the mighty social influences which spread with corrupting force around the great bulk of our youth. We find, as a matter of fact, that complete moral confusion too often meets the young man at the outset of life. Society presents him with no fixed standard of right or wrong, in relation to sex, no clear ideal to be held steadily before him, and striven for. Religious teaching points in one direction, but practical life points in quite a different way. The youth who has grown up from childhood under the guardianship of really wise parents, in a true home with all its ennobling influences, and has been strengthened by enlightened religious instruction, has gradually grown towards the natural human type. He may have met the evils of life as they came to him from boyhood onwards, first of all with the blindness of innocence, which does not realise evil, and then with the repulsion of virtue, which is clear-sighted to the hideous results of vice. Such a one will either pass with healthy strength through life, or he may prove himself the grandest of heroes if beset with tremendous temptations – or again he may fall, after long and terrible struggles with his early virtue. But in the vast majority of cases, the early training through innocence into virtue is wanting. Evil influences are at work unknown to or disregarded by the family, and a gradual process of moral and physical deterioration in the natural growth of sex, corrupts the very young. In by far the larger ranks of life, before the lad has grown into the young man, his notions of right and wrong are too often obscured. He retains a vague notion that virtue is right, but, as he perceives that his friends, his relations, his widening circle of acquaintance, live according to a different standard, his idea of virtue recedes into a vague abstraction, and he begins to think that vice is also right – in a certain way! He is too young to understand consequences; to realise the fearful chain of events in the ever-widening influence of evil acts, results, which if clearly seen would frighten the innocent mind by the hideousness of evil, and make the first step towards it a crime. No one ventures to lift up a warning voice. The parent dares not, or knows not how, to enter upon this subject of vital importance. There are no safeguards to his natural modesty; there is no wise help to strengthen his innocence into virtue.

Here is the testimony in relation to one important class, drawn from experience, by our great English moralist.

> And by the way, ye tender mothers, and sober fathers of Christian families, a prodigious thing that theory of life is, as orally learned at a great public school. Why, if you could hear those boys of fourteen, who blush before mothers, and sneak off in silence in the presence of their daughters, talking among each other – it would be the woman's turn to blush then. Before he was twelve years old, and while his mother fancied him an angel of candour, little Pen had heard talk enough to make him quite awfully wise upon certain points – and so, madam, has your pretty little rosy-cheeked son, who is coming home from school for the ensuing Christmas holidays. I don't say that the boy is lost, so that the innocence has left him which he had from 'Heaven which is our home', but the shades of the prison-house are closing very fast over him, and that we are helping as much as possible to corrupt him.

'Few boys,' says the Head Master of a large school,

> ever remain a month in any school, public or private, without learning all the salient points in the physical relation of the sexes. There are two grave evils in this unlicensed instruction, first, the lessons are learned surreptitiously; second, the knowledge is gained from the vicious experiences of the corrupted older boys, and the traditions handed down by them.

Temptations meet the lad at every step. From childhood onward, an unnatural forcing process is at work, and he is too often mentally corrupted, whilst physically unformed. This mental condition tends to hasten the functions of adult life into premature activity. As already stated, an important period exists between the establishment of puberty and confirmed virility. In the unperverted youth, this space of time marked by the rush of new life, is invaluable as a period for storing up the new forces, needed to confirm young manhood and fit it for the healthy exercise of its important social functions. The very indications of nature's abundant forces at the outset of life are warnings that this new force must not be stimulated, that there is danger of excessive and hasty growth in one direction, danger of hindering that gradual development, which alone ensures strength. If at an early age, thought and feeling have been set in the right direction, and aids to virtue and to health, surround the young man, then this period of time, before his twenty-fifth year, will lead him into a strong and vigorous manhood. But where the mind is corrupted, the imagination heated, and no strong love of virtue planted in the soul, the individual loses the power of self-control, and becomes the victim of physical sensation and suggestion. When this condition of mental and physical deterioration has been produced, it is no longer possible for him to resist surrounding temptations. There are dangers within and without, but he does not recognise the danger. He is young, eager, filled with that excess of activity in blood and nerve, with which nature always flourishes her fresh creative efforts.

At this important stage of life, when self-control, hygiene, mental and moral influence, are of vital importance, the fatal results of his weakened will and a corrupt society, ensue. Opportunity tempts his wavering innocence, thoughtless or vicious companions undertake to 'form' him, laugh at his scruples, sneer at his conscience, excite him with allurements. Or a deadly counsel meets him, meets him from those he is bound to respect. The most powerful morbid stimulant that exists – a stimulant to every drop of his seething young blood – is advised, viz.: the resort to prostitutes. When this fatal step is taken, when the natural modesty of youth, and the respect for womanhood is broken down, when he has broken with the restraints of family life, with the voice of conscience, with the dictates of religion, a return to virtue is indeed difficult – nay often impossible. He has tasted the physical delights of sex, separated from its more exquisite spiritual joys. This unnatural divorce degrades whilst it intoxicates him. Having tasted these physical pleasures, he can no more do without them, than the drunkard without his dram. He ignorantly tramples under foot his birthright of rich compound infinite human love, enthralled by the simple limited animal passion. His Will is no longer free. He has destroyed that grand endowment of Man – that freedom of the youthful Will, which is the priceless possession of innocence and of virtue, and has subjected himself to the slavery of lust. He is no longer his own master – he is the servant of his passions. Those whose interest it is to retain their victim, employ every art of drink, of dress, of excess, to urge him on. The youthful eagerness of his own nature, lends itself to these arts. The power of resistance is lost, until one glance of a prostitute's eye, passing in the street, one token of allurement, will often overturn his best resolutions, and outweigh the wisest counsel of friends! The physiological ignorance and moral blindness, which actually lead some parents to provide a mistress for their sons, in the hope of keeping them from houses of public debauchery, is an effort as unavailing as it is corrupt. Place a youth on the wrong course instead of the right one, lead him into the career of sensual indulgence and selfish disregard for womanhood, instead of manly self-control, and the parent has, by his own act, launched his child into the current of vice, which rapidly hurried him beyond his control.

The evils resulting from a violation of Nature's method of growth by a life of early dissipation are both physical and mental or moral. In some organisations the former, in some the latter, are observable in the most marked degree; but no one can escape either the physical deterioration, or the mental degradation, which results from the irrational and un-human exercise of the great endowment of sex.

Amongst the physical evils, the following may be particularly noted. The loss of self-control re-acting upon the body, produces a morbid irritability (always a sign of weakness) which is a real disease, subjecting the individual to constant excitement and exhaustion from slight causes. The resulting physical evils may be slow in revealing themselves, because they only gradually undermine the constitution. They do not herald themselves in the alarming manner of a fever, or a convulsion, but they are not to be less dreaded, from their masked approach. The chief forms of physical deterioration are, nervous exhaustion; impaired power of resistance to epidemics or other injurious influences; and the development of those germs of disease, or tendencies to some particular form of disease, which exist in the majority of constitutions. The brain and spinal marrow and the lungs, are the vital organs most frequently injured by loose life. But whatever be the weak point of the constitution, from inherited or acquired morbid tendencies, that will probably be the point through which disease or death will enter.

One of the most distinguished hygienists of our age, writes thus:

> The pathological results of venereal excess, are now well known. The gradual derangements of health, experienced by its victims, are not at first recognised by them; and physicians may take the symptoms to be the beginning of very different diseases. How often symptoms are considered as cases of hypochondria or chronic gastritis, or the commencement of heart disease, which are really the results of generative abuse. A general exhaustion of the whole physical force; symptoms of cerebral congestion; or paralysis, attributed to some cerebro-spinal lesion, are often due to the same causes. The same may be said of some of the severest forms of insanity. Many cases of consumption, appearing in young men, who

> suffer from no hereditary tendency to the disease, enter into the same category. So many diseases are vainly treated by medicine or *régime*, which are really caused by abuse of these important functions.

Another of our oldest surgeons writes:

> Amongst the passions of the future man, which at this period should be strictly restrained, is that of physical love; for none wars so completely against the principles which have been already laid down as the most conducive to long life; no excess so thoroughly lessens the sum of the vital power; none so much weakens and softens the organs of life; none is more active in hastening vital consumption; and none so totally prohibits restoration. I might if it were necessary, draw a painful, nay a frightful picture of the results of these melancholy excesses, etc.

Volumes might be filled with similar medical testimony, on the destructive character of early licentiousness.

Striking testimony to the destructive effects of vice, in early manhood, is derived from a very different source – viz., the strictly business calculation of the chances of life, furnished by Life Insurance Companies. These tables show the rapid fall in viability, during the earlier years of adult life. Dr Carpenter has reproduced a striking diagram from the well-known statistician Quetelet, showing the comparative viability of men and women at different ages; and its rapid diminution in the male, from the age of eighteen to twenty-five. He remarks:

> The mortality is much greater in males, from about the age of eighteen to twenty-eight, being at its maximum at twenty-five, when the viability is only half what it is at puberty; this fact is a very striking one, and shows most forcibly that the indulgence of the passions not only weakens the health, but in a great number of instances, is the cause of a very premature death.

The last Annual Report of the Registrar General refers to the same cause of disproportionate early mortality. Dr Bertillon (a well-known French statistician) has shown by the statistics of several European countries, that the irregularities of unmarried life produce disease, crime, and suicide; that the rate of mortality in bachelors of twenty-five is equal to that of married men at forty-five; that the immoral life of the unmarried and the widowed, whether male or female, ages them by twenty years and more.

Many of the foreign health resorts are filled with young men of the richer classes of society, seeking to restore the health destroyed by dissipation. Could the simple truth be recorded, on the tombstones of multitudes of precious youth from imperial families downward, who are mourned as victims of consumption, softening of the brain, etc., all lovers of the race would stand appalled at the endless record of these wasted lives. 'Died from the effects of fornication' would be the true warning voice from these premature graves.

The moral results of early dissipation, are quite as marked as the physical evils. The lower animal nature gains ever-increasing dominion over the moral life of the individual. The limited nature of all animal enjoyments produces its natural effects. First there is the eager search after fresh stimulants, and as the boundaries of physical enjoyment are necessarily reached, come in common sequence, disappointment, disgust, restlessness, dreariness, or bitterness. The character of the mental deterioration differs with the difference of original character in the individual, as in the nation. In some we observe an increasing hardness of character, growing contempt for women, with low material views of life. In others there is a frivolity of mind induced, a constant restlessness and search for new pleasures. The frankness, heartiness, and truthfulness of youth, gradually disappear under the withering influence.[3]

The moral influence of vice upon social character has very wide ramifications. This is illustrated by the immense difficulties which women encounter in the rational endeavour to obtain a complete medical education. Licentiousness, with all its attendant results, is the great social cause of these difficulties.

The dominion of lust is necessarily short-sighted, selfish, or cruel. It is directly opposed to the qualities of truth, trust, self-command, and sympathy; thus sapping the foundations of personal morality. But apart from the individual evils, above referred to, licentiousness inevitably degrades society, firstly from the disproportion of vital force which is thus thrown into one direction, and secondly from the essentially selfish and ungenerous tendency of vice, which, seeking its own limited gratification at the expense of others, is incapable of embracing large views of life, or feeling enthusiasm for progress. The direction into which this disproportionate vital force is thrown is a degrading one, always tending to evil results. Thus the noble enthusiasm of youth, its precious tide of fresh life, without which no nation can grow – life, whose leisure hours should be given to science and art, to social good, to ennobling recreation – is squandered and worse than wasted in degrading dissipation.

This dissipation, which is ruin to man, is also a curse to woman, for in judging the effects of licentiousness upon society, it must never be forgotten, that this is a vice of two, not a vice of one. Injurious as is its influence upon the young man, that is only one half of its effect. What is its influence upon the young woman? This question has a direct bearing on the Moral Aim of Education. The preceding details of physical and moral evils resulting to young men from licentiousness, will apply with equal force to young women subjected to similar influences. One sex may experience more physical evil, the other more mental degradation, from similar vicious habits; but the evil, if not identical, is entirely parallel, and a loss of truthfulness, honour, and generosity, accompanies the loss of purity.

The women more directly involved in this widespread evil of licentiousness are the women of the poorer classes of society. The poorer classes constitute in every country the great majority of the people, they form its solid strength and determine its character. The extreme danger of moral degradation, in those classes of young women who constitute such an immense preponderance of the female population, is at once evident. These women are everywhere; interlinked with every class of society. They form an important part (often the larger female portion) of every well-to-do household. They are the companions and inevitable teachers of infancy and childhood. They often form the chief, or only female influence which meets the young man in early professional, business, or even college life. They meet him in every place of public amusement, in his walks at night, in his travels at home and abroad. By day and by night, the young man away from home is brought into free intercourse, not with women of his own class, but with poor working girls and women, who form the numerical bulk of the female population, who are found in every place, and ready for every service. Educated girls are watched and guarded. The young man meets them in rare moments only, under supervision, and generally under unnatural restraint; but the poor girl he meets constantly, freely, at any time and place. Any clear-sighted person who will quietly observe the way in which female servants (for instance) regard very young men, their superiors in station, can easily comprehend the dangers of such association. The injustice of the common practical view of life is only equalled by its folly. This practical view utterly ignores the fact of the social influence and value of this portion of society. The customs of civilised nations practically consider poor women as subjects for a life so dishonourable, that a rich man feels justified in ostracising wife, sister, or daughter, who is guilty of the slightest approach to such life. It is the great mass of poor women who are regarded as (and sometimes brutally stated to be) the subjects to be used for the benefit of the upper classes. Young and innocent men, it is true, fall into vice or are led into it, or are tempted into it by older women, and are not deliberate betrayers. But the rubicon of chastity once passed, the moral descent is rapid, and the preying upon the poor soon commences. The miserable slaves in houses of prostitution are the outcasts of the poor. The young girls followed at night in the streets are the honest working girl, the young servant seeking a short outdoor relief to her dreary life, as well as the unhappy fallen girl who has become in her turn the seducer. If fearful of health, the individual leaves the licensed slaves of sin and the chance associations of the streets, it is amongst the poor and unprotected that he seeks his mistress; the young seamstress, the pretty shop girl, the girl with some honest employment, but poor, undefended, needing relief in her hard-working life. It is always the poor girl that he seeks. She has no pleasures, he offers them; her virtue is weak, he undermines it; he gains her affection and betrays it, changes her for another and another, leaving each mistress worse than he found her, farther on in the downward road, with the guilt of fresh injury from the strong to the weak on his soul. Any reproach of conscience – conscience which will speak, when an innocent girl has been betrayed, or one not yet fully corrupted has been led farther on in evil life – is quieted by the frivolous answer, 'They will soon marry in their own class.' If, however, this sin be regarded in its inevitable consequences, its effects upon the life of both man and woman in relation to society, the nature of this sophistry will appear in its hideous reality. Is chastity really a virtue, something precious in womanhood? – then, the poor man's home should be blessed by the presence of a pure woman. Does it improve a woman's character to be virtuous? Has she more self-respect in consequence, does she care more for her children, for their respectability and welfare, when she is conscious of her own honest past life? Does she love her husband more, and will she strive to make his home brighter and more attractive to him, exercising patience in the trials of her humble life; being industrious, frugal, sober, with tastes that centre in her home? These are vital questions for the welfare of the great mass of the people, consequently of society and of the nation.

We know on the contrary as a fundamental truth, that unchastity unfits a woman for these natural duties. It fosters her vanity, it makes her slothful or reckless, it gives her tastes at variance with home life, it makes her see nothing in men but their baser passions, and it converts her into a constant tempter of those passions – a corrupter of the young. We know that drunkenness, quarrels, and crimes, have their origin in the wretched homes of the poor, and the centre of those unhappy homes in the unchaste woman, who has lost the restraining influence of her own self-respect, her respect for others, and her love of home. When a pretty vain girl is tempted to sin, a wife and mother is being ruined, discord and misery are being prepared for a poor man's home, and the circumstances created out of which criminals grow. Nor does the evil stop there. It returns to the upper classes. Nurses, servants, bring back to the respectable home the evil associations of their own lives. The children of the upper classes are thus corrupted, and the path of youth is surrounded at every step with coarse temptations. These consequences may not be foreseen, when the individual follows the course of evil customs; but the sequence of events is inevitable, and every man gives birth to a fresh series of vice and misery, when he takes a mistress instead of a wife.[4]

The deterioration of character amongst the women of the working classes is known to all employers of labour; to all who visit amongst the poor; to every housekeeper. The increasing difficulty of obtaining trustworthy servants is now the common experience of civilised countries. In England, France, Germany, and the larger towns of America, it is a fact of wide-spread observation, and has become a source of serious difficulty in the management of family life. The deepest source of this evil lies in the deterioration of womanly character, produced by the increasing spread of habits of licentiousness. The action of sex, though taking different directions, is as powerful in the young woman as in the young man; it needs as careful education, direction, and restraint. This important physiological truth, at present quite overlooked, must nevertheless be distinctly recognised. This strong mental instinct, if yielded to in a degrading way (as is so commonly the case in the poorer classes of society), becomes an absorbing influence. Pride and pleasure in work, the desire to excel, loyalty to duty, and the love of truth in its wide significance, are all subordinated, and gradually weakened, by the irresistible mastery of this new faculty. In all large towns, the lax tone of companions, the difficulty in finding employment, the horrible cupidity of those who pander to corrupt social sentiment and ensnare the young, all these circumstances combined, render vice much easier than virtue – a state of society in which vice must necessarily extend, and virtue diminish. We thus find an immense mass of young women gradually corrupted from childhood, rendered coarse and reckless, the modesty of girlhood destroyed, the reserve of maidenhood changed to bold, often indecent, behaviour. No one accustomed to walk freely about our streets, to watch children at play, to observe the amusements and free gatherings of the poorer classes, can fail to see the signs of degraded sex. The testimony of home missionaries, of those experienced in Benevolent Societies, and long engaged in various ways in helping women, as well as the Reports of Rescue Societies, all testify to the dangerous increase and lamentable results of unchastity, amongst the female population.

We observe in all countries a constant relation also between the prevalence of licentiousness and degradation of female labour; the action and re-action of these two evil facts is invariable. In Paris we see the complete result of these tendencies of modern civilisation in relation to the condition of working women, tendencies which are seen in London and Berlin, in Liverpool, Glasgow – i.e., in all large towns. The revelations made by writers and speakers in relation to the condition of the working women of Paris, are of very serious import to England. Such terrible facts as the following, brought to light by those who have carefully investigated the state of this portion of the population, must arrest attention. In relation to vast numbers of women it is stated:

> In Paris, a woman can no longer live by the work of her own hands; the returns of her labour are so small, that prostitution is the only resource against slow starvation. The population is bastardised to such an extent, that thousands of poor girls know not of any relation that they ever possessed. Orphans and outcasts, their life, if virtuous, is one terrible struggle from the cradle to the grave; but by far the greater number of them are drilled whilst yet children in the public service of debauchery.

The great mass of working women are placed by the present state of society in a position in which there are the strongest temptations to vice. When to lead a virtuous life, often requires the possession of moral heroism.

Of the multitude of those who fall into vice, many ultimately marry, and with injured moral qualities and corrupted tastes, become the creators of poor men's homes. The rest drift into a permanent life of vice. The injurious effects of unchastity upon womanly character already noted, can be studied step by step, to their complete development in that great class of the population – the recognised prostitutes. Their marked characteristics are recklessness, sloth, and drunkenness. This recklessness, and utter disregard of consequences and appearances, with a quarrelsome, violent disposition, the dislike to all labour, and all regular occupation and life; the necessity for stimulants and drink, with a bold address to the lower passions of men – such are the effects of this life upon the character of women. Unchaste women become a most dangerous class of the community. To these bad qualities is added another, wherever, as in France, this evil life is accepted as a part of society, provided for, organised, or legalised; this last result of confirmed licentiousness, is a hardness of character, so complete, so resistent of all improving influences, that the wisest and gentlest efforts to restore are utterly hopeless before the confirmed and hardened prostitute.

The growth of habits of licentiousness amongst us exerts the most direct and injurious influence on the lives of virtuous young women of the middle and upper classes of society. The mode of this influence, demands very serious consideration on the part of parents. It is natural that young women should wish to please. They possess the true instinct, which would guide them to their noble position in society as the centres of pure and happy homes. How do our social customs meet this want? All the young women of the middle and upper classes of society, no matter how pure and innocent their natures, are brought, by these customs of society – into direct competition with prostitutes! The modest grace of pure young womanhood, its simple refined tastes, its love of home pleasures, its instinctive admiration of true and noble sentiments and actions, although refreshing as a contrast, will not compare for a moment with the force of attraction, which sensual indulgence and the excitement of debauch, exerts upon the youth who is habituated to such intoxications. The virtuous girl exercises a certain amount of attraction for a passing moment, but the intense craving awakened in the youth for something far more exciting than she can offer, leads him ever farther from her, in the direction where this morbid craving can be freely indulged. This result is inevitable, if licentiousness is to be accepted as a necessary part of society. Physical passion is not in itself evil, on the contrary it is an essential part of our nature. It is an endowment which like every other *human* faculty, has the power of high growth. It possesses that distinctive human characteristic – receptivity to mental impressions. These impressions blend so completely with itself, as to change its whole character and effect; and it thus becomes an ennobling or a degrading agent in our lives. In either case for good or for evil, sex takes a first place as a motive power, in human education. The young man, inexperienced in life and necessarily crude in thought, but fallen into vice, is mastered by this downward force, and the good girl loses more and more her power over the strong natural attraction of sex, which would otherwise draw him to her. The influence which corrupt young men, on the other hand, exercise upon the young women of their own standing in society, is both strong and often injurious. It being natural that young women should seek to attract and retain them, they unconsciously endeavour to adapt themselves to their taste. These tastes are formed by uneducated girls, and by society of which the respectable young woman feels the effects, and of which she has a vague suspicion, although happily she cannot measure the depth of the evil. The tastes and desires of her young male acquaintance, moulded by coarse material enjoyments, act directly upon the respectable girl, who gives herself up with natural impulse to the influence of her male companion. We thus witness a wide-spread and inevitable deterioration in manners, dress, thought, and habits, amongst the respectable classes of young women. This result leads eventually, as on the Continent, to the entire separation of young men and women in the middle and upper ranks of life, to the arrangement of marriage as a business affair, and to the union of the young with the old.

The faults now so often charged upon young women, their love of dress, luxury, and pleasure, their neglect of economy, and dislike of steady home duties, may be traced directly to the injurious influence, which habits of licentiousness are exercising, directly and indirectly upon marriage, the home, and society. The subject of dress is one of serious importance, for it is a source of extravagance in all classes, and one of the strongest temptations to vice among poor girls. The creation of this morbid excess in dress, by licentiousness, is evident. If physical attraction is the sole or chief force which draws young men to young women, then everything which either enhances physical charms, which brings them more prominently forward, or which supplies the lack of physical beauty, must necessarily be resorted to by women, whose nature it is to draw men to them. The stronger the general domination of physical sensation – over character, sympathy, companionship, mutual help, and social growth – becomes amongst men, the more exclusive, intense, and competitive, must grow this morbid devotion to dress, on the part of women. Did young men seriously long for a virtuous wife and happy home, and fit themselves to secure those blessings, young women would naturally cultivate the domestic qualities which ensure a bright, attractive home. The young man, however, is now discouraged from early marriage; the question soon presents itself to him, 'Why should I marry, and burden myself with wife and family? I am very well off as I am,

I can spend my money as I like on personal pleasures, I can get all that I want from women, without losing my liberty or assuming responsibilities!' The respectable girl is thus forced into a most degrading and utterly unavailing competition with the prostitute or the mistress. Marriage is indefinitely postponed by the young man; at first it may be from necessity, later, from choice. The young woman, unable to obtain the husband suited to her in age, must either lead a single life, or accept the unnatural union with a rich elderly man.

The grave physiological error of promoting marriage between the young and the old, cannot be dwelt on here. It is productive of very grave evils, both to the health and happiness of the individual, and to the growth of the Race. The steady decrease of marriage, and at the same time the late date at which it is contracted, as licentiousness increases, is shown by a comparison of the statistics of Belgium and France with those of England. We find also that the character of the population deteriorates with the spread of vice – the standard of recruiting for the army is lowered, an ever-increasing mass of fatherless children die, or become criminals, and finally, the natural growth of the population of the country, constantly decreases.

The records of History confirm the teaching of Physiology, and Observation, in relation to the fundamental character of sexual virtue, as the secret of durable national greatness. The decline of all the great nations of antiquity is marked by the prevalence of gross social corruption. The complex effects of the same cause, are strikingly observed in the condition of the Mahommedan and other Eastern races, and in all the tribes subject to them. We find amongst these races, as the result of their sexual customs, a want of human charity. This is shown in the absence of benevolent institutions, and other modes of expressing sympathy. A great gulf separates the rich and poor, bridged over by no offices of kindness, no sense of the sacred oneness of humanity, which is deeper than all separations of caste or condition. There is no respect shown for human life, which is lightly and remorselessly sacrificed, and punishment degenerates into torture. There is also an incapacity for understanding the fundamental value of truth and honesty, and a consequent impossibility of creating a good government. We observe that bravery degenerates into fierceness and cruelty, and that the apathy of the masses keeps them victims of oppression. It is the exhibition of a race, where there is no development of the Moral Element in human nature. These general characteristics, and their cause, were well described by the celebrated surgeon, Lallemand, who says: 'The contrast between the polygamous and sensual East, and the monogamous and intellectual West, displays on a large scale the different results produced by the different exercise of the sexual powers. On one side, polygamy, harems, seraglios – the source of venereal excesses – barbarous mutilations, revolting and unnatural vice, with the population scanty, inactive, indolent, sunk in ignorance, and consequently the victim of misery, and of every kind of despotism. On the other side, Monogamy, Christian austerity, more equal distribution of domestic happiness, increase of intelligence, liberty, and general well-being; rapid increase of an active, laborious, and enterprising population, necessarily spreading and dominating.'

The great moral element of society, which contains the power of self-renewal and continual growth, must necessarily be wanting in all nations, where one half of the people – the centre of the family, out of which society must grow – remains in a stunted, or perverted condition. Women, as well as men, create society. Their share is a silent one. It has not the glitter of gold and purple, the noise of drums and marching armies, the smoke and clank of furnaces and machinery. All the splendid din of external life is wanting in the quiet realm of distinctive woman's work, therefore it is often overlooked, misunderstood, or despised. Nevertheless it is of vital importance. It preserves the only germ of society which is capable of permanent growth – the germ of unselfish human love, and innate righteousness – in distinction to which, all dazzling material splendour and intellectual ability divorced from the love of Right, is but sounding brass and tinkling cymbal. It is, for this reason, that no polygamous or licentious customs, which destroy the woman's nature, and dry up the deepest source of human sympathy, can possibly produce a durable, or a noble and happy nation. The value of a nation, its position in the scale of humanity, its durability, must always be judged by the condition of its masses, and the test of that condition is the strength and purity of home virtues – the character of the women of the nation.

No reference to the lessons of history, however brief, should omit the effect produced by religious teaching. The influence exercised by the Christian religion in relation to sex is of the most striking character. Christian teaching is distinguished from all other religious teaching by its justice to women, its tender reverence for childhood, and by the laying down of that great corner-stone, Inward Holiness, as the indispensable foundation of true life. This is all summed up in its establishment of unitary marriage, through the emphatic adoption of the original Law, 'Therefore shall a man leave his father and his mother, and cleave unto his wife, and they twain shall be one flesh.' The development of this Law by Jesus

Christ, into its high significance of spiritual purity, whilst it has been a principle of growth in the past, is the great hope of the future. The study of this Christian type, in its radical effect upon national life, is full of interest and instruction; but is also a study of great difficulty. This teaching of our Lord has never been adopted, as the universal rule of practical life, by any nation. The results of this law of union can only be judged on a large scale, by comparing the condition of so-called Christian countries – where a certain amount of this high teaching has been diffused through the community – with the condition of nations, where no such teaching has existed. The great battle between Christianity and Paganism still continues in our midst. The actual practical type, prevailing in all civilised nations, is not Christian. In these nations the Christian idea of unitary sexual relations is accepted theoretically, as conducive to the best interests of the family, and binding upon the higher classes of woman; but it is entirely set aside as a practical life for the majority of the community. Christ's Law is considered, either as a vague command, applicable only to some indefinite future, or as a theory which it would be positively unwise to put into practice in daily life. The statement is distinctly made, and widely believed, that the nature of men and women differs so radically, that the same moral law is not applicable to the two sexes.

The great lesson derived from History, however, is always this, viz., that moral development must keep pace with the intellectual, or the race degenerates. This moral element is especially embodied by woman; and purity in woman cannot exist without purity in man; this weighty fact being shown by the facts already stated, viz., the action of licentiousness upon the great mass of unprotected women, its reaction upon other classes, and the accumulating influence of hereditary sensuality.

In the indisputable principles brought forward in the preceding pages, and the mass of facts and daily observation which support them, is found the answer to the first question proposed, as a guide to the moral education of youth, viz., What is the true standard for the relations of men and women, the type which contains within itself the germ of progress and indefinite development?

We see that the early and faithful union of one man with one woman is the true Ideal of Society. It secures the health and purity of the family relation, and is the foundation of social and national welfare. It is supported by sound principles of Physiology, by the history of the rise and fall of nations, and by a consideration of the evils of our present age. The lessons of the past and present, our clearer knowledge of cause and effect, alike prove the wisdom of the highest religious teaching, viz., that the faithful union of strong and pure young man and womanhood, is the only element out of which a strong and durable nation can grow.

Appendix

Proofs of the constant increase and diffusion of incentives to licentiousness may be studied in the reports of the Society for the Suppression of Vice, 23 Lincoln's Inn Fields (a society for checking licentious literature, which deserves more active support than it has hitherto received); in the reports of the kindred Society lately established in New York as a branch of the Young Men's Christian Association of that city: in the *Discours sur les Remèdes Secrets et Annoncés Immorales* of Dr Ladame, published at Neufchâtel, Switzerland, 5 Rue de Seyon; *Essay on Licentious Literature* by M. Valleton de Greyon, etc.

It will be found that the amount and variety of obscene incentives is rapidly increasing; that they reach families and schools, as well as colleges, clubs, and places of business; that they are hawked about the country as well as sold in shops; that driven from one place they take refuge in another (as when notorious panderers driven from London have at once gone to Brussels), and export their wares from one country to another; that people in respectable positions in society have carried on an extensive trade in corruption; and that males and females of all classes are applicants for all sorts of obscenities, as shown by the correspondence seized in great quantities on the premises of detected dealers. Thus obscene books, songs, pamphlets, handbills, pictures, and photographs are issued, not by the hundred, but the million. Cards, snuff-boxes, pipes, pensticks, rings, knives, etc., are made the instruments of vice, by picture, shape, or the introduction of some microscopic obscenity, often overlooked by the purchaser. Facts supporting these statements in relation to England may be found in the reports above referred to, as well as through private observation.

The Pastor Quistorp of Pomerania has given a list of more than fifteen firms in Germany which make a specialty of licentious literature and obscene articles; every week they publish detailed descriptions of their wares in hundreds of newspapers. Their trade is so enormous, that in one year the police of Baltimore, US, seized twenty hundredweight of scandalous books and objects which they had exported to that city. Amongst them were quantities of obscene New Year's cards, which are manufactured in Berlin, and coloured by young girls from fourteen to sixteen years of age. But the most successful means of distributing these vile articles is by colporteurage. This system is constantly spreading through the interior of the German Empire, it extends to the country as well as the towns, and within the last few years is spreading through German Switzerland into the French cantons.

A late report of the London Society for the Suppression of Vice, in making an earnest appeal to the public, says,

> Were it once known that we were unable to carry out our operations, the flood-gates of vice would be let loose, and England would find herself in the same state in which America was previous to the formation of the Society in that country, where, according to their reports, obscene books and pictures were traced, not only in schools of girls and boys, but that educated persons, both male and female, were in the habit of acquiring them.

NOTES

1 A late judgement in our Courts allowed the charge of paternity brought against a lad of fourteen to be established.

2 The unhealthiness and indecency of harem life, with its effect upon the boys and girls, its encouragement of abortion, and the unhappy and degraded condition of the women, are sketched with the painful truth of close observation in *The People of Turkey*, edited by S. Lane Poole, a book worthy of careful consideration. See also Lane's *Egyptians*, etc.

3 One of the most powerful causes of the growth of pessimism in Germany is the increasing licentiousness of a race created with a high ideal of virtue and cherishing a love of home. An incident of a carnival held in a garrison and residential town of Germany, where a young man of one of the best families brought eight young girls, his mistresses, dressed in white, bordered with blue à la grecque, to a public ball, is but an illustration of the decay of morality in German-speaking nations. All laws enacted to repress the expressions of popular discontent must be vain, whilst a harsh military system trains the youth of a nation in habits of dreary immorality.

4 The frequent opinion that a limited amount of fornication is a very trivial matter; that the individual may become an excellent father of a family and good citizen in spite of such indulgence, is based on the grave error of regarding sexual relations as the act of one instead of two individuals, and limited in their effects to the moment of occurrence. The moral character of such indulgence is however determined by its effects upon the after-life of two human beings, viz., its effect on the citizen whose judgment becomes injured in relation to this great

subject of national welfare, through early experience, and on the partner in vice whose life is one of growing degradation. These two inevitable facts remain through life.

Annie Besant

Marriage: As It Was, As It Is, and As It Should Be

(1882)

I

Either all human beings have equal rights, or none have any.

Condorcet

The recognition of human rights may be said to be of modern growth, and even yet they are but very imperfectly understood. Liberty used to be regarded as a privilege bestowed, instead of as an inherent right; rights of classes have often been claimed: right to rule, right to tax, right to punish, all these have been argued for and maintained by force; but these are not rights, they are only wrongs veiled as legal rights. Jean Jacques Rousseau struck a new note when he cried: 'Men are born free'; free by birthright was a new thought, when declared as a universal inheritance, and this 'gospel of Jean Jacques Rousseau' dawned on the world as the sun-rising of a glorious day – a day of human liberty, unrestrained by class. In 1789 the doctrine of the 'Rights of Man' received its first European sanction by law; in the August of that year the National Assembly of France proclaimed: 'Men are born, and remain, free and equal in rights. . . . The aim of political association is the conservation of the natural and imprescriptible rights of man; these rights are – liberty, property, safety, and resistance of tyranny.' During savage and semi-civilised ages these 'imprescriptible rights' are never dreamed of as existing; brute force is king; might is the only right, and the strong arm is the only argument whose logic meets with general recognition. In warlike tribes fair equality is found, and the chief is only *primus inter pares;* but when the nomadic tribe settles down into an agricultural community, when the habit of bearing arms ceases to be universal, when wealth begins to accumulate, and the village or town offers attractions for pillage, then strength becomes at once a terror and a possible defence. The weak obey some powerful neighbour partly because they cannot resist, and partly because they desire, by their submission, to gain a strong protection against their enemies. They submit to the exactions of one that they may be shielded from the tyranny of many, and yield up their natural liberty to some extent to preserve themselves from being entirely enslaved. Very slowly do they learn that the union of many individually feeble is stronger than a few powerful, isolated tyrants, and gradually law takes the place of despotic will; gradually the feeling of self-respect, of independence, of love of liberty, grows, until at last man claims freedom as of right, and denies the authority of any to rule him without his own consent.

Thus the Rights of Man have become an accepted doctrine, but, unfortunately, they are only rights of *man*, in the exclusive sense of the word. They are sexual, and not human rights, and until they become human rights, society will never rest on a sure, because just, foundation. Women, as well as men, 'are born and remain free and equal in rights': women, as well as men, have 'natural and imprescriptible rights', for women, as well as for men, 'these rights are – liberty, property, safety, and resistance of tyranny'. Of these rights only crime should deprive them, just as by crime men also are deprived of them; to deny these rights to women, is either to deny them to humanity *quâ* humanity, or to deny that women form a part of humanity; if women's rights are denied, men's rights have no logical basis, no claim to respect; then tyranny ceases to be a crime, slavery is no longer a scandal; 'either all human beings have equal rights or none have any'.

Naturally, in the savage state, women shared the fate of the physically weak, not only because, as a rule, they are smaller-framed and less muscular than their male comrades, but also because the bearing and suckling of children is a drain on their physical resources from which men are exempt. Hence she has suffered from 'the right of the strongest', even more than has man, and her exclusion from all political life has prevented the redressal which man has wrought out for himself; while claiming freedom for himself he has not loosened her chains, and while striking down his own tyrants, he has maintained his personal tyranny in the home. Nor has this generally been done by deliberate intention: it is rather the survival of the old system, which has only been abolished so slowly as regards men. Mrs Mill writes:

That those who were physically weaker should have been

> made legally inferior, is quite conformable to the mode in which the world has been governed. Until very lately, the rule of physical strength was the general law of human affairs. Throughout history, the nations, races, classes, which found themselves strongest, either in muscles, in riches, or in military discipline, have conquered and held in subjection the rest. If, even in the most improved nations, the law of the sword is at last discountenanced as unworthy, it is only since the calumniated eighteenth century. Wars of conquest have only ceased since democratic revolutions began. The world is very young, and has only just begun to cast off injustice. It is only now getting rid of negro slavery. It is only now getting rid of monarchical despotism. It is only now getting rid of hereditary feudal nobility. It is only now getting rid of disabilities on the ground of religion. It is only beginning to treat any *men* as citizens, except the rich and a favoured portion of the middle class. Can we wonder that it has not yet done as much for women? ('Enfranchisement of Women', Mrs Mill, in J. S. Mill's *Discussions and Dissertations*, Vol. II, page 421)

The difference between men and women in all civil rights is, however, with few, although important, exceptions, confined to married women; i.e., women in relation with men. Unmarried women of all ages suffer under comparatively few disabilities; it is marriage which brings with it the weight of injustice and of legal degradation.

In savage times marriage was a matter either of force, fraud, or purchase. Women were merchandise, by the sale of whom their male relatives profited, or they were captives in war, the spoil of the conqueror, or they were stolen away from the paternal home. In all cases, however, the possession once obtained, they became the property of the men who married them, and the husband was their 'lord', their 'master'. In the old Hebrew books – still accounted sacred by Jews and Christians – the wife is regarded as the property of her husband. A man may 'sell his daughter to be a maidservant', i.e., a concubine, as is shown by the following verse (Ex. xxi. 7), and Jacob served seven years for each of his wives, Leah and Rachel; his other two wives were his by gift, and were rather concubines than recognised wives, their children counting to their mistresses. If a Hebrew conquered his enemies, and saw 'among the captives a beautiful woman, and hast a desire unto her, that thou wouldst have her to thy wife', he might take her home, and become her husband, 'and she shall be thy wife'

(Deut xxi, 10–14). After the destruction of Benjamin, as related in Judges xx, it was arranged that the survivors should possess themselves of women as wives by force and fraud:

> Lie in wait in the vineyards, and see and behold if the daughters of Shiloh come out to dance in dances, then come ye out of the vineyards, and catch you every man his wife. . . . And the children of Benjamin did so, and took their wives according to their number, of them that danced, whom they caught. (Judges xxi, 20, 21, 23)

The same plan was adopted by the Romans in their earliest days, when they needed wives. Romulus invited the people of the Sabines and the neighbouring towns to see some public games, and in the midst of the show the Romans rushed in and carried off all the marriageable maidens they could lay hands on (Liddell's *History of Rome*, p. 20). These instances may be objected to as legendary, but they are faithful pictures of the rough wooing of early times. Among some barbarous nations the winning of a bride is still harsher: the bridegroom rushes into the father's house knocks the maiden down, picks up her senseless body, flings it over his shoulder, and runs for his life; he is pursued by the youth of the village, pelted with stones, sticks, etc., and has to win his wife by sheer strength and swiftness. In some tribes this is a mere marriage ceremony, a survival from the time when the fight was a real one, and amongst ourselves the slipper thrown after the departing bridegroom and bride is a direct descendant of the heavier missiles thrown with deadly intent thousands of years ago by our remote ancestors. Amongst many semi-barbarous nations the wives are still bought; in some parts of Africa the wooer pays a certain number of cows for his bride; in other places, money or goods are given in exchange. The point to be noted is that the wife is literally taken by force, or bought; she is not free to choose her husband; she does not give herself to him; she is a piece of property, handed over by her original owner – her father – to her new owner – her husband – in exchange for certain solid money or money's worth; hence she becomes the property of the man who has paid for her.

In an admirable article in the *Westminster Review* for April 1876, the following striking passage is to be found:

> As Aristotle long since remarked, among savages women and slaves hold the same rank. Women are bought primarily as slaves, to drudge and toil for their masters, whilst their function as wives is secondary and subordinate. It is more

> right to say of polygamous people that their slaves are also their wives, than to say that their wives are slaves. They are purchased as slaves, they work as slaves, and they live as slaves. 'The history of uncultivated nations', it has been said, 'uniformly represents the women as in a state of abject slavery, from which they slowly emerge as civilisation advances'. In Canada a strap, a kettle, and a faggot are placed in the new bride's cabin, to indicate that it will be henceforth her duty to carry burdens, dress food, and procure wood for her husband. In Circassia it is the women who till and manure the ground, and in parts of China they follow the plough. A Moorish wife digs and sows and reaps the corn, and an Arabian wife feeds and cleans and saddles her master's horse. Indeed, the sole business of Bedouin wives is to cook and work, and perform all the menial offices connected with tent-life. . . . From the absolute power of a savage over his slaves flow all those rights over a woman from which the marital rights of our own time are the genealogical descendants. . . . A trace of it [purchase] is found in the following customs of old English law: 'The woman at the church-door was given of her father, or some other man of the next of her kin, into the hands of her husband, and he laid down gold and silver for her upon the book, as though he did buy her.'

This custom is still maintained in the Church ritual; the priest asks: 'Who giveth this woman to be married to this man?' and when the man gives the ring to the priest, he gives money with it, receiving back the ring to give the woman, but the money remaining, a survival of the time when wives were literally bought.

By the old Roman laws, the married woman had no personal rights; she was but the head slave in her husband's house, absolutely subject in all things to her lord. As the Romans became civilised, these disabilities were gradually removed. It is important to remember these facts, as these are the origin of our own marriage laws, and our common law really grows out of them.

One other point must be noticed, before dealing immediately with the English marriage laws, and that is the influence exerted over them by ecclesiastical Christianity. The Old Testament expressly sanctions polygamy; but while the New Testament does not proscribe it – except in the case of bishops and deacons – ecclesiastical Christianity has generally been in favour of monogamy; at the same time, both the New Testament and the Church have insisted on the inferiority of the female sex; 'the husband is the head of the wife' (Eph. v, 23); 'wives, submit yourselves unto your own husbands' (Col. iii, 18); 'your women . . . are commanded to be under obedience' (1 Cor. xiv, 34); 'ye wives, be in subjection to your own husbands . . . even as Sara obeyed Abraham, calling him lord, whose daughters ye are as long as ye do well' (1 Pet. iii, 1, 6). The common law of England is quite in accordance with this ancient Eastern teaching, and regards men as superior to women; 'Among the children of the purchaser, males take before females, or, as our male lawgivers have expressed it, the worthiest of blood shall be preferred' (*Comm. on the Laws of England*, J. Stephen, 7th edn, vol. i, p. 402).

The feudal system did much, of course, to perpetuate the subjection of women, it being to the interest of the lord paramount that the fiefs should descend in the male line: in those rough ages, when wars and civil feuds were almost perpetual, it was inevitable that the sex with the biggest body and strongest sinews should have the upper hand; the pity is that English gentlemen today are content to allow the law to remain unaltered, when the whole face of society has changed.

Let us now turn to the disabilities imposed upon women by marriage.

Blackstone lays down, in his world-famous *Commentaries on the Laws of England*, that the first of the 'absolute rights of every Englishman' is 'the legal and uninterrupted enjoyment of his life, his limbs, his body, his health, and his reputation' (9th edn, bk. 1, p. 129). The second right is personal liberty, and he says: 'the confinement of a person in anywise is an imprisonment. So that the keeping a man against his will in a private house. . . . is an imprisonment' (ibid. 136). The third is property, 'which consists in the free use and enjoyment of all his acquisitions, without any control or diminution, save only by the laws of the land' (ibid., 138). A subordinate right, necessary for the enforcement of the others, is 'that of applying to the courts of justice for redress of injuries'. I shall proceed to show that a married woman is deprived of these rights by the mere fact of her marriage.

In the first place, by marriage a woman loses her legal existence; the law does not recognise her, excepting in some few cases, when it becomes conscious of her existence in order to punish her for some crime or misdemeanour. Blackstone says – and no subsequent legislation has in any way modified his dictum:

> By marriage the husband and wife are one person in law; that is, the very being or legal existence of the woman is suspended during the marriage, or at least is incorporated or consolidated into that of the husband; under whose wing,

> protection, and *cover*, she performs every thing; and is therefore called in our law-French a *feme covert*. (p. 442)

'Husband and wife are one person in law' (*Comyn's Digest*, 5th edn, vol. ii, p. 208), and from this it follows that 'by no conveyance at the common law could the husband give an estate to his wife'; that 'a husband cannot covenant or contract with his wife', even for her own advantage, and that any prenuptial contract made with her as to money she shall enjoy for her separate use after marriage, becomes void as soon as she is married. All covenants for the wife's benefit must be made with some one else, and the husband must covenant with some other man or unmarried woman who acts as trustee for the wife. This is the fundamental wrong from which all the others flow: ' "Husband and wife are one person", and that one is the husband.' The wife's body, her reputation, are no longer her own. She can gain no legal redress for injury, for the law does not recognise her existence except under cover of her husband's suit. In some cases more modern legislation has so far become conscious of her, as to protect her against her husband, and if this protection separates her from him, it leaves her the more utterly at the mercy of the world.

Various curious results flow, in criminal law, from this supposition that husband and wife are only one person. They are incompetent – except in a few special instances – to give evidence for or against each other in criminal cases; if a woman's husband be one of several defendants indicted together, the woman cannot give evidence either for or against any of them. Where the wife of an accomplice is the only person to confirm her husband's statement, the statement falls to the ground, as, in practice, confirmation thereof is required; in the case of Rex *v*. Neal (7 C. and P. 168), Justice Park said: 'Confirmation by the wife is, in this case, really no confirmation at all. The wife and the accomplice must be taken as one for this purpose. The prisoners must be acquitted.' They may, however, be severally called as witnesses by the prosecution and the defence, in order that they may contradict each other. Where the wife has suffered personal violence from her husband she is permitted to swear the peace against him, and in divorce suits husband and wife are both admissible as witnesses. A wife who sets fire to her husband's house may escape punishment, as in the case of Rex. *v*. March:

> March and his wife had lived separate for about two years; and, previous to the act, when she applied for the candle with which it was done, she said it was to set her husband's house on fire, because she wanted to burn him to death.

> Upon a case reserved upon the question whether it was an offence within the 7 and 8 George IV., cap. 30, sec. 2, for a wife to set fire to her husband's house for the purpose of doing him a personal injury, the conviction was held wrong, the learned judges thinking that to constitute the offence, it was essential that there should be an intent to injure or defraud some third person, not one identified with herself. (ibid., p. 899)

Identification with one's beloved may be delightful in theory, but when, in practice, it comes to being burned at pleasure, surely the greatest stickler for the 'twain being one' must feel some twinges of doubt. The identity of husband and wife is often by no means advantageous to the husband, for he thereby becomes responsible, to a great extent, for his wife's misdoings.

> For slanderous words spoken by the wife, libel published by her alone, trespass, assault and battery, etc., he is liable to be so sued, whether the act was committed with or without his sanction or knowledge. . . . And wherever the action is grounded on a tort, committed by the wife, it no way affects the necessity of joining the husband, that the parties are living apart, nor even that they are divorced *a mensâ et thoro*, or that the wife is living in adultery. (Lush's *Common Law Practice*, 2nd edn, p. 156)

Pleasant position for a man whose wife may have left him, to be suddenly dragged before a court of justice for some misdeed of hers, of which he may never have heard until he finds himself summoned to answer for it! A large amount of injustice arises from this absurd fiction that two are one; it sometimes injures, sometimes protects the married woman, and it often shields those who have wronged her; but whether it injure or whether it protect, it is equally vicious; it is *unjust*, and injustice is a radical injury to a community, and by destroying the reasonableness and the certainty of the law, it saps that reverence for it which is one of the safeguards of society.

Let us now take Blackstone's 'rights of every Englishman', and see what rights the common law allowed to a married Englishwoman. A married woman is not protected by the law in the 'uninterrupted enjoyment of' her 'limbs', her 'body', or her 'reputation'. On the contrary: 'If a wife be injured in her person, or her property, she can bring no action for redress without her husband's concurrence, and in his name as well as her own' (Blackstone, p. 443). If in a railway accident a married woman has her leg broken, she cannot sue the railway company for damages; she is not a damaged *person;* in the eye of the law, she is a piece of damaged *property*, and the compensation is to be made to her owner. If she is attacked and beaten she cannot at law sue her assailant; her master suffers loss and inconvenience by the assault on his house-keeper, and his action is necessary to obtain redress. If she is libelled, she cannot protect her good name, for she is incapable by herself of maintaining an action. In fact, it is not even needful that her name should appear at all in the matter: 'the husband may sue alone for loss of his wife's society by injury done to her, or for damage to her reputation' (Comyn's Digest, under 'Baron and Feme'). The following curious statement of the law on this head is given in Broom's *Commentaries:*

> Injuries which may be offered to a person considered as a husband, and which are cognisable in a court of common law, are principally three: 1, abduction, or taking away a man's wife; 2, beating her; 3, indirectly causing her some personal hurt, by negligence or otherwise. 1 As to the first sort, abduction, or taking her away, this may either be by fraud and persuasion, or open violence; though the law in both cases supposes force and constraint, the wife having no power to consent, and therefore gives a remedy by action of trespass; and the husband is also entitled to recover damages in an action on the case against such as persuade and entice the wife to live separate from him without a sufficient cause. . . . 2, 3 the second and third injuries above mentioned are constituted by beating a man's wife, or otherwise ill-using her; or causing hurt to her by negligence. For a common assault upon, or battery, or imprisonment, of the wife, the law gives the usual remedy to recover damages, by action of trespass, which must be brought in the names of the husband and wife jointly: but if the beating or other maltreatment be so enormous, that thereby the husband is deprived for any time of the company and assistance of his wife, the law then gives him a separate remedy by action for this ill-usage, *per quod consortium amisit*, in which he may recover a satisfaction in damages. By a provision of the C. L. Proc. Act, 1852, s. 40, in an action by husband and wife jointly for an injury to the wife, the husband is now allowed to add a claim in his own right – as for the loss of the wife's society – or where a joint trespass and assault have been committed on the husband and his wife. (vol. iii, pp. 149, 150)

So far is recognised the husband's complete claim over his wife's person, that anyone who receives a married woman into his house and gives her shelter there after having received notice from her husband that he is not to permit her to remain under his roof, actually becomes liable in damages to the husband. The husband cannot sue for damages if he has turned his wife out of doors, or if he has lost his right of control by cruelty or adultery; short of this, he may obtain damages against any friend or relative of the woman who gives her shelter. The wife has no such remedy against anyone who may induce the husband to live apart, or who may give him house-room at his own wish. The reason for the law being as we find it, is stated by Broom without the smallest compunction:

> We may observe that in these relative injuries notice is only taken of the wrong done to the superior of the parties related, by the breach and dissolution of either the relation itself, or at least the advantage accruing therefrom: while the loss of the inferior by such injuries is, except where the death of a parent has been caused by negligence, unregarded. One reason for which may be, that the inferior has no kind of property in the company, care, or assistance of the superior, as the superior is held to have in that of the inferior; and therefore the inferior can, in contemplation of law, suffer no loss consequential on a wrongful act done to his superior. The wife cannot recover damages for the beating of her husband. The child has no property in his father or guardian. And the servant, whose master is disabled, does not thereby lose his maintenance or wages. (ibid., p. 153)

A man may recover damages equally for the injury done to his servant or to his wife; in both cases he loses their services, and the law recompenses him. A peculiarly disgusting phase of this claim is where a husband claims damages against a co-respondent in the divorce court; if a wife be unfaithful, the husband can not only get a divorce, but can also claim a money payment from the seducer to make up for the damage he has sustained by losing his wife's services. An unmarried girl, under age, is regarded as the property of her father, and the father may bring an action against her seducer for the loss of his daughter's services. It is not the woman who is injured, or who has any redress; it is her male owner who can recover damages for the injury done to his property.

If a wife be separated from her husband, either by deed or by judicial decree, she has no remedy for injury or for libel, unless by the doubtful plan of using her husband's name without his consent. On this injustice Lord Lyndhurst, speaking in the House of Lords in 1856, said:

> A wife is separated from her husband by a decree of the Ecclesiastical Court, the reason for that decree being the husband's misconduct – his cruelty, it may be, or his adultery. From that moment the wife is almost in a state of outlawry. She may not enter into a contract, or if she do, she has no means of enforcing it. The law, so far from protecting, oppresses her. She is homeless, helpless, hopeless, and almost wholly destitute of civil rights. She is liable to all manner of injustice, whether by plot or by violence. She may be wronged in all possible ways, and her character may be mercilessly defamed; yet she has no redress. She is at the mercy of her enemies. Is that fair? Is that honest? Can it be vindicated upon any principle of justice, of mercy or of common humanity?'

A married woman loses control over her own body; it belongs to her owner, not to herself; no force, no violence, on the husband's part in conjugal relations is regarded as possible by the law; she may be suffering, ill, it matters not; force or constraint is recognised by the law as rape, in all cases save that of marriage; the law 'holds it to be felony to force even a concubine or harlot' (Broom's *Commentaries*, vol. iv, p. 255), but no rape can be committed by a husband on a wife; the consent given in marriage is held to cover the life, and if – as sometimes occurs – miscarriage or premature confinement be brought on by the husband's selfish passions, no offence is committed in the eye of the law, for the wife is the husband's property, and by marriage she has lost the right of control over her own body. The English marriage law sweeps away all the tenderness, all the grace, all the generosity of love, and transforms conjugal affection into a hard and brutal legal right.

By the common law the husband has a right to inflict corporal punishment on his wife, and although this right is now much restricted, the effect of the law is seen in the brutal treatment of wives among the rougher classes, and the light – sometimes no – punishment inflicted on wife-beaters. The common law is thus given by Blackstone:

> The husband also (by the old law) might give his wife moderate correction. For as he is to answer for her misbehaviour, the law thought it reasonable to entrust him with this power of restraining her, by domestic chastisement, in the

> same moderation that a man is allowed to correct his apprentices or children. The lower rank of people, who were always fond of the old common law, still claim and exert their ancient privilege.

Blackstone grimly adds, after saying this is all for woman's protection: 'So great a favourite is the female sex of the laws of England' (pp. 444 and 445). This 'ancient privilege' is very commonly exercised at the present time. A man who dragged his wife out of bed (1877), and, pulling off her nightdress, roasted her in front of the fire, was punished (?) by being bound over to keep the peace for a short period. Men who knock their wives down, who dance on them, who drag them about by the hair, etc., are condemned to brief terms of imprisonment, and are then allowed to resume their marital authority, and commence a new course of ill-treatment. In dealing later with the changes I shall recommend in the marriage laws, this point will come under discussion.

Coming to the second 'right', of 'personal liberty', we find that a married woman has no such right. Blackstone says, as we have seen: 'the confinement of a person in any wise is an imprisonment. So that the keeping a man against his will in a private house . . . is an imprisonment' (p. 136). But a husband may legally act as his wife's gaoler; 'the courts of law will still permit a husband to restrain his wife of her liberty, in case of any gross misbehaviour' (Blackstone, p. 445). 'If the wife squanders his estate, or goes into lewd company, he may deprive her of liberty' (Comyn's Digest, under 'Baron and Feme'). Broom says that at the present time

> there can be no question respecting the common-law right of a husband to restrain his wife of her personal liberty, with a view to prevent her going into society of which he disapproves, or otherwise disobeying his rightful authority; such right must not, however, be exercised unnecessarily, or with undue severity: and the moment that the wife by returning to her conjugal duties, makes restraint of her person unnecessary, such restraint becomes unlawful. (vol. i, p. 547)

In the year 1877 a publican at Spilsby chained up his wife to the wall from one day to the afternoon of the following one, in order, he said, to keep her from drink; the magistrates dismissed him without punishment. It may be argued that a woman should not get drunk, go into bad company, etc. Quite so; neither should a man. But would men admit, that under similar circumstances, a wife should have legal power to deprive her husband of liberty? If not, there is no reason in justice why the husband should be permitted to exercise it. Offences known to the law should be punished by the law, and by the law alone; offences which the law cannot touch should entail no punishment on an adult at the hands of a private individual. Public disapproval may brand them, but no personal chastisement should be inflicted by arbitrary and irresponsible power.

The third right, of 'property', has also no existence for married women. Unmarried women have here no ground for complaint: 'A *feme sole*, before her marriage, may do all acts for disposition, etc., of her lands or goods which any man in the same circumstances may do' (Comyn's Digest, under 'Baron and Feme'). The disabilities which affect women as women do not touch property; a *feme sole* may own real or personal estate, buy, sell, give, contract, sue, and be sued, just as though she were of the 'worthier blood'; it is marriage that, like felony and insanity, destroys her capability as proprietor. According to the common law – with which we will deal first – the following results accrued from marriage:

> Whatever personal property belonged to the wife before marriage, is by marriage absolutely vested in the husband. . . . in chattel interests, the sole and absolute property vests in the husband, to be disposed of at his pleasure, if he chooses to take possession of them. (Blackstone, book ii, 443)

If he takes possession, they do not, at his death, revert to the wife, but go to his heirs or to anyone he chooses by will. 'If a woman be seized of an estate of inheritance, and marries, her husband shall be seized of in her right' (Comyn's Digest, under 'Baron and Feme'). If a woman own land in her own right, all rents and profits are not hers, but her husband's; even arrears of rents due before coverture become his; he may make a lease of her land, commencing after his own death, and she is barred, although she survive him; he may dispose of his wife's interest; it may be forfeited by his crime, seized for his debt; she only regains it if she survives him and he has not disposed of it. If a woman, before marriage, lets her land on a lease, the rental, after marriage, becomes her husband's, and her receipt is not a good discharge. If a wife grants a rent-charge out of her own lands (or, rather, what should be her own) without the husband's consent, it is void. All personal goods that 'the wife has in possession in her own right, are vested in her husband by the marriage' (ibid.); gifts to her become his; if he sues for a debt due to his wife, and recovers it, it is his; if a legacy be left her, it goes to him; after his death, all that was her personal property originally, goes to his executors and administrators, and does not revert to her; so absolutely is all she may become possessed of his by law that if, after a divorce *a mensâ et thoro*, the wife should sue another woman for adultery with her husband, and should be awarded her costs, the husband can release the woman from payment.

If a woman own land and lease it, then if, during marriage, the husband reduce it into possession, 'as where rent accruing on a lease granted by the wife *dum sola* is received by a person appointed for that purpose during the husband's life', under such circumstances the husband's 'executors, not his widow, must sue the agent' (Lush's *Common Law Practice*, 2nd edn, p. 27). In a case where

> certain leasehold property was conveyed to trustees upon trust to permit the wife to receive the rents thereof to her sole and separate use, and she after marriage deposited with her trustees part of such rents and died; it was held that her husband might recover the same in an action in his own right. Such money, so deposited, was not a *chose in action* belonging to the wife, but money belonging to the husband, the trust having been discharged in the payment of the rents to the wife. (Ibid., p. 97)

Marriage, to a man, is regarded as a kind of lucrative business:

> The next method of acquiring property in goods and chattels is by marriage; whereby those chattels, which belonged formerly to the wife, are by act of law vested in the husband, with the same degree of property, and with the same powers, as the wife, when sole, had over them . . . A distinction is taken between chattels real and chattels personal, and of chattels personal, whether in possession or reversion, or in action. A chattel real vests in the husband, not absolutely, but *sub modo*. As, in case of a lease for years, the husband shall receive all the rents and profits of it, and may, if he pleases, sell, surrender, or dispose of it during the coverture; if he be outlawed or attainted, it shall be forfeited to the king; it is liable to execution for his debts; and if he survives his wife, it is to all intents and purposes his own. Yet, if he has made no disposition thereof in his lifetime, and dies before his wife, he cannot dispose of it by will: for, the husband having made no alteration in the property during his life, it never was transferred from the wife; but after his death she shall remain in her ancient possession, and it shall not go to his executors. If, however, the wife die in the husband's lifetime, the chattel real survives to him. As to chattels personal (or choses) in

> action, as debts upon bonds, contracts, and the like, these the husband may have if he pleases; that is, if he reduces them into possession by receiving or recovering them at law. And upon such receipt or recovery they are absolutely and entirely his own; and shall go to his executors or administrators, or as he shall bequeath them by will, and shall not revest in the wife. But, if he dies before he has recovered or reduced them into possession, so that, at his death, they still continue choses in action, they shall survive to the wife; for the husband never exerted the power he had of obtaining an exclusive property in them. If the wife die before the husband has reduced choses in action into possession, he does not become entitled by survivorship; nevertheless, he may, by becoming her administrator, gain a title. Chattles in possession, such as ready money and the like, vest absolutely in the husband, and he may deal with them, either whilst living, or by his will, as he pleases. Where the interest of the wife is reversionary, the husband's power is but small: unless it falls into possession during the marriage, his contracts or engagements do not bind it. (*Comm. on the Laws of England*, Broom and Hadley, vol. ii, pp. 618, 619)

So highly does the law value the claims of a husband that it recognises them as existing even before marriage; for if a woman who has contracted an engagement to marry dispose of her property privately, settle it on herself, or on her children, without the congnisance of the man to whom she is engaged, such settlement or disposition may be set aside by the husband as a fraud.

So cruel, as regards property, was felt to be the action of the common law, that the wealthy devised means to escape from it, and women of property were protected on their marriage by 'marriage settlements', whereby they were contracted out of the law. A woman's property was by this means, 'settled on herself'; it was necessary to treat her as incapable, so her property was not in her own power but was vested in trustees for her separate use; thus the principal, or the estate, was protected, but the whole interest or rental, as before, could be taken by the husband the moment in was received by the wife; her signature became necessary to draw it, but the moment it came into her possession it ceased to be hers. The next step was an attempt to protect women's money in their own hands; teribile cases of wrong were continually arising: men who deserted their wives, and left them to maintain the burden of a family, came back after the wife had accumulated a little property, sold the furniture, pocketed the proceeds, and departed, leaving the wife to recommence her labours. Orders of protection were given by magistrates, but these were not found sufficient. At last, parliamentary interference was called for with an urgency that could no longer be resisted, and a Bill to amend the laws relating to married women's property was introduced into the House of Commons. How sore was the need of such amendment may be seen from the following extracts.

Mr Russell Gurney, in moving (14 April 1869) the second reading of the Bill, observed:

> It is now proposed that, for the first time in our history, the property of one half of the married people of this counrty should receive the protection of the law. Up to this time the property of a wife has had no protection from the law, or rather, he should say, in the eye of the law it has had no existence. From the moment of her marriage the wife, in fact, possesses no property; whatever she may up to that time have possessed, by the very act of marriage passes from her, and any gift or bequest made to her becomes at once the property of the husband. Nay, even that which one might suppose to be her inalienable right, the fruit of her mental or bodily toil, is denied her. She may be gifted with powers which enable her to earn an ample fortune, but the moment it is earned, it is not here, it is her husband's. In fact, from the time of her entering into what is described as an honourable estate, the law pronounces her unfit to hold any property whatever.

Mr Jessel (now Master of the Rolls) in seconding the motion, in the course of an able and impassioned speech, said:

> The existing law is a relic of slavery, and the House is now asked to abolish the last remains of slavery in England. In considering what ought to be the nature of the law, we cannot deny that no one should be deprived of the power of disposition, unless on proof of unfitness to exercise that power; and it is not intelligible on what principle a woman should be considered incapable of contracting immediately after she has, with the sanction of the law, entered into the most important contract conceivable. The slavery laws of antiquity are the origin of the common law on this subject. The Roman law originally regarded the position of a wife as similar to that of a daughter who had no property, and might be sold into slavery at the will of her father. When the Roman law became that of a civilised people, the position of the wife

> was altogether changed. . . . The ancient Germans – from whom our law is derived – put the woman into the power of her husband in the same sense as the ancient Roman law did. She became his slave. The law of slavery – whether Roman or English – for we once had slaves and slave-laws in England – gave to the master of a slave the two important rights of flogging and imprisoning him. A slave could not possess property of his own, and could not make contracts except for his master's benefit, and the master alone could sue for an injury to the slave; while the only liability of the master was that he must not let his slave starve. This is exactly the position of the wife under the English law; the husband has the right of flogging and imprisoning her, as may be seen by those who read Blackstone's chapter on the relations of husband and wife. She cannot possess property – she cannot contract, except it is as his agent; and he alone can sue if she is libelled or suffers a personal injury; while all the husband is compellable to do for her is to pay for necessaries. It is astonishing that a law founded on such principles should have survived to the nineteenth century.

A quotation from a later debate finds its fit place here: Mr Hinde Palmer, in moving (19 February 1873) the second reading of the Married Woman's Property Act (1870) Amendment Bill, pointed out that the common law was, that by marriage:

> the whole of a woman's personal property was immediately vested in her husband, and placed entirely at his disposal. By contracting marriage, a woman forfeited all her property. In 1868, the Chancellor of the Exchequer, Mr Lowe, said: 'Show me what crime there is in matrimony that it should be visited by the same punishment as high treason – namely, confiscation, for that is really the fact.' Mr Mill, too, speaking on that question, said that a large portion of the inhabitants of this country were in the anomalous position of having imposed on them without having done anything to deserve it, what we inflicted on the worst criminals as a penalty: like felons, they were incapable of holding property.

Some great and beneficial changes were made by the Acts of 1870 and 1873, although much yet remains to be done. By the Act of 1870, the wages and earnings of married women were protected; they were made capable of depositing money in the savings' banks in their own names; they might hold property in the Funds in their own names, and have the dividends paid to them; they might hold fully-paid up shares, or stock, to which no liability was attached; property in societies might be retained by them; money coming to a married woman as the next-of-kin, or one of the next-of-kin to an intestate, or by deed or will, was made her own, provided that such money did not exceed £200; the rents and profits of freehold, copyhold, or customary-hold property inherited by a married woman were to be her own; a married woman might insure her own or her husband's life; might, under some circumstances maintain an action in her own name; married women were made liable for the maintenance of their husbands and children. The Act of 1873 relates entirely to the recovery of debts contracted by the woman before marriage. It will be perceived that these Acts are very inadequate as regards placing married women in a just position towards their property, but they are certainly a step in the right direction. The Acts only apply to those women who have been married subsequently to their passing.

One great omission in them will have to be promptly remedied, both for the sake of married women and for the sake of their creditors: while a married woman now may, under some circumstances, sue, no machinery is provided whereby she may be used – without joining her husband. In an admirable letter to *The Times* of 4 March 1878, Mrs Ursule Bright, alluding to the 'obscurity and uncertainty of the law', points out

> The effect of that obscurity upon the credit of respectable married women earning their own and their children's bread, in any employment or business carried on separately from their husband; the inconvenience and risk to their creditors is, as you have most ably pointed out, great; but the injury to honest wives is far greater. It puts them at a considerable disadvantage in the labour market and in business. A married woman, for instance, keeping a little shop, may sue for debts due to her, but has no corresponding liability to be sued. If the whereabouts of the husband is not very clearly defined, it is evident she may have some difficulty in obtaining credit.
>
> Again, what employer of labour can with any security engage the services of a married woman? She may leave her work at the mill at an hour's notice unfinished, and her employer has no remedy against her for breach of contract, as a married woman can make no contract which is legally binding. There is no question that such a state of the law must operate as a restriction upon her power to support herself and family.

The state of muddle of the present law is almost inconceiv-

> able. Even now a woman need not pay her debts contracted before marriage out of earnings made after marriage. Suppose an artist or a literary woman to marry when burdened with debts and having no property; should she be earning £1,000 or £10,000 a year by her profession after marriage, these earnings could not be made liable for her debts contracted before marriage.

It cannot too plainly be repeated that non-liability to be sued means non-existence of credit.

The law, as it stands at present, is the old Common Law, modified by the Acts of 1870 and 1873. Archbold says – dealing with indictments for theft:

> Where the person named as owner appears to be a married woman, the defendant must, unless the indictment is amended, be acquitted . . . because in law the goods are the property of the husband; even though she be living apart from her husband upon an income arising from property vested in trustees for her separate use, because the goods cannot be the property of the trustees; and, in law, a married woman has no property. (Archbold's *Criminal Cases*, p. 43)

Archbold gives as exceptions to this general rule, where a judicial separation has taken place, where the wife has obtained a protection order, or where the property is such as is covered by the Married Women's Property Act, 1870.

> Where a married woman lived apart from her husband, upon an income arising from property vested in trustees for her separate use, the judges held that a house which she lived in was properly described as her husband's dwelling-house, though she paid the rent out of her separate property, and the husband had never been in it. R. *v*. French, R *v*. R, 491. (ibid., p. 521)

If a burglary be committed in a house belonging to a married woman, the house must be said to be the dwelling-house of her husband, or the burglar will be acquitted; if she be living separate from her husband, paying her own rent out of money secured for her separate use, it makes no difference; it was decided, in the case of Rex *v*. French, that a married woman could own no property, and that the house must, therefore, belong to the husband. If a married woman picks up a purse in the road and is robbed of it, the property vests in the husband:

> Where goods are in the possession of the wife, they must be

> laid as the goods of her husband; thus, if A is indicted for stealing the goods of B, and it appears that B was a *feme covert* at the time, A must be acquitted. And even if the wife have only received money as the agent of another person, and she is robbed of that money before her husband receives it into his possession, still it is well laid as his money in an indictment for larceny. An indictment charging the stealing of a £5 Bank of England note, the property of E. Wall, averring, in the usual way, that the money secured by the note was due and payable to E. Wall; it appeared that E. Wall's wife had been employed to sell sheep belonging to her father, of or in which her husband never had either possession or any interest, and she received the note in payment for the sheep, and it was stolen from her before she left the place where she received it. It was objected that the note never was the property of E. Wall, either actually or constructively; the money secured by it was not his, and he had no qualified property in it, as it never was in his possession; but it was held that the property was properly laid. (Russell, *On Crimes*, 5th edn, vol. ii, pp. 243, 244)

Yet even a child, in the eye of the law, has property, and if his clothes are stolen it is safer to allege them to be the child's property. The main principle of English law remains unaltered by recent legislation, that 'a married woman has no property'. Married women share incapacity to manage property with minors and lunatics; minors, lunatics, and married women are taken care of by trustees; minors become of age, lunatics often recover, married women remain incapable during the whole of their married life.

Being incapable of holding property, a married woman is of course, incapable of making a will. Here, also, the Common Law may be checkmated. She may make a will

> by virtue of a power reserved to her, or of a marriage settlement, or with her husband's assent, or it may be made by her to carry her separate estate; and the court in determining whether or not such will is entitled to probate, will not go minutely into the question, but will only require that the testatrix had a power reserved to her, or was entitled to separate estate, and will, if so satisfied, grant probate to her executor, leaving it to the Court of Chancery, as the court of construction, to say what portion of her estate, if any, will pass under such will. In this case the husband, though he may not be entitled to take probate of his wife's will, may administer to such of her effects as do not pass under the

> will. (*Comm. on the Laws of England*, Broom and Hadley, vol. iii, pp. 427, 428)

Thus we see that a husband may will away from his wife her own original property, but a wife may not even will away her own, unless the right be specially reserved to her before marriage. And yet it is urged that women have no need of votes, their interests being so well looked after by their fathers, husbands, and brothers!

We have thus seen that the 'rights of every Englishman' are destroyed in women by marriage; one would imagine that matrimony was a crime for which a woman deserved punishment, and that confiscation and outlawry were the fit rewards of her misdeed.

From these three great fundamental wrongs flow a large number of legal disabilities. Take the case of a prisoner accused of misdemeanour; he is often set free on his own recognizances; but a married woman cannot be so released, for she is incapable of becoming bail or of giving her own recognizances; she is here again placed in bad company: 'no person who has been convicted of any crime by which he has become infamous is allowed to be surety for any person charged or suspected of an indictable offence. Nor can a married woman, or an infant, or a prisoner in custody, be bail' (Archbold, p. 88). Let us now suppose that a woman be accused of some misdemeanour, and be committed for trial: she desires to have her case tried by a higher court than the usual one, and wishes to remove the indictment by writ of *certiorari:* she finds that the advantage is denied her, because, as a married woman, she has no property, and she cannot therefore enter into the necessary recognizances to pay costs in the case of a conviction. Thus a married woman finds herself placed at a cruel disadvantage as compared with an unmarried woman or with men.

In matters of business, difficulties arise on every hand: a married woman is incapable of making a contract; if she takes a house without her husband's knowledge and without stating that she is married, the landlord may repudiate the contract; if she states that she is married, the landlord knows that she is unable to make a legal contract, and refuses to let or lease to her, without heavy security. If she buys things she cannot be sued for non-payment without making the husband a defendant, and she consequently finds that she has no credit. If she is cheated, she cannot sue, except in cases covered by the recent Acts, without joining her husband, and so she has often to submit to be wronged.

> A *feme covert* cannot sue without her husband being joined as co-plaintiff, so long as the relation of marriage subsists. It matters not that he is an alien, and has left the country; or

> that, being a subject, he has absconded from the realm as a bankrupt or for other purpose; or that he has become permanently resident abroad; or that they are living apart under a deed of separation; or have been divorced *a mensâ et thoro;* for none of these events dissolve or work a suspension of the marriage contract, and so long as that endures, the wife is unable to sue alone, whatever the cause of action may be. This disability results from the rule of law which vests in the husband not only all the goods and chattels which belonged to the wife at the time of the marriage, but also all which she acquires afterwards. (Lush's *Common Law Practice*, 2nd edn, pp. 33, 34)

The same principle governs all suits against a married woman; the husband must be sued with her:

> In all actions brought against a *feme covert* while the relation of marriage subsists, the husband must be joined for conformity, it being an inflexible rule of law that a wife shall not be sued without her husband. . . . If therefore a wife enters into a bond jointly with her husband, or makes a bill of exchange, promissory note, or any other contract, she cannot be sued thereon, but the action should be brought against, and the bond, bill, etc., alleged to have been made by, the husband. (ibid., p. 75)

The thoughtful author of the *Rights of Women* remarks that the incapacity to sue is 'traceable to the time when disputes were settled by the judgment of arms. A man represents his wife at law now, because in the days of the judicial combat he was her champion-at-arms, and she is unable to sue now, because she was unable to fight then' (p. 22). The explanation is a very reasonable one, and is only an additional proof of the need of alteration in the law; our marriage laws are, as has been shown above, the survival of barbarism, and we only ask that modern civilisation will alter and improve them as it does everything else: trial by combat has been destroyed; ought not its remains to be buried out of sight? The consequence of these business disabilities is that a married woman finds herself thwarted at every turn, and if she be trying to gain a livelihood, and be separated from her husband, she is constantly pained and annoyed by the marriage-fetter, which hinders her activity and checks her efforts to make her way. The notion that irresponsibility is an advantage is an entirely mistaken one; an irresponsible person cannot be dealt with in business matters, and is shut out of all the usual independent ways of obtaining a livelihood.

Authorship and servitude are the only paths really open to married women; in every other career they find humiliating obstacles which it needs both courage and perseverance to surmount.

Married women rank among the 'persons in subjection to the power of others'; they thus come among those who in many cases are not criminally liable; 'infants under the age of discretion', persons who are *non compotes mentis* (not of sound mind), and persons acting under coercion, are not criminally liable for their misdeeds. A married woman is presumed to act under her husband's coercion, unless the contrary be proved, and she may thus escape punishment for her wrongdoings:

> Constraint of a superior is sometimes allowed as an excuse for criminal misconduct, by reason of the matrimonial subjection of the wife to her husband; but neither a son, nor a servant is excused for the commission of any crime by the command or coercion of the parent or master. Thus, if a woman commit theft, or burglary, by the coercion of her husband, or even in his company, which the law *primâ facie* construes a coercion, she is dispunishable, being considered to have acted by compulsion, and not of her own will. (*Comm. on the Laws of England*, Broom and Hadley, vol. iv, p. 27)

> A *feme covert* is so much favoured in respect of that power and authority which her husband has over her, that she shall not suffer any punishment for committing a bare theft, or even a burglary, by the coercion of her husband, or in his company, which the law construes a coercion. (Russell *On Crimes*, vol. i, p. 139)

'Where the wife is to be considered merely as the servant of the husband, she will not be answerable for the consequences of his breach of duty, however fatal, though she may be privy to his conduct. C. Squire and his wife were indicted for the murder of a boy'; he had been cruelly treated by both, and died 'from debility and want of proper food and nourishment';

> Lawrence, J. directed the jury that as the wife was the servant of the husband, it was not her duty to provide the apprentice with sufficient food and nourishment, and that she was not guilty of any breach of duty in neglecting to do so; though, if the husband had allowed her sufficient food for the apprentice, and she had wilfully withholden it from him, then she would have been guilty. But that here the fact was otherwise;

> and therefore, though *in foro conscientiæ* the wife was equally guilty with the husband, yet in point of law she could not be said to be guilty of not providing the apprentice with sufficient food and nourishment. (ibid., pp. 144, 145).

It is hard to see what advantage society gains by this curious fashion of reckoning married women as children or lunatics. Some advantages however, flow to a criminal husband: a wife is not punishable for concealing her husband from justice, knowing that he has committed felony; a husband may not conceal his wife under analogous circumstances:

> So strict is the law where a felony is actually complete, in order to do effectual justice, that the nearest relations are not suffered to aid or receive one another. If the parent assists his child, or the child his parent, if the brother receives the brother, the master his servant, or the servant his master, or even if the husband receives his wife, having any of them committed a felony, the receiver becomes an accessory *ex post facto*. But a *feme covert* cannot become an accessory by the receipt and concealment of her husband; for she is presumed to act under his coercion, and therefore she is not bound, neither ought she, to discover her lord. (ibid., p. 38)

The wife of a blind husband must not, however, regard her coverture as in all cases a protection, for it has been held that if stolen goods were in her possession, her husband's blindness preventing him from knowing of them, her coverture did not avail to shelter her.

Any advantage which married women may possess through the supposition that they are acting under the coercion of their husbands ought to be summarily taken away from them. It is not for the safety of society that criminals should escape punishment simply because they happen to be married women; a criminal husband becomes much more dangerous to the community if he is to have an irresponsible fellow-conspirator beside him; two people – although the law regards them as one – can often commit a crime that a single person could not accomplish, and it is not even impossible that an unscrupulous woman, desiring to get rid easily for awhile of an unpleasant husband, might actually be the secret prompter of an offence, in the commission of which she might share, but in the punishment of which she would have no part. For the sake of wives, as well as of husbands, this irresponsibility should be put an end to, for if a husband is to be held accountable for his wife's misdeeds and debts, it is impossible for the law to refuse him control over her actions; freedom and responsibility must go hand in hand, and women who obtain the rights of freedom must accept the duties of responsibility.

A woman has a legal claim on her husband for the necessaries of life, and a man may be compelled to support his wife. But her claim is a very narrow one, as may be seen by the following case: A man named Plummer was indicted for the manslaughter of his wife; he had been separated from her for several years, and paid her an allowance of 2s. 6d. a week; the last payment was made on a Sunday, and she was turned out of her lodgings on the Tuesday following; she was suffering from diarrhœa, and on the Wednesday was very ill. Plummer was told of her condition, but refused to give her shelter; the evening was wet, and a constable meeting her wandering about took her to her husband's lodgings, but he would not admit her; on Thursday he paid for a bed for her at a public-house, and on Friday she died. Baron Gurney told the jury that the prisoner could not be charged with having caused her death from want of food, since he made her an allowance, and under ordinary circumstances he might have refused to do anything more; the only question was whether the refusal as to shelter had hastened her death. The man was acquitted. A wife has also some limited rights over her husband's property after his death; she may claim dower, her wearing apparel, a bed, and some few other things, including her personal jewellery. Her husband's power to deprive her of her personal ornaments ceases with his life.

To redress the whole of the wrongs as to property, and to enable justice to be done, it is only necessary to pass a short Act of Parliament, ordaining that marriage shall in no fashion alter the civil status of a woman, that she shall have over property the same rights as though she were unmarried, and shall, in all civil and criminal matters, be held as responsible as though she were a *feme sole*. In short, marriage ought no more to affect a woman's position than it does a man's, and should carry with it no kind of legal disability; 'marital control' should cease to exist, and marriage should be regarded as a contract between equals, and not as a bond between master and servant.

Those who are entirely opposed to the idea that a woman should not forfeit her property on marriage, raise a number of theoretical difficulties as to household expenses, ownership of furniture, etc. Practically these would very seldom occur, if we may judge by the experience of countries whose marriage laws do not entail forfeiture on the woman who becomes a wife. In the *Rights of Women*, quoted from above, a very useful summary is given of the laws as to property in various countries; in Germany these laws vary considerably in the different states; one system, known as *Gütergemeinschaft* (community of goods) is a great advance towards equality, although it is not by any means the best resolution of the problem; under this system there is no separate property, it is all merged in the common stock, and 'the husband, as such, has no more right over the common fund than the wife, nor the wife than the husband' (p. 26); the husband administers as 'representative of the community, and not as husband. He is merely head partner, as it were, and has no personal rights beyond that'; he may be dispossessed of even this limited authority if he is wasteful;

> he cannot alienate or mortgage any of the common lands or rights without her consent – a privilege, it must be remembered, which belongs to her, not only over lands brought by herself, but also over those brought by her husband to the marriage. And this control of the wife over the immovable has, for parts of Prussia, been extended by a law of April 16th, 1850, over movables as well; for the husband has been forbidden to dispose not only of immovables, but of the whole or part of the movable property, without the consent of his wife. Nor can the husband by himself make donations *mortis causa;* such arrangements take the form of mutual agreements between the two respecting their claims of inheritance to one another. (p. 27)

In Austria, married couples are more independent of each other; the wives retain their rights over their own property, and can dispose of it

> as they like, and sue or be sued in respect of it, without marital authorisation or control; and just as they have the free disposition of their property, so they can contract with others as they please. A husband is unable to alienate any of his wife's property in her name, or to lend or mortgage it, or to receive any money, institute any law-suits, or make any arrangements in respect of it, unless he has her special mandate. . . . If no stipulation is made at the marriage, each spouse retains his or her separate property, and neither has a claim to anything gained or in any way received by the other during the marriage. (p. 50)

In the New York code (USA),

> beyond the claim of mutual support, neither [husband nor wife] has any interest whatever in the property of the other. Hence either may enter into any engagement or transaction

> with the other or with a stranger with respect to property, just as they might do if they continued unmarried. (p. 95)

The apportionment of household expenses must necessarily be left for the private arrangement of the married pair; where the woman has property, or where she earns her livelihood it would be her duty to contribute to the support of the common home; where the couple are poor, and the care of the house falls directly on the shoulders of the wife, her personal toil would be her fair contribution; this matter should be arranged in the marriage contract, just as similar matters are now dealt with in the marriage settlements of the wealthy. As means of livelihood become more accessible to women the question will be more and more easily arranged; it will no longer be the fashion in homes of professional men that the husband shall over-work himself in earning the means of support, while the wife over-rests herself in spending them, but a more evenly-divided duty shall strengthen the husband's health by more leisure, and the wife's by more work. Recovery of debts incurred for household expenses should be by suit against husband and wife jointly, just as in a partnership the firm may now be sued; recovery of personal debts should be by suits against the person who had contracted them. Many a man's life is now rendered harder than it ought to be, by the waste and extravagance of a wife who can pledge his name and his credit, and even ruin him before he knows his danger: would not the lives of such men be the happier and the less toilsome if their wives were responsible for their own debts, and limited by their own means? Many a woman's home is broken up, and her children beggared, by the reckless spendthrift who wastes her fortune or her earnings: would not the lives of such women be less hopeless, if marriage left their property in their own hands, and did not give them a master as well as a husband? Women, under these circumstances, would, of course, become liable for the support of their children, equally with their husbands – a liability which is, indeed, recognised by the Married Women's Property Act (1870), s. 14.

It is sometimes further urged by those who like 'a man to be master in his own house', that unless women forfeited their property in marriage, there would be constant discord in the home. Surely the contrary effect would be produced. Mrs Mill well says, in the Essay before quoted from:

> The highest order of durable and happy attachments would be a hundred times more frequent than they are, if the affection which the two sexes sought from one another were

> that genuine friendship which only exists between equals in privileges as in faculties.

Nothing is so likely to cause unhappiness as the tendency to tyrannise, generated in the man by authority, and the tendency to rebel, generated in the woman by enforced submission. No grown person should be under the arbitrary power of another; dependence is touching in the infant because of its helplessness; it is revolting in the grown man or woman because with maturity of power should come dignity of self-support.

In a brilliant article in the *Westminster Review* (July 1874) the writer well says: 'Would it not, to begin with, be well to instruct girls that weakness, cowardice, and ignorance, cannot constitute at once the perfection of womankind and the imperfection of mankind?' It is time to do away with the oak and ivy ideal, and to teach each plant to grow strong and self-supporting. Perfect equality would, under this system, be found in the home, and mutual respect and deference would replace the alternate coaxing and commandment now too often seen. Equal rights would abolish both tyranny and rebellion; there would be more courtesy in the husband, more straightforwardness in the wife. Then, indeed, would there be some hope of generally happy marriages, but, as has been eloquently said by the writer just quoted,

> till absolute social and legal equality is the basis of the sacred partnership of marriage (the division of labours and duties in the family, by free agreement, implying no sort of inequality), till no superiority is recognised on either side but that of individual character and capacity, till marriage is no longer legally surrounded with penalties on the woman who enters into it as though she were a criminal – till then the truest love, the truest sympathy, the truest happiness in it, will be the exception rather than the rule, and the real value of this relation, domestic and social, will be fatally missed.

That some marriages are happy, in spite of the evil law, no one will deny; but these are the exception, not the rule. The law, as it is, directly tends to promote unhappiness, and its whole influence on the relations of the sexes is injurious. To quote Mrs Mill once more:

> The influence of the position tends eminently to promote selfishness. The most insignificant of men, the man who can obtain influence or consideration nowhere else, finds one place where he is chief and head. There is one person, often greatly his superior in understanding, who is obliged to

> consult him, and whom he is not obliged to consult. He is judge, magistrate, ruler, over their joint concerns; arbiter of all differences between them. . . . His is now the only tribunal, in civilised life, in which the same person is judge and party. A generous mind in such a situation makes the balance incline against its own side, and gives the other not less, but more, than a fair equality, and thus the weaker side may be enabled to turn the very fact of dependence into an instrument of power, and in default of justice, take an ungenerous advantage of generosity; rendering the unjust power, to those who make an unselfish use of it, a torment and a burthen. But how is it when average men are invested with this power, without reciprocity and without responsibility? Give such a man the idea that he is first in law and in opinion – that to will is his part, and hers to submit – it is absurd to suppose that this idea merely glides over his mind, without sinking into it, or having any effect on his feelings and practice. If there is any self-will in the man, he becomes either the conscious or unconscious despot of his household. The wife, indeed, often succeeds in gaining her objects, but it is by some of the many various forms of indirectness and management.

When marriage is as it should be, there will be no superior and inferior by right of position; but men and women, whether married or unmarried, will retain intact the natural rights 'belonging to every Englishman'.

In dealing with the wrongs of the wife, according to the present English marriage laws, the wrongs of the mother must not be omitted. The unmarried mother has a right to her child; the married mother has none: 'A father is entitled to the custody of his child until it attains the age of sixteen, unless there be some sufficient reason to the contrary' (Russell *On Crimes*, vol. i, p. 898). The 'sufficient reason' is hard to find in most cases, as the inclination of the Courts is to make excuses for male delinquencies, and to uphold every privilege which male Parliaments have conferred on husbands and fathers. In Shelley's case the father was deprived of the custody of his children, but here religious and political heresy caused a strong bias against the poet. The father's right to the custody of legitimate children is complete; the mother has no right over them as against his; he may take them away from her, and place them in the care of another woman, and she has no redress: she may apply to Chancery for access to them at stated times, but even this is matter of favour, not of right. The father may appoint a guardian in his will, and the mother, although the sole surviving parent, has no right over her children as against the stranger appointed by the dead father. If the parents differ in religion, the children are to be brought up in that of the father, whatever agreement may have been made respecting them before marriage; if the father dies without leaving any directions, the children will be educated in his religion; he can, if he chooses, allow his wife to bring them up in her creed, but she can only do so by virtue of his permission. Thus the married mother has no rights over her own children; she bears them, nurses them, toils for them, watches over them, and may then have them torn from her by no fault of her own, and given into the care of a stranger. People talk of maternal love, and of woman's sphere, of her duty in the home, of her work for her babes, but the law has no reverence for the tie between mother and child, and ignores every claim of the mother who is also a wife. The unmarried mother is far better off; she has an absolute right to the custody of her own children; none can step in and deprive her of her little ones, for the law respects the maternal tie when no marriage ceremony has 'legitimated' it. Motherhood is only sacred in the eye of the law when no legal contract exists between the parents of the child.

Looking at a woman's position both as wife and mother, it is impossible not to recognise the fact that marriage is a direct disadvantage to her. In an unlegalised union the woman retains possession of all her natural rights; she is mistress of her own actions, of her body, of her property; she is able to legally defend herself against attack; all the Courts are open to protect her; she forfeits none of her rights as an Englishwoman; she keeps intact her liberty and her independence; she has no master; she owes obedience to the laws alone. If she have a child, the law acknowledges her rights over it, and no man can use her love for it as an engine of torture to force her into compliance with his will. Two disadvantages, however, attach to unlegalised unions; first, the woman has to face social disapprobation, although of late years, as women have been coming more to the front, this difficulty has been very much decreased, for women have begun to recognise the extreme injustice of the laws, and both men and women of advanced views have advocated great changes in the marriage contract. The second disadvantage is of a more serious character: the children proceeding from an unlegalised union have not the same rights as those born in legal wedlock, do not inherit as of right, and have no legal name. These injustices can be prevented by care in making testamentary dispositions protecting them, and by registering the surname, but the fact of the original unfairness still remains, and any carelessness on the parents' part will result in real injury to the child. It must also be remembered that the father, in such a case, has no rights over his children, and this is as unfair to him as the reverse is to the mother. As the law now is, both legal and illegal unions have disadvantages connected with them, and there is only a choice between evils; these evils are, however, overwhelmingly greater on the side of legal unions, as may be seen by the foregoing sketch of the disabilities imposed on women by marriage. So great are these that a wise and self-respecting woman may well hesitate to enter into a contract of marriage while the laws remain as they are, and a man who really honours a woman must reluctantly subject her to the disadvantages imposed on the English wife, when he asks her to take him as literally her master and owner. The relative position is as dishonouring to the man as it is insulting to the woman, and good men revolt against it as hotly as do the most high-spirited women. In happy marriages all these laws are ignored, and it is only at rare intervals that the married pair become conscious of their existence. Some argue that this being so, small practical harm results from the legal injustice; it would be as sensible to argue that as honest people do not want to thieve, it would not be injurious to public morality to have laws on the statute book legalising garotting. Laws are made to prevent injustice being committed with impunity, and it is a curious reversal of every principle of legislation to make laws which protect wrong-doing, and which can only be defended on the ground that they are not generally enforced. If the English marriage laws were univ -sally carried out, marriage would not last for a month in England; as it is, vast numbers of women suffer in silence, thousands rebel and break their chains, and on every side men and women settle down into a mutual tolerance which is simply an easy-going indifference, accepted as the only possible substitute for the wedded happiness which they once dreamed of in youth, but have failed to realise in their maturity.

Things being as they are, what is the best action for those to take who desire to see a healthier and purer sexual morality – a morality founded upon equal rights and diverse duties harmoniously discharged? The first step is to agitate for a reform of the marriage laws by the passing of such an Act of Parliament as is alluded to above. It would be well for some of those who desire to see such a legislative change to meet and confer together on the steps to be taken to introduce such a Bill into the House of Commons. If thought necessary, a Marriage Reform League might be established, to organise the agitation and petitioning which are *de rigueur*, in endeavouring to get a bill passed through the popular House. Side by side with this effort to reform marriage abuses, should go the determination not to contract a legal marriage while the laws remain as immoral as they are. It is well known that the Quakers persistently refused to go through the legal English form of marriage, and quietly made their declarations according to their own conscience, submitting to the disadvantages entailed on them by the illegality, until the legislature formally recognised the Quaker declaration as a legal form of marriage. Why should not we take a leaf out of the Quakers' book, and substitute for the present legal forms of marriage a simple declaration publicly made? We should differ from the Quakers in this, that we should not desire that such declaration should be legalised while the marriage laws remain as they are; but as soon as the laws are moralised, and wives are regarded as self-possessing human beings, instead of as property, then the declaration may, with advantage, seek the sanction of the law. It is not necessary that the declaration should be couched in any special form of words; the conditions of the contract ought to be left to the contracting parties. What is necessary is that it should be a definite contract, and it is highly advisable that it should be a contract in writing – a deed of partnership, in fact, which should – when the law permits – be duly stamped and registered. The law, while it does not dictate the conditions of the contract, should enforce those conditions so long as the contract exists; that is, it should interfere just as far as it does in other contracts, and no further; the law has no right to dictate the terms of the marriage contract; it is for the contracting parties to arrange their own affairs as they will. While, however, the province of the law should be thus limited in respect to the contracting parties, it has a clear right to interfere in defence of the interests of any children who may be born of the marriage, and to compel the parents to clothe, feed, house, and educate them properly: this duty should, if need be, be enforced on both parents alike, and the law should recognise and impose the full discharge of the responsibilities of parents towards those to whom they have given life. No marriage contract should be recognised by the law which is entered into by minors; in this, as in other legal deeds, there should be no capability to contract until the contracting parties are of full age. A marriage is a partnership, and should be so regarded by the law, and it should be the aim of those who are endeavouring to reform marriage, to substitute for the present semi-barbarous laws a scheme which shall be sober, dignified, and practicable, and which shall recognise the vital interest of the

community in the union of those who are to be the parents of the next generation.

Such a deed as I propose would have no legal force at the present time; and here arises a difficulty: might not a libertine take advantage of this fact to desert his wife and possibly leave her with a child, or children, on her hands, to the cold mercy of society which would not even recognise her as a married woman? Men who, under the present state of the law, seduce women and then desert them, would probably do the same if they had gone through a form of marriage which had no legally binding force; but such men are, fortunately, the exception, not the rule, and there is no reason to apprehend an increase of their number, owing to the proposed action on the part of a number of thoughtful men and women who are dissatisfied with the present state of the law, but who have no wish to plunge into debauchery. I freely acknowledge that it is to be desired that marriage should be legally binding, and that a father should be compelled to do his share towards supporting his children; but while English law imposes such a weight of disability on a married woman, and leaves her utterly in the power of her husband, however unprincipled, oppressive, and wicked he may be – short of legal crime – I take leave to think that women have a fairer chance of happiness and comfort in an unlegalised than in a legal marriage. There is many an unhappy woman who would be only too glad if the libertine who has legally married her would desert her, and leave her, even with the burden of a family, to make for herself and her children, by her own toil, a home which should at least be pure, peaceful, and respectable.

Let me, in concluding this branch of the subject, say a word to those who, agreeing with Marriage Reform in principle, fear to openly put their theory into practice. Some of these earnestly hope for change, but do not dare to advocate it openly. Reforms have never been accomplished by Reformers who had not the courage of their opinions. If all the men and women who disapprove of the present immoral laws would sturdily *and openly* oppose them; if those who desire to unite their lives, but are determined not to submit to the English marriage laws, would publicly join hands, making such a declaration as is here suggested, the social odium would soon pass away, and the unlegalised marriage would be recognised as a dignified and civilised substitute for the old brutal and savage traditions. Most valuable work might here be done by men and women who – happy in their own marriages – yet feel the immorality of the law, and desire to see it changed. Such married people might support and strengthen by their open countenance and friendship those who enter into the unlegalised public unions here advocated; and they can do what no one else can do so well: they can prove to English society – the most bigoted and conservative society in the world – that advocacy of change in the marriage laws does not mean the abolition of the home. The value of such co-operation will be simply inestimable, and will do more than anything else to render the reform practicable. Courage and quiet resolution are needed, but, with these, this great social change may safely and speedily be accomplished.

II
Divorce

Any proposed reforms in the marriage laws of England would be extremely imperfect, unless they dealt with the question of divorce. Marriage differs from all ordinary contracts in the extreme difficulty of dissolving it – a difficulty arising from the ecclesiastical character which has been imposed upon it, and from the fact that it has been looked upon as a religious bond instead of as a civil contract. Until the time of the Reformation, marriage was regarded as a sacrament by all Christian people, and it is so regarded by the majority of them up to the present day. When the Reformers advocated divorce, it was considered as part of their general heresy, and as proof of the immoral tendency of their doctrines. Among Roman Catholics the sacramental – and therefore the indissoluble – character of marriage is still maintained, but among Protestants divorce is admitted, the laws regulating it varying much in different countries.

In England – owing to the extreme conservatism of the English in all domestic matters – the Protestant view of marriage made its way very slowly. Divorce remained within the jurisdiction of ecclesiastical courts, and these granted only divorces *a mensâ et thoro* in cases where cruelty or adultery was pleaded as rendering conjugal life impossible. These courts never granted divorces *a vinculo matrimonii*, which permit either – or both – of the divorced persons to contract a fresh marriage, except in cases where the marriage was annulled as having been void from the beginning; they would only grant a separation 'from bed and board', and imposed celibacy on the divorced couple until one of them died, and so set the other free. There was indeed a report drawn up by a commission, under the authority of 3 and 4 Edward VI., c. ii, which was intended as a basis for the re-modelling of the marriage laws, but the death of the king prevented the proposed reform;

the ecclesiastical courts remained as they were, and absolute divorce was unattainable. Natural impatience of a law which separated unhappy married people only to impose celibacy on them, caused occasional applications to be made to Parliament for relief, and a few marriages were thus dissolved under exceptional circumstances. In 1701, a bill was obtained, enabling a petitioner to remarry, and in 1798, Lord Loughborough's 'Orders' were passed.

> By these orders, no petition could be presented to the House, unless an official copy of the proceedings, and of a definitive sentence of divorce, *a mensâ et thoro*, in the ecclesiastical courts, was delivered on oath at the bar of the House at the same time. (Broom's *Comm.*, vol. iii, p. 396)

After explaining the procedure of the ecclesastical court, Broom goes on:

> A definitive sentence of divorce *a mensâ et thoro* being thus obtained, the petitioner proceeded to lay his case before the House of Lords in accordance with the Standing Orders before adverted to, and, subject to his proving the case, he obtained a bill divorcing him from the bonds of matrimony, and allowing him to marry again. The provisions of the bill, which was very short, were generally these: 1 The marriage was dissolved. 2 The husband was empowered to marry again. 3 He was given the rights of a husband as to any property of an after-taken wife. 4 The divorced wife was deprived of any right she might have as his widow. 5 Her after-acquired property was secured to her as against the husband from whom she was divorced. In the case of the wife obtaining the bill, similar provisions were made in her favour. (p. 398)

In 1857, an Act was passed establishing a Court for Divorce and Matrimonial Causes, and thus a great step forward was taken: this court was empowered to grant a judicial separation – equivalent to the old divorce *a mensâ et thoro* – in cases of cruelty, desertion for two years and upwards, or adultery on the part of the husband; it was further empowered to grant an absolute divorce with right of re-marriage – equivalent to the old divorce *a vinculo matrimonii* – in cases of adultery on the part of the wife, or of, on the part of the husband,

> incestuous adultery, or of bigamy with adultery, or of rape, or an unnatural crime, or of adultery coupled with such cruelty as would formerly have entitled her to a divorce *a*

> *mensâ et thoro*, or of adultery coupled with desertion, without reasonable excuse, for two years or upwards. (Broom, vol. i, p. 542)

The other powers held by the court need not now be specially dwelt upon.

The first reform here needed is that husband and wife should be placed on a perfect equality in asking for a divorce: at present if husband and wife be living apart, no amount of adultery on the husband's part can release the wife; if they be living together, a husband may keep as many mistresses as he will, and, provided that he carefully avoid any roughness which can be construed into legal cruelty he is perfectly safe from any suit for dissolution of marriage. Adultery alone, when committed by the husband, is not ground for a dissolution of marriage; it must be coupled with some additional offence before the wife can obtain her freedom. But the husband can obtain a dissolution of marriage for adultery committed by the wife, and he can further obtain money damages from the co-respondent, as a *solatium* to his wounded feelings. Divorce should be absolutely equal as between husband and wife: adultery on either side should be sufficient, and if it be thought necessary to join a male co-respondent when the husband is the injured party, then it should also be necessary to join a female co-respondent where the wife brings the suit. The principle, then, which should be laid down as governing all cases of divorce, is that no difference should be made in favour of either side; whatever is sufficient to break the marriage in the one case should be sufficient to break it in the other.

Next, the system of judicial separation should be entirely swept away. Wherever divorce is granted at all, the divorce should be absolute. No useful end is gained by divorcing people practically and regarding them as married legally. A technical tie is kept up, which retains on the wife the mass of disabilities which flow from marriage, while depriving her of all the privileges, and which widows both man and woman, exiling them from home life and debarring them from love. Judicial separation is a direct incentive to licentiousness and secret sexual intercourse; the partially divorced husband, refused any recognised companion, either indulges in promiscuous lust, to the ruin of his body and mind, or privately lives with some woman whom the law forbids him to marry and whom he is ashamed to openly acknowledge. Meanwhile the semi-divorced wife can obtain no relief, and is compelled to live on, without the freedom of the spinster or the widow, or the social consideration of the married woman. She can only obtain freedom by committing what the law and society brand as adultery; if she has any scruples on this head, she must remain alone, unloved and without home, living a sad, solitary life until death, more merciful than the law, sets her free.

It is hard to see what object there can be in separating a married couple, in breaking up the home, dividing the children, and yet maintaining the fact of marriage just so far as shall prevent the separated couple from forming new ties; the position of those who regard divorce as altogether sinful, is intelligible, however mistaken; but the position of those who advocate divorce, but object to the divorced couple having the right of contracting a new marriage, is wholly incomprehensible. No one profits by such divorce, while the separated couple are left in a dubious and most unsatisfactory condition; they are neither married nor unmarried; they can never shake themselves free from the links of the broken chain; they carry about with them the perpetual mark of their misfortune, and can never escape from the blunder committed in their youth. They would be the happier, and society would be the healthier, if the divorce of life and of interests were also a divorce which should set them free to seek happiness, if they will, in other unions – free technically as well as really, free in law as well as in fact.

If it be admitted that all divorce should be absolute, the question arises: What should be the ground of divorce? First, adultery, because breach of faith on either side should void the contract which implies loyalty to each other; the legal costs of both should fall on the breaker of the contract, but no damages should be recoverable against a third party. Next, cruelty, because where the weaker party suffers from the abuse of power of the stronger, there the law should, when appealed to, step in to annul the contract, which is thus a source of injury to one of the contracting parties; if a man be brought up before the magistrate charged with wife-beating or violence of any kind towards his wife, and be convicted and sentenced, the Divorce Court should on the demand of the wife, the record being submitted to it, pronounce a sentence of divorce; in the rare case of violence committed by a wife on her husband, the same result should accrue; the custody of the children should be awarded to the innocent party, since neither a man nor a woman convicted of doing bodily harm to another is fit to be trusted with the guardianship of a child.[1] The next distinct ground of divorce should be habitual drunkenness; drunkenness causes misery to the sober partner, and is ruinous in its effect, both on the *physique* and on the character of the children proceeding from the marriage. Here, of course, the custody of the children should be committed entirely to the innocent parent.

At present, the usual unfairness presides over the arrangements as to access to the children by the parents: 'In the case of a mother who is proved guilty of adultery, she is usually debarred from such access, though it has not been the practice to treat the offending father with the same rigour' (Broom's *Comm.*, vol. iii, p. 404). In all cases of divorce the interests of the children should be carefully guarded; both parents should be compelled to contribute to their support, whether the guardianship be confided to the father or to the mother.

These glaring reasons for granting a divorce will be admitted by everyone who recognises the reasonableness of divorce at all, but there will be more diversity of opinion as to the advisability of making divorce far more easily attainable. The French Convention of 1792 set an example that has been only too little followed; for the first time in French history divorce was legalised in France. It was obtainable

> on the application of either party [to the marriage] alleging simply as a cause, incompatibility of humour or character. The female children were to be entirely confided to the care of the mother, as well as the males, to the age of seven years, when the latter were again to be re-committed to the superintendence of the father; provided only, that by mutual agreement any other arrangement might take place with respect to the disposal of the children; or arbitrators might be chosen by the nearest of kin to determine on the subject. The parents were to contribute equally to the mainenance of the children, in proportion to their property, whether under the care of the father or mother. Family arbitrators were to be chosen to direct with respect to the partition of the property, or the alimentary pension to be allowed to the party divorced. Neither of the parties could contract a new marriage for the space of one year. (*Impartial History of the Late Revolution*, vol. ii, pp. 179, 180)

This beneficial law was swept away, with many other useful changes, when tyranny came back to France. At the present time the only countries where divorce is easily obtainable are some of the states of Germany and of America. It has been held in at least one American state that proved incompatibility of temper was sufficient ground for separation. And reasonably so; if two people enter into a contract for their mutual comfort and advantage, and the contract issues in mutual misery and loss, why should not the contract be dissolved? It is urged that marriage would be dishonoured if divorce were easily attainable; surely marriage is far more dishonoured by making it a chain to tie together two people who have for each other neither affection nor respect. For the sake of everyone concerned an unhappy marriage should be easily dissoluble; the married couple would be the happier and the better for the separation; their children – if they have any – would be saved from the evil effect of continual family jars, and from the loss of respect for their parents caused by the spectacle of constant bickering; the household would be spared the evil example of the quarrels of its heads; society would see less vice and fewer scandalous divorce suits. In all cases of contract, save that of marriage, those who make can, by mutual consent, unmake; why should those who make the most important contract of all be deprived of the same right?

Mr John Stuart Mill, dealing very briefly with the marriage contract in his essay 'On Liberty', points out that the fulfilment of obligations incurred by marriage must not be forgotten when the contract is dissolved, since these 'must be greatly affected by the continuance or disruption of the relation between the original parties to the contract'. But he goes on to say:

> It does not follow, nor can I admit, that these obligations extend to requiring the fulfilment of the contract at all costs to the happiness of the reluctant party; but they are a necessary element in the question; and even if, as Von Humboldt maintains, they ought to make no difference in the *legal* freedom of the parties to release themselves from the engagement (and I also hold that they ought not to make *much* difference), they necessarily make a great difference in the *moral* freedom. A person is bound to take all these circumstances into account before resolving on a step which may affect such important interests of others; and if he does not allow proper weight to those interests, he is morally responsible for the wrong. I have made these obvious remarks for the better illustration of the general principle of liberty, and not because they are at all needed on the particular question, which, on the contrary, is usually discussed as if the interest of children was everything, and that of grown persons nothing. (p. 61)

The essay of Von Humboldt, referred to by Mr Mill, is that on the 'Sphere and Duties of Government'; Von Humboldt argues that

> even where there is nothing to be objected to the validity of

> a contract, the State should have the power of lessening the restrictions which men impose on one another, even with their own consent, and (by facilitating the release from such engagements) of preventing a moment's decision from hindering their freedom of action for too long a period of life. (p. 134, of Coulthard's translation)

After pointing out that contracts relating to the transfer of *things* should be binding, Von Humboldt proceeds:

> With contracts which render personal performance a duty, or still more with those which produce proper personal relations, the case is wholly different. With these coercion operates hurtfully on man's noblest powers; and since the success of the pursuit itself which is to be conducted in accordance with the contract, is more or less dependent on the continuing consent of the parties, a limitation of such a kind is in them productive of less serious injury. When, therefore, such a personal relation arises from the contract as not only to require certain single actions, but, in the strictest sense, to affect the person, and influence the whole manner of his existence; where that which is done, or left undone, is in the closest dependence on internal sensations, the option of separation should always remain open, and the step itself should not require any extenuating reasons. Thus it is with matrimony. (pp. 134, 135)

Robert Dale Owen – the virtuous and justly revered author of *Moral Physiology;* a man so respected in his adopted country, the United States of America, that he was elected as one of its senators, and was appointed American ambassador at the Court of Naples – Robert Dale Owen, in a letter to Thomas Whittemore, editor of the Boston *Trumpet*, May 1831, deals as follows with the contract of marriage:

> I do not think it virtuous or rational in a man and woman solemnly to swear that they will love and honour each other until death part them. First, because if affection or esteem on either side should afterwards cease (as, alas! we often see it cease), the person who took the marriage-oath has perjured himself; secondly, because I have observed that such an oath, being substituted for the noble and elevating principle of moral obligation, has a tendency to weaken that principle.
>
> You will probably ask me whether I should equally object to a solemn promise to live together during life whatever happens. I do not think this *equally* objectionable, because it

is an explicit promise possible to be kept; whereas the oath to love until death, may become impossible of fulfilment. But still I do not approve even this possible promise; and I will give you the reasons why I do not.

That a man and woman should occupy the same house, and daily enjoy each other's society, so long as such an association gives birth to virtuous feelings, to kindness, to mutual forbearance, to courtesy, to disinterested affection, I consider right and proper. That they should continue to inhabit the same house and to meet daily, in case such intercourse should give birth to vicious feelings, to dislike, to ill temper, to scolding, to a carelessness of each other's comfort and a want of respect for each other's feelings – this I consider, *when the two individuals alone are concerned*, neither right nor proper; neither conducive to good order nor to virtue. I do not think it well, therefore, to promise, at all hazards, to live together for life.

Such a view may be offensive to orthodoxy, but surely, surely it is approved by common sense. Ask yourself, sir, who is – who can be the gainer – the man, the woman, or society at large – by two persons living in discord rather than parting in peace, as Abram and Lot did when their herdsmen could not agree. We have temptations enough already to ill humour in the world, without expressly creating them for ourselves; and of all temptations to that worst of petty vices, domestic bickering, can we suppose one more strong or more continually active than a forced association in which the heart has no share? Do not the interests of virtue and good order, then, imperiously demand (as the immortal author of *Paradise Lost* argued, in his celebrated work *On Divorce*) that the law should abstain from perpetuating any association, after it has become a daily source of vice?

If children's welfare is concerned, and that they will be injured by a separation, the case is different. Those who impart existence to sentient beings are, in my view, responsible to them for as much happiness as it is in their power to bestow. The parent voluntarily assumes this greatest of responsibilities; and he who, having so assumed it, trifles with his child's best interests for his own selfish gratification, is, in my eyes, utterly devoid of moral principle; or, at the least, utterly blind to the most sacred duty which a human being can be called to perform. If, therefore, the well-being and future prosperity of the children are to be sacrificed by a separation of the parents, then I would positively object to the separation, however grievous the evil effects of a continued connection might be to the dissentient couple.

Whether the welfare of children is ever promoted by the continuation of an ill-assorted union, is another question; as also in what way they ought to be provided for, where a separation actually takes place.

But to regard, for the moment, the case of the adults alone. You will remark, that it is no question for us to determine whether it is better or more proper that affections, once conceived, should last through life. We might as well sit down to decree whether the sun should shine or be hid under a cloud, or whether the wind should blow a storm or a gentle breeze. We may rejoice when it does so last, and grieve when it does not; but as to legislating about the matter, it is the idlest of absurdities.

But we *can* determine by law the matter of living together. We may compel a man and woman, though they hate each other as cordially as any of Byron's heroes, to have one common name, one common interest, and (nominally) one common bed and board. We may invest them with the legal appearance of the closest friends while they are the bitterest enemies. It seems to me that mankind have seldom considered what are the actual advantages of such a proceeding to the individuals and to society. I confess that I do not see what is gained in so unfortunate a situation, by keeping up the appearance when the reality is gone.

I do see the necessity, in such a case, if the man and woman separate, of dividing what property they may possess equally between them; and (while the present monopoly of profitable occupations by men lasts) I also see the expediency, in case the property so divided be not sufficient for the woman's comfortable support, of causing the man to continue to contribute a fair proportion of his earnings towards it. I also see the impropriety, as I said before, that the children, if any there be, should suffer. But I cannot see who is the gainer by obliging two persons to continue in each other's society, when heart-burnings, bickerings, and other vicious results, are to be the consequence.

There are cases when affection ceases on one side and remains on the other. No one can deny that this is an evil, often a grievous one; but I cannot perceive how the law can remedy it, or soften its bitterness, any more than it can legislate away the pain caused by unreturned friendship between persons of the same sex.

You will ask me, perhaps, whether I do not believe that, but for the law, there would be a continual and selfish change indulged, without regard to the feelings or welfare of others. What there might be in the world, viciously trained and circumstanced as so many human beings now are, I know not, though I doubt whether things *could* be much worse than they are now; besides that no human power can legislate for the heart. But if men and women were trained (as they so easily might!) to be even decently regardful of each other's feelings, may we not assert positively, that no such result could possibly happen? Let me ask each one of your readers, and let each answer to his or her own heart: 'Are you indeed bound to those you profess to love and honour by the law *alone?*' Alas! for your chance of happiness, if the answer be 'Yes!'

The fact is, as Mr Owen justly says, that a promise to 'love . . . until death us do part' is an immoral promise, because its performance is beyond the power of those who give the promise. To love, or not to love, is not a matter of the will; Love in chains loses his life, and only leaves a corpse in his captive's hand. Love is, of its very nature, voluntary, freely given, drawing together by an irresistible sympathy those whose natures are adapted to each other. Shelley well says, in one of the notes on Queen Mab:

> Love is inevitably consequent on the perception of loveliness. Love withers under constraint; its very essence is liberty; it is compatible neither with obedience, jealousy, nor fear; it is there most pure, perfect and unlimited, where its votaries live in confidence, equality, and unreserve.

To say this, is not to say that higher duty may not come between the lovers, may not, for a time, keep them apart, may not even render their union impossible; it is only to recognise a fact that no thoughtful person can deny, and to show how utterly wrong and foolish it is to promise for life that which can never be controlled by the will.

But marriage, it is said, would be too lightly entered into if it were so easily dissoluble. Why? People do not rush into endless partnerships because they are dissoluble at pleasure; on the contrary, such partnerships last just so long as they are beneficial to the contracting parties. In the same way, marriage would last exactly so long as its continuance was beneficial, and no longer: when it became hurtful, it would be dissolved. Shelley asks,

> How long then ought the sexual connection to last? what

> law ought to specify the extent of the grievances which should limit its duration? A husband and wife ought to continue so long united as they love each other; any law which should bind them to cohabitation for one moment after the decay of their affection, would be a most intolerable tyranny, and the most unworthy of toleration. How odious a usurpation of the right of private judgment should that law be considered which should make the ties of friendship indissoluble, in spite of the caprices, the inconstancy, the fallibility and capacity for improvement of the human mind. And by so much would the fetters of love be heavier and more unendurable than those of friendship, as love is more vehement and capricious, more dependent on those delicate peculiarities of imagination, and less capable of reduction to the ostensible merits of the object. . . . The connection of the sexes is so long sacred as it contributes to the comfort of the parties, and is naturally dissolved when its evils are greater than its benefits. There is nothing immoral in this separation. (Notes on *Queen Mab*)

In spite of this facility of divorce, marriage would be the most enduring of all partnerships; not only is there between married couples the tie of sexual affection, but around them grows up a hedge of common thoughts, common interests, common memories, that, as years go on, makes the idea of separation more and more repulsive. It would only be where the distaste had grown strong enough to break through all these, that divorce would take place, and in such cases the misery of the enforced common life would be removed without harm to any one. Of course, this facility of divorce will entirely sweep away those odious suits for 'restitution of conjugal rights' which occasionally disgrace our courts. If a husband and wife are living apart, without legal sanction, it is now open to either of them to bring a suit for restitution of conjugal rights.

> The decree of restitution pronounces for the marriage, admonishes the respondent to take the petitioner home and treat him or her as husband or wife, and to render him or her conjugal rights; and, further, to certify to the court, within a certain time, that he or she had done so; in default of which, an attachment for contempt of court will be issued against the offending party (Broom's *Comm.*, vol. iii, p. 400)

It is difficult to understand how any man or woman, endued with the most rudimentary sense of decency, can bring such a suit, and, after having succeeded, can enforce the decision. We may hope that, as sexual morality becomes more generally recognised, it will be seen that the essence of prostitution lies in the union of the sexes without mutual love; when a woman marries for rank, for title, for wealth, she sells herself as veritably as her poorer and more unfortunate sister; love alone makes the true marriage, love which is loyal to the beloved, and is swayed by no baser motive than passionate devotion to its object. When no such love exists the union which is marriage by law is nothing higher than legalised prostitution: the enforcement on an unwilling man or woman of conjugal rights is something even still lower, it is legalised rape.

It may be hoped that when divorce is more easily obtainable, the majority of marriages will be far happier than they are now. Half the unhappiness of married life arises from the too great feeling of security which grows out of the indissoluble character of the tie. The husband is very different from the lover; the wife from the betrothed; the ready attention, the desire to please, the eager courtesy, which characterised the lover disappear when possession has become certain; the daintiness, the gaiety, the attractiveness which marked the betrothed, are no longer to be seen in the wife whose position is secure; in society a lover may be known by his attention to his betrothed, a husband by his indifference to his wife. If divorce were the result of jarring at home, married life would very rapidly change; hard words, harshness, petulance, would be checked where those who had won the love desired to keep it, and attractiveness would no longer be dropped on the threshold of the home. Here, too, Shelley's words are well worth weighing:

> The present system of restraint does no more, in the majority of instances, than make hypocrites or open enemies. Persons of delicacy and virtue, unhappily united to those whom they find it impossible to love, spend the loveliest season of their life in unproductive efforts to appear otherwise than they are, for the sake of the feelings of their partner, or the welfare of their mutual offspring; those of less generosity and refinement openly avow their disappointment, and linger out the remnant of that union, which only death can dissolve, in a state of incurable bickering and hostility. The early education of the children takes its colour from the squabbles of the parents; they are nursed in a systematic school of ill-humour, violence and falsehood. Had they been suffered to part at the moment when indifference rendered their union irksome, they would have been spared many years of misery: they would have connected themselves more suitably, and would

> have found that happiness in the society of more congenial partners which is for ever denied them by the despotism of marriage. They would have been separately useful and happy members of society, who, whilst united, were miserable, and rendered misanthropical by misery. The conviction that wedlock is indissoluble, holds out the strongest of all temptations to the perverse; they indulge without restraint in acrimony, and all the little tyrannies of domestic life, when they know that their victim is without appeal. If this conviction were put on a rational basis, each would be assured that habitual ill-temper would terminate in separation, and would check this vicious and dangerous propensity. (Notes on *Queen Mab*)

To those who had thought over the subject carefully, it was no surprise to hear Mr Moncure Conway say – in a debate on marriage at the Dialectical Society – that in Illinois, USA, where there is great facility of divorce, the marriages were exceptionally happy. The reason was not far to seek.

Dealing elsewhere with this same injurious effect of overcertainty on the relations of married people to each other, Mr Moncure Conway writes as follows:

> In England we smilingly walk our halls of Eblis, covering the fatal wound; but our neighbours across the Channel are frank. Their moralists cannot blot out the proverb that 'Marriage is the suicide of love'. Is it any truer here than there that, as a general thing, the courtesies of the courtship survive in the marriage? 'Who is that domino walking with George?' asks Grisette No. 1, as reported by *Charivari*. 'Why,' returns Grisette No. 2, 'do you not walk behind them, and listen to what they say?' 'I have done so, and they do not say a word.' 'Ah, it is his wife.' But what might be George's feeling if he knew his wife might leave him some morning? 'If conserve of roses be frequently eaten,' they say in Persia, 'it will produce a surfeit.' The thousands of husbands and wives yawning in each other's faces at this moment need not go so far for their proverb. If it be well, as it seems to me to be, that this most intimate relation between man and woman should be made as durable as the object for which it is formed will admit, surely the bond should be real to the last, a bond of kindliness, thoughtfulness, actual helpfulness. So long as the strength of the bond lies simply in the disagreeable concomitants of breaking it, so long as it is protected by the very iron hardness which

> makes it gall and oppress, what need is there of the reinforcement of it by the cultivation of minds, the preservation of good temper, and considerate behaviour? Love is not quite willing to accept the judge's mace for his arrow. When the law no longer supplies husband or wife with a cage, each must look to find and make available what resources he or she has for holding what has been won. We may then look for sober second thoughts both before and after marriage. Love, from so long having bandaged eyes, will be all eye. Every real attraction will be stimulated when all depends upon real attraction. When the conserve becomes fatiguing, it will be refreshed by a new flavour, not by a certificate. From the hour when a thought of obligation influences either party to it, the marriage becomes a prostitution. (*The Earthward Pilgrimage*, pp. 289, 290, 291)

A remarkable instance of the permanence of unions dissoluble at pleasure is to be found related by Robert Dale Owen, in an article entitled 'Marriage and Placement', which appeared in the *Free Inquirer* of 28 May 1831. It deals with the unions between the sexes in the Haytian Republic, and the facts therein related are well worthy of serious attention. Mr Owen writes:

> Legal marriage is common in St Domingo as elsewhere. Prostitution, too, exists there as in other countries. But this institution of *placement* is found nowhere, that I know of, but among the Haytians.
>
> Those who choose to marry, are united, as in other countries, by a priest or magistrate. Those who do not choose to marry, and who equally shrink from the mercenary embrace of prostitution, are (in the phraseology of the island) *placés:* that is, literally translated, *placed*.
>
> The difference between *placement* and marriage is, that the former is entered into without any prescribed form, the latter with the usual ceremonies: the former is dissoluble at a day's warning, the latter is indissoluble except by the vexatious and degrading formalities of divorce; the former is a tacit social compact, the latter a legal compulsory one; in the latter the woman gives up her name and her property; in the former, she retains both.
>
> Marriage and placement are, in Hayti, equally respectable, or, if there be a difference, it is in favour of placement; and in effect ten placements take place in the island for one marriage. *Pétion*, the Jefferson of Hayti,[2] sanctioned the custom by his approval and example. *Boyer*, his successor,

the president, did the same;[3] and by far the largest portion of the respectable inhabitants have imitated their presidents, and are *placed*, not married. The children of the placed have, in every particular, the same legal rights and the same standing as those born in wedlock.

I imagine I hear from the clerical supporters of orthodoxy one general burst of indignation at this sample of national profligacy; at this contemning of the laws of God and man; at this escape from the Church's ceremonies and the ecclesiastical blessing. I imagine I hear the question sneeringly put, how long these same *respectable* connections commonly last, and how many dozen times they are changed in the course of a year.

Gently, my reverend friends! it is natural you should find it wrong that men and women dispense with your services and curtail your fees in this matter. But it is neither just nor proper, that because no prayers are said, and no fees paid, you should denounce the custom as a profligate one. Learn (as I did the other day from an intelligent French gentleman who had remained some time on the island) – learn, that *although there are ten times as many placed as married, yet there are actually fewer separations among the former than divorces among the latter*. If constancy, then, is to be the criterion of morality, these same profligate unions – that is, unions unprayed-for by the priest and unpaid for to him – are ten times as moral as the religion-sanctioned institution of marriage.

But this is not all. It is a fact notorious in Hayti, that libertinism is far more common among the married than among the placed. The explanatory cause is easily found. A placement secures to the consenting couple no *legal* right over one another. They remain together, as it were, on good behaviour. Not only positive tyranny or downright viragoism, but petulant peevishness or selfish ill humour, are sufficient causes of separation. As such, they are avoided with sedulous care. The natural consequence is that the unions are usually happy, and that each being comfortable at home, is not on the search for excitement abroad. In indissoluble marriage, on the contrary, if the parties should happen to disagree, their first jarrings are unchecked by considerations of consequences. A husband may be as tyrannical as to him seems good; he remains a lord and master still; a wife may be as pettish as she pleases; she does not thereby forfeit the rights and privileges of a wife. Thus, ill humour is encouraged by being legalised, and the natural results ensue, alienation of the heart, and sundering of the affections. The wife seeks relief in fashionable dissipation; the husband, perhaps, in the brutalities of a brothel.

But, aside from all explanatory theories, the FACT is, as I have stated it, viz.: that (taking the proportion of each into account) *there are ten legal separations of the married, for one voluntary separation of the placed.* If anyone doubts it, let him inquire for himself, and he will doubt no longer.

What say you to that fact, my reverend friends? How consorts it with your favourite theory, that man is a profligate animal, a desperately wicked creature? that, but for your prayers and blessings, the earth would be a scene of licentiousness and excess? that human beings remain together, only because you have helped to tie them? that there is no medium between priestly marriage and unseemly prostitution?

Does this fact open your eyes a little on the real state of things to which we heterodox spirits venture to look forward? Does it assist in explaining to you how it is that we are so much more willing than you to entrust the most sacred duties to moral rather than legal keeping?

You cannot imagine that a man and a woman, finding themselves suited to each other, should agree, without your interference, to become companions; that he should remove to her plantation, or she to his, as they found it most convenient; that the connection should become known to their friends without the agency of banns, and be respected, even though not ostentatiously announced in a newspaper. Yet all this happens in Hayti, without any breach of propriety, without any increase of vice; but, on the contrary, much to the benefit of morality, and the discouragement of prostitution. It happens among the white as well as the coloured population; and the president of the country gives it his sanction, in his own person.

Do you still ask me – accustomed as you are to consider virtue the offspring of restrictions – do you still ask me, what the checks are that produce and preserve such a state of things? I reply, good feeling and public opinion. Continual change is held to be disreputable; where sincere and well-founded affection exists, it is not desired; and as there is no pecuniary inducement in forming a placement, these voluntary unions are seldom ill-assorted.

Where social anarchy is feared, facts like these are worth pages of argument. If the Haytians are civilised enough for this more moral kind of marriage, why should Europeans be on a lower level? For it should not be forgotten that the experiment was tried in St Domingo under great disadvantages, and these unlegalised unions have yet proved more permanent than those tied with all due formality and tightness.

It may be urged: if divorce is to be so easily attainable, why should there be a marriage contract at all? Both as regards the pair immediately concerned, and as regards the children who may result from the union, a clear and definite contract seems to me to be eminently desirable. It is not to be wished that the union of those on whom depends the next generation should be carelessly and lightly entered into; the dignity and self-recollection which a definite compact implies are by no means to be despised, when it is remembered how grave and weighty are the responsibilities assumed by those who are to give to the State new citizens, and to Humanity new lives, which must be either a blessing or a cure. But the dignity of such a course is not its only, nor, indeed, its main recommendation. More important is the absolute necessity that the conditions of the union of the two adult lives should be clearly and thoroughly understood between them. No wise people enter into engagements of an important and durable character without a written agreement; a definite contract excludes all chance of disagreement as to the arrangements made, and prevents misunderstandings from arising. A verbal contract may be misunderstood by either party; lapse of time may bring about partial forgetfulness; slight disagreements may result in grave quarrels. If the contract be a written one, it speaks for itself, and no doubt can arise which cannot be reasonably settled. All this is readily seen where ordinary business partnerships are concerned, but some – unconsciously rebounding from the present immoral system, and plunging into the opposite extreme – consider that the union in marriage of man and woman is too tender and sacred a thing to be thus dealt with as from a business point of view. But it must be remembered that while love is essential to true and holy marriage, marriage implies more than love; it implies also a number of new relations to the outside world which – while men and women live in the world – cannot be wholly disregarded. Questions of house, of money, of credit, etc, necessarily arise in connection with the dual home, and these cannot be ignored by sensible men and women. The contract does not touch with rude hands the sensitive plant of love; it concerns itself only with the garden in which the plant grows, and two people can no more live on love alone than a plant can grow without earth around its roots. A contract which removes occasions of disagreement in business matters shelters and protects the love from receiving many a rude shock. 'Society will ere long,' said Mr Conway, 'be glad enough to assimilate contracts between man and woman to contracts between partners in business. Then love will dispense alike with the bandage on its eyes and the constable's aid.' Some pre-nuptial arrangement seems necessary which shall decide as to the right of inheritance of the survivor of the married pair. As common property will grow up during the union, such property should pass to the survivor and the children, and until some law be made which shall prevent parents from alienating from their children the whole of their property, a provision guarding their inheritance should find its place in the proposed deed. A definite marriage contract is also desirable for the sake of the children who may proceed from the union. Society has a right to demand from those who bring new members into it, some contract which shall enable it to compel them to discharge their responsbilities, if they endeavour to avoid them. If all men and women were perfect, no contract would be necessary, any more than it would be necessary to have laws against murder and theft; but while men and women are as they are, some compulsive power against evil-doers must be held in reserve by the law. Society is bound to guard the interests of the helpless children, and this can only be done by a clear and definite arrangement which makes both father and mother responsible for the lives they have brought into existence, and which shows the parentage in a fashion which could go into a law-court should any dispute arise. Again, if there were no contract, in whom would the guardianship of the children be vested, in case of wrong-doing of either parent, of death, or of separation? Suppose a brutal father: his wife leaves him and takes the children with her; how is she to keep them if he claims and takes them? If she has the legal remedy of divorce, the Court awards her the guardianship and she is safe from molestation. If a wife elope, taking the children with her, is the father to have no right to the guardianship of his sons and daughters, but to remain passive while they pass under the authority of another man? Application for divorce would guard him from such a wrong. If the parents separate, and both desire to have the children, how can such contest be decided, save by appeal to an impartial law? Marriage, as before urged, is a partnership, and where common duties, common interests, and common responsibilites grow up, there it is necessary that either party shall have some legal means of redress in case of the wrong-doing of the other.

To those who, on the other hand, object to facility of divorce being granted at all, it may fairly be asked that they should not forget that to place divorce within the reach of people, is not the same as compelling them to submit to it. Those who prefer to regard marriage as indissoluble could as readily maintain the indissolubility of their own wedded tie under a law which permitted divorce, as they can do at the present time. But those who think otherwise, and are unhappy in their marriages, would then be able to set themselves free. No happy marriage would be affected by the change, for the attainability of divorce would only be welcomed by those whose marriage was a source of misery and of discord; the contented would be no less content, while the unhappy would be relieved of their unhappiness; thus the change would injure no one, while it would benefit many.

It is a pity that there is no way of obtaining the general feminine view of the subject of marriage and divorce; women who study, who form independent opinions are – so far as my experience goes – unanimous in their desire to see the English laws altered; advanced thinkers of both sexes are generally, one might say universally, in favour of change. To those who think that women, if polled to-morrow, would vote for a continuance of the present state of things, may be recommended the following passage from Mrs Mill:

> Women, it is said, do not desire, do not seek what is called their emancipation. On the contrary, they generally disown such claims when made in their behalf, and fall with *acharnement* upon any one of themselves who identifies herself with their common cause. Supposing the fact to be true in the fullest extent ever asserted, if it proves that European women ought to remain as they are, it proves exactly the same with respect to Asiatic Women; for they too, instead of murmuring at their seclusion, and at the restraint imposed upon them, pride themselves on it, and are astonished at the effrontery of women who receive visits from male acquaintances, and are seen in the streets unveiled. Habits of submission make men as well as women servile-minded. The vast population of Asia do not desire or value, probably would not accept, political liberty, nor the savages of the forest, civilisation; which does not prove that either of those things is undesirable for them, or that they will not, at some future time, enjoy it. Custom hardens human beings to any kind of degradation, by deadening the part of their nature which would resist it. And the case of women is, in this respect, even a peculiar one, for no other inferior caste that

> we have heard of have been taught to regard their degradation as their honour.

Mr Conway considers that changed circumstances would rapidly cause women to be favourable to the proposed alteration. He remarks,

> Am I told that woman dreads the easy divorce? Naturally, for the prejudices and arrangements of society have not been adapted to the easy divorce. Let her know that, under the changed sentiment which shall follow changed law, she will meet with sympahty where now she would encounter suspicion; let her know that she will, if divorced from one she loves not, have only her fair share of the burdens entailed by the original mistake; and she who of all persons suffers most if the home be false will welcome the freer marriage. (*The Earthward Pilgrimage*, p. 289)

Both in theory and in practice advanced thinkers have claimed facility of divorce. John Milton, in his essay on 'Divorce', complains that 'the misinterpreting of Scripture . . . hath changed the blessing of matrimony not seldom into a familiar and co-inhabiting mischiefe; at least into a drooping and disconsolate household captivitie, without refuge or redemption' (p. 2), and in his Puritan fashion he remarks that because of this 'doubtes by the policy of the devill that gracious ordinance becomes insupportable', so that men avoid it and plunge into debauchery. Arguing that marriage is not to be regarded merely as a legitimate kind of sexual intercourse, but rather as a union of mind and feeling, Milton says:

> That indisposition, unfitness, or contrariety of mind, arising from a cause in nature unchangable, hindring and ever likely to hinder the main benefits of conjugall society, which are solace and peace, is a greater reason of divorce than natural frigidity, especially if there be no children, and that there be mutual consent. (p. 5)

Luther, before Milton, held the same liberal views. Mary Wolstonecraft acted on the same theory in her own life, and her daughter was united to the poet Shelley while Shelley's first wife was living, no legal divorce having severed the original marriage. Richard Carlile's second marriage was equally illegal. In our own days the union of George Henry Lewes and George Eliot has struck the key-note of the really moral marriage. Mary Wolstonecraft was unhappy in her choice, but in all the other cases the happiest results accrued. It needs considerable assurance to brand these great names with immorality, as all those must do who denounce as immoral unions which are at present illegal.

In the whole of the arguments put forward in the above pages there is not one word which is aimed at real marriage, at the faithful and durable union of two individuals of opposite sexes – a union originated in and maintained by love alone. Rather, to quote Milton once more, is reverence for marriage the root of the reform I urge: he who

> thinks it better to part than to live sadly and injuriously to that cherfull covnant (for not to be belov'd and yet retain'd, is the greatest injury to a gentle spirit), he I say who therefore seeks to part, is one who highly honours the married life, and would not stain it; and the reasons which now move him to divorce, are equall to the best of those that could first warrant him to marry. (p. 10)

In the advocacy of such views marriage is elevated, not degraded; no countenance is given to those who would fain destroy the idea of the durable union between one man and one woman. Monogamy appears to me to be the result of civilisation, of personal dignity, of cultured feeling; loyalty of one man to one woman is, to me, the highest sexual ideal. The more civilised the nature the more durable and exclusive does the marriage union become; in the lower ranges of animal life difference of sex is enough to excite passion: there is no individuality of choice. Among savages it is much the same: it is the female, not the woman, who is loved, although the savage rises higher than the lower brutes, and is attracted by individual beauty. The civilised man and woman need more than sex-difference and beauty of form; they seek satisfaction for mind, heart, and tastes as well as for body; each portion the complex nature requires its answer in its mate. Hence it arises that true marriage is exclusive, and that prostitution is revolting to the noble of both sexes, since in prostitution love is shorn of his fairest attributes, and passion, which is only his wings, is made the sole representative of the divinity. The fleeting connections supposed by some Free Love theorists are steps backward and not forward; they offer no possibility of home, no education of the character, no guarantee for the training of the children. The culture both of father and of mother, of the two natures of which its own is the resultant, is necessary to the healthy development of the child; it cannot be deprived of either without injury to its full and perfect growth.

But just as true marriage is invaluable, so is unreal marriage deteriorating in its effects on all concerned: therefore, where mistake has been made, it is important to the gravest interests of society that such mistake should be readily remediable, without injury to the character of either of those concerned in it. Freed from the union which injures both, the man and woman may seek for their fit helpmeets, and in happy marraiges may become joyful servants of humanity, worthy parents of the citizens of to-morrow. Men and women must know conjugal, before they can know true parental, love; each must see in the child the features of the beloved ere the perfect circle of love can be complete. Husband and wife bound in closest, most durable and yet most eager union, children springing as flowers from the dual stem of love, home where the creators train the lives they have given – such will be the marriage of the future. The loathsome details of the Divorce Court will no longer pollute our papers; the public will no longer be called in to gloat over the ruins of desecrated love; society will be purified from sexual vice; men and women will rise to the full royalty of their humanity, and hand in hand tread life's pathways, trustful instead of suspicious, free instead of enslaved, bound by love instead of by law.

NOTES

1 Since these lines were published in the *National Reformer*, a clause has been inserted in a bill now before Parliament, empowering magistrates to grant an order of separation to a wife, if it is proved that she has been cruelly ill-used by her husband, and further compelling the husband, in such a case, to contribute a weekly sum towards her maintenance. This will be a great improvement on the present state of things, but absolute divorce would be better than mere separation.

2 It may suffice, in illustration of Pétion's character, to quote the touching inscription found on his tomb – 'Here lies Pétion, who enjoyed for twelve years absolute power, and during that period never caused one tear to flow.'

3 Boyer's resolution in this matter is the more remarkable, as he has been urged and pestered to submit to the forms of marriage. Grégoire, archbishop of Blois, and who is well known for the perseverance and benevolence with which he has, for a long series of years, advocated the cause of the African race, wrote to the president of Hayti in the most urgent terms, pressing upon him the virtue – the necessity, for his salvation – of conforming to the sacrament of marriage. To such a degree did the good old archbishop carry his intermeddling officiousness, that when Boyer mildly but firmly declined availing himself of his grace's advice, a rupture was the consequence, greatly to the sorrow of the president, who had ever entertained the greatest respect and affection for his ecclesiastical friend.

Ellice J. Hopkins

from
The Power of Womanhood

(1899)

The modern woman and her future

Up to this point I have dealt only with the great shaping and moulding principles of life, with indirect influence rather than direct. How far direct teaching on matters of sex should be given to our girls has been a far greater perplexity to me than in the case of boys. In the present state of our schools and our streets our boys must get to know evil. Hitherto it was possible to say that our girls *might* get to know evil, and betwen that 'must' and 'might' lay a great and perplexing chasm. We do not want our garden lilies to smell of anything but pure dews and rains and sun-warmed fragrance. But is this ideal possible any longer, except in a few secluded country homes, where, hidden like Keats's nightingale 'among the leaves' they may remain innocent and ignorant of the world's evil?

But with the ordinary conditions of the present day, with the greater freedom accorded to women, the wider range of education, involving a wider range of reading, with modern newspapers left about, I ask, How is it possible for a mother to keep her girls in ignorance and unconscious innocence? A volume of short stories comes into the house from the circulating library; they are clever and apparently absolutely harmless. Yet embedded in the heart of one such volume, which shall be nameless, I came upon a story almost as vile as anything in a French novel, and conveying the most corrupt knowledge. How, I ask, can a busy mother read through every book of short stories before letting it fall into the hands of her girls? or how, if they are to read Latin and Greek, or even carefully to study our own old literature, is she to guard them from a knowledge of evil conveyed in classical allusions, or in the coarse plainness of speech of an earlier age? I know as a fact, whether we recognise it or not, that behind our mature backs our girls are discussing these moral problems with quite an alarming amount of freedom, and some at least, guided by no teaching, and with no practical knowledge of the great laws of human life, are coming to quite startling conclusions, which would make their mothers' hair stand on end. And one most undesirable, and I may add unnatural, result noticeable among the more advanced section is a certain distaste for marriage, a tendency to look upon it as something low and animal, which strikes me as simply a fatal attitude for women to take up.

Have we not, therefore, got clearly to recognise that the old order has changed, giving place to new, and requiring, therefore, new methods? We may or we may not like the new order, but it is *there*. Under the changed conditions of modern life it is inevitable; therefore it must be in the providence of God; it cannot be wholly bad, and if we will work in with it loyally, and not thrust it aside for some old order of our own, it may be, nay, it will be, wholly for good. Let us remember that the two most conservative organic forms, the two that have most resisted progressive evolution, are the donkey and the goose. To ignore the new order, to cling to the old views and methods, is to court moral extinction as a living force. As well think to find safety in escaping from the advance of an express engine by adopting the stately pace of our grandmothers, which was perfectly adapted for getting out of the way of a lumbering stage-coach. May not He

Whose large plan ripens slowly to a whole

be working out a progressive ideal such as we trace in the great spiritual records of our race? The Bible, thank God! neither begins nor ends with sin; but it begins with a sinless garden, it ends with a strong city of God, with evil known and recognised, but cast out beyond its walls. May He not be leading us to form a wider, deeper, stronger ideal; to aim for our girls not so much at Innocence, with her fading wreath of flowers – fading, as, alas! they must ever fade in a world like this – but to aim at Virtue, with her victor's crown of gold, tried in the fire? May it not be that His Divine providence is constraining us to take as our ideal for our womanhood, not the old sheltered garden, but a strong city of God, having foundations, whose very gates are made of pearl, through which nothing that defileth is suffered to enter, and whose common ways are paved with pure gold, gold of no earthly temper, but pure and clear as crystal – a city of refuge for all who are oppressed with wrong, and from which all foul forms of evil are banned by the one word '*Without*'? Sure I am that if we will accept this deeper and larger ideal, and endeavour, however imperfectly, to work it out on the earth, in the midst of it, as in the old garden ideal, will be found the tree of life; but then its very leaves will be for the healing of the nations.

But whether you go with me as far as this or not, I think you will agree with me that we must not leave our girls to their own crude notions on the deepest matters of life, certain to be the cruder owing to their inevitable rebound from the conventions which have shackled them for so long. Still less must we leave them to get their teaching on marriage and matters of sex from some modern novels, which I can only characterise as tuberculosis of the moral sense, but from which, as I have already pointed out, we cannot always guard them. We must give them direct teaching of some kind.

First, I think our girls, as well as our boys, need far more direct teaching than has been customary as to the sanctity of the body. This is especially true of girls who are sent to Boarding Schools, as some of the moral evils of boys' schools are not, I am sorry to say, althogether unknown in girls' schools, though, as far as I can ascertain, the evil is much less in extent, and in many of our best schools is non-existent. Still, all girls need to be taught that the body is the temple of the Lord and giver of life, and that from the crown of their head to the sole of their feet those bodies belong to Christ.

Second, I think that they ought to have some such teaching about life and birth as that which I have already recommended for boys that they may see how through the marital tie and the consequent rise of the parental relation, a world of blind mechanical force gradually developed into a world of life and beauty, and at last crowned itself with a conscious love in an indissoluble union, which makes marriage the very type of the union of the soul with God, of Christ with His Church.

Third, they need to be taught that much in their own physical constitution which they rebel against as handicapping them in the struggle of life is Nature's provision for them that no merely physical function should press upon them as we see it do in the animal creation at certain periods of the year, but that they should be free to serve God, whether in the married or in the unmarried state, in quietness and godly living.

Fourth, above all they need definite teaching on the true nature, the sanctity, and the beauty of marriage. It appears that the line of progress is always a spiral, and it would seem as if we were in the backward sweep of the spiral, which looks like retrogression, but will doubtless bring us out further up in the end. The masculine view that marriage is the one aim and end of a woman's existence, adopted also by some careful mothers, is now exploded. Young men are no longer led to look upon every girl that they meet as furtively, to use a vulgarism, 'setting her cap' at them, and only too ready to fling herself at their feet. So far so good. But have we not suffered our girls to drift into the opposite extreme? In the heyday of their bright young life, with so many new interests and amusements open to them, in the pride of their new freedom, they are no longer so inclined to marry, and are even apt to look down upon the married state. They form so high an ideal of the man to whom they would surrender their independence – an ideal which they fortunately do not apply to their fathers and brothers, whom they find it quite possible to love on a far lower and more human level – that because a man does not fulfil this ideal, and is not a fairy prince, dowered with every possible gift, they refuse men who, though not angels, would have made them happy as wives and mothers. Would not a little sound, sensible teaching be of great good here? Could we not point out that though in so vital and complex a union as the family there must be some seat of ultimate authority, some court of final appeal somewhere, and that the woman herself would not wish it to rest anywhere else than in the man, if she is to respect him, yet there is no subservience on the part of the wife in the obedience she renders, but rather, in South's grand words, 'It is that of a queen to her king, who both owns a subjection and remains a majesty'? Cannot we contend against this falsehood of the age that seems so to underlie our modern life, and which inclines us to look upon all obedience as a slavish thing – that obedience which 'doth preserve the stars from wrong' and through which 'the most ancient heavens are fresh and strong': that obedience which when absolute and implicit to the Divine will is 'a service of perfect freedom'. It is the profession which exacts unquestioning obedience that forms the finest school for character. We do not hear of a Wellington or a Roberts refusing to enter the service because they could not give up their independence. Our military heroes at least know that it is through discipline and obedience that they gain their real independence – the independence of a strong character.

Again, our girls need to be taught not only that there is nothing derogatory in the married relation to the freest and fullest independence of character, but surely in these days of open advocacy by some popular writers of 'les unions libre', and a freedom of divorce that comes to much the same thing, they need to be taught the sanctity of marriage – those first principles which hitherto we have taken for granted, but which now, like everthing else, is thrown into the crucible and brought into question. They need definite teaching as to the true nature of marriage; that it is no mere contract to be broken or kept according to the individual contractor's convenience – I never yet heard of a contract for bringing into existence, not a successful machine, but a moral and spiritual being with infinite possibilities of weal or woe, of heaven or hell – but a sacramental union of love and life, with sacramental grace given to those who will seek it to live happily and endure nobly within its sacred bonds – a union so deep and mystical that even on its physical side our great physiologists are wholly at a loss to account for some of its effects; a union of which permanence is the very essence, as on its permanence rests the permanence and stability of the whole fabric of our life. It can never be treated on an individualistic basis, though that is always the tendency with every man and woman who has ever loved. In Mrs Humphrey Ward's words:

> that is always the way; each man imagines the matter is still for his deciding, and he can no more decide it than he can tamper with the fact that fire burns or water drowns. All these centuries the human animal has fought with the human soul. And step by step the soul has registered her victories. She has won them only by feeling for the law and finding it – uncovering, bringing into light, the firm rocks beneath her feet. And on these rocks she rears her landmarks – marriage, the family, the State, the Church. Neglect them and you sink into the quagmire from which the soul of the race has been for generations struggling to save you.

Fall on this rock, stumble into unhappiness and discontent, as so many do in marriage, and you will be broken. But be faithful to it and the high traditions which generations of suffering men and women have worked out for you, and you will be broken as the bud is broken into the blossom, as the acorn is broken into the oak – broken into a higher and stronger life. On the other hand, rebel against it, attempt to drag it down and cast it from its place, and it will crush you, and grind some part of your higher nature to powder. How strangely and sadly is this shown in the case of one of our greatest writers, who thought that the influence of her writings would far outweigh the influence of her example, but whose name and example is now constantly used by bad men to overcome the virtue of young educated girls struggling alone in London, and often half starving on the miserable pittance which is all they can earn. But still more is it shown in the life of the nation which tampers with the laws of marriage and admits freedom of divorce. Either such suits must be heard *in camera* without the shame of exposure, when divorce would be so facilitated that the family and the State would rest rather on a superstructure of rickety boards on a rock; or they must be heard in public court and form a moral sewer laid on to the whole nation, poisoning the deepest springs of its life, and through that polluted life producing far more individual misery than it endeavours to remedy in dissolving an unhappy marriage. God only knows what I suffered when a *cause celèbre* came on, and I felt that the whole nation was being provided with something worse, and more vitally mischievous, than the most corrupt French novel.

Deeply do I regret – and in this I think most thoughtful minds will agree with me – that the Reformers in their inevitable rebound from the superstitions of Rome, rejected her teaching of the sacramental nature of marriage, which has made so many Protestant nations tend to that freedom of divorce which is carried to so great an extent in some parts of America, and is spreading, alas! to many of our own colonies – a laxity fatally undermining the sanctity and stability of the family. If marriage be not a sacrament, an outward and visible sign of an inward and spiritual life and grace, I ask what is?

I would, therefore, earnestly beseech you to oppose your direct teaching to the whole tendency of modern life, and to much of the direct teaching of modern fiction – even of so great a novelist as George Meredith – which inculcates the subordination of the marriage bond to what is called the higher law of love, or rather, passion. In teaching your sons, and especially your girls, who are far more likely to be led astray by this specious doctrine, base marriage not on emotion, not on sentiment, but on duty. To build upon emotion, with the unruly wills and affections of sinful men, is to build, not upon the sand, but upon the wind. There is but one immovable rock on which steadfast character, steadfast relations, steadfast subordination of the lower and personal desires, to the higher and immutable obligations and trusts and responsibilities of life can be built – duty. When this rock has been faithfully clung to, when in the midst of disillusionment and shattered ideals the noble resolution has been clung to never to base personal happiness on a broken trust, or another's pain, I have over and over again known the most imperfect marriage prove in the end to be happy and contented. Here again I quote some words of Mrs Humphrey Ward, which she puts into the mouth of her hero:

'No,' he said with deep emphasis, 'No – I have come to think

> the most disappointing and hopeless marriage, nobly borne to be better worth having than what people call an "ideal passion" – if the ideal passion must be enjoyed at the expense of one of those fundamental rules which poor human nature has worked out, with such infinite difficulty and pain, for the protection and help of its own weakness'.

I am aware that neither Mr Grant Allen with his 'hill top' novels, nor Mrs Mona Caird need be taken too seriously, but when the latter says, 'There is something pathetically absurd in this sacrifice to their children of generation after generation of grown people,' I would suggest that it would be still more pathetically absurd to see the whole upward-striving past, the whole noble future of the human race, sacrificed to their unruly wills and affections, their passions and desires. If, as Goldwin Smith says in his rough, incisive way, there is not much union of heart in marriage, I do not see that there would be more union of heart in adultery.

I have dwelt thus earnestly upon this point because the sooner we realise for ourselves and our girls that any relaxation of the marriage bond will in its disastrous consequences fall upon us, and not upon men, the better. It is the woman who first grows old and loses her personal attractions while a man often preserves his beauty into extreme old age. It is the burthened mother of a family who cannot compete in companionship with the highly-cultured young unmarried lady, with the leisure to post herself up in the last interesting book or the newest political movement. It is the man who is the more variable in his affections than the woman, more constant as she is by nature, as well as firmly anchored down by the strength of her maternal love. It is therefore on the woman that any loosening of the permanence of the marriage tie will chiefly fall in untold suffering. 'Le mariage c'est la justice,' say the French, who have had experience enough of 'les unions libres' – justice to the wife and mother, securing her the stability to her right of maintenance after she has given up her means of support, above all, the stability of her right to the care of her own children. If we want to study the innate misery to women arising from the relaxation of the married tie, or transient unions, we had better read professor Dowden's *Life of Shelley* – misery not the result of public stigma, for there was no such stigma in the circle in which Shelley moved, but misery brought about by the facts themselves, and producing a state of things which Matthew Arnold could only characterise by the untranslatable French word '*sale*'.

I confess it does fill me with sardonic laughter to find this oldest and stalest of all experiments, this oldest and flattest of all failures, paraded as a brand new and original panacea for all the woes of our family life – woes which, if nobly borne, at least make 'perfect through suffering'.

And now to descend to lower levels. Could we not do a little more to save our young girls from sacrificing their happiness to false ideals by opportunely obtruding a little mature common-sense into their day visions, and their inexperienced way of looking at things? It is all very well in the heyday of life, when existence is full of delight and home affection, to refuse a man who could make them happy, because they don't quite like the shape of his nose, or because he is a little untidy in his dress, or simply because they are waiting for some impossible demigod to whom alone they could surrender their independence. But could we not mildly point out that darker days must come, when life will not be all enjoyment, and that a lonely old age, with only too possible penury to be encountered, must be taken into consideration?

God knows I am no advocate for loveless, and least of all for mercenary, marriages, but I think we want some *viâ media* between the French *mariage de convenance* and our English method of leaving so grave a question as marriage entirely to the whimsies and romantic fancies of young girls. We need not go back to the old fallacy that marriage is the aim and end of a woman's existence and absolutely necessary for her happiness. Some women are doubtless called to be mothers of the race, and to do the social work which is so necessary to our complex civilisation. Some women may feel themselves called to some literary or artistic pursuit, or some other profession, for which they require the freedom of unmarried life. But I think I shall carry most women with me in saying that for the ordinary woman marriage is the happiest state, and that she rarely realises the deepest and highest in her nature except in wifehood and motherhood. Rarely, indeed, can any public work that she can do for the world equal the value of that priceless work of building up, stone by stone, the temple of a good man's character which falls to the lot of his mother. Truly is she called the wife, the weaver, since day and night, without hasting and without resting, she is weaving the temple hangings, wrought about with pomegranates and lilies, of the very shrine of his being. And if our girls could be led to see this, at least it would overcome that adverseness to marriage which many are now so curiously showing, and which inevitably makes them more fastidious and fanciful in their choice. And, on the other hand, without falling back into the old match-making mamma, exposing her wares in the marriage market to be knocked down to the highest bidder, might not parents recognise a little more than they do, how incumbent on them it is to make every effort to give their daughters that free and healthy intercourse with young men which would yield them a wider choice, and which forms the best method for insuring a happy marriage?

At least, let us open our eyes to the fact that we are face to face with some terrible problems with regard to the future of our girls. With interest on savings sinking more and more to Mr Goschen's prediction of one per cent., it must become more and more difficult to make a provision for the unmarried daughters; and if the money is spent instead on training them to earn their own bread, we are still met by the problem of the early superannuation of women's labour, which rests on physical causes, and cannot therefore be removed. This at least is no time to despise marriage, or for women of strong and independent character to adopt an attitude which deprives the nation of many of its noblest mothers.

Now, I come lastly to what I fear will be very debatable ground. I can only ask you to think over what I say, and to give it a careful and as far as you can unprejudiced consideration.

If we are to facilitate marriage, which must form, at any rate, the main solution of the problems of the near future to which I have alluded, if we are to prevent, or even lessen, the degradation of women, if we are to extinguish this pit of destruction in our midst, into which so many a fair and promising young life disappears, and which perpetually threatens the moral and physical welfare of our own sons, if we are to stay the seeds of moral decay in our own nation, we must be content to revolutionise much in the order of our own life, and adopt a lower and simpler standard of living. It is we, and not men, who set the standard; it is we who have been guilty of the vulgar ambition of following the last social fashion, and doing as our richer neighbours do, until we have made our girls such expensive articles, that young men simply dare not indulge in them, and are led to seek in their luxurious clubs the comfort which they should find in a home of their own, with all that relaxation of moral fibre which comes from club-life. Do we really think that this multitude of unmarried men are all monks without the cowl, and without the tonsure? Do we seriously think that we are likely successfully to contend against the degradation of women by our rescue societies and our refuges when we are deliberately bringing about a social condition that ministers to it? 'Oh, of course,' said a near relative of my own, 'no girl can marry comfortably and live in London with less than a thousand a year.' All I can answer is that if this be so, it means the degradation of women writ large.

And have we even secured the happiness of our own daughters

by this high standard of living which prevents so many of them from marrying at all? I confess there is some irony in my anxiety that eligible offers should not be refused on trifling grounds, when so many a charming girl in these days has never had an offer of marriage to refuse. These crowds of unmarried girls, with no worthy object in life to call out the noble energies that lie dormant within them, 'lasting' rather than 'living' – are they really happy? Is not Robert Louis Stevenson right when he says that 'the ideal of the stalled ox is the one ideal that will never satisfy either man or woman?' Are not the hardships of a smaller income and a larger life – a life that would at least satisfy a woman's worst foe, heart hunger – more adapted to their true nature, their true happiness?

And to what further admirable results have we attained by this high standard of comfort and luxury? Nature has carefully provided for the equality of the sexes by sending rather more boys than girls into the world, since fewer boys are reared; but we have managed to derange this order. We have sent our boys out into the world, but we have kept our girls at home, refusing to allow them to rough it with husbands and brothers, or to endure the least hardness. The consequence is that we have nearly a million of surplus women in the old country, while in America, and in our own colonies, we have a corresponding surplus of men, with all the evil moral consequences that belong to a disproportion between the sexes. Truly we may congratulate ourselves!

I would therefore urge that if we are really to grapple with these moral evils, we should simplify our standard of living, and educate our girls very differently to what we are doing. Culture is good, and the more we have of it the better; it gives a woman a wider sphere of influence. But if dead languages are to take the place of living service; if high mathematics are to work out a low plane of cooking and household management; if a first class in moral science is to involve third class performance of the moral duties involved in family life, then I deliberately say it were better that, like Tennyson's mother, we should be

Not learned save in gracious household ways

I protest with the utmost earnestness against the care of human life, of human health, and of human comfort being considered a lower thing and of less importance than good scholarship; or that, when we recognise that months and even years will have to be devoted to the attainment of the one, the arts by which we can fulfil those great human trusts which devolve more or less upon every woman can be practised without ever having been learnt at all.

Only think of the amount of household service that devolved upon our grandmothers in the olden days – the weaving, the spinning, the pharmacy, the pickling and preserving, the brewing, the baking, the getting up of fine linen, and many another household duty which we now shunt upon servants and tradesmen. Do we not instinctively feel that the exclusively book education into which we have almost unconsciously drifted cannot and will not give the same solidity of character as belonged to the women of old, but will incur the 'nemesis of disproportion'? Surely we can choose some nobler type on which to mould our scheme of female education than that of the tadpole, which is all head, no hands, and much active and frivolous tail.

Do not misunderstand me. Do not think I am decrying a classical education; and, as the daughter of a great mathematician, it is not likely that I should underrate mathematics as a mental discipline. I am only urging that they should be subordinated to higher and more practical issues.

May I not, therefore, plead that our girls should not be brought up to be such fine ladies as they largely are at present, but that training in all household management should form an integral part of their education, so that they may be fitted to become the wives of men of modest incomes? They should be taught how to cook, both for the family and for the sick – not a mere smattering of cooking, but a thorough practical knowledge, enabling them to train a young and inexperienced servant, in itself one of the most valuable works that they can do. They must be taught how to cut out, and how to manage a sewing machine, how to iron and get up fine linen. Above all, oh that it may come to be considered part of a woman's education to go for six month's training into a nursing home or a hospital as soon as she is old enough to be admitted! What doctor's bills would be saved, what precious health would be preserved, what skilled nursing would be given, when trained service cannot be afforded! How many a life have I known crippled from a mother's ignorance of the laws of health and the preventives of disease.

Not only would knowledge in these things enable our girls to marry on far smaller incomes, but if from any circumstances they prefer unmarried life, it would open up to them as a means of livelihood many positions for which they are now totally unfitted, especially in relation to our industrial schools, and the orphan children of the State.

Perhaps you will say that your children are being educated at a High School, that all their time is wanted for their lessons, and that you don't see the reason of turning your girls into household drudges. But why, I ask again, should we take this fine lady ideal for our girls, when we take such a much more practical standard for our boys? If an excellent opening offered itself to one of your sons at a bank, would you not agree with his father in expecting him to take it, though it would involve the drudgery of sitting in a cramped attitude on a tall stool for hours and hours every day? Why should we accept life's necessary drudgery for our boys, and refuse it for our girls? No life worth living can be had without drudgery – the most brilliant as well as the dullest. Darwin spent eight of the best years of his life in an exhaustive investigation into the organisation of a barnacle – labour accompanied, as all intellectual work was with him, by a constant sense of physical nausea from which he suffered, till, from sheer weariness and disgust at the drudgery, he ends his researches in his emphatic way with the exclamation 'D – the barnacles!' At least a woman's household drudgery does not end in a barnacle, or in dead coin, but in a living and loved personality whose comfort and health it secures. Blessed is drudgery, the homely mother of Patience, 'that young and rose-lipped cherubim', of quiet endurance, of persistency in well-doing, of all the stablest elements of character.

As to the lack of time, of course I am aware there are periods of the year that are wholly taken up with school education; but in vacation time manual instruction would prove a healthful diversion. Cooking is often a delight to young girls, and the elements of making and cutting out can be taught upon a large doll, and so turned into an agreeable holiday task. Of course I do not say that any household art can be wholly mastered without some drudgery, but I can only repeat the beatitude I have already given, 'Blessed is drudgery'. Do not refuse to your girls the divine hardness which is the very heart of a diviner joy, and of that fuller life 'of which our veins are scant,' nor refuse for them and for ourselves the words of life: 'As the Father has sent Me into the world, even so send I you': but be content to send them into the world to love, to suffer, to endure, to live and die for the good of others.

If you reject the methods that I have suggested for dealing with the difficult problems that are at our very door, work out other better methods of your own. Only remember that with these problems the words may be applied of a General on a battlefield to his soldiers: 'Gentlemen, there are your enemies; if you don't kill them, they will kill you. Up, and at them!'

Emmeline Pethick Lawrence

Education in Love

(1912)

At the outset we must formulate some conception of what love is. Many people, if they think of love at all in its elemental naked form, regard it as a dangerous and destructive force from which the young must be shielded as long as possible. Others regard it as a sort of disease for which marriage or sexual relationships outside marriage are a palliative, if not a cure. Plato, Dante, Shakespeare, Shelley, Whitman, and many others, held to be inspired, offer a different conception. According to their teaching, love is the cosmic creative fire from which all life and forms have been generated, whether it be the life and forms of solar systems, or the life and forms of human beings, or the life and forms of flowers, or the life and forms of the smallest creatures and atoms in existence.

Thus regarded, love is the creative reality for which all religions are seeking: sex its supreme manifestation on this planet: passion is their union in the plane of human life.

As you cannot separate in living man the body from the spirit (for after that separation the man has ceased to be and the corpse alone is left), so you cannot deprive sex of love without destroying living passion. There are, however, infinite degrees by which the human body may become penetrated by spirit; and, even so, there are infinite degrees by which sex can be penetrated by love.

Love is the great creative magic of generation and regeneration operating on every physical and spiritual plane of life. Like other creative forces, love as a human passion, if let loose from direction and control, may sweep away, with irresistible and anarchic violence, human institutions. That is why human beings dread it; so those who hold that the love passion is a dangerous and destructive force are, to a certain extent, right. They have seized the negative side of a great affirmative truth. A creative force must necessarily become, in some conditions, a destructive force too. It vitalises or it shatters the organism brought within the action of its impact. No security from the impact of this force can be found either in ignorance or in convention, or in seclusion from the world. It stands to reason, therefore, that the whole system of education should be directed to the main purpose of training the human body and the human mind to meet this cosmic force without being shattered by it.

The training of the body by every kind of athletic exercise to the attainment of balance and control, and the training of the mind by exercises in concentration and detachment, till both body and mind become obedient to the decrees of the will, are part of the education by which the human organism can be prepared for the awakening within it of the cosmic energy of love.

All that I have said up to this point merely clears the way for a discussion of some of the practical methods by which children can be educated from their earliest years in the elementary science of sex, interpreted at every stage by practice in the art of love.

The first thing that an awakening intelligence wants to know is 'How did I come to be myself, and how did I come to be here?' The moment the question is asked it ought to receive an answer that is a true answer, and an answer sufficiently definite to satisy the intelligence that has prompted the question. It is a part of Nature's beautiful plan that the child's intelligence wakes before his emotions come into play – one of the many indications that in man the brain, from first to last, is meant to be in command of the body.

As the growth of the child's body is stimulated, first by his muscular efforts and later by his play instincts, so the normal development of the child's brain is secured by allowing him to pursue his native methods of inquiry without inhibitions of an artificial kind.

It is better to meet a child's curiosity when it is naturally aroused rather than to make a deliberate attempt to awaken it or to anticipate his desire for knowledge by giving him unsought information. Nor, when a simple question is asked that can be answered shortly and directly, is there any need to improve the occasion by elaborating the answer. A young child's attention lightly wanders. It is often gone in the momentary pause that follows the question before the reply is given. The hint should always be taken by the adult. Nature, the ancient mother and nurse, knows her task well, and has it in hand. The wisest of us are but her reverent observers and obedient votaries. In some circumstances it is even advisable to put an easy test to the keenness of the child's curiosity or interest by suggesting a postponement of the answer until a more convenient specified time during the same day. Then, if the question is forgotten, the matter may be allowed to drop until the next time it crops up, when it should be answered at once. The child should never be made to feel belittled or ashamed for having put out a feeler for the knowledge towards which it is groping. On the contrary, every sign of interest should be wisely stimulated and directed.

To wait for Nature's lead as it is reflected in the sensitive mind of a trustful child and to follow it promptly, is the first adaptation that has to be made by 'the Answerer' who is called upon to initiate by graduated stages the new creature into the mysteries of creation.

'But', you will say, 'such a close following of Nature's lead presupposes an extraordinarily close union between the teacher and the taught.' That is quite true. It is my belief that no child can receive this elementary knowledge, with all its implications (to be unfolded as life goes on) from any teacher so aptly as through the mother, who must herself be an initiate – or, in other words, a great lover – who is aware of every step that has to be taken in the long path that ends in making the creature one with the Creator in the work of generating life.

It is also my belief that no child is rightly prepared for life who has not been led one step at a time to a knowledge of all the elementary laws of sex before he or she is ten years old. More often than not a child will ask his way out of childish bewilderment before he has reached the age of seven or eight years, if the relationship between him and his mother has been one of complete responsive confidence. And though the child's own pace ought not to be forced, except in special circumstances when a child has to be thrown amongst companions from whom he may pick up wrong ideas, the earlier the age when he comes into possession of knowledge the better and safer will be his future.

It is only when the curiosities of the child have been satisfied that he or she will be ready for the next step on the path of initiation which comes with development of *feeling*. A child of seven or eight can begin to know by the development of his affections something of the meaning of friendship, and can begin to appreciate the delight of giving joy to another. He is able also to realise that restraint of his own desires, if exercised out of consideration for the need or the preference of one whom he is anxious to please, brings its compensation in a new kind of pleasure. Not only his affection, but also his powers of imagination, become quickened and ready to accept the stimulus which should come with school life. Romance and drama, song and music, sculpture and painting, all have their part to play in the emotional education of the boy or the girl. Understanding of the body and reverence for it lead to an enthusiasm for physical culture. Thus, the mother first, and in their turn the friend, the teacher, the athlete, the artist, prepare the way for the lover, and, finally, for the child who shall complete the initiation and bring the fully developed human being into conscious fellowship with the Creator of the world.

There are very few to whom this complete education is given; and most children miss the first stage, which gives the right interpretation to the developments that follow later.

Alas! we all know by our own experience and greatly to our own cost, that the usual practice is to withhold from children all knowledge with regard to sex and birth as long as it is possible to do so. Roughly the result is that boys nearly always pick up for themselves amongst their associates some facts and some travesties of fact and that girls of sheltered classes remain very often almost entirely ignorant, until the awakening within them of emotions that they do not understand and have no notion how to control. It is commonly supposed that all well-bred girls can control their emotions. They can, it is true, more often than not, conceal their emotions. That is a very different thing. Distress, and sometimes despair, born of ignorance and fear, can be hidden beneath reserve and correct behaviour. But we are only beginning to learn at what a cost often to health and to happiness this outward reserve is maintained. Those who make this subject a matter of research trace back innumerable nerve and mind disorders to sex repressions, whose effects, though at the time they may have been almost or quite unnoticed by the child, become, when consciously or unconsciously realised, a torture to the mind of the adult. And all of us who meet the great human stream of life in our daily work could tell many stories of the havoc and waste and misery due to this cause. It is the imaginative and the sensitive who suffer most cruelly.

A. was a gifted and sensitive girl in a gifted middle-class family. She knew nothing about the facts of sex until, in her teens, she received instruction kindly and wisely given by her head mistress at school. For her the knowledge came too late to be naturally assimilated. She was at the age when the idealisms of a young and gifted girl have already awakened and have begun to build their own structures. These structures of imagination were shattered; her artistic and sensitive nature was alarmed by an unexpected revelation of facts, concerning which (her childish curiosity having become inhibited) she had pursued no mental inquiries. Being of an age that is physically unstable, her mind became affected by melancholy. She soon recovered, however; her gifts and powers unfolded; all seemed well. Many years later she fell in love with a man whom she expected would want to marry her. One day she heard that he had married. She met this news with perfect outward composure. Not even the members of her own family would have ventured to penetrate her reserve. Suddenly one day the long repressed emotions burst out of her with uncontrollable force, seeping away even her sense of identity. Today she is an an asylum. She will get better again in all probability. But how tragic the prospect that the future has to offer to this sensitive and beautiful nature, wrecked by a torrent of feeling that had never been linked to understanding or related to all the aspects of life! It is nearly always the potentially great lover who comes to grief. The light or the cold or the callous more easily escape the dangers of ignorance and unpreparedness.

There are spiritual as well as physical disasters, due to early inhibitions with regard to sex. Their origins may be entirely forgotten while their effects remain. These effects take as many forms as there are individuals differentiated by temperament. In many a sensitive woman there has grown with her growth a sex shyness that shuts her off almost entirely from men unless they happen to be members of her own family, and induces a reserve that not only entails a loss of friendship amounting sometimes to conscious isolation, not only means a curtailment of her power so that she lives at less than half her potentiality, but means also a deprivation to men which is reflected in much of the drama and literature of the present day.

In the Elizabethan era and in earlier centuries, women of heroic type, with great intellectual and executive qualities, are portrayed in literature with insight and sympathy. Portia, for instance, is none the less a woman, a lover and a friend because with cool audacity and with wit she plays a man's role and handles a difficult situation with masterly decision. The same great qualities of heart and of intellect, the same genius for action, are recognised in modern women by women today. Are men ignorant of it? If they are not, why do we so seldom meet these women on the stage or in the domain of modern literature? Is it not because the barriers of sex-misunderstanding, due to ignorance and fear, are greater than they were in those earlier centuries which coincide with an efflorescence of art. The more sensitive women and men are, the more are they separated by the subconscious effect of these sex misunderstanding and inhibitions. In some cases I know that this is a true explanation. In the delirium that preceded death I learnt once from a great woman who was a great lover (though her whole life had passed without any sex experience whatever) how much a sensitive nature that proudly bears its isolation suffers in secret. 'I had so much to give,' was one cry. 'I had so much to give.' To me and to many other friends and to a great number of people who needed her skill and help, the beauty of her life and her personality had been revealed. By many of her patients she was worshipped. But men had never recognised the lover who lived and worked beside them; had never realised that under the veil of sex reserve she had the passionately loving nature that flung out its arms to life and, in the end, to death.

I believe that is a common occurrence. Men suffer, too, from this super-induced reserve due to inhibitions in childhood. It affects them differently. A man lacking understanding and knowledge, and therefore lacking confidence in himself, will turn in despair from the woman who could be a friend and mate for life, the real lover who knows her own value and therefore is not to be easily won; and, by his physical need, will be beguiled into a facile relationship which may end in lifelong legal union and perhaps lifelong bondage, or which may end in a rupture which leaves the man, if he is sensitive, embittered, and if he is an imaginative writer into the bargain, drives him to belittlement of all womankind.

So on all sides we meet men and women who have been bruised or maimed by the very thing that should have given them fuller and more joyous life. And we can usually trace back the misery to some cause that might have been avoided. We find that boys and girls come entirely unprepared to the deepest and most important of all the experiences and transactions of life. Can we save the men and women of the future from some of these tragic mistake?

Careful and prudent about the equipment of our children to meet the material conditions of their future, it is a matter of astonishment that their guardians can allow them to be flung into the torrent of emotional experience to sink or swim, as luck at the moment may decide. In every other department of practical living common sense decrees that there shall be a graduation in mental knowledge before any call to the serious practice of any craft or avocation can be responded to. The engine driver, for instance, has to be fully qualified for his task before he is allowed to drive an engine. Nobody expects the novice to deal with a crisis and to become expert through experiments where serious issues are at stake. It is only in the most important of all relationships of life that boys and girls are expected to steer themselves through periods of crisis by guesswork or by the help of any advice that may be forthcoming at the moment.

For this strange departure from ordinary rules of practical living there must be some reason. That is the inherent difficulty? Why is it that parents who love their children and are alive to their responsibilities yet dread the 'duty' of talking to them on these matters and put it off until the last possible moment? This reluctance is probably due to a failure to recognise the connection between love and sex which is established in all human relationships. Not only have we allowed hard-and-fast lines to be drawn between sex and love where no hard-and-fast lines exist, but we have disconnected sex as manifested in specialised relationships from the communion of sex in which we all at every period of life move and have our being. Recent scientific investigators in the realm of sex have brought us back to the fact that a child's sex-life begins at birth and that the sex relationship between the mother and her child is a reality as fundamental to all human development as is the sex relationship between the child's parents, and is a force none the less compelling because it is differently manifested. The influence of this deep sex union, more especially in the early years, before the child is capable of response to the more complicated relationships of the social world, a determinative factor in his future development, more potent than has ever yet been generally recognised.

This period of close union between mother and child, at first predominantly physical, but unfolding with the child's awakening intelligence into more and more intelligent love, is the time for gaining his trust and responding with candour to his desire for knowledge. It is strangely and universally true that nothing that intimately affects the body can ever be spoken of naturally except between lovers. It is equally true that between lovers every natural and spontaneous intimacy is delight. Only the lover can impart understanding of the mysteries of love; and the initiation that culminates in parenthood can only rightly be begun in the child by his first lover.

'What was I before I was born, mother?'
'You were a part of me, my darling.'

It was a wise mother who said that to her little girl not six years old, quietly wondering what the effect would be and quite prepared to take the risk of speaking the truth. The child flung her arms round her mother's neck and cried for joy. The wonder and the happiness of this knowledge sufficed to fill the little mind and heart for many months, and from this source of delight sprang the desire subsequently for more and more understanding of the heavenly mystery, together with the growth of intimate friendship between the mother and child.

There comes to my mind the remembrance of another mother not so happy in her own fate and therefore not so wise. 'I found my boy crying bitterly the other day,' she told me. 'I asked him what his trouble was. He said "Oh, mother, I know how children are born." "How did you find out, dear?" "I saw two dogs; it is all so horrible." '

'I didn't know what to say,' said this mother to me. 'I could only put my arms round him and cry too.'

Fortunately, it was not too late for the loving little mother in this case to begin to learn, as she was eager to do, all that could be gleaned from the best scientific books as well as from books of imagination. Had she not done so, the time might have come in her sensitive boy's life when, driven by passionate love of some woman whom he had been taught to regard as 'pure', he might have turned in despair, as so many have done, to women whom he did not love, vainly trying to satisfy cravings which were regarded in himself with disgust, and perpetuating for himself and others the misery of which the world is so unnecessarily full.

A joy akin to the joy in which the child was conceived is felt again by the mother when she takes the adored little body in her arms and, in response to the searching question, answers 'You were part of me, my darling.'

When the child's first lover is his mother she finds delight in every new opportunity that his curiosity or his interest affords her of leading him to an understanding of himself and of the love that brought him into being, and the two are drawn into more and more conscious union as they turn together the pages of Nature's book of life. No woman who has ever known this experience, and no woman who is imaginatively capable of knowing it, would ever dream of letting it slip away and thus missing the chance that can never recur again of getting at the inmost heart of her child.

After the first complete union between mother and child has given place to that separateness of consciousness that must develop later, the difficulty of opening a subject which has been previously ignored and tabooed is great. For sex is so intimately connected with the inmost life that no young creature can rightly be initiated in cold blood into even an elementary knowledge and understanding of the laws that govern the body.

The implications of a right apprehension of sex and love affect vitally every development of our sociological life. We have hardly begun to realise the wonderful possibilities of human relationship, and that means that we have hardly yet entered upon our inheritance of life. There is no problem that is occupying the minds of social reformers today that will not be transformed in its aspects as we begin to throw aside the prejudices and deformities of mind that are the result of past and present repression. A new spirit is knocking today at the door of the human heart. We are all vaguely conscious of it. It seems to some that many of our cherished human institutions are being threatend by it. They dread the new assertion of personality, the new claim of the spirit to full enfranchisement.

Whitman's dream of a city of lovers is a very far-away dream today. And most of the great inspirational poetry in our language might have been written in an unknown tongue. Even amongst social reformers the idea prevails that we can deal with the evils that have been engendered by lack of feeling and by lack of that intelligence in love of which Dante speaks, by repression and punishment, by laws enforced by police courts and prisons. Police courts and prisons are a witness to our lack of religion, our failure to realise the creative principle of life. We run round and round in our cage of repressions. What we need to find is escape from the cage, not only for ourselves but for others.

Freedom is the only condition in which love can develop. Yet we dread freedom. The word 'free-thought' filled our parents with horror as the word 'free-love' fills us with horror today. We never stop to think how thought or love can have any real power until they are free. Of love as a creative power and as a magic working transforming wonders upon a material world, we have never yet laid hold. We have hardly given it place in our imagination. The shortest text in the Bible. 'God is Love' holds for us no actual or workable significance. Some emotion to thrill through us, to quicken us into consciousness, and drive us into activity we must have. And, since we have no hold on the great affirmative, we are driven to the negative passions and energies. We turn from the white magic of love to the black magic of hate. Initiation in hate is so easy; all can obtain it who are prepared to pay a price. Children or adults we are the same. We must have passion. Passion brings us intensification of consciousness and an extension of personality – even the destructive passion of anger or revenge. We revel in it, having missed both knowledge and realisation of the creative passion of love. Partisanship in envy or anger or revenge brings a kind of comradeship. Travesty lays hold of the love spirit to generate enthusiasm for war. We welcome anything that brings release from the isolation from which we all instinctively shrink.

We grow up in the home and the school finding our chief excitement in rivalries and quarrels and revengeful triumphs. We find it stimulating to have our physical energies concentrated in one great emotional effort to put forth power, even if it is destructive power. Hence we have social misery, domination, lust, and war. Hence we have the world tragedy of the present day, and see young men being led in thousands and millions to the slaughter. How far we are from Whitman's definition of a democracy as the rule of lovers! Naming sex as the root he depicts love in a democratic State branching to development in every relationship of personal, civic, and international life. Not only is his greatest city the city that contains the greatest lovers, but cities and States and nations he depicts as interwined in the creative embrace. I will make 'inseparable cities with their arms round each other's necks; by the love of comrades; by the manly love of comrades'.

The child that has not gained from its first lover, its mother, its earliest vision of the delight of friendship and the great creative magic of love has been defrauded of its birthright. We have nearly all been thus defrauded. We know how to hate, as Diderot said, but we have not learned how to love. We have not yet learned; but by making ourselves once more as little children, we can begin to find our way into this Kingdom of Heaven and take possession of it. From the hearts of little children must spring that future era to which we turn with hope from the widespread desolation of today.

Our task it is to prepare the ground and to sow the seed. Let us do it with the realisation that it is by love alone that men and women may be transformed into likeness with the Creator and can enter into vital union with the whole creation of which they are a sentient part. Thus shall we pass on to our children, with the knowledge and understanding of love, their full inheritance of life.

Frances Swiney

The Bar of Isis or The Law of the Mother

(1912)

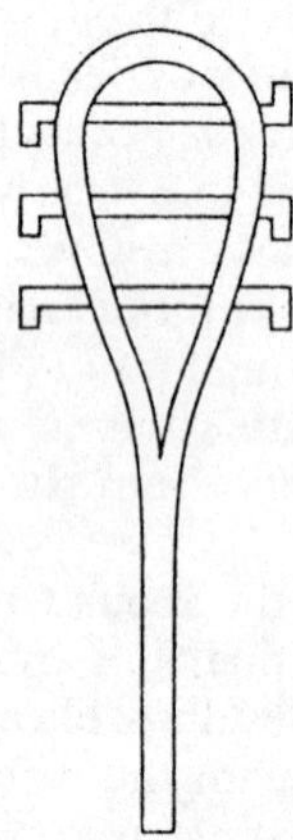

The Bar of Isis, or the Sistrum of Isis, is the Hieroglyph of the Divine Virgin Mother – the Maker of existences (invisible), the Creator of being or forms (visible).

It is the emblem of the creative Power, self-existent, self-contained, self-procreative and inviolable. Moreover, the symbol designates the Law, the Times, and the Seasons of the Mother. For it represents the gravid womb (the sign of fertility), the abode of life, kept inviolate and sacred from all intrusion during the nine months of gestation, and during the period of lactation, that is to say, during the individual mother's supreme task as creatrix, nourisher, and sustainer.

The mother is therefore shown as again the *virgin intacta*, the *alma mater*, unspotted by the world, as in the days of her virginity, and free to develop in peace and sanctity the child-in-the-making, the child of the future, the hope of the race.

Part I The natural law

> The earth mourneth and fadeth away. . . . The earth also is defiled under the inhabitants thereof; because they have transgressed the laws, changed the ordinance, broken the everlasting covenant. Therefore hath the curse devoured the earth, and they that dwell therein are desolate.
>
> (Isaiah xxiv, 4–6)

The subject of race deterioration has become hackneyed. For long it has been one of the chief topics of interest in papers, reviews, and magazines; the object of committees, conferences, debates and scientific discussion, diagnosis and analysis, *ad libitum*.

Yet, with all, the true cause of the curse of being ill-born has never been touched, if one may judge from the various opinions expressed. On the contrary, race degeneracy has been traced to every source but the right one. In turn, insanity, drunkenness, ignorance, poverty, destitution, malnutrition, overcrowding, have borne the brunt of national opprobrium.

Above all, the shortcomings of modern maternity have been anathematised by Church and State, specialist and street-boy, as the main and obvious signs of a decadent womanhood. To the average masculine mind it is always a consolation in adversity to find a scapegoat in the woman, and drive her, naked and ashamed, into the wilderness of inconsequent denunciation.

However, a little consideration reveals the fact that we are here dealing with the effect and not with the cause of the evil; with side-issues, terrible indeed in their varied aspects, but not touching the source of corruption, which appears to be slowly poisoning the race, not only in the United Kingdom, but more or less humanity in general.

If we study the laws of natural phenomena, it becomes apparent that any infringement of them on the part of mankind brings the severest and most condign punishment. In no case is retribution for offence more marked than in the reproduction of species. Biology teaches that 'Life is a series of fermentations', through the dynamic energy of certain chemico-physical combinations. All vital actions are, in brief, the result of ferments set up in the system, causing cell-division, upon which division growth depends. The condition of growth is, therefore, dependent upon the appearance or production or importation of specific ferments at each crucial stage of development.

But destructive ferments can destroy or undo or modify the work accomplished by the constructive, and upset the process of assimilation, or nutrition, or cellular equilibrium on formative lines. Ferments, therefore, are agents of life or death, of health or disease, of growth or decay. Cessation of growth – of development – means simply that the destructive ferment has got the upper hand; it is breaking up, poisoning the constructive *enzymes*. For the characteristic feature of ferments is their extreme potency in relation to their mass. The active principle of malt, for instance, will 'break up a million times its own weight in sugar'.

The process of reproduction of species, whether unisexual or amphigonic (i.e. of two sexual organisms), is thus a matter of fermentation and a consequent series of ferments.

The unicellular maternal organism divides or splits up into two or more daughter-cells, and so on *ad infinitum*, having inherent the active ferments for division and growth.

In sexual reproduction the ovum in the maternal organism first ejects minute portions of ferment in the two polar bodies, and in lieu thereof absorbs the necessary stimulus by the importation of the male sperm, an infinitesimal speck of protoplasm containing the requisite chemical constituents to hasten cell-division. For Nature, though bountiful and prolific, is never wasteful of her elements. She is especially chary in the use of her most potent agents. Moreover, she never duplicates her initial essentials.

Of all ferments, that employed in fertilisation is probably the most powerful and the most complex.[1] Undoubtedly it is the one of which the Great Mother is most careful in expenditure. Though the pollen of plants is produced in vast quantities, only one minute cellule enters the ovule. Though millions of sperms are formed in the male organism, only one penetrates the ovum. With both plant and animal the bar of Isis falls and keeps inviolate the growing seed and embryo. Nature never fertilises twice. She is dealing with a dangerous tool – two-edged – with properties of life and death.

For the action of some ferments is, moreover, under certain conditions, reversible. The enzyme, without losing its distinctive character, is not only able to form a molecule but to pull it apart; the enzyme itself undergoing active chemical changes during the process. The whole battle of life, from the unicellular organism upwards, is fought between the potentialities of the constructive and destructive ferments, i.e. between the anabolic (constructive) and katabolic (destructive) chemico-physical properties of protoplasm.

Thus the object of sex-differentiation is not by any means to further or to assist reproduction; for that function is carried on successfully by myriads of unisexual organisms.[2]

Its aim is variation of type, structure, and characteristics; in fact, to induce variety, by a wider crossing of strains through the dynamics of various chemico-physical combinations, in what may well be termed 'a moving equilibrium' to a given standard of perfectibility in each species.

For Nature never goes off the lines of her own laws of development. All natural advance is by the 'weight and balance and measure' of different elements. She is a strict accountant of the expenditure of energy, and resents an infringement of the law of adjustment. Fertilisation, therefore, is beset by inexorable conditions of time, fitness, quantity, and quality, according to the exigencies of each species. For every flower the seed-time is fixed. For every animal the period for reproduction is limited and controlled by a natural law which admits of no deflection. And the act of fertilisation has but one object, that of aid to the reproduction of kind by the procreatrix, the mother.

Taken broadly, we find that in the subhuman species the interval of latent sexuality is extended with the increasing complexity of the organism. Among the higher mammals the nourishment of the offspring and the recuperation of the mother are ensured by the lengthened periods between the births, roughly calculated to be three to five times that of the months of gestation, as is seen in the whale, elephant, gorilla, etc. Thus reproduction and individual development vary in inverse ratio. As the organism becomes more complex and individuated, there is ever a greater disinclination to exercise the sex-functions, both in the male and female organisms; for self-development and self-preservation take the place of self-reproduction. Fertilisation is for the male an episode, not a habit.

Though among all animals there is sex-attraction, there is no sensual vice – and the female always regulates the sex-function by will and choice. She rejects all males that do not come up to her standard, and whose variability will not be of racial value to the offspring.

> The virtue of the female animal Professor Lester F. Ward writes, is absolute; for virtue does not consist, as many suppose, in refusal but in selection. It is refusal of the unfit, and of all at improper times and places. This definition of

virtue applies to human beings, even the most civilised, as well as to animals.

Also, the continence of all female animals during the periods of gestation and lactation is equally absolute. The gravid womb is inviolate. No mother, *below* the human, submits to any male exactions during the critical times of embryonic growth of her offspring and of its dependence on maternal nutrition. No male, below the human, would dare to infringe on this law of prohibition and of continent maternity. What is more, Nature destined man for a higher purpose than that of a mere fertiliser.

We must, therefore, in considering the present abnormal racial degeneracy, dig deep down into the rotten foundations of human pathology and trace effects to the true cause. Persons, totally ignorant of physiology, write diatribes on the declining birth-rate; and equally hysterical effusions on the fearful mortality of infants fill magazines, reviews, and papers, the onus in each case being thrown on the incapable and ignorant mothers of the race, who are, first, blamed for not producing more infants, and, secondly, upbraided with the loss of those produced.

Yet, in our degenerate, unnatural civilisation, we may well ask, When and where has the human mother had shown to her the consideration imperative in the brute-male? Man, as a rule, has not deemed his offspring worthy of the safeguards of the ape.

Generalising broadly, physiology teaches us that woman, as the most complex and highly functioned of organisms, should, for the natural production of strong, healthy offspring, be limited to three or four children at most, and the interval between the births should be at least four or five years; some physiologists say six should be allowed for full recuperation after the periods of pregnancy and lactation.

Naturally, the rate of reproduction is the lowest in the human species. Allowing for a normal death-rate, the world could never be overpeopled through over-production, if the Law of Nature were followed; for no woman naturally would bear more than four children, six being the maximum in a period of twenty years, and few women would, by choice, endure so long a strain.

Among many primitive peoples the restrictions placed by the natural law on reproduction are more or less strictly observed, and consequently we do not find among them the specific diseases that disgrace and destroy our depraved, civilised (?) humanity, and fill our asylums and hospitals with thousands of victims to sexual excesses. Moreover, the laws of the archaic ages enforced the rights of maternity with exceptional severity. 'Thou shalt respect the times and the condition of the woman.'

'My son,' admonishes Solomon, 'hear the instruction of thy father, and forsake not the law of thy mother'; thus plainly showing that the man had to be taught the strict discipline of the mother's rule in the primitive days of the matriarchate. But now it may well be said, 'It is time for Thee, Lord, to work: for they have made void Thy law' (Psalm cxix, 126).

Part II The child in the making

> The reformation of the world can never be accomplished except through cheerful obedience to prenatal laws. All the educational institutions in the world, all the benevolent industrial, and reform societies, and all the divines in the world, combined and working harmoniously together, cannot do as much in a lifetime of effort in the elevation of mankind as can a mother in nine months of prenatal effort.
>
> (*The Science of a New Life*, John Cowan, M.D., p. 137)

We will take first the proved and terrible results of incontinence during pregnancy, as they affect the offspring.

I have before observed that organic life and growth depend upon a series of ferments. Fertilisation is fermentation. The single sperm contains all that is necessary in stimulating properties for the embryonic development of the fœtus. Limited, its power is for good; in excess, it is a virulent poison.

It has been found that among primitive people the new-born infant is seldom if ever covered with the sebaceous deposit known as *vernix caseosa*, the chief cause of eczema, of a number of peculiar forms of skin diseases, of diseased sweat-glands, or early baldness, of scurf on the head, of inflammatory diseases of the eyes – notably the worst and most incurable form, *ophthalmia neonatorum* – of *crusta lactea* (milk crust, tetter), of blennorrhœa, and kindred incurable diseases that baffle all medical science.[3]

In former times it was erroneously asserted that *vernix caseosa* was a natural lubricant to aid parturition, but, unfortunately for this hypothesis, no animal below the human shows a trace of this supposititious emollient, while even in civilised life all children are not covered with the unctuous material. Instead of being beneficial, it is an excrescence and parasitic in its nature. In the words of the author of *Modern Researches:*

> Those parents who have well-defined and positive convictions on the subject of sex-relations that there should not be any co-habitation after pregnancy is assured, who believe at that period the pregnant woman should not only have complete rest from excitement of the sex organs during that time, but also that such excitation produces deleterious effects on the character of the future offspring which she is nourishing – in such cases there is no *vernix caseosa* found on the child at birth. . . . I believe it to be an indication of a disturbance in the maternal organism, that it is a signal-light which Nature holds out so that he who runs may read, to warn mankind that there has been something at work which is detrimental to the race. . . . I repeat, that cheesy mess is not found on infants born to parents who believe that motherhood is a sacred and, as it were, a holy state.

Now, when one considers that the delicate epithelial cells are formed in the fifth month of fœtal life, it is obvious that no foreign substance or ferment should be injected into the maternal organism, and allowed to make its way to the skin, thus injuring its growth and development. *Vernix caseosa* is in no sense a product of the maternal organism: it is an importation from the male, and is formed of 'inanimate decomposed zoosperms', actively poisonous to both mother and child. The eminent obstetrician, Professor Parvin of the Jefferson Medical College, laid great stress on the inviolability of the prospective mother, as have many of the foremost American doctors who have made a study of the pernicious effects of *vernix caseosa*. For 'any effete matter which remains in the system, after it has performed its function, is injurious', and even a healthy fertiliser is dangerous when unnecessary. But what of the unhealthy?

For instance, the germ-plasm of a confirmed drunkard is saturated with alcohol, the most injurious and deadly of protoplasmic poisons. The initial fertilising sperm, therefore, brings disease to the ovum: and if sexual relations continue during gestation, the embryo becomes covered with toxic matter of the most deleterious composition, prejudicial to the growing tissues of the fœtus, especially those of the heart and brain. Nicotine poison also retards the growth of healthy tissue. Tobacco blindness in adults is a recognised disease. The offspring of a confirmed smoker is handicapped at birth.

'The direct paternal transmission of syphilis without preliminary infection of the mother may be classed among the established facts of medical science,' is the statement in the *Journal of Cutaneous and Genito-Urinary Diseases.*

> The spermatozoa of a syphilitic father, carried into the uterus, then drawn into the liquor amnii and deposited or settling on the forming epidermis of the unborn child, does more or less injury to the skin. . . . Were the skin perfectly constructed, as it might have been had there been no vernix on it during its uterine existence, it would have been immune to the unhealthy or infectious germs

of many forms of epidermic disorders. Again, in cases of blindness and eye diseases,

> the infected fluid of a syphilitic father has been doing its malignant work while those tender and delicate cells which were to form the eyes and its enclosure were under construction, sowing the germs of disease, which, if it does not appear at once, may produce weak and disordered eyes early in the lifetime of the helpless victim. A father, who is but slightly tainted with some blood disorder which may not be looked upon as serious, may have added to his own tainted discharges the infection of alcohol, tobacco, opium, gluttony, etc. Nearly all medical writers say, The germs may be infected by excesses of any kind – that they weaken the system. So, just in that proportion would the spermatozoa be likely to affect the normal development of the eyes of the offspring. If the seminal fluid be heavily laden with the germs of disease, the resulting disorder would be proportionately of a more malignant type.[4]

Dr Ernest Fuchs, the Vienna eye specialist, estimates that there are 30,000 blind people in Europe whose misfortune is due to prenatal effects. 'In the city of New York there is one blind person to every 2500 inhabitants.' In every paper throughout the civilised world may be seen specious advertisements of cures for skin diseases, showing how prevalent are the disorders and how numerous are the victims of parental disobedience to Nature's law.

Nature in vain warns and protests against any infringement of her decrees. Inexorably she demands the penalty to the third and fourth generation. The mortality of infants is thus more than accounted for. They are often conceived in iniquity, of drunken, lustful parents; and, developed in the rankest poison; they become stunted, malformed, diseased, and prematurely old before they see the light.[5] Dr C. E. Page writes that 'one-third of the children in the United States die before they are one year old'; while in France and England the massacre of the innocents is continuous, increasing, and abnormal, though the general death-rate is decreasing, but this is owing to greater care and attention to the sick and defective.

In 1905, 120,000 babies died in England and Wales alone. In Manchester, Birmingham, and Liverpool the infant death-rate is 19.2, or 20 per cent of the births. Burnley and Preston have an infant death-rate of 208 per thousand: London numbers 129 per thousand, but in certain parts, Finsbury, for instance, the rate is 148.6. Sir William Broadbent avers that not only the big cities but small country towns have their high infant mortality, sometimes 500 babies dying out of every thousand born. And for every child that dies six are incapacitated for life, mostly through prenatal injuries and malformations.

For if we study the reports of the various committees, societies, and organisations interested in physical culture, race degeneracy, and pathological statistics, we find the same retributive scale of victims. Of the children of the National Schools 68 per cent have unhealthy skins, all children over ten have decayed teeth, 10 per cent have sore or defective eyes, 29 per cent have defective hearing, 49 per cent have pathological conditions of the nose and throat with poor lung development, and, above all, the number of the feeble-minded is increasing. Among these the atavistic traits are very pronounced: as the absence of the pleat ridge from the outside ear, and the presence of horizontal furrows on the brows, formed by the working of the frontal muscles after the habit of our simian ancestors. These defects are five times more numerous among boys than among girls, and all point to arrested prenatal development. The percentage of cases of heart disease among children is abnormally high, and 24 per cent are more or less anæmic; the result of nicotine and alcoholic poisons.

The residue who grow up to man's estate present equally defective organisms.

In 1904, out of 70,000 youths who presented themselves for enlistment in the army, 24,782 were rejected as unfit. The proportion works out at 352.29 per 1000. The defects are mainly due to poor physical development, deficiences in weight and chest measurement, weak constitutions, unsound organs, flat feet, malformations, and general debility. In 1903, the British army spent most of its time in bed in the various military hospitals. It may be urged that these recruits were of the poorer classes; but the standard of efficiency is nearly as low in the upper. The report of the War Office on the Sandhurst Cadets is not reassuring, in that the medical officer a year back informed the board that 'the last batch of Cadets was physically the weakest for many years past'.

Of our soldiers, 70 per cent in times of peace are on the sick-list in the course of the year. According to Maj.-Gen. Sir Frederick Maurice, K.C.B., out of every five men enlisted, by the end of two years' service only two remain in the army.

On all sides and in every civilised country we find an alarming increase of epilepsy, insanity, idiocy, and congenital disease. We are brought face to face with a steady deterioration of the masses, and the survival of the fittest is in truth that bad is the best. And again we ask, What solution is there to this problem?

Undoubtedly, the answer is plain. Return to the natural law governing reproduction. For, as yet, I have only dealt with the question as regards the offspring. We have now to consider the matter from the point of view and the welfare of the mother. The consequences of disobedience there are but too apparent.

Part III The creative periods

We deplore the pangs of childbirth, and consider them inevitable in the climax of the maternal function. As a rule, we mildly acquiesce in the man-inspired dictum, that sorrow and motherhood are synonymous; thus casting upon the Divine Nature the most terrible of reproaches and the most iniquitous of libels. The Natural Law has again been flagrantly set aside by man to his own undoing.

'Childbirth without pain or danger is entirely natural. Pain and danger come from artificial and diseasing habits and conditions,' writes Dr T. L. Nichols. In *Esoteric Anthropology*, the same authority declares, 'Women are everywhere outraged and abused. When the full chapter of woman's wrongs and suffering is written, the world will be horrified at the hideous spectacle.' For 'the so called Diseases of Women' are due 'directly or collaterally to one form or another of *masculine* excess or abuse'.

I have before alluded to the respect shown to the female of their kind by the most powerful and savage of beasts. There are consequently no specific and exclusive female diseases; among the lower animals parturition is painless, and devoid of danger to either mother or offspring. It is only among domesticated animals that man has been able to introduce unnatural suffering and increased chances of death.

'It seems to be a legitimate view that every disease to which animals (and probably plants also) are liable, excepting as a transient and very exceptional occurrence, is due to man's interference,' is the indictment of Ray Lankester.

Of civilised women thousands die in childbed, 5000 annually in England alone. We do not find this death-roll among the primitive peoples who observe the natural law of continence during the gestative period. For instance, among many African tribes, as pointed out by Winwood Reade and other travellers, no sexual union is permitted during pregnancy and lactation. The same rule holds good among the nobler of the American Indians, and the Fiji and various South Pacific Islanders.[6] The venereal diseases rampant among Europeans were unknown until introduced by civilised Christians. The annual baby is also an abnormality so deservedly censured that few parents would dare to face the odium of producing it. There is no greater shame attached to a man among many primitive tribes than that of infringing on the seclusion of the wife during the period of prohibition, lasting from the time of conception to the weaning of the child, often extending four years; consequently parturition is easy and painless, and the women strong, healthy, and long-lived, though the conditions of life may appear hard in other respects.[7]

To what a state has civilised man reduced a natural, simple function when we consider that 40 per cent of childbirths are, in truth, surgical operations; that 80 per cent of tortured women are placed under anæsthetics; and that childbed is regarded by many as the dreaded prelude to the deathbed and the portal of the grave!

The cause of this phenomenal suffering is obvious to those who honestly seek it. Bayer traces it conclusively to the pathological complications induced by ill-timed sexual intercourse. He attributes to this source alone the unnatural inflamed condition of the tissues of the uterine cavity, the adhesion of the placenta and consequent flooding, long and agonising labour,[8] and retarded recovery.

It is truly said that 'in medical history there has been much groping in the dark', and naturally women above all has suffered from the ignorance of male practitioners, who, at the best, have only an objective knowledge of the mysteries of the female organism. Puerperal fever, one of the most terrible scourges of childbed, has been the subject of much guesswork as to its cause and inexplicable appearance. Yet from this disease alone it is computed that within the last thirty years 48,374 women in England and Wales have died after childbirth.[9] And, again, we find that Nature's law has been outraged, and the mother suffers in consequence the penalty of death due to an abnormal inflammatory condition of the system.

Bayer puts the indictment very plainly:

> I maintain that in the case of puerperal fever there has been excessive excitation of the parturient tract and the uterus by congress. It has produced a weakened state of the membranes. When the generative fluid is in a healthy condition the result will be difficult, painful labour, but no feverish complications. If, in addition, the male germs are diseased, fever and convulsions will likely occur. . . . I maintain that the causes of parturient disorders are, first and foremost, incontinence during the latter part of pregnancy. It is useless to ignore the law of continence which prevails throughout the animal world, excepting man in civilisation. As long as the State allows ignorance of the law of Nature and sensuality to mate, there will be, must be, as a consequence, disease and degeneracy. . . . I have also found that married primiparas (women in first confinement) who have obeyed the law of continence during the larger part of the gestative period, rarely suffer from lying-in complications. . . . I am driven to the conclusion that puerperal fevers, eclampsia, etc., arise from infection of the uterine organs, and are largely caused by the disordered condition of the father's system; that comparatively few young men enter the married state in a perfectly healthy condition; consequently their wives are broken down in health. . . . If the organs and connective tissues had been kept inflamed by excessive congress and diseased spermatozoa . . . puerperal fever would be likely. . . . The danger of infection from syphilitic or gonorrhœal zoosperms must be an ever present one. Such infection may be the direct producing factor in the cause of most, if not all, of these puerperal complications. . . . Puerperal fever attacks women in the best and in the worst surroundings. No class, except one, is immune: and that is the class which observes natural law relating to pregnancy. . . . Nor do I believe that any course of fruit diet, dress, exercise, or any system of hygiene, will indemnify Nature for the outrage committed against its decrees.

Well may Dr Rentoul declare that 'the health of woman is our greatest national asset, that the physically and mentally healthy woman represents the best thing in life – motherhood'. Well, too, may he condemn man's inhumanity to woman. No female animal has been so ruthlessly, so brutally, so generally mercilessly exploited by the male, as woman. She has in truth borne the travail of the world's motherhood. She stands the martyr of organised and systematic sexual wrong-doing on the part of the man who should be her mate, and whom she alone has evolved to the human plane.

Church and State, religion, law, prejudice, custom, tradition, greed, lust, hatred, injustice, selfishness, ignorance, and arrogance have all conspired against her under the sexual rule of the human male. Vices, however, like curses, come back to roost. In his own enfeebled frame, in his diseased tissues, in his weak will, his gibbering idiocy, his raving insanity, and hideous criminality, he reaps the fruits of a dishonoured motherhood, an outraged womanhood, an unnatural abnormal stimulated childbirth, and a starved, poison-fed infancy. For after diseasing the child in the womb and torturing the mother in her life-giving function, what further disability has proceeded from man's disregard of Nature's wise and just restraints?

Severe is man's indictment on the inability of civilised women to nurse their children. But physiology proves how intimate is the inter-connection between gestation and lactation. Simultaneously the womb and the breast prepare for the child's development and welfare. And no artificial substitute can be found for the nourishment Nature has provided for the young of the mammalia. It has all the necessary dietetic constituents for the health, strength, and growth of the tender, helpless offspring. But the mother gives much more than nutriment with her milk. 'She gives of her nervous power, her vital force, her heart, and mind, and soul.' The supply of milk is the register of her physical and mental capacity.

Children, breast-fed, have, as a rule, no serious complications in teething, no digestive troubles, and no infantile diarrhœa, that dread enemy of infancy, mowing down thousands of artificially-reared children.

The primitive human mother can suckle her child from three to five years; the civilised mother, under natural conditions, can easily prolong the nursing of her infant to two years at the least, with benefit to herself and the child. But such is the perverted, diseased state in which civilised humanity is engulfed, few women are capable of this exercise of maternal duty. The curse has fallen upon them and on their offspring as it fell upon the sensual Semites.

> Give them, O Lord; what wilt thou give? give them a miscarrying womb and dry breasts.

Says Dr Saleeby: 'The history of organic evolution teaches that the mammalia have conquered the earth just because they are mammalia, and the race the women of which cease to be mammals will assuredly have to yield and make way for its betters.' But the human nursing mother must be under the same law as the ewe and the heifer. She must rule supreme in sex-relations.

How little has the consciousness of man developed when we find that the majority of so-called civilised men, freed from the rigid rule of *Tabu* existing among primitive races for the regulation of sexual relations, are incapable of imagining objectively the grave physical and psychical condition of the nursing mother! They appear to be too dense and callous to appreciate the great peril and self-sacrifice entailed in childbirth on the part of the woman. They are more careful of their breeding animals than of the mother of their children. They impose upon the most highly strung and complex of organisms a strain and excitation that they are fully aware would be fatal to their milch-cows. They extort from women unwilling acquiescence to a three-fold demand – nourishment for the infant, self-gratification of the male,[10] and the development of an embryo.

Nature refuses to respond.

First, the woman suffers. The delicate mechanism of the reproductive organs is not given time for rehabilitation; her strength is not recuperated, and is still being exhausted in nourishing her infant. Instead of growing stronger and healthier, she becomes weaker and pathologic, and less able to undergo another pregnancy.

Second, the child suffers. Its natural supply of food waxes less and less, becomes less nutritious in quality, and at last is a veritable poison, its constituents being changed by the noxious ferment of fertilising chemicals absorbed in the mother's system.

Third, the embryo suffers. The maternal organism does its best; but it cannot achieve what is by natural law impossible. It cannot construct and expend at the same time with equal facility. The embryo is starved in proportion as the infant is fed, and vice versa. At the most critical stages of cell-formation in both born and unborn the mechanism slows down, becomes stationary, or stops altogether; the various parts are badly formed, the tissues, the brain-cells, the teeth, the circulation, the heart, lungs, and digestive organs become defective, and the annual baby is handicapped from the moment of its conception. But often it never reaches the gates of life. The miscarriages, the abortions, the still-births, that make up the sum total of the holocaust of unconsidered offspring due to man's perverted sexuality, are the fell results of a merciless exploitation of the supreme rights of motherhood and the extorted price the woman pays for her sex-prerogative of creatrix.

It is evident, therefore, that the education of the fathers is much more deficient than the education of the mothers. The degeneracy we deplore lies at the door of a selfish, lustful, diseased manhood. Men have sought in woman only a body. They have possessed that body. They have made it the refuse-heap of sexual pathology, when they should have reverenced it as the Temple of God, the Holy Fane of Life,[11] the Fountain of Health to the human race.

Instead of anathematising the mother for her rebellion against undesired motherhood, for her awakened conscience that refuses to sanction repeated painful, unhealthy, unnatural and futile pregnancies, the quidnuncs – clerical, medical, social, philanthropic, and political – had better turn their attention to a profounder study of Nature's wise and beneficient laws. Let them first teach their own sex in particular the science of life, the supreme lesson, that 'the development of the individual and the reproduction of the species, stand in an inverse ratio to each other', a truth strongly emphasised by Carpenter, Darwin, Spencer, etc.

Man has not developed, because he has 'wasted his substance in riotous living'. He has expended his life-force, the complex chemico-physics which, retained in the system, are reabsorbed and transmuted for the formation of

> the finest brain, nerve, and muscular tissue. By its aid a man can become the most powerful athlete, or exercise the highest intellectual power of which he is capable. . . . If wasted, it leaves him . . . intellectually and physically debilitated.

Expelled from the organism it is, under *every* condition, only excrementitious in character and properties.

Let those who go periodically into hysterics over birth-rate statistics, practise a little common-sense or study the instinctive wisdom of the wild animal. They will then be better prepared to instruct the human race in the responsibilities marriage entails; they will possess greater knowledge of the glory of motherhood and the obligatory self-control and continence of fatherhood.

Dr Taylor plaintively asks, in deploring a decreasing birth-rate,

> If we see, and we believe, in addition to disease, grave moral and social dangers arising and growing are we to be dumb and hold our peace? We [physicians] are placed in positions of trust; we are, in some special sense . . . guardians of the sanctity and honour of English family life, and we have social as well as professional rights and responsibilities.

But women may well ask in return, Where was this high sense of honour and responsibility during the hideous slaughter of women in forced and undesired childbirth? When in the past did the majority of medical practitioners prescribe moderation, self-control, and the natural instinctive chivalry of the brute when the husband had rendered the wife a life-long invalid, a worn-out machine, broken down under the strain and stress, mental and physical, of repeated sexual exactions?[12]

Did an appreciable number of these honourable gentlemen then preach moral responsibility and the sanctity of motherhood? Never! For every child born of a mother's agony, every miscarriage due to overstrain of the maternal functions, every disease to which the reproductive organs are liable through over-excitation and abuse, brought so many fees to their grasping hands, and were, in fact, the main source of their incomes. Many now see, with dismay, this mine of gold, dug from the depths of diseased humanity, of exploited and outraged womanhood, becoming exhausted, and they fill the air with self-interested, sinister lamentations over a decreasing birth-rate and a wisely controlled maternity. Their science is as false as their morality, and as ineffective. For woman, herself, is happily learning the natural law of reproduction with the natural restrictions placed on sexual relations, and she is gradually teaching man self-respect, self-reverence, self-control, and the exercise of a love that worketh no evil. She sees plainly through the awful hypocrisy that can look back on the over-production of the race, as under the supreme sanction of the Divine, and regards with loathing the sanctimonious fulminations of bishops, senators, presidents and politicians, whose abysmal ignorance of physiology is only equalled by their utter disregard of elementary ethics. Little do they know of the Love that worketh no ill, of the divine Fatherhood that is perfect in purity.

For the morality of family life has been insidiously undermined by a system of legalised prostitution, so fearful, so deadly, so debasing in its character and consequences that only because, as Lester Ward asserts, 'woman is the race', could the mother of mankind have survived the terrible ordeal.

Mr John Burns is reported to have said that 'it is to the mothers of the race that we must look for the improvement of the race'. And this statement is in a measure true, if our would-be reformers will also turn their attention, with the same assiduity to the fathers and husbands of the mothers. We need good fathers as well as good mothers. According to Sir James Crichton Browne, 'We are gratuitously tossing into the graveyard upwards of 50,000 infants every year. Then the mothers as well as the infants are needlessly sacrificed. Upwards of 1600 of them die every year.' Where does he lay the blame? Who places the mother on the altar of sacrifice?

Who is the self-elected priest who girds the victim with cords and bonds, who is deaf to her cries and blind to her tears? Is it not her 'own familiar friend', her mate?

Dr C. W. Saleeby has arrived at the self-evident conclusion that 'no nation or race ever yet survived the decadence of motherhood within it'. He advocates a practical scheme of feeding the nursing mother, 'because it is obeying Nature, beginning at the beginning. . . . It involves teaching the mother that her motherhood, in all its functions, is indispensable for the child.' He appears to forget that the beginning in sexual reproduction is the absorption by the ovum of an imported sperm, preferably of a healthy composition.

But this involves also the education of the fathers in the dignity, prerogatives, rights, and sanctity of fatherhood and womanhood. They too must go back to the beginning. Are they also willing to be taught? Will they become obedient to Nature's wise law and discipline? Will they reverence the Temple of Creative Life, the abode of the child-in-the-making, the matrix of humanity?

'We must subjugate the passions,' writes the author of *Are We a Declining Race?* 'before we can retrieve our position today. Temperance and chastity are the two virtues to be adopted, if we want to hold our own, and the sooner we recognise this fact the better it will be for the race.'

> There is no other way to strike at the root of many evils, Bayer writes, not only in the physical nature of man, but in his sociological and ethical nature, except through an education of the coming parenthood upon the mental and physical relation of the sexes, and until that is done there can be no improvement or permanent cure for the varied evils which afflict mankind. The laws which govern health, sanitation, and hygiene are considered of great importance, but the most important of all laws, indicating how to bring good brains and bodies into existence, are totally disregarded. The laws of Nature governing reproduction are not taught. We spend millions to produce good hogs and cattle, but not one dollar to produce good children. . . . The first and strongest plea is for the observance of Nature's laws, for purity of motive, as this is the foundation of good morals. But false modesty and prudery are criminal.

Let us mark well the grand words of Dr Nichols:

> For evils of ignorance we want knowledge, for those of false notions we want truth.

When the great law of Nature – which is the law of God – respecting the reproductive function is clearly known, and the consequences of its disorders and abuses, and the health and happiness that may come from purity and holiness of health and life, men and women will aid each other in avoiding the evil and enjoying the good. Men will no longer injure themselves and destroy women; women will no longer give the sanction of their tolerance, and even approval, to men of profligate and dishonest lives, wasting their own energies, and making women the wretched slaves of their lusts.

With a wider, deeper knowledge of physiology, biology, and embryology, men will no longer boast of being members of large families, and the survivors of twelve or fifteen death struggles of their mothers.

Their individual psychology will have so far developed that they will be able to realise the position, above all, of the working mothers,

> of those sad women crushed by the triple burden of poverty, of ceaseless procreation, and too often of bad treatment – breeding women, whom a brutal male, in a savage, drunken fit, impregnates without a thought, who up to the last moment have to work hard, despite the pains of pregnancy, for all the family, waiting on the man and the children, and who, after undergoing on the pallet-bed of their garret, without air in summer and without fire in winter, the trials of childbirth, resume, quite broken down, at the end of three or four days, their task of beasts of burden, awaiting with anguish their next pregnancy, which comes so soon.

Deep down in the heart of humanity has ever been a rebellion against the abnormal and fostered sensuality of the human male. It is at length, and not too soon, finding expression in speech and action. All that is best and noble in manhood is in harmony with the awakened conscience of the race.

It is realised that only

> Where the city of the cleanliness of the sexes stands,
> Where the city of the healthiest fathers stands,
> Where the city of the best bodied mothers stands,
> There the great city stands.
>
> *Walt Whitman*

Thousands of men and women, with enlightened eyes and

understanding hearts, are pledged to the betterment of mankind, and are treading that upward path which will lead humanity to heights of which the majority now have little conception, but have been ever the glorious vision of the poet and the seer.

> I have climbed to the snows of Age, and I gaze at a field in the Past,
> Where I sank with the body at times in the sloughs of a low desire;
> But I hear no yelps of the beast, and the man is quiet at last,
> As he stands on the heights of his life with a glimpse of a height that is higher.
>
> *Tennyson*

NOTES

1 According to Meisher, 'The semen (human) is composed of 82 to 90 parts water; the remainder is serum, albumen, alkali albuminate, hemial-bumose, nuclein, lecithin, guanin, hypoxanthin, protomin, fat, cholestrin, inorganic salts, and phosphoric acid, muriatic acid in combination with inorganic bases.' (*Modern Researches*, Bayer (US), p.192.)

2 'The experiments on artificial parthenogenesis indicate clearly enough that the development of the egg can be caused without even the presence of a sperm nucleus.' (*The Dynamics of Living Matter*, Prof. Jacques Loeb, p.179.)

Again, to show that the direct and essential effect of the spermatozoon is the starting of a definite chemical process, Professor Delage found that a fragment of egg protoplasm which has no nucleus can develop when fertilised, for the creative property is potential in each particle.

3 Want or absence of oxygen prevents cell-division, and tends to be liquefaction of the existing cell-walls; but 'Budgett found that a number of poisons, such as potassium cyanide, morphine, quinine, antipyrin, nicotine, and atrophine, produce structural changes of the same character as those described for lack of oxygen.' (*Dynamics of Living Matter*, Prof. Jacques Loeb, p.21.)

'Looking soley to the effects of drugs when taken by the pregnant woman, I conclude that congenital epilepsy, imbecility, chorea, and other pronounced nervous disorders are, in most cases, attributable to the administration of chemicals or drugs, ingested by the mother, through whom they enter the fœtal system. In that manner they arrest or retard its development, and produce or modify the chemical changes in the blood and in the cellular structure.' (*Modern Researches*, Bayer (US) p.150.)

4 *Ibid.*, p.207. All seminal fluid, being of the nature of excreta, decom-

poses in the system of the woman. To show its virulence, Dr J. H. Tressel writes:

> I took decomposed human generative fluid and injected it into the vascular system of guinea-pigs and rabbits. The most of them died within twenty-four hours. . . . I also took the fluid of putrid meat and tried it in the same manner; but found that it was not so deadly as the semen; it proved to be a much less active poison. Some of the animals did not die from the effects of the putrid meat infection, and those which did lived longer than any inoculated with the spermatozoic poison. (See *Modern Researches*, p.269.)

5 Regarding the ability of spermatozoa to penetrate the membrane inclosing the *liquor amnii*, it is acknowledged that they penetrate the membrane which surrounds the ovum. If they have that power, it is logical to assume they can penetrate the *amnii* as well. . . . If one were to ask, 'What force is there in a fœtal structure which enables it to eliminate the deleterious male excretions?' I would answer that it is the same force (excretory function) that eliminates other effete matter which is disposed of, or the organism of both mother and child would become involved. . . . I therefore assume that there is some power in the fœtal organism to attract *vernix caseosa*, or, more properly, spermatozoa, to it, because it is found there; and it is not there if there are no male germs deposited during that period. . . . I conclude that the attraction to the fœtus is utilised to enable the maternal organism to rid itself of that which is unnecessary and which has become a septic product. (*Modern Researches*, Bayer (US) pp. 211, 212)

Biology refutes the old fallacy that 'the seed' is with the male. The sperm is simply the stimulating fertiliser to the 'seed' of the female. 'For fertilisation in its essence has nothing to do with reproduction,' writes Prof. Winterton C. Curtis in *Science*.

6 The human female is in no degree inferior to the male; the cause of inferiority is attributable to a violation of natural law. (*Modern Researches*, Bayer (US) p.225)

'With the advent of the androcratic stage, while woman lost her power of selection, so that man could develop no further, the abuses to which he subjected her soon began to tell upon her and produce degeneracy.' (*Pure Sociology*, Lester F. Ward, p.370.)

7 'It is not the ordinary wear and tear of daily life which breaks down woman's health. It is the subtle, insidious drain on her generative organs.' (*Modern Researches*, p.241).

8 'Sex-relation during pregnancy is a large factor in cases of difficult labour' (Dr A. C. Krum Eric). The same opinion is now held by the most enlightened members of the medical profession; but the average practitioner, male or female, is fearful of encroaching on 'the rights of the husband', enforced by Church and State, to condone sexual indulgence. The day, however, is dawning when no reputable medico will countenance any infringement of Nature's law; and the law of reproduction will be as necessarily taught as the first rules of arithmetic.

The law of Nature is beautiful, just, and pure. The shame is with the infringement.

9 From 1871 to 1893, 50,211 women died from diseases of childbirth: victims to man, not to Nature. In many cases the husband has exercised 'his rights' on the wife after the pains of labour have begun – often, among the poorer classes, sex-relations continue up to the last day of gestation. And the medical profession is silent, has been silent, during these countless years! The Churches, moreover, have glorified in and flourished on the subjection and degradation of woman. The Roman Catholic Church, for instance, makes it obligatory on the wife to 'submit' herself to her husband at all times, whatever may be her own state of health or disinclination. Hence the depth of woman's degradation in all the southern countries of Europe, where the priest has sway.

10 One fortnight after confinement some men will insist on resuming sexual relations with their wives. They are below the brutes. To term them *human* is a misapplication of a definition.

11 Every woman will begin with her own redemption . . . She is, so to speak, battered and rolled out by very rough forces. Whilst her will is annihilated and enslaved, and her heart often remains an undiscovered country, she assists, with pain and disgust, at the downfall of her flesh – that flesh which has become the abode of pain, a body of death, to give birth to life. (*The Women of the Renaissance*, De Maulde, p.19)

12 We must remember that the diseased state of the spermatozoa and, consequently, of the embryo, proceed primarily from the vices of the male. Alcoholic, nicotic, and syphilitic poisons were first engendered in the male organism and then transmitted to the offspring. The first drunken woman was the daughter of the male drunkard. The ferments of male animals are not poisons to the female – they are potent, not noxious. The human race is suffering from over-fertilisation and enforced reproduction. Man, the destroyer, has been at work, not woman, the constructor. When man is continent, the mysterious origin of cancer will be solved, and cancer, with other kindred horror, will disappear. Sexual germs are not confined to the reproductive organs; they permeate the whole body. Assimilation and absorption by the female organism cannot divest them of their potential properties of stimulation and disintegration, of decay and corruption. Hence the terrible increase of cancer among the Western races, who, for so long, have ignored the Law. See *Cancer: A Working Theory for its Prevention and Cure*, by John Shaw, M.D.

'Situations, where fœtal rests are abundant, are the favourite seats of cancer' (p.15).

'Fœtal rests' are 'cells which have failed to develop, like their fellows, into structures organically and functionally complete.' They have, in a word, been retarded in organic growth by disturbed vibrations.

Beatrice Webb

The Teaching of Children as to the Reproduction of Life

(1918)

Ladies,

I am keenly alive to the fact that you who are mothers have a great fund of knowledge and of wisdom in all matters relating to children, but there are certain points as to which a medical woman, from her special knowledge as a doctor, may be able to help you to clear your minds, so that you may see plainly what it is you want to say to your children as to reproductive processes and how you want to say it.

It will be well to begin by a short account of matters with which you are, of course, familiar, the structure and the working of the reproductive organs in the female, so laying a clear foundation for further considerations.

The female reproductive organs consist of:

1 The uterus, a small, pear-shaped, hollow, muscular organ about three inches long and two inches broad, lying behind the bladder and in front of the rectum, that is, the end of the bowel. It lies with the small end pointing downwards and opening by a narrow neck into a passage, the vagina.
2 The vagina is a passage about three inches long and an inch and a half across, which, at its upper end, fits on to the small end of the uterus and which opens to the exterior just behind the opening from the bladder and in front of that from the bowel. The outlet of the vagina is protected by two sets of lips, an outer and an inner, and in the case of the single girl by a ring of tissue with a small opening in the centre.
3 The ovaries, or egg-forming organs, which are about the size of an almond in its shell, lie one of each side of the uterus at a distance of about three inches from it.

4 The Fallopian tubes are narrow passages about four inches long, which lead off from the interior of the uterus at its upper end, one to the right and one to the left, and which open into the body cavity close to the ovaries.

The working of these organs is briefly as follows: The organs are present, complete and perfect, in a baby girl when born, including even the ova or eggs, of which there are 32,000 each ovary – a fact which links us on to a far distant ancestry. After monthly periods have been established one egg breaks away from an ovary every month, passes into the open mouth of the Fallopian tube and along it into the uterus. If the egg there meets and unites with a male reproductive germ it grows into a child. If it does not meet with a male germ it passes out through the vagina, a minute particle of living matter. Once a month the lining of the uterus becomes much swollen, because its blood vessels are widely distended and full of blood. A part of the lining membrane detaches itself from the thick muscular walls of the uterus and comes away in fine shreds, and in so doing tears many little blood vessels and so causes a loss of blood, which goes on for a few days.

The exact relation of the setting free of an ovum and the coming away of the lining of the uterus is not clear, but it is no longer thought that these two processes happen at the same time. The purpose served by the loss of blood is unknown, and all we can say is that it does serve some good end or it would not occur.

In addition to their functions as reproductive organs, the uterus and ovaries serve a general purpose as regards the well-being of the body. They make and pour into the blood secretions which have valuable effects on general health, especially in the direction of keeping the blood vessels properly toned up for their work.

When the climacteric period comes, bringing reproductive possibilities to an end, there are often certain discomforts which are due to the loss of the secretions from the uterus and ovaries. These discomforts, such as flushings, sudden heats, headaches, indigestion, constipation and poor sleep, arise from difficulties in the circulation, which come to an end when other organs in the body have taken over the share formerly done by the uterus and ovaries in keeping up the tone of the blood vessels.

This short account having cleared our minds as to the structure and working of the reproductive organs, we begin to consider the question of telling the children.

The whole subject has for long been shrouded in mystery. It was almost unmentionable to our grandmothers if they had any pretensions to delicacy of mind. Now it is being brought out into the light of day. It has been a mystery primarily because all the great things of life are mysteries – life itself, religion, love of all kinds – because it pertains to a great force linked with the deepest and strongest and best in us, linked with the other mysteries of love and of religion. It has been a mystery, secondarily, from the idea that children's minds should be kept from matters with which they have no present concern; a laudable aim, but one with results which are often unfortunate.

The causes which have led to the subject now being brought out into the light are various. There is a general tendency in the age to try to get to the bottom of things; there is a growing realisation that evils may come from ignorance. The public conscience is being aroused to certain special disasters linked with race problems; there is a growing sense of responsibility to children and to our fellows. There is a truer view as to the dignity of the body and a sense that it is better to know the actual facts than to be at the mercy of chance words, which often produce incorrect impressions. But if there is to be less mystery there must still be reticence, because speech on the greatest things is never easy, and this is particularly true of the British. It is easy to make it clear to a child that reticence is observed on these matters for the same reason as in the case of religion, of love, of patriotism, because the subject is a very deep and sacred one, not because there is anything low or unworthy about it.

When we come to the question as to who is to explain, there is in my mind no doubt about it. It is the mother's duty and privilege as regards her girls and her little boys, with help from the father for the latter as they grow to be about twelve. No one else, neither teachers, nor clergy, nor doctors, should take over this duty except by the express wish of the parents. The duty must not be shirked, for it is not a question of the child being told or left untold. If the mother does not explain the child will learn in some other way, perhaps from another child, perhaps from a low-minded adult, perhaps from an undesirable story, and may learn in such a way as to sadden its whole outlook on life.

The time for teaching the child is clear. It is as soon as the child asks. The child who is old enough to ask an intelligent question is old enough to have an intelligent answer. The age must vary with the make of the child's mind. The dull, unobservant child may not want to know till eight or ten or later, and such a child needs helping to see and leading to think. The quick, interested child may want to know at four, or even at three, where the new baby came from. The earlier such teaching can be given the better, for the little child 'the world is so full of a number of things', so many of them mysteries, that it takes them all simply and without astonishment. This mystery of birth and new life is accepted quite calmly as just one among the rest and put away in the mind with the others.

What is to be taught is also clear. The truth and nothing but the truth. There must be no lies. Lies about doctors' bags, about storks, about gooseberry bushes, about falling from the sky, are insulting and disastrous. The little child is very logical and also keenly instinctive: it knows when lies are being told to it, and so it comes to distrust the grown-ups and becomes increasingly curious and sets about getting knowledge in some other way and saying nothing to those who have deceived it. Therefore the child's questions should be answered as simply and as fully as it wishes.

When we come to consider how to teach, our best initial text is the hen. Every toddler of two who lives in the country knows that hens lay eggs, knows all about it, and even the town child has country holidays or is familiar with hens in gardens and backyards. The child playing about the farmyard or garden sees the empty nest, sees the hen go in to sit there, then the hen comes away with loud rejoicings, and someone comes and takes the child's hand and says 'Let's run and get the egg!' Follows the triumphant entry of the child with a warm egg in its hand 'to be boiled for my tea!' The child knows perfectly that the egg came from inside the hen. Then comes a spring-time when it learns that eggs become chickens, after the hen has sat on them for a very long time, for there comes an exciting day when the nest is found full of broken shells and little chickens. So the child is quite clear. Hens lay eggs and eggs grow into chickens. Cats and kittens come into the lives of even the most towny of town children, and little children know where kittens come from. A tiny boy said to me, gently stroking his cat, 'We must be very careful not to hurt pussy, she's going to have some kittens!' When the kittens had arrived he added, 'We'll give pussy some warm milk and leave her quiet, because she is tired.' They know the cat does not lay hard eggs with kittens in them, needing to be sat on for weeks while they grow. The cat lays just kittens, kittens ready made.

Then there is the joy, the ever-recurring joy, of the first lamb of the year. One day there are only sheep in the field, the next there is a lamb, and you can see the lamb belongs to a sheep; she is its mother and feeds it and cuddles it. The child knows quite well where the lamb comes from – if no one has previously lied to it – the sheep has laid the lamb.

Some day comes the great joy and excitement of a new baby at home! The little child's mind is very clear and logical. It thinks for itself and it reasons, from eggs and chickens, new kittens, new lambs, to the new baby, and it says to itself, 'Mothers lay babies.' Quite simple, nothing very wonderful about it. The rather dull or unobservant child may not carry on this line of interest and of reasoning unless helped, but can easily be led in this direction if chances are taken as they arise. The question as to why one does not chatter as to the coming of the new baby can be met by telling that it is a great and solemn thing to start a new little life, the greatest thing mother can do. The little child has a natural fund of reverence to which we can appeal with confidence. Such teaching is not incompatible with that which most mothers like to give as to the baby having come from Heaven or as to its having been sent by God, for the baby has a soul as well as a body, and if God did not send the soul, the body would not grow. God wants more chickens, more kittens, more lambs, and more babies in the world, so He sends the life, the soul, and makes the mothers able to grow the bodies. A very little girl I know said: 'We've got a new little brother! He's just dropped, and I do think it was clever of mother to catch him!' And she looked up to the sky to see if more babies were dropping. Beautiful, but no more beautiful than that the little soul has come from Heaven, and that God has helped mother to make a little body for it.

Such teaching at three or four or five will carry the child on serenely till the time comes to think of fathers. It is best to teach the father's share early, before self-consciousness and shyness have arisen, to get the facts known and put away at the back of the mind while the child is a child, not during the difficult transition period between fourteen and eighteen years. We can make no rule beyond that of answering when the child asks. If she does not ask, it is wise to lead up to the question when she is ten or twelve or so, according to the make of the child's mind. Children in general accept a father as part of the scheme of things, but there are children like a little girl I knew who said, sitting on the knee of an affectionate father: 'It's very nice to have a father, but I don't see that it's much use.' It is well to explain that every living thing above the lowliest has a father as well as a mother, though the fathers of chickens, kittens, puppies, and lambs take no share in bringing them up. In this way qualities are inherited from two parents, and so there can be great variety among people, whereas if there were mothers only there would be a great sameness.

In the human family, to have a father and a mother to bring up the children, to share the work, the joys, and the troubles, gives the best home, as the children learn some things from the father and some from the mother, and so are better balanced than if brought up by a mother only. The mother is needed to be with the young children while the father goes out into the world to make a living. The child must belong to them both. Part of the child must come from the mother, part from the father. So it links them together.

In explaining the father's share in producing the new life, it is common to begin by showing and telling about plants. I think this is not the best plan. If the male and female germs were always on separate plants, if we could say this is a father rose bush, this other is a mother rose bush, it might be simple and helpful. But with the male and female organs in one flower, as they commonly are, the issue becomes confused and indirect. It is a possible way. We can say, taking, for instance, the sweet pea or the edible pea, the pollen stalks are fathers, the pod is a mother, the petals are the little house in which they live; the father germ unites with the mother germ, which is a tiny white egg in the pod, and makes it able to grow into a big green seed, which is really a new little pea plant. Germ is the best word for the living matter contributed by the father. All children are now used to the word 'germ' as meaning a tiny, invisible speck of living matter. They are constantly hearing of influenza germs, of germs of colds, of good germs which help us, as well as bad germs which harm us; so although the word 'germ' is not strictly accurate, it is near enough and better than anything else, unless we use the proper term 'sperm' which would convey an unfamiliar idea and is therefore better avoided. A term sometimes used, 'father seed' will not do at all, as children learn in their botany lessons that the seed is the complete new little plant derived from the union of male and female elements. It is probably best to leave plants alone at first and begin with animal life.

The fish gives a good starting point. Fish roe is familiar to a child as an occasional part of its breakfast herring – just a mass of little eggs. Then children read in natural history books and stories about animals – how the mother salmon leaves the sea and goes up the river to find a safe, quiet place to lay her eggs; how the father salmon goes up with her and, when the eggs have been laid, lays germs among them; how the eggs and the germs unite and grow to fishes in the water, with the mother salmon watching them for a time.

Many children see at school or in their own homes a little aquarium in which frogs' eggs are growing into frogs, and we can tell them how, when the mother frog lays eggs, the father lays germs at the same time, each egg meeting a germ as it leaves the mother's body. The eggs grow into tadpoles, and the tadpoles into frogs. If when the mother frog lays her eggs there is no father frog to lay germs, the eggs just die and never become frogs.

But kittens are *not* eggs when laid. They have grown in a warm, safe place inside the mother cat till quite big, so the father germ and the egg have had to meet inside that safe place in the mother cat. The father germs have gone in through the passage which afterwards lets the kittens come out – the passage between the opening from the bladder and the opening from the bowel.

'Where did the new baby come from?' said a very small boy to his father. 'Till it was big enough to come out, mother kept it inside under her heart,' was the answer. The baby has to grow from a tiny egg smaller than a pin's head to a full-sized baby before it can live in the world, so the father germ and the egg must meet inside the special place in the mother in which the baby grows for nine months before it is born.

Such simple teaching as this will clear the air, will lay to rest wonderings and secrets. The child who knows, clearly and fully, is not a victim to another child or an adult of unclean mind. Such a child would tend to be a little scornful and superior, and to take the tone, 'I know all about that! Mother told me, and I don't like your way of talking about it.'

Reverence and reticence on these matters are not difficult to teach to a child of ten or twelve. Such children have still a fund of instinct, of spirituality about them, and can be led to see the greatness of our linking ourselves of today with the eternal procession of life – now we so come nearest to a conscious carrying on of the Divine Will for our world. They can see how this part of our life more than any other stands for the upward struggle from the lower life of self to the higher life of service. When they come to early youth they will be ready to see how it stands for all we mean by

> What's life but just our chance of learning the prize of love!
> Love, the spark from God's life at strife with death.

They will be ready to respond to

> Rejoice, we are allied
> To that which doth provide
> and not partake, effect and not receive!
> A spark disturbs our clod
> Nearer we hold of God,
> Who gives, than of His tribes that take.

Having dealt simply with the main questions as to what is to be told to children and how and when it may best be told, we pass on to the consideration of special problems, of certain difficulties and of certain safeguards concerning the growing girl.

The little child has been taught where the baby comes from; the child of ten or twelve has been taught the father's share in the baby; the girl of twelve should have teaching as to menstruation, lest it should begin early and alarm and distress her because she had had no warning. Why the onset of menstruation should come at fourteen instead of eighteen or twenty, which would seem more reasonable, we are not able to tell her because we do not know. We say vaguely that it is a survival from times when maternity was common at an earlier age than at present; but this does not help us much, knowing as we do that the children of immature mothers are inferior to those of mothers of twenty-three, when maturity has been reached.

We may well approach the subject of menstruation by saying to the girl of twelve that we hope that every healthy girl will some day be a mother, because that will give her the most natural life, usually the happiest life, and certainly the life which most tends to help in a spiritual direction by reason of the unselfishness it calls for. Most little girls have a natural affection for babies, and are ready to look forward happily to having babies of their own. We can tell them that Nature takes a long time over getting a girl ready to be a mother, that she begins when the girl is about fourteen and goes on till she is about twenty-three, by which time she should be really ready. There is no need for more than a very brief statement as to the structure of the organs concerned – just that the uterus or womb is the name of the part of the body within which the baby grows, and that two small glands, something like big tonsils, called the ovaries, form the eggs which grow into babies. Once a month, after about the age of fourteen, these parts are supplied with an extra good circulation of blood, just as the leg muscles are supplied with an extra good circulation when a girl is playing a hard game of hockey, and as the brain is so supplied when she is working at a hard lesson. The blood which passes through the uterus is not all needed, and some of it comes away through the passage leading from the uterus, which is just behind the passage leading from the bladder, coming away gradually for a few days. This is not an accident, and there is nothing alarming about it. How it helps the body we do not know, but it does help or it would not happen. We cannot always understand Nature, but she knows her work and is doing the right thing. Sometimes a great deal of blood circulates through the nose, perhaps when a girl has a bad headache, and if some of this blood comes away from the nose her headache is relieved. It has been a help to lose that blood. Menstruation is not an illness, and we should never speak of the monthly loss as a time of 'being unwell', of 'being poorly'. Unfortunately it often *is* a time of being unwell, but it has no business to be; it is no part of Nature's plan that a girl should suffer at monthly periods, and it is a mistake to suggest the idea of being unwell. A little vague pain or discomfort, as from a mild toothache or headache, for an hour or two any sensible girl will put up with pluckily. Anything more, anything affecting appetite or sleep, or causing headache, faintness, a feeling of sickness or of being miserable is wrong, and should mean prompt medical advice. There is far too much needless pain and weariness borne with silent endurance, and often making a girl dread the next period as soon as the last has passed.

There are simple aids to the normal monthly period, some of them general, some of them special. The best general aids are found in an ordinary healthy life, providing for daily outdoor games, long nights in bed at a wide, open window, plenty of good simple food and a strict avoidance of constipation or of stimulants.

When the period of the monthly loss arrives, certain special aids come in. The daily bath is then more needed than ever, and should never be omitted, but it should not during that time be either a cold bath or a hot bath, but should be a tepid one – that is, at a temperature of about 90 degrees Fahrenheit. Exercise may need modification, and in the matter of games and gymnastics every good school has its rules for the monthly period, and mothers and girls must loyally fall in with these rules. Speaking for girls who are not at such schools, it may be said that jumping and violent trunk movements should be avoided, but that mild exercise will be helpful rather than harmful. It is not possible to lay down general rules, and the individual girl and her mother can arrive at a working basis. If exercise in games or gymnastics leaves a girl unduly tired and increases the loss from the uterus, such exercise should be stopped. If the girl feels well, enjoys the games or gymnastics, and does not find the loss increased, she is safe in doing anything which does not involve violent movements. The question turns largely on the type of girl; there are girls who tend to do too much, and there are lazy, self-indulgent girls who tend to do too little at all times and are glad of an excuse for doing still less. It is best for the girl physically if the period can go by hardly noticed, with no disturbance of the routine of life, but not if this means the girl is suffering in silence.

Clear teaching is needed as to sex relations, and certain points should be definitely made. Reproductive processes should not be carried out until a girl is at least twenty-one, and, better, twenty-three. Complete development is not reached until twenty-three as is shown by the fact that research into the problem proves that first babies born when the mother is twenty-three are better than first babies born when the mother is either under or over twenty-three.

Reproductive processes should not be carried on without the sanction of matrimony. It is not enough to say because it is wrong, or because it is wicked, or irreligious. This statement would satisfy the great majority of girls, but there will always be a thinking minority of girls who want to know why it is wrong, and it is best that all girls, thinking or unthinking, should see clearly where the wrong lies. (1) It is wrong because it is an offence against the spiritual progress of the race. (2) It is an offence between man and woman, and it is always the woman who pays the penalty in loss of position, in pain, suffering, and pecuniary damage. (3) It is also wrong because it is not fair to the baby. The history of the human race has proved by every kind of experiment carried out through countless ages that children grow up best in families, with father and mother to care for them and brothers and sisters to give them the discipline which no grown-up person can give – that most valuable discipline which comes of judgement by one's peers. So it has come about that the father and mother make an undertaking, a legal promise to the State, to live together so as to bring up their children, and this is marriage. Most people wish to add a religious ceremony, to make a promise to God as well as to the State, but the essence of marriage is the mutual promise to live together in permanent union, and in civil marriage this promise is made before the State. It follows that all children born to married parents are lawful or legitimate children – children born according to the law of the land. It follows that all children born to unmarried parents are unlawful or illegitimate children – children born against the law of the land.

It is also wrong because it is not fair to the mother. The unmarried mother generally has to bring up her child without proper help from the father. It is a very mean and selfish thing for a man to become the father of a child unless he is married to the mother, and it is selfish to them both to become the parents of a child who will not have a proper home and an honourable place according to the law of the land.

As to when this should be taught there can be no rule. Certainly it should be whenever the child or the growing girl asks, and probably the earlier the better, once a child can understand, before the emotional side of life is much developed. In any case, it should be somewhere between fourteen and eighteen, according to the type of girl.

There are many helps which can be given during girlhood, during the difficult years from fourteen to eighteen or twenty, when so many changes are taking place, changes of body, of mind, of soul. It is a time in which internal activities, impulses and vague emotions connected with reproduction are developing, while yet there is no scope for their exercise. An immense amount of energy is linked to reproductive processes and for this energy there must be provided alternative outlets in all directions, physical, mental and psychical.

The best physical help is given by organised open-air games of all kinds – hockey, cricket, lacrosse, netball – or, where these are impossible, by walking, tennis, cycling, swimming, golf. The organised games are much the most helpful, because they give so much and in all directions – hard physical exercise; healthy excitement which is the best safeguard against morbid excitement; happy comradeship. In addition, they teach the highest of all lessons – to 'play the game' and not to play for oneself, the lesson which seems to be one of the most valuable contributions the British Race can make to the world. Such games should form part of the daily life of all growing girls.

Plain living helps. Plenty of good nourishing food, such as milk, cheese, butter, eggs, home-made bread and cake, porridge, puddings, sugar, vegetables and fruits. In war-time one can only speak guardedly of foods and we must all take what we can get, but in normal times such a diet is possible. Little meat or fish is needed – not more than one small helping a day – and the less tea and coffee the better.

There should be long nights in bed, going to bed early, with a hard mattress and light bed clothes, light and only just warm enough to prevent a sensation of cold. The bed should be drawn up alongside a wide open window, and the girl should sleep on her side with her face to the window, and as near as possible to the window sill. Even in our maligned climate there are few nights when it really rains in, and on such nights it is easy to get up and pull a light bed a few feet away from the window. It is also easy next morning to mop a boarded or linoleum-covered floor.

A daily cold bath is one of the best helps, and there are few girls for whom some form of this is not possible. It should be a regular part of every girl's daily life, and in the case of girls with special circulatory difficulties a doctor will know what can be done to make a cold splash or cold sponge safe.

Among the best mental helps are interesting but really hard

school lessons, which mean that the girl must think for herself. It is a duty to the growing girl to see that she has not a dull life, and we need to help her in every way to have hobbies and amusements which are to her taste though not necessarily to ours. She needs, too, good standard novels, both classical and modern, and free time in which to read. It is important, in the interests of individuality, that every girl should have some part of the day, even if only an hour, which is really her own, with no claims upon it, a time she can give to her own special interest.

Psychically, a girl can be helped by having a good many friends or friendly acquaintances, and we do well to encourage variety in this respect and not to encourage sentimental and morbid devotions to an individual. The staffs of all good schools do everything possible to discourage wholesale devotions to some one mistress or Sixth Form girl and to encourage breadth of sympathy by every means in their power.

Simple frank friendship between girls and boys from nursery days is a help to both, giving both a better balanced view of life, wider sympathies and a safeguard against the fascinations of the unknown. We can help the girl who is growing, the girl between seventeen and twenty-one, to see how mean and unkind flirtation may be, exciting feelings and desires in a boy or man for which there is to be no normal realisation. A fair-minded girl will see she should help a man and not make it harder for him to keep to a high ideal of parenthood.

So far we have dealt with the normal development of reproductive activities, from early childhood to grown-up life, and it is along normal lines that almost all children in good homes develop. But in a few cases there are certain abnormal activities of the reproductive organs, and it is necessary to be alive to possible danger from these, both in little children and in growing girls. All natural functions, eating, exercising, resting, are attended by a sense of satisfaction, and reproductive functions are no exception to this rule. Sometimes children find this out, accidentally or from other children, or from bad nurses. Local irritation of the external reproductive organs is apt to follow any want of perfect cleanliness; this sets up rubbing to remove the irritation, the little child finds pleasure results and so acquires a habit, which may happen very early. Other children, knowing no harm, may teach the habit. A baby or small child who is cross and difficult finds itself soothed and lulled by such excitation of the reproductive organs, and a bad nurse may deliberately or even ignorantly teach a baby or small child the habit in order to keep it quiet, which it may do for an hour or two at a time. The growing girl may fall into the habit, thinking no harm.

What we need to teach is the habit of thorough daily cleanliness, every accessible part of the external organs being well cleansed by a brisk application of soap, to be followed by a plunge into a cold bath and water dashed vigorously against the parts time after time. Apart from this daily bath the very little child should be taught there is to be no handling whatever. At night each child should from the first have a bed to itself, and if there is any suspicion that a child has acquired bad habits, it should be put into a warm sleeping suit, and brought up to sleep with hands outside the bed clothes. To children old enough, if it is necessary to say anything, which could only be if the habit existed, one could explain that it is very exhausting, makes them dull and stupid, and is a waste of powers given them for the good of the world, for the good of their children. If the habit has become fixed, or has arisen in a young girl, it may be very difficult to get rid of. A girl may be intensely unhappy when she finds she has dropped into a bad habit unwittingly. Then a good medical woman can often help.

Travelling is often a source of anxiety to mothers of young girls. It is best to avoid as far as possible train journeys alone for every child and young girl. She cannot always choose her company in a train, and until all carriages are corridor carriages, or better still, are on the American open-car system, there will be a certain amount of risk. Trams and omnibuses are much better whenever possible for daily school journeys, and cycling any reasonable distance is better for the average girl than either trains or trams.

If a girl is obliged to take a long journey alone and to change trains at junctions we need to be sure that she is clear on certain points, such as that at stations she must ask direction only of officials of the railway company, in towns only of policemen; that she must go nowhere, not even to a refreshment room, with anyone, man or woman, whom she does not know; that she must never sit down on the seat of a public lavatory, in train, waiting room, restaurant, or any public place, but should take up a position which avoids any contact of the skin with the seat.

The last problem, a very difficult one, is as to whether young girls shall be told anything as to venereal diseases. They must be told, because they read freely, allusions are everywhere now, and true knowledge is safer than a medley of scraps, some true, some false. At the same time, we must darken their young lives as little as possible. What they have been told as to unlawful children has shown them that sex intercourse does sometimes occur between unmarried persons, and this has prepared the way for what must be said. There is no need to frighten young people, but it is best to say quite simply: Certain infectious diseases affect particularly the reproductive organs, are very serious and damaging, much worse than scarlet fever, pneumonia, or diptheria, in their long-lasting effects. These are called venereal diseases. If a person in whom the reproductive organs are affected by a venereal disease comes into close personal contact with another person the infection may be handed on – as scarlet fever and diptheria may be handed on and the reproductive organs of that second person become diseased. This is why a girl must never sit down on the seat of a public lavatory, as she may be following someone suffering from venereal disease. These diseases never arise except by infection from someone suffering and would die out entirely if all girls and boys, all women and men, would keep to a rule that reproductive activities should never be exercised except between husband and wife. For as neither the man nor the woman had been exposed to infection they would come to their married life free from venereal disease, and by remaining faithful to one another would keep free. This puts the matter on a hopeful footing in the girl's mind and is probably the least trying presentation which can be made.

B *The Impact of Sex Reform*

Havelock Ellis

Love and Pain

(1913)

I

The Chief Key to the Relationship between Love and Pain to be Found in Animal Courtship – Courtship a Source of Combativity and of Cruelty – Human Play in the Light of Animal Courtship – The Frequency of Crimes Against the Person in Adolsecence – Marriage by Capture and its Psychological Basis – Man's Pleasure in Exerting Force and Woman's Pleasure in Experiencing it – Resemblance of Love to Pain even in Outward Expression – The Love-bite – in what Sense Pain may be Pleasurable – The Natural Contradiction in the Emotional Attitude of Women Toward Men – Relative Insensibility to Pain of the Organic Sexual Sphere in Women – The Significance of the Use of the Ampallang and Similar Appliances in Coitus – The Sexual Subjection of Women to Men in Part Explainable as the Necessary Condition for Sexual Pleasure.

The relation of love to pain is one of the most difficult problems, and yet one of the most fundamental, in the whole range of sexual psychology. Why is it that love inflicts, and even seeks to inflict, pain? Why is it that love suffers pain, and even seeks to suffer it? In answering that question, it seems to me, we have to take an apparently circuitous route, sometimes going beyond the ostensible limits of sex altogether; but if we can succeed in answering it we shall have come very near one of the great mysteries of love. At the same time we shall have made clear the normal basis on which rest the extreme aberrations of love.

The chief key to the relationship of love to pain is to be found by returning to the consideration of the essential phenomena of courtship in the animal world generally. Courtship is a play, a game; even its combats are often, to a large extent, mock-combats; but the process behind it is one of terrible earnestness, and the play may at any moment become deadly. Courtship tends to involve a mock-combat between males for the possession of the female which may at any time become a real combat; it is a pursuit of the female by the male which may at any time become a kind of persecution; so that, as Colin Scott remarks, 'Courting may be looked upon as a refined and delicate form of combat.' The note of courtship, more especially among mammals, is very easily forced, and as soon as we force it we reach pain.[1] The intimate and inevitable association in the animal world of combat – of the fighting and hunting impulses – with the process of courtship alone suffices to bring love into close connection with pain.

Among mammals the male wins the female very largely by the display of force. The infliction of pain must inevitably be a frequent indirect result of the exertion of power. It is even more than this; the infliction of pain by the male on the female may itself be a gratification of the impulse to exert force. This tendency has always to be held in check, for it is of the essence of courtship that the male should win the female, and she can only be won by the promise of pleasure. The tendency of the male to inflict pain must be restrained, so far as the female is concerned, by the consideration of what is pleasing to her. Yet, the more carefully we study the essential elements of courtship, the clearer it becomes that, playful as these manifestations may seem on the surface, in every direction they are verging on pain. It is so among animals generally; it is so in man among savages. 'It is precisely the alliance of pleasure and pain,' wrote the physiologist Burdach, 'which constitutes the voluptuous emotion.'

Nor is this emotional attitude entirely confined to the male. The female also in courtship delights to arouse to the highest degree in the male the desire for her favours and to withhold those favours from him, thus finding on her part also the enjoyment of power in cruelty. 'One's cruelty is one's power,' Millament says in Congreve's *Way of the World*, 'and when one parts with one's cruelty one parts with one's power.'

At the outset, then, the impulse to inflict pain is brought into courtship, and at the same time rendered a pleasurable idea to the female, because with primitive man, as well as among his immediate ancestors, the victor in love has been the bravest and strongest rather than the most beautiful or the most skilful. Until he can fight he is not reckoned a man and he cannot hope to win a woman. Among the African Masai a man is not supposed to marry until he has blooded his spear, and in a very different part of the world, among the Dyaks of Borneo, there can be little doubt that the chief incentive to head-hunting is the desire to please the women, the possession of a head decapitated by himself being an excellent way of winning a maiden's favour. Such instances are too well known to need multiplication here, and they survive in civilisation, for, even among ourselves, although courtship is now chiefly ruled by quite other considerations, most women are in some degree emotionally affected by strength and courage. But the direct result of this is that a group of phenomena with which cruelty and the infliction of pain must inevitably be more or less allied is brought within the sphere of courtship and rendered agreeable to women. Here, indeed, we have the source of that love of cruelty which some have found so marked in women. This is a phase of courtship which helps us to understand how it is that, as we shall see, the idea of pain, having become associated with sexual emotion, may be pleasurable to women.

Thus, in order to understand the connection between love and pain, we have once more to return to the consideration, under a somewhat new aspect, of the fundamental elements in the sexual impulse. In discussing the 'Evolution of Modesty' we found that the primary part of the female in courtship is the playful, yet serious, assumption of the role of a hunted animal who lures on the pursuer, not with the object of escaping, but with the object of being finally caught. In considering the 'Analysis of the Sexual Impulse' we found that the primary part of the male in courtship is by the display of his energy and skill to capture the female or to arouse in her an emotional condition which leads her to surrender herself to him, this process itself at the same time heightening his own excitement. In the playing of these two different parts is attained in both male and female that charging of nervous energy, that degree of vascular tumescence, necssary for adequate discharge and detumescence in an explosion by which sperm-cells and germ-cells are brought together for the propagation of the race. We are now concerned with the necessary interplay of the differing male and female roles in courtship, and with their accidental emotional by-products. Both male and female are instinctively seeking the same end of sexual union at the moment of highest excitement. There cannot, therefore, be a real conflict.[2] But there is the semblance of a conflict, an apparent clash of aim, an appearance of cruelty. Moreover – and this is a significant moment in the process from our present point of view – when there are rivals for the possession of one female there is always a possibility of actual combat, so tending to introduce an element of real violence, of undisguised cruelty, which the male inflicts on his rival and which the female views with satisfaction and delight in the prowess of the successful claimant. Here we are brought close to the zoological root of the connection between love and pain.[3]

In his admirable work on play in man Groos has fully discussed the plays of combat (*Kampfspiele*), which begin to develop even in childhood and assume full activity during adolescence; and he points out that, while the impulse to such play certainly has a wider biological significance, it still possesses a relationship to the sexual life and to the rivalries of animals in courtship which must not be forgotten.[4]

Nor is it only in play that the connection between love and combativity may still be traced. With the epoch of the first sexual relationship, Marro points out, awakes the instinct of cruelty, which prompts the youth to acts which are sometimes in absolute contrast to his previous conduct, and leads him to be careless of the lives of others as well as of his own life.[5] Marro presents a diagram showing how crimes against the person in Italy rise rapidly from the age of 16 to 20 and reach a climax between 21 and 25. In Paris, Garnier states, crimes of blood are six times more frequent in adolescents (aged 16 to 20) than in adults. It is the same elsewhere.[6] This tendency to criminal violence during the age-period of courtship is a by-product of the sexual impulse, a kind of tertiary sexual character.

In the process of what is commonly termed 'marriage by capture' we have a method of courtship which closely resembles the most typical form of animal courtship, and is yet found in all but the highest and most artificial stages of human society. It may not be true that, as MacLennan and others have argued, almost every race of man has passed through an actual stage of marriage by capture, but the phenomena in question have certainly been extremely widespread and exist in popular custom even among the highest races today. George Sand has presented a charming picture of such a custom, existing in France, in her *Mare au Diable*. Farther away, among the Kirghiz, the young woman is pursued by all her lovers, but she is armed with a formidable whip, which she does not hesitate to use if overtaken by a lover to whom she is not favourable. Among the Malays, according to early travelers, courtship is carried on in the water in canoes with double-bladed paddles; or, if no water is near, the damsel, stripped naked of all but a waist-band, is given a certain start and runs off on foot followed by her lover. Vaughan Stevens in 1896 reported that this performance is merely a sport; but Skeat and Blagden, in their more recent and very elaborate investigations in the Malay States, find that it is a rite.

Even if we regard 'marriage by capture' as simply a primitive human institution stimulated by tribal exigencies and early social conditions, yet, when we recall its widespread and persistent character, its close resemblance to the most general method of courtship among animals, and the emotional tendencies which still persist even in the most civilized men and women, we have to recognize that we are in presence of a real psychological impulse which cannot fail in its exercise to introduce some element of pain into love.

There are, however, two fundamentally different theories concerning 'marriage by capture'. According to the first, that of MacLennan, which, until recently, has been very widely accepted, and to which Professor Tylor has given the weight of his authority, there has really been in primitive society a recognized stage in which marriages were effected by the capture of the wife. Such a state of things MacLennan regarded as once world-wide. There can be no doubt that women very frequently have been captured in this way among primitive peoples. Nor, indeed, has the custom been confined to savages. In Europe we find that even up to comparatively recent times the abduction of women was not only very common, but was often more or less recognized. In England it was not until Henry VII's time that the violent seizure of a woman was made a criminal offense, and even then the statute was limited to women possessed of lands and goods. A man might still carry off a girl provided she was not an heiress; but even the abduction of heiresses continued to be common, and in Ireland remained so until the end of the eighteenth century. But it is not so clear that such raids and abductions, even when not of a genuinely hostile character, have ever been a recognized and constant method of marriage.

According to the second set of theories, the capture is not real, but simulated, and may be accounted for by psychological reasons. Fustel de Coulanges, in *La Cité Antique*, discussing simulated marriage by capture among the Romans, mentioned the view that it was 'a symbol of the young girl's modesty,' but himself regarded it as an act of force to symbolize the husband's power. He was possibly alluding to Herbert Spencer, who suggested a psychological explanation of the apparent prevalence of marriage by capture based on the supposition that, capturing a wife being a proof of bravery, such a method of obtaining a wife would be practised by the strongest men and be admired, while, on the other hand, he considered that 'female coyness' was 'an important factor' in constituting the more formal kinds of marriage by capture ceremonial. Westermarck, while accepting true marriage by capture, considers that Spencer's statement 'can scarcely be disproved'.[7] In his valuable study of certain aspects of primitive marriage Crawley, developing the explanation rejected by Fustel de Coulanges, regards the fundamental fact to be the modesty of women, which has to be neutralized, and this is done by 'a ceremonial use of force, which is half real and half make-believe.' Thus the manifestations are not survivals, but 'arising in a natural way from normal human feelings. It is not the tribe from which the bride is abducted, nor, primarily, her family and kindred, but her *sex*'; and her 'sexual characters of timidity, bashfulness, and passivity are sympathetically overcome by make-believe representations of male characteristic actions.'[8]

It is not necessary for the present purpose that either of these two opposing theories concerning the origin of the customs and feelings we are here concerned with should be definitely rejected. Whichever theory is adopted, the fundamental psychic element which here alone concerns us still exists intact. It may be pointed out, however, that we probably have to accept two groups of such phenomena: one, seldom or never existing as the sole form of marriage, in which the capture is real; and another in which the 'capture' is more or less ceremonial or playful. The two groups coexist among the Turcomans, as described by Vámbéry, who are constantly capturing and enslaving the Persians of both sexes, and side by side with this, have a marriage ceremonial of mock-capture of entirely playful character. At the same time the two groups sometimes overlap, as is indicated by cases in which, while the 'capture' appears to be ceremonial, the girl is still allowed to escape altogether if she wishes. The difficulty of disentangling the two groups is shown by the fact that so careful an invetigator as Westermarck cites cases of real capture and mock-capture together without attempting to distinguish between them. From our present point of view it is quite unnecessary to attempt such a distinction. Whether the capture is simulated or real, the man is still playing the masculine and aggressive part proper to the male; the woman is still playing the feminine and defensive part proper to the female. The universal prevalence of these phenomena is due to the fact that manifestations of this kind, real or pretended, afford each sex the very best opportunity for playing its proper part in courtship, and so, even when the force is real, must always gratify a profound instinct.

This association between love and pain still persists even among the most normal civilized men and women possessing well-developed sexual impulses. The masculine tendency to delight in domination, the feminine tendency to delight in submission, still maintain the ancient traditions when the male animal pursued the female. The phenomean of 'marriage by capture,' in its real and its simulated forms, have been traced to various causes. But it has to be remembered that these causes could only have been operative in the presence of a favorable emotional aptitude, constituted by the zoological history of our race and still traceable even today. To exert power, as psychologists well recognize, is one of our most primary impulses, and it always tends to be manifested in the attitude of a man toward the woman he loves.[9]

It might be possible to maintain that the primitive element of more or less latent cruelty in courtship tends to be more rather than less marked in civilized man. In civilization the opportunity of dissipating the surplus energy of the courtship process by inflicting pain on rivals usually has to be inhibited; thus the woman to be wooed tends to become the recipient of the whole of this energy, both in its pleasure-giving and its pain-giving aspects. Moreover, the natural process of courtship, as it exists among animals and usually among the lower human races, tends to become disguised and distorted in civilization, as well by economic conditions as by conventional social conditions and even ethical prescription. It becomes forgotten that the woman's pleasure is an essential element in the process of courtship. A woman is often reduced to seek a man for the sake of maintenance; she is taught that pleasure is sinful or shameful, that sex-matters are disgusting, and that it is a woman's duty, and also her best policy, to be in subjection to her husband. Thus, various external checks which normally inhibit any passing over of masculine sexual energy into cruelty are liable to be removed.

We have to admit that a certain pleasure in manifesting his power over a woman by inflicting pain upon her is an outcome and survival of the primitive process of courtship, and an almost or quite normal constituent of the sexual impulse in man. But it must be at once added that in the normal well-balanced and well-conditioned man this constituent of the sexual impulse, when present, is always held in check. When the normal man inflicts, or feels the impulse to inflict, some degree of physical pain on the woman he loves he can scarcely be said to be moved by cruelty. He feels, more or less obscurely, that the pain he inflicts, or desires to inflict, is really a part of his love, and that, moreover, it is not really resented by the woman on whom it is exercised. His feeling is by no means always according to knowledge, but it has to be taken into account as an essential part of his emotional state. The physical force, the teasing and bullying, which he may be moved to exert under the stress of sexual excitement, are, he usually more or less unconsciously persuades himself, not really unwelcome to the object of his love.[10] Moreover, we have to bear in mind the fact – a very significant fact from more than one point of view – that the normal manifestations of a woman's sexual pleasure are exceedingly like those of pain. 'The outward expressions of pain,' as a lady very truly writes – 'tears, cries, etc. – which are laid stress on to prove the cruelty of the person who inflicts it, are not so different from those of a woman in the ecstasy of passion, when she implores the man to desist, though that is really the last thing she desires.'[11] If a man is convinced that he is causing real and unmitigated pain, he becomes repentant at once. If this is not the case he must either be regarded as a radically abnormal person or as carried away by passion to a point of temporary insanity.

The intimate connection of love with pain, its tendency to approach cruelty, is seen in one of the most widespread of the occasional and non-essential manifestations of strong sexual emotion, especially in women, the tendency to bite. We may find references to love-bites in the literature of ancient as well as of modern times, in the East as well as in the West. Plautus, Catullus, Propertius, Horace, Ovid, Petronius, and other Latin writers refer to bites as associated with kisses and usually on the lips. Plutarch says that Flora, the mistress of Cnæus Pompey, in commending her lover remarked that he was so lovable that she could never leave him without giving him a bite. In the Arabic *Perfumed Garden* there are many references to love-bites, while in the Indian *Kama Sutra* of Vatsyayana a chapter is devoted to this subject. Biting in love is also common among the South Slavs. The phenomenon is indeed sufficiently familiar to enable Heine, in one of his *Romancero*, to describe those marks by which the ancient chronicler states that Edith Swanneck recognized Harold, after the Battle of Hastings, as the scars of the bites she had once given him.

It would be fanciful to trace this tendency back to that process of devouring to which sexual congress has, in the primitive stages of its evolution, been reduced. But we may probably find one of the germs of the love-bite in the attitude of many mammals during or before coitus; in attaining a firm grip of the female it is not uncommon (as may be observed in the donkey) for the male to seize the female's neck between his teeth. The horse sometimes bites the mare before coitus and it is said that among the Arabs when a mare is not apt for coitus she is sent to pasture with a small ardent horse, who excites her by playing with her and biting her. It may be noted, also, that dogs often show their affection for their masters by gentle bites. Children also, as Stanley Hall has pointed out, are similarly fond of biting.

Perhaps a still more important factor is the element of combat in tumescence, since the primitive conditions associated with tumescence provide a reservoir of emotions which are constantly drawn on even in the sexual excitement of individuals belonging to civilization. The tendency to show affection by biting is, indeed, commoner among women than among men and not only in civilization. It has been noted among idiot girls as well as among the women of various savage races. It may thus be that the conservative instincts of women have preserved a primitive tendency that at its origin marked the male more than the female. But in any case the tendency to bite at the climax of sexual excitement is so common and widespread that it must be regarded, when occurring in women, as coming within the normal range of variation in such manifestations. The gradations are of wide extent; while in its slight forms it is more or less normal and is one of the origins of the kiss, in its extreme forms it tends to become one of the most violent and antisocial of sexual aberrations.

A correspondent writes regarding his experience of biting and being bitten:

> I have often felt inclination to bite a woman I love, even when not in coitus or even excited. (I like doing so also with my little boy, playfully, as a cat and kittens.) There seem to be several reasons for this: (1) the muscular effect relieves me; (2) I imagine I am giving the woman pleasure; (3) I seem to attain to a more intimated possession of the loved one. I cannot remember when I first felt desire to be bitten in coitus, or whether the idea was first suggested to me. I was initiated into pinching by a French prostitute who once pinched my nates in coitus, no doubt as a matter of business; it heightened my pleasure, perhaps by stimulating muscular movement. It does not occur to me to ask to be pinched when I am very much excited already, but only at an earlier stage, no doubt with the object of promoting excitement. Apart altogether from sexual excitement, being pinched is unpleasant to me. It has not seemed to me that women usually like to be bitten. One or two women have bitten and sucked my flesh. (The latter does not affect me.) I like being bitten, partly for the same reason as I like being pinched, because if spontaneous it is a sign of my partner's amorousness and the biting never seems too hard. Women do not usually seem to like being bitten, though there are exceptions; 'I should like to bite you

> and I should like you to bite me,' said one woman; I did so hard, in coitus, and she did not flinch.

'She is particularly anxious to eat me alive,' another correspondent writes, 'and nothing gives her greater satisfaction than to tear open my clothes and fasten her teeth into my flesh until I yell for mercy. My experience has generally been, however,' the same correspondent continues, 'that the cruelty is *unconscious*. A woman just grows mad with the desire to squeeze or bite something, with a complete unconsciousness of what result it will produce in the victim. She is astonished when she sees the result and will hardly believe she had done it.' It is unnecessary to accumulate evidence of a tendency which is sufficiently common to be fairly well known, but one or two quotations may be presented to show its wide distribution. In the *Kama Sutra* we read: 'If she is very exalted, and if in the exaltation of her passionate transports she begins a sort of combat, then she takes her lover by the hair, draws his head to hers, kisses his lower lip, and then in her delirium bites him all over his body, shutting her eyes': it is added that with the marks of such bites lovers can remind each other of their affections, and that such love will last for ages. In Japan the maiden of Ainu race feels the same impulse. A. H. Savage Landor (*Alone with the Hairy Ainu*, 1893, p. 140) says of an Ainu girl:

> Loving and biting went together with her. She could not do the one without the other. As we sat on a stone in the twilight she began by gently biting my fingers without hurting me, as affectionate dogs do to their masters. She then bit my arm, then my shoulder, and when she had worked herself up into a passion she put her arms around my neck and bit my cheeks. It was undoubtedly a curious way of making love, and, when I had been bitten all over, and was pretty tired of the new sensation, we retired to our respective homes. Kissing, apparently, was an unknown art to her.

The significance of biting, and the close relationship which, as will have to be pointed out later, it reveals to other phenomena, may be illustrated by some observations which have been made by Alonzi on the peasant women of Sicily.

> The women of the people especially in the districts where crimes of blood are prevalent, give vent to their affection for their little ones by kissing and sucking them on the neck and arms till they make then cry convulsively; all the while they say: 'How sweet you are! I will bite you, I will gnaw you all over,' exhibiting every appearance of great pleasure. If a child

> commits some slight fault they do not resort to simple blows, but pursue it through the street and bite it on the face, ears, and arms until the blood flows. At such moments the face of even a beautiful woman is transformed, with injected eyes, gnashing teeth, and convulsive tremors. Among both men and women a very common threat is 'I will drink your blood.' It is told on ocular evidence that a man who had murdered another in a quarrel licked the hot blood from the victim's hand. (G. Alonzi, *Archivio di Psichiatria*, vol. vi, fasc. 4.)

A few years ago a nurse girl in New York was sentenced to prison for cruelty to the baby in her charge. The mother had frequently noticed that the child was in pain and at last discovered the marks of teeth on its legs. The girl admitted that she had bitten the child because that action gave her intense pleasure (*Alienist and Neurologist*, August, 1901, p. 558). In the light of such observations as these we may understand a morbid perversion of affection such as was recorded in the London police news some years ago (1894). A man of 30 was charged with ill-treating his wife's illegitimate daughter, aged 3, during a period of many months; her lips, eyes, and hands were bitten and bruised from sucking, and sometimes her pinafore was covered with blood. 'Defendant admitted he had bitten the child because he loved it.'

It is not surprising that such phenomena as these should sometimes be the stimulant and accompaniment to the sexual act. Ferriani thus reports such a case in the words of the young man's mistress:

> Certainly he is a strange, maddish youth, though he is fond of me and spends money on me when he has any. He likes much sexual intercourse, but, to tell the truth, he has worn out my patience, for before our embraces there are always struggles which become assaults. He tells me he has no pleasure except when he sees me crying on account of his bites and vigorous pinching. Lately, just before going with me, when I was groaning with pleasure, he threw himself on me and at the moment of emission furiously bit my right cheek till the blood came. Then he kissed me and begged my pardon, but would do it again if the wish took him. (L. Ferriani, *Archivio di Psicopatie Sessuale*, vol. i, fasc. 7 and 8, 1896, p. 107)

In morbid cases biting may even become a substitute for coitus. Thus, Moll (*Die Konträre Sexualempfindung*, second edition, p. 323) records the case of a hysterical woman who was sexually anesthetic, though she greatly loved her husband. It was her chief delight to bite him till the blood flowed, and she was content if, instead of coitus, he bit her and she him, though she was grieved if she inflicted much pain. In other still more morbid cases the fear of inflicting pain is more or less abolished.

An idealized view of the impulse of love to bite and devour is presented in the following passage from a letter by a lady who associates this impulse with the idea of the Last Supper:

> Your remarks about the Lord's Supper in 'Whitman' make it natural to me to tell you my thoughts about that 'central sacrament of Christianity'. I cannot tell many people because they misunderstand, and a clergyman, a very great friend of mine, when I once told what I thought and felt, said I was carnal. He did not understand the divinity and intensity of human love as I understand it. Well, when one loves anyone very much – a child, a woman, or a man – one loves everything belonging to him: the things he wears, still more his hands, and his face, every bit of his body. We always want to have all, or part, of him as part of ourselves. Hence the expression: I could *devour* you, I love you so. In some such warm, devouring way Jesus Christ, I have always felt, loved each and every human creature. So it was that he took this mystery of food, which by eating became part of ourselves, as the symbol of the most intense human love, the most intense Divine love. Some day, perhaps, love will be so understood by all that this sacrament will cease to be a superstition, a bone of contention, an 'article' of the church, and become, in all simplicity, a symbol of pure love.

While in men it is possible to trace a tendency to inflict pain, or the simulacrum of pain, on the women they love, it is still easier to trace in women a delight in experiencing physical pain when inflicted by a lover, and an eagerness to accept subjection to his will. Such a tendency is certainly normal. To abandon herself to her lover, to be able to rely on his physical strength and mental resourcefulness, to be swept out of herself and beyond the control of her own will, to drift idly in delicious submission to another and stronger will – this is one of the commonest aspirations in a young woman's intimate love-dreams. In our own age these aspirations most often only find their expression in such dreams. In ages when life was more nakedly lived, and emotion more openly expressed, it was easier to trace this impulse. In the thirteenth century we have found Marie de France – a French poetess living in England who has been credited with 'an exquisite sense of the generosities and delicacy of the heart,' and whose work was certainly highly appreciated in the best circles and among the most cultivated class of her day – describing as a perfect, wise, and courteous knight a man who practically commits a rape on a woman who has refused to have anything to do with him, and, in so acting, he wins her entire love. The savage beauty of New Caledonia furnishes no better illustration of the fascination of force, for she, at all events, has done her best to court the violence she undergoes. In Middleton's *Spanish Gypsy* we find exactly the same episode; and the unhappy Portuguese nun wrote: 'Love me for ever and make me suffer still more.' To find in literature more attenuated examples of the same tendency is easy. Shakespeare, whose observation so little escaped, has seldom depicted the adult passion of a grown woman, but in the play which he has mainly devoted to this subject he makes Cleopatra refer to 'amorous pinches,' and she says in the end: 'The stroke of death is as a lover's pinch, which hurts and is desired.' 'I think the Sabine woman enjoyed being carried off like that,' a woman remarked in front of Rubens's *Rape of the Sabines*, confessing that such a method of love-making appealed strongly to herself, and it is probable that the majority of women would be prepared to echo that remark.

It may be argued that pain cannot give pleasure, and that when what would usually be pain is felt as pleasure it cannot be regarded as pain at all. It must be admitted that the emotional state is often somewhat complex. Moreover, women by no means always agree in the statement of their experience. It is noteworthy, however, that even when the pleasurableness of pain in love is denied it is still admitted that, under some circumstances, pain, or the idea of pain, is felt as pleasurable. I am indebted to a lady for a somewhat elaborate discussion of this subject, which I may here quote at length:

> As regards physical pain, though the idea of it is sometimes exciting, I think the reality is the reverse. A very slight amount of pain destroys my pleasure completely. This was the case with me for fully a month after marriage, and since. When pain has occasionally been associated with passion, pleasure has been sensibly diminished. I can imagine that, when there is a want of sensitiveness so that the tender kiss or caress might fail to give pleasure, more forcible methods are desired; but in that case what would be pain to a sensitive person would be only a pleasant excitement, and it could not be truly said that such obtuse persons liked pain, though they

might appear to do so. I cannot think that anyone enjoys what is pain *to them*, if only from the fact that it detracts and divides the attention. This, however, is only my own idea drawn from my own negative experience. No woman has ever told me that she would like to have pain inflicted on her. On the other hand, the desire to inflict pain seems almost universal among men. I have only met one man in whom I have never at any time been able to detect it. At the same time most men shrink from putting their ideas into practice. A friend of my husband finds his chief pleasure in imagining women hurt and ill-treated, but is too tender-hearted ever to inflict pain on them in reality, even when they are willing to submit to it. Perhaps a woman's readiness to submit to pain to please a man may sometimes be taken for pleasure in it. Even when women like the idea of pain, I fancy it is only because it implies subjection to the man, from association with the fact that physical pleasure must necessarily be preceded by submission to his will.

In a subsequent communication this lady enlarged and perhaps somewhat modified her statements on this point:

I don't think that what I said to you was quite correct. *Actual* pain gives me no pleasure, yet the *idea* of pain does, *if inflicted by way of discipline and for the ultimate good of the person suffering it.* This is essential. For instance, I once read a poem in which the devil and the lost souls in hell were represented as recognizing that they could not be good except under torture, but that while suffering the purifying actions of the flames of hell they so realized the beauty of holiness that they submitted willingly to their agony and praised God for the sternness of his judgment. This poem gave me decided physical pleasure, yet I know that if my hand were held in a fire for five minutes I should feel nothing but the pain of the burning. To get the feeling of pleasure, too, I must, for the moment, revert to my old religious beliefs and my old notion that mere suffering has an elevating influence; one's emotions are greatly modified by one's beliefs. When I was about fifteen I invented a game which I played with a younger sister, in which we were supposed to be going through a process of discipline and preparation for heaven after death. Each person was supposed to enter this state on dying and to pass successively into the charge of different angels named after the special virtues it was their function to instill. The last angel was that of Love, who governed solely by the quality whose name he

bore. In the lower stages, we were under an angel called Severity who prepared us by extreme harshness and by exacting implicit obedience to arbitrary orders for the acquirement of later virtues. Our duties were to superintend the weather, paint the sunrise and sunset, etc., the constant work involved exercising us in patience and submission. The physical pleasure came in inventing and recounting to each other our day's work and the penalties and hardships we had been subjected to. We never told each other that we got any physical pleasure out of this, and I cannot therefore be sure that my sister did so; I only imagine she did because she entered so heartily into the spirit of the game. I could get as much pleasure by imagining myself the angel and inflicting the pain, under the conditions mentioned; but my sister did not like this so much, as she then had no companion in subjection. I could not, however, thus reverse my feelings in regard to a man, as it would appear to me unnatural, and, besides, the greater physical strength is essential in the superior position. I can, however by imagining myself a man, sometimes get pleasure in conceiving myself as educating and disciplining a woman by severe measures. There is, however, no real cruelty in this idea, as I always imagine her liking it.

I only get pleasure in the idea of a woman submitting herself to pain and harshness from the man she loves when the following conditions are fulfilled: 1 She must be absolutely sure of the man's love. 2 She must have perfect confidence in his judgment. 3 The pain must be deliberately inflicted, not accidental. 4 It must be inflicted in kindness and for her own improvement, not in anger or with any revengeful feelings, as that would spoil one's ideal of the man. 5 The pain must not be excessive and must be what when we were children we used to call a 'tidy' pain; i.e., there must be no mutilation, cutting, etc. 6 Last, one would have to feel very sure of one's own influence over the man. So much for the idea. As I have never suffered pain under a combination of all these conditions, I have no right to say that I should or should not experience pleasure from its infliction in reality.

Another lady writes:

I quite agree that the idea of pain may be pleasurable, but must be associated with something to be gained by it. My experience is that it [coitus] does often hurt for a few moments, but that passes and the rest is easy; so that the little

> hurt is nothing terrible, but all the same annoying if only for the sake of a few minutes' pleasure, which is not long enough. I do not know how my experience compares with other women's, but I feel sure that in my case the time needed is longer than usual, and the longer the better, always, with me. As to liking pain – no, I do not really like it, although I can tolerate pain very well, of any kind; but I like to feel force and strength; this is usual, I think, women being – or supposed to be – passive in love. I have not found that 'pain at once kills pleaure.

Again, another lady briefly states that, for her, pain has a mental fascination, and that such pain as she has had she has liked, but that, if it had been any stronger, pleasure would have been destroyed.

The evidence thus seems to point, with various shades of gradation, to the conclusion that the idea or even the reality of pain in sexual emotion is welcomed by women, provided that this element of pain is of small amount and subordinate to the pleasure which is to follow it. Unless coitus is fundamentally pleasure the element of pain must necessarily be unmitigated pain, and a craving for pain unassociated with a greater satisfaction to follow it cannot be regarded as normal.

In this connection I may refer to a suggestive chapter on 'The Enjoyment of Pain' in Hirn's *Origins of Art.*

> If we take into account the powerful stimulating effect which is produced by acute pain, we may easily understand why people submit to momentary unpleasantness for the sake of enjoying the subsequent excitement. This motive leads to the deliberate creation, not only of pain-sensations, but also of emotions in which pain enters as an element. The violent activity which is involved in the reaction against fear, and still more in that against anger, affords us a sensation of pleasurable excitement which is well worth the cost of the passing unpleasantness. It is, moreover, notorious that some persons have developed a peculiar art of making the initial pain of anger so transient that they can enjoy the active elements in it with almost undivided delight. Such an accomplishment is far more difficult in the case of sorrow. . . . The creation of pain-sensations may be explained as a desperate device for enhancing the intensity of the emotional state.

The relation of pain and pleasure to emotion has been thoroughly discussed, I may add, by H. R. Marshall in his *Pain, Pleasure, and*

Æsthetics. He contends that pleasure and pain are 'general qualities, one of which must, and either of which may, belong to any fixed element of consciousness'. 'Pleasure,' he considers, 'is experienced whenever the physical activity coincident with the psychic state to which the pleasure is attached involves the use of surplus stored force.' We can see, therefore, how, if pain acts as a stimulant to emotion, it becomes the servant of pleasure by supplying it with surplus stored force.

This problem of pain is thus one of psychic dynamics. If we realize this we shall begin to understand the place of cruelty in life. 'One ought to learn anew about cruelty,' said Nietzsche (*Beyond Good and Evil*, 229), 'and open one's eyes. Almost everything that we call "higher culture" is based upon the spiritualizing and intensifying of *cruelty*. . . . Then, to be sure, we must put aside teaching the blundering psychology of former times, which could only teach with regard to cruelty that it originated at the sight of the suffering of *others;* there is an abundant, superabundant enjoyment even in one's own suffering, in causing one's own suffering.' The element of paradox disappears from this statement if we realize that it is not a question of 'cruelty', but of the dynamics of pain.

Camille Bos in a suggestive essay (Du Plaisir de la Douleur, *Revue Philosophique*, July 1902) finds the explanation of the mystery in that complexity of the phenomena to which I have already referred. Both pain and pleasure are complex feelings, the resultant of various components, and we name that resultant in accordance with the nature of the strongest component. 'Thus we give to a complexus a name which strictly belongs only to one of its factors, *and in pain all is not painful*.' When pain becomes a desired end Camille Bos regards the desire as due to three causes: (1) the pain contrasts with and revives a pleasure which custom threatens to dull; (2) the pain by preceding the pleasure accentuates the positive character of the latter; (3) pain momentarily raises the lowered level of sensibility and restores to the organism for a brief period the faculty of enjoyment it had lost.

It must therefore be said that, in so far as pain is pleasurable, it is so only in so far as it is recognized as a prelude to pleasure, or else when it is an actual stimulus to the nerves conveying the sensation of pleasure. The nymphomaniac who experienced an orgasm at the moment when the knife passed through her clitoris (as recorded by Mantegazza) and the prostitute who experienced keen pleasure when the surgeon removed vegetations from her vulva (as recorded by Féré) took no pleasure in pain, but in one case the intense craving for strong sexual emotion, and in the other the long-blunted nerves of pleasure, welcomed the abnormally strong impulse; and the pain of the incision, if felt at all, was immediately swallowed up in the sensation of pleasure. Moll remarks (*Konträre Sexualempfindung*, third edition, p. 278) that even in man a trace of physical pain may be normally combined with sexual pleasure, when the vagina contracts on the penis at the moment of ejaculation, the pain, when not too severe, being almost immediately felt as pleasure. That there is no pleasure in the actual pain, even in masochism, is indicated by the following statement which Krafft-Ebing gives as representing the experiences of a masochist (*Psychopathia Sexualis*, English translation, p. 201):

> The relation is not of such a nature that what causes physical pain is simply perceived as physical pleasure, for the person in a state of masochistic ecstasy feels no pain, either because by reason of his emotional state (like that of the soldier in battle) the physical effect on his cutaneous nerves is not apperceived, or because (as with religious martyrs and enthusiasts) in the preoccupation of consciousness with sexual emotion the idea of maltreatment remains merely a symbol, without its quality of pain. To a certain extent there is over-compensation of physical pain in psychic pleasure, and only the excess remains in consciousness as psychic lust. This also undergoes an increase, since, either through reflex spinal influence or through a peculiar coloring in the sensorium of sensory impressions, a kind of hallucination of bodily pleasure takes place, with a vague localization of the objectively projected sensation. In the self-torture of religious enthusiasts (fakirs, howling dervishes, religious flagellants) there is an analogous state, only with a difference in the quality of pleasurable feeling. Here the conception of martyrdom is also apperceived without its pain, for consciousness is filled with the pleasurably colored idea of serving God, atoning for sins, deserving Heaven, etc., through martyrdom.

This statement cannot be said to clear up the matter entirely; but it is fairly evident that, when a woman says that she finds pleasure in the pain inflicted by a lover, she means that under the special circumstances she finds pleasure in treatment which would at other times be felt as pain, or else that the slight real pain experienced is so quickly followed by overwhelming pleasure that in memory the pain itself seems to have been pleasure and may even be regarded as the symbol of pleasure.

There is a special peculiarity of physical pain, which may be well borne in mind in considering the phenomena now before us, for it helps to account for the tolerance with which the idea of pain is regarded. I refer to the great ease with which physical pain is forgotten, a fact well known to all mothers, or to all who have been present at the birth of a child. As Professor von Tschisch points out ('Der Schmerz', *Zeitschrift für Psychologie und Physiologie der Sinnesorgane*, Bd. xxvi, ht. 1 and 2, 1901), memory can only preserve impressions as a whole; physical pain consists of a sensation and of a feeling. But memory cannot easily reproduce the definite sensation of the pain, and thus the whole memory is disintegrated and speedily forgotten. It is quite otherwise with moral suffering, which persists in memory and has far more influence on conduct. No one wishes to suffer moral pain or has any pleasure even in the idea of suffering it.

It is the presence of this essential tendency which leads to a certain apparent contradiction in a woman's emotions. On the one hand, rooted in the maternal instinct, we find pity, tenderness, and compassion; on the other hand, rooted in the sexual instinct, we find a delight in roughness, violence, pain, and danger, sometimes in herself, sometimes also in others. The one impulse craves something innocent and helpless, to cherish and protect; the other delights in the spectacle of recklessness, audacity, sometimes even effrontery.[12] A woman is not perfectly happy in her lover unless he can give at least some satisfaction to each of these two opposite longings.

The psychological satisfaction which women tend to feel in a certain degree of pain in love is strictly co-ordinated with a physical fact. Women possess a minor degree of sensibility in the sexual region. This fact must not be misunderstood. On the one hand, it by no means begs the question as to whether women's sensibility generally is greater or less than that of men; this is a disputed question and the evidence is still somewhat conflicing. On the other hand, it also by no means involves a less degree of specific sexual pleasure in women, for the tactile sensibility of the sexual organs is no index to the specific sexual sensibility of those organs when in a state of tumuscence. The real significance of the less tactile sensibility of the genital region in women is to be found in parturition and the special liability of the sexual region in women to injury. The women who are less sensitive in this respect would be better able and more willing to endure the risks of childbirth, and would therefore tend to supplant those who were more sensitive. But, as a by-product of this less degree of sensibility, we have a condition in which physical irritation amounting even to pain may become to normal women in the state of extreme tumescence a source of pleasurable excitement, such as it would rarely be to normal men.

To Calmann appear to be due the first carefully made observations showing the minor sensibility of the genital tract in women. (Adolf Calmann, 'Sensibilitätsprufungen am weiblicken Genitale nach forensichen Gesichtspunkten', *Archiv für Gynäkologie*, 1898, p. 454.) He investigated the vagina, urethra, and anus in eighteen women and found a great lack of sensibility, least marked in anus, and most marked in vagina. (This distribution of the insensitiveness alone indicates that it is due, as I have suggested, to natural selection.) Sometimes a finger in the vagina could not be felt at all. One woman, when a catheter was introduced into the anus, said it might be the vagina or urethra, but was certainly not the anus. (Calmann remarks that he was careful to put his questions in an intelligible form.) The women were only conscious of the urine being drawn off when they heard the familiar sound of the stream or when the bladder was very full; if the sound of the stream was deadened by a towel they were quite unconscious that the bladder had been emptied. (In confirmation of this statement I have noticed that in a lady whose distended bladder it was necessary to empty by the catheter shortly before the birth of her first child – but who had, indeed, been partly under the influence of chloroform – there was no consciousness of the artificial relief; she merely remarked that she thought she could now relieve herself.) There was some sense of temperature, but sense of locality, tactile sense, and judgment of size were often widely erroneous. It is significant that virgins were just as insensitive as married women or those who had had children. Calmann's experiments appear to be confirmed by the experiments of Marco Treves, of Turin, on the thermoesthesiometry of mucous membranes, as reported to the Turin International Congress of Physiology (and briefly noted in *Nature*, 21 November 1901). Treves found that the sensitivity of mucous membranes is always less than that of the skin. The mucosa of the urethra and of the cervix uteri was quite incapable of heat and cold sensations, and even the cautery excited only slight, and that painful, sensation.

In further illustration of this point reference may be made to the not infrequent cases in which the whole process of parturition and the enormous distention of tissues which it involves proceed throughout in an almost or quite painless manner. It is sufficient to refer to two cases reported in Paris by Macé and briefly summarized in the *British Medical Journal*, 25 May 1901. In the first the patient was a primipara 20 years of age, and, until the dilation of the cervix was complete and efforts at expulsion had commenced, the uterine contractions were quite painless. In the second case, the mother, aged 25, a tripara, had previously had very rapid labors; she awoke in the middle of the night without pains, but during micturition the fetal head appeared at the vulva, and was soon born.

Further illustration may be found in those cases in which severe inflammatory processes may take place in the genital canal without being noticed. Thus, Maxwell reports the case of a young Chinese woman, certainly quite normal, in whom after the birth of her first child the vagina became almost obliterated, yet beyond slight occasional pain she noticed nothing wrong until the husband found that penetration was impossible (*British Medical Journal*, 11 January 1902, p. 78). The insensitiveness of the vagina and its contrast, in this respect, with the penis – though we are justified in regarding the penis as being, like organs of special sense, relatively deficient in general sensibility – are vividly presented in such an incident as the following, reported a few years ago in America by Dr G. W. Allen in the *Boston Medical and Surgical Journal:* A man came under observation with an edematous, inflamed penis. The wife, the night previous, on advice of friends, had injected pure carbolic acid into the vagina just previous to coitus. The husband, ignorant of the fact, experienced untoward burning and smarting during and after coitus, but thought little of it, and soon fell asleep. The next morning there were large blisters on the penis, but it was no longer painful. When seen by Dr Allen the prepuce was retracted and edematous, the whole penis was much swollen, and there were large, perfectly raw surfaces on either side of the glans.

In this connection we may well bring into line a remarkable group of phenomena concerning which much evidence has now accumulated. I refer to the use of various appliances, fixed in or around the penis, whether permanently or temporarily during coitus, such appliance being employed at the woman's instigation and solely in order to heighten her excitement in congress. These appliances have their great center among the Indonesian peoples (in Borneo, Java, Sumatra, the Malay peninsula, the Philippines, etc.), thence extending in a modified form through China, to become, it appears, considerably prevalent in Russia; I have also a note of their appearance in India. They have another widely diffused center, through which however, they are more sparsely scattered, among the American Indians of the northern and more especially of the southern continents. Amerigo Vespucci and other early travelers noted the existence of some of these appliances, and since Miklucho-Macleay carefully described them as used in Borneo their existence has been generally recognized. They are usually regarded merely as ethnological curiosities. As such they would not concern us here. Their real significance for us is that they illustrate the comparative insensitiveness of the genital canal in women, while at the same time they show that a certain amount of what we cannot but regard as painful stimulation is craved by women, in order to heighten tumescence and increase sexual pleasure, even though it can only be procured by artificial methods. It is, of course, possible to argue that in these cases we are not concerned with pain at all, but with a strong stimulation that is felt as purely pleasurable. There can be no doubt, however, that in the absence of sexual excitement this stimulation would be felt as purely painful, and – in the light of our previous discussion – we may, perhaps, fairly regard it as a painful stimulation which is craved, not because it is itself pleasurable, but because it heightens the highly pleasurable state of tumescence.

Borneo, the geographical center of the Indonesian world, appears also to be the district in which these instruments are most popular. The *ampallang, palang, kambion*, or *sprit-sail yard*, as it is variously termed, is a little rod of bone or metal nearly two inches in length, rounded at the ends, and used by the Kyans and Dyaks of Borneo. Before coitus it is inserted into a transverse orifice in the penis, made by a painful and somewhat dangerous operation and kept open by a quill. Two or more of these instruments are occasionally worn. Sometimes little brushes are attached to each end of the instrument. Another instrument, used by the Dyaks, but said to have been borrowed from the Malays, is the *palang anus*, which is a ring or collar of plaited palm-fiber, furnished with a pair of stiffish horns of the same wiry material; it is worn on the neck of the glans and fits tight to the skin so as not to slip off. (Brooke Low, 'The Natives of Borneo', *Journal of the Anthropological Institute*, August and November 1892, p. 45; the *ampallang* and similar instruments are described by Ploss and Bartels, *Das Weib*, Bd. i, chapter xvii; also in *Untrodden Fields of Anthropology*, by a French army surgeon, 1898, vol. ii, pp. 135–41; also Mantegazza, *Gli Amori degli Uomini*, French translation, p. 83 *et seq.*) Riedel informed Miklucho-Macleay that in the Celebes the Alfurus fasten the eyelids of goats with the eyelashes round the corona of the glans penis, and in Java a piece of goatskin is used in a similar way, so as to form a hairy sheath (*Zeitschrift für Ethnologie*, 1876, pp. 22–5), while among the Batta, of Sumatra, Hagen found that small stones are inserted by an incision under the skin of the penis (*Zeitschrift für Ethnologie*, 1891, ht. 3, p. 351).

In the Malay peninsula Stevens found instruments somewhat similar to the *ampallang* still in use among some tribes, and among others formerly in use. He thinks they were brought from Borneo. (H. V. Stevens, *Zeitschrift für Ethnologie*, 1896, ht. 4, p. 181.) Bloch, who brings forward other examples of similar devices (*Beiträge zur Aetiologie der Psychopathia Sexualis*, pp. 56–8), considers that the Australian mica operation may thus in part be explained.

Such instruments are not, however, entirely unknown in Europe. In France, in the eighteenth century, it appears that rings, sometimes set with hard knobs, and called 'aides', were occasionally used by men to heighten the pleasure of women in intercourse. (Dühren, *Marquis de Sade*, 1901, p. 130.) In Russia, according to Weissenberg, of Elizabethsgrad, it is not uncommon to use elastic rings set with little teeth; these rings are fastened around the base of the glans. (Weissenberg, *Zeitschrift für Ethnologie*, 1893, ht. 2, p. 135.) This instrument must have been brought to Russia from the East, for Burton (in the notes to his *Arabian Nights*) mentions a precisely similar instrument as in use in China. Somewhat similar is the 'Chinese hedgehog', a wreath of fine, soft feathers with the quills solidly fastened by silver wire to a ring of the same metal, which is slipped over the glans. In South America the Araucanians of Argentina use a little horsehair brush fastened around the penis; one of these is in the museum at La Plata; it is said the custom may have been borrowed from the Patagonians; these instruments, called *geskels*, are made by the women and the workmanship is very delicate. (Lehmann-Nitsche, *Zeitschrift für Ethnologie*, 1900, ht. 6, p. 491.) It is noteworthy that a somewhat similar tuft of horse-hair is also worn in Borneo. (Breitenstein, *21 Jahr in India*, 1899, pt. i, p. 227.) Most of the accounts state that the women attach great importance to the gratification afforded by such instruments. In Borneo a modest woman symbolically indicates to her lover the exact length of the ampallang she would prefer by leaving at a particular spot a cigarette of that length. Miklucho-Macleay considers that these instruments were invented by women. Brooke Low remarks that 'no woman once habituated to its use will ever dream of permitting her bedfellow to discontinue the practice of wearing it,' and Stevens states that at one time no woman would marry a man who was not furnished with such an apparatus. It may be added that a very similar appliance may be found in European countries (especially Germany) in the use of a condom furnished with irregularities, or a frill, in order to increase the woman's excitement. It is not impossible to find evidence that, in European countries, even in the absence of such instruments, the craving which they gratify still exists in women. Thus, Mauriac tells of a patient with vegetations on the glans who delayed treatment because his mistress liked him so best (art. 'Végétations', *Dictionnaire de Médecine et Chirurgie pratique*).

It may seem that such impulses and such devices to gratify them are altogether unnatural. This is not so. They have a zoological basis and in many animals are embodied in the anatomical structure. Many rodents, ruminants, and some of the carnivora show natural developments of the penis closely resembling some of those artificially adopted by man. Thus the guinea-pigs possess two horny styles attached to the penis, while the glans of the penis is covered with sharp spines. Some of the Caviidæ also have two sharp, horny saws at the side of the penis. The cat, the rhinoceros, the tapir, and other animals possess projecting structures on the penis, and some species of ruminants, such as the sheep, the giraffe, and many antelopes, have, attached to the penis, long filiform processes through which the urethra passes. (F. H. A. Marshall *The Physiology of Reproduction*, pp. 246–8.)

We find, even in creatures so delicate and ethereal as the butterflies, a whole armory of keen weapons for use in coitus. These were described in detail in an elaborate and fully illustrated memoir by P. H. Gosse ('On the Clasping Organs Ancillary to Generation in Certain Groups of the Lepidoptera', *Transactions of the Linnæan Society*, second series, vol. ii, Zoology, 1882). These organs, which Gosse terms *harpes* (or grappling irons), are found in the Papilionidæ and are very beautiful and varied, taking the forms of projecting claws, hooks, pikes, swords, knobs, and strange combinations of these, commonly brought to a keen edge and then cut into sharp teeth.

It is probable that all these structures serve to excite the sexual apparatus of the female and the promote tumescence.

To the careless observer there may seem to be something visious or perverted in such manifestations in man. That opinion becomes very doubtful when we consider how these tendencies occur in people living under natural conditions in widely separated parts of the world. It becomes still further untenable if we are justified in believing that the ancestors of men possessed projecting epithelial appendages attached to the penis, and if we accept the discovery by Friedenthal of the rudiment of these appendages on the penis of the human fetus at an early stage (Friedenthal, 'Sonderformen der menschlichen Leibesbildung', *Sexual-Problems*, Feb. 1912, p. 129). In this case human ingenuity would merely be seeking to supply an organ which nature has ceased to furnish, although it is still in some cases needed, especially among peoples whose aptitude for erethism has remained at, or fallen to, a subhuman level.

At first sight the connection between love and pain – the tendency of men to delight in inflicting it and women in suffering it – seems strange and inexplicable. It seems amazing that a tender and even independent woman should maintain a passionate attachment to a man who subjects her to physical and moral insults, and that a strong man, often intelligent, reasonable, and even kind-hearted, should desire to subject to such insults a woman whom he loves passionately and who has given him every final proof of her own passion. In understanding such cases we have to remember that it is only within limits that a woman really enjoys the pain, discomfort, or subjection to which she submits. A little pain which the man knows he can himself soothe, a little pain which the woman gladly accepts as the sign and forerunner of pleasure – this degree of pain comes within the normal limits of love and is rooted, as we have seen, in the experience of the race. But when it is carried beyond these limits, though it may still be tolerated because of the support it receives from its biological basis, it is no longer enjoyed. The natural note has been too violently struck, and the rhythm of love has ceased to be perfect. A woman may desire to be forced, to be roughly forced, to be ravished away beyond her own will. But all the time she only desires to be forced toward those things which are essentially and profoundly agreeable to her. A man who fails to realize this has made little progress in the art of love. 'I like being knocked about and made to do things I don't want to do,' a woman said, but she admitted, on being questioned, that she would not like to have *much* pain inflicted, and that she might not care to be made to do important things she did not want to do. The story of Griselda's unbounded submissiveness can scarcely be said to be psychologically right, though it has its artistic rightness as an elaborate fantasia on this theme justified by its conclusion.

This point is further illustrated by the following passage from a letter written by a lady:

> Submission to the man's will is still, and always must be, the prelude to pleasure, and the association of ideas will probably always produce this much misunderstood instinct. Now, I find, indirectly from other women and directly from my own experience, that, when the point in dispute is very important and the man exerts his authority, the desire to get one's own way completely obliterates the sexual feeling, while, conversely, in small things the sexual feeling obliterates the desire to have one's own way. Where the two are nearly equal a conflict between them ensues, and I can stand aside and wonder which will get the best of it, though I

encourage the sexual feeling when possible, as, if the other conquers, it leaves a sense of great mental irritation and physical discomfort. A man should command in small things, as in nine cases out of ten this will produce excitement. He should *advise* in large matters, or he may find either that he is unable to enforce his orders or that he produces a feeling of dislike and annoyance he was far from intending. Women imagine men must be stronger than themselves to excite their passion. I disagree. A passionate man has the best chance, for in him the primitive instincts are strong. The wish to subdue the female is one of them, and in small things he will exert his authority to make her feel his power, while she knows that on a question of real importance she has a good chance of getting her own way by working on his greater susceptibility. Perhaps an illustration will show what I mean. I was listening to the band and a girl and her *fiancé* came up to occupy two seats near me. The girl sank into one seat, but for some reason the man wished her to take the other. She refused. He repeated his order twice, the second time so peremptorily that she changed places, and I heard him say: 'I don't think you heard what I said. I don't expect to give an order three times.'

This little scene interested me, and I afterward asked the girl the following questions:

'Had you any reason for taking one chair more than the other?'

'No.'

'Did Mr – 's insistence on your changing give you any pleasure?'

'Yes' (after a little hesitation).

'Why?'

'I don't know.'

'Would it have done so if you had particularly wished to sit in that chair; if, for instance, you had had a boil on your cheek and wished to turn that side away from him?'

'No; certainly not. The worry of thinking he was looking at it would have made me too cross to feel pleased.'

Does this explain what I mean? The occasion, by the way, need not be really important, but, as in this imaginary case of the boil, if it *seems important* to the woman, irritation will outweigh the physical sensation.

I am well aware that in thus asserting a certain tendency in women to delight in suffering pain – however careful and qualified the position I have taken – many estimable people will cry out that I am degrading a whole sex and generally supporting the 'subjection of women'. But the day for academic discussion concerning the 'subjection of women' has gone by. The tendency I have sought to make clear is too well established by the experience of normal and typical women – however numerous the exceptions may be – to be called in question. I would point out to those who would deprecate the influence of such facts in relation to social progress that nothing is gained by regarding women as simply men of smaller growth. They are not so; they have the laws of their own nature; their development must be along their own lines, and not along masculine lines. It is as true now as in Bacon's day that we only learn to command nature by obeying her. To ignore facts is to court disappointment in our measure of progress. The particular fact with which we have here come in contact is very vital and radical, and most subtle in its influence. It is foolish to ignore it; we must allow for its existence. We can neither attain a sane view of life nor a sane social legislation of life unless we possess a just and accurage knowledge of the fundamental instincts upon which life is built.

NOTES

1 Various mammals, carried away by the reckless fury of the sexual impulse, are apt to ill-treat their females (R. Müller, *Sexualbiologie*, p. 123). This treatment is, however, usually only an incident of courtship, the result of excess of ardor. 'The chaffinches and saffron-finches (*Fringella* and *Sycalis*) are very rough wooers,' says A. G. Butler (*Zoologist*, 1902, p. 241); 'they sing vociferously, and chase their hens violently, knocking them over in their flight, pursuing and savagely pecking them even on the ground; but when once the hens become submissive, the males change their tactics, and become for the time model husbands, feeding their wives from their crop, and assisting in rearing the young.'

2 Marro considers that there may be transference of emotion – the impulse of violence generated in the male by his rivals being turned against his partner – according to a tendency noted by Sully and illustrated by Ribot in his *Psychology of the Emotions*, part i, chapter xii.

3 Several writers have found in the facts of primitive animal courtship the explanation of the connection between love and pain. Thus, Krafft-Ebing (*Psychopathia Sexualis*, English translation of tenth German edition, p. 80) briefly notes that outbreaks of sadism are possibly atavistic. Marro (*La Pubertà*, 1898, p. 219 *et seq.*) has some suggestive pages on this subject. It would appear that this explanation was vaguely outlined by Jäger. Laserre, in a Bordeaux thesis mentioned by Féré,

has argued in the same sense. Féré (*L'Instinct Sexuel*, p. 134), on grounds that are scarcely sufficient, regards this explanation as merely a superficial analogy. But it is certainly not a complete explanation.

4 Schäfer (*Jahrbücher für Psychologie*, Bd. ii, p. 128, and quoted by Drafft-Ebing in *Psychopathia Sexualis*), in connection with a case in which sexual excitement was produced by the sight of battles or of paintings of them remarks:

> The pleasure of battle and murder is so predominantly an attribute of the male sex throughout the animal kingdom that there can be no question about the close connection between this side of the masculine character and male sexuality. I believe that I can show by observation that in men who are absolutely normal, mentally and physically, the first indefinite and incomprehensible precursors of sexual excitement may be induced by reading exciting scenes of chase and war. These give rise to unconscious longings for a kind of satisfaction in warlike games (wrestling, etc.) which express the fundamental sexual impulse to close and complete contact with a companion, with a secondary more or less clearly defined thought of conquest.

Groos (*Spiele der Menschen*, 1899, p. 232) also thinks there is more or less truth in this suggestion of a subconscious sexual element in the playful wrestling combats of boys. Freud considers (*Drei Abhandlungen zur Sexualtheorie*, p. 49) that the tendency to sexual excitement through muscular activity in wrestling, etc., is one of the roots of sadism. I have been told of normal men who feel a conscious pleasure of this kind when lifted in games, as may happen, for instance, in football. It may be added that in some parts of the world the suitor has to throw the girl in a wrestling-bout in order to secure her hand.

5 A minor manifestation of this tendency, appearing even in quite normal and well-conditioned individuals, is the impulse among boys at and after puberty to take pleasure in persecuting and hurting lower animals or their own young companions. Some youths display a diabolical enjoyment and ingenuity in torturing sensitive juniors, and even a boy who is otherwise kindly and considerate may find enjoyment in deliberately mutilating a frog. In some cases, in boys and youths who have no true sadistic impulse and are not usually cruel, this infliction of torture on a lower animal produces an erection, though not necessarily any pleasant sexual sensations.

6 Marro, *La Pubertà*, 1898, p. 223; Garnier, 'La Criminalité Juvenile', *Comptes-rendus Congrès Internationale d'Anthropologie Criminelle*, Amsterdam, 1901, p. 296; *Archivio di Psichiatria*, 1899, fasc, v-vi, p. 572.

7 Westermarck, *Human Marriage*, p. 388. Grosse is of the same opinion; he considers also that the mock-capture is often an imitation, due to admiration, of real capture; he does not believe that the latter has ever been a form of marriage recognized by custom and law, but only 'an

occasional and punishable act of violence.' (*Die Formen der Familie*, pp. 105–7.) This position is too extreme.

8 Ernest Crawley, *The Mystic Rose*, 1902, p. 350 *et seq.* Van Gennep rightly remarks that we cannot correctly say that the woman is abducted from 'her sex', but only from her 'sexual society'.

9 Féré (*L'Instinct Sexuel*, p. 133) appears to regard the satisfaction, based on the sentiment of personal power, which may be experienced in the suffering and subjection of a victim as an adequate explanation of the association of pain with love. This I can scarcely admit. It is a factor in the emotional attitude, but when it only exists in the sexual sphere it is reasonable to base this attitude largely on the still more fundamental biological attitude of the male toward the female in the process of courtship. Féré regards this biological element as merely a superficial analogy, on the ground that an act of cruelty may become an equivalent of coitus. But a sexual perversion is quite commonly constituted by the selection and magnification of a single moment in the normal sexual process.

10 The process may, however, be quite conscious. Thus, a correspondent tells me that he not only finds sexual pleasure in cruelty toward the woman he loves, but that he regards this as an essential element. He is convinced that it gives the woman pleasure, and that it is possible to distinguish by gesture, inflection of voice, etc. and hysterical, assumed, or imagined feeling of pain from real pain. He would not wish to give real pain, and would regard that as sadism.

11 De Sade has already made the same remark, while Duchenne, of Boulogne, pointed out that the facial expressions of sexual passion and of cruelty are similar.

12 De Stendhal (*De l'Amour*) mentions that when in London he was on terms of friendship with an English actress who was the mistress of a wealthy colonel, but privately had another lover. One day the colonel arrived when the other man was present. 'This gentleman has called about the pony I want to sell,' said the actress. 'I have come for a very different purpose,' said the little man, and thus aroused a love which was beginning to languish.

Margaret Sanger

Family Limitation

(1914)

Introduction

Birth Control or family limitation has been recommended by some of the leading physicians of the United States and of Europe. While the medical profession as a whole has not yet taken a united stand upon the subject, we know that the practice of birth control has already been incorporated into the private moral code of millions of the most intelligent and respected families in every country.

There is little doubt but that its general practice among married persons will shortly win full acceptation and sanction by public authorities, who will encourage the practice among the diseased and unfit and help to direct the movement into its proper channels.

In cases of women suffering from serious ailments, such as Bright's disease, heart disease, or tuberculosis the physician usually warns the woman to guard herself against pregnancy. It is an established fact that two-thirds of the women who die from the above named diseases do so because they have become pregnant. Therefore, it is imperative that physicians should not only warn women suffering from these diseases against pregnancy, but they should see that they are properly instructed in methods to prevent conception. Such responsibility on the part of physicians would reduce the maternal mortality of the world tremendously.

While the above-named diseases are not considered transmissible from the mother to the child, there are certain other diseases and conditions such as insanity, syphilis, idiocy and feeble-mindedness which are passed to the next generation.

When either the man or the woman is afflicted with any one of these diseases, it is absolutely wrong to allow a child to be born. In such cases the man or the woman should be sterilised.

The patient should understand that such an operation does not deprive him or her of sexual desire or expression. It simply renders the patient incapable of producing children.

To conserve the lives of mothers and to prevent the birth of diseased or defective children are objects for which we need a sound educational campaign for Birth Control.

We hold that children should be:

1 Conceived in love.
2 Born of the mother's conscious desire.
3 And only begotten under conditions which render possible the heritage of health.

We want parents to be conscious of their responsibility to the race in bringing children into the world. Instead of being a blind and haphazard consequence of uncontrolled instinct, parenthood must be made the responsible and self-directed means of human expression and regeneration.

To the working woman

The need for safe practical information of birth control is more urgent today among women that it has ever been before.

The working man and woman have begun to realise the difficulty of supporting a family of eight or ten children on a wage scarcely sufficient to decently keep two or three. They have begun also to realise that no increase of wages, obtained through long days of toil or through strikes or lock-outs, can keep pace with the increased cost of living or the cost of an ever-increasing family.

It is the big battalions of unwanted babies that make life so hard for the wife of the working man. It is the ever-increasing number of children, coming year after year into her life, that perpetuates poverty and misery and ignorance from generation to generation.

The working mother knows through her natural instinct that she should not have more children than her husband's wages can support, yet she does not know what she can do to prevent conception. When she asks her friends or neighbours for advice, she is given remedies, usually unscientific, unauthoritative and unreliable, which her experience or knowledge warns her may be injurious.

So she is thrust back upon the possibility of taking drugs for producing abortion, or resigning herself to all the children nature will give her, which can mean from ten to twenty in one woman's lifetime.

These women resent the fact that the educated women are able to obtain safe, scientific, harmless information of birth control, while Society condemns its use among the working women. Present-day Society is generous in doling out pittances for the unfit and diseased, thus encouraging their multiplication and perpetuation, while it prevents and discourages the use of scientific knowledge which would enable women to avoid bringing into the world children they cannot feed, clothe, or care for.

I give herewith the knowledge obtained through study and through more than fourteen years' experience as a trained nurse in USA.

My own experience as a mother of three children has modified some of the advice given in books.

It is my intention to present the facts to the reader in the simplest language, leaving out dogmas or religious accompaniment.

While there are various mechanical instruments often used to prevent conception, I will not give them here, because my experience has taught me that they are likely to cause irritation and trouble to the woman. There is sufficient information given here, which, if followed, will prevent a woman from becoming pregnant unless she wishes to do so. It must not be forgotten that the best results can be obtained only when the woman will see that, in every case, she follows directions. She must not get careless even once, for it needs only one union in twelve months, unprotected, to give a woman a baby each year. Therefore, to protect herself from pregnancy the woman must use care constantly.

While it may be troublesome to get up to douche, and a nuisance to have to watch the date of the menstrual period, and to some it may seem sordid and inartistic to insert a pessary or a suppository in anticipation of the sexual act, it may be far more sordid and the condition far worse than inartistic a few years later for the mother to find herself burdened down with half a dozen 'accidental' children, unwanted, helpless, shoddily clothed, sometimes starved or under-nourished, dragging at her skirt, while she becomes a worn-out shadow of the woman she once was.

It takes but a few years of continued pregnancies to break a woman's health. The drain on the family income is continually increasing and the standard of the whole family is lowered.

Mothers – do not be over-sentimental in this important phase of hygience. Learn the facts of pregnancy. The inevitable fact is that, unless you prevent the male sperm from entering the womb, you are liable to become pregnant.

Women of the working class should not have more than two children today. The conditions of society do not render possible the proper care of more than this number. The average wage-earner can take care of no more than this in decent fashion.

It has been my experience that women desire only the number of children they can properly care for, but that they are compelled to have them from carelessness, or through ignorance of the methods to prevent conception.

It is only the workers who are ignorant of the means to prevent bringing children into the world. It is also mainly their children who fill the child labour records, the factories, mills, jails, hospitals, poor-houses. It is the workers' children who compete with their parents in the labour market for their daily bread, thereby reducing the wages of the parents – an inevitable consequence when the supply is greather than the demand.

Women of the world arise – let us close the gates of our bodies against the diseased, the unfit, and bring to birth only the best, as we know it, which should be at least, a child with a sound body and a sound mind.

Is there a safe period?

There is current among people an idea that conception does not take place at certain times of the month. For instance: the interval between ten days after the menstrual period, and four or five days before the next period. This is not to be relied upon at all, for it has been proven again and again that some women conceive at any time in the month. Do not depend upon this belief, for there is no scientific foundation for it. There is also the knowledge that nursing, after child-birth, prevents the return of the menstrual flow for several months and conception does not take place. It is well not to depend upon this too much, especially after the fifth month, for often a woman conceives again without having 'seen anything', or without her realising that she has become pregnant. She thus finds herself with one at the breast and another in the womb. Use some preventive.

Coitus interruptus

Perhaps the most commonly used preventive, excepting the use of the condom, is 'Coitus Interruptus' or withdrawal of the penis from the vagina shortly before the ejection of the semen. No one can doubt that in theory this should be a perfectly safe method; and we also find authorities who claim it is not injurious to the man, but who object to it on the grounds of lack of satisfaction to the woman.

The claim is that if she has not completed her desire, she is under a highly nervous tension, her whole being is perhaps on the verge of satisfaction and she is left in a dissatisfied state. This, without doubt, does her injury. A mutual and satisfied sexual act is of great benefit to the average woman, the magnetism of it is health-giving.

When it is not desired on the part of the woman and she gives no response, it should not take place. The submission of her body without love or desire is degrading to the woman's finer sensibility, all the marriage certificates on earth to the contrary notwithstanding.

During several years past, however, I have come in contact with thousands of men and women who have given me their confidence and experience along these lines. The consensus of experience seems to be that there are many men who prefer to practise the method of withdrawal and have been able to control the ejaculation until after the woman's orgasm. If this is done all objections affecting the woman's satisfaction are of course removed. But the fact remains that even in such cases, with the strongest control on the part of the man, we find that pregnancy does take place. This is often due to some slight disposition on the part of the man to a seminal leakage, in which the spermatazoa escape from the male organs without the man's knowledge and before the ejaculation.

A woman physician examined a vaginal passage and found sperm deposits when absolutely no ejaculation had taken place. The results of these inquiries are sufficient for us to say that the practice of withdrawal cannot always be counted upon as a safe preventive.

Again, while in the quest of information regarding this practice, I have had many men say that their nervous system had suffered decidedly bad effects from this method, and upon using another, at once an improved condition was felt.

Here we see how very individual all methods of birth control really are. What may give happiness and good results to one may prove injurious to another. But coitus interruptus, or withdrawal, is by no means to be counted upon as either the safest or the best method of preventing conception. There are other methods more to be recommended.

Douche a cleanser – not a preventive

Although an antiseptic douche is an important factor in preventing conception, it should not be relied upon as a preventive measure in itself. A douche is a cleanser, but it is not of itself to be advised as a reliable method to prevent conception. When one understands how conception takes place, it can be seen at once that it is quite possible for a woman to be in a state of pregnancy before she leaves the bed, or before she can reach a douche, unless the womb has been previously covered with the rubber pessary, or by the ingredients of a suppository.

Nevertheless, every woman should learn to cleanse herself thoroughly by means of the vaginal douche. Some women object to the use of the suppository because of its lubricant effect; this can be modified greatly by the use of a warm salt douche, taken just previously to inserting the suppository, cleansing the parts thoroughly of any secretion already there.

Every woman should posses a good two-quart douche bag, called a fountain syringe. Hang it high enough to secure a good, strong steady flow.

Bulb syringes, such as the whirling spray syringes have been found satisfactory by many women for the purpose, especially where there is no bathroom or toilet conveniences, as the bulb syringe can easily be used in the privacy of one's bedroom over a vessel. Directions for use come with each syringe.

How to take a douche

If you have bathing conveniences, go as quickly as possible to the bathroom after the sexual act and prepare a douche. Lie down upon the back in the bath tub. Hang the filled douche bag high over the tub, and let the water flow freely into the vagina, to wash out the male sperm which was deposited during the act.

Do not be afraid to assist the cleansing by introducing the first finger with the tube and washing out the semen from the folds of the membrane. One can soon learn to tell by the feeling when it is sufficiently clean. It is said, that the French women are the most thorough douchers in the world, which helps greatly in keeping the organs in a clean and healthy condition, as well as preventing the male sperm from reaching the womb to mate with the ovum.

When there are no bathroom conveniences – a douche can be taken over the toilet, or when that is impossible, it can be taken over a vessel in a squatting position.

Douches

Many women have been advised by physicians to use an antiseptic douche as a means to prevent conception. I do not advise any woman, who desires to avoid pregnancy, to rely upon a douche for a contraceptive. I wish to emphasise again that a douche used alone is not a contraceptive, because the germ from the male may already have entered the mouth of the womb before a woman can use a douche. Therefore it is absolutely necessary that some method be used to cover the womb.

A douche is a cleanser. It is a means of hygiene rather than a preventive. Do not depend upon a douche to prevent conception. Some women have been successful in using this for many years, and then later on, to their surprise, find that pregnancy has occurred. The explanation is as follows:

When the womb is placed high out of the vagina it is not so easy for the germ from the man to reach directly into the womb. In such cases it is possible for a woman to get up and prepare a douche before the germ from the male enters the womb. There are times, however, when a woman has been standing on her feet, washing or ironing or working, and becomes overtired. At such times the womb is pulled or dragged down into the canal of the vagina. At such times, if intercourse takes place, it is much easier for the seed from the male to enter directly into the womb, unless there is some protection. It is at such times that a woman who has previously depended upon a douche as a preventive finds it has failed.

My advice is – never depend upon a douche alone. It should be used after the use of a suppository or any other preventive.

Cold water douches are not advised, as there is a tendency to chill and shock the nervous system. A warm or moderate douche is advised.

Warm soapsuds as a douche are used by women in France in

the rural districts, just plain common soap, as a cleansing douche after the act.

Solutions for douching

Following are some of the solutions to be used for the douche which, when carefully used, will kill the male sperm or prevent its entering the womb:

Cresol is said to be the equivalent chemically of lysol and is likely to be obtained at a lower cost. Directions are much the same as those for the use of lysol.

Salt solution – Mix four tablespoons of table salt in one quart of warm water and dissolve thoroughly. This is good, and cheap.

Vinegar solution – Many peasants in Europe use vinegar as an antiseptic almost exclusively. One glassful to two quarts of water is the strength usually desired. Douche afterwards with clear water.

Acetic acid being the sperm-killing agent in vinegar, may also be used and with the certainty of more uniformity than can be depended upon in the various grades of vinegar. A good solution is one and a half teaspoonfuls of 36 per cent acetic acid to two quarts of warm water.

Plain water douche – This will sometimes remove the semen quite effectively without the aid of an antiseptic. But as the semen can hide itself away in the wrinkled lining of the vaginal cavity, the plain water will only impede its progress for a time. Some ingredient which will kill the sperm is to be more relied upon.

Some women use the douche before the sexual act as a preventive. If this is done, any astringent such as boric acid, alum, hydrochlorate of quinine used in the solution will do. Only a pint of solution is needed for this purpose, following the act a larger douche is used as a cleanser. This can also be done with the regular antiseptic douche.

The use of the condom or 'sheath'

These are made of soft tissues which envelope the male organ (penis) completely and serve to catch the semen at the time of the act. In this way the sperm does not enter the vagina nor the womb.

The condoms are obtainable at all drug stores at various prices. There are some of skin gut and some of rubber tissue. While the rubber condom is best known, there is found to be least objection to the use of those made of soft skin gut. The skin condom is made more durable and more agreeable to use, if kept in denatured alcohol. Alcohol sterilises and toughens the membrane. The condom should be washed before and after putting it into the jar of alcohol and should be kept tightly corked. It is almost impossible to keep skin condoms satisfactorily if they are dried. If properly adjusted they will not break. Fear of breaking is the main objection to their use. If space has not been allowed for expansion of the penis, at the time the semen is expelled, the tissue is likely to split and the sperm finds its way into the uterus. The woman becomes pregnant without being conscious of it. If on the other hand care is given to the adjustment of the condom, not fitting it too close, it will act as a protector against both conception and veneral disease. Care must be exercised in withdrawing the penis after the act, not to allow the condom to peel off, thereby allowing the semen to pass into the vagina.

It is desirable to discard the condom after it has been used once unless with certain precautions. If it is to be used again care must be taken to wash the condom in an antiseptic solution before drying it and placing it away for further use. A weak solution of lysol is excellent for the rubber condom.

The condom should be well lubricated with oil before penetration. It should always be tested for holes or breaks before using.

The condom is one of the most commonly known preventives in the United States. It has another value quite apart from prevention in decreasing the tendency in the male to arrive at the climax in the sexual act before the female.

There are few men and women so perfectly mated that the climax of the act is reached together. It is usual for the male to arrive at this stage earlier than the female, with the consequence that he is further incapacitated to satisfy her desire for some time after. During this time the woman is in a highly nervous condition, and it is the opinion of the best medical authorities that a continuous condition of this unsatisfied state brings on or causes disease of her generative organs, besides giving her a horror and repulsion for the sexual act.

Thousands of well-meaning men ask the advice of physicians as to the cause of the sexual coldness and indifference of their wives. Nine times out of ten it is the fault of the man, who through ignorance or selfishness and inconsiderateness, has satisfied his own desire and promptly gone off to sleep. The woman in self-defence has learned to protect herself from the long hours of sleeplessness and nervous tension by refusing to become interested.

The condom will often help in this difficulty. There are many girls who have had no education on this subject, no idea of the physiology of the act, who upon any contact of the semen have a disgust and repulsion, from which it takes some time to recover. Much depends upon the education of the girl, but more depends upon the attitude of the man toward the relation.

The pessary – rubber womb cap

One of the best means of prevention is the pessary or the rubber womb cap. These come in various forms and sizes, the Dutch Mensinga with its ten or twelve sizes, the Matrisalus, used also in Holland and Germany, the French cap-shaped, the Haire pessary used largely in England, and the Mizpah largely used in USA. While the French pessary (see below) may be conveniently used in many cases with satisfaction, I find the Mizpah still better fitting and more convenient for the average use. The fact that the cap can be removed and replaced at a very small cost adds greatly to its preference among working women. There is also an inner lip which prevents its slipping from its hold, when once it is in place. The loose, large detachable cap makes one size (the medium) practically universal for any womb, whether the woman has had one or ten children. This cannot be said of the French pessary, which comes in three sizes and must be fitted to accommodate every change. If, however, one desires the French pessary, it is best to get the medium size, as the small ones are only for very small boned women and easily get out of place during intercourse.

In my estimation a well-fitted pessary is one of the surest methods of preventing conception. I have known hundreds of women who have used it for years with the most satisfactory results. The trouble is women are afraid of their own bodies, and are of course ignorant of their physical construction. They are silly in thinking the pessary can go up too far, or that it could get lost, etc., etc., and therefore discard it. It cannot get into the womb, neither can it get lost. The only thing it can do is to come out. And even that will give warning by the discomfort of the bulky feeling it causes, when it is out of place.

Before inserting a pessary inject into the cap a small amount of boric ointment or a small quantity of bicarbonate of soda. This will act as a cement to help seal the mouth of the womb for the time being and thus doubly insures prevention.

In inserting the pessary it is well to get into a position which will make the entrance easy. One foot resting on a low chair opens the parts considerably, also a squatting position brings the uterus lower and makes the fitting of the pessary easier. Do not use vaseline or oils on rubber, they decay it. Glycerine or soap rubbed on its surface makes it smooth enough to slip easily into place.

After the pessary has been placed into the vagina deeply, it can be fitted well over the neck of the womb. One can feel it is fitted by pressing the fingers around the soft part of the pessary, which should completely cover the mouth of the womb.

If you do not feel the head of the womb through the rubber, then the pessary is not on right. It should be moved backward a little or forward until the head can be felt covered. If you still cannot feel it, then remove and use some other preventive, or take it to your physician and ask for instructions. The uterus may be turned or tipped back so far that a pessary could not cover the cervix.

If it is properly adjusted there will be no discomfort, the man will be unconscious that anything is used, and no germ or semen can enter the womb.

It is not always necessary to take a douche until the following morning, but it is always SAFER to douche immediately after the act. Take part or about a quart of antiseptic douche BEFORE the pessary is removed; after removing it continue the douche and cleanse thoroughly.

There are some well-meaning advocates of birth control who have more theories than practical knowledge, who urge or advise that the pessary be left in the body for several days and claim that in this way a douche is not necessary.

The theory may work well in women who belong to the class where standing long hours on the feet is not necessary and where a daily bath in a tub of clear water helps to keep the parts clean. But my experience in the nursing field among working women has given evidence that the pessary cannot remain in place long when a woman stands on her feet, as in washing or ironing. The strain pulls the muscles of the womb down into the vagina and the pessary loses its hold and position. Also the constant contact of the rubber with the natural secretions causes an odour to emanate from the parts, which is not pleasant. It is not advisable to wear the pessary all the time. Take it out after using, and wear it only when needed. A little experience will teach one that to place it is a simple matter.

Wash the pessary in warm soapsuds or soapy water, dry well and place away in the box. One should last two years, if cared for.

I consider the use of the pessary as one of the most convenient, as well as the cheapest and the safest method of prevention. Any nurse or doctor will teach one how to adjust it.

The use of the pessary has many advantages over other methods of prevention. There are few women whose generative organs are in a healthy, normal condition, who cannot find one of the various kinds of pessaries to fit her convenience.

While the pessary can be used *only* in cases where the womb is in its normal position – the sponge can be used to great advantage even when the womb is tipped back or out of its usual position.

Contraceptalene is an entirely new contraceptive jelly intended to be used in conjunction with the Dutch Mensinga Pessary. It is made according to a prescription furnished by Dr Norman Haire, who states that he has found it to be very reliable when used in combination with the Dutch Mensinga Pessary. The price is 2/6 per tube.

The usual sponge used for the purpose of preventing conception has a tape attached to it. These are to be had at nearly all drug stores. They should be soaked in an antiseptic solution for a few minutes before coitus and then introduced into the vagina far up as they can be placed. Some physicians have recommended the use of the cotton plug, instead of the sponge, to be soaked into a solution of three per cent. carbolic and glycerine, before the act. The male sperm is destroyed by the weakest solution of carbolic acid. Some of the peasants in Europe use the sponge soaked in vinegar for the same purpose and find it satisfactory. In this country a boric acid solution has been used with satisfactory results. Of course this requires a saturated solution, as, for instance, one teaspoonful of the powder to a cup of water stirred until dissolved.

Sponges and cotton plugs can be recommended as safe, if followed by an antiseptic douche before the removal of the plug or sponge, thus preventing the sperm from entering the womb. The problem is to kill the male sperm upon entering the vagina, or to wash it out or to kill it directly afterwards. A weak solution of alum may also be used for cotton plugs and sponges, also carbolated vaseline.

Any objection to the use of the small tape sponge can be overcome by the use of a large sponge, divided into parts three or four inches in diameter and a half inch in thickness. Cut into parts while new – boil for ten minutes, as the sponge is never considered hygienically clean until boiled. Push one part up into the vagina as far as it will go, pack it tight around the mouth of the womb so that it covers completely. Douche thoroughly after its removal. Always keep these parts in a solution of vinegar half and half of quinine. As soon as one sponge is removed and the vaginal canal cleansed – insert another sponge and leave for a few days. This will not have the same bad effects as the rubber pessary.

One of the cheapest methods of birth control is the use of a large sponge.

Suppositories or soluble pessaries

These are becoming more generally used than any other method of prevention. There is reason to believe these can be greatly improved upon, and the results obtained far more satisfactory than is at present prevalent in England especially.

These may be found at any reliable pharmacy. The majority of them are made from cocoa butter or gelatine, which makes it necessary that they be deposited in the vagina several minutes before the act, in order for them to melt. Special ingredients negate the effect of the male seed.

One of the objections to the suppository is the greasy feeling the cocoa butter gives. This can be overcome by douching the parts thoroughly before the suppository is inserted.

While some women object to the suppository because of the lubricant effect, other women who have a tendency to a 'dry vagina' approve of the suppository because of this tendency and effect.

Get your druggist to make up any of the following:

Vaginal Suppository
(Sufficient for three)
Acid citric, 6 grains.

2 gr. Quinine bisulphate.
Acid boracic, ½ dram.
Cocoa butter, 120 grains.

Another suppository found reliable is (sufficient for one):

Boric acid, 10 grains.
Salicylic acid, 2 grains.
Quinine bisulphate, 3 grains.
Cocoa butter, 60 grains.

(for one):

Chinosol, 3 grains.
Salicylic acid, 2 grains.
Quinine bisulphate, 3 grains
Cocoa butter, 60 grains.

A simple recipe which anybody can easily make is as follows (for twenty):

1 ounce cocoa butter.
60 grains quinine.

Melt the cocoa butter, mix the quinine with it, and form into suppositories by letting mixture harden into cake, and then cutting it up into pieces.

It is advisable, in the use of the suppositories, which must be injected before every sexual act, that immediately after the completion of the act a mild antiseptic douche be used to cleanse out the secretions. This is a procedure in the use of all suppositories, and while it is true that a douche is troublesome, it is certain to give better results in preventing pregnancy, than to depend upon the suppository alone.

The Contrap is a modern and up-to-date contraceptive pessary. It is spherical and 1⅛ inches in diameter, and dissolves slowly in contact with moisture. When wet it has a smooth soapy surface and can be inserted without the aid of a lubricant. In ten minutes it begins to disintegrate and is effective. Its shape avoids the risk of misplacement and its size obstructs the vagina and prevents the semen from reaching the mouth of the womb. On dissolving, it becomes creamy in consistence and occludes the mouth of the womb, and fills all the irregularities of the mucous surface. As no oil or vaseline is present it is not messy. No douching is required. Sold in boxes of one dozen at 3/6 per box.

Some questions often asked

1 *What is the best preventive?*

There is no one preventive to be recommended for everyone in every case. There are good and harmless preventives, any one of which can be made safe, according to the intelligence applied in using them.

I would advise the use of a recommended suppository for the first few months in the case of a bride, until the parts are in a condition where a pessary may be inserted and worn with comfort. Sometimes it is advisable to use suppositories during the early months of marriage, using the pessary only after children have been born.

2 *Is a douche necessary after the use of the suppository?*

To be certain of good results, I would advise a douche as soon as convenient.

3 *Are any of these methods recommended injurious to the health of the man or woman?*

The only method which physicians claim may be injurious to one or both is the continued practice of withdrawal. This method is not generally recommended, though it is practiced largely in France and England.

4 *Which method is safest?*

All are safe if you use care and intelligence in applying them.

5 *Which the least troublesome?*

The pessary can be recommended as the least troublesome, as after it is inserted it may be left to cover the cervix until the next day.

6 *Is there a safe period?*

There is no absolutely safe period between the menstrual periods where intercourse can take place without pregnancy occurring, at least not for all women. Some women claim this period exists in themselves, but unless you know this positively I would not advise a woman to depend upon it.

7 *How soon after menstruation ceases should intercourse occur?*

This should be left, as in all cases, to the natural desire of the woman.

8 *Does nursing a baby prevent pregnancy?*

It is claimed that pregnancy does not so easily occur during the nursing period, especially during the first three or four months. There are many women, however, who have conceived, immediately giving birth to another baby eleven months after the other. I would not advise depending upon this at all. Use some preventive at once and control intelligently the time for the next baby's arrival, instead of leaving it to chance.

9 *Does fear of pregnancy affect the child?*

Fear affects everything. We do not yet know the effect upon the human race which the fear of pregnancy has caused.

10 *Is it harmful to take drugs during the first few weeks after menstruation has stopped?*

It is considered especially harmful, not only to the mother, but to the child in cases where the drugs have not the desired effect. It stands to reason that a drug which is powerful enough to eject the fertilized ovum out of the uterus must have power to affect other organs. We often find children wetting the bed up to a late age, as well as suffering from other organic weaknesses, which may be traced back to the mother's frantic attempt to 'come around'. Women will not need to endanger their lives by taking drugs after conception if they will carefully carry out the advice here given.

11 *Should the woman or the man take the precautions?*

Either or both, but preferably the woman. The methods to be used by the man – withdrawal and the condom – have their objections for many people. While it is true that the employment of either of these methods lessen the trouble for the woman, they also deprive her of that great sacred closeness or spiritual union which the full play of magnetism gives when not checked by fear, as in withdrawal, or interfered with, as in the use of the condom. Some sensitive men object to the use of these methods, as also do many women. It is for each couple to decide. Many men prefer to use the condom in consideration of the woman, to lessen her trouble in douching.

12 *Should a woman have joy in the union?*

Yes.

13 *Why does she not?*

Either because her mind is occupied with fear of the results, or because of the awkwardness and ignorance of the man.

14 *Can this be overcome?*

Yes; first, by using a contraceptive which gives confidence so there shall be freedom from fear of pregnancy; second, by making the husband understand that a greater love and joy is created in the relation when the union is consummated only when the woman desires it naturally.

I have given in the foregoing pages the most commonly known means of prevention. Personally I recommend every poor woman who has had at least one child to use a well-fitted pessary and learn to adjust it.

Marie C. Stopes

from
Married Love

(1918)

Woman's 'contrariness'

> Oh! for that Being whom I can conceive to be in the world, though I shall not live to prove it. One to whom I might have recourse in all my Humours and Dispositions: in all my Distempers of Mind, visionary Causes of Mortification, and Fairy dreams of Pleasure. I have been trying to train up a Lady or two for these good offices of Friendship, but hitherto I must not boast of my success.
>
> *Herrick*

What is the fate of the average man who marries, happily and hopefully, a girl well suited to him? He desires with his whole heart a mutual, lifelong happiness. He marries with the intention of fulfilling every injunction given him by father, doctor, and friend. He is considerate in trifles, he speaks no harsh words, he and his bride go about together, walk together, read together, and perhaps, if they are very advanced, even work together. But after a few months, or maybe a few years of marriage they seem to have drifted apart, and he finds her often cold and incomprehensible. Few men will acknowledge this even to their best friends. But each heart knows its own pain.

He may at times laugh, and in the friendliest spirit tease his wife about her contrariness. That is taken by every one to mean nothing but a playful concealment of his profound love. Probably it is. But gnawing at the very roots of his love is a hateful little worm – the sense that she *is contrary*. He feels that she is at times inexplicably cold; that, sometimes, when he has 'done nothing' she will have tears in her eyes, irrational tears which she cannot explain.

He observes that one week his tender lovemaking and romantic advances win her to smiles and joyous yielding, and then perhaps a few days later the same, or more impassioned, tenderness on his part is met by coldness or a forced appearance of warmth, which, while he may make no comment upon it, hurts him acutely. And this deep, inexplicable hurt is often the beginning of the end of his love. Men like to feel that they understand their dearest one, and that she is a rational being.

After inexplicable misunderstanding has continued for some time, if the man is of at all a jealous nature he will search his wife's acquaintances for some one whom she may have met, for some one who may momentarily have diverted her attention. For however hard it is for the natural man to believe that any one could step into *his* shoes, some are ready to seek the explanation of their own ill success in a rival. On some occasion when her coldness puzzles him the man is perhaps conscious that his love, his own desires, are as ardent as they were a few days before; then, knowing so intimately his own heart, he is sure of the steadiness of its love, and he feels acutely the romantic passion to which her beauty stirs him; he remembers perhaps that a few days earlier his ardour had awakened a response in her; therefore, he reaches what appears to him to be the infallible logical deduction – that either there must be some rival or his bride's nature is incomprehensible, contrary, capricious. Both thoughts to madden.

With capriciousness, man in general has little patience. Caprice renders his best efforts null and void. Woman's caprice is, or appears to be, a negation of reason. And as reason is man's most precious and hard-won faculty, the one which has raised mankind from the ranks of the brute creation, he cannot bear to see it apparently flouted.

That his bride should lack logic and sweet reasonableness is a flaw it hurts him to recognise in her. He has to crush the thought down.

It may then happen that the young man, himself pained and bewildered at having pained his bride by the very ardour of his affection, may strive to please her by placing restraint upon himself. He may ask himself: Do not religious and many kinds of moral teachers preach restraint to the man? He reads the books written for the guidance of youth, and finds 'restraint', 'self-control', in general terms (and often irrationally) urged in them all. His next step may then be to curtail the expression of his tender feelings, and to work hard and late in the evenings instead of kissing his bride's fingers and coming to her for sweet communion in the dusk.

And then, if he is at all observant, he may be aggrieved and astonished to find her again wistful or hurt. With the tender longing to *understand*, which is so profound a characteristic in all the best of our young men, he begs, implores, or pets her into telling him some part of the reason for her fresh grievance. He discovers to his amazement that *this* time she is hurt because he had not made those very advances which so recently had repelled her, and had been with such difficulty repressed by his intellectual efforts.

He asks himself in despair: What is a man to do? If he is 'educated', he probably devours all the books on sex he can obtain. But in them he is not likely to find much real guidance. He learns from them that 'restraint' is advised from every point of view, but according to the character of the author he will find that 'restraint' means having the marriage relations with his wife not more than three times a week, or once a month – or never at all except for the procreation of children. He finds no *rational* guidance based on natural law.

According to his temperament then, he may begin to practise 'restraint'.

But it may happen, and indeed it has probably happened in every marriage once or many times, that the night comes when the man who has heroically practised restraint, accidentally discovers his wife in tears on her solitary pillow.

He seeks for advice indirectly from his friends, perhaps from his doctor. But can his local doctor or his friends tell him more than the chief European authorities on this subject? The famous Professor Forel (*The Sexual Question*, Engl. trans. 1908) gives the following advice:

> The reformer, Luther, who was a practical man, laid down the average rule of *two or three connections a week* in marriage, at the time of highest sexual power. I may say that my numerous observations as a physician have generally confirmed this rule, which seems to me to conform very well to the normal state to which *man*[1] has become gradually adapted during thousands of years. Husbands who would consider this average as an imprescriptible right would, however, make wrong pretensions, for it is quite possible for a normal man to contain himself much longer, and it is his duty to do so, not only when his wife is ill, but also during menstruation and pregnancy.

Many men will not be so considerate as to follow this advice, which represents a high standard of living; but, on the other hand, there are many who are willing to go not only so far, but further than this in their self-suppression in order to attain their heart's desire, the happiness of their mate, and consequently their own life's joy.

However willing they may be to go further, the great question for the man is: Where?

There are innumerable leaders anxious to lead in many different directions. The young husband may try first one and then the other, and still find his wife unsatisfied, incomprehensible – capricious. Then it may be that, disheartened, he tires, and she sinks into the dull apathy of acquiescence in her 'wifely duty'. He is left with an echo of resentment in his heart. If only she had not been so capricious, they would still have been happy, he fancies.

Many writers, novelists, poets and dramatists have represented the uttermost tragedy of human life as due to the incomprehensible contrariness of the feminine nature. The kindly ones smile, perhaps a little patronisingly, and tell us that women are more instinctive, more childlike, less reasonable than men. The bitter ones sneer or reproach or laugh at this in women they do not understand, and which, baffling *their* intellect, appears to them to be irrational folly.

It seems strange that those who search for natural law in every province of our universe should have neglected the most vital subject, the one which concerns us all infinitely more than the naming of planets or the collecting of insects. Woman is *not* essentially capricious; some of the laws of her being might have been discovered long ago had the existence of law been suspected. But it has suited the general structure of society much better for men to shrug their shoulders and smile at women as irrational and capricious creatures, to be courted when it suited them, not to be studied.

Vaguely, perhaps, men have realised that much of the charm of life lies in the sex-*differences* between men and women; so they have snatched at the easy theory that women differ from themselves by being capricious. Moreover, by attributing to mere caprice the coldness which at times comes over the most ardent woman, man was unconsciously justifying himself for at any time coercing her to suit himself.

Circumstances have so contrived that hitherto the explorers and scientific investigators, the historians and statisticians, the poets and artists have been mainly men. Consequently woman's side of the joint life has found little or no expression. Woman, so long coerced by economic dependence, and the need for protection while she bore her children, has had to be content to mould herself to the shape desired by man wherever possible, and she has stifled her natural feelings and her own deep thoughts as they welled up.

Most women have never realised intellectually, but many have been dimly half-conscious, that woman's nature is set to rhythms over which man has no more control than he has over the tides of the sea. While the ocean can subdue and dominate man and laugh at his attempted restrictions, woman has bowed to man's desire over her body, and, regardless of its pulses, he approaches her or not as is his will. Some of her rhythms defy him – the moon-month tide of menstruation, the cycle of ten moon-months of bearing the growing child and its birth at the end of the tenth wave – these are essentials too strong to be mastered by man. But the subtler ebb and flow of woman's sex has escaped man's observation or his care.

If a swimmer comes to a sandy beach when the tide is out and the waves have receded, leaving sand where he had expected deep blue water – does he, baulked of his bathe, angrily call the sea 'capricious'?

But the tenderest bridegroom finds only caprice in his bride's coldness when she yields her sacrificial body while her sex-tide is at the ebb.

There is another side to this problem, one perhaps even less considered by society. There is the tragic figure of the loving woman whose love-tide is at the highest, and whose husband does not recognise the delicate signs of her ardour. In our anæmic artificial days it often happens that the man's desire is a surface need, quickly satisfied, colourless, and lacking beauty, and that he has no knowledge of the rich complexities of love-making which an initiate of love's mysteries enjoys. To such a man his wife may indeed seem petulant, capricious, or resentful without reason.

Welling up in her are the wonderful tides, scented and enriched by the myriad experiences of the human race from its ancient days of leisure and flower-wreathed love-making, urging her to transports and to self-expressions, were the man but ready to take the first step in the initiative or to recognise and welcome it in her. Seldom dare any woman, still more seldom dare a wife, risk the blow at her heart which would be given were she to offer charming love-play to which the man did not respond. To the initiate she will be able to reveal that the tide is up by a hundred subtle signs, upon which he will seize with delight. But if her husband is blind to them there is for her nothing but silence, self-suppression, and their inevitable sequence of self-scorn, followed by resentment towards the man who places her in such a position of humilation while talking of his 'love'.

So unaware of the elements of the physiological reactions of women are many modern men that the case of Mrs G. is not exceptional. Her husband was accustomed to pet her and have relations with her frequently, but yet he never took any trouble to rouse in her the necessary preliminary feeling for mutual union. She had married as a very ignorant girl, but often vaguely felt a sense of something lacking in her husband's love. Her husband had never kissed her except on the lips and cheek, but once at the crest of the wave of her sex-tide (all unconscious that it was so) she felt a yearning to feel his head, his lips, pressed against her bosom. The sensitive interrelation between a woman's breasts and the rest of her sex-life is not only a bodily thrill, but there is a world of poetic beauty in the longing of a loving woman for the unconceived child which melts in mists of tenderness toward her lover, the soft touch of whose lips can thus rouse her mingled joy. Because she shyly asked him, Mrs G.'s husband gave her one swift unrepeated kiss upon her bosom. He was so ignorant that he did not know that her husband's lips upon her breast melt a wife to tenderness and are one of a husband's first and surest ways to make her physically ready for complete union. In this way he inhibited her natural desire, and as he never did anything to stir it, she never had any physical pleasure in their relation. Such prudish or careless husbands, content with their own satisfaction, little know the pent-up aching, or even resentment, which may eat into a wife's heart, and ultimately may affect her whole health.

Often the man is also the victim of the purblind social customs which make sex-knowledge taboo.

It has become a tradition of our social life that the ignorance of woman about her own body and that of her future husband is a flower-like innocence. And to such an extreme is this sometimes pushed, that not seldom is a girl married unaware that married life will bring her into physical relations with her husband fundamentally different from those with her brother. When she discovers the true nature of his body, and learns the part she has to play as a wife, she may refuse utterly to agree to her husband's wishes. I know one pair of which the husband, chivalrous and loving, had to wait years before his bride recovered from the shock of the discovery of the meaning of marriage and was able to allow him a natural relation. There have been not a few brides whom the horror of the first night of marriage with a man less considerate has driven to suicide or insanity.

That girls can reach a marriageable age without some knowledge of the realities of marriage would seem incredible were it not a fact. One highly educated lady intimately known to me told me that when she was about eighteen she suffered many months of agonising apprehension that she was about to have a baby because a man had snatched a kiss from her lips at a dance. And another girl told me she also not only suffered in the same way mentally, but that this fear of the results of a mere kiss so affected her that menstruation was suppressed for months.

When girls so brought up are married it is a *rape* for the husband to insist on his 'marital rights' at once. It will be difficult or impossible for such a bride ever after to experience the joys of sex-union, for such a beginning must imprint upon her consciousness the view that the man's animal nature dominates him.

In a magazine I came across a poem which vividly expresses this peculiarly feminine sorrow:

> To mate with men who have no soul above
> Earth grubbing; who, the bridal night, forsooth,
> Killed sparks that rise from instinct fires of life,
> And left us frozen things, alone to fashion
> Our souls to dust, masked with the name of wife –
> Long years of youth – love years – the years of passion
> Yawning before us. So, shamming to the end,
> All shrivelled by the side of him we wed,
> Hoping that peace may riper years attend,
> Mere odalisques are we – well housed, well fed.
>
> *Katherine Nelson*

Many men who enter marriage sincerely and tenderly may yet have some previous experience of bought 'love'. It is then not unlikely that they may fall into the error of explaining their wife's experiences in terms of the reactions of the prostitute. They argue that, because the prostitute showed physical excitement and pleasure in union, if the bride or wife does not do so, then she is 'cold' or 'undersexed'. They may not realise that often all the bodily movements which the prostitute makes are studied and simulated because her client enjoys his climax best when the woman in his arms simultaneously thrills.

As Forel says (*The Sexual Question*, Engl. trans. 1908):

> The company of prostitutes often renders men incapable of understanding feminine psychology, for prostitutes are hardly more than automata trained for the use of male sensuality. When men look among these for the sexual psychology of woman they find only their own mirror.

Yet the simulated transports of the prostitute have their meretricious value only because they imitate something real, something which should sweep over every wife each time she and her husband unite. The key which unlocks this electric force in his wife must reverently be sought by every husband, and its place varies in different women.

Fate is often cruel to men, too. More high-spirited young men than the world imagines strive for and keep their purity to give their brides; if such a man then marries a woman who is soiled and has lost her reverence for love, or, on the other hand, one who is so 'pure' and prudish that she denies him union with her body, his noble achievement seems bitterly vain. On the other hand, it may be that after years of fighting with his hot young blood a man has given up and gone now and again for relief to prostitutes, and then later in life has met the woman who is his mate, and whom, after remorse for his soiled past, and after winning her forgiveness for it, he marries. Then, unwittingly, he may make the wife suffer either by interpreting her in the light of the other women or perhaps (though this happens less frequently) by setting her absolutely apart from them. I know of a man who, after a loose life, met a woman whom he reverenced and adored. He married her, but to preserve her 'purity', her difference from the others, he never consummated his marriage with her. She was strangely unhappy, for she loved him passionately and longed for children. She appeared to him to be pining 'capriciously' when she became thin and neurotic.

Perhaps this man might have seen his own behaviour in a truer light had he known that some creatures simply *die* if unmated.

The idea that woman is lowered by sex-intercourse is very deeply rooted in our present society. Many sources have contributed to this mistaken idea, not the least powerful being the ascetic ideal of the early Church and the fact that man has *used* woman as his instrument so often regardless of her wishes. Women's education, therefore, and the trend of social feeling have largely been in the direction of freeing her from this, and thus mistakenly enouraging the idea that sex-life is a low, physical, and degrading necessity which a pure woman is above enjoying.

In marriage the husband has used his 'marital right'[2] of intercourse when *he* wished it. Both law and custom have strengthened the view that he has the right to approach his wife whenever he wishes, and that she has no wishes and no fundamental needs in the matter at all.

That woman has a rhythmic sex-tide which, if its indications were obeyed, would ensure not only her enjoyment and an accession of health and vitality, and would explode the myth of her capriciousness, seems not to be suspected. We have studied the wave-lengths of water, of sound, of light; but when will the sons and daughters of men study the sex-tide in woman and learn the laws of her Periodicity of Recurrence of desire?

The fundamental pulse

> The judgments of men concerning women are very rarely matters of cold scientific observation, but are coloured both by their own sexual emotions and by their own moral attitude toward the sexual impulse. . . . [Men's] Statements about the sexual impulses of woman often tell us less about women than about the persons who make them.
>
> *H. Ellis*

By the majority of 'nice' people woman is supposed to have no spontaneous sex-impulses. By this I do not mean a sentimental 'falling in love', but a physical, a physiological state of stimulation which arises spontaneously and quite apart from any particular man. It is in truth the *creative* impulse, and is an expression of a high power of vitality. So widespread in our country is the view that it is only depraved women who have such feelings (especially before marriage) that most women would rather die than own that they *do* at times feel a physical yearning indescribable, but as profound as hunger for food. Yet many, many women have shown me the truth of their natures when I have simply and naturally assumed that of course they feel it – being normal women – and have asked them only: *When?* From their replies I have collected facts which are sufficient to overturn many ready-made theories about women.

Some of the ridiculous absurdities which go by the name of science may be illustrated by the statement made by Windscheid in *Centralblatt für Gynäkologie:*

> In the normal woman, especially of the higher social classes, the sexual instinct is acquired, not inborn; when it is inborn, or awakens by itself, there is *abnormality*. Since women do not know this instinct before marriage, they do not miss it when they have no occasion in life to learn it. (Ellis trans.)

The negation of this view is expressed in the fable of Hera quoted by Ellen Key. Hera sent Iris to earth to seek out three virtuous and perfectly chaste maidens who were unsoiled by any dreams of love. Iris found them, but could not take them back to Olympus, for they had already been sent for to replace the superannuated Furies in the infernal regions.

Nevertheless it is true that the whole education of girls, which so largely consists in the concealment of the essential facts of life from them; and the positive teaching so prevalent that the racial instincts are low and shameful; and also the social condition which places so many women in the position of depending on their husband's will not only for the luxuries but for the necessaries of life, have all tended to inhibit natural sex-impulses in women, and to conceal and distort what remains.

It is also true that in our northern climate women are on the whole naturally less persistently sitrred than southerners, and it is further true that with the delaying of maturity, due to our ever-lengthening youth, if often happens that a woman is approaching or even past thirty years before she is awake to the existence of the profoundest calls of her nature. For many years before that, however, the unrealised influence, diffused throughout her very system, had profoundly affected her. It is also true that (partly due to the inhibiting influences of our customs, traditions and social code) women may marry before it wakes, and may remain long after marriage entirely unconsicous that it surges subdued within them. For innumerable women, too, the husband's regular habits of intercourse, claiming her both when she would naturally enjoy union and when it is to some degree repugnant to her, have tended to flatten out the billowing curves of the line of her natural desire. One result, apparently little suspected, of using the woman as a passive instrument for man's need has been, in effect, to make her that and nothing more. Those men – and there are many – who complain of the lack of ardour in good wives, are often themselves entirely the cause of it. When a woman is claimed at times when she takes no *natural* pleasure in union, and claimed in such a way that there is no *induced* romantic pleasure, the act reduces her vitality, and tends to kill her power of enjoying it when the love-season returns.

It is certainly true of women as they have been made by the inhibitions of modern conditions, that most of them are only fully awake to the existence of sex after marriage. As we are human beings, the social, intellectual, spiritual side of love-choice have tended to mask the basic physiological aspect of women's sex-life. To find a woman in whom the currents are not all so entangled that the whole is inseparable into factors, is not easy, but I have found that wives (particularly happy wives whose feelings are not complicated by the stimulus of another love) who have been separated from their husbands for some months through professional or business duties – whose husbands, for instance, are abroad – are the women from whom the best and most definitive evidence of a fundamental rhythm of feeling can be obtained. Such women, yearning daily for the tender conradeship and nearness of their husbands, find, in addition, at particular times, an accession of longing for the close physical union of the final sex-act. Many such separated wives feel this; and those I have asked to keep notes of the dates, have, with remarkable unanimity, told me that these times came specially just before and some week or so after the close of menstruation, coming, that is, about every fortnight. It is from such women that I got the first clue to the knowledge of what I call the law of Periodicity of Recurrence of desire in women. For some years I have been making as scientific and detailed a study as possible of this extremely complex problem. Owing to the frank and scientific attitude of a number of women, and the ready and intimate confidence of many more, I have obtained a number of most interesting facts from which I think it is already possible to deduce a generalisation which is illuminating, and may be of great medical and sociological value. As may be imagined, since this book was first published a great deal of further evidence has been sent to me: this remarkably confirms the original charts, so that I see no reason to revise the general statement for the average healthy type of woman. A more detailed and scientific consideration of my data will be published elsewhere.

My law of Periodicity and Recurrence of desire in women it is possible to represent graphically as a curved line; a succession of crests and hollows as in all wave-lines. Its simplest and most fundamental expression, however, is generally immensely complicated by other stimulations which may bring into it diverse series of waves, or irregular wave-crests. We have all, at some time, watched the regular ripples of the sea breaking against a sand-bank, and noticed that the influx of another current of water may send a second system of waves at right angles to the first, cutting athwart them, so that the two series of waves pass through each other.

Woman is so sensitive and responsive an instrument, and so liable in our modern civilised world to be influenced by innumerable sets of stimuli, that it is perhaps scarcely surprising that the deep, underlying waves of her primitive sex-tides have been obscured, and entangled so that their regualr sequence has been masked in the choppy turmoil of her sea, and their existence has been largely unsuspected, and apparently quite unstudied.

As it bears intimately on the subject of the present chapter, a short and simple account of my conclusions on woman's rhythmic life must be given here.

It is first necessary to consider several other features of woman's life, however.

The obvious moon-month rhythm in woman, so obvious that it *cannot* be overlooked, has been partially studied in its relation to some of the ordinary functions of her life. Experiments have been made to show its influence on the rate of breathing, the muscular strength, the temperature, the keenness of sight, etc., and these results have even been brought together and pictured in a single curved diagram supposed to show the variability in woman's capacities at the different times in her twenty-eight-day cycle.

But it brings home to one how little original work even in this field has yet been done, that the same identical diagram is repeated from book to book, and in Marshall's *Physiology* it is 'taken from Sellheim', in Havelock Ellis 'from Von Ott', and in other books is re-copied and attributed to still other sources, but it is always the same old diagram.

This diagram is reproduced by one learned authority after another, yet nearly every point on which this curve is based appears to have been disputed.

According to this curve, woman's vitality rises during the few days before menstruation, sinks to its lowest ebb during menstruation and rises shortly after, and then runs nearly level till it begins to rise again before the next menstrual period. This simple curve may or may not be true for woman's temperature, muscular strength, and the other relatively simple things which have been investigated. My work and observations on a large number of women all go to show that this curve does *not* represent the waves of woman's sex-vitality.

The whole subject is so complex and so little studied that it is difficult to enter upon it at all without going into many details which may seem remote or dull to the general reader. Even a question which we must all have asked, and over which we have probably pondered in vain – namely, what is menstruation? – cannot yet be answered. To the lay mind it would seem that this question should be answerable at once by any doctor; but many medical men are still far from being able to reply to it even approximately correctly.

There are a good many slight variations among us, ranging from a three-to a five-weeks 'month', but the majority of the women of our race have a moon-month of twenty-eight days, once during which comes the flow of menstruation. If we draw out a chart with succeeding periods of twenty-eight days each, looking on each period as a unit: When in this period is it that a normal healthy woman feels desire or any up-welling of her sex-tides?

The few statements which are made in general medical and physiological literature on the subject of sex-feeling in women are generally very guarded and vague. Marshall (*Physiology of Reproduction*, p. 138), for instance, says: 'The period of most acute sexual feeling is generally just after the close of the menstrual period.' Ellis speaks of desire being stronger before and sometimes also after menstruation, and appears to lean to the view that it is natural for desire to coincide with the menstrual flow.

After the most careful inquiries I have come to the conclusion that the general confusion regarding this subject is due partly to the great amount of variation which exists between different individuals, and partly to the fact that very few women have any idea of taking any scientific interest in life, and partly to the fact that the more profound, fundamental rhythm of sex-desire which I have come to the conclusion exists, or is potential, in every normal woman, is covered over or masked by the more superficial and temproary influences due to a great variety of stimuli or inhibitions in modern life. For the present consideration I have tried to disentangle the profound and natural rhythm from the more irregular surface waves.

The chart given overleaf may assist in making graphically clear what has been said in these last few pages. It is compounded from a number of individual records, and shows a fair average chart of the rhythmic sequence of superabundance and flagging in woman's sex-vitality. The tops of the wave-crests come with remarkable regularity, so that there are two wave-crests in each twenty-eight-day month. The one comes on the two of three days just *before* menstruation, the other after; but after menstruation has ceased there is a nearly level interval, bringing the next wave-crest to the two or three days which come about eight or nine days after the close of menstruation – that is, just round the fourteen days, or half the moon-month, since the last wave-crest. If this is put in its simplest way, one may say that there are fortnightly periods of desire, arranged so that one period comes always just *before* each menstrual flow. According to her vitality at the time, and the general health of the woman, the length of each desire-period, or, as we might say, the size and complexity of each wave-crest, depends. Sometimes for the whole or as much as, or even more than, three days, she may be ardently and quite naturally stimulated, while at another time the same woman, if she is tired and overworked, may be conscious of desire for only a few hours, or even less.

The effects of fatigue, city life, bad feeding, and, indeed, of most outward circumstances may be very marked, and may for years, or all her life, so reduce her vitality that a woman may never have experienced any spontaneous sex-impulse at all.

The effects of fatigue, which reduces the vital energy, even in a normal, strongly sexed woman, can be seen in the second chart, where at *a* the intermediate wave-crest is very much reduced. This is not a generalised chart, but a detailed record of an actual individual case.

Curves similar to those shown in Chart 1 represent in general terms a simplified view of what my research leads me to believe to be the normal, spontaneous sex-tide in women of our race. As one young married woman confided to me, her longing for bodily union with her husband, as distinct from her longing for his daily companionship, seemed to well up naturally like 'clockwork', and this during his long absence. But human beings vary remarkably in every particular, and just as no two people have the same features, so no two people would have *absolutely* identical curves were they recorded in sufficient detail. Many a woman is particularly conscious of only one sex-impulse in each moon-month. Of such women, some feel the period which comes before menstruation, and some feel the one which follows it. In those who generally feel only one, the second period is sometimes felt when they are particularly well, or only when they read exciting novels, or meet the man they love at a time coinciding with the natural, but suppressed, time of desire. There are a very few women, who seem to be really a little abnormal, who feel the strongest desire actually during the menstrual flow.

If any one who reads this thinks to test my view by questioning a number of women, the result will probably appear very conflicting, partly because it is not often that women will tell the truth about such a thing, and partly because in the larger number of women either one or the other period is the more acute and is the one they observe in themselves – if they have observed anything. But a delicate and more accurate investigation of such cases will often bring to light the existence of the second crest of vitality. Once the fundamental idea is grasped, much that appeared obscure or of no significance becomes plain and full of meaning. A lady doctor with whom I discussed my view at once said that it illuminated many observations she had made on her patients, but had not brought together or explained.

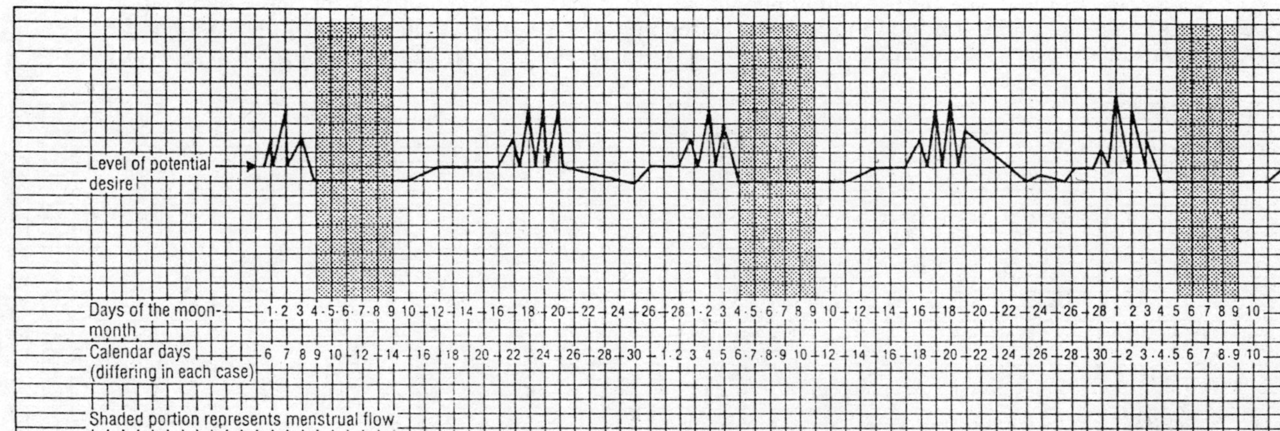

Chart I Curve showing the Periodicity of Recurrence of natural desire in healthy women. Various causes make slight irregularities in the position, size, and duration of the 'wave-crests', but the general rhythmic sequence is apparent.

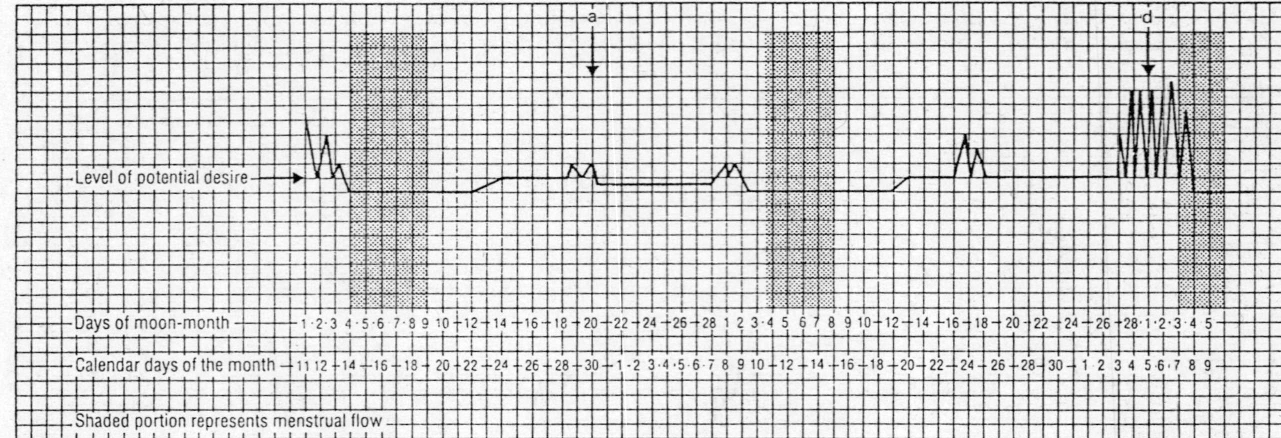

Chart II Curve showing the depressing effects on the 'wave-crests' of fatigue and overwork. Crest *a* represented only by a feeble and transient up-welling. Shortly before and during the time of the crest *d* Alpine air restored the vitality of the subject. The increased vitality is shown by the height and number of the apices of this wave-crest.

There is but little evidence of such observation to be found in scientific works on sex, but an interesting instance is mentioned by Forel (*The Sexual Question*, Engl. trans., page 92) in another connection. He says: 'A married woman confessed to me, when I reproached her for being unfaithful to her husband, that she desired coitus at least once a fortnight, and that when her husband was not there she took the first comer.' Forel did not see any law behind this. We may perhaps all see in her want of self-control a grievous *moral* abnormality, but in her fortnightly periods of desire she fits perfectly into the physiological law which, it appears to me, governs the normal sex-tides of our race.

In this connection it is of interest to note the decrees of the Mosaic Law regarding marriage intercourse. Not only was all intercourse with a woman during her menstruation period very heavily punished (see Leviticus xx. 18: 'If a man lie with a woman having her sickness . . . both of them shall be cut off from among their people'), but the Mosaic Law provided that women should be protected from intercourse for some days *after* each such period. The results obtained by my independent investigation thus find some support in this ancient wisdom of the East. Modern writers are inclined to deride the Mosaic Law on the ground that it prohibits intercourse just at the time when *they think* sex-feeling should be strongest. But it does not appear on what grounds they make the latter statement, nor do they give any scientific data in support of it. Thus Galabin in his *Manual of Midwifery* says:

> In the Jewish law women are directed to abstain[3] from coitus during menstruation and for seven days after its cessation. Strict observers of the law are said to go beyond what is commanded in Leviticus, and even if discharge lasts only for an hour or two, to observe five days during which the discharge might last, for the period itself, and add to these seven clear days, making twelve in all. It is much to be doubted whether a whole nation was ever induced to practise abstinence at the period of most acute sexual feeling.

But, as will readily be recognised, the old Jewish plan of having twelve clear days after the beginning of menstruation before the next union is in almost exact harmony with the law of Periodicity of Recurrence of women's desire shown in my charts (pp. 565, 566.)

These comparatively simple curves represent what I would postulate as the normal spontaneous up-welling of natural desire in woman. These are the foundations on which the edifice of the physical expression of love may be built. It must not be forgotten, however, that, particularly in modern luxurious life, there are innumerable excitements which may *stimulate* sexual feeling, just as there are many factors in our life which tend to inhibit or retard it. A woman may be, like a man, so swayed by a great love that there is not a day in the whole month when her lover's touch, his voice, the memory of his smile, does not stir her into the thrilling longing for the uttermost union. Hence it is often difficult, particularly for a woman dwelling with the man she loves, to recognise this rhythm in herself, for she may be perpetually stimulated by her love and by his being.

I am convinced, however, that ordinarily, whether she recognises it by outward signs or not, a fortnightly rhythm profoundly influences the average woman, and hence that it fundamentally affects the marriage relation in every way. The burning magnificence of an overpowering lifelong love is not given to many, and a husband who desires lasting and mutual happiness in his marriage will carefully study his wife, observe how far she has a normal rhythm, and in what she has little personal traits. He will then endeavour to adapt his demands on her so that they are in harmony with her nature.

She will not conceal from him the return of her longing for him, although, if she is wise, she will wreath it with enhancing mystery and enchantment; nor will she deprive him of the natural joy of knowing that he is giving her delight. A husband who thus feels himself *successful* is far more likely to be willing to modify and adapt his demands on his wife to suit her nature than one who is repressed and deadened by a uniform lack of response, or one whose wife often pretends to feelings she does not experience in order 'not to put him off'. True feeling cannot be stimulated, but when each considers the other it grows and blossoms in both.

NOTES

1 The italics are mine. – M. C. S.
This pronouncement by an exceptionally advanced and broad-minded thinker serves to show how little attention has hitherto been paid to the woman's side of this question, or to ascertaining *her* natural requirements.

2 'Conjugal Rights', *Notes and Queries*, 16 May 1891, p. 383. 'S. writes from the Probate Registry, Somerset House: "Previous to 1733 legal proceedings were recorded in Latin, and the word then used where we now speak of *rights* was *obsequies*. For some time after the substitution of English for Latin the term *rites* was usually, if not invariably adopted; *rights* would appear to be a comparatively modern error." '
'Mr T. E. Paget writes (*Romeo and Juliet*, Act V., Scene III):

What cursed foot wanders this way to-night
To cross my obsequies, and true lovers rite?

Well may Lord Esher say he has never been able to make out what the phrase "conjugal rights" means. The origin of the term is now clear, and a blunder, which was first made, perhaps, by a type-setter in the early part of the last century, and never exposed until now, has led to a vast amount of misapprehension. Here, too, is another proof that Shakespeare was exceedingly familiar with "legal language".'

3 In Leviticus xv. it is the *man* who is directed to abstain from touching the woman at this period, and who is rendered unclean if he does – M.C.S.

C *Mothers, Spinsters, Lesbians*

Ellen Key

from

The Woman Movement

(1912)

The influence of the woman movement upon motherhood

Because it has increased the culture of woman and her feelings of personal responsibility, the woman movement has had its influence, both directly and indirectly, upon the postponement of the legal and customary marriage age. Since young girls have exercised their brains as much as the boys have, they are no longer so far in advance of the boys in physical development. But when modern girls finish their studies they are physically as well as psychically more universally developed that their grandmothers were. They know much more of the difficulties and realities of life, not least of the sexual life. And this knowledge has instilled in them a reluctance to undertake too early the serious and difficult task of motherhood. They have greater need of truth and culture, and less tendency to erotic visionary dreaming than girls of their age in the middle of the previous century; their desire for work and their social feeling fix goals, and they work with all their might to attain them. And because, as already explained, both sexes have for each other a more many-sided attraction than the merely erotic, young people are more careful, more choice, in their erotic decisions. The finest young girls of today are penetrated by the Nietzchean idea, that marriage is the combined will of two people to create a new being greater than themselves. But their joy does *not* consist in the fact 'that the man wills'; they are themselves 'will', and above all they have the will to choose the right father for their children, not only for their own sake but for the sake of the children.

If it be true that immediate, 'blind', erotic attraction is most instinctively correct in choice, then the present comrade life of young people and the increased clear-sightedness which it gives, as well as the increasing erotic idealism of young girls, are not unconditionally advantageous to the new race. The question is, however, still undecided. Here it may only be emphasised that the young girl of today, in spite of all intellectual development, is still won always by powerful spiritual sensual love, which the woman movement has too long considered as a negligible quantity. Under the influence of the doctrine of evolution, young girls begin to understand that their value as members of society depends essentially upon their value for the propagation of mankind; all the more they realise the duty of physical culture which will enable them to fulfil this function better; they no longer consider their erotic longing as impure and ugly but as pure and beautiful. It is out of this soul condition that the different movements for the protection of mothers and children, theoretically considered, have proceeded. These are at present the most important 'woman movements', although unrecognised by the older woman movement. And this older movement has not yet recognised the fact that, because of present marriage conditions, the degenerate, uneducated, decrepit, have greater opportunity for propagating the race, both within and outside of marriage, than the young, sound, pure-minded, and loving; that it can therefore *be no sin* from the point of view of the race, if the latter become parents without marriage, nor should it be a subject of shame from the social point of view. All women's rights have little value, until this one thing is attained: that a woman who through her illegitimate motherhood has lost nothing of her personal worth, but on the contrary has proved it, does not forfeit social esteem.

Our time can point to women who have been typical of the reform tendencies of the century in this respect. Some of these women, if they really accomplished the unprecedented task of 'a child and a work', have drawn their strength for the task out of precisely the commonplace, homely qualities and sterling virtues, contrary to which they believed they were acting when they became mothers, driven by a power greater than their *conscious* personality. Others again became mothers with the consent of their whole personality. They were clear that they thus made use of the masculine rights and freedom which feminism first brought home to women. And although many advocates of women's rights refrain from such consequences of their ideas, the women who in other respects determine their conduct of life by their free personal choice recognise that this, their *real* 'emancipation', is a fruit of the woman movement.

In Europe, however, most women under thirty still dare to dream of motherhood in a love marriage as the greatest happiness and the highest duty of life.[1]

But, as direct and indirect result of the woman movement, the fact none the less remains that there is found *among women an increasing disinclination for maternity*, a reluctance which deprives mankind of many superior mothers, while at the same time woman's commercial work for self-support in all classes increases her sterility or makes her incapable of the suckling so vitally important for the children.

That the modern woman, because of individual fate or her own choice, often remains unmarried is no danger in and for itself. This fact, as I have emphasised above, is connected with a number of cultural and material conditions, which sometime will be altered, and then woman's desire for marriage will again increase. The real danger has appeared only since women have begun to strengthen the tendency to celibacy by the amaternal theory, which now confuses the feminine brain and leads the feminine instinct astray.

The woman movement in and with this influence upon maternity sinks to the lowest point of the scale according to the criterion of worth employed here: the elevation of the life of the individual and of the race. In this we stand in our time before a twofold mystery, which lies in the circumstance that not only women – women 'with breasts made right to suckle babes' – emphasise this stultifying influence, but that there are men, each the son of a mother, who also propagate it. These men have allowed themselves to be blinded by the false logic concerning women, which declares that since rich mothers do not wish to fulfil the duties of a mother and the poor cannot fulfil them, superior social organisations must be created for that purpose; in other words, instigated by a mere temporary unpleasant discrepancy, we will create a new, a different order of things. But, if this is obtained universally, it would inflict imcomparably greater injury upon mankind than do present unhappy conditions.

It is precisely as a result of this tendency that the deepest hostility of men against feminism has developed. The fact that the idea of evolution is now beginning to enter into the flesh and blood of man also contributes its share to this feeling. Just as formerly a man wished heirs for his personal and real estate and for his name, he now desires inheritors of his being; he desires an eternal life, which becomes a certainty only by means of parenthood, whereby the individual as father or mother loves on physically and spiritually, in body and soul, in his children and grandchildren down to the last of his descendants. This conception has made the sex instinct again holy, as it was for the pagans. This new reverence for their duty as beings of sex now induces many young men to guard their sexual health and strength by an ascetisicm the motive of which is the exact opposite of that which determined the asceticism called forth by Christianity, the asceticism which was fear of the sex instinct as impure and as a temptation to sin. Now the innermost aim of youg men's creative desire is the higher development of mankind. Love becomes for them the condition by which they can most perfectly redeem their religious certainty of being part of a great design, their religious longing for harmony with life's creative desire, with the infinite.

There are now men who work most zealously for the ennoblement of the race – 'eugenics', as this effort is called in England – as well as for the protection of mother and child – 'puericulture', as this endeavour is called in France. There are men who write excellent works upon the psychology of the child, and upon sexual instruction; men, who, in art and poetry, give expression to the new veneration of the sanctity of generation, for motherhood, for the child. The finest thing written about the child as a cultural power is written by an American. Painting has now new devotional pictures of the Mother with her Child, especially those conceived by a Frenchman and an Italian. The most beautiful representation of youth's new desire for love is by a German sculptor. Likewise a German, Nietzsche, has the most profound conception of parenthood and education as the means whereby humanity will cross over the bridge of the men of today to the superman.

Only when all this is realised can one conceive what the feelings of these new men must be when they meet those new women 'who are no longer willing to be slaves of the instrinct for the propagation of the race'; who see in motherhood 'a loss of time from their work'; 'an attack upon their beauty'; an obstacle to the refined conduct of life; – a conduct of life certain to debase woman's worth as a child-bearing being, but to elevate her to that exquisite, perfect product of culture, a 'woman of the world'; an obstacle also for woman as creator of other objective cultural values. If a man with a father's desires finds himself united with such a woman, he finds himself in marriage quite as much a prostitute as innumerable wives have felt themselves to be when they were mere tools of a man's desire. On the contrary the desire for the elevation of mankind on the part of the new woman and the new man, is evinced in the idea that not the quantity but the quality of the children they give to humanity is most significant; that a land of fewer but more perfect men is a higher culture ideal than the principle still always maintained from the point of view of national competition, that the inhabitants of a country must only be numerous however inferior they may be.

To this wholly new evolutionary conception of life the amaternal women oppose the following train of thought which greatly influences the feeling and desire of women today:[2]

Culture now sets new duties for woman, more significant than exclusively natural ones. The more the individual life increases in value, the more the interest for the mere functions of sex declines, and with it also the value of woman *as woman* for a society where, because of motherhood, she has become a being of secondary rank. It evinces lack of ideality if one censures this tendency of the modern woman to renounce maternity for the sake of more spiritual interests. While the mother concentrates herself upon her own child only, the woman who renounces motherhood can extend her being to embrace children as children in general. As a mother, woman is only a being of nature. But the personality, with its multiplicity of feeling and endeavours, demands an independent activity as well as maternity.

To put her entire personality into the education of her children is a two fold error. First and foremost, most mothers are *bad* educators and serve their children better if they entrust them to a born teacher; in the second place, *gifted* children educate themselves best and should be spared all educational arts. The mediocre child, who is more susceptible to education, has ordinarily also only mediocre parents, who likewise benefit the children most if they put them in the care of excellent teachers. Children who are *below* mediocrity can also be best educated by specialists. So there remains for the mother, after the first years' care and training, no especial task as educator, at least none in which she can really put her personality. To talk to a mother about the possibilities of a richer office of mother, as educator of her children, she calls lulling her into an illusion under which she must labour only to suffer. A woman who can exercise her personality in another way should not therefore put it into the education of her children.

The amaternal advocates deny that motherliness is the criterion of womanliness; they find this criterion in the form, the external being of woman, in her manner and physical appearance – in a word, in the *outer* expression of the inner disposition, which they deny as typical of womanliness! 'Womanliness' is thus reduced to an 'æsthetic principle', while woman's spiritual attributes are considered as 'universally human'; and the right is granted to the feminine sex to emancipate herself from the result of the heresy that *motherliness* should be the ethical norm for the 'being' or 'essence' of womanhood. The suitability of woman's *psychic* constitution for her work as mother is not acknowledged as proof that motherliness is the distinguishing characteristic of womanliness. For this constitution is less conspicuous in the higher stages of differentiation. Its suitability was then a phenomenon of adaptation and changed with the conditions of life. Thus this constitution cannot be cited as a reason for limiting woman's personal exercise of her powers. Motherliness is no social instinct. How can motherliness, which we have in common with beasts and savages, be considered as higher than, for example, justice, truth, and other gradually won spiritual values, which woman can promote by her personal activity? The higher the forms of life woman attains, the less will her personality be determined by motherliness. Why then should women bring to the domestic life the sacrifice of their personality, while no one demands this of men? Why shall not woman, just as man, satisfy her demands as a sex-being in marriage and, as for the rest, follow her profession, attend to her spiritual development, her social tasks? Why condemn woman to remain a half-being – that is, with unexercised brain – only because certain of her instincts attract her to man, while he is not constrained to suppress his personality because he in like manner felt attracted to woman? It is the old superstition of the family life as 'woman's sphere', which still confuses the conception. By the present form of family life woman is 'oversexed'. Her higher development, as well as that of her husband and children, will be promoted if woman guards her independence by earning her own living, in commercial work conducted beyond the portal of the home; if housekeeping becomes co-operative; if the education of the children is carried on outside the home, in which now the motherly tenderness emasculates the children and fosters in them family sentiment of an egoistic nature and not social feelings. Thus are solved the difficulties which are entailed when the wife's work is carried on outside the home; equipoise between her intellectual and emotional, her sexual and social nature follows, and her worth, as that of a man, will be measured by her human personality, not by her womanliness, her efficacy in the family, for the exercise of which she is now constrained to renounce her personality.

So runs in brief the programme of the amaternals.

It has already been indicated that the woman movement, in its *inception*, could gather strength only by combating with all its power the prejudice that *woman is incapable of the same kind of activity as man*. But now the whole woman movement has for a long time been emphasising the fact that woman is entitled, not only on her own behalf but more especially in her capacity as homekeeper, wife, and mother, to the full development of her powers and to equality with man in the family and in society. In the amaternal programme sketched above, however, the fanaticism, which characterised the entire woman movement a generation ago, now evinces itself in the error that *equal rights* for the sexes must mean also *equal functions;* that the development of women's powers involves also their application in the same spheres of activity in which man is engaged; that *equality* of the sexes implies *sameness* of the sexes. While moderate feminism begins to see that, if man and wife compete, this rivalry can benefit[3] neither the woman, the man, nor the children, amaternal feminism urges the keenest competition. And if this is once accepted as advantageous to woman's personality and to society, then it is obvious that she must, with all the energy of the attacked, defend herself from the duties of maternity, because of which she would obviously come off second-best in the competition.

From the point of view of individualism it is obvious that the *law* must set no limitations to woman's practice of a vocation, unless evident hygienic dangers menace either her or the coming generation. Women must, for their own sake as well as for that of society, have free *choice of work*, for life and nature possess innumerable unforeseen possibilities. Nevertheless, it does happen that a woman who gives superior children to humanity may, neverthess, feel herself incapable of educating them; likewise it sometimes happens that a husband and wife who have exceptional children, cannot endure to live together. In neither case has law or custom a right to force upon a mother or a father a yoke that is intolerable or to demand of a mother or a father unreasonable sacrifices.

But the right to limit the choice of work, the law does not possess; nature assumes that right herself: first of all from the axiom that no one can be in two places at the same time, and in the second place because no one can respond simultaneously and with full energy to two different spiritual activities. One cannot, for example, count even to one hundred and at a certain number give a simple grasp of the hand without suspending the counting momentarily. Although no one has ever been denied the privilege of solving a mathematical problem and of following carefully at the same time a piece of music, yet it is certain that the effectiveness of both intellectual activities would be thereby diminished. These extremely simple observations can be continued until the most complex are reached. If the observation be directed to the sphere of domestic life, every wife and mother who *is willing to institute impartial observations of self,* will affirm the difficulty of working with a divided mind.

If a mother carries on her work at home and must put it away in order to be beside the sick-bed of her child, or to make those arrangements which assure domestic comfort, or to help her husband, then she feels that her book or her picture suffers, that the activity which binds her more intimately to the home relaxes for a time the intimacy of her connection with her work. One can by day carry on a dull industrial task, and by night produce an achievement of the soul; but one cannot let one's soul radiate in one direction without impairing its energy in another. A work needs exclusive devotion. And this is, viewed externally, difficult to attain in joint action; viewed from within, it requires a renunciation that in the case of a loving soul evokes a continual inner struggle. For that reason, also, literature with woman as its subject has for some decades been filled with the great conflict of modern woman's life: the conflict between vocation and parents, between vocation and husband, between vocation and child. Certainly the family has often been a torture chamber for individuality, as a consequence of laws and customs, which the future will regard as we now do the rack and the thumbscrew. But nature is more severe than law and custom when she confronts us with a choice which, however it may turn out, tears a piece from our heart.

And now neither custom nor man demands of woman the 'sacrifice of the personality'. This sacrifice is required only by the law of limitations which rules over us all.

The creative man or the man working objectively must often condemn the emotional side of his personality to a partial development; he must for the sake of his work renounce many family values important for this emotional side of his being. Even if shorter working hours could partially diminish this cultural offering, the *inner* conflict, for the man or the woman, is not settled thereby.

Even if a man, in the consciousness of his wife's endowment of talent, assumed a number of domestic duties, especially those pertaining to the children, the inner conflict would still continue. And this conflict is in no way solved by the amaternal theory that the personal life must be placed above the instinct life. For, as has been emphasised, the choicc is not between the personal and the instinct life, but between the intellectual and the emotional side of woman's personality. And the solution of this choice has not been discovered by the amaternals, who would combine commercial work with marriage and maternity. Women who remain unmarried or who give up commercial activity which they cannot carry on in the home, have not *settled the conflict either*, but have only reduced its difficulties.

The fundamental error of the amaternal solution of the problem is that it characterises motherliness as a *non-social* instinct, but, on the other hand, defines the 'personal' activity of woman as an expression of the social instinct. *For all social instincts have been developed by culture out of primitive instincts.* All cultural development lies between the sex impulse of the Australian negress and the erotic sentiment of Elizabeth Barrett Browning's sonnets. And when the amaternals assert that motherliness, which 'we have in common with beasts and savages', cannot be an expression of the personality, their argument has the same validity as that which would deny to the Sistine Chapel the quality of an expression of personality because beasts and savages also exhibit the decorative instinct.

The development of the mother instinct into motherliness is one of the greatest achievements in the progress of culture, a development by which the maternal functions have continually become more complex and differentiated. Already in the case of the higher animals maternity involves much more that the mere act of giving birth; an animal not only faces death for her young, she gives them also a training which often indicates power of judgment. A cat, for instance, which sought in vain to prevent her kitten from entering the water and which finally threw the kitten in and then pulled it out, thus obtaining the desired result of her pedagogy, had not, as have so many modern mothers, read Spencer, but could, nevertheless, put many of these mothers to shame. Even the initial maternal functions, nursing and physical care, involve a culture of the spiritual life of the mother, not only through an increase in tenderness, but also in observation, discrimination, judgment, self-control; a woman's character often develops more in a month during which she is occupied with the care of children, than in years of professional work. Mother love and the reciprocal love which it awakens in the child, not only exercise the first deep influence upon the individual's life of feeling, but this love is *the first form of the law of mutual help – it is the root of altruism, the cotyledon* of a now widely ramified tree of 'social instincts'.

Although woman through the mere *physical* functions of motherhood makes a great social contirbution, the importance of her contribution is greatly enhanced if one also takes into consideration her *spiritual* nature. And notwithstanding the fact that fatherhood has also, to a certain degree, developed in man the qualities of tenderness, watchfulness, patience, yet the enormous predominance of woman's *physical* share in parenthood, in comparison with man's, is in itself enough to create, in course of time, the intimate connection which still exists today between mother and child, as well as the difference between the personality of woman and man. The physical functions of motherhood were the fundamental reasons for the earliest division of labour. And this division of labour, the aim of which, next to self-preservation, was for both sexes the protection of posterity, augmented and strengthened the qualities which each sex employed for its special functions. All human qualities lie latent in each. But they have been so specialised by this division of labour, or, on the other hand, suppressed by it, that they now appear in varying proportions: in woman, a careful, managing, supervising, life-guarding, inward-directed sense of love; in man, courage, desire for action, force of will, power of thought, an activity subduing nature and life, became the distinguishing characteristics; and fatherhood became psychologically, as it is physiologically, something different from motherhood. Even if culture continues to efface the sharp lines of demarcation, so that it becomes more and more impossible to generalise about 'woman' and 'man', and increasingly more necessary for each and every woman to solve the 'woman question' individually, yet from the point of view of the race, the *division of labour must on the whole remain the same as that which hitherto existed*, if the higher development of mankind shall continue in uninterrupted advance to more perfect forms. It is necessary for *these higher ends of culture* that woman *in an ever more perfect manner shall fulfil what has hitherto been her most exalted task:* the bearing and rearing of the new generation.

The amaternal assertion, that motherliness can be no higher than justice and truth, is an infuriating antithesis. It is as if one should assert that 'air is better than water, or both better than bread'. Both assertions place the fundamental condition of life counter to other needs of life! Who shall exercise justice and truth when no new men are born? And, moreover, how shall justice and truth increase in mankind if children are not trained to a greater reverence for justice and a deeper love of truth? In order to fulfil this one office *of education* well, mothers need their *universal human culture in its entirety*. But even if this were not so, if motherhood did not require the concentration of woman's personality; even if motherliness remained only 'primitive instinct', yet this instinct, in the women who have guarded it, is more valuable for mankind that the universal human development of power of the women who have lost this instinct. No social nor individual activity of women could compensate for the extinction of this 'instinct', which only recently in Messina drove hundreds of mothers to shield their children with their own bodies; this 'instinct', which recently impelled a mother, who learned before she gave birth to her child that her own life must be the price for the saving of that of the child, to cry: 'I have lived, but the life of my child belongs now to mankind – save the child!' So the mother died without even having seen the beautiful being for whom she gave her life. In the world of 'personally' developed women, however, after a new Messina catastrophe the mothers would be found with their manuscript and their pictures in their arms. And confronted with a choice like that related above, the mother would answer: 'Let the child die, I will live my personal life to the end.'

The amaternal type must persist for the present. There are in reality in our time many women who with unresponsive eyes can pass by a lovely child, among them even mothers who do not feel the pure sensuousness, the wise madness, the intoxicating delight which such a child awakens in every motherly woman; mothers who have no conception what a fascinating subject for study the soul of a child can offer. Jean Paul, who scourged worthless mothers and tried to awaken the repressed maternal instinct of this time with the charge that a woman who is bored when she has children, is a contemptible creature, would find today many mothers who are bored only if they have their children about them.

And these cerebral, amaternal women must obviously be accorded the freedom of finding the domestic life, with its limited but intensive exercise of power meagre, beside the feeling of power which they enjoy as public personalities, as consummate women of the world, as talented professionals. But they have not the right to *falsify life values* in their own favour so that they themselves shall represent the highest form of life, the 'human personality' in comparison with which the 'instinctively feminine' signifies a lower stage of development, a poorer type of life.

Women who have produced books and works of art, to be compared, as respects permanence of value, to confetti at a carnival, have, according to this viewpoint, proved themselves human individualities, while a mother who has contributed an endless amount of clear thought, rich understanding, warm feeling, and strong will to the education of a fine group of children, requires a public office in order to prove herself a 'human personality'! The brain work which a woman employs in a commercial concern bears witness to her individuality, but the brain work which a large, well-managed household demands, does not. The woman physician who delivers a mother expresses her 'personality', but the mother has put no 'personality' into the feelings with which she has borne the child, the dreams with which she has consecrated it, the ideas in accordance with which she has educated it! The girl who has passed her examination has proved herself a developed human being; but her grandmother, who is now filled with the kindness and wisdom which she had won in a life dedicated to domestic duties, a life in which the restricted sphere of her duties did not prevent the comprehensiveness of her cultural interests, nor her all-embracing sympathy with humanity – such a woman is not a personality!

When men advance as an argument against women's rights the fear that women will lose their womanliness in public life, the older feminists answer that womanliness, especially motherliness, is rooted too firmly in nature to make it possible for this danger to exist. Nothing has, however, become more clear in this amaternalistic time than that motherliness is *not* an indestructible instinct. Just as our time produces in increasing numbers sterile women and women incapable of nursing their children, so it produces more and more psychically amaternal women. We can pass in silence the cases of children martyred in families or in children's homes, for sexual perversity and religious fanaticism often play a role in such connections; we can also pass by the millions of mothers who bring about the abortion of their offspring, for the poor are driven to such practices largely by necessity, the rich mostly by love of pleasure. There still remain a sufficient number of women in whom the mother instinct has faded away because of a course of thought like that just described. Our time furnishes manifold proofs of the fact that the mother instinct can easily be weakened, or even entirely disappear, although the erotic impulse continues to live; that motherliness is not a spontaneous natural instinct, but the product of thousands of years not merely of *child-bearing*, but also of *child-rearing;* and that it must be strengthened in each new generation by the personal care which mothers bestow upon their children. A woman learns to love the strange child whom she nurses as if it were her own; a father who can devote himself to the care of his little children is possessed by an almost 'motherly tenderness' for them, as are also older brothers and sisters for the little ones whom they care for. But while those who advocate the cause of the amaternal women draw from such facts the conclusion that motherliness cannot be used as a criterion of womanliness, yet an entirely different conclusion forces itself upon everyone who sees in the united uplift of the individual and of mankind the criterion of the life-enhancing effect of the woman movement, the conclusion that the amaternal soul not only confirms the worst apprehensions of men in regard to the results of the woman movement, but also constitutes the greatest danger to the woman movement itself. For the amaternal ideas will evoke a violent reaction *on the part of men*, in case such a reaction does not appear at an early stage on the part of women.

This latter reaction might also include a rebellion against the methods of industrial production, which exhaust the strength of mothers and children. For the objection of industrialism, that 'it cannot exist without women', falls to the ground in face of the fact that a race cannot exist without sound and moral mothers. And 'moral' means, here, mothers capable and willing to bear sound children and to train children along moral lines. If, on the contrary, Europe and America adhere to the economic and ethical principles which prevent a number of able and willing women of this type from becoming mothers, and if numbers of other women who could be mothers continue unwilling to assume the burden of motherhood, then this problem will finally become the problem of *a future for the European-American people*.

The woman movement must now with resolute determination abandon the narrow, biased attitude, psychologically natural a generation ago when the zealots of feminism had no other standard of value for an idea, an investigation, or a book, than whether they *advanced or did not advance* the cause of woman; whether they *proved or did not prove* woman's equality with man. For woman's work, studies, and other accomplishments, no other standard was applied than that of equality with man's work, man's studies, and the accomplishments of man. In a word, the proposition was that woman should be enabled to perform at the same time the life-work of a woman and of a man!

It is through these hybrids that the feminine sex transgresses against the masculine. And this is one reason why our time is so filled with the tragic vicissitudes of women. Truly, every progressive person must agree with Goethe's aphorism, 'I love him whom the impossible lures'. For, thus allured, man has elevated his particular generation above the generation preceding. But *in action* every one must go down who is not imbued with the consciousness that whoever exceeds his limits is liable to tragic consequences, in the modern psychological view of the guilt attaching to one who undertakes more than his strength will allow.

But our time exhibits also other less convulsively strained conditions of the feminine soul and therefore also brighter fates for woman. It shows not infrequently wives united with their husbands, not only by the sympathy which the human personality of each inspires, but also by the erotic attraction which the sex character of each exercises. And they have both won thereby that unity through which all the best and highest powers of their being are liberated and elevated as by religion. And their parenthood will then be the highest expression of this religion.

Only religious natures are – in the deepest meaning of the word – loving or faithful or creative. It is the same soul which in one person reveals itself in ecstasy of belief, in a second in ardour of creation, in a third in a great erotic passion, in the fourth as parental love, in others again as love of country, as enthusiasm for freedom, desire for reform. At times one and the same soul, a woman's or a man's, is kindled by all these passions. But never has the same soul been able *at the same time* to feed all these passions in their highest potency. Whether it be God, a work, or a human being that the soul embraces with its entire devotion, the religious character of this devotion always evinces itself in increasing longing, an endless susceptibility, a more persistent search after means of expression, a continual service, an inexhaustible patience in waiting for reciprocal activity from the object of love. The religious strength of a feeling consists of this, that the soul in every work, every sorrow, every joy – in a word, in every spiritual condition, every experience – is, consciously as well as unconsciously, more closely united with God, with the work, with the beloved, until every finest fibre of one's being reaches down to the profound depths which the object of love represents for the lover.

In this necessary condition of concentration of the spiritual life is found the truth of woman's complaint that the man, absorbed by his work, 'no longer loves her'; the truth of the experience that earthly love indisputably detracts from the love of God; the truth of the frequent experience of husband and wife that with children the wealth of their spiritual life together is in certain respects inevitably diminished; the truth of man's fear that woman's absorption in a life-work personally dear to her must to a certain degree detract from her devotion to the home; the truth of the experience that the office of mother often interferes with the development of woman's intellectual power.

Only persons who distinguish themselves by what Heine called 'exuberance of mental poverty', or what I might call analogously an 'abyss of superficiality', have not experienced the severe and beautiful psychic truth of Jesus' glorification of *simplicity*. The quiet harkening to the voice of God or to the inspiration of work or to the delicate vibrations of another soul, which daily, hourly, momentarily, are the conditions that enable the soul to live wholly in its belief, its work, its love, so that these feelings may grow stronger and the soul grow greater through these feelings – all this has 'simplicity' as a condition; in a word, symmetrical unity, longing for completeness, inner poise, the swift emotion. Fidelity – to a belief, a work, a love – is no product of duty. It is a process of growth.

These are the conditions to which many modern women, womanly at heart but divided, restless, groping, attempting much, will not submit. They could even learn to reverence these conditions in the child for whom play is such sacred seriousness; but instead they transform the most sacred earnest into play.

Other women, on the contrary, are beginning to understand these conditions of growth and to comprehend that it was exactly the protected position of woman in the home, which has made it possible for her family feeling to acquire that depth which is to be attained only by concentration. But if this is no longer possible, then woman will love those that belong to her with less religious warmth. Nothing can better illustrate the difference still existing between man and woman in this respect, than the fact that most men would consider themselves unfortunate if their entire exercise of power were concentrated upon the family, while most women still feel themselves fortunate when they have been given the opportunity to exercise to the uttermost the tendency inherent in them. For most women love best *personally* and *in propinquity*, while the potency of love in man often seeks distant goals. Woman is happy in the degree to which she can bestow her love upon a person closely connected with her; if she cannot do that, then she may be useful, resigned, content, but never happy.[4] The very fact that woman's strongest *primitive instinct* coincided with her *greatest* cultural *office* has been an essential factor in the harmony of her being.

The modern developed mother feels with every breath of grateful joy in that she lives the most perfect life when she can contribute her developed human powers, her liberated human personality, to the establishment of a home and to the vocation of motherhood. These functions conceived and understood as social, in the embracing sense in which the word is now used, give the new mother a richer opportunity to exercise her entire personality that she could find in modern commercial work. In one such occupation she must suppress either the intellectual or the emotional side of her nature; in another, the life either of the imagination or of the will. In domestic duties, on the contrary, these powers of the soul can work in unison. This is undoubtedly the deepest reason why, taken as a whole, women have become more harmonious, and men stronger in any special crisis, women more soulful, men more gifted. On this account men offer their great sacrifice more readily for an idea, or for the accomplishment of a work; women, for persons closely connected with them. And yet this co-operation of woman's spiritual powers was in earlier times partly repressed by man's demand for passivity on the part of woman as a thinking and willing personality, but for her unceasing activity as promoter of his comfort and that of the entire home. The mother of today can, on the contrary, exercise, as distributer, her culture, her thought, her supervision, her judgment, and her criticism, in order to make fully effective the faculty of her sex for foresight and organisation. She applies a great amount of spiritual energy to the selection of the essentials and the subordination of secondary things, to the creation of such facilities in the material work that time and means are left for the spiritual values, which, alas, are still neglected in the domestic economy of small, private households, as well as in national housekeeping. And as mother, modern woman is offered the first fitting opportunity to assert herself as a thinking and willing personality.

The significance of the vocation of mother has been underrated in its significance even by moderate feminists. But these were right when they demonstrated that the 'sanctity' of this office had become a mere phrase, so badly or amateurishly was this vocation fulfilled – an indictment in which Nietzsche and feminism for one rare moment are on common ground. Mothers needed the spur of this contempt; it was necessary that their feeling of responsibility, their universal human culture, their personal self-reliance, should be aroused by the woman movement. Only so could the new generation acquire the new type of women who for the present seek to qualify themselves by self-culture for the office of mother, in the expectation that for all women an obligatory education for motherhood will be realised. So long as this vocation *can* be practised without any training, nothing can be known of the possibilities whereby ordinary mothers may become good educators – unless they place the mother love and the intuitive understanding of the nature of the child that it affords above even the best outside teachers. Just as a glorious voice makes a country girl a 'natural singer', so nature has at all times made certain mothers – and not least the women of the people – natural educators of children.

The biography of nearly every great man shows the place the mother through her personality occupied in the life of her son, the atmosphere which she diffused about her in the home, her direct and indirect influence. But only the culture of their natural gifts with conscious purpose will make of mothers artists.

When Nietzsche wrote: '*There will come a time when we shall have no other thought than education*', and when he placed this education specifically in the hands of mothers, least of all did he mean those 'arts of education', from which amaternals believe they 'guard' children by rejecting an 'artistically creative' home training by the mother, as a violence to the peculiar characteristic of the child!

The *new mother*, as the doctrine of evolution and the true woman movement have created her, stands with deep veneration before the mystic depths she calls her child, a being in whom the whole life of mankind is garnered. The richer the nature of the child is, the more zealously she endeavours to preserve for him that simplicity which he needs, and at the same time to provide for him the material that will enable him to work for himself. She insures to the child the pleasures adapted to his age, pleasures which at no later time can be enjoyed so intensely. The effect upon him of his playfellows and books, of nature, art, music, conversation, of the entire home *milieu* which the child receives, above all the influence of the personality and interests of the father and mother – all these the mother who is an artist in education observes in order to learn the natural proclivity of the child and then *directly to strengthen and encourage it*. At the same time she endeavours to find out what *restraints* are necessary *in order that the natural bent be not impeded in its growth by secondary qualities*. But the new type of mother does not seek to *eradicate;* she recognises the likeness between wheat and tares. The Christian education, which has thus far prevailed, has exercised a restraining oppression or has done violence to the 'sinful nature', which must be broken and bent; this education was dermatological, not psychological, in method.

The new mother is especially characterised by the fact that she has rejected this earlier method. She allows her child, within certain bounds, full freedom, and demands, beyond those bounds, unconditional obedience. She helps the child to find for himself ever nobler motives for repression. This she can do because from the very beginning she has taken care of him; year by year she has persevered in the effort to establish good habits; she has tried to enlist as aids, food, bath, bed, dress, air, and play in the effort to keep him strong, sound, sexually pure – conditions fundamental to the whole later conduct of life. Such a methodical physical care *can* be performed by the mother herself, while, on the other hand, in the first years of childhood paid hands might, through carelessness, stupidity, cruelty, laxity, or over-indulgence, destroy the glorious possibilities. If the prevention of *the possibilities of nature being warped or destroyed* constituted all that a mother could give, this one task would, nevertheless, be more important than any social relief work.

What characterises the new mother is that she understands the enormous significance of the *first years*, when the indispensable 'training' takes place, in which the future life of the child is determined by the methods employed – whether they be those of torture or of culture, irrational or rational. Then the great problem must be solved of establishing willing obedience from within in place of the hitherto *enforced* obedience from without; of maintaining self-control, won by self, in place of self-control *imposed* from without; of evoking voluntary renunciation in place of enforcing renunciation. For the capacity for obedience, for self-control, for renunciation, is one of the qualities fundamental to the whole later conduct of life. The new mother knows this as well as the mother of former times. But she endeavours to create this capacity by slow and sure means. The same thing obtains in regard to physical and psychical courage, which in the early years can often be so demoralised by fright that it can never emerge again. The training which hitherto was customary – based on *compelling* and *forbidding* – had its effect only upon the surface and *prevented* the child from experiencing *the results of his own choice*.

It is this *indirect* education by results which is the new mother's method. Her unceasing vigilance and consistency are required in order that the child shall actually bear the results of his actions. What she needs for this is first and foremost, *time*, *time*, and again *time*. Apparently good effects can be obtained much quicker by intervening, preventing, punishing, but thus are turned aside the *real* results. By this method the child is deprived of the *inner* growth, which only the fully experienced reality with its components of bitter and sweet can give; and this growth the new mother endeavours to advance. Much more time still is necessary to play the psychological game of chess, which consists in the checkmating of black by white; in other words, the conquest of negative characteristics by positive, through the child's own activity – a task in which the child at first must be guided, just as in the assimilation of the elements of every other accomplishment, but in which he can later perfect himself. Modern investigation in the realm of the soul enables us to see the dangers which sometime will demand quite as new methods in spiritual hygiene as bacteriology has created in the hygiene of the body. But we still leave unexercised powers of the soul, still misunderstand spiritual laws which sometime will radically transform the means of education.

At some future day the new mothers will institute legal protection for children to an extent incomprehensible to us and therefore provocative only of smiles. For example, legal prohibition of corporal punishment by parents as well as teachers; legal prohibition of child labour, of certain tenement conditions, certain 'amusements', certain improper uses of the press. For the present every individual educator must *set these laws over himself;* must sedulously create counter influences to cope with the destructive influences which great cities, especially, exert upon children.[5] The new mothers lead children out into nature and endeavour to satisfy their zeal for activity by appropriate tasks as well as to encourage by suitable means their love of invention and their impulse for play. In the country children provide much for themselves. But what both city and country children need is a mother familiar with nature, who can answer the questions which the child is by his own observations prompted to ask; and the number of such mothers is continually increasing. Both city and country children need also a mother who can tell stories. Just as the settlement gardens most clearly demonstrate how sundered the working people of the great cities are from nature, so the 'story evenings', which are now established for children, show how far children have been permitted to stray from the mother, who formerly gathered them about her for the hour of story, play, and song. What, finally, children need is the mother's delicate revelation of the sexual 'mystery', which often early exercises the thoughts of the child and in which he should be initiated quietly and gradually by the mother.

All the educational influences here outlined emanate not only from the enlightened, exceptional mother; they are exercised by the average mother of today to better advantage than by the spiritually significant mother of fifty years ago. And they are *quite as essential*, in order that the highest possibility within the reach of each may be attained, in the education of the genius as in that of the ordinary child. Such influences in like degree strengthen the innate bent of the genius and raise the average, from generation to generation, to a level where man can live according to higher standards than those of the present time. The new mothers understand that for the utilisation of all these opportunities that make their appearance in the first seven years of the child's life, their motherly tenderness, gentleness, and patience do not suffice; that they need in addition all the intelligence, imagination, fine feeling, scientific methods of observation, ethical and æsthetic culture and other spiritual acquisitions they possess, as direct and indirect fruits of the woman movement.

When student and comrade life begin to claim the children, when the influence of the mother – that is of the new mother who has respect for the peculiar characteristic, the human worth, and the right of the child to live his own life – becomes more indirect, she nevertheless bears in mind that it is of the utmost importance that the son and the daughter should *find the mother*, when they return to the parental roof; that they should be able to breathe there an atmosphere of peace and warmth; that they should find the attentive eye, the listening ear, the helpful hand; that the mother should have the repose, the fine feeling, the observation requisite for following, without interfering with, the conflicts of youth; that she should not demand confidences but be always at hand to receive them; that she should show vital sympathy for the plans of work, the disappointments, the joys, of the young people; that she should always have time for caresses, tears, smiles, comfort, and care; that she should divine their moods, and anticipate their desires. By all these means the mother perpetuates in the soul of the child, unknown to him and to herself, her own personality. The talent which she has not redeemed by a productive work of her own, perhaps often for that very reason, benefits mankind in a son or a daughter, in whose soul the mother had implanted the social ideas, the dreams, the rebellion, which later become in them social deeds or works of art. Above all, in the restless, sensitive, life-deciding years when the boy is becoming a youth and the little girl a maiden, the mother needs quiet and leisure to be able to give the ineffably needy children 'the hoarded, secret treasure of her heart', as the beautiful saying of Dūrer runs.

When such a mother is found, and such mothers are already found, she is the most splendid fruit of the woman movement's sowing upon the field of woman's nature.

Because the new mother created for herself an open space about her own personality, she understands her son or her daughter when they in their turn push her aside in order to create that same open space about themselves. For in every generation the young renounce the ideals and the aims of their parents. The knowledge of this does not prevent the new mother, any more than it did the mother of earlier times, from feeling the pain incident to being set aside. But the former looks forward to a day when the son and daughter will freely choose her as a friend, having discovered what a significant pleasure the mother's personality can afford them.

As the bird's nest is made of nothing but bits of straw and down, so the feeling of home is fashioned out of soft, simple things; out of little activities that are neither ponderable nor measurable as political or as economic factors. When Segantini painted the two nuns looking wistfully into the bird's nest, he gave expression to the deepest pain that many modern women experience, the pain resulting from the consciousness that their life, notwithstanding its freedom, is lonely, because it has denied them the privilege of making a home and as a consequence has failed to afford them the joy of creation, which nature intended they should have, and of continuity of life in children to whom they gave birth.

Here we stand at a point where the woman movement parallels the other social revolutions, undeviatingly as the rails of a track, and leads to the same objective. Modern men and women, and especially women, have forfeited an opportunity for happiness in the loss of the feeling of homogeneity and security. Just as formerly the property-holding family felt a secure sense of proprietorship in the ancestral estate, so every member of the home group felt himself safe in the family. Now the children cannot depend with certainty upon the parents, nor the parents upon the children; the wife upon the husband, nor the husband upon the wife. Each in extremity relies only upon himself. The character of man is thus altered quite as much as trees are changed when they are left standing alone in the denuded forest of which they once formed a part. If they can withstand the storms, they have produced more 'character' than they had when they stood close together, under a mutual protection that nevertheless enforced uniformity.

From their earliest youth innumerable women must now care for themselves, as well as decide for themselves. Thus the feeling of independence of modern woman has increased through the sacrifice of her peace; her individual characteristics, at the expense of her harmony. Her feeling of loneliness is mitigated to a certain degree by the growing feeling of community with the whole. But this feeling cannot compensate certain natures for the forfeiture of the advantages which women of earlier times possessed, when they sat secure and protected within the four walls of the home, sucked the juice from family chronicles, guarded family traditions, maintained the old holiday customs, lived at the same time in the past and in the present.

The new woman lives in the present, sometimes even in the future – her land of romance! The enthusiasm of the old romanticism about a 'hut and a heart' has little charm for her. For she knows reality and that prevents her from giving credence to the feminine illusion that twice two can be five. What she does know, on the contrary, is that out of fours she can gradually work out sixteen. While the women of former times could only save, the new woman can acquire. Woman's beautiful, foolish superstition regarding life has vanished, but her eagerness to achieve can still remove mountains, her daring has still often the splendour of a dream. Intellectual values are for her no longer pastimes but necessities of life; with her culture has developed her feeling for truth and justice. This does not secure the new woman immunity at all times from new illusions and errors of feeling, nor does it prevent her developing passions whose value, to say the least, is questionable. But in and through her determination 'to be some one', to have a characteristic personality, she has acquired a love of life, in its diverse manifestations, both good and evil; a new capacity to enjoy her own and others' individuality, as well as a new joy – sometimes an unblushing, insolent joy – in expressing her own being. In place of the earlier resignation toward society, the expression of rebellion is found even in the sparkling eye of the school-girl, with red cap upon her curly hair.

The young women of today, married or single, mothers as well as those who are childless, are still more vigorous in soul, more courageous, more eager for life than are men. Because all that which for men has so long been a matter of course, is for women new, rich, enchanting, comprising, as it does, free life in nature, scientific studies, serious artistic work, economic independence. Even in a fine and soulful woman there is found something of the inevitable hardness toward herself and others of which an observer is instinctively conscious when he speaks of some woman as one who 'will go far' upon the course she has chosen. The modern young woman desires above all else the elevation of her own personality. She experiences the same feeling of joy a man is conscious of when she realises that her strength of will is augmented, her ability becoming more certain, her depth of thought greater, her association of ideas richer. She stands ready to choose *her* work and follow *her* fate; in sorrow as in joy she experiences the blessedness of growth, and she loves her view of life and the work to which she has dedicated herself, often as devotedly as man loves his.

If we compare the seventeen-year-old girl of today with her progenitor living in the middle of the foregoing century, we find that the girl of earlier times was to a larger extent swayed by feeling, and that the modern girl is to a larger extent determined by ideas. The former was directed more to the centre of life, the latter remains often nearer the periphery; the former was warmer, the latter is more intelligent; the former was better balanced, the latter is more interesting.

The restlessness, the uncertainty, the feeling of emptiness, the suffering, that is sometimes experienced by the young woman of today, is primarily traceable to the disintegration of religious belief, which gave to the older generation of emancipated women an inner stability, resignation, and self-discipline. Scientific study has deprived many modern women of their belief and those who can create a new one, suited to their needs, are still very few. Thus to the outer homelessness an inner estrangement is added. The woman movement has, it is true, contributed indirectly to this spiritual distress by making the road to man's culture accessible to woman. For men also suffer in like manner, and suffer above all perhaps because our culture is unstable, aimless, and lacks style, owing to the very fact that it is at present without a religious centre. And even the future can give to mankind no such new centre as the Middle Ages had, for example, in Catholicism. The attainment of individualism has shut out that possibility forever.

But *one* factor in the religion of the past, the adoration of motherhood as divine mystery; *one* factor in the religion of the Middle Ages, the worship of the Madonna, has meanwhile been given back to the present by the doctrine of evolution, with that universal validity which the thought must possess which seeks to give again to culture a centre. Great, solitary individuals – prophets more often than sibyls – have proclaimed the religion of this generation. But the word will become flesh only when fathers and mothers instil into the blood and soul of children their devout hope for a higher humanity. When women are permeated by this hope, this new devout feeling, then they will recover the piety, the peace, and the harmony which for the present, and partly owing to feminism, have been lost.

The innumerable new relations which the woman movement has established between woman and the home, between woman and society, and all of the interchanges of new spiritual forces which have been put in operation because of these relations, cannot possibly take fixed form, at least not so long as the woman movement remains 'a movement'; in other words, as long as everything is in a condition of flux, in a state of becoming, all spiritual relationships between individuals must change their form. Continual new, fine shades of feeling, not to be expressed in words, determine every woman's soul and every woman's fate. And even ancient feelings receive continually different nuances, different intonations. I am, therefore, laying down no laws but merely recapitulating certain suggestions based on what has previously been said in regard to the soul of the modern woman, as seen in that portion of the present generation whose age ranges between twenty and thirty years – that is to say, that part of the generation which is decisive for the immediate future.

Since co-education is becoming more and more general, each

sex is beginning to have more esteem for the other, and woman, as well as man, is beginning to found self-respect upon work. When all women by culture and capacity for work have finally become strong-willed, self-supporting co-workers in society, then no woman will give or receive love for any extraneous benefit whatsoever. No outward tie and no outward gain through love – this is the ultimate aim of the new sex morale as the most highly developed modern young woman sees it.

The new woman is deeply convinced that the relation between the sexes attains its true beauty and sanctity only when every external privilege disappears on both sides, when man and woman stand wholly equal in what concerns their legal right and their personal freedom.

She demands that the contrasts between legal and illegal, rich and poor, boy and girl, shall disappear, and that society shall show the same interest in the complete human development of all children. She knows that when both sexes awake to a feeling of responsibility toward the future generation, then the real concern of sexual morale becomes the endeavour to give the race an ever more perfect progeny. And in order to feel in its fulness this command, maidens as well as youths must henceforth demand scientific instruction in sexual duties.

The new woman is deeply convinced that only when she feels happy – and happiness signifies the development of the powers inherent in the personality – can she properly fulfil her duties as daughter, wife, and mother. She can consciously sacrifice a part of her personality, for example forego the development of a talent, but she can never subjugate nor surrender her whole personality and at the same time remain a strongwilled member of the family or of society, in the broadest meaning of the word. She must assert her conception of life, her feeling of right, her ideals. And no special considerations for children, husband, or family life are, for her, above the consideration which, in this respect, she owes to her own personality. When conflicts arise, she seeks, wherever possible, a solution that will permit her to fulfil her duty without annihilating herself. But if this is not possible, then she feels that it is her first duty not to fall below her ideal, either physically or spiritually. For this would prevent her from fulfilling precisely those duties for which she has so sacrificed herself; duties which she can perhaps perform later under other conditions, provided she has saved herself from being extinguished by brutality or despotism.

But along with this individualism there exists in the new woman a feeling for the unity of existence, the unity in which all things are parts and in which nothing is lost. She does not, then, look upon husband and children as continually demanding sacrifice and upon herself as being always sacrificed; she sees herself and them, as in the antiquity of the race, always existing *by means of one another*. She is not consumed by her love, for she knows that under such circumstances she would deprive her loved ones of the wealth of her personality. But although she will not, like the women of earlier times, abandon her ego *absolutely*, she will not, on the other hand, like certain modern feminists, keep it *unreservedly*. She will preserve upon a higher plane the old division of labour which made man the one who felled the game, fought the battles, made conquests, achieved advancement through victories; and which made woman the one who rendered the new domains habitable, who utilised the booty for herself and hers, who transmitted what was won to the new generation – all that of which woman's ancient tasks as guardian of the fire and cultivator of the fields are beautiful symbols. She feels that when each sex pursues its course for the happiness of the individual and of mankind, but at the same time and as an equal helps the other in the different tasks, then each is most capable, then society is most benefited.

The fact that there is still so much masculine brutality and despotism, and that there are so many legal means at man's disposal whereby he may put into practice with impunity this brutality and despotism, is the reason why the new woman is still always a 'feminist', why she still maintains the fundamental tenets of the woman movement. But she is not a feminist in the sense that she turns *against* man. Her solution is always that of Mary Wollstonecraft: 'We do not desire to rule over men but to rule over ourselves.' She often exhibits now in deliberation and in determination the characteristics which were formerly called 'masculine': practical knowledge, love of truth, courage of conviction; she desists more and more from unjust imputations and empty words; she proposes a greater number of well-considered suggestions for improvements. The woman movement has now in a word a more universally human, a less onesidedly feminine character. It emphasises more and more the fact that the right of woman is a necessity in order that she may fulfil her duties in the small, individual family, and exercise her powers in the great, universal human family for the general good. The new woman does not wish to displace man nor to abolish society. She wishes to be able to exercise *everywhere* her most beautiful prerogative to help, to support, to comfort. But this she cannot do so long as she is not free as a citizen and has not fully developed as a human personality. She knows that this is the condition not only of her own happiness, but also, in quite as high a degree, of the happiness of man. For every man who works, struggles, and suffers there is a mother, a wife, a sister, a daughter, who suffers with him. For every woman who in her way works and struggles, there is a father, a husband, a brother, or a son for whom her contribution directly or indirectly has significance. Above all, the modern woman understands that in every marriage wherein a wife still suffers under man's misuse of his legal authority, it is in the last analysis *the man who sustains the greatest injury*, for under present conditions he needs exercise neither kindness nor justice nor intelligence to be ruler in the family. These humane characteristics he must, therefore, begin to develop when the wife is legally his equal.

The sacred conviction of the new woman is that man and woman *rise together*, just as they *sink together*.

The masculine and the feminine characteristics, which exist side by side in the poet soul, produce work in co-operation. Alternately, however, they seek to usurp the entire power, whereby is occasioned the disharmony which enters into the life of those who endeavour to fulfil at one and the same time the universal, human duties as well as those of sex. Indeed it may be that one of the reasons why great poetic geniuses, masculine as well as feminine, have often had no progeny at all, and in other cases one of little significance, is that their nature was not capable of a double production, that poetic creation received the richest part of their physical and psychical power.

Whether the opinion of genius expressed here is correct or not, does not, however, affect the general situation. For the genius will always go his own way, which is never that of the average man. From the point of view of the ordinary individual an effacement of the spiritual sex-character would be in still higher degree a misfortune for culture and nature. For it is the difference in the spiritual as well as in the physical sex-characteristics that makes love a fusion of two beings in a higher unity, where each finds the full deliverance and harmony of his being. With the elimination of the *spiritual* difference *psychical* love would vanish. There would be left, then, upon the one side, only the mating instinct, in which the same points of view as in animal breeding must obtain; on the other, only the same kind of sympathy which is expressed in the friendship between persons of the same sex, the sympathy in which the human, individual difference instead of sexual difference forms the attraction. In love, on the other hand, sympathy grows in intensity, the more universally human and at the same time sexually attractive the individual is: the 'manly' in man is charmed by the 'womanly' in woman, while the 'womanly' in man is likewise captivated by the 'manly' in woman, and vice versa. But when neither needs the *spiritual sex* of the other as his complement, then man, in erotic respects, returns to the antique conception of the sex relationship, of which Plato has drawn the final logical conclusion.

The 'humanity' in the soul of man was strengthened when he felt himself necessary to mother and child. When woman by sweetness and tenderness taught man to love, not only to desire, then his humanity increased immeasurably.

In our time the average man is beginning to learn that woman does not desire him as man, that she looks down upon him as a lower kind of being, that she does not need him as supporter. He does not at all grasp what it is the woman of highest culture seeks, demands, and awaits from his sex. But he learns that even the mediocre woman rejects the best he has to give her erotically; that imbued as she is with ideals of 'universal humanity', she no longer needs him as the supplement to her sexual being. Then brutality awakes in him anew; then his erotic life loses what humanity it had won; then he begins to hate woman. And not with the imaginative, theoretical hatred of thinkers and poets; but with the blind-rage which the contempt of the weaker for the stronger arouses in him. And here we encounter what is, perhaps, the deepest reason for the present war between the sexes, appearing already in the literary world as well as in the labour market.

Here the extreme feminists play unconsciously about an abyss – the depths in the nature of man out of which the elementary, hundred-thousand-year-old impulses arise, the impulses which all cultural acquisitions and influences cannot eradicate, so long as the human race continues to subsist and multiply under present conditions.

The feminism which has driven individualism to the point where the individual asserts her personality in opposition to, instead of within, the race; the individualism which becomes self-concentration, anti-social egoism, although the watchword inscribed upon its banner is 'Society instead of the family' – this feminism will bear the blame should the hatred referred to lead to war.

It would be a pity to conclude a survey of the influence of the woman movement with an expression of fear lest this extreme feminism should be victorious. I believe not; no more than I believe that the sun will for the present be extinguished or streams flow back to their sources.

No 'culture' can annul the great fundamental laws of nature; it can only ennoble them; and motherhood is one of these fundamental laws. I hope that the future will furnish a new and a more secure protection for motherhood than the present family and social organisation affords. I place my trust in a new society, with a new morality, which will be a synthesis of the being of man and that of woman, of the demands of the individual and those of society, of the pagan and Christian conceptions of life, of the will of the future and reverence for the past.

When the earth blooms with this beautiful and vigorous flower of morality, there will no longer be a woman movement. But there will always be a woman question, not put by women to society but by society to women: the question whether they will continue in a higher degree to prove themselves worthy of the great privilege of being the mothers of the new generation.

In the degree in which this new ethics permeates mankind, women will answer this question in life-affirmation. And the result of their life-affirmation will be an enormous enhancement of life, not only for women themselves but for all mankind.

NOTES

1 An inquiry instituted among English women as to whether they would prefer to be men or women gave as a result the fact that, out of about 7000 who answered, two-thirds wished to remain women and this above all in order to be mothers, while a third wished to be men. This indicated probably the highest figure of the disinclination for maternity which such a *European* inquiry could elicit. But even these women who wish to marry and to become mothers feel the pressure of the idea created by the zealots of the woman movement which finds expression often in the following conversation between two former schoolmates about a third: 'And A – what is she doing now?' – 'Nothing – she is married and has children.'

The old folk legend about the girl who trampled on the bread she was carrying to her mother because she wished to go dry-shod, can serve as symbol of many modern women zealots: life's great, sound values are offered for the meal; vanity sits down alone to partake of them.

2 This amaternal idea is advanced with great ability in some works of Charlotte Perkins Stetson and Rosa Mayreder. The word amaternal coined by me is used to characterise the theory subsequently advanced, because the word unmaternal (unmotherly) signifies a *spiritual condition*, the antithesis to 'motherliness'. The maternal as opposed to the amaternal theory is this: that a woman's life is lived most intensively and most extensively, most individually and most socially; she is for her own part most free, and for others most fruitful, most egoistic and most altruistic, most receptive and most generous, in and with the *physical and psychic exercise of the function of maternity, because of the conscious*

desire, by means of this function, to uplift the life of the race as well as her own life.

3 It can even be shown that, if man invades the so-called woman's spheres (for example the art of cooking or of dress-making), it is most frequently he who makes new discoveries and attains great success!

4 The best proof of this is that many women who, in a life free from care in an outward sense, were comparable only to geese or peacocks, nevertheless, when hard times came and gave them opportunity to develop their power of love, not only proved themselves heroines, but asserted that their 'happy' years were those in which they had so 'sacrificed' themselves.

5 How many children have had their idea of right debased by the manner in which the 'Captain of Köpernick' was received at his liberation – to cite only one example.

The Spinster

By One *The Freewoman*

23 November 1911

I write of the High Priestess of Society. Not of the mother of sons, but of her barren sister, the withered tree, the acidulous vestal under whose pale shadow we chill and whiten, of the Spinster I write. Because of her power and dominion. She, unobtrusive, meek, soft-footed, silent, shamefaced, bloodless and boneless, thinned to spirit, enters the secret recesses of the mind, sits at the secret springs of action, and moulds and fashions our emasculate Society. She is our social Nemesis. For the insult of her creation, without knowing it she takes her revenge. What she has become, she makes all. To every form of social life she gives its complexion. Every book, every play, every sermon, every song, each bears her inscription. The Churches she has made her own. Their message and their conventions are for her type, and of their Ideal she has made a Spinster transfigured. In the auditorium of every theatre she sits, the pale guardian. What the players say and do, they say and do never forgetting her presence. She haunts every library. Her eye will pierce the cover of every book, and her glance may not be offended. In our schools she takes the little children, and day by day they breathe in the atmosphere of her violated spirit. She tinges every conversation, she weights each moral judgment. She rules the earth. All our outward morality is made to accommodate her, and any alien, wild life-impulse which clamours for release is released in secret, in shame, and under the sense of sin. A restive but impotent world writhes under her subtle priestly domination. She triumphs, and we turn half expecting to see in her the joy of triumph. But no, not that even. She has no knowledge of it. All is pure fatality. She remains at once the injured and the injuring. Society has cursed her and the curse is now roosting at home.

The indictment which the Spinster lays up against Society is that of ingenious cruelty. The type of intelligence which, in its immaturity, conceived the tortures of a Tantalus might have essayed the creation of a spinster as its ripe production. See how she is made, and from what. She is mothered into the world by a being, who, whatever else she may be, is not a spinster, and from this being she draws her instincts. While yet a child these instincts are intensified and made self-conscious by the development, in her own person, of a phenomenon which is unmistakable, repellent, and recurrent with a rapid and painful certainty. This development engenders its own lassitude, and in this lassitude new instincts are set free. Little by little, the development of her entire form sets towards a single consummation, and all the while, by every kind of device, the mind is set towards the same consummation. In babyhood, she begins, with her dolls. Why do not the parents of a prospective spinster give her a gun or an engine. If Society is going to have spinsters, it should train spinsters. In girlhood, she is ushered into an atmosphere charged with sex-distinctions and sex-insinuations. She is educated on a literature saturated with these. In every book she takes up, in every play she sees, in every conversation, in every social amusement, in every interest in life she finds that the pivot upon which all interest turns is the sex interest. So body, mind, training, and environment unite to produce in her an expectation which awaits definite fulfilment. She is ready to marry, ripe to marry, needing marriage, and up to this point Society has been blameless. It is in the next step that she sins. Did Society inculcate nothing more, Nature would step in to solve her own difficulties, as she does where Society and its judgments have little weight. Among the very poor there is no spinster difficulty, because the very poor do not remain spinsters. It is from higher up in the social scale, where social judgments count, where the individual is a little more highly wrought, better fashioned for suffering, that we draw the army of actual spinsters. It is in the classes where it is not good form to have too much feeling, and actual bad form to show any; where there is a smattering of education, and little interests to fill in the time, that their numbers rally and increase. It is here that Society, after having fostered just expectations, turns round arbitrarily on one perhaps in every four and says, 'Thou shalt not.' No reason given, only outlawry prescribed if the prohibition is disregarded. And because Society has a dim consciousness of its own treachery – for its protection and like a coward – it lays down the law of silence, and in subtle fashion makes the poor wretch the culprit. (It is probably this sense of self-defection which keeps these cheated women from committing rape. Imagine an equal proportion of any male population under similar circumstances!) Probably, one will ask, What is all the fuss about? Is it all because a man did not turn up at the right time? Well, partly yes and partly no. Not *any* man; *any* man was not what she had been led to expect. She had, in fact, been specially warned against *any* man. It was the right man she was expecting, HER man. Rightly or wrongly, the theory of the right man has been dinned into the consciousness of the ordinary middle-class woman. It may be merely a subtle ruse on the part of a consciously inadequate society to prepare its victims for the altar. However that may be, the result is the same. The Spinster stands the racket. She pays the penalty. She is the failure, and she closes her teeth down and says nothing. What can she say? Is she not the failure? And so the conspiracy of silence becomes complete. Then, mind and body begin. *They* get their pound of flesh, and the innermost Ego of the Soul, the solitary Dweller behind the Mind, stands at bay to meet their baiting. Day by day, year by year, the baiting goes on. To what end – for what temporal or final good is all this? This is the question to which Society, in sheer amends, has to find an answer. This unfair war waged by instinct and training against poor ordinary consciousness can only be rendered decent by some overwhelming good accruing to someone or something. To whom and for what? These are questions to which we demand an answer as a right. Then, being answered, if any woman considers the benefit conferred upon Society great enough to outweigh the suffering entailed upon herself she may possibly undertake it in the spirit of some magnanimous benefactor. Because this inward warfare cannot truthfully be considered for one moment as benefiting the Spinster herself. Her character for instance, is not in need of that kind of tonic. For, be it noted, the Spinster does not overcome Sex as a Saint overcomes Sin. She does not, save rarely, crush out of existence that part of her which is threatening her life's reasonable calm. Driven inward, denied its rightful ordained fulfilment, the instinct becomes diffused. The field of consciousness is charged with an all-pervasive unrest and sickness, which changes all meanings, and queers all judgments, and which, appearing outwardly, we recognise as sentimentality. It is to this sentimentality that all reason and intelligence has to bow. It is by this means that we are all made to pass under the yoke. It is not, however, to be believed that every spinster will thus suffer mind and body to enter into bondage. Some are finding a way of escape. Some women have taken this way, and more will take it. It is the final retort. It is the way of the Saint. It would be the right way in overcoming sin. But in overcoming the life instinct itself, who shall say it is right? The way is to destroy the faculty. With a strong will and a stern régime it can be done. Women are doing it with a fierce joy that would have gladdened the heart of some old Puritan. You take the body and tire it out with work, work, work. In any crevice of time left over you rush here and there, up and down, constantly active. And for the mind, you close down the shutters on that field. No image, no phrase, no brooding, nothing there which speaks of emotions which produce life. And this sort of Spinster, more and more, is bringing up the younger generation. Another unconscious revenge! But this is the way of the few. As for the many, they go the sentimental way. For there is no shuffling possible in this matter. The Spinster must either keep her womanhood at the cost of suffering inordinate for the thing it is, and be compelled to turn what should be an incidental interest into the basis of all interest; or she must destroy the faculty itself, and know herself atrophied. There is no alternative. To offer work, pleasure, 'doing good', in lieu of this is as much to the point and as sensible as to offer a loaf to a person who is tortured with thirst.

Let the social guardians remember that in the fulness of time physical developments show themselves, and that as they appear, so must they be provided for. This social slaughter can no longer pass without challenge, and they may remember for their comfort that if prurience has slain its thousands, chastity has slain its tens of thousands. In this matter, it remains for Society to justify itself.

Stella Browne

Studies in Feminine Inversion

(1923)

I must apologise for what I feel to be a misleading title chosen for reasons of brevity and economy of effort in the framing of notices; for, what I have to put before you today are only very fragmentary data, and suggestions of a peculiarly obscure subject. They have, however, this validity; that they are the result of close and careful observation, conducted so far as I am consciously aware, without any prejudice, though they would probably be much more illuminating had they been recorded by an observer who was herself entirely or predominantly homosexual. I hope that the endless omissions will be to some extent supplied by comment and criticism, from our members, in the course of debate.

My material would have been both less limited and much more definite and intimate had I been able to include cases which have been told me in confidence. Those, of course, I have omitted.

The cases which I will now briefly describe to you are all well-known to me; they are all innate, and very pronounced and deeply rooted, not episodical. At the same time though I am sure there has been, in some of them at least, no definite and conscious physical expression, they are absolutely distinguishable from affectionate friendship. They have all of them in varying degrees, the element of passion: and here I should like to quote a definition of passion by Desmond McCarthy, which seems to me very apt and very true:

> It differs from lust in the intensity with which the personality of the object is apprehended, and in being also an excitement of the whole being, and, therefore, not satisfied so simply: from other kinds of love, in that it is intensely sexual and not accompanied, necessarily, by any contemplation of the

object as good, or any strong desire for his or her welfare apart from the satisfaction of itself.

Now for my cases, and then a few comments and conclusions.

Case A. Member of a small family, but numerous cousins on both sides. The mother's family is nervous, with a decided streak of eccentricity of varying kinds, and some of its members much above the average in intelligence. The father's family much more commonplace, but robust. She is of small-boned frame, but childish rather than feminine in appearance, the liberating and illuminating effect of some definite and direct physical sex-expression, have had, and still have, a disastrous effect on a nature which has much inherent force and many fine qualities. Her whole outlook on life is subtly distorted and dislocated, moral values are confused and a false standard of values is set up. The hardening and narrowing effect of her way of life is shown in a tremendous array of prejudices on every conceivable topic: caste prejudices, race prejudices, down to prejudices founded on the slightest eccentricity of dress or unconventionality of behaviour; also in an immense intolerance of normal passion, even in its most legally sanctioned and certificated forms. As to unlegalised sex-relationships, they are of course considered the very depth alike of depravity and of crass folly. And all the while, her life revolves round a deep and ardent sex-passion, frustrated and exasperated through functional repression, but entirely justified in her own opinion as pure family affection and duty! Though the orthodox and conventional point of view she takes on sex-questions, generally, would logically condemn just *that* form of sex-passion, as peculiarly reprehensible.

Case B. Also the member of a small family though with numerous cousins, paternal and maternal. Family of marked ability – on both sides, especially the mother's. Of very graceful and attractive appearance, entirely feminine, beautiful eyes and classical features, but indifferent to her looks and abnormally lacking in vanity, self-confidence and animal vitality generally, though no one is quicker to appreciate any beauty or charm in other women. I think she is a pronounced psychic invert whose intuitive faculties and bent towards mysticism have never been cultivated. Keen instinctive delicacy and emotional depth, enthusiastically devoted and generous to friends; much personal pride (though no vanity) and reserve. Too amenable to group suggestions and the influences of tradition. Artistic and musical tastes and a faculty for literary criticism which has lain fallow for want of systematic exercise. Rather fond of animals and devoted to children, especially to young relatives and the children of friends. Has done good philanthropic work for children, but is essentially interested in *persons* rather than in theories, or institutions. Is a devout Christian and I think gets much support and comfort from her religious beliefs. A distaste, even positive disgust, for the physical side of sex, which is tending more and more to manifest itself in conventional moral attitudes and judgements. General social attitude towards men less definitely *hostile* than that of Case A, but absolutely aloof. Devoted to women friends and relatives, yet has had no full and satisfying expression of this devotion. This inhibition of a whole infinitely important set of feelings and activities has weakened her naturally very sound judgment, and also had a bad permanent effect on her bodily health.

Case C. The sixth, and second youngest of a large and very able and vigorous family. Tall, and of the typical Diana build; long limbs, broad shoulders, slight bust, narrow hips. Decidedly athletic. Voice agreeable in tone and quite deep, can whistle well. Extremely energetic and capable, any amount of initiative and enthusiasm, never afraid to assume responsibility; very dominating and managing, something of a tyrant in practice, though an extreme democrat in theory, and most intolerant towards different emotional temperaments. Scientific training; interested in politics and public affairs; logical and rationalistic bent of mind. Emotionally reserved, intense, jealous and monopolistic. Will always try to express all emotion in terms of reason and moral theory, and is thus capable of much mental dishonesty, while making a fetich of complete and meticulous truthfulness. An agnostic and quite militant and aggressive. The episode in her life which I observed fairly closely was a long and intimate friendship with a young girl – ten years her junior – of a very attractive and vivacious type, who roused the interest of both men and women keenly. Cleverness and physical charm in girls appealed to her, but she instinctively resented any independent divergent views or standard of values. For years she practically formed this girl's mental life, and they spent their holidays together. When the girl fell in love with and impulsively married a very masculine and brilliantly gifted man, who has since won great distinction in his special profession, C's agony of rage and desolation was terrible and pitiable, though here again, she tried to hide the real nature of her loss by misgivings as to the young man's 'type of ethical theory' – her own phrase! I cannot for a moment believe that she was ignorant of her own sex-nature, and I hope she has by now found free and full personal realisation with some beloved woman – though, unless the beloved woman is exceptionally understanding or exceptionally docile, it will be a stormy relationship. She is a very strong personality, and a born ruler. Her attitude towards men was one of perfectly unembarrassed and equal comradeship.

Case D. Is on a less evolved plane than the three aforementioned, being conspicuously lacking in refinement of feeling and, to some extent, of habit. But is well above the average in vigor, energy and efficiency. A decided turn for carpentry, mechanics and executive manual work. Not tall; slim, boyish figure; very hard, strong muscles, singularly impassive face, with big magnetic eyes. The dominating tendency is very strong here, and is not held in leash by a high standard of either delicacy or principle. Is professionally associated with children and young girls, and shows her innate homosexual tendency by excess of petting and spoiling, and intense jealousy of any other person's contact with, or interest in the children. I do not definitely know if there is any physical expression of her feelings, beyond the kissing and embracing which is normal, and even, in some cases conventional, between women or between women and children. But the *emotional tone* is quite unmistakable; will rave for hours over some 'lovely kiddy', and injure the children's own best interests, as well as the working of the establishment, by unreasonable and unfair indulgence.

Her sexual idiosyncracy in the post which she occupies is extremely harmful, and together with her jealous and domineering nature, leads to a general atmosphere of slackness and intrigue, and the children under her care, of course, take advantage of it. As she has had medical training, I cannot suppose she is ignorant on the subject of her own sex nature. Member of a large family, mostly brothers.

Case E. This was a case which at one time was fairly well-known to me, and is very well-marked. Two assistant mistresses at a girl's boarding-school were completely inseparable. They took all their walks together, and spent all their time when they were 'off duty' and not walking, in one another's rooms – they occupied adjoining rooms.

One of them was a slim, graceful, restless, neurotic girl with a distinct consumptive tendency; quick in perception and easy in manner, but it seemed to me then, and it seems still, decidedly superficial and shallow. The other partner was an invert of the most pronounced physical type. Her tall, stiff, rather heavily muscular figure, her voice, and her chubby, fresh-coloured face, which was curiously eighteenth-century in outline and expression, were so like those of a very young and very well-groomed youth, that all the staff of the school nick-named her 'Boy', though I do not believe any of them clearly realised what this epithet – and her intimacy with a woman of such strongly contrasted type, implied. 'Boy' was extremely self-conscious and curiously inarticulate; she had musical tastes and played rather well – not in the colourless and amateurish style of the musical hack. I think music was an outlet for her. She was also fond of taking long walks, and of driving, and of dogs and horses. Beyond these matters I don't think I ever heard her express an opinion about anything. The intimacy with her restless, tricky adored one ran its course, unhindered either by circumstances, or by unconscious public opinion. There was some idealism in the relationship, at least on 'Boy's' side.

There was no community of intellectual interests – or rather there was community in the mutual absence of intellectual interests. I lost sight of them completely, but heard later that the friend had taken a post in South Africa, and 'Boy' was planning to join her there, but I do not know whether this plan materialised.

I have omitted from consideration that episodical homosexuality on the part of women who are normally much more attracted to men, of which every experienced observer must know instances.

I have also left out of consideration here, various instances known to me of passionate but unconscious inversion in girls whose sex-life is just beginning. All of these are important, and may throw helpful light not only on the problem inversion, but on the sexual impulse of women generally.

There exists no document in modern English literature comparable in authenticity or artistic merit, as a study of the female homosexual or bi-sexual temperaments, with the hauntingly beautiful verse of Renee Vivien (Pauline Tarn) or the vivid autobiographical novels of Colette Willy (Gabrielle Gautheir Villars).

I know of two modern English novels in which the subject is touched on with a good deal of subtlety, and in both cases in association with school life. *Regiment of Women* by Clemence Dane – a brilliant piece of psychology, and a novel by an Australian writer, cruder and shorter, but unmistakably powerful, *The Getting of Wisdom* by Henry Handel Richardson. There is frank and brilliant description of the feminine intermediate and homosexual temperaments in *I, Mary MacLane*, (New York, Stokes & Co).

I would draw your attention to one quality which two of my cases have in common, and to a very marked degree: the maternal instinct. Two of the most intensely maternal women I know are cases A and B, both congenital inverts.

A friend has suggested to me that in such cases in the future, the resources of developed chemistry and biology will be made use of, in artificial fertilisation. And I now see in reading Dr Marie

Stopes's interesting Essay 'Married Love', that she makes a similar suggestion, though not with reference to inversion.

This problem of feminine inversion is very pressing and immediate, taking into consideration the fact that in the near future, for at least a generation, the circumstances of women's lives and work will tend, even more than at present, to favour the frigid, and next to the frigid, the inverted types. Even at present, the social and affectional side of the invert's nature has often fuller opportunity of satisfaction than the heterosexual woman's, but often at the cost of adequate and definite physical expression. And how decisive for vigour, sanity and serenity of body and mind, for efficiency, for happiness, for the mastery of life, and the understanding of one's fellow-creatures – just this definite physical expression is! The lack of it, 'normal' and 'abnormal', is at the root of most of what is most trivial and unsatisfactory in women's intellectual output, as well as of their besetting vice of cruelty. How can anyone be finely or greatly creative, if one's supreme moral law is a negation! Not to *live*, not to *do*, not even to try to understand.

In the cases which I have called A and B, sexual experience along the lines of their own psychic idiosyncracy would have revealed to them definitely where they stood, and as both are well above the average in intelligence, would have been a key to many mysteries of human conduct which are now judged with dainty shrinking from incomprehensible folly and perversity.

I am sure that much of the towering spiritual arrogance which is found, e.g., in may high places in the Suffrage movement, and among the unco guid generally, is really unconscious inversion.

I think it is perhaps not wholly uncalled-for, to underline very strongly my opinion that the homosexual impulse *is not in any way superior* to the normal; it has a fully equal right to existence and expression, it is no worse, no lower; *but no better.*

By all means let the invert – let all of us – have as many and varied 'channels of sublimation' as possible; and far more than are at present available. But, to be honest, are we not too inclined to make 'sublimation' an excuse for refusing to tackle fundamentals? The tragedy of the repressed invert is apt to be not only one of emotional frustration, but complete dislocation of mental values.

Moreover, our present social arrangements, founded as they are on the repression and degradation of the normal erotic impulse, artificially stimulate inversion and have thus forfeited all right to condemn it. There is a huge, persistent, indirect pressure on women of strong passions and fine brains to find an emotional outlet with other women. A woman who is unwilling to accept either marriage – under present laws – or prostitution, and at the same time refuses to limit her sexual life to auto-erotic manifestations, will find she has to struggle against the whole social order for what is nevertheless her most precious personal right. The right sort of woman faces the struggle and counts the cost well worth while; but it is impossible to avoid seeing that she risks the most painful experiences, and spends an incalculable amount of time and energy on things that should be matters of course. Under these conditions, some women who *are not innately or predominantly homosexual* do form more or less explicitly erotic relations with other women, yet these are makeshifts and essentially substitutes, which cannot replace the vital contact, mental and bodily, with congenial men.

No one who has observed the repressed inverted impulse flaring into sex-antagonism, or masked as the devotion of daughter or cousin or the solicitude of teacher or nurse, or perverted into the cheap, malignant cant of conventional moral indignation, can deny its force. Let us recognise this force, as frankly as we recognise and reverence the love between men and women. When Paris was devouring and disputing over Willy and Colette Willy's wonderful Claudine stories, another gifted woman-writer, who had also touched on the subject of inversion, defended not only the artistic conception and treatment of the stories (they need no defence, and remain one of the joys and achievements of modern French writing), but also their ethical content: Mme Rachilde wrote '*une amoureuse d'amour n'est pas une vicieuse*'.

After all: every strong passion, every deep affection, has its own endless possibilities, of pain, change, loss, incompatibility, satiety, jealousy, incompleteness: why add wholly extraneous difficulties and burdens? Harmony may be incompatible with freedom; we do not yet know, for few of us know either. But both truth and the most essential human dignity are incompatible with things as they are.

Biographical Notes

William Acton (1814–1875)

Trained at St Bartholomew's Hospital between 1830 and 1835 before going to Paris to study at the venereal hospital for women. He was elected Secretary of the Parisian Medical Society in 1839 but returned to Britain a year later to practise surgery in London. He was a contentious figure who was famous for his theories of masculinity and virility but challenged by Elizabeth Blackwell, amongst others, for denying female sexuality.

Annie Besant (1847–1933)

Born Annie Wood in London, she married the Reverend Frank Besant in 1867 and was legally separated from him six years later. She was the co-editor, with Charles Bradlaugh, of the *National Reformer*. In 1874 she was elected Vice-President of the National Secular Society after publicly declaring her atheism. After publishing *The Fruits of Philosophy* in 1875, a treatise advocating preventive checks to the population, both she and Bradlaugh were sentenced to six months' imprisonment and fined £200. The sentence was reversed on appeal but Annie lost the custody of her daughter. She was converted to socialism and joined the Fabian Society in 1885. Three years later she was the chief organiser of the Match Girls' Strike at Bryant and Mays in London's East End. In 1889, under the guidance of Helena Blvatsky, she was converted to theosophy and left for India. In 1898 she founded the Hindu

College in Benares. She learned Sanskrit and became interested in Indian politics. She was elected President of the Indian National Congress from 1917 to 1923. In 1925 she advertised the merits of the Commonwealth of India Bill and won the backing of the Labour Party. She died in India.

Elizabeth Blackwell (1821–1910)

English-born, she emigrated to the USA with her family at the age of eleven. In 1847 she moved to Philadelphia and studied anatomy at private schools. She applied to Geneva College, New York, and in 1849, became the first woman to gain a medical degree in the USA. After further study in Paris, at La Maternité, she set up practice in New York, securing from the state a charter for a small hospital, the New York Infirmary for Indigent Women and Children. With her sister, EMILY BLACKWELL, she planned to attach a medical college to the hospital: it opened in 1868 and functioned for over twenty years until, in 1899, women were accepted by Cornell University to study medicine. In 1869 she settled in England and founded the National Health Society of London and helped to form the London School of Medicine for Women, accepting the Chair of Gynaecology there in 1874. She was a Christian Socialist and fought for the legal control of prostitution.

Isaac Baker Brown (1812–1873)

Trained at Guy's Hospital, London, after which he established a general practice in partnership with Samuel Griffith in 1834. Twelve years later he gave up general practice for that of surgeon *accoucher* at St Mary's Hospital, Paddington. It was here that he became interested in gynaecological surgery and started to practise and recommend clitoridectomy as a cure for epilepsy, hysteria, sterility and insanity believing that all of these were produced by sexual arousal and assuming that women were dominated by their reproductive systems. In 1867 he was expelled from the Obstetrical Society for neglecting to inform his patients or their families of the nature of the operation; his career ended abruptly.

Stella Browne (1882–1955)

Became an active worker for socialist feminism on the eve of the First World War. She campaigned for women's right to contraception and abortion and, from 1914, was involved in the Malthusian League informing workers of contraceptive methods. She remained active in the League throughout the 1920s and was a founder member of the Abortion Law Reform Association in 1936. She joined the Communist Party at its inception and, later, the Labour Party. Browne knew HAVELOCK ELLIS and her ideas on sexuality were greatly influenced by his works. For two of her published pieces and further biographical information see *A New World for Women: Stella Brown – Socialist Feminist* (Pluto, London, 1977).

Josephine Butler (1828–1906)

One of seven children, she was born in Dilston, Northumberland. Her father, John Grey, was a radical agricultural reformer and abolitionist. Her mother was a devout Moravian Christian. In 1850 she married George Butler, a lecturer at Durham University. She had a daughter who died from a fall at five years old. In Liverpool she established a refuge for ill prostitutes and in 1869 was elected the President if the Ladies' National Association and campaigned against the state regulation of prostitution under the Contagious Diseases Acts (1866–9). In 1886 her campaign won the repeal of the Acts. She was a founder member of the National Viligance Association although she retired from the social purity movements of the 1890s.

Frances Power Cobbe (1822–1904)

The daughter of strict Evangelical Protestants, she was educated at home with two years' schooling in Brighton. After her father's death in 1856 she travelled in Italy and Greece and became the Italian correspondent of the *London Daily News*. She was involved in many welfare causes, advocating special care for the insane and the incurably sick, she worked in Bristol's 'ragged schools' with Mary Carpenter, reformed workhouses and appealed for the care of working girls. An early suffrage campaigner, she advocated a radical view of women's rights and wrote for several periodicals.

Katherine Dixon

No biographical information available.

Havelock Ellis (1859–1939)

Was the most influential sexologist of the twentieth century, seen by many as the 'father' of sex advice literature. The first volume of his *Studies in the Psychology of Sex*, 'Sexual Inversion', was published in 1897. He trained as a doctor in the 1880s and began to write about a range of subjects, including literature, science, religion, philosophy, travel and politics. He became involved in the radical political, moral and philosophical discussion that was emerging with the socialist revival. Biological assumptions about innate differences between men and women governed his thinking. He aimed, through his writings, to eliminate prejudice so that men's and women's 'real' sexuality could emerge. He believed men's 'real' sexuality to be aggressive and sadistic and women's to be passive and masochistic. These ideas were central to the development of 'sexual liberation'.

Elizabeth C. Wolstenholme Elmy

She worked for fifteen years for the Married Women's Property Acts of 1870 and 1882 and for three years for the 1886 Custody of Infants Act. She took a radical stand on sexuality, working alongside JOSEPHINE BUTLER and CHRISTABEL PANKHURST. Writing under the name Ellis Ethelmer, she wrote two books on sex education for children, *The Human Flower* and *Baby Buds*. The central theme of her writings was the right of women to control their own bodies; she wrote of the horror of sexual coercion of the wife by her husband and advocated celibacy other than for purposes of reproduction. Her aim was to free women from sexual vulnerability and she encouraged sexual self-control and 'psychic love' as a means by which women could liberate themselves.

Ellice J. Hopkins (1836–1904)

She was involved in the social purity campaigns and attacked the Church of England for its hypocrisy and indifference to the elimination of prostitution. She demanded that the Church should not be content to set up penitentiaries for prostitutes but should deal with the root of the problem and establish men's chastity leagues. From her efforts the White Cross Army, whose purpose was to circulate literature and enlist the support of men, and the Church of England Purity Society were set up. She was instrumental in starting The Ladies' National Association for the Care and Protection of Friendless Girls, associations which were established in towns all over Britain to provide a home for girls who had come looking for work and who might be lured into prostitution. The girls were trained in domestic work, clothed and helped to find jobs. Her books include *Rose Turquand, a novel* (1876); *Notes on Penitentiary Work* (1879); *Grave Moral Questions addressed to Men and Women of England* (1882); *The Present Moral Crisis* (1886).

Ellen Key

Was a Swedish spinster and schoolteacher who began, late in life, to publish works on sex reform which were translated into many languages and influential in 'progressive' circles throughout the western world. HAVELOCK ELLIS promoted her ideas because she saw women's destiny as limited to motherhood and went so far as to suggest that mothers should not work outside the home. Key believed that the highest human unit was 'triune', i.e. father, mother and child, with marriage becoming the central point of life. Her main works, *The Century of the Child, The Woman Movement*, and *Love and Marriage* were all published just before the outbreak of the First World War.

Maria Adelaide Lowndes (1868–?)

The only daughter of a French barrister, Louis Belloc, and Bessie Rayner Parkes, one of the founding editors of the *Englishwoman's Journal* and early suffrage campaigner. Maria was educated at a convent and studied French history and literature; in 1899 she was recognised as an authority in matters of French contemporary biography. In 1889 she published *The Life and Letters of Charlotte Elizabeth, Princess Palatine* and edited the correspondence of Edmond and Jules de Goncourt in 1894. She was one of London's leading female journalists and regularly wrote for the *Observer* and the *Daily News*. In 1896 she married another journalist, Frederick Sawrey Lowndes.

Harriet Martineau (1802–1876)

In her twenties, her father, brother and fiancé all died and she resolved to become independent as a professional writer. In 1831, after winning prizes for her essays in the *Unitarian Journal*, she decided to write a series which illustrated the principles of political economy which was, at this time, a new subject. Her *Illustrations of Political Economy* (1832–4), influenced by John Stuart Mill, were an instant success and established her a journalist. Between 1839 and 1844 she was ill and wrote children's stories and two novels. *Deerbrook* (1839) and *The Hour and the Man* (1841). When she recovered she travelled to Egypt and to Palestine, returning to England as a regular contributor to the *London Daily News* from 1852 to 1866 covering a range of subjects from agricultural economics to the evil of licensed prostitution. She supported the Married Women's Property Bill in 1857 and had become Secretary of Bedford College for Women in 1849. After being told that she was incurably ill, published until after her death in 1877.

Christabel Pankhurst (1880–1958)

In 1901, while studying Law at Victoria University, Manchester, she was a member of the North of England Society for Women's Suffrage and of the Manchester Women's Trade Union Council, but she grew impatient with the Independent Labour Party and decided, with her mother, Emmeline Pankhurst, to form a Women's Branch. In 1903, the Women's Social and Political Union was founded with the slogan 'Votes for Women'. After two years of local campaigning, she was arrested, with Annie Kenney, after their protest at a Liberal election meeting in Free Trade Hall, Manchester. In their coverage of the story, the *Daily Mail* coined the term 'suffragette'. Christabel's militancy had been inflamed further by the refusal of Lincoln's Inn to accept her in 1904 because she was first in the 1906 LLB. The following year she moved to London and spent the next six years campaigning for women's suffrage for which she was arrested several times. Threatened with a conspiracy charge in 1912, she escaped to Paris where she joined the lesbian feminist group around the Princess de Polignac and continued to direct the British campaign through *The Suffragette*. She attacked sexual as well as political oppression and wrote articles on venereal disease and prostitution which were reprinted as *The Great Scourge*. She stopped her work for suffrage to help her mother's recruiting drive for the First World War in 1914.

Emmeline Pethick Lawrence (1867–1954)

Committed to social reform and disinterested in marriage, she met William Lawrence in 1899 and refused his proposal on the grounds that she would lose her independence. They met two years later, when she was thirty-four, and she agreed to marry him, retaining her own name in addition to his as a symbol of her own identity. In 1905 they travelled to South Africa were they met Olive Schreiner and read about CHRISTABEL PANKHURST and Annie Kenney's arrest. On her return to England, Emmeline became treasurer of the WSPU and played a prominent role in the cause for women's enfranchisement and in peace movements.

Lucy Re-Bartlett and Ursula Roberts

No biographical information available.

Margaret Sanger (1883–1966)

Born in New York, she trained as a nurse working in the Lower East Side and lecturing on health to young mothers. She was distressed by the connections she saw between poverty, numerous pregnancies, infant and maternal death and backstreet abortions. She wrote for the socialist paper, *The Call* (including an article on venereal disease which was suppressed by the government) and became friends with Emma Goldman and the radical journalist Agnes Smedley. In 1913 she went to Paris where she met Malthusian reformers and, on her return to the USA, she was prosecuted for her pamphlet *Family Limitation*. She was also publishing a journal, *Women Rebel*, which later became *Birth Control Review*. The case against her was dismissed in 1916 after she had been forced to leave America to escape prosecution. In Britain, she met MARIE STOPES and HAVELOCK ELLIS. When she returned to New York, she opened a clinic in Brooklyn but it was closed down and she was sentenced to thirty days in a workhouse for causing a 'public nuisance'. She founded the American Birth Control League in 1921 and organised the first World Population Conference in Geneva in 1927 out of which a national lobby group was created which pressed for changes in legislation throughout the 1930s. By 1932 over eighty birth control clinics were operating in the USA. She retired from active leadership in 1938 but continued to lecture and was the first President of the International Planned Parenthood Federation in 1953, going on to work for birth control in India and the Far East.

Marie C. Stopes (1880–1958)

Born Charlotte Carmichael in Edinburgh, she studied geology, geography and botany at University College, London. After a year's research she went to Munich and obtained a PhD in 1904 and was the first woman to join the Science Faculty at Manchester University in the same year. In 1911 she married a Canadian botanist, Reginald Ruggles Gates. The inadequacy of their sexual relations prompted her to read widely on the subject and after their marriage was annulled in 1916, on the ground of non-consummation, she concentrated on campaigning for birth control and sex education. Unlike MARGARET SANGER who saw her contraception campaign as an attack on poverty, Marie felt that it was an aid to sexual fulfilment because it reduced women's fear of pregnancy and gave them control of their bodies. In 1918 she married Humphry Verdon-Roe, an aircraft manufacturer, and they campaigned together. She started a birth control clinic in Islington in 1921, against fierce opposition from the medical establishment and the Catholic Church. After the Second World War she campaigned for birth control in the Far East.

Helena M. Swanwick (1864–1939)

Born in Munich, she moved to England when she was four. She graduated from Girton College in 1885 and became a psychology lecturer at Westfield College, London. In 1888 she married Frederick Swanwick and moved to Manchester where she joined the Women's Trade Union Council. In 1900 she became a member of the North of England Suffrage Society and advocated constitutional as opposed to militant tactics. In 1909 she became the editor of *The Common Cause* but returned to freelance writing in 1912, contributing to the *Manchester Guardian*, the *Observer*, *The Nation* and the *Daily News*. In 1913 she attended the International Suffrage Congress in Budapest and published *The Future of the Women's Movement*. She violently opposed the First World War and became President of the British branch of the Women's International League for Peace. After the war she was adviser to the Labour Party on international affairs and was sent as a delegate to the League of Nations in 1924 and in 1929. During the 1930s she wrote on pacifism and disarmament in Women's International League pamphlets. She died after the outbreak of the Second World War following an overdose of sleeping pills.

Frances Swiney

She began writing in the 1890s and continued to publish numerous pamphlets and books up until the First World War. Her ideas were influential in the women's movement and her books were reviewed and advertised in *The Suffragette* and other suffrage journals. She became friendly with ELIZABETH WOLSTENHOLME ELMY – both women believed that the sexual subjection of women was fundamental to the oppression of women by men. She thought that this subjection was abusive, particularly so during pregnancy and immediately after childbirth, and she gathered evidence from biological, medical and anthropoligical sources to prove her point. She advocated the 'Natural Law' or the 'Law of Continence' – that sexual intercourse should be permitted only for purposes of reproduction and that women should not be expected to bear children under four or five yearly intervals. She codified the 'Natural Law' into a religious system for the theosophical society she administered, the League of Isis. The most famous convert to theosophy was ANNIE BESANT who ceased to advocate free love and argued for celibacy in its place.

Beatrice Webb (1858–1943)

Born Beatrice Potter, she was raised in liberal political and intellectual circles. In 1884 she became a visitor with the Charity Organisation Society and a rent collector in London before working on the survey *Life and Labour of the People of London* (1887). She published her research into East End dock life and gave evidence to the House of Lords Committee on the Sweating System in 1888. She met Fabian theorist, Sidney Webb, when she was thirty-four and together they produced over a hundred books and articles on the labour movement. In 1913 they founded the *New Statesman* and supported the new labour party. During the First World War, Beatrice wrote her classic *Wages of Men and Women – should they be Equal?*

Ellen Webb

No biographical information available.

Index